RIGHTS
WATCH

WORLD REPORT

2019

EVENTS OF 2018

ISBN-13: 978-1-60980-884-6

Cover photo: *Anti-government protestors in Venezuela take to the streets for a candlelight vigil in honor of protesters killed in clashes with security forces.*
© 2017 Associated Press

Back cover photo: *Immigrant children, many of whom have been separated from their parents under a new "zero tolerance" policy by the Trump administration, are being housed in tents next to the Mexican border in Tornillo, Texas, US, June 18, 2018.*
© REUTERS/Mike Blake

Cover and book design by Rafael Jiménez

www.hrw.org

Human Rights Watch defends the rights of people worldwide.

We scrupulously investigate abuses, expose facts widely, and pressure those with power to respect rights and secure justice.

Human Rights Watch is an independent, international organization that works as part of a vibrant movement to uphold human dignity and advance the cause of human rights for all.

Human Rights Watch began in 1978 with the founding of its Europe and Central Asia division (then known as Helsinki Watch). Today it also includes divisions covering Africa, the Americas, Asia, Europe and Central Asia, the Middle East and North Africa, and the United States. There are thematic divisions or programs on arms; business and human rights; children's rights; disability rights; the environment and human rights; health and human rights; international justice; lesbian, gay, bisexual, and transgender rights; refugees; terrorism and counterterrorism; women's rights; and emergencies.

The organization maintains offices in Amman, Amsterdam, Beirut, Berlin, Bishkek, Brussels, Chicago, Geneva, Goma, Hong Kong, Johannesburg, Kiev, Kinshasa, London, Los Angeles, Miami, Moscow, Nairobi, New York, Paris, San Francisco, São Paulo, Seoul, Silicon Valley, Stockholm, Sydney, Tokyo, Toronto, Tunis, Washington DC, and Zurich, and field presences in more than 50 other locations globally.

Human Rights Watch is an independent, nongovernmental organization, supported by contributions from private individuals and foundations worldwide. It accepts no government funds, directly or indirectly.

HUMAN RIGHTS WATCH

This 29th annual World Report is dedicated to the memory of our beloved colleague David Mepham OBE, UK director, who died of cancer on October 21 at age 50. David was a superb advocate, combining a piercing intellect, an extraordinary eloquence, and a deep personal commitment to the human rights cause. Colleagues around the world recall the depth and scope of his knowledge, his willingness to go the extra mile, and his determination to challenge those in power—always with unfailing courtesy. Perhaps most of all, we miss his genuine warmth, evident in his deep love for his family, and his steadfast support of colleagues and friends.

Table of Contents

Foreword

World Report 2019 is Human Rights Watch's 29th annual review of human rights practices around the globe. It summarizes key human rights issues in more than 90 countries and territories worldwide, drawing on events from late 2017 through November 2018.

In his keynote essay, "World's Autocrats Face Rising Resistance," Human Rights Watch Executive Director Kenneth Roth argues that while autocrats and rights abusers often captured headlines in 2018, rights defenders pushed back and gained strength in unexpected ways.

Drawing on analysis of a series of human rights successes in international fora, often led by unlikely government coalitions, and of powerful activism by civic groups at national and regional levels, he shows that defense of rights worldwide is resilient and multi-faceted. Even though many once-influential governments have been missing in action on human rights or even switched sides, effective coalitions emerged to "raise the price of abuse and shift the cost-benefit calculus that convinces governments that repression pays."

The mounting resistance to autocracy, cautions Roth, is not always successful in the short term, and this remains in some ways a dark time for human rights. But recent events also show "the promise of rights-respecting democracy … remains a vital, mobilizing vision." Roth emphasizes that important battles are being won, re-energizing the global defense of human rights.

The rest of the volume consists of individual country entries, each of which identifies significant human rights abuses, examines the freedom of local human rights defenders to conduct their work, and surveys the response of key international actors, such as the United Nations, European Union, African Union, United States, China, and various regional and international organizations and institutions.

The book reflects extensive investigative work that Human Rights Watch staff undertook in 2018, usually in close partnership with human rights activists and groups in the country in question. It also reflects the work of our advocacy team, which monitors policy developments and strives to persuade governments and international institutions to curb abuses and promote human rights. Human

Rights Watch publications, issued throughout the year, contain more detailed accounts of many of the issues addressed in the brief summaries in this volume. They can be found on the Human Rights Watch website, www.hrw.org.

As in past years, this report does not include a chapter on every country where Human Rights Watch works, nor does it discuss every issue of importance. The absence of a country or issue often simply reflects staffing or resource limitations and should not be taken as commentary on the significance of the problem. There are many serious human rights violations that Human Rights Watch simply lacks the capacity to address.

The factors we considered in determining the focus of our work in 2018 (and hence the content of this volume) include the number of people affected and the severity of abuse, access to the country and the availability of information about it, the susceptibility of abusive forces to influence, and the importance of addressing certain thematic concerns and of reinforcing the work of local rights organizations.

The World Report does not have separate chapters addressing our thematic work but instead incorporates such material directly into the country entries. Please consult the Human Rights Watch website for more detailed treatment of our work on children's rights; women's rights; arms and military issues; business and human rights; health and human rights; disability rights; the environment and human rights; international justice; terrorism and counterterrorism; refugees and displaced people; and lesbian, gay, bisexual, and transgender people's rights; and for information about our international film festivals.

The book was edited by Danielle Haas, senior editor at Human Rights Watch, with assistance from Aditi Shetty, senior coordinator, and Delphine Starr, associate. Grace Choi, director of publications and information design, oversaw production of visual elements and layout.

World's Autocrats Face Rising Resistance

By Kenneth Roth, *Executive Director, Human Rights Watch*

In some ways this is a dark time for human rights. Yet while the autocrats and rights abusers may capture the headlines, the defenders of human rights, democracy, and the rule of law are also gaining strength. The same populists who are spreading hatred and intolerance are spawning a resistance that keeps winning its share of battles. Victory in any given case is never assured, but it has occurred often enough in the past year to suggest that the excesses of autocratic rule are fueling a powerful counterattack.

Unlike traditional dictators, today's would-be autocrats typically emerge from democratic settings. Most pursue a two-step strategy for undermining democracy: first, scapegoat and demonize vulnerable minorities to build popular support; then, weaken the checks and balances on government power needed to preserve human rights and the rule of law, such as an independent judiciary, a free media, and vigorous civic groups. Even the world's established democracies have shown themselves vulnerable to this demagoguery and manipulation.

Autocratic leaders rarely solve the problems that they cite to justify their rise to power, but they do create their own legacy of abuse. At home, the unaccountable government that they lead becomes prone to repression, corruption, and mismanagement. Some claim that autocrats are better at getting things done, but as they prioritize perpetuating their own power, the human cost can be enormous, such as the hyperinflation and economic devastation in once oil-rich Venezuela, the spree of extrajudicial killings as part of the "drug war" in the Philippines, or China's mass detention of upwards of 1 million Turkic Muslims, primarily Uyghurs.

Because they dislike human rights scrutiny, autocratic leaders also tend to retreat from the defense of human rights beyond their borders. This retrenchment has made it easier for brutal leaders to get away with large-scale atrocities, such as Syria's war on civilians in areas held by anti-government forces, the Saudi-led coalition's indiscriminate bombing and blockade that are killing and starving Yemeni civilians, and the Myanmar army's mass murder, rape, and arson against Rohingya Muslims.

In response to these disturbing trends, new alliances of rights-respecting governments, often prompted and joined by civic groups and the public, have mounted an increasingly effective resistance. Political leaders decide to violate human rights because they see advantages, whether maintaining their grip on power, padding their bank accounts, or rewarding their cronies. This growing resistance has repeatedly raised the price of those abusive decisions. Because even abusive governments weigh costs and benefits, increasing the cost of abuse is the surest way to change their calculus of repression. Such pressure may not succeed immediately, but it has a proven record over the long term.

Much of this pushback has played out at the United Nations—a noteworthy development because so many autocrats seek to weaken this multilateral institution and undermine the international standards that it sets. The UN Human Rights Council, for example, took important—sometimes unprecedented—steps in the past year to increase pressure on Myanmar, Saudi Arabia, and Venezuela. The opponents of human rights enforcement, such as China, Russia, Egypt, and Saudi Arabia, traditionally carry considerable weight in these settings, so it was impressive to see how often they lost this past year. Given the recent reluctance of many large Western powers to promote human rights enforcement, the leaders of this resistance were often coalitions of smaller- and medium-sized states, including some non-traditional allies.

Significant pressure in defense of rights was also asserted outside the UN. Within the past year, that included efforts to prevent a bloodbath in Syria, to resist autocratic trends in Europe, to defend the longstanding ban on chemical weapons, to convince an African president to accept constitutional limits on his reign, and to press for a full investigation into the murder of Saudi journalist Jamal Khashoggi.

This mounting pressure illustrates the possibility of defending human rights—indeed, the responsibility to do so—even in darker times. The promise of rights-respecting democratic rule—of accountable governments that answer to the needs of their citizens rather than the power and wealth of high-level officials—remains a vital, mobilizing vision. The past year shows that battles in its defense remain very much worth waging.

The Dark Side of Autocratic Rule

Despite the mounting resistance, the forces of autocracy have been on the rise. For example, Brazil elected as president Jair Bolsonaro—a man who, at great risk to public safety, openly encourages the use of lethal force by the military and police in a country already wracked by a sky-high rate of police killings and more than 60,000 homicides per year.

Established autocrats and their admirers continued their disregard for basic rights. Turkey's President Recep Tayyip Erdoğan and Egypt's President Abdel Fattah al-Sisi persisted in silencing independent voices and civic groups and locking up thousands for their presumed political views. Philippines President Rodrigo Duterte encouraged more summary executions, supposedly of drug suspects, but often of people guilty of no more than being poor young men. Hungary's Prime Minister Viktor Orbán implemented his brand of "illiberal democracy." Poland's de facto ruler, Jarosław Kaczyński, sought to stack his country's courts with his preferred judges, undermining the judiciary's independence. Italy's interior minister and deputy prime minister, Matteo Salvini, closed ports to refugees and migrants, scuttled efforts to save migrants' lives at sea, and stoked anti-immigrant sentiment. India's Prime Minister Narendra Modi failed to halt the demonizing of Muslims while attacking civic groups that criticized his rights record or environmental policies. The Cambodian prime minister, Hun Sen, tightened his grip on power by holding sham elections from which the opposition party was banned. US President Donald Trump disparaged immigrants and minorities and tried to bully judges and journalists whom he deemed to stand in his way. Russia under President Vladimir Putin continued its multiyear crackdown on independent voices and political opposition. China closed off any possibility of organized opposition to the increasingly one-man rule of Xi Jinping.

Beyond the immediate victims, some of the economic costs of autocratic rule became more visible over the course of the year. Oil-rich Venezuela once enjoyed one of Latin America's highest standards of living but today, under the autocratic rule of President Nicolás Maduro, Venezuelans suffer severe shortages of food and medicine, causing millions to flee the country. President Erdogan, persisting with large-scale building projects that often benefited his allies, oversaw a plummeting currency and a skyrocketing cost of living in Turkey. Mozambique discovered that $2 billion in government funds had disappeared from its treasury.

China's much-touted "One Belt, One Road" initiative to develop trade infrastructure fostered autocratic mismanagement in other countries. In keeping with Beijing's longstanding practice, Belt and Road loans come with no visible conditions, making Beijing a preferred lender for autocrats. These unscrutinized infusions of cash made it easier for corrupt officials to pad their bank accounts while saddling their people with massive debt in the service of infrastructure projects that in several cases benefit China more than the people of the indebted nation.

In Malaysia, Prime Minister Mahathir bin Mohamad cancelled three major infrastructure projects financed by Chinese loans amid concerns that his predecessor, Najib Razak, had agreed to unfavorable terms to obtain funds to cover up a corruption scandal. Unable to afford its enormous debt burden, Sri Lanka was forced to surrender control of a port to China, built with Chinese loans but without an economic rationale in the home district of former President Mahinda Rajapaksa. Kenya came to rue a Chinese-funded railroad that offered no promise of economic viability. Pakistan, Djibouti, Sierra Leone, and the Maldives all expressed regret at having agreed to certain Chinese-funded projects. Talk of a Chinese "debt trap" became common.

The Pushback

The growing pushback against autocratic rule and the corruption it frequently fueled took various forms over the past year. Sometimes elections or public pressure were the vehicle. Malaysian voters ousted their corrupt prime minister, Najib Razak, and the ruling coalition in power for almost six decades, for a coalition running on an agenda of human rights reform. Maldives voters rejected their autocratic president, Yameen Abdulla Gayoom. In Armenia, whose government was mired in corruption, Prime Minister Serzh Sargsyan had to step down amid massive protests. Czech Prime Minister Andrej Babis faced growing protests against his alleged corruption. Ethiopia, under popular pressure, replaced a long-abusive government with a new one led by Prime Minister Abiy Ahmed, who embarked on an impressive reform agenda. US voters in the midterm elections for the House of Representatives seemed to rebuke President Trump's divisive and rights-averse policies.

Sometimes independent institutions of government resisted the overreach of their country's leaders. Poland's independent judges refused to abandon their jobs in the face of Kaczyński's efforts to purge them; the European Court of Justice later backed their refusal. Guatemala's Constitutional Court reversed President Jimmy Morales's attempt to bar from the country the chief investigator of a UN-backed anti-corruption body after it started probing his own alleged financial wrongdoing. US Chief Justice John Roberts, appointed by former President George W. Bush, publicly berated President Trump for disparaging "an Obama judge" who had ruled against Trump's efforts to limit migrants' right to seek asylum.

In many cases, the public led the resistance in the streets. Large crowds in Budapest protested Orbán's moves to shut Central European University, an academic bastion of liberal inquiry and thought. Tens of thousands of Poles repeatedly took to the streets to defend their courts from the ruling party's attempts to undermine their independence. People across the United States and dozens of companies protested Trump's forcible separation of immigrant children from their parents.

Multilateral Resistance

New governments had to pick up the defense of human rights because several important governments faltered. President Trump preferred to embrace autocrats whom he viewed as friendly, even if parts of the US government often tried to work around the White House. The British government, worried about Brexit, appeared willing to publicly advocate for human rights mainly in countries where British trade or commercial interests were limited. French President Emmanuel Macron defended democratic values rhetorically, but too often found reasons to avoid applying those principles when they implicated efforts to curb migration, fight terrorism, or secure commercial opportunities. Germany's Chancellor Angela Merkel spoke against anti-rights policies emanating from Moscow and Washington but was often beset by political challenges at home. China and Russia did all they could to undermine global rights enforcement, while at home they imposed the most repressive rule in decades.

UN Human Rights Council

Against this challenging backdrop, a critical mass of human rights supporters has regularly risen to the occasion. The 47-member UN Human Rights Council was an especially important venue. It proved significant even though the Trump administration ordered the United States to withdraw from it—the first country ever to do so—in a failed effort to discredit the council's regular criticism of Israel. Washington objected to the council's focus on Israel, which occurs in part because many US administrations, including that of President Trump, use the US veto at the UN Security Council to shield Israel from any criticism there. The Human Rights Council has repeatedly taken important steps to defend rights in North Korea, Syria, Myanmar, Yemen, Sudan, South Sudan, Burundi, and the Democratic Republic of Congo—all countries with deeply problematic human rights records that the US government has long said it wants addressed. Yet President Trump was willing to jeopardize that in the name of weakening the council because it denounces such Israeli policies as the crippling closure of Gaza and the discriminatory and illegal settlement regime in the West Bank.

The Human Rights Council made major advances despite—and in one case arguably because of—the US absence. For example, the possibility of a Chinese, Russian, or even American veto at the UN Security Council appeared to doom any effort to refer Myanmar to the International Criminal Court (ICC) for its army's mass atrocities—foremost the crimes against humanity that sent 700,000 Rohingya fleeing for their lives to Bangladesh. In response, the Human Rights Council, where there is no veto, stepped in to create a semi-prosecutorial investigative mechanism to preserve evidence, identify those responsible, and build cases for the day when a tribunal becomes available to judge these crimes. That effort won overwhelmingly, with 35 in favor and only 3 against (7 abstained), sending the signal that these atrocities cannot be committed with impunity, even as senior leader Aung San Suu Kyi and the army continued to deny they occurred.

The European Union co-presented the council's resolution on the Rohingya along with the Organisation of Islamic Cooperation (OIC), which until Myanmar's attacks on the Rohingya had opposed all resolutions criticizing any particular country other than Israel. And in what may be an alternative route to the International Criminal Court (ICC) that does not depend on the Security Council, the ICC prosecutor opened a preliminary examination into the alleged deportation of Rohingya from Myanmar, using for jurisdiction the fact that the crime was completed when the Rohingya were pushed into Bangladesh, an ICC member state.

With the Netherlands, Belgium, Luxembourg, Ireland, and Canada taking the lead, the Human Rights Council also rejected a heavy-handed Saudi effort to avoid scrutiny of war crimes in Yemen, such as the Saudi-led coalition's repeated bombing and devastating blockade of Yemeni civilians that have left millions on the brink of starvation in what UN officials describe as the world's worst humanitarian crisis. One month before the vote, apparently to signal the possibility of broader retaliation, Saudi Arabia lashed out at and imposed sanctions on Canada for Foreign Minister Chrystia Freeland's wholly justified criticism of its crackdown on women's rights activists. (Saudi Arabia's crown prince, Mohamed bin Salman, preferred to portray his concessions on women's rights, such as granting the right to drive though not lifting the "guardianship" rules that treat women as children, as matters of royal grace rather than as acquiescence to popular demand). Yet the Human Rights Council resolved to continue an international investigation started last year of war crimes in Yemen by a vote of 21 to 8 with 18 abstentions.

For the first time, the Human Rights Council condemned the severe repression in Venezuela under President Maduro. A resolution, led by a group of Latin American nations, won by a vote of 23 to 7 with 17 abstentions. This followed the US government's departure from the council, making it easier for resolution sponsors to show they were addressing Venezuela as a matter of principle rather than as a tool of Washington's ideology.

In addition, five Latin American governments and Canada urged the International Criminal Court to open an investigation of crimes in Venezuela—the first time that any governments have sought an ICC investigation of crimes that took place entirely outside their territory. Other governments, including France and Germany, supported the move. A group of Latin American governments led by Argentina also organized in the context of the Human Rights Council the first joint statement, signed by 47 countries, on the worsening repression in Nicaragua, as President Daniel Ortega responded with violence to growing protests against his repressive rule.

European Institutions and the Chemical Weapons Agency

Beyond the Human Rights Council, governments mounted important defenses of human rights in other venues as well. One was the Organisation for the Prohibition of Chemical Weapons (OPCW), which had been empowered to determine in any given case only whether chemical weapons have been used, not who used them. Russia opposed empowering any international investigation to attribute responsibility, given its backing of and cover for the Syrian government as it repeatedly used chemical weapons, and its own apparent use of the Novichok nerve agent in an attempted assassination of a former spy in Britain. For example, Moscow vetoed renewal in the UN Security Council of a separate investigation that could identify perpetrators, the UN-OPCW Joint Investigative Mechanism on Syria. The pushback came in an initiative led by France and Britain, over the opposition of Russia, which resulted in the member states of the OPCW voting 82 to 24 to grant it the mandate to begin identifying the users of chemical weapons. A Russian effort to block funding for this new mandate was also rejected.

In the European Union, in response to the Polish government's efforts to undermine the independence of the judiciary and Orbán's implementation of his "illiberal democracy" in Hungary, the EU launched a process that could end with the imposition of political sanctions under article 7 of the EU Treaty; the European Commission acted in the case of Poland and a two-thirds majority of the European Parliament acted in the case of Hungary. Although Poland and Hungary have the power under unanimity rules to shield each other from the actual imposition of such sanctions, the article 7 process lays the groundwork for using the leverage provided by the EU's next five-year budget, which should be adopted by the end of 2020. Poland is the largest recipient of EU funds, and Hungary is among the largest per capita recipients. Both the Polish and Hungarian governments have used these funds to their political advantage, so it is reasonable to ask whether the EU should continue to generously fund their attacks on the EU's core democratic values.

Europe's top intergovernmental human rights body, the Council of Europe, pushed back against attempts by Azerbaijan's authoritarian government to improperly influence members of the council's Parliamentary Assembly (PACE) to soften criticism of the country's human rights record. Following reports by journalists and activists, the Council of Europe launched an investigation that found "a strong suspicion" of "activity of a corruptive nature" by certain current and former PACE members due to illicit Azerbaijani government lobbying. The investigation led to resignations, various penalties, and the introduction of new lobbying rules.

Syria and Saudi Arabia

The multilateral action that may have saved the most lives over the past year focused on Syria. In recent years, as the Syrian military—with backing from Russia, Iran, and Hezbollah—gradually retook one enclave after another held by anti-government forces, many of the residents who feared retaliation or detention in the government's notorious torture and execution chambers were given the option of moving to Idlib province and surrounding areas in northwest Syria, where anti-government forces retained control. Today, an estimated three million people live there, at least half of them displaced from elsewhere in Syria.

But with Turkey having closed its border (after having received 3.5 million Syrian refugees) and the Syrian-Russian military alliance threatening an offensive against Idlib, a bloodbath seemed likely, given the indiscriminate way that the Syrian and Russian militaries have fought the war to date. The Kremlin held the keys to whether this feared slaughter of civilians proceeded because the Syrian military was incapable of sustaining an offensive without Russian aerial support. Intensive international pressure on the Russian government ultimately persuaded President Putin to agree with Turkish President Erdogan to a ceasefire in Idlib, beginning in September. Whether that ceasefire fails, as others have, or holds remains to be seen at time of writing in early December, but its existence shows that even in as complicated a situation as wartime Syria, concerted pressure can save lives.

The aftermath of the Saudi government's gruesome murder of Jamal Khashoggi at its Istanbul consulate provided another example of widespread though still selective multilateral pressure. It is unfortunate that it took the killing of a prominent journalist, rather than of countless unknown Yemeni civilians, to mobilize global outrage at Riyadh's human rights record, but this single murder turned out to be galvanizing. The Saudi government advanced a series of changing cover stories, each refuted with evidence released piece-by-piece by the Turkish government (which continued to persecute its own journalists, activists, academics, and politicians who dared to criticize President Erdogan).

Gradually, the United States and Canada imposed targeted sanctions against many of the Saudis implicated in the murder. In Europe, Germany took the unprecedented step of barring 18 Saudi officials from entering the 26-nation Schengen Zone, while Germany, the Netherlands, Denmark, and Finland stopped arms sales to the kingdom. Yet President Trump pointedly refused to endorse the CIA's reported finding that the Saudi crown prince had likely ordered Khashoggi's murder, offering a cavalier and effectively exculpatory, "Maybe he did and maybe he didn't!" Trump, like his British and French counterparts, refused to stop lucrative arms sales to Saudi Arabia, as if an indeterminate number of domestic jobs outweighed the large-scale loss of Yemeni civilian lives. Many members of the US Congress from both parties—along with members of the US media and public—denounced this callous calculation.

Africa

Pressure from a group of African states was key to finally persuading President Joseph Kabila of the Democratic Republic of Congo to schedule elections for his successor. Barred from seeking re-election by constitutional term limits yet reluctant to give up power, Kabila had deployed security forces to detain and even fire upon pro-democracy activists. He relented only after coordinated pressure from African states—foremost Angola and South Africa—as well as such Western governments as the United States and Belgium. At time of writing, it was unclear whether the elections scheduled for December 23 would take place and whether conditions would be free and fair.

The threat of mass African withdrawal from the International Criminal Court continued to ebb in the wake of pushback from African governments and civic groups supporting the ICC. To date, the only African state to have withdrawn is Burundi, whose president, Pierre Nkurunziza, hopes to avoid criminal charges for his brutal repression of opposition to his amending constitutional term limits on his tenure. The UN Human Rights Council repudiated Nkurunziza's quest for immunity by reaffirming UN scrutiny of Burundi's rights record by a vote of 23 to 7 with 17 abstentions.

China

Multilateral pressure also began building on the Chinese government, which represents a dangerous challenge to human rights not only because of the severity of its repression—the worst since the violent suppression of the Tiananmen Square democracy movement of 1989—but also because it represents an autocrat's dream: the prospect of long-term power and economic gain without human rights, democracy, or the rule of law.

But the last year saw greater scrutiny of the downside of such unaccountable government. Some critics focused on Chinese authorities' mass-surveillance ambitions—the deployment of systems that use facial-recognition software, artificial intelligence, and big data to more effectively monitor the population and predict, among other things, political loyalty. International businesses also came under growing pressure not to become complicit in these intrusive practices.

The issue receiving the most attention was the Chinese government's mass arbitrary detention for "re-education" of upwards of 1 million Muslims in the Xinjiang region, mostly ethnic Uyghurs, to force them to disown their Muslim faith and ethnic identity. This brainwashing effort is not limited to China's burgeoning detention facilities: the government has deployed some 1 million officials to live in Muslims' homes and spy on them to ensure their political and cultural loyalty.

In response, China faced tough questions from many countries during a periodic review at the UN Human Rights Council, and a coalition of 15 Western ambassadors, spearheaded by Canada, sought to challenge Xinjiang's party secretary, Chen Quanguo, over these abuses. Speaking to the Human Rights Council just one week after her appointment, the new UN high commissioner for human rights, former Chilean President Michelle Bachelet, expressed concern at the crackdown on Uyghurs and called for access to the region.

However, having come to the defense of Muslims persecuted by Myanmar, the 57 Muslim-majority countries of the OIC at time of writing had yet to speak out in defense of China's Muslims, other than Turkey raising the issue at the UN and Malaysia's Anwar Ibrahim, the leader of the country's ruling coalition, speaking publicly about it.

Immigration and Asylum

In the West, the most divisive issue seized upon by autocratic politicians was immigration, even in such places as Poland and eastern Germany that have relatively few immigrants. Some centrist politicians calculated that the best way to defeat this autocratic threat was to ape it, even at the cost of mainstreaming its rhetoric of hate and divisiveness. That strategy failed miserably, for example, for Germany's interior minister, Horst Seehofer, whose Christian Social Union fared poorly in elections in its Bavarian home, while the far right gained. By contrast, the most outspoken German opponents of the far right, the Greens, enjoyed unprecedented success. The results of local elections in the Netherlands and Belgium and general elections in Luxembourg sent similar messages.

But the pushback against the xenophobic response to immigration—and the Islamophobia that often accompanied it—was not as strong as needed. European governments, for example, have expended too little energy assessing policies that have poorly integrated longstanding immigrant communities. That failure, in turn, facilitates the demonizing of newcomers. Instead, European leaders sought to close their borders even to asylum seekers, who are entitled to an opportunity to make the case that they deserve protection.

They also sought to make it easier to deny asylum even to those who do arrive, on the grounds they could have sought protection in a country outside the EU that it considers "safe," even though many lack the capacity to process asylum claims or to provide effective protection. And the deportations of migrants who arrived seeking economic opportunities, who mostly have no right to enter or remain, were often not conducted humanely or safely. Hungary, Bulgaria, Croatia, Poland, Spain, and Greece forced people back to non-EU countries, in some cases violently. Italy led efforts to get the Libyan Coast Guard to return migrants to nightmarish conditions of detention in Libya and blocked humanitarian rescue efforts in the Mediterranean Sea, apparently with the callous hope that more drownings at sea would deter further migration. The EU also enlisted problematic governments such as Sudan and Mali to reduce the number of migrants and asylum seekers reaching Europe.

In the United States, President Trump used the perceived threat of a caravan of asylum seekers fleeing Central American violence to mobilize his political base just before the US congressional elections. He went so far as to deploy 5,000 US troops along the Mexican border in a wasteful political stunt. He also ordered the separation of immigrant children from their parents and illegally restricted the right of asylum seekers to present their case upon arrival at the border.

Despite widespread criticism of the family separation policy, Trump's political opponents largely failed to articulate an alternative positive vision on immigration—for example, one that distinguishes between long-time immigrants who have effectively become Americans in all but papers (often with US citizen children and spouses and established places in the workplace and the community) and recent arrivals who are not seeking asylum and typically have no strong claim to stay.

Despite the divisiveness of US politics, a broad consensus for immigration reform has been forged in the past, so it should be possible to articulate a vision that facilitates strong border enforcement while respecting asylum for refugees and the human equities that should protect most long-term immigrants from deportation.

Beyond an Anniversary

The challenges of the past year arose as the world celebrated the 70th anniversary of the Universal Declaration of Human Rights—as well as the 20th anniversary of the treaty founding the ICC and the 40th anniversary of Human Rights Watch. Clearly this is no moment for complacency. Just as human rights standards have become deeply entrenched as a way of measuring how governments treat their people, human rights are under threat.

Despite the unfavorable winds, the past year shows that defending human rights remains a worthy imperative. When governments see political or economic advantage in violating rights, rights defenders still can raise the price of abuse and shift the cost-benefit calculus to convince governments that repression does not pay. The terrain for the fight has shifted, with many long-time participants missing in action or even switching sides. But effective coalitions have emerged to oppose governments that are not accountable to their people and respectful of their rights. With this report, Human Rights Watch seeks to expand this re-energized global defense of a rights-respecting future.

HUMAN
RIGHTS
WATCH

"By Day We Fear the Army,
By Night the Jihadists"

Abuses by Armed Islamists and Security Forces in Burkina Faso

WORLD REPORT

2019

COUNTRIES

HUMAN
RIGHTS
WATCH

"No Safe Place"
Insurgent Attacks on Civilians in Afghanistan

Afghanistan

As military operations by insurgents, international, and government forces in Afghanistan intensified in 2018, insurgent attacks in urban areas sharply increased. The widening armed conflict killed or injured more than 10,000 civilians between January and December. Insurgents targeting civilians and carrying out indiscriminate attacks were responsible for the vast majority of these, but an increase in airstrikes by US and Afghan forces also caused hundreds of civilian casualties during the year. Neither the US nor the Afghan governments conducted adequate investigations into airstrikes that represented possible war crimes.

Although the Afghan government acceded to the United Nations Optional Protocol to the Convention against Torture in April 2018, it failed to hold police and National Directorate of Security (NDS) personnel accountable for systematic torture, extrajudicial executions, and enforced disappearances. Entrenched impunity for perpetrators of violence against women meant that girls and women still rarely saw justice in courts, as prosecutors and police pressured them to accept mediation rather than prosecution of their assailants. For the first time since 2002, the number of children in school fell; 60 percent of Afghan girls were not in school during the year.

Widespread violence marked preparations for the October parliamentary elections, with insurgents carrying out numerous attacks on candidates and facilities used for voter registration, including schools. Targeted attacks on voters, roadways, and poll facilities on election days killed or injured over 400 civilians. Evidence of fraud and vote-buying undermined the credibility of the parliamentary elections, and cast doubt on prospects for credible presidential elections in 2019. The worst drought in decades and the deportation of thousands of Afghans from Iran added to the hundreds of thousands internally displaced by conflict, taxing existing humanitarian aid resources.

Violations of International Humanitarian Law

The Islamic State of Khorasan Province (ISKP), the Afghan branch of the Islamic State (the extremist armed group, also known as ISIS), sharply escalated its attacks in urban areas, including bombings that targeted Afghanistan's minority Shia population.

Dasht-e Barchi, a predominantly Shia neighborhood of western Kabul, suffered multiple attacks during 2018: on August 15, a bombing at a university preparatory course killed 34 and injured 70, many of them children; on September 6, twin bombings at a sports club in Kabul killed at least 20 civilians. ISKP also increasingly attacked humanitarian and healthcare facilities: a suicide attack on January 24 on the Save the Children office in Jalalabad killed six civilians and injured 27; an attack on a midwife training school on July 28 killed three; and a July 31 attack on the Nangarhar province's refugee office killed 13. ISKP also targeted media: on April 30, a suicide bomber posing as a cameraman blew himself up among journalists who were reporting on an earlier suicide attack, killing nine. Two Tolo TV news reporters covering the September 6 bombing in Dasht-e Barchi were killed by a second suicide attack.

The Taliban claimed to target only Afghan government and foreign military facilities, but they used indiscriminate means that killed and injured hundreds of civilians. In the deadliest incident, on January 28, 2018, a Taliban car bomb disguised as an ambulance killed over 100 in Kabul. A Taliban attack on a NATO convoy in Kandahar on April 30, killed 11 children at a nearby school. The Taliban were believed to be responsible for a car bomb near a sports facility in Lashkar Gah, Helmand province, that killed 15 civilians and injured 40 on March 23. That incident launched the Helmand Peace March, a group of survivors and relatives of victims of suicide bombings and airstrikes who began walking across Afghanistan, stopping in cities along the way, to call for an end to the war. As of November, they had reached Mazar-e-Sharif, more than 500 kilometers from where they had started.

Air operations by US forces and the Afghan Air Force (AAF) killed and injured over 600 civilians. On April 2, AAF helicopters strafed a madrasa graduation ceremony in northern Kunduz province, killing 30 children and injuring 51. An airstrike in Chardara district, Kunduz province in July, reportedly killed 14 members of one family, including five women and seven children aged 2 to 14. The US conducted only internal reviews of a limited number of incidents of civilian casualties, and did not carry out site visits or interview witnesses. The Afghan government carried out few internal reviews of incidents causing civilian casualties. During a six-day Taliban assault on Ghazni city, both insurgents and

government security forces launched indiscriminate attacks in densely populated areas, killing and injuring more than 300 civilians.

Afghan special forces conducting search operations and night raids were responsible for summary executions. During the raid of a Taliban stronghold in
Maiwand village, Kandahar province, Afghan special forces reportedly executed
20 civilians on the night of January 31, 2018. NDS helicopter units shot dead
eight farmers in their fields in Chaparhar district, Nangarhar province, on March
17.

On April 30, unidentified gunmen shot dead Ahmad Shah, a BBC reporter in
Khost, who had written critical articles about the CIA-controlled Khost Protection
Force, a counterinsurgency militia that operates under CIA control. No one was
held accountable for any of these killings.

Election-Related Violence

Both the Taliban and ISKP carried out attacks on election facilities and threatened election staff. On April 22, an ISKP suicide bomber killed 69 and injured
138, many of them women and children, at a voter registration center in the predominantly Shia neighborhood of Dasht-e Barchi. An ISKP bombing at a voter
registration center in Khost killed at least 14 civilians on May 6. On July 1, ISKP
attacked a delegation from the minority Hindu and Sikh communities that was
meeting the governor in Jalalabad, killing 19—10 from Afghanistan's Sikh community, including the sole Sikh parliamentary candidate.

On April 18, as voter registration began across Afghanistan, the Taliban issued a
statement denouncing the elections and warning people not to participate. The
UN Assistance Mission to Afghanistan (UNAMA) reported that on April 23, Taliban officials in Alishang district, Laghman province, warned community elders
that anyone who registered to vote would face serious consequences. However,
the elders told the Taliban not to interfere in the process. On May 3, Taliban
forces in Mardyan district, Jawzjan province, abducted and threatened to kill 20
election staff members, releasing 17 after they agreed not to work on the elections. The fate of the other three was unknown at time of writing.

There were multiple attacks by the Taliban across Afghanistan on the election
days of October 20-21, which killed and injured more than 400 civilians.

Women's and Girls' Rights

Entrenched impunity for perpetrators of violence against women continued. Police routinely refuse to register cases, instead telling women who have been the victims of domestic violence to return to their husbands. In May 2018, UNAMA reported that even cases of murder and rape often never reach the courts. Afghan authorities routinely turn victims away or pressure them to accept mediation, a process in which the abuser merely promises not to repeat the crime. UNAMA also reviewed murders of women in so-called honor killings; the vast majority of these were never prosecuted but instead settled through mediation.

Despite a 2016 pledge from President Ashraf Ghani to end the imprisonment of women accused of running away from their families, in 2018 Afghan police and prosecutors continued to jail women and girls for "moral crimes" that include "running away" from home, and committing or attempting to commit *zina* (sex outside of marriage).

Police and prosecutors also continued to subject girls and women to invasive and scientifically invalid vaginal and anal examinations by Afghan government doctors, purportedly to determine whether a woman or girl is a virgin. Afghan officials claim the government banned the examinations, but officials told Human Rights Watch that the practice remains widespread, with many judges, prosecutors, and police officials routinely ordering "virginity tests."

Women with disabilities in Afghanistan face formidable obstacles gaining access to education and health care. In interviews with Human Rights Watch in March and June 2018, women with disabilities reported being sexually harassed when seeking assistance from the Ministry of Labor, Social Affairs, Martyrs and Disabled. Although the ministry offered limited financial assistance to those injured in the conflict, psychosocial services for survivors or people with disabilities are extremely limited.

Torture

A June 2018 report by the Afghanistan Independent Human Rights Commission noted that while Afghanistan had ratified the UN Optional Protocol on the Convention against Torture, enacted legislation criminalizing torture, and established a government commission on torture, the government had not significantly reduced torture since it assumed office in 2014, and did not prosecute any senior officials accused of torture.

On July 22, First Vice President Abdul Rashid Dostum returned to Afghanistan after more than a year abroad evading charges on the abduction, illegal imprisonment, and sexual assault of a rival Uzbek politician, Ahmad Ishchi. Although a Kabul criminal court, in 2017, convicted seven of Dostum's bodyguards in absentia of sexual assault and illegal imprisonment, and sentenced them to five years in prison, none had been imprisoned at time of writing.

A report by Integrity Watch Afghanistan in late 2017 documented inhumane conditions in Afghan prisons and detention centers, with severe overcrowding and insufficient toilets, potable water, mattresses, and other facilities. Through the first half of 2018, prisoners in Pul-e-Charkhi prison carried out a hunger strike to protest conditions. The situation remained particularly poor for female prisoners, many of whom have been imprisoned for so-called morality crimes and who are often imprisoned with their children, far from home.

In Afghanistan, same-sex relations are punishable by 5 to 15 years in prison under a law that bans all sex between unmarried individuals.

Access to and Attacks on Education, Military Recruitment of Children

According to UNAMA, in 2018 schools and mosques used for voter registration were the target of dozens of attacks by insurgents, particularly ISKP.

On May 2, 2018, Taliban officials in Shrana district, Paktika province, warned teachers that they would target schools used for elections purposes. As of October, many schools in the district remained closed. In June in Nangarhar province, ISKP forced 80 girls' schools to close in retaliation for US and AAF airstrikes; some schools remained closed during the October 20 elections. The group also attacked the provincial education office in Jalalabad on July 11, 2018, killing 11 and injuring 17. In March 2018, the Taliban closed 29 schools in Logar province in retaliation for an attack by pro-government militias on one of their commanders' houses. Although the government, in 2016, criminalized military recruitment of Afghans under 18 years old, the practice continued, notably among the

Afghan Local Police (ALP) and pro-government militias. UNAMA also documented recruitment of child soldiers by ISKP and Taliban.

A June 2018 UNICEF report found that for the first time since 2002, the number of Afghan children in school was falling, with girls most affected. Up to 3.7 million children in Afghanistan—nearly half the children in the country—are out of school, compared with 3.5 million in 2016, 60 percent of them girls. In many provinces, fewer than 15 percent of students are girls.

Government and insurgent forces also continued to use schools for military purposes.

Key International Actors

Under the Trump administration's South Asia strategy, announced in 2017, US troop levels increased to 15,000, including an elite brigade of 800 military advisers who deployed with Afghan forces in March. The US expanded airstrikes and covert drone attacks, releasing over 5,000 bombs and missiles in Afghanistan between January and November, the highest number since 2011.

The US agreed for the first time to participate in direct talks on a peace settlement with the Taliban; a meeting between Taliban officials and Alice Wells, US principal deputy assistant secretary for South and Central Asia, took place in Doha in July.

Although President Ghani told donor countries in 2017 that the torture and rape case involving Vice President Dostum was a make-or-break challenge for his government to demonstrate that it would prosecute officials accused of human rights violations, only Norway and the European Union issued statements about the need to conclude proceedings against Dostum after he returned to Kabul but faced no legal consequences.

In December 2017, the European Parliament expressed concern about the deteriorating security situation in Afghanistan, and called on governments to refrain from repatriating Afghans. In May 2018, the EU deployed a team of international police experts to work with Afghanistan's Ministry of Interior Affairs and National Security Council staff.

The actions of Australian special forces who served in Uruzgan province in 2006-2013, came under investigation by a special war crimes inquiry headed by New

South Wales Supreme Court Judge Paul Brereton. The alleged crimes include summary executions and abuses against Afghan civilians.

In November 2017, the prosecutor of the International Criminal Court (ICC) had asked the court's judges for permission to open an investigation into possible war crimes and crimes against humanity committed by the Taliban, Afghan government forces, and US forces since May 1, 2003, when Afghanistan became a member of the court. On September 10, the US threatened to punish individuals who cooperated with the ICC in a potential investigation of US wartime actions in Afghanistan.

Algeria

2018 saw no overall improvement in human rights conditions in Algeria. Authorities curtailed free speech and the rights to freedom of association, assembly, and peaceful protest, and arrested and prosecuted bloggers and human rights activists under various charges such as "inciting an unauthorized gathering," "intelligence with a foreign country," and defamation of public officials. Authorities also deported thousands of migrants without due process, and prosecuted members of the Ahmadiyya religious minority on charges related to the exercise of their religion.

Authorities continued to block the legal registration of Algerian human rights nongovernmental organizations and maintained its non-acceptance of country visits requests from several United Nations human rights experts and mechanisms, such as the special rapporteurs on torture and on freedom of peaceful assembly and of association, and the UN Working Groups on Enforced or Involuntary Disappearances and on Arbitrary Detention.

Freedom of Assembly

Authorities continued to routinely violate the right to freedom of assembly. The penal code punishes organizing or participating in an unauthorized demonstration in a public place with up to one year in prison (article 98).

A court in the city of Ghardaia in October 2017 filed various charges against six human rights and political activists for protesting in front of the courthouse the trial of a human rights lawyer in 2016. On June 26, the court acquitted them of all the charges.

Throughout August and September, the authorities blocked meetings planned for Algiers, Constantine, and Bejaia organized by the Mouwatana movement, a group that presses for democratic reforms and opposes a fifth term for President Abdelaziz Bouteflika.

Freedom of Association

A 2012 law on associations, requires associations, even if they have successfully registered previously, to apply anew for a registration receipt from the Interior Ministry in order to operate legally.

On February 27, 2018, Algerian authorities sealed the premises of two women's rights associations, the Feminist Association for Personal Development and Exercise of Citizenship (Association Fèministe pour l'Epanouisement de la Personne et l'Exercice de la Citoyennetè, AFEPEC) and Algerian Women Claiming their Rights (Femmes Algériennes Revendiquant leurs Droits, FARD), on the pretext that they were not registered. Authorities had issued neither a receipt for their re-registration, leaving them in legal limbo. A week later, authorities provisionally permitted the organizations to resume work. On May 20, an administrative court ordered the governor to issue FARD a registration receipt, which it did in September 29.

Other associations such as the Algerian League for Human Rights (Ligue Algérienne de Défense des Droits de l'Homme, LADDH), Youth Action Rally (Rassemblement Action Jeunesse, RAJ), Algeria's Amnesty International section, are among formerly registered associations whose applications for re-registration received no answer.

Freedom of Speech

On June 21, an appeals court in Bejaia sentenced blogger Merzoug Touati to seven years in prison for incitement to an illegal gathering, for urging public protests against a new finance law, and for "intelligence with a foreign country aiming at harming Algeria." The latter charge relates to an interview he published with an Israeli government spokesperson. Touati has been held since January 22, 2017, in Oued Ghir prison in Bejaia.

The appeals court in Relizane, on June 6, upheld a two-year prison sentence against blogger Abdullah Benaoum for social media publications accusing the authorities and the Algerian army of being responsible for several massacres of civilians and the disappearance of thousands during the internal armed conflict of the 1990s. The charges were based both on penal code articles prohibiting the defamation of public institutions and article 46 of the Charter for Peace and

National Reconciliation, which prohibits exploiting the wounds of the "'National Tragedy' to harm the institutions of Algeria" or tarnish its image internationally. Benaoum was serving his term at time of writing.

On August 7, 2018, a court in Ghardaia sentenced Salim Yezza, a blogger and member of the Rally for Amazigh in France, to a suspended one-year prison term on charges of inciting a public gathering and disseminating calls to hatred and discrimination for a Facebook post he wrote in 2014 criticizing government discrimination against the Mozabites, who are part of Algeria's Amazigh ethnic population. Authorities arrested Yezza on July 14 at the Biskra airport as he was returning to Paris after a visit. He spent three weeks in prison before being released.

Women's Rights

While Algeria's 2015 law on domestic violence criminalized some forms of domestic violence, it contained loopholes that allow convictions to be dropped or sentences reduced if victims pardon their perpetrators. Despite some amendments in 2005 that improved women's access to divorce and child custody, Algeria's Family Code still discriminates against women by requiring them to apply to the courts for a divorce on specified grounds whereas men have a unilateral right to divorce without explanation.

Article 326 of the penal code allows a person who abducts a minor to escape prosecution if he marries his victim. The penal code does not define rape but does refer to it as an attack on honor. During Algeria's fourth periodic review of its obligations under the International Covenant on Civil and Political Rights, the UN Human Rights Committee in July 2018 recommended that Algeria amend its penal code to include a comprehensive definition of rape, repeal article 326, and remove the pardon clauses in the domestic violence law.

Freedom of Religion

Algeria continues to prosecute members of the Ahmadiyya religious minority for the exercise of their faith. More than 315 Ahmadis stood trial between June 2016 and March 2018. Sentences ranged from fines to a year in prison. Authorities frequently discriminate against the Ahmadi community of about 2,000 adherents, prosecuting members of the group for denigrating the dogma or precepts of Islam; participating in an unauthorized association; collecting donations without a license and possessing and distributing documents from foreign sources threatening national security.

Migrants

Since at least December 2016, Algeria has rounded up and expelled en masse thousands of Sub-Saharan migrants, including women and children. In 2018, Algerian authorities continued to raid areas where migrants are known to live, arresting them on the streets or on construction sites, bussing them south and then expelling them at the border with Niger or Mali, in most instances with no food and little water.

Authorities prohibited the Algerian League for the Defense of Human Rights and other associations that have denounced the arbitrary deportations of migrants, from holding an annual National Meeting of the Migratory Platform, set to take place on July 20 and 21 in Oran, because authorities alleged they had no authorization to organize a public event. Algerian NGOs founded the platform in 2015 to enhance the protection of migrants.

Sexual Orientation and Gender Identity

Same-sex relations are punishable under article 338 of the penal code by up two years in prison. At a press conference in September during a visit by German Chancellor Angela Merkel, a journalist asked Prime Minister Ahmed Ouyahia about the rights of homosexuals. Ouyahia replied that "Algerian society has its own traditions, which will continue to evolve according to its values."

Accountability for Past Crimes

During the armed conflict of the 1990s, the security forces, allied militias, and armed Islamist groups battling the government killed more than 100,000, according to estimates, and forcibly disappeared several thousand whose fate remains unknown.

The 2006 law implementing the Charter on Peace and National Reconciliation granted legal immunity to perpetrators of grave abuses. It also criminalized acts of speech that "denigrate" state institutions or security forces in relation to their conduct during that conflict.

The law promised compensation for families of "disappeared" persons but brought them no closer to learning what happened to their missing relatives.

Key International Actors

During its fourth Periodic Review of Algeria in July, the UN Human Rights Committee pressed Algeria to open serious investigations into forced disappearances, halt arbitrary detention and expulsion of migrants and refugees, release and compensate all persons imprisoned for exercising their right to freedom of expression, and end discrimination against religious minorities, among other recommendations.

In April 2018, the UN committee that reviews compliance of states with the International Convention on the Protection of the Rights of All Migrant Workers and Members of Their Families recommended that Algeria prohibit collective expulsions and deportations of migrants and members of their families. It also recommended that Algeria ensure migrants facing deportation the right to challenge the measure.

Angola

Angola registered significant progress on various fronts in 2018, as the political and civil rights environment became less restrictive, and the courts appeared to operate without political interference. Authorities continued to forcibly evict people without the necessary procedural protections or the provision of alternative housing or adequate compensation.

Security forces were implicated in extrajudicial killings and other serious human rights violations. The lesbian, gay, bisexual, and transgender (LGBT) movement celebrated the legalization of the country's only gay rights lobby group. President João Lourenço launched an anti-corruption campaign that led to the arrest and investigation of several former government and ruling party officials, including relatives of former President Jose Eduardo Dos Santos.

Extrajudicial Killings

Angolan security forces were implicated in several cases of extrajudicial killings of young men suspected of crimes. In June, footage recorded by a woman who said she witnessed an incident of extrajudicial killing showed an agent of the Angola Criminal Investigation Service (SIC) firing several shots at a criminal suspect. On June 1, the Angolan Ministry of Interior confirmed the incident recorded on the video, condemning the action as "ignoble" and pledged to take disciplinary actions against the agents.

Earlier in February, investigative journalist and human rights activist Rafael Marques published a report documenting over 50 cases of extrajudicial executions by Angolan security forces. In response, the government promised to investigate. The outcome of the investigations, if any, have not been made public.

Arbitrary Arrests

Angolan police continued to arbitrarily arrest peaceful protesters and activists. On February 3, police arrested and accused five men of plotting to kill the deputy president, Bornito de Sousa, after they parked their car near his official residence.

On April 4, three youth activists were arrested after allegedly participating in a protest against the governor of Malange province during a visit of the vice president to the province. Police accused them of throwing stones at the vice president's convoy. On April 9, the Malange Provincial court sentenced the three activists to seven months in prison. In July, the Angola Supreme Court ruled that there was insufficient evidence to prove that the three were involved in throwing stones at the vice president's convoy.

On August 10, police arrested 13 separatists agitating for the independence of the oil-rich enclave of Cabinda, during a meeting in Cabinda to organize a public debate on the enclave's autonomy. A week later, a court acquitted the group of charges of crimes against state security, ruling that the meeting was not illegal.

Housing Rights

Angolan authorities continued to forcibly evict people without the necessary procedural guarantees or the provision of alternative housing or adequate compensation. In May, Human Rights Watch wrote a letter to the president urging him to stop the forced evictions. In response, the Ministry of Justice claimed that evictions in Angola only occur in a judicial manner and that the government had made efforts to properly resettle residents who have built housing units in state's land reserves. However, Human Rights Watch has documented cases that contradict the government. For example, on July 4, police fired live bullets against residents of a neighborhood in Viana, in the capital, Luanda, during a protest against demolitions, killing a pregnant woman. Four other people were injured by bullets allegedly fired by police. According to Angolan nongovernmental organization SOS Habitat, on August 1, police shot and wounded an 18-year-old man and detained four people without charge during a peaceful protest against house demolitions in Viana.

Freedom of the Media and Expression

On July 6, a court in Luanda acquitted investigative journalist Rafael Marques and the editor of weekly paper *O Crime*, Mariano Bras, on accusations of insulting the state, a ruling that was considered a huge victory for press freedom in a country where media have often been the target of government repression. The two journalists had been charged on June 21, 2017, with "outrage to a body of sovereignty and injury against public authority," under Angola's Law on Crimes against State Security, after publishing an article about an alleged illegal land acquisition involving the attorney general, João Maria de Sousa. State prosecutors could not convince the court that the journalists acted in bad faith and violated the ethical principles of journalism.

Despite this ruling, Angolan journalists continued to work under a repressive media law signed in January 2017, introduced by the administration of former President Dos Santos. In response to Human Rights Watch's concerns over the law and defamation clauses, the Angolan government said in a July 18 letter that the limitations imposed by the law only intend to protect the interests, honor, and good name of citizens who have been affected, and it cannot be interpreted that the government has the intention to violate or restrict the right to freedom of expression.

Sexual Orientation and Gender Identity

In June, the Angolan government gave legal status to Iris Angola, the country's only gay rights lobby group, which was established in 2013. Iris Angola has often complained that its members face discrimination accessing health and education services, mainly because of the lack of recognition from the state institutions. The group called the decision an "historic moment" that will allow the organization to defend the rights of homosexuals in Angola. Angola is currently revising its penal code and may scrap the article that characterizes homosexuality as "vices against nature." The country inherited the penal code from the colonial era but there are no public records of law enforcement reinforcing the homosexuality laws.

In September, the Angolan Ministry of Health organized a meeting in Luanda to discuss the country National Strategy for HIV, with a special focus on the LGBT community.

Fight Against Corruption

Angola law enforcement delivered the first results of the anti-corruption campaign launched by President Lourenco, with several officials linked to former president Dos Santos being arrested and investigated. On September 19, the

Supreme Court ordered that Norberto Garcia, the former spokesman of the ruling MPLA party and former director of the defunct Technical Unit for Private Investment, a state institution, be placed under house arrest in Luanda. He was charged with fraud, money laundering and document falsification in March 2018. The case dates back to November 2017 when Garcia and six foreigners were said to have tried to set up a fake state project worth US$50 million.

On September 21, former transport minister Augusto Tomas was arrested on charges of embezzlement and corruption. On September 24, Jose Filomeno dos Santos, son of former President Dos Santos and the former head of Angola's sovereign fund, was arrested in Luanda, on accusations of misappropriation of $1.5 billion of public funds. His business partner, Jean-Claude Bastos de Morais, was also arrested on a charge of misappropriating over a $500 million, with the help of the former governor of the National Bank of Angola, Valter Filipe, who is under investigation.

Treatment of Migrants

In October, Angola expelled over 400,000 largely Congolese migrants, who thereafter sought refuge mostly in the Kasai, Kasai Central, and Kwango provinces of the Democratic Republic of Congo. The mass expulsion was a result of "Operation Transparency," reportedly aimed at reducing diamond smuggling, as part of President Lourenço's drive to diversify the economy. Angolan authorities said the smuggling and illegal mining were organized and controlled by "irregular migrants," with no evidence to back up this claim. Many Congolese migrants targeted in the operation accused the Angolan forces of killing dozens of people, burning down homes, looting property, and using excessive force. They also described an environment of fear and intimidation following the expulsion.

Key International Actors

In June, then-United Kingdom Foreigner Secretary Boris Johnson revealed on Twitter that Angola had expressed interest in joining the Commonwealth. He welcomed the decision and President Lourenço's commitment to long-term reform, tackling corruption, and improving human rights. In August, the International Monetary Fund (IMF) confirmed that Angola had requested talks on a bailout in return for more structural reforms. The IMF did not specify if the reforms would include human rights and rule of law. Also in August, President Lourenço visited Germany, where he reiterated his country's plans to purchase German warships. The Berlin visit agenda was mostly focused on business, but German Chancellor Angela Merkel offered to assist Angola's reform process.

In September, UN Secretary-General António Guterres held a meeting with Lourenço during the Forum on China-Africa Cooperation (FOCAC) in Beijing. During the meeting, Guterres highlighted the role of Angola in the effort to maintain peace and stability in Southern Africa and the Great Lakes region.

In October, UN High Commissioner for Human Rights Michelle Bachelet condemned the mass deportation of Congolese nationals from Angola.

Argentina

Long-standing human rights problems in Argentina include police abuse, poor prison conditions, endemic violence against women, and obstacles keeping indigenous people from enjoying the rights that Argentine and international law afford them. Restrictions on abortion and difficulty accessing reproductive services remain serious concerns; an attempt in 2018 to decriminalize abortion did not pass the Senate.

Impunity for the 1994 bombing of the AMIA Jewish center in Buenos Aires, vaguely defined criminal provisions that undermine free speech, and delays in appointing permanent judges are other concerns.

Argentina continues to make significant progress protecting lesbian, gay, bisexual, and transgender (LGBT) rights and prosecuting officials for abuses committed during the country's last military dictatorship (1976-1983), although trials have been delayed.

Confronting Past Abuses

As of November 2018, the Attorney General's Office reported 3,007 people charged, 867 convicted, and 110 acquitted of crimes allegedly committed by Argentina's last military junta. Of 599 cases alleging crimes against humanity, judges had issued rulings in 203.

Prosecutions were made possible by a series of actions taken in the early 2000s by Congress, the Supreme Court, and federal judges annulling amnesty laws and striking down pardons of former officials implicated in the crimes. As of November 2018, 128 people who were illegally taken from their parents as children during the 1976-1983 dictatorship had been identified. Many were reunited with their families.

In May, an appeals court upheld the criminal conviction of 12 people accused of participating in Operation Condor, a regional strategy to coordinate repressive efforts by dictatorships in several Latin American countries. They were sentenced to up to 25 years in prison for participating in an illicit association that kidnapped 103 people.

The large number of victims, suspects, and cases makes it difficult for prosecutors and judges to bring those responsible to justice while respecting their due process rights. Argentine law allows judges to send inmates age 70 and older to serve their time under house arrest. The Attorney General's Office reported in September that 641 pretrial detainees and convicted prisoners were under house arrest. In 2016, the government said it would not appeal judicial rulings granting house arrest to pretrial detainees and convicted prisoners.

Freedom of Expression

In January 2016, police detained Milagro Sala, a prominent social leader in Jujuy province, in connection with her participation in street protests. Sala and others had gathered in the provincial capital to protest a decree the governor had issued purporting to regulate organizations like Sala's, which implement government-funded housing and other welfare programs.

Sala was charged with instigating protesters to commit crimes and with sedition. Sala was also under investigation for alleged corruption. In August 2018, the Supreme Court ordered that Sala, whom a local judge had ordered returned from house arrest to prison, be returned to house arrest. The ruling cited provisional measures that the Inter-American Court of Human Rights (IACHR) had issued in her favor in November 2017.

In April 2017, the Argentine government committed to reforming the criminal code to modify and narrow the definition of sedition. However, it had yet to present a formal proposal to Congress at time of writing.

Upon taking office, President Mauricio Macri adopted a temporary set of decrees to regulate media and created a temporary agency to implement the new rules. The agency reports to the Modernization Ministry and so is not independent from the executive branch, compromising its ability to act independently from government interests. In 2016, the government said it was drafting a communications law that it claimed would respect free speech. At time of writing, the law had not been presented to Congress and the supposedly temporary agency had issued rulings regulating media.

In 2016, the Macri administration issued a resolution establishing transparent criteria to prevent favoritism in government purchases of media advertising. In

2017, the president appointed the head of a national agency to ensure public access to information held by government bodies, implementing a 2016 law approved by Congress. The agency is also charged with protecting personal data. Between September 2017, when the law entered into force, and October 2018, the number of information requests reached 3,582.

Authorities responded to most requests within a month, but citizens filed 204 appeals before the agency, in most cases after authorities failed to respond to the original requests. However, some provinces and municipalities lack freedom of information laws, undermining transparency at those levels of government.

Prison Conditions and Abuses by Security Forces

Overcrowding, ill-treatment by guards, inadequate facilities, and inmate violence continue in Argentina's prisons. The National Penitentiary Office, which Congress created in 2003 to supervise federal prisons and protect detainees' rights, reported the violent deaths of six federal prisoners during the first semester of 2018, but did not identify the individuals responsible. The office also documented 301 alleged cases of torture or ill-treatment in federal prisons between January and June 2018, after 615 cases in 2017.

In December 2017, the federal government created the National Committee to Prevent Torture, charged with monitoring the situation of people in detention.

In July 2018, the UN Working Group on Arbitrary Detention (UNWAD) reported that police forces often conduct criminal arrests in a discriminatory and subjective manner. Approximately 60 percent of all people behind bars in Argentina are in pretrial detention, and the period of such detention sometimes lasts up to six years. Largely due to overcrowding, some pretrial detainees are being held in police stations. Prison guards have taken "disobedient" detainees to isolation cells without following predetermined sanction procedures. Security forces have detained children and subjected them to abuse.

Police and other security forces occasionally employ excessive force against protesters, despite a 2011 commitment by authorities in at least 19 of Argentina's 23 provinces to ensure that force is used proportionately.

In September, a court sentenced six policemen to up to 10-and-a-half years in prison for the arbitrary arrest and torture of two teenagers in 2016. The officers had detained the two, 15- and 18-years-old at the time, while they walked in a low-income community in Buenos Aires. One of them told the court the officers severely beat him on the back and head, kicked him as he was lying on the floor, and threatened to kill him while placing a knife at his throat.

In February, Security Minister Patricia Bullrich said the government would modify the criminal code to protect police officers who shoot at a person they believe to be committing a crime. The minister claimed that all actions by police officers should be "presumed" legal. The minister's pledge followed a well-known case in which an officer killed a man who was running away after stabbing a tourist in Buenos Aires. At time of writing, the proposal had not been filed.

In July, President Macri announced the Armed Forces would "collaborate in interior security" operations linked to combatting drug trafficking at Argentina's borders. He later adopted a decree outlining a new defense policy that includes some vague language that would, for example, allow the Armed Forces to respond to threats that do not come from another state and to protect unspecified "strategic objectives." Defense Minister Oscar Aguad said troops would not be deployed in public security operations.

Judicial Independence

The delayed appointment of permanent judges by the Council of the Judiciary has led to temporary appointments of judges who lack security of tenure, which the Supreme Court ruled in 2015 undermines judicial independence. As of November 2018, 260 of 985 lower-court judgeships remained vacant.

Impunity for the AMIA Bombing

Twenty-three years after the 1994 bombing of the Argentine Israelite Mutual Association (AMIA) in Buenos Aires that killed 85 people and injured more than 300, no one has been convicted of the crime.

The investigation stalled when Iran, which Argentina's judiciary suspects of ordering the attack, refused to allow Argentine investigators to interview Iranian suspects in Argentina. In 2013 Argentina and Iran signed a memorandum of understanding (MOU) that allowed an international commission of jurists to review evidence and question Iranian suspects—but only in Tehran—likely rendering the interviews inadmissible in an Argentine court. A federal court declared the MOU unconstitutional; the Macri administration did not appeal.

Red notices—a form of international arrest warrant—that the Argentine government requested from Interpol to detain several Iranians implicated in the attack remain in force. In September, President Macri called on Iranian authorities to collaborate with the investigations during his speech at the UN General Assembly.

In January 2015, Alberto Nisman, the prosecutor in charge of investigating the bombing, was found dead in his home with a single gunshot wound to the head and a pistol beside him matching the wound. His death came just days after he had filed a criminal complaint accusing then-President Cristina Fernández de Kirchner and her foreign affairs minister of conspiring with Iran to undermine the investigation.

A federal court dismissed Nisman's complaint, but, following an appeal, in 2016 the judiciary ordered the case reopened. In March 2018, an appeals court upheld a decision ordering the pretrial detention of Fernández de Kirchner for her alleged role in the cover-up. It has not been implemented because she has parliamentary immunity as a senator. As of November, courts had not determined whether Nisman's death was suicide or murder.

In 2015, several officials—including former President Carlos Menem, his head of intelligence, and a judge—were put on trial for alleged interference with the initial investigation into the bombing. The trial continued at time of writing.

Indigenous Rights

Indigenous people in Argentina face obstacles in accessing justice, land, education, health care, and basic services. Argentina has failed to fully implement existing laws to protect indigenous peoples' right to free, prior, and informed consent when the government adopts decisions that may affect their rights—a right provided for in international law.

In July, the UNWAD reported that demonstrations by members of indigenous communities had been "violently repressed," that these groups had been subject to abuse by security forces and private security guards, and that members had been detained without respect for their basic rights.

In November 2017, Congress approved a law extending the deadline for completing a survey of indigenous lands to 2021. The survey is being conducted, but slowly.

Women's Rights

Abortion is illegal in Argentina, except in cases of rape or when the life or health of the woman is at risk. But even in such cases, women and girls are sometimes subject to criminal prosecution for seeking abortions and have trouble accessing reproductive services, such as contraception and voluntary sterilization.

In May 2018, a 10-year-old girl who had been raped by her stepfather faced obstacles to obtaining an abortion in Salta province. A decree by the governor only allowed abortion during the first 12 weeks of pregnancy, and a provincial protocol required an interview by a team of psychologists, despite a Supreme Court protocol asserting that a woman's statement that she has been raped is enough to allow an abortion. Although the governor lifted the decree in response to the public outcry generated by this case and the girl was eventually allowed to have an abortion, the family decided that she should not.

In June, following massive protests, the House of Representatives passed a bill intended to decriminalize abortion completely during the first 14 weeks of pregnancy and, after that period, to allow women and girls to end pregnancies when they are the result of rape, when the life or health of the woman or girl is at risk, or when the fetus suffers from severe conditions not compatible with life outside the womb. The Senate rejected the bill in August.

Despite a 2009 law setting forth comprehensive measures to prevent and punish violence against women, the unpunished killing of women remains a serious concern. The National Registry of Femicides, administered by the Supreme Court, reported 251 femicides—the murder of women based on their gender—but only 12 convictions, in 2017. In May 2018, the Attorney General's Office adopted a special protocol for investigating and prosecuting femicides.

Sexual Orientation and Gender Identity

In 2010, Argentina became the first Latin American country to legalize same-sex marriage. The Civil Marriage Law allows same-sex couples to enter civil mar-

riages and affords them the same legal marital protections as different-sex couples, including adoption rights and pension benefits. Since 2010 more than
18,000 same-sex couples have married nationwide.

Key International Actors and Foreign Policy

In January 2018, the UN Committee on Enforced Disappearances closed its urgent action on the disappearance of Santiago Maldonado, an artisan who had
gone missing in August 2017 while visiting a Mapuche indigenous community in
Chubut province. Community members had told authorities they saw federal security forces take Maldonado away from a demonstration. His body was found
two months later near a local river. Forensic examiners concluded that he had
drowned and his body showed no evidence of abuse. Also in January, the Inter-
American Commission on Human Rights closed the precautionary measures it
had granted requesting that the Argentine government protect Maldonado's life
and physical integrity when he went missing. The criminal investigation into the
circumstances of his death remained open at time of writing.

The UNWAD's July 2018 report on Argentina, based on an in-country visit in 2017,
outlined concrete recommendations to address the abuses against detainees
that it had documented.

President Macri has repeatedly and publicly criticized Venezuela's poor human
rights record and called for the release of its political prisoners. His administration
has allowed Venezuelans to apply for the same permits to stay in Argentina
granted to residents of Mercosur member countries, despite Venezuela's expulsion from the regional trade bloc. The number of Venezuelans moving legally to Argentina has constantly increased since 2014, reaching over 135,000 in October.

Armenia

Former opposition leader Nikol Pashinyan became Armenia's prime minister following weeks of popular protests in April and May 2018 against the outgoing president, Serzh Sargsyan. After serving the maximum two presidential terms, Sargsyan tried to hold onto power by securing his party's backing so he would be elected as prime minister, before he stepped down amid the protests.

Pashinyan inherited a country plagued with corruption and myriad human rights problems, including lack of accountability for law enforcement abuses, domestic violence, violence and discrimination against lesbian, gay, bisexual, and transgender (LGBT) people, lack of access to quality education for children with disabilities, and institutionalization of people with psychosocial and intellectual disabilities. In October, Pashinyan stepped down to trigger snap parliamentary elections, set for December 2018.

Yerevan Municipal Elections

Hayk Marutyan, the candidate from Pashinyan's "My Step" alliance, won a landslide victory in Yerevan's September mayoral election. The former mayor resigned amid strong public pressure in July. Previous elections had been marred by vote-buying and intimidation of public servants and private employees, another theme of the spring's public protests. In September, the parliament adopted a package of bills, initiated by the government, which made buying and selling votes a criminal offense punishable by up to six years' imprisonment.

Accountability for Abuses by Law Enforcement Officials

Armenian authorities have a long record of using excessive force to break up largely peaceful protests, in some cases causing serious injury to protest participants and journalists. The April and May protests were mostly peaceful, but there were sporadic clashes between police and protesters, including on April 16 when police allegedly used stun grenades, leaving 46 people injured, including six policemen. Police also arbitrarily arrested hundreds of protest participants, including protest leader Pashinyan, based on accusations of participation in mass riots or holding rallies in violation of the established rules. They were all released within a few hours or days.

In a commendable move, the new authorities made progress in existing investigations into abuses that had been stalled for years. In June, they brought charges against a policeman accused of seriously ill-treating, in a court basement, four defendants in a trial concerning the violent takeover of a Yerevan police station in July 2016.

Authorities also revived the investigation into the March 2008 deadly clashes between protesters and security forces, that left 10 people dead, including two policemen. The previous investigation was one-sided, with 52 protesters sent to prison. Following the renewed investigation, authorities brought criminal charges against three former high-level officials, including ex-President Robert Kocharyan, and two commanders, Michael Harutyunyan and Yuri Khachaturov, accusing them of attempting to overthrow the constitutional order. A court initially remanded Kocharyan to pretrial detention, but he was released upon appeal, pending completion of the investigation.

In September, authorities suspended the investigation into the July 2016 police violence against protesters. Courts previously convicted 21 protesters, while no officials faced criminal charges. However, in July, authorities brought criminal charges against one policeman for abuse of office. At time of writing, the investigation was pending.

Disability Rights

The government continues to transform some residential institutions for children into community centers and to support family-based care, but these programs do not include children with disabilities on an equal basis with other children. Existing legislation allows for deprivation of legal capacity of persons with psychosocial or intellectual disabilities and there are no supported decision-making mechanisms in place. As a result, some people with disabilities remain in institutions indefinitely.

As a follow up to the May 2017 United Nations (UN) Committee on the Rights of Persons with Disabilities concluding observations, authorities in May informed the committee that the 2018 state budget included funds to support 94 children in 90 foster families, but did not specify how many of those children have disabilities.

Authorities continue to implement their commitment to full inclusive education by 2025. Inclusive education involves children with and without disabilities studying together in community schools. Despite some progress, children with disabilities continue to face segregation and stigma, and do not always receive reasonable accommodation in schools to enable them to study on an equal basis with other children.

Women's Rights

Domestic violence persists as a serious problem in Armenia. According to police, during the first five months of 2018 they recorded 864 incidents of violence against women, of which 223 were cases of domestic violence. Authorities brought charges against 31 persons for domestic violence through July, and courts convicted seven. Women's rights activists believe domestic violence is widely underreported.

In January, a new law on violence in the family entered into force, providing a definition of domestic violence, but including notions of "strengthening traditional values" and "restoring family harmony" as key principles. Women's rights activists raised concerns that those principles could be used to reinforce obsolete and problematic gender roles and stereotypes, and to pressure women to remain in abusive relationships.

In February, the government approved the action plan for the implementation of the law, and in June set up the Council on Prevention of Violence in the Family, the coordination body for policies on prevention of domestic violence. Authorities also drafted relevant decrees regulating requirements for shelter staff members, and for establishing a centralized record on domestic violence cases. At time of writing, the decrees had not been adopted.

Authorities still need to increase the number of shelter spaces and establish state-run shelters, and conduct campaigns to educate the public about the new law, how to file complaints, and the availability of services.

In January, Armenia signed, but still has to ratify, the Council of Europe (CoE) Istanbul Convention on Prevention and Combating Violence against Women and Domestic Violence (Istanbul Convention).

Sexual Orientation and Gender Identity

LGBT people face harassment, discrimination, and violence. Hateful and deroga-tory comments circulated on social media regarding the private visit to the coun-try in May of musician Elton John and his husband.

In August, a crowd of about 30 people attacked nine LGBT activists in a southern Armenian village. The assailants ran after Hayk Hakobyan and his fellow ac-tivists, as they tried to escape, hitting, kicking, throwing stones, and shouting profanities, injuring six. Police questioned several of the attackers. At time of writing, no one had been charged.

Earlier in April, Hakobyan was the victim of another homophobic assault. He re-ported it, but authorities failed to effectively investigate.

The LGBT rights organization PINK Armenia documented physical attacks against at least 17 individuals based on sexual orientation or gender identity between January and August.

New Generation, a nongovernmental organization, had to cancel an LGBT Chris-tian Groups' conference planned in November, amid uproar by the public and government officials over the event.

Fear of discrimination and public disclosure of their sexual orientation prevents many LGBT people from reporting crimes. The criminal code does not recognize homophobia as an aggravating criminal circumstance, and a government bill on equality does not include sexual orientation and gender identity as grounds for protection from discrimination.

Openly gay men fear for their physical security in the military, and some seek ex-emption from serving in the army. An exemption, however, requires a medical conclusion finding them "psychologically or mentally unfit" to serve. In Armenia, a finding of "psychological or mental disorder" could be an obstacle to employ-ment or obtaining a driver's license.

Key International Actors

In April, Armenia's parliament ratified the European Union-Armenia Comprehen-sive and Enhanced Partnership Agreement, signed in November 2017, triggering its provisional application as of June 1. The agreement aims to strengthen political dialogue, increase economic cooperation, and promote reforms, including on human rights and the rule of law.

In June, the EU published an assessment report on EU-Armenia relations in the framework of the European Neighbourhood Policy, welcoming some progress, particularly "improvements on the respect of human rights and on checks and balances" as part of the 2015 constitutional reforms. The EU assessment also highlighted ill-treatment and police abuse, disproportionate use of force by the police against peaceful demonstrators, lack of a mechanism to protect LGBT rights, inequality and a gender gap, and overrepresentation of children with disabilities in residential institutions.

In his April report, the UN special rapporteur on right to health, Dainius Pūras, noted the need to provide legal protection against discrimination in healthcare services regardless of health status, sexual orientation, and gender identity. Among other things, he urged Armenian authorities to introduce comprehensive infrastructure for the healthcare of children with disabilities to support families, instead of large institutions for children. He also called on authorities to stop prioritizing investments in large psychiatric hospitals and residential institutions for people with mental health conditions, and increase investments in alternative mental health services.

In its May 2017 combined periodic report on Armenia, the United Nations Committee on the Elimination of Racial Discrimination welcomed the constitutional reform, and urged authorities to further amend the legislation to bring it in line with the Convention on Elimination of Racial Discrimination, including by introducing a new definition of hate crime in state law, and reviewing the quota system to allow for greater representation of minorities in parliament.

During a September visit, CoE Human Rights Commissioner Dunja Mijatovic called on the government to guarantee legal capacity, phase out institutions, and ensure quality, inclusive education for persons with disabilities.

A joint declaration following the Francophonie summit hosted by Armenia in October reiterated the member states' commitments to the protection of human rights, rule of law, and gender equality.

Australia

Australia has a strong record of protecting civil and political rights, but serious human rights issues remain. In 2018, the government continued to hold refugees and asylum seekers who arrived by boat in Australian waters on Manus Island in Papua New Guinea and on Nauru, marking more than five years since the reintroduction of its draconian offshore processing and settlement policy.

In October, the Queensland government introduced a human rights act, becoming the third jurisdiction in Australia to do so behind the Australian Capital Territory and Victoria.

Asylum Seekers and Refugees

At time of writing, 570 refugees and asylum seekers remained in Papua New Guinea and around 600 on Nauru. Countries of origin include Afghanistan, Myanmar, Iran, Pakistan, Somalia, and Sudan.

Many refugees and asylum seekers suffer from poor mental health or mental illness due to, or exacerbated by, years of detention and uncertainty about their futures. Self-harm and suicide attempts are frequent. At least 12 refugees and asylum seekers have died on Manus Island and Nauru since 2013. Two refugees with mental health conditions reportedly committed suicide on Manus and Nauru in 2018.

In October, the Nauruan government ordered Médecins Sans Frontières (MSF) to end its work providing mental healthcare services on Nauru, claiming MSF had "conspired" against it to advance political agendas. MSF described the mental health situation of asylum seekers and refugees on Nauru as "beyond desperate."

Civil society and medical professionals coordinated a successful campaign in 2018 to draw attention to the plight of refugee children in Nauru and the need to evacuate them. At time of writing, the government, reacting to the change in popular opinion, had relocated more than 100 children from Nauru to Australia between August and November.

But most cases required legal intervention. Australian courts have ordered the government to transfer more than 90 refugees and asylum seekers in poor health from Nauru and Manus to receive medical treatment in Australia. More than 150 other refugees and asylum seekers have been transferred only after lawyers threatened urgent court proceedings. These cases include children as young as 10 who suffer from acute mental health conditions, some of whom have attempted suicide.

In July, a Queensland inquest found that the death of Iranian asylum seeker Hamid Khazaei on Manus Island in 2014 was preventable.

Progress under the resettlement deal to send some refugees to the United States has been slow, with less than 450 sent to the US at time of writing.

The hypocrisy of Australia's professed "non-discriminatory" immigration policy was evident when it was revealed that then-Immigration Minister Peter Dutton intervened to grant tourist visas to foreign nannies on "public interest" grounds in 2015, while his office denied medical transfers to Australia for asylum seekers in offshore detention. In March 2018 Dutton also commented that persecuted white South African farmers deserved "special attention" on humanitarian grounds from a "civilised country" like Australia.

In August the government removed income support and housing from asylum seekers living in Australia, in a move described by UN Special Rapporteur for Extreme Poverty and Human Rights Philip Alston as "ruthless."

Indigenous Rights

Indigenous Australians are significantly overrepresented in the criminal justice system, often for minor offenses like unpaid fines. Aboriginal and Torres Strait Islander people comprise 28 percent of Australia's adult prison population, but just 2 percent of the national population. Indigenous women make up 34 percent of Australia's women prison population and Indigenous children make up over 50 percent of the youth prison population.

In March, the Australian Law Reform Commission recommended that the government develop national criminal justice targets to reduce incarceration rates of indigenous people, and abolish discriminatory laws like mandatory sentencing and end the practice of imprisonment for unpaid fines—which disproportionately impacts indigenous women.

In August, the *Guardian* reported that more than 407 Aboriginal and Torres Strait Islander people had died in custody since a 1991 royal commission was established to look into the issue.

Children's Rights

In April, the Northern Territory government acknowledged the November 2017 royal commission's finding of "shocking and systemic failures" in the youth justice and protection systems, but claimed it lacked funding to implement all of the commission's 227 recommendations.

Australian states and territories set the age of criminal responsibility at 10-years-old. Across Australia, around 600 children under the age of 14 are imprisoned each year, mostly Indigenous. In March, the Northern Territory announced support "in principle" for the royal commission recommendation to raise the age from 10 to 12, but at time of writing had yet to implement it. In July, a review of Queensland's youth justice system also recommended increasing the age to 12.

In April, the inspector of custodial services released a report into conditions at Banksia Hill youth detention center in Western Australia, and found that two boys were "probably" held in solitary confinement in breach of the United Nations Convention against Torture.

Freedom of Expression

In June, Australia enacted new espionage and foreign interference legislation, increasing penalties for unauthorized disclosure of information without providing a strong public-interest defense across all offenses and defining national security in overly broad terms.

In May, former Australian spy "Witness K" and his lawyer were charged with conspiracy to communicate information from the Australian Secret Intelligence Service. Information about the trial is likely to be suppressed, despite strong public interest in knowing the reasons for prosecuting two people who exposed wrongdoing by the Australian government in Timor Leste.

Cybersecurity and Surveillance

In February, the government introduced an identity-matching services bill that would create a nationwide database of people's physical characteristics and identities, linking facial images and data from states and territories and integrating them with a facial recognition system. The proposed law lacks adequate safeguards against abuse. The bill had yet to pass into law at time of writing.

In September, the government introduced legislation that would undermine strong encryption and cybersecurity, allowing law enforcement and security agencies to order technology companies and even individuals to facilitate access to encrypted data and devices. The law would give officials wide discretion to decide whether an order is "reasonable and proportionate."

Disability Rights

More than half the Australian prison population has a physical, sensory, psychosocial (mental health), or cognitive disability. In particular, Aboriginal and Torres Strait Islander people are 13 times more likely to be imprisoned than the rest of the Australian population and are more likely to have a disability. People with disabilities struggle to cope in often- overcrowded prisons without adequate access to support services, and are particularly at risk of neglect and abuse.

Human Rights Watch research in 14 prisons across Western Australia and Queensland found that prisoners with disabilities routinely experience bullying, harassment, racism, and physical and sexual violence from fellow prisoners as well as staff. Due to a lack of staff sensitivity and training, prisoners with disability are frequently punished for behavior associated with their disability and end up disproportionately represented in punishment units. Prisoners with psychosocial or cognitive disability can spend weeks, months, or even years locked in solitary confinement for 22 hours or more a day.

Rights of Older People

In February, the attorney-general announced a national plan to address abuse of older people, a key recommendation of the 2017 Australian Law Reform Commis-

HUMAN
RIGHTS
WATCH

"I Needed Help,
Instead I Was Punished"
Abuse and Neglect of Prisoners with Disabilities in Australia

sion report that detailed cases of serious physical abuse, financial manipulation, neglect, and exploitation of older people.

In September, the prime minister announced the establishment of a royal commission into care for the aged following numerous reports of abuse in Australian nursing homes.

Women's Rights

In October, the Queensland government decriminalized abortion. In June, the New South Wales government passed legislation to provide safe access zones around clinics that provide abortions.

Forced Labor

In June, the Australian government introduced a modern slavery bill that would require companies above a certain size to submit annual statements regarding their supply chains. The bill, however, does not set out penalties for non-compliance.

Foreign Policy

In 2018, Australia started its term on the UN Human Rights Council, but beyond Geneva continued to shy away from publicly raising concerns about human rights in other countries—including neighboring Cambodia, the Philippines, and Vietnam, where rights violations are rife but with whom Australia works closely on border security and trade. In March, Australia and Vietnam upgraded ties under a new strategic partnership; the joint statement makes no reference to human rights apart from passing mention of the annual rights dialogue.

When Cambodian Prime Minister Hun Sen publicly threatened to beat up protesters in Australia who burned effigies of him in connection with an Association of Southeast Asian Nations (ASEAN) summit in Sydney in March, the Australian prime minister failed to publicly condemn the statement and said little publicly about larger human rights concerns in ASEAN countries.

In October, the government announced targeted sanctions, including travel bans and asset freezes, against five Myanmar military officers involved in atrocities against the Rohingya, following the release of a UN report on Myanmar.

Key International Actors

The UN special rapporteur on the situation of human rights defenders released a report on Australia in February 2018 highlighting efforts to undermine the Australian Human Rights Commission, and how activists face "enormous pressure" and vilification from public officials and media outlets.

In July, the UN Committee on the Elimination of Discrimination against Women expressed concern over the rate of gender-based violence against women in Australia, the treatment of asylum seeker and refugee women in offshore detention on Nauru, and the lack of harmonization in state and territory legislation on abortion.

In September, incoming UN High Commissioner for Human Rights Michelle Bachelet referred to Australia's offshore processing centers as an "affront to the protection of human rights."

Azerbaijan

Azerbaijan's appalling human rights record did not improve in 2018. In April, President Ilham Aliyev was elected for a fourth term in elections that international observers found lacked competition, and "took place in a restrictive political environment and under laws that curtail fundamental rights and freedoms."

At least 43 human rights defenders, journalists, political and religious activists remained wrongfully imprisoned, while dozens more were detained or under criminal investigation, faced harassment and travel bans, or fled Azerbaijan. Restrictive laws continued to prevent nongovernmental organizations (NGOs) from operating independently. Other persistent human rights problems included systemic torture, undue interference in the work of lawyers, and restrictions on media freedoms.

Azerbaijan's international partners criticized abuses, but did not condition ties with Azerbaijan on improvements.

Prosecuting Government Critics

Authorities released some political activists, but continued to imprison other critics on politically motivated charges.

In August, authorities released prominent political activist Ilgar Mammadov subject to a suspended two-year term, after he spent over five years in prison on charges that the European Court of Human Rights (ECtHR) found to be unlawful and in retaliation for his activism. In December 2017, the Council of Europe's (CoE) Committee of Ministers had triggered unprecedented proceedings against Azerbaijan for failing to implement the court's judgment in Mammadov's case.

Elnur Farajov, an opposition party member imprisoned on bogus drug charges, died from cancer shortly after his May release by presidential pardon, having been denied adequate medical treatment in prison.

Authorities continued to target leading and rank-and-file members of opposition political parties. In January, a court sentenced Azerbaijan Popular Front Party (APFP) Deputy Chairwoman Gozel Bayramli to three years on false smuggling charges. In September, a court sentenced Orkhan Bakhishli, another leading APFP member, to six years in prison on bogus drug possession charges. In Sep-

HUMAN
RIGHTS
WATCH

HARASSED, IMPRISONED, EXILED

Azerbaijan's Continuing Crackdown on Government Critics, Lawyers,
and Civil Society

tember, Mammad Ibrahim, advisor to the APFP's chairman, was to be released after serving a three-year-term on bogus hooliganism charges, but on the day of his expected release, officials brought additional charges against him, claiming they found a knife under his pillow. If convicted, he could face up to six additional months in jail.

Among nine other APFP members in prison are Fuad Ahmadli, Fuad Gahramanli, and Murad Adilov.

In March, a court sentenced Ahsan Nuruzade, senior member of Muslim Unity, an unregistered, conservative Shiite movement, to seven years in jail on bogus drug charges. At least 17 other members of Muslim Unity remained in prison on dubious extremism and other charges.

In May, a court convicted Alikram Khurshidov, an active member of the opposition Musavat party, on bogus hooliganism charges and sentenced him to five years' imprisonment, reduced by six months upon appeal in August. He actively criticized government corruption on social media.

Many others continued to serve long prison terms on politically motivated charges, including youth activists Ilkin Rustamzadeh, Elgiz Gahraman, Giyas Ibrahimov, and Bayram Mammadov.

Authorities also held dozens of critics in jail for up to 30 days following pro forma court hearings on bogus misdemeanor charges, including six members of the opposition REAL political party after they organized a peaceful march in Baku in May to mark Azerbaijan republic's centennial anniversary.

Attacks on the Judiciary

Pressure mounted against lawyers who work on human rights-related cases.

In April, the Azerbaijan Bar Association, which is closely tied to the government, suspended the licenses of Asabali Mustafayev and Nemet Karimli, lawyers who often worked on cases involving political persecution. The move came after the prosecutor's office lodged complaints about public statements the lawyers made concerning the politically motivated cases on which they were working. Earlier in January, based on a similar complaint, the Bar Association suspended the license of another lawyer, Fakhraddin Mehdiyev.

In June, human rights lawyer Irada Javadova was disbarred pursuant to a complaint that authorities allegedly pressured her client to file against her.

In November 2017, Yalchin Imanov lost his license after going public about his defendants' torture in prison.

Following December 2017 legislative amendments, lawyers without Bar Association membership may no longer represent clients in civic or administrative proceedings, further restricting the work of the handful of independent lawyers working on politically motivated cases.

In July, the Bar Association reprimanded Fuad Agayev, who represents several prominent political prisoners, based on a bogus complaint that he had insulted a prison guard.

Freedom of Media

All mainstream media remained under tight government control. Defamation is a criminal offense. People who publicly criticize the authorities faced arrest and threats aimed at silencing them; at least 10 remained behind bars.

In January, a court convicted journalist Afghan Mukhtarli to six years on bogus smuggling charges after he was kidnapped in May 2017 from Georgia, where he had lived in exile out of fear for his security, and illegally transferred to Azerbaijan.

Opposition journalist Seymur Hazi, satirical poet Tofig Hasanli, and prominent blogger Mehman Huseynov remained in prison on bogus charges.

In June, the Communications Ministry permanently blocked three news websites following the prosecutor general's accusations that they "supported terrorism" with their "incorrect coverage" of an assassination attempt on a public official and the ensuing public unrest.

In August, courts in Baku ruled to block three local news websites, az24saat.org, xural.com, and monitortv.info, after officials brought defamation charges against them.

Fifteen journalists working in Azerbaijan for the Berlin-based Meydan TV have remained under criminal tax evasion investigation since 2016. Eight of them remained under travel bans. Authorities continued to block Meydan TV's website in Azerbaijan.

Torture and Ill-Treatment in Detention

In July, the Council of Europe's Committee for the Prevention of Torture and Inhuman or Degrading Treatment or Punishment (CPT) published reports on six visits to Azerbaijan, between 2004 and 2017. The CPT found that torture and other ill-treatment by the police and other law enforcement agencies, and impunity for it, remain systemic and endemic. Detainees are often denied access to lawyers of their choosing.

In February, Elgiz Sadigli, brother of an outspoken exiled activist, was abducted and held for four days in incommunicado police custody, where he said police beat him and subjected him to electric shocks in retaliation for his brother's activism; he was then sentenced to 30 days on disobedience charges. Authorities failed to conduct an effective investigation into his allegations of torture.

No progress was made in the investigation into the 2017 suspicious death in custody of blogger Mehman Galandarov, whom authorities said they found hanged in his prison cell and swiftly buried with no witnesses.

Key International Actors

International financial institutions funded Azerbaijani state hydrocarbon projects, despite their institutional mandates that require them to ensure project partners respect principles of pluralism and transparency. The US, European Union, and Azerbaijan's other bilateral and international partners continued to criticize the government's targeting of critics.

In March 2018, the European Investment Bank (EIB) approved a €932 million loan for the construction of the Trans-Anatolian Natural Gas Pipeline (TANAP), which brings natural gas from Azerbaijan across Turkey to western Europe. Azerbaijan's state-owned company SOCAR is a 58 percent partner of the pipeline. The EIB did not condition the loan on the improvement of human rights, even though its obligations under the EU Charter of Fundamental Rights mean it should not finance projects that would encourage or support human rights violations.

In October 2017, the European Bank for Reconstruction and Development (EBRD) approved a US$500 million loan for TANAP, despite the bank's commitment to transparency and Azerbaijan's suspension from a key extractive revenue transparency initiative.

In May, Azerbaijan underwent the third cycle of the Universal Periodic Review at the United Nations Human Rights Council, during which it continued to deny allegations of rights violations. Several states expressed concerns about new restrictions on civil society.

In April, an independent body published a report finding that Azerbaijan exerted undue influence on members of the Parliamentary Assembly of the Council of Europe (PACE) to minimize criticism of its human rights record. The report said that this improper influence resulted or "contributed to" the voting down of a PACE report on political prisoners in Azerbaijan. In June, the PACE appointed a new rapporteur on the political prisoners issue.

A July, European Parliament resolution threatened not to ratify a partnership deal with Azerbaijan, under negotiation since 2017, unless it freed political prisoners and allowed nongovernmental groups and lawyers to work without undue government interference.

In August, the EU welcomed Mammadov's conditional release and called for the release and rehabilitation of all others detained on political grounds.

In August, during her first visit to Azerbaijan, German Chancellor Angela Merkel raised human rights issues with President Aliyev, arguing that "strong civil society must be part of an open, secular society." In a show of support, Merkel also met with civil society activists.

In August, the US administration welcomed the release of Ilgar Mammadov and urged Baku to release "all other individuals who have been imprisoned for exercising their fundamental freedoms."

In August, after the government blocked news websites, the Organization for Security and Co-operation in Europe (OSCE) Representative on Freedom of the Media, Harlem Désir, called on the authorities to reform the laws and regulations affecting media, and to encourage pluralistic debate on all issues of public importance, both off and online.

Bahrain

Civilian and military courts continue to convict and imprison peaceful dissenters, including prominent human rights defenders and opposition leaders, under the guise of national security.

Authorities have failed to hold officials accountable for torture and other ill-treatment despite the installation of oversight mechanisms as recommended by the Bahrain Independent Commission of Inquiry (BICI), which King Hamad Al-Khalifa established following mass protests in 2011.

Courts since January 2018 have stripped at least 243 people of their citizenship, including activists, leaving most of them effectively stateless. Authorities also deported at least eight people after stripping their citizenship.

The government announced general elections for November 2018 despite serious restrictions on free speech and assembly.

Freedom of Expression, Association, and Peaceful Assembly

Bahraini authorities continue to detain and harass scores of activists, journalists, and photographers since nationwide anti-government protests in 2011. Thirteen prominent dissidents are serving varying lengthy prison terms since their arrest in 2011. They include leading human rights advocate, Abdulhadi al-Khawaja, and Hassan Mushaima, leader of the unrecognized opposition group Al Haq, both serving life terms.

Authorities in Bahrain have used overly broad definitions of terrorism in the Terrorist Act to detain protesters and convict opposition leaders, including people who participated in anti-government demonstrations in 2011. The definition extends to non-violent acts, the aim of which are "disrupting the public order," "threatening the Kingdom's safety and security," and "damaging national unity."

The Interior Ministry on March 25 threatened to punish harshly those who criticized the government online, saying it was already tracking accounts that "departed from national norms, customs and traditions."

On March 27, the Bahrain Cassation Court upheld a 10-year prison sentence and stripping of citizenship for Sayed Ahmed Al-Mousawi, a photographer, arrested in 2014 after covering anti-government protests.

On June 11, King Hamad signed into law an amendment to the Exercise of Political Rights Law that would disqualify many potential opposition and independent candidates from running for office, including in general elections slated for late 2018. The amendments prohibit individuals from running if they are "felons and persons previously convicted to a prison sentence of six months or more;" or "leaders and members of dissolved political organizations who committed a serious violation of the provisions of the Kingdom's Constitution or laws;" and persons who "destroy or disrupt the conduct of constitutional or parliamentary life or whose membership were revoked."

The Information Affairs Ministry suspended *Al Wasat*, the last independent newspaper in the country, in 2017. The same year, the government also dissolved the last opposition political formation, the secular-left National Democratic Action Society (Wa'ad), accusing members of "incitement of acts of terrorism and promoting violent and forceful overthrow of the political regime."

In his report to the United Nation Human Rights Council's 39th session, UN Secretary-General António Guterres on August 13 condemned long-standing travel bans imposed on many civil society representatives that prevented them from participating in sessions of the council in Geneva between June 2017 and June 2018.

On November 4, the Bahrain High Court of Appeals overturned a lower court's decision from June 2018 to acquit of all charges three senior members of Bahrain's largest now-dissolved political opposition party Al-Wifaq, including the group's leader Sheikh Ali Salman, and sentenced them to life in prison for allegedly spying on behalf of Qatar. While Salman has remained in detention in Bahrain since December 2014, the two other members of the group who were also sentenced, Sheikh Hassan Sultan and Ali Alaswad, were tried in absentia.

Arbitrary Citizenship Revocations

Courts stripped 258 persons of their citizenship for alleged offenses that include "terrorism," "national security," and "offending the country," between January and November, bringing the total since 2012 to 764 people, according to the London-based Bahrain Institute for Rights and Democracy (BIRD). Most Bahraini nationals stripped of their citizenship were rendered effectively stateless.

All known citizenship revocations since January have been handed down by civil or military courts. In 108 cases prior to 2018, authorities directly revoked a person's citizenship through a royal decree or order of the Interior Ministry.

Between January 29 and February 1, the government deported to Iraq eight stateless Bahrainis whose citizenship it had previously stripped.

Security Forces

Since 2011, authorities have failed to credibly investigate and prosecute officials and police officers who allegedly committed violations, including torture. Despite numerous complaints by detainees and their family members, the Interior Ministry's Ombudsman Office and Special Investigations Unit failed to hold prison guards and officers to account.

Hajer Mansoor Hasan, who was sentenced on dubious terrorism charges and is the mother-in-law of exiled rights defender, Sayed Ahmed Al-Wadaei, filed complaints in March, July, and August, claiming that Isa Town Prison personnel had mistreated her. The Ombudsman's Office responded to each of the complaints denying accusations.

In September, Hasan and two other female detainees said prison officials assaulted them after they complained that authorities denied them the right to participate in religious commemorations on the occasion of the Shi'ite religious festival of Ashoura. According to Hasan's relatives, prison authorities have since restricted the inmates' access to family visits, phone calls, and time spent outside their cells.

Despite commitments to implement substantive recommendations of the Bahrain Independent Commission of Inquiry (BICI) pursuant to mass anti-government protests in 2011, authorities in 2017 reversed two such recommendations it had previously implemented, by restoring arrest and detention authority to the abusive and unaccountable National Security Agency (NSA) and by giving military courts jurisdiction over civilians.

Death Penalty

Bahrain ended a de facto seven-year moratorium in January 2017 when it executed three Shia men for a bomb attack that resulted in the deaths of three police officers amid allegations that they had been tortured into confessing.

On April 26, King Hamad commuted the sentences of four men among a group of six who a military court had sentenced to death in December 2017. The other two were tried in absentia.

As of November, Bahraini prisons held 14 people on death row.

Human Rights Defenders

On March 21, authorities sentenced in absentia, to two months in prison, Duaa Al-Wadaei, wife of prominent exiled activist Sayed Ahmed Al-Wadaei, for allegedly insulting an officer at Manama airport in 2016. Three of Al-Wadaei's other relatives are serving prison terms after authorities sentenced them in October 2017 on dubious terrorism-related charges that appear to have been filed in reprisal against his human rights work.

Nabeel Rajab, one of Bahrain's preeminent human rights defenders and head of the Bahrain Center for Human Rights, completed a two-year prison term for "spreading false news and rumors about the internal situation in the Kingdom, which undermines the state prestige and status." He then immediately began a five-year prison term for his Tweets criticizing alleged torture in Bahrain's Jaw Prison and the Saudi-led military operations in Yemen. The Manama Appeals Court on June 5 upheld the latter conviction, finding that Rajab "deliberately disseminated in wartime false or malicious news, statements or rumors […] so as to cause damage to military preparations;" "publicly offended a foreign country," in this case Saudi Arabia; and "insulted a statutory body."

Rajab, who suffers from a serious skin condition, has been in detention since June 2016.

On August 13, the United Nations Working Group on Arbitrary Detention called for Rajab's immediate release, saying his detention was not only arbitrary, because it resulted from his exercise of the right to freedom of opinion and expression, but also constituted "discrimination based on political or other opinion, as well as on his status as a human rights defender."

Women's Rights, Gender Identity, and Sexual Orientation

Bahraini law discriminates against women in the right to divorce and transmission of Bahraini nationality to their children on an equal basis to men.

Article 353 of the penal code exempts perpetrators of rape from prosecution and punishment if they marry their victims. Bahrain's parliament proposed a full repeal of that article in 2016, but the cabinet rejected the proposal. Article 334 of the penal code reduces the penalties for perpetrators of so-called honor crimes.

Adultery and sexual relations outside marriage are criminalized. No law prohibits discrimination on the grounds of sex, gender identity, or sexual orientation.

Key International Actors

Bahrain continued to participate in the Saudi Arabia-led coalition military operations in Yemen.

On March 23, the Department of State stressed the key role Bahrain played in the security architecture of the Gulf region, saying the kingdom was a vital United States partner in major defense initiatives as well, as providing support for countering terrorism. The US maintains a major naval base in Bahrain.

The State Department approved two major weapons sales to Bahrain in 2018. On April 27, it approved the sale of AH-1Z attack helicopters, missiles, and other military equipment to the kingdom, for an estimated US$911.4 million. On May 17, the State Department approved a deal worth up to US$45 million, which included 3,200 bomb bodies to arm Bahrain's F-16 fighters fleet.

As of November, the State Department had approved five major weapons sales to Bahrain in 2018 worth an estimated US$1.4 billion. This resumption of arms sales came after the US lifted in March 2017 the human rights conditions that the Obama administration had attached to a sale to Bahrain of F-16 fighter jets worth $2.8 billion.

The European Parliament passed a resolution on June 14 on the human rights situation in Bahrain that called on the government to release all political activists and human rights defenders, including Nabeel Rajab. It also called for an official moratorium on all executions, and for an end to the military trials of civilians. It condemned the high number of death sentences and criticized the stripping of citizenship "as a means of reprisal."

In his last address on June 18 to the UN Human Rights Council (HRC), during its 38th session, former UN High Commissioner for Human Rights Zeid Ra'ad Al Hussein said that Bahrain continued to refuse his office and the Special Procedures unconditional access to the country "amid continued crackdowns on civil society and additional legislation which further restricts the people's fundamental rights."

Zeid's successor, High Commissioner Michelle Bachelet, decried on September 10 during her opening statement at the 39th Session of the HRC, the "large number of cases of revocation of citizenship" and called for the release of all human rights defenders who are currently arbitrarily detained, including Nabeel Rajab.

Bangladesh

Ahead of national elections scheduled for end December 2018, Bangladesh authorities detained or jailed senior members of main opposition parties, lodged politically motivated trumped-up cases against thousands of opposition supporters, and violated international standards on freedom of speech by cracking down on media and civil society critical of government abuses.

Despite an international outcry, authorities detained photographer-activist Shahidul Alam for 107 days. Alam had criticized human rights violations in an interview with Al Jazeera television and on Facebook in August. Bangladesh also enacted an overly broad and vague law that affects various forms of speech, particularly through the use of social media and other internet-based devices.

The government deployed humanitarian, medical, and other services to ensure the safety and welfare of Rohingya refugees who fled crimes against humanity by the military in neighboring Myanmar beginning in late August 2017. Bangladesh is now host to nearly 1 million Rohingya refugees, a population which includes both recent refugees and those who have been there longer. The continued influx of Rohingya refugees from Myanmar is creating a severe strain on humanitarian and government aid agencies.

April marked the five-year anniversary of the collapse of Rana Plaza garment factory, leading to the deaths of over 1,100 workers. The prime minister promised that reforms will continue to ensure the safety of workers but was resistant to continuing to receive external international oversight through the Bangladesh Accord and the Bangladesh Alliance, which were set up with the assistance of international brands following the collapse of Rana Plaza.

Attacks on Political Opposition, Peaceful Protesters, Students, and Media

Bangladesh continued a harsh crackdown to suppress those that disagree or are critical of the ruling Awami League. These included members and supporters of the political opposition, journalists, prominent members of civil society, as well as students, and even school children.

HUMAN
RIGHTS
WATCH

NO PLACE FOR CRITICISM
Bangladesh Crackdown on Social Media Commentary

The leader of the Bangladesh Nationalist Party, Khaleda Zia, was convicted and jailed in February, after the courts finally moved long-standing pending cases against her. Zia's supporters said that the corruption cases against her were brought by the same military-backed government that had filed allegations against the current prime minister, Sheikh Hasina; however, after the Awami League came to office, all cases against Hasina were dropped, but those against Zia proceeded.

Thousands of opposition supporters, including senior leaders, faced trumped-up cases. Newspapers reported that even names of individuals who are dead or critically ill in the hospital were included in these arbitrary actions.

In July, university and school students launched a protest demanding road safety following the death of two students by a speeding bus. Eyewitnesses credibly alleged that members of the Awami League and their student wing had attacked the students with sticks and machetes. Authorities took no action against those carrying out the abuses, but instead detained the protesting students. Police also arrested scores on vague allegations of "instigating" violence, based on their comments on social media either supporting the protests or criticizing the crackdown on students.

Photojournalist Shahidul Alam, who was covering the protests, was detained in early August. He was arrested by members of the Detective Branch hours after he gave a media interview describing the violence he witnessed during the protests. He said he was beaten in custody. Other journalists covering the protests also reported being attacked. Several protesters faced secret detentions, in effect amounting to enforced disappearances. Alam was eventually released on bail in late November, although he continues to face charges against him.

Freedom of Expression and Association

In September, the government passed the Digital Security Act, designed to monitor all electronic communications. This new law was supposed to address abusive provisions in the Information and Communication Technology Act. However, the new law still retains similar provisions and contains new sections to criminalize free expression. Meanwhile, hundreds continued to face charges for their social media commentary.

HUMAN
RIGHTS
WATCH

"Bangladesh Is Not My Country"
The Plight of Rohingya Refugees from Myanmar

Human rights groups remained under pressure, due to restrictions on accessing foreign funding. Journalists reported threats and intimidation to prevent any crit icism of the government.

Impunity for RAB and other Security Forces

In May, the government announced a war on drugs, and within a short period of time, nearly 100 persons had been killed by the security forces. Sheikh Hasina also announced that an additional 10,000 suspects had been arrested. Despite allegations of violations, including an audio recording of an extrajudicial execution by members of the Rapid Action Battalion (RAB), authorities failed to investigate and prosecute those responsible.

Enforced disappearances and extrajudicial killings continued. Security forces persisted with a long-standing pattern of covering up unlawful killings, by claiming the deaths occurred during a gun-fight or in crossfire.

Refugees

A year after a brutal crackdown by the Myanmar army, almost 1 million Rohingya refugees remained in camps in Bangladesh.

Humanitarian agencies, the government, and the refugees themselves, struggled to shore up the hastily built, severely overcrowded camps. The government obstructed certain infrastructure improvements, particularly in shelter and education, because it insisted the camps are temporary, and the solution to the refugee problem is return to Myanmar.

Vulnerable groups, such as people with disabilities and older people, are particularly at risk and have difficulty accessing basic services and humanitarian assistance.

The Bangladesh government, after failing to negotiate the safe return of the refugees to Myanmar, and in an attempt to resolve the overcrowded camp conditions, announced a plan to relocate 100,000 in the first phase to an island in the Bay of Bengal called Bhasan Char. The government hired external contractors to build embankments around the island, but there are serious concerns about risk of floods and tidal surges, particularly during the monsoon and cyclone seasons, as well as lack of livelihoods and freedom of movement for refugees who would be transferred there.

Labor Rights

The Bangladesh High Court ordered that the two international initiatives on fire and building safety—the Bangladesh Accord on Fire and Building Safety and the Alliance for Bangladesh Worker Safety—should finish their work and hand over their operations to government authorities by November 2018. The government has yet to publicly report on all its fire and building safety inspections and progress in a manner comparable to the transparent reporting adopted by the Accord and the Alliance. The government increased workers' minimum wage in the apparel industry, but workers continued to protest this as being inadequate.

Women's and Girls' Rights

Bangladesh continues to have one of the highest rates of child marriage in the world. In spite of the government's stated pledge to end the practice by 2041, it has yet to make meaningful progress. A law remained on the books allowing girls to get married before the age of 18 under special circumstances.

Authorities failed to properly enforce laws to protect women in cases of sexual violence, rape, domestic abuse, and acid attacks.

Sexual Orientation and Gender Identity

Although the government took some steps in recent years, such as declaring legal recognition of a third gender category for hijras (sometimes referred to as transgender women), policy implementation on access to state benefits were weak, and sexual and gender minorities remained under constant pressure and threat.

Sexual and gender minorities fear for their safety, amid a climate of impunity for attacks on minorities by religious extremists, and feared that, if they were targeted, authorities would deny that they were targeted because of their sexual orientation or gender identity, rather than come to their defense.

Key International Actors

The Bangladesh government ignored or dismissed numerous key recommendations, particularly around its crackdown on speech, and the increasing cases of enforced disappearances and killings during its Universal Periodic Review in May 2018.

After months of increasing interest for a visiting mission to Bangladesh and Myanmar, the Security Council traveled to both countries in April. In Bangladesh, council members visited refugee camps in Cox's Bazar, where they assessed efforts to provide assistance for Rohingya refugees.

In July, Secretary-General Antonio Guterres and World Bank President Jim Yong Kim conducted a joint visit to Bangladesh. They met with government authorities in Dhaka and visited Cox's Bazar. During and following his mission, the secretary-general expressed deep concern about the situation in the camps and urged donor countries to increase humanitarian assistance to Bangladesh host communities.

Relations with India was placed under strain when the Indian government announced plans to detain and deport those deemed to be illegal settlers from Bangladesh in Assam state. India failed to speak up against human rights violations in Bangladesh, including against the political opposition.

China resisted international efforts to hold the Myanmar military accountable for abuses against the Rohingya, and instead offered to mediate refugee repatriation. Bangladesh authorities said those mediation attempts had failed, with Myanmar refusing to accept the Rohingya as citizens. China's proposal on refugees seemed to minimize the engagement of various other international players in Myanmar.

International donors, including the European Union and its members states, focused mostly on conditions for the Rohingya refugees, and were restrained on publicly criticizing the Bangladesh authorities for human rights violations.

In April, during the yearly bilateral human rights consultations, the EU raised concerns over reports of extrajudicial killings and enforced disappearances, urged Bangladesh to abide by its labor legislation with international labor conventions, and underlined the urgency of addressing the issue of violence and harassments against trade unionists.

In September, the EU delegation and the missions of EU member states Switzerland and Norway reiterated concerns on provisions in the Digital Security Act, which can be used to unduly restrict freedom of expression and the freedom of media and undermine judicial procedural guarantees.

After the United States called for free and fair elections and criticized the crackdown on the student protests, alleged supporters of the ruling Awami League attacked the US ambassador's convoy in Dhaka in early August, throwing stones at her car.

Since August 2017, the United States has provided more than US$389 million in humanitarian assistance to displaced people in and from Burma, primarily in Bangladesh.

Belarus

In 2018, civil society activists, lawyers, rights groups, and independent media continued to face government harassment and pressure. Authorities prosecuted dozens of journalists on a variety of arbitrary grounds and adopted new restrictions on internet freedoms.

Belarus remains the only European country to use the death penalty. Those condemned to death are executed by a shot to the head. Authorities do not inform families of the execution date or the burial place.

Death Penalty

In October 2017, authorities executed Kiryl Kazachok, sentenced on murder charges in December 2016. In mid-May, they executed Viktar Liotau and Aliaksei Mikhalenia, both sentenced on murder charges in 2017.

In December 2017 and May 2018 respectively, appeal courts upheld death sentences for Ihar Hershankou and Siamion Berazhnou, sentenced on fraud and murder charges in 2017, and Viachaslau Sukharka and Aliaksandr Zhylnikau, sentenced on murder charges in 2015.

Freedom of Expression and Attacks on Journalists

According to the Belarusian Association of Journalists, between January and August, authorities arbitrarily detained 29 journalists, including while covering Freedom Day protests.

In December 2017, a court fined Anatol Bukas, chief editor of Naviny.by, 345 Belarusian rubles (roughly US$158) for writing about an unauthorized rally in Minsk. In November, the Justice Ministry issued the outlet a warning for violating mass media legislation. Under Belarusian law, two warnings may lead to an outlet's closure.

In February, the police beat Belsat cameraman Andrus Koziel for live-streaming vote counting during local elections and jailed him for one night. In March, a court fined him 735 Belarusian rubles (US$338) for disobeying police.

In February, 19-year old blogger Stsiapan Sviatlou became a target for police for allegedly posting videos that insulted President Aliaksandr Lukashenka. Police searched Siatlou's parents' apartment and seized his laptop and video camera.

Authorities intensified the prosecution of freelance journalists for cooperating with unregistered foreign media, bringing 33 cases against 17 journalists from September through December 2017, and 85 cases against 31 journalists from January through September 2018, an increase over the same period in 2017. All resulted in fines ranging from 490 to 1,225 Belarusian rubles (US$230 to US$575).

In February 2018, Belarusian courts handed down suspended sentences of five years' imprisonment to Yuri Pavlovets, Dimitri Alimkin, and Sergei Shiptenko, bloggers with the Russian-language websites Regnum, Lenta.ru and EADaily, on bogus charges of inciting extremism and sowing social discord between Russia and Belarus. Yuri Pavlovets and Sergei Shiptenko appealed to the Supreme Court, which upheld the verdict.

In April, authorities arrested Dzmitri Halko, editor of *Belarussian Partisan* on dubious charges of assaulting police officers in November 2017 in an incident when police interrupted his son's birthday party. In July, a court sentenced Halko to four years in prison and a fine of 930 Belarusian rubles (US$430). At time of writing, Halko's appeal was pending.

In June, authorities began investigating Ales Lipai, head of the independent BelaPAN news agency, on criminal tax evasion charges. Investigative authorities searched Lipai's apartment and banned him from leaving Belarus pending trial. Following Lipai's death in August, authorities closed the case.

In August, authorities launched a criminal probe against several publications for allegedly using passwords for the state news agency, BelTA, without authorization in order to access it for free. The disproportionate response raised concerns that the government was using the issue to punish news outlets. Police searched the offices of BelaPAN and TUT.by, an independent news website, as well as the editorial offices of several other media outlets (including some state-owned) and the homes of several journalists. At least 18 journalists were arrested on charges of "unauthorized access to computer information causing significant

harm." All were released by August 10; criminal proceedings against them continued at time of writing.

After admitting she was aware that her staff was using login data for BelTA's paid
subscription, TUT.by's chief editor was charged with negligence, punishable by
up to five years in prison.

Freedom of Information

In December 2017 and January 2018, the Information Ministry ordered the blocking of independent news websites Belarusian Partisan and Charter '97 for "disseminating prohibited information."

June amendments to the Law on Mass Media introduced additional, excessive
restrictions requiring that all online media outlets keep public records of the
names of people who submit comments online and disclose that information to
authorities. The amendments also provided for holding owners of registered online media criminally liable for any content posted on their website.

Human Rights Defenders and Lawyers

Authorities refused to investigate police mistreatment of Aliaksei Loika during a
police raid at Viasna Human Rights Center in March 2017. In October 2017, border
officials arbitrarily detained and searched another Viasna member, who was returning to Belarus after attending a human rights forum, before ultimately releasing him.

In February, human rights lawyer Elena Tonkacheva returned to Belarus after the
expiration of an arbitrarily imposed three-year entry ban.

Authorities pressured lawyers working on politicized cases. In September, the
Justice Ministry suspended the license of Anna Bakhtina, a defense lawyer with
more than 38-years' experience, alleging that she was "insufficiently competent" to practice law. In October, a court upheld the decision. Bakhtina was one
of eight lawyers the authorities forced to take an "extraordinary certification"
exam. All eight were representing defendants allegedly associated with White
Legion, a disbanded nationalist group. The seven other lawyers were declared
"partially compliant" and had to re-take the examination in March 2018. They all
passed.

Freedom of Assembly

Police arbitrarily detained at least 110 people in connection with peaceful protests held in Minsk and other cities on March 25, traditionally celebrated by the opposition as Freedom Day.

In the lead-up to the rally in Minsk, police arrested opposition leader Mikalay Statkevich and rally organizers Uladzimir Niakliayeu, Viachaslau Siuchyk, and Maksim Viniarski. Courts sentenced them to up to 10-days' detention.

Police detained seven members of the Belarusian Helsinki Committee and Viasna while they monitored the rally in central Minsk, charging six with "participating in unauthorized mass events" and additionally charging one with "disobeying a police officer." All were released the same day, and in April, filed appeals against unlawful actions by police. An official inquiry found no police misconduct. In August, the charges against the activists were dropped due to the statute of limitations.

In May, police charged lesbian, gay, bisexual, and transgender (LGBT) activist Vika Biran for staging single-person pickets near three governmental buildings to protest the Interior Ministry's statement decrying the British embassy for flying a rainbow flag to mark the International Day Against Homophobia. Courts convicted her of two offenses of violating rules on public gatherings and fined her a total of 735 Belarusian rubles (US$335).

Freedom of Association

In May, the Belarusian Council of Ministers submitted a draft law to repeal Article 193.1 of the criminal code, which criminalizes participation in the activities of unregistered organizations, and to replace criminal liability for that offense with an administrative fine of up to 1,225 Belarusian rubles (US$600).

Authorities continued to deny registration to independent groups and opposition parties on arbitrary pretexts.

In April, the Justice Ministry rejected the seventh registration application filed by the Belarusian Christian Democracy party citing minor errors in the application. In May, the Supreme Court dismissed the party's appeal.

In October 2017, the Supreme Court upheld the Justice Ministry's second refusal to register the Social Christian Movement.

In August, a court in Minsk sentenced the head of the Belarusian Radio and Electronics Workers' Union and its accountant to a five-year curfew and other restrictions on dubious tax evasion charges.

Key International Actors

The government continued to refuse to cooperate with United Nations Special Rapporteur on Belarus Miklos Haraszti, appointed in 2012. In his final report to the UN Human Rights Council (UNHRC) as special rapporteur in June, he stated that Belarus is "governed by a purposefully repressive legal framework, aggravated by regularly recurring, centrally planned violent crackdowns." In June, the UNHRC renewed the the mandate of the special rapporteur on Belarus for another year.

In December 2017, in its concluding observations to Belarus' periodic report to the UN Committee on the Elimination of Racial Discrimination, the committee urged the government to investigate all cases of racial discrimination, take measures to prevent discrimination against Roma, and promote independence of the judiciary.

In its June review of Belarus' fifth periodic report to the UN Committee against Torture (CAT), the committee urged Belarus to put in place a moratorium on executions, with a view to abolishing the death penalty, highlighted "widespread" use of torture in Belarus, called for an end to the use of torture in detention, and warned against the use of psychiatric hospitalization for non-medical reasons.

In an April resolution, the European Parliament deplored the continued harassment of Belarusian activists, politicians, and journalists and urged the authorities to unblock the website of Charter '97, abandon amendments to the Law on the Media, and end persecution of independent bloggers.

The European Union decried shortcomings in the February local elections and spoke out against Belarus' continued use of the death penalty and against the Freedom Day crackdown, stressing that respect for human rights is key in shaping the EU's future relationship with Belarus. In February, EU member states extended for one year the EU's restrictive measures against Belarus in response to continued human rights violations, including an arms embargo and targeted sanctions against four individuals. Despite Belarus's lack of progress on human rights, the European Commission continued talks with the government on visa facilitation and readmission.

Bolivia

Impunity for violent crime and human rights violations remain serious problems in Bolivia. The administration of President Evo Morales has created a hostile environment for human rights defenders that undermines their ability to work independently.

Despite recent legal reforms, extensive use of pretrial detention—combined with trial delays—undermine defendants' rights and contribute to prison overcrowding. Threats to judicial independence, violence against women, and child labor are other major concerns.

A 2013 Constitutional Court ruling allowed President Evo Morales to run for a third term, although the constitution, at the time, limited presidential re-election to two five-year terms. In a 2016 national referendum, voters rejected changing the constitution to allow President Morales to run a fourth time, but in November 2017, the Constitutional Court struck down limits on re-election altogether, which will allow President Morales to run for a fourth term in 2019.

Impunity for Abuses and Violent Crime

Bolivia has prosecuted only a few of the officials responsible for human rights violations committed under authoritarian governments from 1964-1982, partly because the armed forces have at times refused to give information to judicial authorities about the fate of people killed or forcibly disappeared.

A truth commission established by the government in August 2017 to carry out non-judicial investigations of grave human rights abuses committed during that period continued to operate in 2018. The commission, which will provide information to prosecutors and judges trying to convict those responsible for abuses, was originally required by law to publish a report on its findings by August 2019, but in May the Plurinational Assembly—the country's legislature—allowed the president to extend the deadline by one year.

Impunity has led to mob attacks, or lynchings, of alleged criminals. In May, a mob of motorcycle taxi drivers in Cochabamba killed 19-year-old Edson Soria, whom they believed had stolen several motorcycles, according to press reports.

Judicial Independence

The government has sought to reform the Bolivian justice system, which has been plagued by corruption, delays, and political interference for years. While reforms are certainly called for, current efforts pose a serious risk to judicial independence in the country.

In 2016, members of the three branches of government, as well as civil society groups and other stakeholders, discussed proposals during a "National Justice Summit." The summit's recommendations included reforming the selection process for high court judges, creating a new body to supervise judges, and assessing the work of current judges and prosecutors.

In 2017, Congress created a commission to oversee implementation of the recommendations. The commission has broad powers, including "controlling" the appointment of new judges and carrying out "all other actions necessary" to implement the recommendations. Five of the commission's nine members are either supporters of Morales in the Plurinational Assembly or government officials directly appointed by him.

In March 2018, the commission participated in a process to appoint 77 appellate court judges, although the Bolivian Constitution assigns that task to a magistrate's council that is required to be independent of the executive branch.

In 2017, the Magistrate's Council ruled that all the judges who were appointed before the 2009 constitution was enacted were to be considered transitory and could be summarily removed by the council. In May 2017, the council summarily removed 88 judges.

In December 2017, voters elected high court judges and members of the Magistrate's Council from lists created by the Plurinational Assembly, where the Morales's Movement for Socialism party has a two-thirds majority. According to the Due Process of Law Foundation (DPLF), more than half of the elected judges and officials had worked for the Morales administration.

A Supreme Electoral Tribunal decision on whether President Morales could register as a candidate for the 2019 presidential election remained pending at time of writing. In November, Gerardo García, the vice president of the Movement for Socialism, said that the court would have to "bear the consequences" if it did not allow Morales to run.

Due Process and Prison Conditions

Around 70 percent of all Bolivians in detention have not been convicted of a crime. Extended pretrial detention and trial delays overcrowd prisons and lead to poor and inhumane conditions. By mid-2018, more than 16,000 inmates were packed into prisons built to hold a maximum of around 5,000.

In March 2018, seven prisoners died during a police operation in Palmasola prison in Santa Cruz. The government said the operation sought to recover control of the prison from criminal organizations.

Presidential decrees adopted between 2012 and 2018 allow the president to reduce the sentences of those convicted of minor crimes and drop charges against those held in pretrial detention for minor crimes. Official figures reveal that more than 5,000 people have benefited from such decrees.

The Attorney General's Office has repeatedly used a 2010 anti-corruption law to prosecute alleged crimes committed before the law was enacted. International human rights law, however, prohibits such retroactive application of changes to criminal law, unless doing so is beneficial to the defendant.

In October 2016, the Attorney General's Office used the law to charge businessman and opposition leader Samuel Doria Medina with "anti-economic conduct" for allegedly transferring US$21 million from the government to a private foundation when he was planning minister in the government of President Jaime Paz Zamora in 1992.

In May 2015, Jorge "Tuto" Quiroga, former president of Bolivia and current opposition leader, was charged with "anti-economic conduct." Prosecutors argued that officials in his administration harmed the "interests of the state" by signing four oil agreements with foreign companies.

In July 2018, the Attorney General's Office asked the Plurinational Assembly to try Carlos Mesa, also a former president of Bolivia and current opposition leader, for harming the "interests of the state" when his administration expelled the Chilean company Quirobax from the country in 2004. In 2015, the International Centre for Settlement of Investment Disputes (ICSID) had awarded Quirobax compensation for being expelled from Bolivia.

In September, President Morales granted amnesty to former Presidents Quiroga and Mesa.

Human Rights Defenders

Human rights defenders continue to face harassment, including from government officials, which undermines their ability to work independently.

A law and decree that President Morales signed in 2013 grants the government broad powers to dissolve civil society organizations. Under the decree, any government office may request that the Ministry of Autonomy revoke the permit of a nongovernmental organization (NGO) if it performs activities other than those listed in its bylaws, or if the organization's legal representative is criminally punished for carrying out activities that "undermine security or public order."

The decree also allows the Plurinational Assembly to request the revocation of an NGO's permit in cases of "necessity or public interest." These measures give the government inappropriately wide latitude to interfere with the operation of independent civil society groups.

Bolivian officials have repeatedly accused rights groups of engaging in an international conspiracy against the government, but have failed to present evidence to support such claims.

Freedom of Expression

While public debate is robust, the Morales administration periodically lashes out at journalists, accusing them, without presenting evidence, of publishing lies and politically motivated distortions. The government has repeatedly accused media of participating in an international conspiracy against Bolivia and the president.

Bolivia lacks transparent criteria for using government funds to purchase media advertisements—an important source of media revenue—and some media outlets have accused the government of discriminating against those who criticize government officials by withholding advertising from them.

Indigenous Rights

The 2009 constitution includes comprehensive guarantees for indigenous groups' rights to collective land titling, intercultural education, prior consultation on development projects, and protection of indigenous justice systems.

Indigenous peoples' right to free, prior, and informed consent (FPIC) regarding legislative or administrative measures that may affect them is not fully enshrined in Bolivian legislation. One current mining law limits FPIC to the exploitation phase of land concessions, but international standards call for FPIC through all stages of projects that affect indigenous peoples' rights to land and natural resources.

In May 2017, President Morales signed a bill that authorizes the building of a highway in the Isiboro Secure National Park and Indigenous Territory. The law is based on a 2012 consultation with local indigenous groups, which some rights groups say was not fully free or fair.

Gender-Based Violence and Reproductive Rights

Women and girls in Bolivia remain at high risk of gender-based violence, despite a 2013 law that sets forth comprehensive measures to prevent and prosecute violence against women. The law created the crime of "femicide" (the killing of a woman in certain circumstances, including of domestic violence) and called for the establishment of shelters for women as well as special prosecutors and courts for gender-based crimes. The National Police reported over 100 "femicides" in 2017.

Women and girls face numerous obstacles to accessing sexual and reproductive health services, including contraceptives.

Under Bolivian law, abortion is not a crime when the pregnancy is due to rape or if the procedure is necessary to protect the life or health of a pregnant woman or girl. In December 2017, the Plurinational Assembly passed government-sponsored criminal reform that would significantly eased abortion restrictions.

But, in response to protests, the assembly abrogated the bill in January 2018, before it took force. The law would have fully decriminalized abortion for girls. It would have allowed women to end pregnancies in a range of circumstances, including if their lives or health are at risk; if the pregnancy is the result of rape; and if the fetus suffers from severe conditions not compatible with life outside the womb.

Child Labor

In February 2018, the Constitutional Court abrogated a provision in a 2014 law that had allowed children as young as 10 to work in activities that are not deemed "dangerous" or "unhealthy." The law contravened international standards and had made Bolivia the first country in the world to legalize employment at such a young age.

Sexual Orientation and Gender Identity

In 2016, the Plurinational Assembly passed a bill that allows people to revise the gender listed on their identification documents without prior judicial approval.

However, in November 2017, the Constitutional Court ruled that revision of gender did not grant the right to marry a person of the same biological sex.

Same-sex couples are not allowed to marry or engage in civil unions. Bolivia's 2009 constitution defines marriage as the union of a man and a woman.

Key International Actors

In April 2018, the UN Human Rights Committee found that Bolivia violated the human rights of two former members of the Bolivian parliament by disqualifying them as candidates for the positions of mayors in 2015 subnational elections.

Also in April, the Inter-American Commission on Human Rights accepted a case concerning the April 2009 killing of two Hungarians (one of Bolivian birth) and an Irishman, whom the government alleged were mercenaries involved in a separatist plot. Police shot them dead after storming their hotel rooms in Santa Cruz. President Morales tweeted that admitting the case meant that the commission "was a defender of terrorism and separatism."

In June, the Morales administration nominated Nardi Suxo, its former minister of transparency and ambassador to the United Nations, to become a judge on the Inter-American Court of Human Rights, but her candidacy was defeated in the General Assembly of the Organization of American States.

Bosnia and Herzegovina

Bosnia and Herzegovina made limited progress in 2018 towards addressing long-standing human rights problems. Members of national minorities were ineligible to stand for the presidency in the 2018 general elections because of the ongoing failure to amend discriminatory provisions of the constitution. Authorities did not provide basic support to thousands of asylum seekers and migrants who arrived in 2018. Journalists continued to face threats and interference in their work. War crimes cases continued to be resolved at a slow rate.

Ethnic and Religious Discrimination

Despite multiple rulings of the Bosnian Constitutional Court and the European Court of Human Rights (ECtHR) that the constitution discriminates against ethnic and religious minorities, there was no progress during the year towards amending it to allow Roma, Jewish, and other minorities to run for the presidency in 2018 October general elections.

Authorities in Mostar failed again to change the city's electoral statute ordered by the Bosnian Constitutional Court in 2010 to reflect the one person, one vote principle, scuppering an idea to hold local elections in Mostar in 2018 at the same time as the October general elections. Political disagreements mean the city has not held local elections since 2008, disenfranchising its voters.

A survey conducted in April 2018 by the United Nations Development Programme showed Roma in Bosnia and Herzegovina continue to face many difficulties accessing and enjoying, health care, education, housing, and employment, notwithstanding some improvements in living standards. Many Roma lack identification documents necessary to access services.

Asylum Seekers and Internally Displaced Persons

The numbers of asylum seekers and migrants entering the country increased significantly during the year. According to the Service for Foreigners' Affairs of Bosnia and Herzegovina, between January and November 2018, 21,163 asylum seekers, most of whom have either lodged claims or indicated an intention to lodge asylum claims, entered Bosnia and Herzegovina, compared to only 755 in the whole of 2017. The three largest nationalities were Pakistan, Iran, and Syria.

The state did not provide adequate shelter, food, and access to medical assistance to the new arrivals, particularly in Velika Kladusa and Bihac municipalities. In November 2018 there were only two state-managed centers for migrants and refugees—an open asylum center with capacity of about 154, and an open refugee reception center with capacity of around 290—and two temporary accommodation centers for migrants set up with support of international organizations. The lack of accommodation and services forced thousands to live in the streets, abandoned buildings, or tents.

The lack of official accommodation means that many would-be asylum seekers cannot register a place of residence upon arrival, a requirement to apply for asylum. This leaves many without access to asylum procedures even after they register their intention to apply. Among the 2018 arrivals, over 19, 900 asylum seekers expressed intention to apply for asylum, but only 1,314 applied.

Twenty-three years after the end of the war in Bosnia, only 42 percent of Bosnian refugees have returned to Bosnia, according to the Ministry for Human Rights and Refugees, and 91,813 remained internally displaced at the end of June 2018, many still living in 156 collective centers. At time of writing, 737 homes for internally displaced had been built under the Regional Housing Programme. A plan to build housing for displaced people living in 121 collective centers by 2020 under a Council of Europe Development Bank-funded project had started but was moving slowly in most municipalities.

Accountability for War Crimes

In July 2018, Bosnia and Herzegovina signed a joint Declaration on War Crimes at a summit meeting on the Western Balkans with regional and EU leaders, committing to assist efforts to bring perpetrators of human rights crimes to justice. However, the Bosnian government did not support a civil society-backed initiative to establish a regional truth commission, known as RECOM.

With the closure of the International Criminal Tribunal for the former Yugoslavia (ICTY) in December 2017, the prosecution of war crimes in domestic courts took on a new importance. But in practice, progress in Bosnia remains slow.

A revised National War Crimes Processing Strategy has been waiting approval by the Council of Ministers since February 2018. The revised strategy aims to improve the process of determining which cases merit handling by the State Court War Crimes Chamber and prosecutor, and which can be dealt with in entity, district, and cantonal courts.

There were 114 cases for war crimes before the State Court involving 296 defendants as of September 2018. Between January and September 2018, the court delivered 29 verdicts, 14 convictions, 12 acquittals, and three partial acquittals. The court delivered seven verdicts for conflict-related sexual violence, five of which were convictions. Between January and September 2018, the Supreme Court of Republika Srpska, which tries war crimes cases in that entity, received seven war crime cases, four of which resulted in convictions and three of which were being processed at time of writing. One of the four convictions was for conflict-related sexual violence. Statistics for cantonal courts in the federation were not available at time of writing.

In January 2018, the State Court confirmed a genocide indictment against former Bosnian Serb Interior Minister Tomislav Kovac. He is accused of controlling the police forces involved in capturing, detaining, and executing up to 8,000 Bosniak men in Srebrenica in 1995.

Several cases were dealt with during the year by the residual Mechanism for International Criminal Tribunal (MICT) set up to deal with any outstanding issues arising from the ICTY caseload. In April 2018, former Bosnian Serb wartime President Radovan Karadzic in the appeal hearings at the MICT against his March 2016 conviction at the ICTY for genocide, crimes against humanity and war crimes, denied the charges and demanded a new trial. Prosecutors urged the judges at the MICT to reject Karadzic's appeal and change his sentence to life in prison.

Human Rights Defenders and Civil Society

In 2018, civil society groups reported intensified state efforts to discourage public protests by issuing fines for public disorder, making it increasingly difficult and slow to obtain necessary permits, restricting protests to specific and less central areas, and over-policing peaceful events.

Despite existing laws that regulate civil society's reporting of income, officials in Republika Srpska drafted a new law on foreign donations which, if passed by the Republika Srpska assembly, would allow authorities to categorize NGOs who receive foreign donations as "foreign agents" and monitor their work and income in unwarranted ways that could discourage their independent work.

Freedom of Media

Attacks on journalists and freedom of media continued at high rate in 2018. Bosnian journalists' association BH Novinari registered 41 attacks against journalists, including five death threats, seven physical attacks, and eight direct threats by politicians. The Human Rights Ombudsman's office received nine complaints regarding attacks on journalists. Some cases were investigated by police and handed over to the Prosecutor's Office, but no-one was convicted for attacks on journalists at time of writing.

In August 2018 Vladimir Kovacevic, a journalist at BN TV, was attacked in Banja Luka after covering a protest over the failure of authorities to investigate or solve the suspicious death of a 21-year-old man. He was hospitalized, and at time of writing the attack was being investigated by police as an attempted murder. In response to the attack, the public and other journalists organized protest walks demanding better safety and protection standards for journalists.

Sexual Orientation and Gender Identity

Between January and September 2018, Sarajevo Open Center, a lesbian, gay, bisexual, transgender, and intersex (LGBTI) and women's rights group, recorded 27 hate-motivated incidents against LGBTI people, including 10 involving domestic violence, and 136 cases of hate speech, mostly online. Five cases were reported to police, one of which was referred to a prosecutor. However, the status of the investigation was unknown at time of writing.

According to Foundation CURE, a feminist activist organization, politicians in Bosnia and Herzegovina still do not publicly discuss LGBT rights and concerns, police often dismiss hate crimes against LGBT people, and acquiring permits for LGBT events and peaceful gatherings was significantly more difficult in 2018 than in previous years.

In a notable development, Republika Srpska amended its criminal law to include an offence of public incitement to violence and hatred based on sex, sexual orientation, and gender identity.

Key International Actors

In May 2018, Council of Europe (CoE) Commissioner for Human Rights Dunja Mijatovic urged the minister for human rights and refugees and the minister for security to address the migration crisis in a way that is compliant with human rights.

In June 2018, the Council of the European Union told Bosnian authorities to ensure that any changes to electoral law not further complicate efforts to implement the European Court of Human Rights' judgement on discrimination against minorities running for political office (Sejdic-Finci case) but did not insist on immediate implementation of the 2009 ruling.

The EU, the Organization for Security and Co-operation in Europe, and the United States Embassy jointly urged the Council of Ministers in Bosnia and Herzegovina to prioritize adopting the revised National War Crimes Processing Strategy.

In April 2018, the OSCE reviewed the draft law on Public Assembly in the Federation of Bosnia and Herzegovina and concluded that if adopted it would violate freedom of assembly, unduly burden organizers of assemblies, and pose severe restrictions on venues for assemblies.

In their August 2018 concluding observations of the periodic report of Bosnia and Herzegovina, the United Nations Committee on the Elimination of Racial Discrimination called on Bosnian authorities to include in its criminal code all grounds for discrimination, ensure that local laws enable equal rights for all, and end "two schools under one roof," the practice of ethnic-based segregation within a single school.

HUMAN
RIGHTS
WATCH

"You Don't Want to Breathe
Poison Anymore"
The Failing Response to Pesticide Drift in Brazil's Rural Communities

Brazil

Jair Bolsonaro, a member of Congress who has endorsed torture and other abusive practices, and made openly racist, homophobic and misogynist statements, won a run-off election in October. Political violence and threats against journalists marred the presidential contest.

Violence reached a new record in Brazil, with some 64,000 killings in 2017. Police solve just a small fraction of homicides. Unlawful killings by police feed the wave of violence. Weak state control of many prisons facilitates gang recruitment.

Domestic violence remains widespread; thousands of cases each year are not properly investigated.

Tens of thousands of Venezuelans poured into Brazil in 2018 fleeing repression, hunger, and inadequate medical care. Brazil has kept its borders open, but there have been several serious xenophobic attacks against Venezuelans.

Many rural Brazilians are exposed to pesticides sprayed near their homes, schools, and workplaces, and they fear reprisals if they report poisonings.

Public Security and Police Conduct

A large-scale study by criminologists and journalists estimates that prosecutors file charges in only two out of every ten homicides.

Abuses by police, including extrajudicial executions, contribute to a cycle of violence that undermines public security and endangers the lives of police officers and civilians.

The federal government has failed to publish a yearly report about killings by and of police officers, as ordered by the Inter-American Court of Human Rights in a 2017 ruling. Data compiled by the nonprofit Brazilian Forum on Public Security from official sources show that 367 on- and off-duty police officers were killed in 2017, the latest available information. Police officers, including off-duty officers, killed 5,144 people in 2017, 20 percent more than in 2016.

While some police killings are in self-defense, research by Human Rights Watch and other organizations shows that some are extrajudicial executions. In São

Paulo, the police ombudsman examined hundreds of police killings in 2017, concluding that police used excessive force in three-quarters of them, sometimes against unarmed people.

A 2017 law moved trials of members of the armed forces accused of unlawful killings of civilians from civilian to military courts. The law also moved trials of military police—the state police force that patrols the streets in Brazil—accused of torture and other crimes to military courts, although homicides by them remain in civilian jurisdiction. This means that the armed forces and military police investigate their own members who are accused of crimes. Under international norms, extrajudicial executions and other grave human rights violations by police and the military must be investigated by civilian authorities and tried in civilian courts.

Less than a month after the law was enacted, eight civilians were killed during a joint civil police and army operation in Rio de Janeiro's metropolitan area. At time of writing, neither armed forces investigators nor federal military prosecutors had interviewed any civilian witnesses.

Then-President Michel Temer in February transferred responsibility for public security and prisons in Rio de Janeiro to the army, until December 2018, with the stated aim of improving citizens' safety. Yet from March to October, homicides went up by 2 percent in Rio State, while police killings increased by 44 percent, compared to the same period in 2017.

Among the Rio homicide victims were councilwoman and human rights defender Marielle Franco and her driver, Anderson Gomes, gunned down in a professional killing in March. At time of writing, police had made no arrests in the case.

Prison Conditions, Torture, and Ill-Treatment of Detainees

In June 2016, more than 726,000 adults were behind bars in facilities built to hold half that number, Ministry of Justice data show. The federal government expected another 115,000 by the end of 2018.

Overcrowding and understaffing make it impossible for prison authorities to maintain control within many prisons, leaving detainees vulnerable to violence and recruitment into gangs.

Fewer than 15 percent of inmates have access to educational or work opportunities, and health services are often deficient. Rio's Public Defenders' Office reported that in that state alone, 266 people died in detention in 2017, most of such treatable conditions as diabetes, hypertension, or respiratory ailments.

In February, the Supreme Court ruled that pregnant women, mothers of children under 13, and mothers of children and adults with disabilities who are in pretrial detention for non-violent crimes should instead await trial under house arrest, except for "very exceptional cases." Although the Ministry of Justice said the order could apply to 10,693 incarcerated women, judges had released to house arrest only 426 by May 1, the Supreme Court's deadline for compliance. Judges made widespread use of a "very exceptional cases" exception to retain women in jail.

Many people awaiting trial are routinely held with convicted prisoners, in violation of international standards and Brazilian law.

The National Council of Justice ordered that by May 2016 all detainees should be taken, within 24 hours of arrest, to a hearing to determine if they should be in preventive detention or set free pending trial. But more than two years later, many jurisdictions outside state capitals still do not hold such "custody hearings." In the absence of those hearings, detainees often wait months to see a judge for the first time.

At custody hearings, judges can detect police abuse, yet some do not ask detainees about their treatment. In most cases, police officers are present during the hearing, which can be intimidating. Still, about 5 percent of detainees report abuse during the hearings, according to the National Council of Justice. Several studies have shown that their allegations are often not properly investigated.

At time of writing, Congress was examining a bill to make custody hearings mandatory countrywide. But the bill would allow some to be held via videoconference with people in their places of detention, which would make the hearings far less useful as a genuine opportunity to discover allegations of police abuse.

Children's Rights

Brazil's juvenile detention facilities housed 24,345 children and young adults in January 2018, official data show.

Police accused 13 staff members of negligent homicide for delay in responding to a fire that killed 10 children in a detention center in Goiânia State in May. And in Ceará State, federal prosecutors blamed the "actions and omissions" of state authorities for the deaths of seven children and young adults in 2017 and 2018.

In a 2018 study of children and young adults detained in São Paulo State by a nonprofit Instituto Sou da Paz with the cooperation of state authorities, 90 percent said military police had mistreated them during arrest, and 25 percent said juvenile detention staff had beaten them. Investigations by the National Mechanism for the Prevention and Combatting of Torture and Human Rights Watch have revealed scores of cases of mistreatment in various states. Abuses are often not properly investigated or punished.

Freedom of Expression

More than 140 reporters covering the elections were harassed, threatened, and in some cases physically attacked, the Brazilian Association of Investigative Journalism (Abraji) found. After winning the election, Bolsonaro said he would withdraw state advertising from news media that are "unworthy."

During the campaign, electoral court judges ordered universities to clamp down on what they considered illegal political campaigning, including an event against fascism and publications "in defense of democracy." In a unanimous decision, the Supreme Court decided those restrictions violated freedom of expression and struck them down.

The ruling comes as Bolsonaro and his allies push a bill that would prohibit teachers from promoting their own opinions in the classroom or using the terms "gender" or "sexual orientation," and would order that sex and religious education be framed around "family values."

In March, in the case of a man sentenced to six months in prison for insulting a soldier, three Supreme Court justices upheld a legal provision called *desacato* that punishes the "disrespecting" of public officials with up to two years in prison. A fourth justice maintained that punishing "disrespect" violates freedom of expression. The Brazilian Bar Association has petitioned the Supreme Court to rule the *desacato* provision unconstitutional. That case was pending at time of writing.

Military police have abused *desacato* to quell criticism, for example, detaining people participating in protests, saying they disrespected officers.

Military police officers face broad restrictions on their own freedom of speech. State disciplinary codes and the military criminal code subject officers to expulsion from the force and prison sentences for offenses, such as criticizing a superior officer or a government decision.

Women's and Girls' Rights

At the end of 2017, more than 1.2 million cases of domestic violence were pending before the courts. Implementation of Brazil's anti-domestic violence legislation, the 2006 "Maria da Penha" law, is lagging. Official data show that 23 shelters that housed women and children in desperate need closed in 2017 due to budget cuts. Only 74 shelters remain, in a country of more than 200 million people. Each year, police do not properly investigate thousands of domestic violence cases, with the result that they are never prosecuted.

Unchecked domestic abuse typically escalates and may lead to death. In 2017, the last year for which data is available, 4,539 women were killed in Brazil, the Brazilian Forum on Public Security reports. Police registered 1,133 as femicides, defined under Brazilian law as the killing of a woman "on account of being persons of the female sex." The real number is likely higher, as police do not record as femicides killings for which the motives are initially unclear.

Abortion is legal in Brazil only in cases of rape, when necessary to save a woman's life, or when the fetus suffers from anencephaly, a fatal congenital brain disorder. Women and girls who have clandestine abortions not only risk injury and death but face up to three years in prison, while people convicted of performing unlawful abortions face up to four years. In August, the Supreme Court held a two-day hearing on a pending petition to decriminalize abortion in the first 12 weeks of pregnancy.

An outbreak of the Zika virus in 2015-2016 caused particular harm to women and girls. When a pregnant woman is infected, Zika can cause complications in fetal development, including of the brain. Ministry of Health data from June showed that two-thirds of children born with Zika syndrome had not received the specialized early stimulation that is crucial for their development.

Disability Rights

Thousands of people with disabilities, including children and infants, are needlessly confined in institutions, where they may face neglect and abuse, sometimes for life. At the request of a relative or an institution's director, courts can strip people with disabilities of their legal capacity—the right to make decisions for themselves, with support if they ask for it. A person stripped of legal capacity can only leave an institution with the consent of their guardian, which constitutes unlawful deprivation of liberty according to the Convention on the Rights of People with Disabilities, which Brazil has ratified.

In June, the Senate approved a bill that recognizes a right to legal capacity for some adults with disabilities. The bill does not establish universal legal capacity or a system that allows all people with disabilities access to supported decision-making.

Migrants, Refugees, and Asylum Seekers

Thousands of Venezuelans have crossed the border into Brazil fleeing hunger, lack of basic health care, and persecution. UNHCR data shows that from January 2014 to April 2018, 25,311 Venezuelans requested a residency permit in Brazil. From January 2014 to July 2018, 57,575 requested asylum. Brazil granted asylum to 14 Venezuelans in 2016, and denied it to 28. In October, the head of Brazil's refugee agency (CONARE) told Human Rights Watch the agency had not made any decisions about asylum requests from Venezuelans "in the last years."

By October, the federal government and the UNHCR had opened 13 shelters in Roraima State that housed more than 5,500 Venezuelans. The government has been slow to integrate them into society; most children in shelters do not go to school, and many Venezuelans still lack legal papers. By November, more than 3,100 Venezuelans had benefited from a federal program that relocates them to other states.

In March, a mob expelled Venezuelans from an improvised shelter in Roraima, the Brazilian state that borders Venezuela, and burned their belongings; in August, after another attack, a mob pushed about 1,200 Venezuelans back across the border while police looked on, making no arrests; and in September, several Brazilians lynched a Venezuelan whom they accused of a killing.

Sexual Orientation and Gender Identity

In September 2017, a federal judge overruled a 1999 decision by the Federal Council of Psychology that banned conversion therapy, which attempts to change an individual's sexual orientation or gender identity. The council's appeals to a federal court and to the Supreme Court were pending at time of writing.

In March, the Supreme Court ruled that the government can no longer require transgender people who want their name and gender marker on identification documents changed to undergo medical procedures or subject their decisions to judicial review.

Brazilian media reported about dozens of cases of threats and attacks against lesbian, gay, bisexual, and transgender people during the presidential campaign, many of them allegedly by Bolsonaro supporters.

Labor Rights

From January to October, the Ministry of Labor identified 1,246 cases of workers subjected to abusive conditions that under Brazilian law rise to the level of "slave-like," such as forced labor or degrading working conditions. In response to a judicial order, the Ministry of Labor in April released a list of 166 employers on whom it had imposed penalties since 2010 for employing people in "slave-like" conditions.

Environment and Land-Related Conflicts

Many rural residents are exposed to pesticides sprayed near their homes, schools, and workplaces. They fear reprisals from large landowners if they denounce poisonings.

The government does not adequately monitor pesticide exposure and pesticide residues in drinking water and food. At time of writing, Congress was considering a bill that would weaken the regulatory framework for pesticides, including by reducing the role of the Health and Environment Ministries in authorizing new pesticides.

In 2017, 71 people involved in land conflicts died violently, the highest number since 2003, the Pastoral Land Commission of the Catholic Church reported.

In March, then-President Temer issued three decrees implementing a 2017 federal law that would grant titles to people occupying land illegally. Environmental and landless peasant organizations argue that the law would benefit large landowners and illegal loggers. The attorney general has warned that it could increase the number of killings as a result of land conflicts. Three pending petitions ask the Supreme Court to declare the law unconstitutional.

Confronting Military-Era Abuses

The perpetrators of human rights abuses during military rule from 1964 to 1985 are shielded from justice by a 1979 amnesty law that the Supreme Court upheld in 2010, a decision that the Inter-American Court of Human Rights ruled violated Brazil's obligations under international law.

Since 2012, federal prosecutors have charged more than 40 former military officers and other agents of the dictatorship with killings, kidnappings, and other serious human rights abuses. Lower courts dismissed most of the cases, while the Supreme Court halted two, pending re-examination of the amnesty law.

In July, the Inter-American Court of Human Rights condemned Brazil's handling of the case of journalist Vladimir Herzog, whom state agents tortured and killed in 1975. The court ruled that killing should be considered a crime against humanity and ordered Brazilian institutions to recognize that type of crime is not subject to statutes of limitation. In compliance with the ruling, federal prosecutors re-opened the Herzog investigation.

In October, an appeals court reversed a lower court's decision to order a former army colonel to pay about US$25,000 to the family of a man who was tortured and killed by the units under the colonel's command during the dictatorship. The court found the statute of limitation had expired.

Key International Actors

The Inter-American Commission on Human Rights (IACHR) and the United Nations Office of the High Commissioner for Human Rights (OHCHR) expressed "deep concern" over then-President Temer's decision to put public security in the hands of the armed forces in Rio de Janeiro. The UN special rapporteur on ex-trajudicial, summary, or arbitrary executions criticized the 2017 law that shields members of the armed forces from trial in civilian courts for unlawful killings of civilians. In November, after its first visit to Brazil since 1995, the IACHR found systematic violations of human rights by state agents, such as extrajudicial killings by police and "deplorable" prison conditions.

Foreign Policy

The Brazilian government condemned violations of human rights in Venezuela, urged the administration of President Nicolás Maduro to allow humanitarian aid to enter the country, and called for the re-establishment of democracy. Brazil did not co-sponsor a resolution condemning abuses in Venezuela that the so-called Lima Group countries introduced to the UN Human Rights Council—but it voted in favor.

A Saudi-led coalition has used Brazilian-made cluster munitions in Yemen on at least four occasions in the past few years. Cluster munitions are prohibited by a 2008 treaty joined by 104 countries, but not by Brazil.

Brazil is a strong supporter of a prohibition on fully autonomous weapons. To-gether with Austria and Chile, Brazil called, in August, for negotiating a treaty to retain meaningful human control over weapons systems and the use of force.

Burundi

Burundi's security services and members of the Imbonerakure, the ruling party youth league, carried out widespread human rights abuses throughout 2018, including summary executions, rapes, abductions, beatings, and intimidation of suspected political opponents. Many of the worst abuses occurred in the lead-up to a May 17 constitutional referendum, which enables President Pierre Nkurunziza to potentially remain in power until 2034.

The humanitarian situation remains dire; the country's once vibrant civil society and media landscape has been decimated since the crisis began in April 2015, when Nkurunziza announced his bid for a disputed third term. On May 11, just before the referendum, unidentified assailants, suspected of entering Burundi from the Democratic Republic of Congo, launched one of the deadliest attacks in Burundi in recent years, killing 26 people, including 11 children, in Ruhagarika, Cibitoke Province.

A United Nations Human Rights Council-mandated commission of inquiry reported in September that serious violations, including crimes against humanity, continued in 2017 and 2018.

On September 27, 2017, Burundi's National Security Council announced a three-month suspension of international nongovernmental organizations. As a result, the operations of around 130 international NGOs, some of them providing life-saving assistance, were seriously hampered.

Abuses by Security Forces and Ruling Party Youth

The Commission of Inquiry confirmed new cases in 2018 of summary execution, enforced disappearance, arbitrary arrest and detention, sexual violence, torture and other cruel, inhuman or degrading treatment. The commission concluded that the perpetrators of these crimes—the National Intelligence Services, the police, and the Imbonerakure—operate in "a climate of impunity perpetuated by the lack of an independent judiciary." The commission for the first time implicated Nkurunziza directly in "repeated hate speech and calls for violence."

When announcing the referendum on December 12, 2017, President Pierre Nkurunziza warned that those who dared to "sabotage" the project to revise the constitution "by word or action" would be crossing a "red line." In the months leading up to the referendum, police, intelligence services, and members of the Imbonerakure killed, raped, abducted, beat, and intimidated suspected opponents of the ruling party, the National Council for the Defense of Democracy-Forces for the Defense of Democracy (Conseil national pour la défense de la démocratie-Forces de défense de la démocratie, CNDD-FDD). Beatings and intimidation of suspected opponents continued after the vote.

Political violence tied to the May referendum claimed at least 15 lives, according to Human Rights Watch research, but the actual number killed is likely much higher. Dozens of dead bodies were found across the country in suspicious circumstances. Many of them were never identified and the circumstances around the deaths never confirmed.

Numerous political opponents were arrested, intimidated, or held incommunicado in unknown locations, including members of the National Liberation Forces (Forces nationales de libération, FNL), the Movement for Solidarity and Democracy (Mouvement pour la solidarité et la démocratie, MSD), and other opposition parties. Some were accused of having told their members to vote against the referendum.

The Commission of Inquiry found that CNDD-FDD and Imbonerakure members "stepped up their efforts to recruit members from among the general public" before and during the referendum campaign, including through forced recruitment. The commission also found that Imbonerakure members can act freely due to their dependence "on the discretion of State power structures and on the impunity accorded by the latter."

Refugees

At time of writing, approximately 378,000 refugees lived outside Burundi, including in Tanzania, Rwanda, Uganda, and Congo. Following a peak of around 431,000 Burundian refugees in March, as of early October, about 40,000 refugees had returned to Burundi from Tanzania under a voluntary repatriation program involving Tanzania, Burundi, and the United Nations High Commissioner for Refugees (UNHCR). Some refugees said they had no choice but to return to Burundi after Tanzanian local authorities had banned them from trading

HUMAN
RIGHTS
WATCH

"We Will Beat You to Correct You"

Abuses Ahead of Burundi's Constitutional Referendum

inside the closed camps they had been living in and cash-strapped aid agencies had reduced daily food rations to one meal a day.

In April, around 2,500 Burundian refugees, most of whom are members of a religious sect known as the "Zebiya followers," returned from Rwanda to Burundi. They had originally fled to Kamanyola, in eastern Congo's South Kivu province in 2015. In September 2017, Congolese security forces used excessive force to quash a protest led by the Burundian refugees in Kamanyola, killing around 40 refugees and wounding more than 100 others. As conditions deteriorated further, those who survived the massacre fled to Rwanda in March. After several of their leaders were arrested in Rwanda, and because many refused certain procedures on religious grounds, including biometric registration, most of the refugees then returned to Burundi, where some may have faced persecution.

Civil Society and Freedom of Media

Space for civil society and media has become much narrower in 2018, and many civil society activists and independent journalists remained in exile. Many of those who remained in Burundi faced intimidation, detention, or trials on trumped up charges. Human rights activist Germain Rukuki, a member of Action by Christians for the Abolition of Torture (ACAT), was sentenced to 32 years in prison in April on charges of "rebellion," "threatening state security," "participation in an insurrectional movement," and "attacks on the head of state." In August, activist Nestor Nibitanga, an observer for the Association for the Protection of Human Rights and Detained Persons (APRODH), was sentenced to five years for "threatening state security." The government closed ACAT and APRODH in October 2016, along with several other human rights groups.

In March, three members of Parole et Action pour le Réveil des Consciences et l'Évolution des Mentalités (PARCEM), were sentenced to 10 years in prison for having "prepared actions likely to disrupt security." PARCEM is one of the few remaining independent NGOs operating in the country. The activists were arrested in 2017 while organizing a workshop on arbitrary arrests.

The National Communication Council (CNC) suspended the online readers' forum of Burundi's main independent newspaper Iwacu in April for three months, for "violation of professional standards." In early May, the CNC suspended the British Broadcasting Corporation for six months for "violating press laws" and "unprofessional conduct" after inviting a leading Burundian human rights activist, Pierre Claver Mbonimpa, to its program on March 12. The CNC claimed Mbonimpa's remarks were "inappropriate, exaggerated, non-verified and damaged the reputation of the head of state." At the same time, the CNC banned the Voice of America (VOA), also for six months, for the technical reason that it was using a banned frequency. BBC and VOA remain off the air at time of writing.

Sexual Orientation and Gender Identity

Burundi punishes consensual same-sex sexual relations between adults with up to two years in prison under article 567 of the penal code. This violates the rights to privacy and freedom from discrimination.

Right to Education

In June, the government banned girls who are pregnant or have a child from attending school. About four weeks later, the government reversed the decision without giving a reason.

Constitutional Reform

The new constitution, adopted during the May referendum, replaced the 2005 constitution, which came into force after the signing of the 2000 Arusha Peace Accords, which helped to end a civil war. The new constitution increased presidential terms from five to seven years, renewable only once, and reset the clock on terms already served, enabling Nkurunziza to potentially stand for two new seven-year terms, one in 2020 and another in 2027.

Beyond changing the law around term limits, the new constitution was designed to strengthen the CNDD-FDD's grip by reducing the majority needed to adopt legislation. The changes could lead to a dismantling of the power sharing components that were central to the Arusha Accords, and put into question guarantees that the ethnic Tutsi minority hold some government posts.

Key International Actors

The Inter-Burundi dialogue, which began in 2014 under the leadership of the East African Community (EAC), continued to stall, hampered by an apparent unwillingness among regional leaders to press Nkurunziza to make real concessions. The inter-Burundi dialogue's Facilitator, former Tanzanian President Benjamin Mkapa, called for a fifth and final round of talks between the government and the political opposition. The consultations took place from October between October 24 and 29in Arusha, Tanzania. Little was accomplished, as the Burundian government did not attend the session.

In February, the Sub-Committee on Accreditation of the Global Alliance of National Human Rights Institutions, which assesses the effectiveness and independence of national human rights institutions, downgraded Burundi's National Independent Human Rights Commission from a status "A" to "B" for a lack of independence.

The International Criminal Court continued investigations into crimes committed in Burundi since 2015. The UN commission held an interactive dialogue at the UN General Assembly 73rd Session on October 24, 2018. In an August press statement, the UN Security Council urged Burundi "to take further steps to respect, protect and guarantee human rights and fundamental freedoms for all, in line with the country's Constitution and its international obligations."

The Human Rights Council renewed the commission of inquiry's mandate for another year, despite Burundi's continued refusal to cooperate with the commission and declaring its members persona non-grata in September. In April, the government also revoked the visas of three UN experts tasked by the high commissioner for human rights to gather information on abuses to share with local judicial authorities, despite Burundi having endorsed the experts and their assignment in September 2017.

The Security Council continues to hold regular meetings on the situation in Burundi but has remained paralyzed on the matter, mostly because Burundi is not a priority due to other competing interests, such as the crisis in Syria and other conflicts.

Cambodia

In anticipation of national elections in July 2018, the government of Prime Minister Hun Sen and his Cambodian People's Party (CPP) intensified its onslaught on the political opposition, civil society groups, and independent media. In late 2017, the CPP-controlled Supreme Court dissolved the main opposition party, the Cambodia National Rescue Party (CNRP). Former opposition leader Sam Rainsy remained in exile after being convicted on politically motivated charges, while party chief Kem Sokha was jailed for a year on dubious charges and has since been under house arrest. The CPP, facing no major opposition party, won all 125 seats in the National Assembly, effectively creating a one-party state. Hun Sen, in power since 1985, announced he wants to be the world's longest-serving leader in history.

Cambodia's politicized and corrupt judiciary continued to target individuals for peacefully criticizing the government, including online. During 2018, large numbers of opposition party members and activists fled the country to avoid arbitrary arrest. The number of political prisoners rose to more than 30 in July 2018, but 16 were released after the election on royal pardons sought by Hun Sen to deflect international criticism of the elections.

Media freedoms, already under pressure, collapsed in 2018. Threatening a massive, bogus tax bill, the government coerced the owners of the highly regarded *Phnom Penh Post* to sell to a Malaysian businessman with reportedly close ties to Hun Sen, making future critical reporting unlikely. By the end of 2018, Cambodia no longer had any local independent newspapers or radio and TV channels. Social media also came under assault, with criminal charges filed for posts to Facebook critical of the government.

The government frequently resorted to repressive laws, such as the Law on Associations and Non-Governmental Organizations (LANGO), to arbitrarily restrict the activities of human rights organizations and silence them. Democratic space in Cambodia has reached its lowest level since before the intervention over 25 years ago by the international community through the United Nations Transitional Authority in Cambodia (UNTAC), established to facilitate the implementation of the 1991 Paris Peace Accords. UNTAC assisted in ending the Cambodian

HUMAN
RIGHTS
WATCH

CAMBODIA'S DIRTY DOZEN
A Long History of Rights Abuses by Hun Sen's Generals

civil war, created an environment conducive for civil society, and established a state that pledged to uphold democracy, rule of law, and human rights.

Attacks on Human Rights Defenders

On January 4, 2018, a Phnom Penh investigating judge charged labor rights advocate Moeun Tola, director of the Center for Alliance of Labor and Human Rights (CENTRAL); free media advocate Pa Nguon Teang, director of the Cambodian Center for Independent Media (CCIM); and social activist Venerable But Buntenh, a Buddhist monk, with embezzlement in retaliation for being members of the funeral committee for Kem Ley, a popular political commentator who was assassinated in 2016. In July, the charges were dropped against Moeun Tola under pressure from global apparel brands, but charges remained against the two others at time of writing.

On August 20, the king pardoned longtime land rights activist Tep Vanny after two years in prison for protesting for justice in a land dispute involving a Chinese company granted a concession in Phnom Penh's Boeung Kak Lake community. However, immediately afterwards, a court convicted her of making death threats in what started out as an internal community dispute in 2012. While the complainant had dropped her lawsuit, the prosecutor decided to pursue it on his own accord, leading to Tep Vanny and five other Boeung Kak Lake community members being sentenced to six months' imprisonment; the judge suspended the sentence for five years.

The courts also proceeded with cases against other activists. On September 26, a Phnom Penh court convicted five former and current senior staff members of the Cambodian Human Rights and Development Association (ADHOC) of bribery of a witness, in a case that was widely criticized as being politically motivated, and imposed a five-year suspended prison sentence. An investigating judge had released them on bail in June 2017 after 427 days in pretrial detention.

Attacks on Political Opposition

Elections on July 29 were fundamentally flawed, denying Cambodians their right to freely choose their representatives. In addition to dissolving the CNRP, the

Supreme Court-imposed a ban on 118 senior CNRP members from all political activity for five years.

Other serious problems with the electoral process included a lack of fair and equal access to the media; a pro-government national election commission; and surveillance, intimidation, detention, and politically motivated prosecution of key opposition members. The CPP based its crackdown on unsubstantiated claims that the CNRP intended to lead a "color revolution" to overthrow the government.

The CNRP's founder Sam Rainsy and other leading opposition figures remained in exile to avoid enforcement of threatened prosecutions and pending prison sentences. His successor as leader of the CNRP, Kem Sokha, remained in pretrial detention on bogus treason charges.

CNRP lawmaker Um Sam An was royally pardoned and released on August 25, 2018, after having spent over two years in prison for an incitement conviction that arose out of his accusations against the government that the Cambodia-Vietnam border had been wrongfully demarked. On May 20, the appeals court upheld the conviction of 11 CNRP activists for "insurrection." The 11 had already served three years of their 7 to 20-year prison terms on baseless charges for a 2014 demonstration in Phnom Penh, in which police were attacked after security forces assaulted peaceful protesters. On August 28, all 11, plus three more CNRP activists who had been sentenced separately on the same charges, were pardoned and released.

Freedom of Media

The government further curtailed freedom of media, including online publications. In May 2018, the government coerced the sale of the last independent local newspaper, the *Phnom Penh Post*, to a Malaysian businessman with reported ties to the Cambodian government by leveling the newspaper with a questionable unpaid tax bill of US$3.9 million. The *Post*, along with the previously shuttered local independent newspaper, the *Cambodia Daily*, had long provided investigative reporting frequently critical of the government.

On August 21, two former Radio Free Asia (RFA) journalists, Yeang Sothearin and Uon Chhin, were released on bail. They had been arbitrarily arrested on November 14, 2017, on fabricated espionage charges for allegedly having continued to report for RFA after the closure of RFA's Cambodia office. The two remain under surveillance and on September 18, 2018, the Supreme Court ruled that the judicial investigation against them would continue.

On August 31, after 14 months of pretrial detention, an Australian filmmaker was convicted on trumped-up espionage charges and sentenced to six years in prison. He received a royal pardon on September 21, and was deported to Australia soon after.

Social media networks faced increased government surveillance and interventions. On May 28, the government issued a national decree, allowing the Ministries of Interior, Information, and Posts and Telecommunications to take down content on social media outlets and websites that the government deems to be "incitement, breaking solidarity, discrimination and willfully creating turmoil that undermines national security, public interest and social order."

New Repressive Laws

In March 2018, the government introduced a new *lese majeste* (insulting the monarchy) provision into Cambodia's penal code, with a punishment of up to five years in prison and a $2,500 fine. Two months later, authorities arrested two people under the provision, who remained in detention at time of writing.

A series of repressive new laws and amendments were passed in 2018 that further restricted freedom of association. These included amendments to articles 34 and 42 of Cambodia's Constitution to require that every Cambodian "defend the motherland" and empower the government to take action against political parties if they do not "place the country and nation's interest first." The repressive and controversial amendments to Cambodia's Law on Political Parties, allowing for the arbitrary dissolution of political parties and the banning of party leaders without due process, remained in place.

Key International Actors

The United States responded to attacks on the opposition and an increasingly repressive environment for elections by ending all electoral assistance and suspending other assistance programs amounting to $8.3 million. Ahead of the elections, the US State Department imposed new visa restrictions against Cambodian officials responsible for "anti-democratic" actions.

On June 12, 2018, the US Treasury Department imposed Global Magnitsky Act sanctions against the head of Hun Sen's bodyguard unit, Hing Bun Hieng, for being the leader of an entity involved in serious human rights abuses. On July 25, US Congress passed the Cambodia Democracy Act to impose "sanctions on all members of Hun Sen's inner circle for their role in undermining democracy in Cambodia and committing serious human rights violations." The UN special rapporteur on Cambodia and the UN high commissioner for human rights also expressed concern about the elections.

After the dissolution of the CNRP, Sweden—Cambodia's longest-standing Western donor—stopped new state-to-state development aid, except in the areas of education and research. The European Union and its member states, South Korea, Australia, and other democratic countries cut election assistance and/or did not send election observers. Several countries condemned the elections as falling far short of international standards.

In February, the EU's 28 foreign ministers threatened targeted sanctions and the suspension of trade preferences in response to the government's crackdown on rights. In July, the European Commission deployed a mission to Cambodia to assess the country's compliance with its human rights obligations. In September, the European Parliament reiterated its strong concerns over the human rights situation, calling on the commission to report on the mission's findings. EU Trade Commissioner Cecilia Malmström notified Cambodia in October that the EU was launching its procedure for withdrawal of the trade preferences.

Japan, which is competing with China for influence in Cambodia, maintained its $7.5 million electoral support. A week before the election, it decided not to deploy official election observers. In February, Japan said it would provide $168 million in development aid in 2018.

China, despite its own lack of competitive elections, sent election observers and praised the elections. China was the biggest aid donor of Cambodia in 2018. In June, China provided more than $100 million in military aid to Cambodia. Under China's "One Belt, One Road" initiative, Cambodia has received about $5.3 billion in investment and loan agreements between 2013 and 2018. China is pledging another $7 billion in new projects. Cambodia's public external debt was at $9.6 billion by 2017 and may rise to $17 billion by 2020.

In January 2018, China's Foreign Ministry announced that bilateral trade would reach $6 billion by 2020. China has sought to expand its political influence and economic power in Cambodia amid Cambodia's dwindling support from Western governments. Cambodia has supported China's territorial claims to the Spratly Islands in Southeast Asia's regional dispute over the South China Sea.

HUMAN RIGHTS WATCH

"These Killings Can Be Stopped"
Government and Separatist Groups Abuses in Cameroon's Anglophone Regions

Cameroon

Cameroon, a country previously known for its stability, faced violence and serious human rights abuses in 2018. The country endured abusive military operations against a secessionist insurgency in three Anglophone regions, attacks by the Islamic militant group, Boko Haram, in the Far North, and a worsening humanitarian crisis. President Paul Biya, 85, won a seventh seven-year term on October 7.

In the South West and North West, government security forces have committed extrajudicial executions, burned property, carried out arbitrary arrests, and tortured detainees. A Human Rights Watch report documented a range of abuses by both sides in the Anglophone regions, including arson attacks on homes and schools. According to the International Crisis Group, government forces and armed separatists killed over 420 civilians in the regions since the crisis escalated in 2017.

The humanitarian consequences of the Boko Haram attacks and separatist insurgency are of growing concern. As of August, the United Nations estimated that more than 235,000 civilians were displaced in the Far North and 255,000 in the Anglophone North West and South West regions. About 25,000 Cameroonians took refuge in Nigeria. Also, Cameroon has continued to forcibly return Nigerian asylum seekers, fleeing Boko Haram attacks in northeastern Nigeria.

While the government maintained it did not tolerate serious crimes committed by security forces, it failed to demonstrate progress in investigating and punishing them.

On October 22, Cameroon's Constitutional Council validated Paul Biya's reelection, with 71.28 percent of the votes. The council's decision was immediately contested by one of Biya's rivals, Maurice Kamto, who claimed the results had been altered. In early November, dozens of pro-Kamto protesters were arrested in Bafoussam, Western region. Biya was sworn-in for a seventh term as president on November 6.

The Anglophone Crisis: Abuses on Both Sides

In the Anglophone North West and South West regions, the absence of a genuine political process to address decades-old grievances against the Biya government contributed to the radicalization of the discourse and tactics of Anglophone activists. Since late 2016, Anglophone separatists have attacked government institutions and threatened, kidnapped, and killed civilians perceived to side with the government.

In 2016 and 2017, government security forces used excessive force against at least five largely peaceful demonstrations organized by members of the country's Anglophone minority who were calling for the region's independence. Equipped with anti-riot gear, including shields, helmets and tear gas, government forces used live ammunition, including from helicopters, against demonstrators and bystanders, killing at least a dozen people and injuring scores. Some individuals detained in the context of the demonstrations were subjected to torture and ill-treatment.

In October 2017, separatist leaders unilaterally declared independence of the North West and South West regions, and the formation of a new nation, Ambazonia. The following month, President Biya announced that Cameroon was under attack from terrorists and vowed to "eradicate these criminals." The pace and scale of separatists' attacks against security forces, government workers, and state institutions increased, especially following the arrest and deportation of 47 secessionist activists from Nigeria in January 2018.

Violations by Government Forces

Human Rights Watch found that government forces responded to the growing separatist insurgency by carrying out abusive security operations against communities suspected of supporting secessionist groups. Security forces committed extrajudicial executions, used excessive force against civilians, tortured and abused suspected separatists and other detainees, and burned homes and other property in scores of villages.

During attacks documented by Human Rights Watch, security forces allegedly shot and killed over a dozen civilians, including at least seven people whom witnesses said had intellectual, psychosocial or physical disabilities who did not flee because they were unable or refused to. At least four older women died, burned alive, after security forces set fire to their homes.

Human Rights Watch also documented three cases where security forces detained people suspected of supporting the secessionist cause, and then tortured and killed them in detention. In a fourth case, Human Rights Watch analyzed evidence of torture filmed by perpetrators, who appear to be gendarmes. On September 24 and 27, a total of nine men were allegedly executed by security forces in the town of Buea, according to videos reviewed by Human Rights Watch and a report by the Centre for Human Rights and Democracy in Africa, a local non-governmental organization (NGO).

Abuses by Separatists: Attacks on Students, Teachers and Schools

To enforce boycotts of schools following protests by Anglophone teachers against perceived discrimination by the Francophone-dominated national government, separatist groups attacked and burned dozens of schools, threatened teachers, students and parents, kidnapped principals and violently attacked teachers and students. In March, people believed to be armed separatists attacked a high school dormitory in Widikum, North West region, and shot dead Emmanuel Galega, a student.

The pressure tactics forced the majority of schools to close during the 2016-2017 academic year, and as of May 2018 an estimated 42,500 children were still out of school, according to UN Office for Humanitarian Affairs (OCHA). Many schools did not re-open in 2018.

On April 30, Father William Neba, principal of St. Bede's College, in Ashing near Belo, North West region, was reported abducted while celebrating mass with students. He was released two days later. The school suspended classes on the day of the abduction. In September, unidentified gunmen attacked a girl's school in Bafut, North West region, kidnapping five pupils and severely wounding the principal.

In September, the government endorsed the Safe Schools Declaration, an international political agreement to protect education during armed conflict.

On November 5, up to 78 schoolchildren were reportedly kidnapped in Bamenda, North West region, by unknown gunmen. They were released two days later.

Refugee Rights

Cameroon hosts more than 350,000 refugees and asylum seekers, including 260,000 from the Central African Republic and at least 90,000 from Nigeria. Despite its long history of hosting refugees, Cameroon has forcibly returned tens of thousands of Nigerian asylum seekers since 2015. A 2017 Human Rights Watch report documented how soldiers used violence and abuse, including torture, against asylum seekers in remote border regions. Authorities also imposed unlawful restrictions on movement in Cameroon's only official camp for Nigerian refugees. In August 2018, the UN High Commissioner for Refugees reported that between January and July, Cameroon unlawfully returned at least 800 refugees and asylum seekers to Nigeria.

Sexual Orientation and Gender Identity

Cameroon's penal code punishes "sexual relations between persons of the same sex" with up to five years in prison. Police and gendarmes continued to carry out arrests and harassment of people they believe to be lesbian, gay, bisexual or transgender (LGBT). In April, police arrested four activists and a security guard at the office of AJO, an organization that works on HIV education with men who have sex with men (MSM), and other vulnerable groups. They spent a week in jail on spurious homosexuality charges before a lawyer secured their release. Cameroonian human rights organizations documented the arrest of at least 25 other men and at least two women on homosexuality charges in the first half of 2018. They also reported numerous cases of physical violence by private citizens targeting LGBT people.

Justice and Accountability

While the government has repeatedly promised to investigate crimes committed by security forces, it has not done so transparently or systematically.

Government officials told Human Rights Watch in June that while they conducted investigations, they did not want to make them public to avoid undermining the morale of government troops. However, the visible lack of accountability appears to have fueled abuses, like arson and torture, rather than ending them.

In July, the government finally granted access to the 47 prominent Anglophone leaders who had been detained and deported from Nigeria to Cameroon in January. The individuals, held incommunicado for over six months, were permitted to meet their lawyers and the International Committee of the Red Cross.

The government dismissed video footage that emerged in July showing two women and two children being executed by men in uniform in Cameroon's Far North as "fake news." Only after an investigation conducted by Amnesty International demonstrated the killings took place in Cameroon did the government announce it had arrested six soldiers suspected of executing the civilians in the video.

Key International Actors

France, the United States, and the United Kingdom are Cameroon's principal partners, primarily in the context of the counter Boko Haram operations in the country's Far North region. Both France and the US provide Cameroon with military and security assistance and training.

The US has continued to provide military aid to Cameroon.

In February, the European Union called for proportionate use of force and accountability for abuses in the Anglophone region.

In September 2017, as the pace and scope of abuses continued to escalate in Cameroon's Anglophone regions, the UN and African Union issued a joint communiqué calling on the government to facilitate access to humanitarian and human rights organizations and engage in an inclusive dialogue to address the root causes of the crisis.

The UN Security Council in August expressed concern about the situation in Cameroon's Anglophone regions.

Canada

Since assuming office in 2015, the government of Prime Minister Justin Trudeau has made notable efforts to advance human rights in Canada. Domestically, the Trudeau government has been a vocal advocate for a pluralistic and multicultural society that respects the rights of immigrants, lesbian, gay, bisexual, and transgender (LGBT) people, and other minorities.

Despite these efforts, Canada continues to struggle to address issues, including discrimination, against Indigenous peoples and abuses by Canadian companies operating overseas. The Trudeau government has also not suspended arms sales to the Saudi-led coalition despite policy guidelines urging close control over exports of military equipment to countries with a record of human rights violations.

Rights of Indigenous Peoples

Prime Minister Trudeau promised a "renewed, nation-to-nation relationship with Indigenous peoples," but there remain considerable challenges to undoing decades of systemic discrimination. In February 2018, the government announced fundamental changes to how the federal government recognizes Indigenous rights and land title, vowing to work with Indigenous communities across Canada to develop a new legal framework to advance self-determination and self-governance. In May, parliament passed a private member's bill aimed at ensuring that Canada's laws are in harmony with the United Nations Declaration on the Rights of Indigenous Peoples.

However, the water crisis in First Nations communities continues to impede efforts to advance Indigenous rights in Canada. While the Trudeau government lifted long-term boil water advisories (issued when drinking water is or could be contaminated) between November 2015 and October 2018, 68 First Nations communities across the country remained subject to such water advisories, several of which were new, at time of writing.

The 2018 budget provides an additional CDN$172.6 million over three years for infrastructure projects to support high risk water systems. The government has committed to end all drinking water advisories on First Nations reserves by March 2021. The drinking water crisis extends beyond these advisories to include problems related to wells, insufficient operations and maintenance funding, and lack of source water protection.

Violence Against Indigenous Women

In 2016, the Trudeau government announced the establishment of a National Inquiry into Missing and Murdered Indigenous Women and Girls, with a mandate to examine the systemic causes of violence against Indigenous women and make concrete recommendations for action.

Since its establishment, the inquiry has been plagued by delays and complaints from victims' families about inadequate communication and transparency. In March, the inquiry requested a two-year extension to finalize its work. In June, the government announced it would extend the process by only six months, with the inquiry's final report due in April 2019.

In April, after a visit to Canada, the UN special rapporteur on violence against women called for improvements in Canada's legal framework, and urgent action on systemic violence against indigenous women.

Corporate Accountability

Since 2011, Human Rights Watch has urged the Canadian government to establish an ombudsperson's office with a mandate to independently investigate and publicly report on human rights abuses involving Canadian extractive companies. In January, the Trudeau government announced the creation of a new Canadian Ombudsperson for Responsible Enterprise (CORE) tasked with investigating "allegations of human rights abuses linked to Canadian corporate activity abroad." The ombudsperson will focus on the mining, oil and gas, and garment sectors. The government announced that it may withhold support, including financial support, from companies that are found to have committed violations.

In March and April, Citizen Lab, a University of Toronto-based technical research group, published two reports alleging that Canadian-made web-filtering technology is being exported to several repressive governments around the world where it is used to censor political speech, news, and dissident websites, and to block searches for keywords related to LGBT identities.

In response, a spokesperson for Global Affairs Canada said the government was "concerned by allegations of the misuse of Canadian-made technology, including reports of its use in inappropriately preventing free access to the internet."

In June, the Senate Committee on Human Rights released a report concluding that Canada's export laws have enabled the federal government to prioritize economic and other foreign policy interests over human rights. The report recommended that the minister of foreign affairs introduce amendments to the Export and Import Permits Act (1947) requiring the government to put greater emphasis on human rights concerns in issuing export permits. The report also called on Global Affairs Canada to work with industry and civil society to establish a monitoring mechanism to help prevent Canadian-made goods and services from ending up in the hands of human rights abusers.

Sexual Orientation and Gender Identity

In May, the Senate passed Bill C-66, which expunges the records of individuals who were prosecuted because of their sexuality when homosexuality was criminalized in Canada. The bill follows Prime Minister Trudeau's 2017 apology in the House of Commons for the historic mistreatment of sexual minorities by the Canadian government.

Foreign Policy

Throughout 2018 the Canadian government actively addressed the Rohingya crisis. In May, the government announced it would support a referral to the International Criminal Court (ICC) and measures to preserve evidence of crimes by the Myanmar military. By June, Canada had imposed targeted sanctions against eight senior Myanmar military officials for their involvement in the violence and persecution of Rohingya Muslims in Rakhine State.

In August, following a tweet by Canada's Foreign Ministry calling for the immediate release of detained Saudi women's rights activists, Saudi Arabia announced it would expel the Canadian ambassador to Riyadh, freeze all new trade and investments with Canada, suspend state airline flights to Canada, and withdraw all Saudi students from Canadian universities. Following the announcements by the Saudi Foreign Ministry, Foreign Minister Chrystia Freeland said that "Canada will always stand up for the protection of human rights, including women's rights and freedom of expression around the world."

Despite widespread evidence of abuses in Yemen and Canadian policy guidelines that urge close control over exports of military equipment to countries with a record of human rights violations, the Canadian government continues to allow Canadian arms manufacturing companies to sell arms to the Saudi-led coalition. Human Rights Watch has documented repeated laws of war violations by the coalition in Yemen, some likely war crimes, and has repeatedly urged the Canadian government and others to stop selling weapons to Saudi Arabia until it credibly investigates and curtails its unlawful attacks.

In February 2018, Foreign Minister Freeland announced that a government probe "found no conclusive evidence that Canadian-made vehicles were used in human-rights violations." The government did not publicly release the report on this investigation but announced that, despite the findings, it would amend Canadian arms export legislation to legally require the foreign minister to refuse to issue export permits if there is a substantial risk that equipment could be used to commit human rights violations.

Key International Actors

In August, the UN Human Rights Committee concluded that Canada violated the rights of an undocumented irregular migrant by denying her access to essential health care. The committee asked the government to review national legislation to ensure that irregular migrants have access to basic health care.

In May, Canada underwent its third Universal Periodic Review by the UN Human Rights Council. States urged Canada to improve its treatment of Indigenous people, including women and girls.

In April, following a mission to Canada, the UN working group on business and human rights noted the absence of a coherent national policy framework "to protect against business-related human rights abuses and promote effective business respect for human rights…." The working group's report followed expressions of concern by several other UN bodies about abuses linked to Canadian company operations abroad and the lack of access to remedies for victims.

Central African Republic

Armed groups continued to commit serious human rights abuses, expanding their control to an estimated 70 percent of the country, while the central government, led by President Faustin-Archange Touadéra, controlled the capital, Bangui, and surrounding areas to the west.

Fighting between predominantly Muslim Seleka rebels, anti-balaka militias, and other armed groups in the central, northwestern, and eastern parts of the Central African Republic forced thousands to flee their homes. Armed groups killed civilians, raped and sexually assaulted women and girls, attacked displacement camps, recruited and used children as soldiers, burned down villages, and took civilians hostage. Access to justice for serious crimes remained difficult or impossible for many people.

A political dialogue between the African Union (AU) and armed groups, aimed at reaching a political agreement to end the fighting, resumed in August but did not stop the violence and abuses against civilians. While there was some success in restoring order, particularly in Paoua, United Nations peacekeepers generally struggled to protect civilians from attack by armed groups, some committed around UN bases.

While some local courts rendered convictions of armed group leaders implicated in serious crimes, overall impunity for past abuses and war crimes continued. The Special Criminal Court, a hybrid court in the national justice system comprised of national and international judges and prosecutors, officially began to function in October.

The International Criminal Court (ICC) appeals chamber overturned the conviction of Jean-Pierre Bemba, a former vice-president of the Democratic Republic of Congo, for crimes committed in the Central African Republic in 2002 and 2003. The ICC continued its second investigation of crimes committed in the country, related to the more recent conflict, and in November, took Alfred Yékatom, an anti-balaka leader, into custody for crimes committed between December 2013 and August 2014.

Attacks on Civilians

Between December 2017 and February 2018, fighting between Revolution Justice (RJ) and the National Movement for the Liberation of the Central African Republic (*Mouvement national pour la libération de la Centrafrique,* MNLC) and indiscriminate attacks killed scores of civilians in the Ouham-Pendé province, near the town Paoua. The violence caused the displacement of up to 60,000 people around Paoua from December 2017 to February 2018. While many of the displaced later returned to their homes, MNLC and RJ fighters remained in the area and continued to threaten civilians.

Anti-balaka and the Union for Peace in the Central African Republic (*l'Union pour la Paix en Centrafrique* UPC), a Seleka faction, clashed multiple times on the road between Bambari and Ippy, in the Ouaka province, and attacked civilians in the area. In March, anti-balaka fighters killed at least 15 civilian Peuhl herders, including women and children. In revenge, the UPC twice attacked a church in Seko, killing an estimated 40 internally displaced people who had sought shelter there.

In April, a joint operation between the UN and national security forces in the PK5 neighborhood of Bangui, dubbed "Sukula," exacerbated tensions between UN peacekeepers and the "self-defense" groups. The operation aimed to dismantle bases of "self-defense" groups, some affiliated with the Seleka that had taken control of parts of the neighborhood, but the ensuing violence lasted two months, flaming tensions between Muslims and non-Muslims. An escalation of fighting led to the death of at least 70 people, some of them civilians. Following the "Sukula" operation militia fighters from PK5 attacked a religious service at Fatima church in May, killing at least 30 people, including a priest. The operation did not dismantle the bases of "self-defense" groups, but instead led to the groups' strengthening their position in PK5.

Fighters from the Popular Front for the Renaissance in the Central African Republic (Front Populaire pour la Renaissance de la Centrafrique, FPRC), a Seleka faction, killed at least 24 civilians in and around Bria from August 25 to September 16, in Haute-Kotto province. They executed nine of the victims about five kilometers from a UN base. Anti-balaka groups also killed civilians in the area from June onwards, executing at least seven non-Muslim civilians outside of Bria for having done business with Muslims in the town.

The Ugandan rebel group the Lord's Resistance Army (LRA) remained active in the southeast with allegations of killings and increased abductions of civilians.

Attacks against humanitarian workers increased across the country. In February, six aid and education workers were killed by unidentified assailants near Markounda, in Ouham province.

Three Russian journalists were killed by unidentified people in July outside of Sibut, in Kemo province. The men were allegedly investigating Russia's increased role in the country and the possible role of Russian mercenary outfits on the ground.

Refugees and Internally Displaced Persons

Fighting and attacks by armed groups forced tens of thousands of people to flee their homes throughout 2018. The total number of internally displaced people in the country, based on UN figures, reached over 642,800, and the total number of refugees to 574,600, the highest numbers since 2014. Conditions for IDPs and refugees, most of whom stay in camps, remained harsh. Many displaced people had little or no access to humanitarian assistance. Persons with disabilities at displacement sites faced barriers to access sanitation, food, and medical assistance.

About 2.5 million people, out of a population of 4.6 million, needed humanitarian assistance. The humanitarian response plan was less than half-funded, with a budget gap of around US$268 million.

Regional and International Forces

The UN peacekeeping mission, MINUSCA, deployed about 11,650 military peacekeepers and 2,080 police across many parts of the country. In November 2017, the UN Security Council approved an additional 900 troops for MINUSCA, but not all troops were in place by the end of 2018.

Under Chapter VII of the UN Charter, the mission is authorized to take all necessary means to protect the civilian population from threat of physical violence and to "implement a mission-wide protection strategy."

Russian civilian and military advisers arrived in the country in December 2017 to train the national armed forces. Some Russian instructors were stationed with national forces outside Bangui.

National and International Justice

While there was some progress in ensuring justice for serious crimes, impunity continued to be a key challenge and a driver of abuses in conflict.

Two armed group leaders, along with several other fighters, were convicted in a Bangui criminal court. In January, anti-balaka leader Rodrique Ngaïbona, alias "Andilo," was found guilty on four charges, including murder, and given a life sentence. Human Rights Watch, in a 2017 report documented cases of rape by men under Ngaïbona's command. In August, Idriss Ahmned el Bachar, the political head of the Central African Patriotic Movement (Mouvement Patriotique pour la Centrafrique, MPC), a Seleka faction, was convicted of "associating with criminals" and "possession of illegal weapons and ammunition" and was sentenced to five years in prison. Human Rights Watch has documented multiple war crimes committed by MPC fighters since 2016.

The Special Criminal Court, a hybrid court with national and international judges and prosecutors that will focus on grave international crimes committed since 2003, began functioning, with judges, investigators and other staff taking up their positions. In May, parliament passed the rules of procedure and evidence necessary for the court to proceed with investigations and prosecutions.

In June, an appeals chamber at the ICC overturned the war crimes and crimes against humanity convictions of Jean-Pierre Bemba, a former vice-president of Congo and leader of the Movement for the Liberation of the Congo (*Mouvement pour la Libération du Congo*). Bemba was found guilty of rape, murder, and pillage in March 2016 for crimes committed in the Central African Republic in 2002 and 2003. In September, the appeals chamber sentenced Bemba to 12 months for a related conviction of witness tampering, but this time had already been served. Bemba returned to Congo in August.

The Office of the Prosecutor at the ICC continued its second investigation into the situation in the Central African Republic, into alleged war crimes and crimes against humanity committed in the country since 2012. On November 17, the ICC took Alfred Yékatom, known as "Rombhot," into custody. Yékatom is an anti-balaka leader who has been charged with crimes against humanity and war crimes committed between December 2013 and August 2014.

Three peacekeepers from the Republic of Congo were convicted in the Appeals Court in Brazzaville of the murder of 11 civilians in Boali in March 2014. At the time of the killing, the peacekeepers were serving in an African Union peacekeeping mission known as MISCA. The court found the men guilty of war crimes, which can carry a life sentence under Congolese law. The peacekeepers, however, were given three-year sentences. Representatives from an association of family members of the victims expressed interest in pursuing civil claims against the perpetrators.

In September, the UN Human Rights Council decided to continue the mandate of the UN independent expert on the Central African Republic for another year.

Chile

After Sebastian Piñera took office in March 2018 for his second, although non-consecutive, presidential term, his administration took steps that could impact the rights of several vulnerable groups within Chile. The Piñera government supported a bill granting transgender individuals the right to change their name and gender in the civil registry, took steps to replace the flawed National Service for Minors (SENAME), established protections for thousands of migrants with irregular immigration status, and announced an ambitious plan to improve the standard of living of indigenous communities in La Araucanía.

Despite Chile's successful passage of a law decriminalizing abortion in certain circumstances in 2017, women still face significant barriers to access. Many doctors and private institutions continue to refuse to provide abortions on moral grounds even when permissible under the law. The Piñera government promulgated rules that would have made it easier for medical providers and publicly funded hospitals to refuse to provide any abortion services, but Chile's comptroller general declared the rules unlawful.

Confronting Past Abuses

Chilean courts continue to prosecute former police and military officers responsible for human rights abuses during Augusto Pinochet's dictatorship from 1973 to 1990.

Notable convictions in 2018 include three former agents of the Chilean secret police (DINA) for the murder of the leader of the Revolutionary Left Movement, Miguel Enríquez Espinosa, on October 5, 1974; eight ex-military officers for the kidnapping, torture, and murders of pop singer Víctor Jara and former prison director Littré Quiroga Carvajal, during the coup in September 1973; and 24 former DINA agents for their participation in the enforced disappearances of 119 leftist collaborators between 1974 and 1975, known as "Operation Colombo."

In November 2018, Juan Emilio Cheyre, an officer under Pinochet and the commander-in-chief of the Chilean army from 2002-2006, was convicted for his role in the murder of 15 people following the 1973 coup. Juan Emilio Cheyre is the most senior official to be held accountable for human rights abuses during the Pinochet years.

Chile continues to maintain a 50-year veil of secrecy over victim's testimony given to the National Commission on Political Prison and Torture from November 2003 to May 2004. The testimony revealed places of detention and torture methods used by the dictatorship, and identified former political prisoners and torture victims. The Bachelet administration submitted a bill to lift the secrecy order in 2017, which generated heated debate between those who believe revealing the testimony would violate victims' rights to privacy, and those who believe revealing it is necessary to fully punish the guilty and bring justice to victims.

In a controversial decision in July 2018, the Supreme Court granted conditional release to seven former police and military officers who had been serving sentences for human rights abuses committed during the Pinochet dictatorship. Members of opposition parties attempted to remove the three Supreme Court judges responsible for the decision, but Chile's congress rejected the attempt.

Women's Sexual and Reproductive Rights

Chile's 28-year ban on abortion came to an end in 2017 when the Constitutional Court upheld a new law decriminalizing abortion in three circumstances: when the pregnancy is the result of rape, the life of the mother is at risk, or the fetus is unviable. Although passage of the law signaled progress for reproductive rights in Chile, significant barriers to access remain even for legally permissible abortions.

The law in its current form allows doctors, as well as private institutions, to refuse to provide abortions on moral grounds. Chilean research organizations and the Ministry of Health have recently reported that high percentages of providers in Chile are "conscientious objectors" in one or more of the three circumstances. Nearly 50 percent of all medical providers in Chile object to providing abortions after rape, and some public hospitals lack a single provider willing to perform an abortion in that circumstance.

In March 2018, a new threat to women's access to abortion arose when the Piñera administration eliminated the requirement that hospitals give a reason for refusing to provide abortions. Under Piñera's regulatory change, hospitals could simply tell the Health Ministry that their doctors would not perform abortions. Likewise, doctors who were conscientious objectors no longer had to register as such in advance, which meant that clinics and hospitals could no longer ensure that they would always have a doctor available to provide an abortion. In May, Chile's comptroller general abrogated the new regulations, restoring prior rules requiring doctors and institutions raising conscientious objections to opt out in writing in advance.

Indigenous Rights

Chilean courts continue to prosecute Mapuche land-rights activists under the country's counterterrorism law for violence and destruction of property during protests. The law has faced criticism for its overly broad definition of terrorism and insufficient due process guarantees. Both the Bachelet and Piñera administrations proposed modifications to update the law and clarify its scope, but the changes remained pending at time of writing.

In May 2018, three Mapuche land-rights activists were found guilty of arson under the counterterrorism law in connection with the deaths of prominent landowners, Werner Luchsinger and Vivianne Mackay, in May 2013. Two of the three were sentenced to life in prison. The activists had been acquitted for lack of evidence in an initial trial in October 2017 that was subsequently annulled.

The Piñera administration announced an ambitious plan to boost development and promote peace in the predominantly indigenous region of La Araucanía. The plan proposes US$24 billion in public and private investments between 2018 and 2026 for development projects, increased dialogue between indigenous communities and the state, and a constitutional reform recognizing and protecting the history, identity, culture, languages, institutions, and traditions of the indigenous population.

Sexual Orientation and Gender Identity

In September 2018, Chile's congress voted to allow transgender individuals over 14 years of age to legally change their name and gender in the civil registry, with no requirement for surgery or change in physical appearance. The passage of the bill, which has been before Congress since 2013, marks an important step forward for the transgender community in Chile. The bill was pending final approval from President Piñera at time of writing.

The Bachelet administration's bill to legalize same-sex marriage and allow same-sex couples the right to adoption or other reproductive options, submitted in August 2017, remains pending in the Senate.

Migrants' Rights

In April 2018, the Piñera administration introduced amendments to the 2013 immigration bill. The changes, still pending at time of writing, aim to further regulate and systematize the immigration process to address the growing migrant population. Immigration laws have not been updated since 1975.

The amendments were accompanied by a series of administrative measures, including reforms to temporary residence permits and visas and the initiation of an "extraordinary regularization" process. The extraordinary regularization process allows anyone with an irregular immigration status who entered Chile before April 8, 2018, to remain in the country legally until their immigration status is resolved, provided they do not have a criminal background. As of June, 140,000 migrants, primarily from Haiti, Venezuela, and Peru, had registered for the regularization process.

While the regularization process helps and protects many migrants, Haitian and Venezuelan migrants who did not enter Chile before the April 8 deadline may face significant barriers to entry under the new rules. Haitian and Venezuelan migrants must now obtain visas from the Chilean consulates in their respective countries to be granted access.

Children's Rights

In March 2018, President Piñera introduced a bill establishing new child protection and youth reintegration services and eliminating the National Service for Minors (SENAME). SENAME had been the subject of scrutiny for several years due to reports of abuse, ill-treatment, and death in its centers throughout the country.

Prison Conditions

Chile's National Human Rights Institute (INDH) has filed dozens of lawsuits on behalf of inmates living in undignified and unhealthy conditions. The Santiago Court of Appeals ruled in favor of INDH in two such lawsuits in 2018 regarding Penal Colony I and II, establishing that it is unacceptable for prisoners to live in environments that do not provide clean water, mattresses, clothing, and proper sanitation. The court also ordered Chile's national prison service to take steps to ensure prisoners' rights to health and hygiene.

The Supreme Court released a report in February 2018 analyzing 53 prisons in Chile and documenting a serious problem with overcrowding, with some prisons at 140 percent capacity or more.

Key International Actors

As a member of the United Nations Human Rights Council (HRC), Chile supported UN efforts in 2018 to put human rights violations in Venezuela, Myanmar, North Korea, Belarus, Eritrea, Syria, Iran, the Occupied Palestinian Territories, and South Sudan under scrutiny.

Chile was one of six governments to make the unprecedented request that the International Criminal Court open an investigation into the situation in Venezuela.

Chile has supported resolutions condemning abuses in Venezuela and Nicaragua before the Organization of American States.

The UN Committee Against Torture released a report in August urging Chile to lift the 50-year veil of secrecy on victims' testimony, update the counterterrorism law, thoroughly investigate all abuses reported at SENAME centers, and take necessary steps to reduce overcrowding and improve conditions in prisons.

The UN Committee on the Elimination of Discrimination against Women released a report in March recommending that Chile decriminalize abortion in all circumstances and apply strict justification requirements for conscientious objection.

In August 2018, former Chilean President Michelle Bachelet was appointed UN high commissioner for human rights.

China

President Xi Jinping, born in 1953, has indicated his intent to rule indefinitely after China's legislature amended the constitution in March 2018 to scrap term limits for the presidency. This move was also emblematic of the increasing repression under Xi's rule.

The Chinese Communist Party (CCP) also strengthened its power over the government bureaucracy in a major overhaul of central government structure in March. The party oversees a powerful new government body, the National Supervisory Commission, which is empowered to detain incommunicado anyone exercising public authority for up to six months without fair trial procedures in a system called "liuzhi."

In October, Meng Hongwei, then-president of Interpol, the international police organization, and China's vice minister for Public Security, disappeared upon return to China and was assumed to be held in "liuzhi." The CCP also subsumed state bodies in charge of religious, ethnic, and overseas Chinese affairs under a party agency, the United Front Work Department.

Authorities dramatically stepped up repression and systematic abuses against the 13 million Turkic Muslims, including Uyghurs and ethnic Kazakhs, in China's northwestern Xinjiang region. Authorities have carried out mass arbitrary detention, torture, and mistreatment of some of them in various detention facilities, and increasingly imposed pervasive controls on daily life. New regulations in Tibet now criminalize even traditional forms of social action, including community mediation by religious figures. In Hong Kong, a region promised "a high degree of autonomy" under the Sino-British Joint Declaration, the Chinese and Hong Kong governments hastened their efforts in 2018 to undermine people's rights to free speech and political participation.

Human rights defenders continue to endure arbitrary detention, imprisonment, and enforced disappearance. The government maintains tight control over the internet, mass media, and academia. Authorities stepped up their persecution of religious communities, including prohibitions on Islam in Xinjiang, suppression of Christians in Henan province, and increasing scrutiny of Hui Muslims in Ningxia.

Authorities increasingly deploy mass surveillance systems to tighten control over society. In 2018, the government continued to collect, on a mass scale, biometrics including DNA and voice samples; use such biometrics for automated surveillance purposes; develop a nationwide reward and punishment system known as the "social credit system"; and develop and apply "big data" policing programs aimed at preventing dissent. All of these systems are being deployed without effective privacy protections in law or in practice, and often people are unaware that their data is being gathered, or how it is used or stored.

In 2018, animated by the global #MeToo movement, a number of Chinese women stepped forward exposing people who they said had sexually harassed them. Government censorship dampened subsequent public outrage.

In one of its only human rights concessions all year, Chinese authorities allowed Liu Xia, an artist and the widow of 2010 Nobel Peace Prize winner Liu Xiaobo, to leave for Germany in July after eight years of legally baseless house arrest. However, the decision of authorities to bar her family members from also leaving reflects Beijing's campaign to punish dissent and restrict expression globally.

China's growing global power makes it an exporter of human rights violations, including at the United Nations, where in 2018 it sought to block participation of its critics. China again ranked among countries singled out for reprisals against human rights defenders, and in March successfully advanced a Human Rights Council (HRC) resolution on a retrograde approach that it calls "win-win" or "mutually beneficial" cooperation. In this view, states do not pursue accountability for serious human rights violations but engage merely in "dialogue"; moreover, there is no role for independent civil society, only governments, and a narrow role for the UN itself.

Few governments spoke forcefully against these developments, even in the face of Chinese government harassment of people in their own countries or pressure on foreign companies to publicly support Chinese government positions.

Human Rights Defenders

The case of human rights lawyer Wang Quanzhang is emblematic of authorities' ruthlessness toward human rights defenders and those activists' fortitude. Beijing police detained Wang amid a national crackdown on human rights lawyers and activists in August 2015; while detained he was reportedly tortured with electric shocks and forced to take medications. In July, Wang was finally allowed to meet his lawyer for the first time. Charged with "subversion of state power," he could face life imprisonment if convicted. During Wang's detention, Li Wenzu, his wife, along with families of other lawyers and activists detained during the crackdown, have campaigned relentlessly for his release despite having to endure incessant intimidation and harassment.

Authorities continued politically motivated prosecutions and disbarments of human rights lawyers. In January, police detained lawyer Yu Wensheng, charging him with "inciting subversion of state power" and "obstructing public duties." Judicial authorities revoked or suspended the licenses of over a dozen human rights lawyers, and even some who retain licenses have been unable to find work due to police pressure on employers.

In 2018, the courts handed down lengthy prison terms to a number of prominent human rights activists after protracted and sham prosecutions. In July, a Wuhan court sentenced veteran democracy activist Qin Yongmin to 13 years in prison for "subversion of state power." Qin, 64, has previously spent a total of 22 years in prison or in "Re-education Through Labor."

Also in July, a Chongqing court sentenced political cartoonist Jiang Yefei to six-and-a-half years in prison for "subversion of state power" and "illegally crossing a national border." In 2015, Thai authorities forcibly repatriated Jiang and human rights activist Dong Guangping to China even after the pair had been granted UNHCR refugee status. Dong, who was tried alongside Jiang, was given a three-and-a-half-year sentence for inciting subversion and illegal border crossing.

Other defenders continue to face long detentions without trials or verdicts. Liu Feiyue, founder of the human rights news website Civil Rights and Livelihood Watch, was detained in November 2016 and charged with "inciting subversion of state power." He was tried in August 2018 but had not yet been sentenced at time of writing. Veteran activist and founder of the human rights website "64," Tianwang Huang Qi, has been detained since November 2016 but not yet tried. Huang suffers from several health conditions for which he has not received adequate treatment, including possible imminent kidney failure and lung inflammation.

More human rights defenders were detained in 2018. In July, authorities detained Dong Yaoqiong after she poured ink over a poster of President Xi in Shanghai. Police later held her in a psychiatric hospital and prevented her father from seeing her. In August, Guangxi police detained activist and a leader in the Tiananmen Square protests Zhou Yongjun for possessing materials related to Falun Gong, a banned religious group in China. Also in August, Shenzhen police detained dozens of labor and student activists after they gathered to show support to factory workers at the welding machinery company Jasic International, who were fired for trying to form a union. Some were later released but 14 remained in custody or under house arrest at time of writing.

Authorities also tried to silence Chinese human rights defenders abroad by harassing and detaining their families in China. In January 2018, Guangzhou authorities forcibly disappeared Li Huaiping, wife of Chen Xiaoping, a US-based journalist for the Chinese-language Mirror Media Group. The disappearance came shortly after Chen interviewed Guo Wengui, a Chinese billionaire fugitive who exposed corruption among China's ruling elite. Authorities continually harassed the China-based family members of Canadian human rights activist Anastasia Lin, banning them from travel abroad and threatening to persecute them "like in the Cultural Revolution."

In 2018, authorities continue to subject various activists and lawyers to travel bans, surveillance, detention, and ill-treatment for their efforts to engage with the UN. Using human rights treaties for advocacy was cited in the criminal indictment against activist Qin Yongmin, who was sentenced to 13 years in prison.

Freedom of Expression

Chinese authorities continue to harass and detain journalists who cover human rights issues, as well as their interviewees. In May, Beijing police physically assaulted and briefly detained a cameraperson for the Hong Kong broadcaster Now TV reporting on a human rights lawyer's court hearing. In July, Hunan police detained independent blogger Chen Jieren after he wrote articles alleging corruption by provincial party officials; state media repeatedly attacked Chen as an "internet pest" who had "polluted the online space." In August, Shandong police broke into the home of retired professor Sun Wenguang as he was giving a live interview with the US broadcaster Voice of America (VOA). Sun was subsequently put under house arrest. Police later also briefly detained VOA journalists who attempted to interview Sun again.

Authorities expanded their internet censorship regime to suppress politically sensitive information and "vulgar" content. In January 2018, social media platform Weibo suspended several of its most popular programs after authorities ordered it to clean up "wrong-oriented" and "vulgar" information. In April, regulators shut down Neihan Duanzi, a parody and meme app with over 38 million monthly users.

In January 2018, Chinese authorities forcibly disappeared Swedish citizen and bookseller Gui Mihai while he was traveling with Swedish diplomats. Gui, a publisher of books about China's political intrigues, had been imprisoned for two years from 2015 to 2017 after being abducted from Thailand.

In August, media reports revealed that Google, which suspended its search service in China in 2010 citing censorship concerns, had been developing a censored search engine app for the Chinese market. The app would reportedly comply with China's expansive censorship requirements by automatically identifying and filtering sites blocked by the Great Firewall, China's internet filtering system.

The government also tightened its ideological grip over universities. A number of professors, including foreigners, were punished for making comments critical of the government. In July, the University of Nottingham Ningbo China removed Stephen Morgan from its management broad after he wrote an online essay critical of the Chinese Communist Party. In August, Guizhou University dismissed economics professor Yang Shaozheng, alleging him of "disseminating politically incorrect views." Peking University did not renew the contract of American professor Christopher Balding, who had previously launched a campaign calling on Cambridge University Press to resist the Chinese government's pressure to censor academic articles.

The Chinese government also pressured foreign companies to adhere to disputed terms and policies. In January, US-based Marriott International apologized for listing Taiwan and Tibet as separate countries on its website after authorities shut down the website and app in China for a week. In March, Marriott fired an employee for "liking" a pro-Tibet tweet. After Chinese authorities threatened to ban them from operating in China, dozens of international airlines made changes on their websites to refer to Taiwan as part of China.

Freedom of Religion

The government restricts religious practice to five officially recognized religions in officially approved premises. Authorities retain control over religious bodies' personnel appointments, publications, finances, and seminary applications. The government classifies many religious groups outside its control as "evil cults," and subjects members to police harassment, torture, arbitrary detention, and imprisonment.

In February, revised Regulations on Religious Affairs came into effect. Designed to "curb extremism" and "resist infiltration," they ban unauthorized teaching about religion and going abroad to take part in training or meetings.

In March, a Yunnan court sentenced Christian pastor John Sanqiang Cao to seven years in prison for "organizing others to illegally cross the border" between China and Myanmar. Cao had been involved in educational projects for impoverished minority groups in Myanmar.

A crackdown on Christian churches intensified in Henan province during the year, as authorities demolished dozens of church buildings or the crosses atop of them, prevented believers from gathering in house churches, and confiscated bibles and other religious materials.

In September, the Vatican and Beijing reached a historic deal, ending a decades-long standoff over authority to appoint bishops in China. China's estimated 12 million Roman Catholics are divided between an underground community that pledges allegiance to the Pope and a government-run association where bishops are state appointed. Under the accord, Beijing will propose names for future bishops and the Pope will have veto power over the appointments.

In August, in the heavily-Hui Muslim Ningxia region, thousands of Huis gathered to protest the demolition of the Grand Mosque in the town of Weizhou. Ningxia authorities have reportedly also moved Islamic icons and Arabic signs from streets across the region.

Hong Kong

Beijing's assault on Hong Kong's freedoms, particularly the rights to free expression, association and political participation, worsened considerably in 2018.

The Hong Kong government has continued to disqualify pro-democracy figures from running for seats on Hong Kong's Legislative Council (LegCo). In January and October, the Hong Kong Electoral Affairs Commission disqualified Demosisto Party candidate Agnes Chow and Labor Party candidate Lau Siu-lai, respectively, stating that their promotion of "self-determination" for Hong Kong is "inconsistent" with the Basic Law.

The Hong Kong and Chinese governments have harassed people for peaceful pro-independence speech. In March, they denounced pro-democracy scholar Benny Tai, equating his hypothetical discussion of Hong Kong independence with "a threat to national security." In August, Chinese Ministry of Foreign Affairs officials had requested that the Hong Kong Foreign Correspondents Club cancel a talk by Andy Chan, a pro-independence activist. After the club refused, Hong Kong authorities rejected without explanation its vice-president's application to renew his work visa.

In August, Demosisto reported that police had briefly detained and interrogated two members in the mainland in March and August. In September, a pro-independence group, Studentlocalism, said police in the mainland had harassed relatives of two members for their political activities in Hong Kong.

In September, new regulations went into effect allowing mainland law to prevail in Hong Kong's West Kowloon railway terminus and all operating trains going between Hong Kong and mainland China—a significant step in China's erosion of Hong Kong's autonomy.

In an unprecedented move, the Hong Kong government in September banned a political party—the pro-independence Hong Kong National Party. Authorities stated that the party "poses a real threat to national security," against which they had to take "preventive measures."

Xinjiang

Chinese authorities are hostile to many expressions of Uyghur identity, and have in recent years justified sweeping repression as a necessary response to threats of terrorism.

The Chinese government began waging a "Strike Hard Campaign against Violent Extremism" in Xinjiang in 2014. But the level of repression increased dramatically after Communist Party Secretary Chen Quanguo was transferred from the Tibet Autonomous Region to assume leadership of Xinjiang in late 2016.

Since then, authorities have stepped up mass arbitrary detention, including in pretrial detention centers and prisons, both of which are formal facilities, and in "political education" camps, which have no basis under Chinese law. Credible estimates indicate that 1 million people are being indefinitely held in the camps, where Turkic Muslims are being forced to learn Mandarin Chinese, praise the government and party, and abandon many aspects of their distinct identity. Those who resist or are deemed to have failed to "learn" are punished.

Outside these detention facilities, authorities subject Turkic Muslims in Xinjiang to extraordinary restrictions on personal life. Authorities have recalled passports throughout the region, and to travel from one town or another, people have to apply for permission and go through checkpoints. They are subjected to persistent political indoctrination, including compulsory flag-raising ceremonies and political or denunciation meetings. With unprecedented levels of control over religious practices, authorities have effectively outlawed the practice of Islam in the region.

They have also subjected people in Xinjiang to pervasive surveillance. Authorities employ high-tech mass surveillance systems that make use of QR codes, biometrics, artificial intelligence, phone spyware, and big data. And they have mobilized over a million officials to monitor people, including through intrusive programs in which officials regularly stay in people's homes.

The campaign has divided families, with some family members in Xinjiang and others abroad caught unexpectedly by the tightening of passport controls and border crossings. Children have at times been trapped in one country without their parents. The government has barred Turkic Muslims from contacting people abroad, and has pressured some Uyghurs and ethnic Kazakhs living outside the

country to return to China, while requiring others to provide detailed personal information about their lives abroad.

The collective punishment of families was particularly striking in the case of five US-based Radio Free Asia Uyghur Service journalists. Media reports in February said their relatives in Xinjiang have been detained in retaliation for their journalism about the region.

Tibet

Authorities in Tibetan areas continue to severely restrict religious freedom, speech, movement, and assembly, and fail to redress popular concerns about mining and land grabs by local officials, which often involve intimidation and arbitrary violence by security forces. Authorities intensified surveillance of online and phone communications.

There were clear findings by UN human rights experts that the charges were baseless. Nonetheless, courts sentenced former political prisoner Tsegon Gyal in January to three years in prison and language activist Tashi Wangchuk in May to five years.

Several hundred Tibetans traveling on Chinese passports to India for a January 2018 teaching by the Dalai Lama were forced to return early when officials in Tibetan areas threatened retaliation against those traveling abroad and their family members back home.

Intensified political education has been reported in monasteries and schools, and for the public at large. Tibetan authorities have used a nationwide anti-crime campaign to encourage people to denounce members of their communities on the slightest suspicion of sympathy for the exiled Dalai Lama or opposition to the government.

Several more cases were reported in 2018 of land grabs by local officials for construction projects, both in the Tibet Autonomous Region and other Tibetan areas. In Driru county, 30 villagers were detained in May for allegedly sharing with international media information about the arrest of a village leader who had led popular opposition to a mining project on a sacred mountain.

Tibetans continue to self-immolate to protest Chinese policies; four more such protests took place between November 2017 and time of writing.

Women's and Girls' Rights

In 2018, the #MeToo movement gained momentum in China as a slew of prominent academics, journalists, and activists were accused on social media of sexual misconduct. After a prominent state media TV host and a senior Buddhist monk at a government-controlled temple were accused of sexual harassment, censors deleted social media posts about those cases. In June, China University of Petroleum authorities held Ren Liping, a student who had accused an ex-boyfriend of raping her on campus, for six days in a hotel room after she protested against the university and police for mishandling her allegations.

While women in China may be more willing to speak out against sexual harassment, seeking legal redress is still very difficult. Chinese law prohibits sexual harassment, but its failure to define the term makes meaningful legal action nearly impossible.

Women continue to face widespread discrimination in the job market. In the 2018 national civil service job list, 19 percent specified a requirement or preference for men, up from 13 percent from the previous year. Technology giants including Alibaba and Tencent pledged to ensure gender equality in their recruitment.

As China faces an unprecedented sex ratio imbalance and aging population, authorities promoted traditional roles for women, encouraging them to marry early and have children. The "bride shortage" in China has triggered trafficking of women from a number of neighboring countries, an abuse largely ignored by the Chinese government. Although the "one-child policy" has been relaxed to a "two-child policy," women and girls continue to face violations of their reproductive rights.

The Chinese government remains hostile to women's rights activism. In March, social media platforms Weibo and WeChat permanently suspended the accounts of Feminist Voices, a social media publication run by outspoken feminists.

Sexual Orientation and Gender Identity

While China decriminalized homosexuality in 1997, it lacks laws protecting people from discrimination on the basis of sexual orientation or gender identity, and same-sex partnership is not legal.

"ONLY MEN NEED APPLY"

Gender Discrimination in Job Advertisements in China

HUMAN RIGHTS WATCH

In March, the Beijing International Film Festival pulled an award-winning film featuring a homosexual relationship, "Call Me By Your Name," after it failed to pass government approval. In April, Chinese social media platform Weibo announced that posts related to gay culture would be taken down, as part of a "cleanup" effort. The move prompted widespread protest: many people posted messages with the hashtag "I am gay" and rainbow emoticons. Weibo subsequently dropped the restriction.

In Hong Kong, the territory's highest court in July ruled that the government's denial of a visa and associated benefits to the same-sex spouse of a legal resident amounted to discrimination. Around the same time, Hong Kong authorities decided to move a selection of 10 children's books with LGBT themes to the "closed stacks" in public libraries.

A gay teacher in September filed a suit against his former school, alleging that he was fired because he posted information on social media about a lesbian, gay, bisexual, and transgender (LGBT)-themed event that he had attended.

Refugees and Asylum Seekers

China continued to arrest and forcibly return hundreds, and perhaps thousands, of North Koreans, who Human Rights Watch considers refugees sur place, to North Korean state security services, who has long tortured, sexually abused, and imprisoned them. Beijing refused to consider fleeing North Koreans as refugees and would not grant UNHCR access to them or areas on the North Korea-China border, further violating its obligations as a party to the 1951 Refugee Convention.

Key International Actors

While some governments and parliaments publicly expressed concerns about Beijing's human rights violations, and continued to try to observe trials and meet with human rights defenders in China, few took forceful action to end abuses or press for accountability.

In March, China proposed a resolution at the UN Human Rights Council, focusing on its vision for "win-win cooperation" while omitting any consequences for non-cooperation, any mention of accountability, and other core parts of the council's mandate. The resolution, ultimately renamed "mutually beneficial cooperation", was adopted by a wide margin with the US as the only no vote. Throughout the year, members of the US Congress and the administration called for sanctions and export controls.

In July, Germany secured the release of Liu Xia. In September, Malaysia's new premier, Anwar Ibrahim, publicly called for talks with China about violations in Xinjiang. Sweden did not secure the release of bookseller Gui Minhai; Australia adopted new laws to counter Chinese political interference at home, but took few meaningful steps to challenge the root cause of political repression in China. The European Parliament and the European Union's External Action Service repeatedly called for release of jailed and disappeared human rights lawyers, dissenters, and activists and expressed concerns about the situation in Xinjiang, but their efforts were partly frustrated by the EU leaders' failure to echo these concerns and calls publicly at a summit in July.

UN Secretary-General Antonio Guterres visited China in April and September without publicly expressing his concern about these issues. However, new UN High Commissioner for Human Rights Michelle Bachelet, the Committee to Eliminate Racial Discrimination, and the assistant secretary-general for human rights expressed concern particularly about Xinjiang and abuses of human rights defenders.

China continues to use its permanent seat on the UN Security Council to block important discussions of human rights issues. In March 2018, China and Russia successfully mobilized other council members to prevent then-High Commissioner for Human Rights Zeid Ra'ad al-Hussein from addressing the council on Syria. In October 2018, it circulated a letter expressing its opposition to the "internationalization" of efforts to address the Rohingya crisis in Myanmar and its opposition has stymied stronger Security Council action to react to the crisis.

Foreign Policy

Throughout the year China pressed ahead with its "One Belt, One Road" initiative despite the lack of safeguards or respect for human rights in many participating countries. Some governments, including Myanmar and Malaysia, backed away from previously agreed bilateral investment arrangements, citing unsustainable debt and concerns about sovereignty.

China also pressed other governments, including Egypt, Kazakhstan, and Malaysia, to forcibly return asylum seekers to China.

Major Chinese technology companies, including Huawei, iFlytek, and ZTE, all of which enjoy close relations with the government and contribute to the police's mass surveillance efforts, tried to expand abroad in 2018. Some were rebuffed by Australia, Canada, and the US due to security concerns.

HUMAN
RIGHTS
WATCH

RECYCLED VIOLENCE
Abuses by FARC Dissident Groups in Tumaco
on Colombia's Pacific Coast

Colombia

The 52-year armed conflict between the Revolutionary Armed Forces of Colombia (FARC) and the government officially ended with a peace accord in 2016, but violence associated with armed groups increased again in 2018 after initial declines after a 2015 FARC ceasefire. Civilians have suffered serious abuses at the hands of the National Liberation Army (ELN) guerrillas, FARC dissidents, and paramilitary successor groups. Human rights defenders, journalists, indigenous and Afro-Colombian leaders, and other community activists have faced death threats and violence. Violence associated with the conflict has forcibly displaced more than 8.1 million Colombians since 1985.

Impunity for past serious human rights crimes, barriers to land restitution for displaced people, limits on reproductive rights, and conditions faced by Wayuu and other indigenous communities also remain important human rights concerns in Colombia.

In June 2018, Iván Duque was elected president after defeating Gustavo Petro in a run-off election.

Guerrillas and FARC dissidents

In June 2017, the United Nations political mission in Colombia verified that FARC guerrillas who accepted the peace agreement with the government had handed in their weapons to the mission. The demobilized guerrilla group later announced it was forming a political party, the Revolutionary Alternative Force of the Common People.

In September 2018, the UN political mission announced that six former FARC commanders in southwest Colombia had abandoned the sites where they were to be reincorporated into Colombian society. These include Iván Márquez, the FARC's second-in-command and chief peace negotiator, whose location remained unknown at time of writing.

A minority of dissident guerrilla fighters rejected the terms of the peace agreement, have not disarmed, and continue to commit abuses. Others joined or created new groups after disarming, partly in reaction to inadequate reintegration programs. In February, the government estimated that FARC dissident groups had more than 1,400 members.

In the southern municipality of Tumaco, FARC dissident groups have engaged in serious abuses against civilians, including murder, rape, child recruitment, kidnappings, and disappearances.

In March, one of these groups, the Oliver Sinisterra Front, kidnapped three employees of the Ecuadorian newspaper *El Comercio* who were reporting on the group's operations in Mataje, Ecuador. The group held the men hostage for two weeks, demanding that the Ecuadorian government release three imprisoned Front members. On April 11, the group released a pamphlet announcing that the three hostages were dead. Their bodies were found in rural Tumaco in mid-June.

The ELN continued in 2018 to commit serious abuses against civilians, including killings, forced displacement, and child recruitment. In its fighting with the Popular Army of Liberation (EPL)—a hold-out from a guerrilla group that demobilized in the 1990s—the groups forced over 12,000 people to leave their houses in the northeast area of Catatumbo.

The ELN continued to engage in kidnappings in 2018. On September 7, ELN members kidnapped Mayerli Cortés Rodríguez, 15, whom the group accused of being a government informant. They released her on September 19.

Paramilitaries and Successors

Between 2003 and 2006, right-wing paramilitary organizations with close ties to security forces and politicians underwent a deeply flawed government demobilization process in which many members remained active and simply reorganized into new groups. These successor groups continue to commit serious abuses, including killings, disappearances, and rape.

Fighting between the Gaitanist Self-Defenses of Colombia (AGC), the largest successor group, and the Caparrapos, a group that splintered from the AGC, caused over 2,000 people to flee from their houses in the Bajo Cauca zone, northern Colombia, between January and March 2018.

In July, Congress passed a law significantly reducing sentences of armed group members who demobilize, recognize the crimes with which they are charged, and provide information about how their groups operate. Then-President Juan

Manuel Santos said that the AGC had agreed to demobilize under the new law, but its demobilization had yet to take place at time of writing.

Implementation of the Justice and Peace Law of 2005, which offers reduced sentences to demobilized paramilitary members who confess their crimes, has been slow. Of more than 30,000 paramilitary troops who demobilized, 4,000 have sought to exchange a confession for a lighter sentence. As of March 2018, 215—or about 5 percent—had been sentenced.

Santiago Uribe, brother of former President Alvaro Uribe, continued to face trial on charges of murder and conspiracy for his alleged role in the paramilitary group "The 12 Apostles" in the 1990s.

In July, the Supreme Court summoned former President Uribe to answer allegations that he tampered with witnesses who implicated him in paramilitary atrocities in the 1990s. The hearing was postponed in August and Uribe had not been questioned at time of writing.

Abuses by Public Security Forces

From 2002 through 2008, army brigades across Colombia routinely executed civilians in what have come to be known as "false positive" killings. Under pressure from superiors to show "positive" results and boost body counts in their war against guerrillas, soldiers, and officers abducted victims or lured them to remote locations under false pretenses—such as promises of work—shot them dead, placed weapons on their bodies, and reported them as enemy combatants killed in action. The number of allegations of unlawful killings by security forces has fallen sharply since 2009, though credible reports of some new cases continue to emerge.

As of March 2018, the Attorney General's Office was investigating more than 3,600 alleged unlawful killings by army personnel from 2002 through 2008, and had achieved convictions in cases against more than 1,600 mid and low-level soldiers, including convictions against the same individual in different cases.

Authorities have largely failed, however, to prosecute senior army officers involved in the killings and instead have promoted many of them through the military ranks. Cases against 19 army generals under investigation for false-positive killings have seen scant progress.

In April 2018, the Colombian magazine *Semana* revealed that in 2017 General Rodríguez Barragan, who at the time commanded the Colombian armed forces, asked other officers to establish cyber surveillance and monitoring of Human Rights Watch Americas Director José Miguel Vivanco and discussed ways to censor his tweets.

In October 2017, eight farmers were killed in the southern municipality of Tumaco during a peaceful protest against delays in the implementation of programs to replace illicit crops. The Defense Ministry initially said that FARC dissidents had shot at protesters; survivors blamed the police. At time of writing, no one had been charged in relation to the killings.

Violence Against Community Activists, Trade Unionists, and Journalists

Indigenous, Afro-Colombian, and other community activists continue to be targeted with threats and attacks. Despite an Interior Ministry program that assigns protection to human rights defenders, trade unionists, and journalists, the Office of the UN High Commissioner for Human Rights (OHCHR) documented the killings of 53 prominent activists from January through September 2018.

In April, a group of armed men kidnapped three relatives of community leader Iber Angulo Zamora. On May 5, as employees of the human rights ombudsman's office were taking Angulo Zamora by boat up the Naya River to a safe haven, armed men grabbed him. In June, men claiming to belong to a FARC dissident group called the "United Force of the Pacific" released a video announcing that all of the kidnapped men had been killed.

Most of these killings have occurred in five areas where illegal economic activities, such as drug production and trafficking, are common: the southern provinces of Cauca and Nariño; the northeastern zone of Catatumbo, on the border with Venezuela; and the northwestern areas of Bajo Cauca and Urabá.

In July, the Attorney General's Office reported it had issued arrest warrants against individuals believed responsible for about half of the murders of indigenous, Afro-Colombian, and other community activists reported by the OHCHR since January 2016. The Attorney General's Office said 71 people were detained in connection with these abuses and perpetrators had been convicted in five cases.

In August, President Duque announced that the government would introduce new programs to prevent such murders and ensure that those responsible are held to account.

Peace Negotiations and Accountability

The peace agreement between the Colombian government and the FARC provided for the creation of a "Special Jurisdiction for Peace" to try those responsible for gross human rights violations committed during the conflict. FARC guerrillas and members of the armed forces responsible for crimes against humanity and serious war crimes who fully cooperate with the new jurisdiction and confess their crimes are subject to as much as eight years of "effective restrictions on freedoms and rights," but no prison time.

Throughout 2018, Special Jurisdiction magistrates prioritized four situations for analysis: kidnappings committed by the FARC; false-positive killings; army and FARC abuses against Afro-Colombian and indigenous people in three municipalities in the southern province of Nariño between 1990 and 2016; and FARC and army abuses committed in the northern zone of Urabá between 1986 and 2016.

In July, lawmakers passed a law containing a provision that suspends, unless defendants request otherwise, Special Jurisdiction prosecutions of soldiers of the Colombian Armed Forces until the government creates a "special and differentiated process" for them. The provision, which was proposed by the Democratic Center—the party of Uribe and Duque—and was being reviewed by the Constitutional Court at time of writing, could halt prosecutions for false positive killings.

Throughout 2018, the Democratic Center introduced in Congress other bills that would seriously undermine prosecutions against members of the armed forces, including by allowing soldiers to receive sentencing benefits regardless of whether they confess their crimes. But these proposals had for the most part been withdrawn or fixed by lawmakers at time of writing.

The Democratic Center has falsely accused Special Jurisdiction for Peace magistrates of being biased against the armed forces. A bill that would name 14 additional judges in the Special Jurisdiction remained pending in Congress at time of writing.

Internal Displacement and Land Restitution

Conflict-related violence has displaced more than 8.1 million Colombians since 1985, government figures reveal. More than 48,000 were displaced between January and September 2018.

The government's implementation of land restitution under the 2011 Victims' Law continues to move slowly. The law was enacted to restore millions of hectares of land that were left behind by or stolen from internally displaced Colombians during the many years of conflict. As of November 2018, the courts had issued rulings in only 8,200 of more than 116,000 claims received.

In September, a Democratic Center senator introduced a bill in Congress that would limit land restitution to land that was stolen and in the meantime sold.

Migration from Venezuela

The continuing human rights and humanitarian crisis in Venezuela has generated the largest migration crisis in recent Latin American history. Colombia has received by far the largest number of Venezuelan migrants. At least a million people moved from Venezuela to Colombia between March 2017 and June 2018 alone.

In July 2017, the Colombian government created a special permit that allows Venezuelan citizens who enter the country legally but overstay their visas to regularize their status and obtain work permits and access to basic public services. In 2017 and during the first months of 2018, 180,000 Venezuelans were granted such a permit. In July 2018, the Colombian government granted more than 400,000 Venezuelan irregular immigrants who had registered in a government survey access to basic public services, work permits, and school enrollment for their children.

Women's and Girls' Rights

Gender-based violence is widespread in Colombia. Lack of training and poor implementation of treatment protocols impede timely access to medical services and create obstacles for women and girls seeking post-violence care and justice. Perpetrators of violent, gender-based crimes are rarely held accountable.

Abortion is illegal in Colombia except when the life or health of the women or girl is at risk, the pregnancy is the result of rape, or the fetus suffers complications incompatible with life outside the womb. In October, a majority of Constitutional Court magistrates rejected a magistrate's proposal to limit legal abortion to the first 24 weeks of pregnancy.

Women and girls often face barriers accessing legal abortion, including long delays and a shortage of doctors willing to provide abortions.

Sexual Orientation and Gender Identity

In recent years, authorities have taken several steps to recognize the rights of lesbian, gay, bisexual, and transgender (LGBT) people. In June 2015, the Justice Ministry issued a decree allowing people to revise the gender noted on their identification documents without prior judicial approval. In November 2015, the Constitutional Court ruled that Colombians cannot be barred from adopting a child because of their sexual orientation. In 2016, the court upheld the right of same-sex couples to marry.

Indigenous Rights

Indigenous people in Colombia suffer disproportionate levels of poverty that greatly impede their ability to fulfill their social and economic rights. From January through early-November 2018, at least 43 children under age five—the majority of them belonging to Wayuu indigenous communities—died in the province of La Guajira of causes associated with malnutrition. Many of these deaths are caused by limited access to drinking water. The Inter-American Commission of Human Rights (IACHR) had asked the government as early as December 2015 to take measures to prevent such deaths.

Key International Actors

The United States remains the most influential foreign actor in Colombia. In March 2018, the US Congress approved more than US$390 million in aid, mostly for development and drug enforcement. A portion of US military aid is subject to human rights conditions. The US Department of State has not rigorously enforced these conditions.

The Office of the Prosecutor (OTP) of the International Criminal Court (ICC) continues to monitor Colombian investigations of crimes that may fall within the court's jurisdiction. OTP staff visited Colombia in March, May, and November 2018 to obtain information about relevant national proceedings.

In 2016, at the request of the government of then-President Juan Manuel Santos, the UN Security Council established a political mission in Colombia to monitor and verify implementation of the FARC peace accord. In September 2018, the Security Council extended the mandate of the UN Verification Mission in Colombia until September 25, 2019.

The Office of the UN High Commissioner for Human Rights continues to play a key role in defending and promoting human rights in Colombia. In March 2018 Alberto Brunori was named the new representative of the office in Colombia. Initially, the government granted him a short-term work permit, which limited his capacity to work in Colombia. The permit was extended in May.

The Colombian government continues to support regional efforts to address the human rights crisis in Venezuela. In 2018, Colombia remained a member of the Lima Group—a coalition of governments in the region that is monitoring Venezuela's crisis.

On September 26, the governments of Colombia, Argentina, Canada, Chile, Peru, and Paraguay referred the situation in Venezuela to the ICC prosecutor, Fatou Bensouda, for investigation.

Cote d'Ivoire

Côte d'Ivoire enjoyed relative stability in 2018, particularly given the absence of the army mutinies that had characterized the prior year. The government has still, however, made limited progress in tackling impunity and has not addressed the other root causes of past political violence, notably an undisciplined army and politicized judiciary. Côte d'Ivoire held local elections in October, with pockets of violence between rival political factions leaving several people dead.

Although Ivorian judges continued to investigate the crimes of the 2010-11 post-election crisis, President Alassane Ouattara's August announcement of an amnesty for crimes related to the 2010-11 crisis raised concerns that victims will not get justice in Ivorian courts. The ICC is currently prosecuting Laurent Gbagbo, the former president, and Charles Blé Goudé, a former youth minister and leader of a pro-Gbagbo militia, for crimes against humanity allegedly committed during the 2010-11 post-election crisis. The ICC is also investigating crimes committed by pro-Ouattara forces.

A new press law thst provides some protection against the detention of journalists was adopted in December 2017. However, it sets out fines for defamation-related offences that could be used to suppress free speech. The Ivorian Constitution protects freedom of assembly, but Ivorian law requires demonstrators to request permits for public rallies. Security forces on occasion forcibly broke up largely peaceful opposition protests that had been denied a permit.

Accountability for Past Crimes

Côte d'Ivoire's Special Investigative and Examination Cell continued its investigations into the human rights abuses of the 2010-11 post-election crisis, which left more than 3,000 dead and more than 150 women raped. The cell, established in 2011, has charged more than two dozen senior military officers and political leaders with crimes against humanity or war crimes.

However, the August amnesty announcement "for national reconciliation" for 800 people implicated in crimes related to the post-election crisis and subsequent political violence raised major doubts about whether those responsible for the crisis' worst abuses would be tried in Ivorian courts.

A government-order implementing the amnesty stated that it would not apply to individuals who are "members of the military and armed groups." But the list of people released or exonerated under the amnesty included individuals accused of serious human rights violations during the 2010-11 crisis, both from pro-Ouattara and pro-Gbagbo forces.

Those released due to the amnesty included former first lady Simone Gbagbo. Her acquittal in an Ivorian court for crimes against humanity during the post-election crisis was overturned by the Supreme Court on July 26, but the amnesty means that she will not now be retried. Simone Gbagbo is also wanted by the ICC on four counts of crimes against humanity, but the Ivorian government has refused to transfer her to The Hague.

The amnesty did at least result in the release of hundreds of pro-Gbagbo sympathizers who had languished for years in pretrial detention without trial, or who had been convicted of "threats against state security" in trials that often lacked basis due process.

The ICC continued the trial of Gbagbo and Blé Goudé for crimes against humanity committed during the 2010-11 crisis. The prosecution closed its case in early 2018, and the defense filed a no-case-to-answer submission in July, arguing that the changes against the two should be dismissed. At time of writing, a decision on the submission was pending.

The ICC continued its investigations into crimes committed by pro-Ouattara forces during the crisis, but has yet to issue arrest warrants. President Ouattara has said that no further individuals will be transferred to The Hague. Neither Côte d'Ivoire's Special Cell nor the ICC are investigating crimes committed during election-related violence in 2000 or the 2002-2003 armed conflict.

Security Force Abuses and Security Sector Reform

Members of the security forces continued to engage in racketeering and extortion, particularly at checkpoints on secondary roads. A gendarme was killed by a mob on February 17 after shooting to death a taxi driver at a checkpoint in Bloléquin, western Côte d'Ivoire, allegedly for refusing to pay a bribe. Senior army commanders also continued to be implicated in the illicit exploitation of natural resources.

The lack of progress in accountability for past human rights violations means that commanders allegedly implicated in serious abuses remain in positions of authority within the armed forces.

There was no repeat of the large-scale army mutinies of 2017, although the mutinies' underlying causes, particularly the lack of effective control over thousands of ex-rebels now serving in the army, remained largely unaddressed. In an effort to reduce the size of the security forces, more than 3,000 soldiers accepted payouts of 15 million CFA (US$26,000) to voluntarily leave the army.

Freedom of Assembly and Expression

The National Assembly in December 2017 adopted a new law on the press that, in principle, prohibits detaining or imprisoning journalists, although it leaves open the possibility that journalists might be detained or imprisoned under other laws. The new press law also includes several defamation-related offenses, punishable by fines, including the crime of "offending the President."

An online news editor was fined 10 million CFA ($17,500) in January for "divulgation of fake news" in relation to a May 2016 interview with former-President Gbagbo's son, Michel. The latter was sentenced to six months imprisonment for alleging in the interview that the government had unjustly detained, mistreated, and even disappeared pro-Gbagbo supporters, although the sentence against him had not been enforced at time of writing.

The government on several occasions prohibited opposition rallies and used tear gas and other non-lethal force to disperse largely peaceful demonstrators. Dozens of largely peaceful protesters were arrested during a March 22 opposition demonstration, 18 of which were on April 6 sentenced to 12 days' imprisonment for disturbing public order.

Land Reform and Instability in the West

Recurring disputes over land ownership remain an important source of intercommunal tension, particularly in western Côte d'Ivoire, although 2018 witnessed fewer reported deaths in land-related conflicts than previous years. A rural land agency, created in 2016 but only operational in 2018, began to accelerate efforts to facilitate land registration and demarcate village boundaries. Overall, however, implementation of a 1998 land law, which could reduce conflicts by registering customary land ownership and issuing legal title, remains extremely slow, in large part due to the lengthy and expensive land registration process.

In Abidjan, local government officials in July forcibly evicted thousands of people from the Port Bouët neighborhood without adequate prior notice. Ivorian forestry officials also in some areas continued to forcibly evict farmers from protected forests and national parks. Past government-led forestry reclamation efforts, such as the 2016 eviction of farmers from Mont Péko national park, left thousands of evicted families without access to adequate food, water, or shelter.

Judiciary and Detention Conditions

As in 2017, the organization of *cour d'assises* sessions in Abidjan and regional courts went some way to addressing the backlog of serious criminal cases. The criminal justice system still faces longstanding and fundamental challenges, however, including a lack of judicial independence, excessive use of pretrial detention, and prison overcrowding.

As of July, some 16,000 people were detained within a prison system designed for less than 9,000. Some 5,800 detainees were in pretrial detention. Detainees lack adequate access to medical care and suffer extortion by prison guards and fellow inmates. Partly to help ease prison overcrowding, President Ouattara pardoned more than 4,000 prisoners accused of non-political crimes in January 2018, another 4,000 in September.

Gender-Based Violence

Sexual and gender-based violence remain frequent, with social stigma and widespread impunity preventing many victims from reporting abuses and obtaining medical care or counseling. Although female genital mutilation has been criminalized since 1998, it is still practiced widely, affecting more than a third of women aged between 15 and 49. Child marriage is also still common, with more than a quarter of women now aged 20 to 24 having been married by age 18.

Key International Actors

Côte d'Ivoire's international partners, including China, the European Union, France, and the United States, failed to publicly comment on the August amnesty, consistent with their failure to meaningfully pressure the government to hold to account those implicated in past human rights violations.

France, the US, and the EU remained major donors in the justice and security sector. The lack of adequate progress made by Cote d'Ivoire in security sector reform was cited in an April leaked EU memorandum that underscored the precariousness of Côte d'Ivoire's political stability.

Cuba

The Cuban government continues to repress and punish dissent and public criticism. The number of short-term arbitrary arrests of human rights defenders, independent journalists, and others was significantly less in 2018 than in 2017, but still remained high, with more than 2,000 reports of arbitrary detentions between January and August. The government continues to use other repressive tactics, including beatings, public shaming, travel restrictions, and termination of employment against critics.

On April 19, Cuba inaugurated a new president, Miguel Díaz-Canel, who took over from Raúl Castro. Castro remained as the leader of the Communist Party and retained his seat in the National Assembly.

On July 22, the National Assembly unanimously approved a proposal for a new constitution, to be voted on in a national referendum on February 24, 2019. The new constitution, which would replace one adopted in 1976, would eliminate the objective of "achieving a Communist society" but retain the assertion that the Communist Party is the "superior leading force of society and the State."

Arbitrary Detention and Short-Term Imprisonment

The Cuban government continues to employ arbitrary detention to harass and intimidate critics, independent activists, political opponents, and others. The number of arbitrary short-term detentions, which increased dramatically between 2010 and 2016—from a monthly average of 172 incidents to 827—started to drop in 2017, according to the Cuban Commission for Human Rights and National Reconciliation, an independent human rights group that the government considers illegal.

The number of reports of arbitrary detentions continued to drop in 2018, with 2,024 from January through August, a decrease of 45 percent compared to the 3,706 reports during the same period in 2017.

Security officers rarely present arrest orders to justify detaining critics. In some cases, detainees are released after receiving official warnings, which prosecutors can use in subsequent criminal trials to show a pattern of "delinquent" behavior.

Detention is often used preemptively to prevent people from participating in peaceful marches or meetings to discuss politics. Detainees are often beaten, threatened, and held incommunicado for hours or days. Police or state security agents routinely harass, rough up, and detain members of the Ladies in White (Damas de Blanco)—a group founded by the wives, mothers, and daughters of political prisoners—before or after they attend Sunday mass.

In March, a former political prisoner, Ivan Hernández Carrillo, reported having been violently beaten and detained when he intervened to stop the arrest of his mother, Asunción Carrillo, a Ladies in White member, who was leaving her home to attend mass. Hernández said he was charged—after shouting "Down with Raul Castro!"—and fined for "contempt for the figure of the maximum leader." The Carrillos were released the same day.

On August 3, dissident José Daniel Ferrer, who founded the Patriotic Union of Cuba (UNPACU) in 2011—upon his release from eight years in prison—was arrested along with activist Ebert Hidalgo and charged with "attempted murder" when the car he was driving struck a Ministry of Interior official. Activists have said the charges are a farce and witnesses allege that the official threw himself in front of the car intentionally, only to get up and ride off on his motorcycle. Upon his release 12 days later, Hidalgo reported having been psychologically tortured and held in harsh conditions in a dark, dirty cell.

In September, dissident Arianna López Roque was briefly detained after burning a copy of the proposal for new constitution. According to Lopez, she was charged with public disorder, disobedience, resistance, and contempt and an official threatened with retaliating against her husband, who is currently imprisoned.

Freedom of Expression

The government controls virtually all media outlets in Cuba and restricts access to outside information. A small number of independent journalists and bloggers manage to write articles for websites or blogs, or publish tweets. The government routinely blocks access within Cuba to these websites, and only a fraction of Cubans can read independent websites and blogs because of the high cost of, and limited access to, the internet. In September 2017, Cuba announced it would gradually extend home internet services.

Independent journalists who publish information considered critical of the government are subject to harassment, smear campaigns, raids on their homes and offices, confiscation of their working materials, and arbitrary arrests. The journalists are held incommunicado, as are artists and academics who demand greater freedoms. *Desacato* laws continue to be enforced against opponents.

On January 30, Iris Mariño García, a journalist for *La Hora de Cuba*, was criminally charged with engaging in journalism without authorization. The manager of the newspaper said a woman accused Mariño of interviewing her on the street and that when police interviewed Mariño they focused on the paper's opinion surveys, showing the political motivation behind the arrest. Mariño was detained again when attempting to take a picture of a May 1 workers' parade. Officers took her to a police station and interrogated her.

In July, Roberto de Jesús Quiñones, an independent journalist whose work is published on the news site Cubanet, was detained for 58 hours and held incommunicado. Police raided his home and confiscated computers, phones, and other goods.

In April 2018, President Díaz-Canel signed Decree 349, expected to enter into force in December 2018, establishing broad and vague restrictions on artistic expression. Under the regulation, artists cannot "provide artistic services" in public or private spaces without prior approval from the Ministry of Culture. Those who hire or make payments to artists for artistic services which lacked proper authorization are subject to sanctions, as are the artists themselves. The decree provides different sanctions, including fines, confiscation of materials, cancellation of artistic events and revocation of licenses. Local independent artists have been protesting the decree. On August 11, police detained and beat Luis Manuel Otero Alcántara and at least three other artists when trying to organize a concert to protest the decree, according to press reports.

Political Prisoners

In May 2018, the Cuban Commission for Human Rights reported that Cuba was holding 120 political prisoners, including more than 40 members of the Cuban Patriotic Union. The government denies independent human rights groups access to its prisons. The groups believe that additional political prisoners, whose cases they have been unable to document, remain locked up.

Cubans who criticize the government continue to face the threat of criminal prosecution. They do not benefit from due process guarantees, such as the right to fair and public hearings by a competent and impartial tribunal. In practice, courts are subordinate to the executive and legislative branches, denying meaningful judicial independence.

Dr. Eduardo Cardet Concepción, leader of the Christian Liberation Movement, remained in prison at time of writing. Cardet, who had been threatened with jail because of his support for the "One Cuban, One Vote" campaign, was sentenced to three years in prison on March 2017. As of August 2018, he was being held in solitary confinement, and denied visits and any contact with family members, even by phone. Authorities argued that family visits were not "contributing to his re-education."

In May, Dr. Ruíz Urquiola, a former biology professor and an outspoken environmentalist, was sentenced to a year in prison for disrespecting a park ranger. During his imprisonment he went on a hunger strike. In July 2018, he was granted a conditional release for health reasons. In August 2018, he reported irregularities in the handling of his case, and the imposition of travel restrictions.

Travel Restrictions

Since reforms in 2003 to travel regulations, many people who had previously been denied permission to travel have been able to do so, including human rights defenders and independent bloggers. The reforms, however, gave the government broad discretionary powers to restrict the right to travel on the grounds of "defense and national security" or "other reasons of public interest," and authorities have repeatedly denied exit to people who express dissent.

The government restricts the movement of citizens within Cuba through a 1997 law known as Decree 217, which is designed to limit migration to Havana. The decree has been used to harass dissidents and prevent those from elsewhere in Cuba from traveling to Havana to attend meetings.

In April, dissidents and human rights defenders Dulce Amanda Duran, Roseling Peñalvar, and Wendis Castillo were barred from traveling to Lima for a civil society meeting. Castillo, a human rights defender and member of the Dignity Movement, had also been barred from traveling in November 2017, when she intended to fly to Lima for a conference on corruption and human rights in Latin America.

In July 2018, Rene Gómez Manzano, a prominent dissident who has been imprisoned several times, was intercepted at the airport before boarding a plane to attend a human rights meeting in Montevideo. Agents informed him that he was not authorized to travel.

Prison Conditions

Prisons are overcrowded. Prisoners are forced to work 12-hour days and are punished if they do not meet production quotas, according to former political prisoners. Inmates have no effective complaint mechanism to seek redress for abuses. Those who criticize the government or engage in hunger strikes and other forms of protest often endure extended solitary confinement, beatings, and restrictions on family visits, and are denied medical care.

While the government allowed select members of the foreign press to conduct controlled visits to a handful of prisons in 2013, it continues to deny international human rights groups and independent Cuban organizations access to its prisons.

On August 9, Alejandro Pupo Echemendía died in police custody at Placetas, Villa Clara, while under investigation for a crime related to horse racing. Family members say his body showed signs of severe beatings; authorities contend he threw himself against a wall and died of a heart attack. Allegations have surfaced of family members and witnesses being coerced to withdraw their initial statements and to confirm the official version.

Labor Rights

Despite updating its Labor Code in 2014, Cuba continues to violate conventions of the International Labour Organization that it ratified, specifically regarding freedom of association and collective bargaining. While the law technically allows the formation of independent unions, in practice Cuba only permits one confederation of state-controlled unions, the Workers' Central Union of Cuba.

Human Rights Defenders

The Cuban government still refuses to recognize human rights monitoring as a legitimate activity and denies legal status to local human rights groups. Government authorities have harassed, assaulted, and imprisoned human rights defenders who attempt to document abuses.

Sexual Orientation and Gender Identity

The proposed new constitution would redefine marriage to include same-sex couples. It provides in article 68 that marriage is "the voluntarily concerted union of two people," eliminating the current reference to "a man and a woman."

Key International Actors

In November, the US government reinstated restrictions on Americans' right to travel to Cuba and to do business with any entity tied to the Cuban military, security, or intelligence services. The US also voted against a United Nations resolution condemning the US embargo on Cuba, a sharp break from its 2016 abstention.

In March, former Colombian President Andres Pastrana and former Bolivian President Jorge Quiroga were detained at Havana airport and denied entry. They had flown to Cuba to receive an award on behalf of the Democratic Initiative of Spain and the Americas, a forum of 37 former presidents and heads of state.

In April 2018, Secretary General of the Organization of American States Luis Almagro criticized the election of Díaz-Canel, calling it "an attempt to perpetuate a dynastic-familial autocratic regime. It is called a dictatorship."

In January 2018, the foreign policy chief of the European Union met in Havana with Cuban authorities to accelerate the implementation of their Political Dialogue and Cooperation Agreement. On May 15, the EU and Cuba held their first-ever ministerial-level Joint Council meeting in Brussels.

Cuba is a current member of the Human Rights Council, having been reelected for the 2017-2019 term.

Democratic Republic of Congo

Throughout 2018, government officials and security forces carried out widespread repression and serious human rights violations against political opposition leaders and supporters, pro-democracy and human rights activists, journalists, and peaceful protesters. At time of writing, elections were scheduled for December 23, 2018, but serious concerns remained about the credibility, fairness, and inclusivity of the electoral process, and the potential for further delays.

In central and eastern Congo, numerous armed groups, and in some cases government security forces, attacked civilians, killing and wounding many. Much of the violence appeared linked to the country's broader political crisis. The humanitarian situation remained alarming, with 4.5 million people displaced from their homes, and more than 120,000 refugees fled to neighboring countries. In April, government officials denied any humanitarian crisis and refused to attend an international donor conference to raise US$1.7 billion for emergency assistance to over 13 million people in need in Congo.

Freedom of Expression and Peaceful Assembly

Throughout 2018, government officials and security forces banned peaceful demonstrations; used teargas and in some cases live ammunition to disperse protesters; restricted the movement of opposition leaders; and arbitrarily detained hundreds of pro-democracy and human rights activists, opposition supporters, journalists, peaceful protesters, and others, most of whom were eventually released.

During three separate protests led by the Lay Coordination Committee (CLC) of the Catholic Church in December 2017, and January and February 2018, security forces used excessive force, including teargas and live ammunition, against peaceful protesters within and around Catholic churches in the capital, Kinshasa, and other cities. Security forces killed at least 18 people, including prominent pro-democracy activist Rossy Mukendi. More than 80 people were injured, including many with gunshot wounds.

Catholic Church lay leaders had called for peaceful marches to press Congo's leaders to respect the church-mediated "New Year's Eve agreement" signed in late 2016. The agreement called for presidential elections by the end of 2017 and confidence-building measures, including releasing political prisoners, to ease political tensions. These commitments were largely ignored, however, as Kabila held on to power through repression and violence.

On April 25, security forces brutally repressed a protest led by the citizens' movement Lutte pour le Changement (Struggle for Change, LUCHA) in Beni, in eastern Congo, arresting 42 people and injuring four others. On May 1, security forces arrested 27 activists during a LUCHA protest in Goma, in eastern Congo. Leading democracy activist Luc Nkulula died under suspicious circumstances during a fire in his house in Goma on June 9. Fellow activists and others believe he was the victim of a targeted attack.

In July, two journalists and two human rights activists were threatened and went into hiding following the release of a documentary about mass evictions from land claimed by the presidential family in eastern Congo.

In early August, Congolese security forces fired teargas and live ammunition to disperse political opposition supporters, killing at least two people—including a child—and injuring at least seven others with gunshot wounds, during the candidate registration period for presidential elections. Authorities also restricted the movement of opposition leaders, arrested dozens of opposition supporters, and prevented one presidential aspirant, Moïse Katumbi, from entering the country to file his candidacy.

Congolese police arbitrarily arrested nearly 90 pro-democracy activists and injured more than 20 others during peaceful protests on September 3. The protesters had called on the national electoral commission to clean up the voter rolls after an audit by the Organisation Internationale de la Francophonie (OIF) found that over 16 percent of those on the lists had been registered without fingerprints, raising concerns about potentially fictitious voters. They also called on the commission to abandon the use of controversial voting machines, which are untested in Congo and could potentially be used to tamper with results.

A Congolese court sentenced four members of the Filimbi ("whistle" in Swahili) citizens' movement to one year in prison in September. Carbone Beni, Grâce

Tshunza, Cédric Kalonji, Palmer Kabeya, and Mino Bompomi were arbitrarily arrested or abducted in December 2017 as they mobilized Kinshasa residents for nationwide protests on December 31, 2017. Kabeya was freed in September.

In November, authorities arrested and detained for a few days 17 pro-democracy activists in Kinshasa. They also abducted and tortured a LUCHA activist in Goma, who was released after three days.

Attacks on Civilians by Armed Groups and Government Forces

More than 140 armed groups were active in eastern Congo's North Kivu and South Kivu provinces, and many continued to attack civilians, including the largely Rwandan Democratic Forces for the Liberation of Rwanda (FDLR) and allied Congolese Nyatura groups, the Ugandan-led Allied Democratic Forces (ADF), the Nduma Defense of Congo-Renové (NDC-R), the Mazembe and Yakutumba Mai Mai groups, and several Burundian armed groups. Many of their commanders have been implicated in war crimes, including ethnic massacres, rape, forced recruitment of children, and pillage.

According to the Kivu Security Tracker, which documents violence in eastern Congo, assailants, including state security forces, killed more than 780 civilians and abducted, as well as kidnapped for ransom, more than 1,200 others in North Kivu and South Kivu in 2018.

In Beni territory, North Kivu province, around 300 civilians were killed in nearly 100 attacks by various armed groups, including the ADF.

In May, unidentified assailants killed a park ranger and kidnapped two British tourists and their Congolese driver in eastern Congo's Virunga National Park. The park has since been closed for tourism. The tourists and driver were later freed.

Between December 2017 and March 2018, violence intensified in parts of northeastern Congo's Ituri province, where armed groups launched deadly attacks on villages, killing scores of civilians, raping or mutilating many others, torching hundreds of homes, and displacing an estimated 350,000 people.

Also, in northeastern Congo, the Ugandan-led Lord's Resistance Army continued to kidnap large groups of people and commit other serious abuses.

Justice and Accountability

The trial of Bosco Ntaganda, accused of 13 counts of war crimes and five counts of crimes against humanity allegedly committed in northeastern Congo's Ituri province in 2002 and 2003, continued at the International Criminal Court (ICC) in the Hague.

In June, an ICC appeals chamber overturned the war crimes and crimes against humanity convictions against former Congolese Vice President Jean-Pierre Bemba for crimes committed in neighboring Central African Republic. In September, the court sentenced Bemba on appeal to 12 months for a related conviction of witness tampering. Interpreting witness tampering as a form of corruption prohibited by the Congolese electoral law for presidential candidates, Congo's electoral commission later invalidated Bemba's presidential candidacy in what appears to be a politically motivated decision.

Sylvestre Mudacumura, military commander of the FDLR armed group, remained at large. The ICC issued an arrest warrant against him in 2012 for nine counts of war crimes.

The Congolese trial into the murders of UN investigators Michael Sharp and Zaida Catalán and the disappearance of the four Congolese who accompanied them in 2017 in the central Kasai region was ongoing at time of writing. A team of experts mandated by the United Nations secretary-general to support the Congolese investigation had not been granted the access or cooperation needed to effectively support a credible and independent investigation. Human Rights Watch research implicates government officials in the murders.

A UN Human Rights Council-mandated investigation into the broader, large-scale violence in the Kasai region since 2016 found that Congolese security forces and militia committed atrocities amounting to war crimes and crimes against humanity. In July, the council called on the UN High Commissioner for Human Rights to dispatch a team of two international human rights experts to monitor and report on the implementation by Congolese authorities of the Kasai investigation's recommendations.

The trial against Congolese security force members arrested for allegedly using excessive force to quash a protest in Kamanyola, eastern Congo, in September

2017, during which around 40 Burundian refugees were killed, and more than 100 others wounded, had yet to begin at time of writing.

The trial of militia leader Ntabo Ntaberi Sheka, who surrendered to the UN peacekeeping mission in Congo (MONUSCO), began on November 27. Sheka was implicated in numerous atrocities in eastern Congo, and he had been sought on a Congolese arrest warrant since 2011 for crimes against humanity for mass rape.

In July, Kabila promoted two generals, Gabriel Amisi and John Numbi, despite their long involvement in serious human rights abuses. Both generals have also been sanctioned by the United States and the European Union.

Key International Actors

In 2018, the UN Security Council, which visited Kinshasa in October, the UN secretary-general, the African Union, the Southern African Development Community (SADC), the US, the EU, and many individual states called for the electoral calendar to be respected. They emphasized the need for full respect of the New Year's Eve agreement, including the confidence building measures, and for the elections to be credible and inclusive.

Angolan Foreign Minister Manuel Domingos Augusto said in August that Kabila's decision not to make an unconstitutional bid for a third term was "a big step," but that more needed to happen "for the electoral process to succeed and achieve the objectives that have been set by the Congolese." At a SADC summit in Namibia in August, the Namibian president and new SADC chairman, Hage Geingob, said that the crisis in Congo could lead to more refugees fleeing to neighboring countries if it was not resolved.

In December 2017, the US sanctioned Israeli billionaire Dan Gertler, one of Kabila's close friends and financial associates who "amassed his fortune through hundreds of millions of dollars' worth of opaque and corrupt mining and oil deals" in Congo, as well as several individuals and companies associated with Gertler. In June 2018, the US announced the cancellation, or the denial, of the visas of several Congolese officials, due to their involvement in human rights violations and significant corruption related to the country's electoral process.

Belgium announced in January 2018 that it was suspending all direct bilateral support to the Congolese government and redirecting its aid to humanitarian and civil society organizations.

Ecuador

Ecuador faces chronic human rights challenges, including poor prison conditions, laws that give authorities broad powers to limit free speech and judicial independence, and far-reaching restrictions on women's and girls' access to reproductive health care.

President Lenín Moreno, who took office in May 2017, has implemented policy changes that have fostered a climate of open debate and are aimed at repairing damage suffered by democratic institutions during former President Rafael Correa's decade in power. Although some measures have been adopted and other initiatives are underway, structural changes are needed, such as repealing key provisions of the Communications Law that severely undermine free speech.

In February 2018, Ecuadoreans voted on a proposal by President Moreno to amend the constitution. The electorate supported all proposals, including reversing indefinite re-election of public officials, ending statutes of limitations for sexual crimes against children, and appointing a new Transition Council of Citizen Participation tasked with evaluating the performance of key state institutions and authorities, and empowered to replace them. At time of writing, the Transition Council had suspended several authorities and designated their temporary replacements, including the attorney general, the ombudsman, and the prosecutor general.

Freedom of Expression

President Moreno has undertaken important changes to restore freedom of expression, including by ending government pressure to determine the editorial line of public media outlets and by ending President Correa's practice of publicly threatening and harassing independent journalists, human rights defenders, and critics.

In May, President Moreno announced that a 2013 communications law, which gives the government broad powers to limit free speech, would be amended, recognizing that "international standards have been breached in the past decade." The law requires that all information disseminated by media be "verified" and "precise," opening the door to retaliation against media critical of the government. It also prohibits "media lynching," defined as "repeatedly disseminating information with the purpose of discrediting or harming the reputation of a person or entity." And it prohibits "censorship," defined as the failure of private media outlets to cover issues the government considers to be of "public interest."

The proposal includes positive changes that could strengthen free speech, such as repealing the "media lynching" provision and media outlets' obligation to cover information considered by authorities to be of "public interest." However, it also includes problematic provisions, such as an obligation to rectify information that does not comply with a vague requirement to produce "quality information" and a requirement to allow the government to broadcast "mandatory statements" without specifying that it should only apply in emergency situations.

In March 2018, the Transition Council removed the head of Superintendency of Information and Communication (SUPERCOM), a government regulatory body created by the 2013 law, and appointed his temporary replacement. Under President Correa, SUPERCOM had been used to harass and sanction independent media outlets. Since President Moreno took office, sanctions imposed by SUPERCOM have declined steeply. His amendment proposal would eliminate SUPERCOM, the enforcement powers of which would be transferred to the Ombudsman Office.

Provisions that criminalize expressions and opinions, including slander and the misdemeanor of "discrediting expressions," which have been used in the past to punish government critics, remain on the books but are rarely used.

In April, President Moreno confirmed that three Ecuadoreans working for *El Comercio* newspaper had been killed. Javier Ortega, Paúl Rivas, and Efraín Segarra had been investigating increased violence along the Ecuador-Colombia border when Colombian guerrillas abducted them. In June, the bodies were found in Colombia and repatriated to Ecuador. In July, the Inter-American Commission on Human Rights (IACHR) created a special team, with the support of the Colombian and Ecuadorean governments, to support investigations, which were still underway at time of writing.

Freedom of Association

During his time in office, President Correa issued decrees granting the executive broad powers to intervene in the operations of nongovernmental organizations (NGOs). Several organizations critical of the government were dissolved, or threatened with dissolution, under these provisions.

In October 2017, President Moreno replaced Correa's decree with a new one that limits some of the previous decree's vaguely worded language but maintains some ambiguous grounds for dissolving civil society organizations.

A proposal to adopt a law that could make Correa's decree permanent was pending before the National Assembly at time of writing and may be modified during debate in Congress.

Judicial Independence

Corruption, inefficiency, and political interference have plagued Ecuador's judiciary for years. During the Correa administration, high-level officials and Judiciary Council members interfered in the resolution of cases that touched on government interests, and in the appointment and removal of judges.

After taking office, President Moreno said that judges would be free to "make decisions without any pressure whatsoever" and vowed "never to call a judge to influence him."

In April, the Transition Council suspended all pending designations of judges and prosecutors by the Judiciary Council, while evaluating its performance. In June, it found all council members were responsible of actions including establishing a system to favor government interests through its decisions and removed them. The Transition Council designated temporary authorities to carry out the Judiciary Council's activities until permanent authorities are appointed. However, following strong public criticism, in September, the Transition Council suspended their power to evaluate the performance of the judiciary, including the National Court of Justice, to ensure such review was carried out by a permanent body.

In August, the Transition Council removed all nine members of the Constitutional Court, arguing, among other things, that they lacked independence and that there were irregularities in the use of public funds related to their functions. Civil society groups have questioned the legality of these removals and their impact on judicial independence. The court has not operated since.

The legal framework that allowed for political interference in the judiciary under President Correa remains in place. Ecuador's Organic Code on Judicial Function allows the Judiciary Council to suspend or remove justice officials, including judges, for acting with "criminal intent, evident negligence or inexcusable error." Between 2013 and August 2017, 145 judges were suspended or removed for committing "inexcusable errors," according to the council. This broad rule allows for the removal of judges for legal errors, and exposes them to political pressure and undermines judicial independence.

Prosecutions of Indigenous Leaders

The Correa administration used the criminal justice system to target environmentalists and indigenous leaders. Since taking office, President Moreno has opened a dialogue with them. In July, he met with leaders of the indigenous umbrella group CONAIE, who later reported they would submit a new request for an amnesty for indigenous people whom they say have been arbitrarily prosecuted in recent years. The National Assembly rejected a previous amnesty request for 200 people in 2017, when a former interior minister of Correa's administration was presiding.

In May, a court found indigenous leader Agustin Wachapá not guilty on charges of "inciting discord" through a Facebook post calling on the Amazonia people to mobilize against the military presence ordered by then-President Correa in Morona Santiago province. The military was deployed there after a police officer died and several people were injured during clashes between the police and indigenous Shuar people who were attempting to take over a mining camp that they said was built on ancestral lands without their consent.

In January, the Shuar indigenous leader Pepe Acacho was sentenced to eight months in prison for promoting a 2009 indigenous protest against a bill that would have granted the State powers to manage hydrological resources and eliminated indigenous boards that had such powers in ancestral territories. During the protest, a person was killed. Shuar activists argued the law deprived them of control of water in their territories. All of the evidence supporting Aca-

cho's prosecution was dubious, and nothing said by him in several radio interviews cited as evidence by prosecutors could reasonably be construed as incitement to violence. Though initially arrested in 2011, Acacho was freed a few days later, after filing a habeas corpus. Acacho was detained again in September and released 17 days after his arrest when President Moreno granted him a presidential pardon.

Prison Conditions

Prison overcrowding, poor prison conditions, and violence inside prisons are longstanding human rights problems in Ecuador.

Video recordings leaked to the public in 2016 showed prison guards beating inmates at the prison, some of them naked, and subjecting them to electric shock. In 2017, the Attorney General's Office changed the grounds for investigation from torture to "overreaching in the execution of an act of service," and declined to accuse 34 of the 49 officers implicated. A judge then dismissed charges against all of the officers. But an appellate court annulled the dismissal of charges. In September, the trial against 42 officers accused of torture began, and was ongoing at time of writing.

Accountability for Past Abuses

A truth commission set up by the Correa administration to investigate government abuses from 1984 to 2008 (from the beginning of the repressive presidency of León Febres Cordero until Correa took office) documented 136 cases of gross human rights violations involving 456 victims, including 68 extrajudicial executions and 17 disappearances. A special prosecutorial unit created in 2010 to investigate the cases has initiated judicial procedures in less than 10 of them, and final rulings were rendered in only two. Both the investigation and judicialization of the remaining cases appears to be completely stalled.

Women's Rights

In Ecuador's criminal code, the right to seek an abortion is limited to instances in which a woman's health or life is at risk, or when a pregnancy results from the rape of a "woman with a mental disability." Women who have abortions in other cases face prison sentences of up to two years. Fear of criminal prosecution drives some women and girls to have illegal and unsafe abortions and impedes access to health care and services for survivors of sexual violence.

Research by an academic institution and civil society organizations, citing official data, reported 243 abortion-related criminal cases in Ecuador between 2013 and 2017. A proposal to decriminalize abortion in cases of rape, which was supported by civil society groups, remained pending before the Justice Commission at time of writing.

According to government statistics released in 2012, when the latest national survey on gender-based violence was conducted, 6 out of every 10 women and girls had suffered gender-based violence, and 1 out of every 4, sexual violence.

From 2014 through February 2018, the government recorded 288 femicides in the country. Ecuador's criminal code punishes femicide, defined as the exercise of power relations resulting in the death of a woman for "being a woman," with prison sentences ranging from 22 to 26 years. According to civil society organizations, there were 64 cases of femicides between January and October 2018.

Sexual Violence Against Children

In March, a special legislative commission created to analyze information on sexual violence against children reported that ministers of education in office from 2013 until 2017 were negligent in processing reports of sexual abuse in schools. The commission was established after a series of cases were made public in 2017—and after President Moreno's Education Ministry revealed that 882 cases had occurred in schools between 2014 and 2017. Impunity in those cases remains the norm.

Sexual Orientation and Gender Identity

Same-sex couples are not allowed to marry in Ecuador. Since 2008, civil unions have been recognized but do not accord the full range of rights enjoyed by married couples, including the ability to adopt children.

In July, two Cuenca lower courts issued historic decisions in favor of two same-sex couples who had challenged the civil registry office, which refused to register their marriages. The courts cited Ecuador's international obligations and ordered the marriages registered. The civil registry appealed. In September, a provincial appeals court overturned the Cuenca courts' decisions, ruling that the Ecuadorean Constitution defines marriage as the union between a man and a woman.

In May, Ecuador's Constitutional Court ruled that a girl, born in Ecuador, with two British mothers should be registered as an Ecuadorean citizen, and that the registry office should record the names of her two mothers as her parents.

In October, a family judge in Quito ruled in favor of a girl and her parents, who were requesting the change of name and gender in her identity document, to match her self-perceived gender identity. The Civil Registry appealed the decision.

Refugees

In September, President Moreno affirmed before the United Nations General Assembly that Ecuador was receiving more than 6,000 Venezuelan migrants a day. Many pass through Ecuador to other countries, but at least 250,000 have stayed. Several xenophobic attacks against Venezuelans have been reported in 2018.

In August, Ecuador declared a state of emergency in three provinces on the northern border, to attend to Venezuelan migrants' urgent needs. In August, Ecuador announced that Venezuelans would need to present a valid passport to enter the country. But the measure, opposed by the ombudswoman, was suspended. As of October, Ecuador required Venezuelans who wished to enter the country with their Venezuelan ID to present a certificate ensuring the ID's validity, issued by a regional or international body or by the Venezuelan government. These measures make it effectively much harder for Venezuelans to enter Ecuador.

In September, Ecuador hosted a summit to address the region's response to the Venezuelan exodus.

Foreign Policy

President Moreno has criticized excessive use of force against protestors, detention of political opponents, and a lack of democratic guarantees in Venezuela. In June, Ecuador abstained from voting on an Organization of American States

(OAS) resolution on Venezuela's crisis. But in September, it supported a resolution at the UN Human Rights Council, departing from former President Correa's staunch support for the Maduro government. In October, it expelled Venezuela's ambassador to Ecuador after Venezuela's information minister called Moreno a "liar."

In July, the Ecuadorean government condemned violence by security forces in Nicaragua against students and members of the Catholic Church. It expressed concern about human rights violations, calling on the Nicaraguan government to investigate and punish those responsible.

Key International Actors

President Moreno has taken important steps to rebuild relations with the Inter-American human rights system. In May, he visited the Inter-American Court and expressed support for it. In June, Ecuador participated in a hearing before the IACHR on judicial independence in the country, reversing the previous administration's practice—which had continued through 2017—of refusing to participate in such hearings.

In October, the commission hosted a hearing in which several human rights organizations criticized the government's handling of official statistics on how many people had gone missing since 2014, and how the Attorney General's Office was investigating the hundreds of reported cases of people whose whereabouts remain unknown.

In August, the OAS special rapporteur for freedom of expression visited Ecuador for the first time in more than a decade. In October, the UN special rapporteur for freedom of expression visited Ecuador following an invitation from President Moreno.

Egypt

Since President Abdel Fattah al-Sisi secured a second term in a largely unfree and unfair presidential election in March, his security forces have escalated a campaign of intimidation, violence, and arrests against political opponents, civil society activists, and many others who have simply voiced mild criticism of the government. The Egyptian government and state media have framed this repression under the guise of combating terrorism, and al-Sisi has increasingly invoked terrorism and the country's state of emergency law to silence peaceful activists.

The government continued to silence critics through arrests and unfair prosecutions of journalists and bloggers, and the parliament issued severely restrictive laws that further curtail freedom of speech and access to information. The intensified crackdown also includes lesbian, gay, bisexual, and transgender (LGBT) activists, artists, and alleged or self-described atheists. Authorities have placed hundreds of people and entities on the country's terrorism list and seized their assets for alleged terrorism links without any hearing or proper due process.

In addition to using the exceptional State Security Courts, for which court decisions cannot be appealed, authorities continue to prosecute thousands of civilians before military courts. Both court systems are inherently abusive and do not meet minimum due process standards.

In North Sinai, where government forces have been fighting an ISIS-affiliated group called Sinai Province (*Wilayat Sinai*), the army committed flagrant abuses of residents' rights that amount in certain cases to collective punishment. Beginning in January, the army launched the most intensive wave of home demolitions in Sinai in years.

Security Forces Abuses

The Interior Ministry's National Security Agency (NSA) continues to operate with near-absolute impunity. Judicial authorities have investigated very few officers and even fewer have been prosecuted for abuses, including enforced disappearances and torture. Prosecutors continued to use detainee confessions despite credible allegations they were coerced through torture. Authorities announced in late 2017 that they were investigating Human Rights Watch claims of police and

NSA forces' use of torture, but at time of writing, these investigations had not led to the prosecution of any alleged perpetrators.

The Stop Enforced Disappearance campaign has documented 1,530 cases from July 2013 to August 2018. At least 230 of those occurred between August 2017 and August 2018. The whereabouts of at least 32 of those disappeared in 2018 remained unknown as of August 2018.

According to Hafez Abu Seada, a member of the National Council for Human Rights, the Ministry of Interior acknowledged that 500 out of 700 people whose families reported their disappearance since 2015 remain in detention. Although he claimed enforced disappearances are not systematic in Egypt, he failed to explain why the Interior Ministry did not report the whereabouts of 500 people to families who had submitted official complaints.

In late January and February, security forces carried out a series of arbitrary arrests in an escalating crackdown against al-Sisi's peaceful political opponents ahead of the presidential vote. The arrests included those who called for boycotting the process, such as the 2012 presidential candidate and the head of the Strong Egypt Party, Abd al-Moneim Abu al-Fotouh. Following his arrest, a court placed Abu al-Fotouh and others on the country's terrorism list. He remains in pretrial detention despite a heart condition. Security forces also arrested two potential presidential candidates: former Gen. Ahmed Shafiq, whom authorities placed for weeks under de facto house arrest, and former army chief of staff, Sami Anan, who remained in prison at time of writing on trumped up charges.

In May 2018, Egyptian police and NSA forces carried out another wave of arrests of critics of President al-Sisi in dawn raids. Those arrested included Hazem Abd al-Azim, a political activist; rights defender, Wael Abbas; Shady al-Ghazaly Harb, a surgeon; Haitham Mohamadeen, a lawyer; Amal Fathy, an activist; and Shady Abu Zaid, a satirist. Another series of arrests launched in August included former ambassador Ma'soum Marzouk, who called for a public referendum on whether al-Sisi should resign.

Authorities have not investigated a single official or member of the security forces more than five years after the mass killings of the largely peaceful protesters in the Rab'a Square in Cairo, where supporters of former President Mohamed Morsy gathered for weeks after his ouster by the army in July 2013. At least 817 protesters were killed in one day, in what most likely amounted to a crime against humanity.

Death Penalty

Since July 2013, Egyptian criminal courts have sentenced hundreds of people to death in cases stemming from alleged political violence. Many of those were convicted in flawed trials. While Egypt's Cassation Court overturned hundreds of them, it upheld others. Egypt ranked sixth in highest numbers of executions and third in the largest number of death sentences in the world in 2017. In September 2018 alone, a Cairo Criminal Court handed down 75 death sentences, in a mass trial, stemming from the Raba' dispersal events in August 2013.

According to the Cairo Institute for Human Rights Studies (CIHRS), as of September, at least 29 Egyptians remain at imminent risk of execution after losing all of their appeal chances. Between December 2017 and March 2018, CIHRS has documented the execution of 39 individuals, most of them civilians, whom military courts convicted. Military trials of civilians in Egypt are inherently unfair as all officials in military courts, including judges and prosecutors, are serving members of the military.

Freedom of Expression

Egypt remains one of the worst jailers of journalists in the world with roughly 20 journalists behind bars. Egypt's press freedom deteriorated further, ranking 161 out of 180 countries according to Reporters Without Borders. On August 18, President al-Sisi approved a new law regulating the internet called the Anti-Cyber and Information Technology Crimes Law (Cybercrime Law). The Egyptian parliament had passed the law on July 5, granting the government broader powers to restrict freedom of expression, violate citizens' privacy, and jail online activists for peaceful speech. In late July, parliament also passed a new law regulating the press, the Media Regulation Law, which further restricts journalistic freedoms, allows censorship without judicial orders, and levies severe monetary fines for violating the law's articles, in addition to prison sentences for cases related to "inciting violence." Despite objections from Egypt's Journalists' Syndicate, parliament approved the law largely unamended.

Egyptian authorities have been using counterterrorism and state-of-emergency laws and courts to unjustly prosecute bloggers, activists, and critics for their peaceful criticism. Some cases have been transferred to the Emergency State Security Courts, a parallel judicial system operating since October 2017, under the state of emergency that the government claims is being used only against terrorists and drug traffickers. These courts do not guarantee a fair trial and their decisions are not subject to appeal.

Hundreds of news and rights organizations and political websites remain blocked in Egypt without judicial orders, including Human Rights Watch's website.

Freedom of Assembly

The government has not released the implementing regulations of the 2017 NGO law, but has issued scores of decrees based on this law. In November, President al-Sisi ordered the law revised but the government did not announce a timeline for such revision.

Prosecutions in the protracted "Case 173 of 2011" into nongovernmental organizations' foreign funding continued, despite calls from the United Nations, United States, and European Union to end them. At least 28 leading rights activists have been banned from leaving the country as part of this case and could be arrested at any moment. At least 10 individuals and 7 organizations have had their assets frozen.

Sinai Conflict

Military operations in Sinai have escalated over the last five years. In February, the army announced a new campaign against militants of the ISIS-affiliated group known as Sinai Province. Since then, the Egyptian army has destroyed hundreds of hectares of farmland and at least 3,000 homes and commercial buildings, together with 600 buildings destroyed in January—the largest number of demolitions since the army officially began evicting Rafah city in 2014. The army began another security buffer zone around al-Arish Airport, however authorities issued no laws to establish compensation for those whose properties have been damaged or destroyed and the exact area to be evicted. In addition, the army has demolished without judicial orders several houses in al-Arish that belong to families of dissidents, including, in September, the family home of journalist Hossam al-Shorbagy.

From February, the army also intensified its restrictions on freedom of movement, isolating North Sinai from the mainland, North Sinai cities from each other for weeks, and imposing a complete ban on several essential commodities, including car fuel. The restrictions caused a severe shortage of food, cooking gas, and other essential commercial goods in March and April. A new governor, Abdel Fadil Shousha, eased some restrictions beginning in October but residents were allowed only a few liters of car fuel every month and had to line up for hours to obtain it.

Telecommunications and electricity are still sometimes shut for days or weeks in some areas. Thousands of residents in the east rely on rain water. The security forces have committed widespread abuses during the protracted campaign including enforced disappearances, torture, extrajudicial executions, and military trials of civilians, as well as home demolitions. Sinai Province militants have also targeted civilians they perceive to be government collaborators or sympathizers, as well as security forces, and routinely executed their captives. Militants also used improvised landmines that struck civilians on several occasions.

A North Sinai mosque was attacked in November 2017 during Friday prayers. The attack killed 305 worshippers including 27 children. No group claimed responsibility for the attack, but witnesses said they carried ISIS flags.

Freedom of Religion

Egypt's Christian community, which comprises roughly 10 percent of the population and is the largest Christian minority in the Middle East, has suffered legal and social discrimination for decades. Authorities have regularly failed to protect Christians from sectarian attacks and to prosecute perpetrators. In one incident of sectarian violence on August 31, mobs ransacked and looted five homes in Minya's Dimshau Hashim village, after rumors circulated that Christian villagers were planning to build a church. Authorities pressured victims to accept a government-mediated "reconciliation" that allows perpetrators to evade prosecutions, while authorities offered no concrete future protections to the worshippers and their families.

The restrictive Law 80 of 2016 on the construction of churches allowed for conditionally legalizing a small number of churches that were operating without an official permit, but restrictions remain largely in place. Over 90 percent of over 3,700 churches and buildings still work without a permit and lack legal protection. The rights group Egyptian Initiative for Personal Rights (EIPR) documented the closure by the authorities of 14 churches.

Authorities continue to arrest those who describe themselves as non-believers or atheists and jail them under "insulting religions" charges.

Social and Labor Rights

Authorities held in May the first trade union elections in Egypt in 12 years. However, while state officials claimed the elections were transparent and fair, results only reflected the former status quo, with the government-affiliated Egyptian Trade Union Federation (ETUF) emerging from the process effectively in control of the unions. The Center for Trade Union and Workers Services, the oldest independent labor rights group in Egypt, said that the elections were marred by violations such as the exclusion from the electoral process of hundreds of candidates not aligned with the government.

The elections were held on the backdrop of a new trade union law that parliament passed in December 2017 after the International Labour Organization (ILO) put Egypt back on its blacklist over the country's failure to issue a new trade union law in keeping with ILO Convention 87 concerning the right of workers to organize. However in the view of trade unionists and labor activists, the law "was only issued to win favor with the International Labor Organization," and it kept in place several restrictions on the right to organize.

Authorities arrested dozens of people who peacefully protested in May in response to increases in Cairo's subway fare prices.

Violence and Discrimination Against Women, Girls, and LGBT People

The government has failed to adequately protect women and girls from sexual and gender-based violence, and, in some cases, even punished them for speaking out on this issue. On May 9, activist Amal Fathy posted a video on her Facebook page in which she spoke about the prevalence of sexual harassment in Egypt and criticized the government's failure to protect women. The next day, pro-government and state-owned media outlets initiated a smear campaign against Fathy and then on May 11, authorities arrested her. On September 29, a criminal court sentenced Fathy to two years' imprisonment for "publishing false news," as well as a fine of 10,000 Egyptian pounds (US$560) for making "public insults." She continues to face charges in a separate case on trumped-up allegations of belonging to a terrorist organization.

Other women's rights groups and women's rights activists continue to face trial for their women's rights activism including Mozn Hassan, head of Nazra for Feminist Studies, and Azza Soliman, head of the Center for Egyptian Women's Legal Assistance, who remain under travel bans.

Though amendments to the penal code introduced harsher penalties against female genital mutilation (FGM) in August 2016, application of the law is still flawed. In May, the Task Force to Combat FGM issued a statement condemning the extremely lax efforts made to advance the National Strategy Against FGM (2016-2020) and the law's inadequate protection of girls' lives and health.

Egypt continues to prosecute dozens of people based on their sexual orientation or gender identity. Unlike other countries in the region, Egypt has taken no steps to ban forced anal examinations of people accused of homosexual conduct.

Refugee Rights

Egypt hosts refugees and asylum-seekers from more than 60 countries, including Eritrea, Ethiopia, Iraq, Somalia, South Sudan, Sudan, Syria, and Yemen. There is limited public information on the implementation of Egypt's 2016 law on combating "irregular" immigration.

Egyptian authorities have arrested scores of documented and undocumented migrants and kept them in inhumane detention conditions, referring some of them to trials. Authorities have also either returned or threatened to return Sudanese, including those with refugee status, despite the likelihood that they may face persecution in Sudan.

Disability and Health Rights

In February, Egypt passed a new law on the rights of persons with disabilities, 10 years after it ratified the United Nations Convention on the Rights of Persons with Disabilities. At time of writing, the government had yet to adopt by-laws required for implementation. Egypt's also passed the country's first comprehensive law for health insurance for citizens in January and legalized the situation of some scores of churches that the government had previously not approved for building. Yet restrictions on freedom of religion remain largely in place. In 2017-2018, Egypt achieved substantial progress in fighting the endemic Hepatitis C virus through a national health program that included treatment care and new steps for systematic screening.

Key International Actors

Egypt's international allies continue to support Egypt's government and rarely offer public criticism. US President Donald Trump, during al-Sisi's September visit to New York, said that al-Sisi has done "an outstanding job" in fighting terrorism.

In July, the Trump administration announced that it would reinstate Foreign Military Financing funds to Egypt after withholding some funds in August 2017 pending improving democracy and human rights benchmarks, which were not published. The funds were released despite the ongoing and worsening crackdown on human rights in Egypt.

In February, the European Parliament adopted a strongly-worded resolution against Egypt's use of death penalty, which also criticized the country's crackdown on human rights. In May, the European Union spokesperson decried the wave of arrest of human rights defenders in the country.

During the September session of the UN Human Rights Council, the EU expressed concerns over the situation of civil society in the country and about the new cybercrime and media laws.

Three years after the abduction, torture, and murder of the Italian PhD student, Giulio Regeni, in Cairo, prosecutors failed to charge anyone despite the government saying security was monitoring Regeni and investigated his activities before his death.

Several UN experts, including the high commissioner for human rights and UN special procedure mandate holders, have on several occasions individually or collectively condemned abuses in Egypt, including the systematic targeting of human rights defenders, verdicts against protesters, and death sentences following unfair trials.

El Salvador

El Salvador has one of the world's highest homicide rates.

Gangs continued in 2018 to exercise territorial control and extort residents in municipalities throughout the country. They forcibly recruit children and subject some women, girls, and lesbian, gay, bisexual, and transgender (LGBT) individuals to sexual slavery. Gangs kill, disappear, rape, or displace those who resist them, including government officials, security forces, and journalists.

Security forces have been largely ineffective in protecting the population from gang violence and have committed egregious abuses, including the extrajudicial execution of alleged gang members, sexual assaults, and enforced disappearances.

Girls and women alleged to have had abortions have been imprisoned for homicide and aggravated homicide, including during the year. LGBT individuals also face discrimination and violence. These conditions have resulted in internal and cross-border displacement.

Government Accountability

While impunity for government abuses and corruption continue to be the norm, in recent years, El Salvador has taken some steps to bring former officials to justice.

In July 2016, the Supreme Court declared unconstitutional a 1993 amnesty law that prohibited the prosecution of war crimes and crimes against humanity, committed overwhelmingly by state security forces, according to the United Nations Truth Commission, during the country's civil war (1979-1992). In March 2017, former military commanders were brought to trial for their alleged responsibility for the 1981 El Mozote massacre, in which 978 civilians died, including 553 children, and soldiers committed mass rapes. The trial was ongoing at time of writing.

Four other cases remained open but had not reached trial, including one related to the assassination of Archbishop Oscar Romero as he celebrated mass in a hospital chapel in March 1980, a day after his radio homily begging soldiers to stop their repression and killings. In October, a judge ordered the arrest of ex-Cpt. Alvaro Saravia for his alleged role in planning the crime.

In September, a court sentenced former President Antonio Saca and various members of his administration to 5-10 years in prison for embezzling more than US$301 million of public funds to enrich themselves and bribe officials and journalists during his presidency (2004-2009). The ruling followed the attorney general's arrest of 32 people in former President Mauricio Funes' (2009-2014) circle for allegedly embezzling $351 million through the same mechanism. In January 2016, former President Francisco Flores (1999-2004) died while he was being investigated for similar crimes.

Abuses by Security Forces

Since taking office in 2014, President Salvador Sánchez Cerén has expanded the military's role in public security operations, despite a 1992 peace accord stipulation that it not be involved in policing. Killings of alleged gang members by security forces in supposed "armed confrontations" increased from 142 in 2013 to 591 in 2016. In her June 2018 report, the UN special rapporteur on extrajudicial killings found a "pattern of behavior … amounting to extrajudicial executions and excessive use of force" by state security.

A 2017 investigative report in the Salvadoran online newspaper Revista Factum documented evidence of a "death squad" within an elite unit of the Salvadoran police that engaged in killings, sexual assault of teenage girls, robbery, and extortion. At the funeral of a female police officer in September, the National Civil Police (Policia Nacional Civil) director stated that another, now-defunct elite unit participated in her December 2017 disappearance and "femicide," which Salvadoran law defines as a killing motivated by hatred or contempt for women.

In their 2017 and 2018 visits, the UN special rapporteurs on internal displacement and extrajudicial killings documented threats and harassment by security forces against members of the LGBT population, individuals who work toward gang members' rehabilitation, and adolescent children and young adults.

Prison Conditions

In August, the Legislative Assembly made permanent a "state of emergency" that put inmates at seven prisons on lockdown and suspended their family visits. El Salvador first declared the emergency state in March 2016, then extended it as part of its "extraordinary measures" to combat crime in April 2016.

Designed to hold up to 11,400 inmates, the country's penal institutions held more than 38,700 in January. Approximately 30 percent are in pretrial or remand detention.

Cases of tuberculosis among inmates increased from 96 in March 2016 to 1,272 in January 2018. Access to visit prisons has been restricted, but international journalists allowed to enter have noted prisoners' skeletal appearance. More were killed or died in the prisons in 2018 than in 2017.

Gangs

According to widely reported figures, approximately 60,000 gang members are present in at least 247 of the country's 262 municipalities. They enforce their territories' borders and extort and gather intelligence on residents and those transiting these areas, particularly around public transport, schools, and markets.

Numerous security and elected officials have collaborated with gangs in criminal operations, according to international and national media. According to media reports, all political parties have negotiated with them for conducting campaigns, voting, and daily operations and on a truce begun in 2012 between national government, 11 municipal governments, and the two largest gangs.

In April 2016, the Legislative Assembly modified an existing counterterrorism statute to explicitly classify gangs as terrorist organizations and reformed its penal code to impose prison sentences of up to 15 years on anyone who "solicits, demands, offers, promotes, formulates, negotiates, convenes or enters into a non-persecution agreement" with gangs. The UN special rapporteur on extrajudicial killings noted a large discrepancy between charges for membership in a terrorist organization and convictions for it. The Attorney General's Office used the reforms to retroactively prosecute current and former officials who participated in truce negotiations from 2012 to 2014.

Children's Rights

Various local and international officials believe child abuse is widespread. In 2017, 46 girls and 311 boys were murdered, according to the Institute of Legal

Medicine, and at least 20 girls and 14 boys were disappeared, according to the Attorney General's Office. Judges absolved rapists of children as young as 12, if they "formed a home" or had a child together.

In August 2017, the Legislative Assembly prohibited marriage below the age of 18 in all circumstances, ending an exception for pregnant girls.

Women's Sexual and Reproductive Rights

Since 1998, abortion is illegal under all circumstances. Providers and those who assist with the procedure face prison sentences of between six months and 12 years.

In 2018, the Legislative Assembly considered two proposals for modifications to the penal code to permit abortion in cases of rape, grave fetal malformations, or risks to the health of the mother. Support was insufficient to bring either to a vote.

More than 150 girls and women were prosecuted in the past two decades. The courts accepted as evidence a floating lung test that forensic pathologists deemed unreliable over a century ago.

At least 20 women remained imprisoned at time of writing on charges of manslaughter, homicide, or aggravated homicide for allegedly having abortions. In February, the Supreme Court determined there was not enough evidence to prove Teodora Vasquez harmed her fetus and released her 10 years into her 30-year sentence. In March, Maira Figueroa was released 15 years into her 30-year sentence, after the Supreme Court decided charges for aggravated homicide were "excessive and immoral," given that the then-19-year-old became pregnant from rape and had obstetric complications.

LGBT Rights

LGBT individuals are targets of homophobic and transphobic violence, including by police and gang members. Since 1994, over 600 have been killed, according to four Salvadoran LGBT rights organizations.

El Salvador introduced hate crimes into its penal code in September 2015. To date, no cases have been prosecuted as hate crimes. Human Rights Watch is not aware of any bias-related murders of known LGBT individuals that have resulted in conviction.

Attacks on Journalists

Journalists reporting on abuses of power or corruption at various outlets are targets of death threats, as are journalists living in gang-controlled neighborhoods.

In the past decade, at least seven journalists have been murdered. In three cases between 2011 and 2016, Salvadoran courts convicted gang members, who had targeted journalists because of their reporting.

Key International Actors

For fiscal year 2018, the United States disbursed over $42 million in bilateral aid to El Salvador.

In her April report, the UN special rapporteur for internal displacement noted a "striking disparity between government figures [in the hundreds] on those internally displaced by [State and gang] violence and those of civil society and international organizations [in the tens or hundreds of thousands]."

In August, El Salvador broke diplomatic relations with Taiwan to open them with China.

In October, Pope Francis canonized Archbishop Oscar Romero, who before his assassination used his pulpit to preach peace and to denounce state killings and abuses of power.

Equatorial Guinea

Corruption, poverty, and repression of civil and political rights continued to undermine human rights in Equatorial Guinea under President Teodoro Obiang Nguema Mbasogo, who has been in power since 1979, making him the world's longest serving president. Vast oil revenues funded lavish lifestyles for political elite, while little progress was made improving access to health care and primary education.

Mismanagement of public funds, credible allegations of high-level corruption, and serious human rights violations persist, including repression of civil society groups and opposition politicians, torture, and unfair trials. In December 2017, police arrested 147 members of the political party that holds the sole opposition seat in parliament following a confrontation with police officers in Aconibe, a town in the east of the mainland. A court later sentenced 28 of them to 30 years in prison and ordered the party's dissolution. Their lawyers allege authorities physically abused or tortured all the detainees, leading to two deaths. In October, the president pardoned and freed these prisoners. The international community largely remained reluctant to criticize the government about these events.

In a positive step, Equatorial Guinea in May ratified the United Nations Convention Against Corruption, a move the International Monetary Fund required as a pre-condition for a loan. However, the government has held only one meeting with civil society this year to advance its commitment to join the Extractive Industries Transparency Initiative (EITI), an anti-corruption initiative that requires governments and natural resource companies to disclose key information related to governance of oil, gas, and mining.

Equatorial Guinea began a two-year term on the Security Council in January 2018, after campaigning as a champion of sustainable development, despite its poor record on economic and social rights.

Economic and Social Rights

Equatorial Guinea is among the top five oil producers in sub-Saharan Africa and has a population of approximately 1 million people. Although its two-year term

on the Security Council was won campaigning as a champion of sustainable development, it ranks 141 out of 189 countries in the Human Development Index,
by far the world's largest gap between per capita wealth and human development score.

Despite its natural resource wealth, Equatorial Guinea has failed to provide crucial public services, and does not produce reliable data relevant to economic
and social rights. The latest available reliable data is from a household survey
conducted in 2011, which then showed extremely poor outcomes for access to
clean water and childhood malnutrition. 2016 data indicates that at 42 percent,
Equatorial Guinea has the seventh highest proportion of children not registered
in primary schools in the world, according to UNICEF.

In May, Equatorial Guinea ratified the UN Convention Against Corruption, but it
made little progress on its commitment to rejoin EITI, an initiative from which it
was expelled in 2010, in part due to its failure to guarantee an "enabling environment" for civil society to fully participate in EITI's implementation. However,
Equatorial Guinea's EITI steering committee, made up of government officials,
industry representatives, and civil society, met just once in 2018, in July. The
country's leading human rights organization, CEID, withdrew from its role representing civil society on the committee after authorities held its president and
vice president in detention without charge for two weeks.

Freedom of Expression and Due Process

The few private media outlets in the country are largely owned by persons close
to Obiang. Freedoms of association and of assembly are severely curtailed, and
the government imposes restrictive conditions on the registration and operation
of nongovernmental organizations. The few local activists who work on human
rights-related issues often face intimidation, harassment, and reprisals.

On February 27, a judge dismissed the case brought against political cartoonist,
Ramón Nsé Esono Ebalé, whose drawings frequently lampoon President Obiang
and other senior officials. State security officials arrested Ebalé on September
16, 2017, and arraigned him on charges of counterfeiting around US $1,800 in
local currency. Police interrogated him about his art, produced no credible evidence of his involvement in counterfeiting, and at trial, the government's sole
witness admitted that authorities ordered him to make the claims.

Police arrested Julián Abaga, 44, a teacher, on December 12, 2017, soon after an audio message he sent to a friend living abroad denouncing corruption in Equatorial Guinea was uploaded on the internet, according to a news release published by a political opposition party. A lawyer who met with Abaga said he was accused of "insulting the president," although he was never brought to trial. He was released on July 4, as a "gesture of goodwill" following an event Obiang initiated that purported to bring the government into dialogue with political opposition groups.

A magistrate judge, José Esono Ndong Bindang, died while in police custody on July 21, three days after he was arrested for allegedly misappropriating funds, according to a lawyer familiar with his case. The lawyer said that Esono was diabetic and was brought to a clinic when he fell ill soon after his arrest, but police then returned him to the prison against medical advice. He died several hours later.

Political Repression

In 2018, Obiang and the ruling Democratic Party (PDGE) further solidified their monopoly over political life after a court dissolved the political party that held the sole seat belonging to the opposition in the 170-member bicameral parliament. In December 2017, police arrested 147 members of Citizens for Innovation (CI), including its member of parliament, Jesús Mitogo, after a confrontation in the city of Aconibe between CI supporters attending a rally for which it held a permit and police. One of the lawyers who worked on the case, Maria Jesus Bikene, said the confrontation began after police ordered CI to disperse the rally. During the confrontation, CI members harmed three police officers and seized four guns from them, according to news reports.

Authorities appear to have used the incident to crack down on CI. Bikene maintained that the vast majority of the 147 arrested were not in Aconibe, and that nearly all the detainees were repeatedly beaten, and in many cases tortured. A second lawyer, Ponciano Mbomio Nvó, who represented Mitogo, similarly said his client was not in Aconibe on the day of the altercation and that he was tortured while in detention in Malabo, the country's capital. One of the detainees, Santiago Ebee Ela, who was not represented by a lawyer, was tortured to death while in detention, Bikene said. On February 23, a court ordered the dissolution of CI and sentenced 21 of the detainees, including Mitogo, to 30 years in prison for "sedition" and other crimes, and released the others. On July 2, one of those sentenced, Juan Obama Edu, died. Bikene alleges that the death was due to torture.

Beginning July 16, the government held a five-day "National Dialogue and Political Interaction," an event Obiang initiated to bring political opposition activists and groups, including those in exile, into dialogue with the government and ruling party. Obiang promised amnesty to political prisoners and opposition members who were sentenced by an Equatoguinean court while living in exile. However, most opposition groups and leaders remained wary of this promise and did not attend the dialogue. Moreover, the imprisoned CI members were not released until October 22, when Obiang issued a pardon for them and 48 other prisoners. Obiang did not provide any official reason for the pardon.

On October 27, four armed men forced Alfredo Okenve, the vice president of CEID, from his car by gunpoint and took him to a remote area where they severely beat and then abandoned him. The car the men drove indicated they were security officials. The men appear to have mistaken Okenve for his brother, who leads a political party, although they continued to beat him after ascertaining his correct identity.

International Corruption Investigations

On September 14, Brazil seized $15 million worth of watches and $1.5 million in cash from Teodorin, Obiang's eldest son and the vice president, whom authorities said brought the valuables to the country in a private plane without declaring them in accordance with the law.

These allegations are the latest in a string of investigations into Teodorin for corruption, money-laundering, and embezzlement. In October 2017, a French court convicted Teodorin in absentia of laundering tens of millions of dollars in France. He received a suspended sentence, €30 million (US$35 million) fine, and his assets were seized. He has appealed the case.

In a separate case, in 2014, the US Department of Justice seized a $30 million Malibu mansion and a $38.5 million private jet from Teodorin, alleging it was purchased with stolen funds. Teodorin settled that case by agreeing to forfeit

$30 million to US authorities that would be repatriated for the benefit of Equatoguineans. The US is expected to determine which charities will receive the funds.

A corruption case before a Spanish court implicating several senior Equatoguinean government officials is ongoing. A trial is expected next year. The complaint alleges that the officials purchased homes in Spain through a private company that a US Senate investigation revealed had received $26.5 million in government funds at around the same time of the purchases.

Eritrea

After decades of near total diplomatic isolation, 2018 was a year of significant change in Eritrea's relationship with its neighbors. In July, the leaders of Eritrea and Ethiopia signed a five-point declaration to usher in "a new era of peace and friendship," formally ending a border war that began 20 years earlier. A month later, Eritrea and Somalia resumed diplomatic relations after 15 years, and Djibouti and Eritrea did the same shortly after. In November, the United Nations Security Council lifted its nine-year arms embargo against Eritrea. Despite these changes, there was no sign of Eritrea ending its severe repression of basic rights.

For two decades, President Isaias Afewerki used the absence of peace with Ethiopia to justify authoritarianism. Forced conscription into "national service" was prolonged indefinitely despite a decree limiting service to 18 months. Political opponents—anyone who questions Isaias' rule—are jailed infinitely without trial, often incommunicado. Independent media is prohibited, and journalists imprisoned. Political parties and nongovernmental organizations are also prohibited; elections, a legislature, and an independent judiciary are all not permitted because Isais argued they would weaken Eritrea's defenses. Some religious groups are forbidden altogether, and others strictly regulated by government appointees. Implementation of a constitution approved by a constituent assembly in 1997, before the war, was deferred indefinitely.

The change in rapport with Ethiopia ended Isais' many excuses for repressive policies but not, so far, the harshness of his rule. Two weeks before the Eritrea-Ethiopia declaration, the United Nations Human Rights Council lamented the government's "systematic, widespread and gross human rights violations" committed "in a climate of generalized impunity." Among the abuses were "arbitrary detention, enforced disappearances, torture and sexual violence and forced labor," as described in the latest report of the council's special rapporteur on Eritrea. Symptomatic of the government's approach to critics was its foreign minister's diatribe that the rapporteur was "morally bankrupt" and "willfully distort[ed] reality" to further a "wicked agenda."

By year's end, conditions had not changed. Nevertheless, in October, the UN General Assembly elected Eritrea to the Human Rights Council.

Indefinite Military Service and Forced Labor

The rights of all Eritrean citizens remain severely restricted, but younger generations conscripted into national service are especially impacted. A UN commission of inquiry on human rights in Eritrea in 2016 characterized national service as "enslavement." And despite its agreement with Ethiopia, the government has not released any long-term national service conscripts.

All 18-year-olds are conscripted into national service. They serve indefinitely, some as long as 18 years. National service is not the sole reason thousands, including unaccompanied children, flee Eritrea each month but it remains a primary factor. Almost 15 percent of the population has fled since the 1998 war. After the Eritrea-Ethiopia border opened, the number of fleeing Eritreans, especially unaccompanied minors, increased significantly, according to the United Nations High Commissioner for Refugees (UNHCR).

Conscripts have long been subject to inhuman and degrading punishment, including torture, without recourse. Although pay was increased in recent years, it remains nominal and insufficient to support a family, especially as such increases are offset by higher deductions for food.

Eritrea's information minister acknowledged in a 2018 interview that fewer than one-fifth of conscripts have military roles. The rest are farm laborers, teachers, construction workers, civil servants, lower-level judges, and other civilian laborers. Conscripts assigned to government-owned construction firms work on building infrastructure at foreign-owned mineral mines.

Right to Education

The Eritrean government uses the high school system to forcibly channel thousands of young people into national service, requiring them to spend their final year at the abusive Sawa military camp. Instead of developing a pool of well-trained and voluntary secondary school teachers, the government relies on national service conscripts, with little to no choice in their assignment and no end to their deployment in sight.

Decades of forced conscription have created a teaching corps lacking qualifications and motivation, severely impacting young Eritreans' right to education. Because of inadequate pay and indefinite service, teachers are often absent from classes and many emigrate. Students are unmotivated by poor teaching and their belief that education has little benefit in the face of a future of endless forced national service.

Freedom of Speech, Expression, and Association

The government has not allowed the private press—destroyed in 2001 when 10 journalists were arrested and detained without trial indefinitely—to resume operations, nor has it permitted nongovernmental organizations.

The government neither released nor improved the conditions of its most prominent prisoners, government officials and reporters arrested in 2001 and incarcerated incommunicado ever since. Because of government secrecy and the absence of independent monitoring, it is impossible to determine how many political prisoners remain behind bars.

In March, the government released the body of the 90-year-old honorary president of a private Islamic school in Asmara, Al Diaa, jailed in October 2017 for protesting a planned government takeover of the school. Thousands, including minors, were arrested as they marched through Asmara to attend his funeral. Most were released during the next three months, but some school leaders remain imprisoned at the time of writing.

Former finance minister and critic of the president, Berhane Abrehe, was arrested in September and his location remains unknown. Berhane had authored a book that detailed problems with Isais's rule and calling on young people to rise against his regime. The government arrested Berhane's wife, Almaz Habtemariam, in February and she has been held incommunicado ever since.

Freedom of Religion

The government refuses to recognize all but four religious groups: Sunni Islam, Eritrean Orthodox, Roman Catholic, and Evangelical (Lutheran) churches. Eritrean Orthodox Patriarch Antonios, deposed by the government in 2007, remains under house arrest.

Security personnel continue to raid private homes where devotees of unrecognized religions meet for communal prayer. Repudiation of their religion is typically the price of release. In March, a newly married couple was arrested at a wedding-related ceremony.

Fifty-three Jehovah's Witnesses remain in detention, including three arrested and sent to the Sawa military training camp in 1994. Prison conditions improved somewhat for them in 2017 when they were all transferred to the Mai Serwa prison. For a brief time there, they were allowed visitors for the first time since being incarcerated; in late 2018, however, visits were again barred.

Refugees

Eritrean refugees faced the prospect of repatriation from some countries in light of improved relations with Ethiopia. While Ethiopia shut down Eritrean opposition outlets, it took no steps to expel the 164,000 Eritrean refugees in Ethiopia.

Israel calls Eritrean (and Sudanese) asylum seekers "infiltrators" and continually subjects them to harsh measures to pressure them to leave Israel "voluntarily." In January, Israeli authorities said they would indefinitely detain thousands if they refused to leave for Rwanda or Uganda. In March, the Israeli High Court ruled the policy unlawful after the third-countries said they would refuse anyone deported from Israel. Israel's justice minister warned repatriation would be likely if Eritrea "canceled" national service.

In September 2017, the United States announce it would repatriate about 700 Eritreans who were denied asylum. Some of them fled to Canada. One committed suicide at the Cairo airport while being repatriated.

In July, the Swiss Federal Administrative Court ruled that conditions in Eritrean national service were not so severe as to make deportation unlawful. The ruling came despite a 2017 report by the European Asylum Support Office that Eritreans returned involuntarily risked punishment, including imprisonment in inhumane conditions, forced labor, and torture.

Key International Actors

Eritrea's resumption of diplomatic relations with Ethiopia and Somalia led both countries to support lifting the UN arms embargo, originally instituted in response to Eritrean support of Al-Shabab and Eritrea's aggression against Djibouti. Djibouti later concurred with lifting sanctions, but reluctantly, because the border with Eritrea remains unsettled and Eritrea has not accounted for missing Djibouti prisoners-of-war.

The United Arab Emirates, which played a role in back-channel negotiations between Eritrea and Ethiopia, and which rents a military base near Eritrea's port of Assab that it uses in the Yemeni civil war, announced an agreement with Ethiopia to build an oil pipeline linking Assab with Ethiopia's capital. Russia in September announced plans to build a "logistics center" at an Eritrean port but gave no details about the project.

US Deputy Assistant Secretary for African Affairs Ambassador Donald Yamamoto visited Eritrea in April. Despite the visit and the rapprochement with Ethiopia, Eritrea continued to detain three Eritrean staff of the United States Embassy imprisoned since 2001.

Chinese firms maintain significant investments in Eritrea's mining sector. The mines are required to use government-owned construction firms for infrastructure development and thereby indirectly profit from conscript labor. One mine, at Bisha, was long majority-owned by Canada's Nevsun Mining. In September, Nevsun agreed to a buyout by China's Zijin Mining Group Company. The sale cleared regulatory hurdles in Canada and China in November.

Eswatini (formerly Swaziland)

In 2018, Swaziland's absolute monarch, King Mswati III, who has ruled Swaziland since 1986, unilaterally changed the country's name to Eswatini, but has done little to change the policy of political repression and disregard for human rights and rule of law.

Candidates for the national elections held on September 21 were elected based on "individual merits," without any affiliation to political parties. The State of Emergency decree, which bans political parties, has been in force since 1973. Despite the adoption of the 2005 constitution which guarantees basic rights, and the country's international human rights commitments, the government has not reviewed the decree or changed the law to allow the formation, registration, and participation of political parties in elections.

During 2018, amid reports of the king's lavish lifestyle, Eswatini continued to struggle to fulfill the socio-economic rights of its estimated 1.4 million population. Despite improved access to HIV testing services and the provision of free antiretroviral treatment to those who need it, the country has the highest HIV adult prevalence rate in the world at 27.2 percent. Women and girls continued to be disproportionately affected by the epidemic.

Freedom of Association and Assembly

Restrictions on freedom of association and assembly continued in 2018. Although Eswatini signed the African Charter on Democracy, Elections and Governance in January, the government has not taken steps to ratify and implement the charter.

A few days before the September elections, public sector workers, including teachers and nurses under the umbrella of the Trade Union Congress of Swaziland (TUCOSWA), embarked on protests over salaries across the country. Police responded in a heavy-handed manner, beating and injuring protesters in Manzini. Earlier in June, police injured at least four workers protesting alleged corruption in government. These incidents occurred despite the new Police Service Act of 2018 that provides that "the police shall respect and protect human dignity and human rights," and that "police officers are prohibited from inflicting or tolerating any act of torture or cruel, inhuman or degrading treatment."

Forced Evictions

In April, armed police and the Mbabane High Court Deputy Sheriff evicted 61 people in Malterns town, rendering them homeless. Although the eviction was carried out on the orders of the country's Supreme Court, those evicted were not given adequate notice prior to the demolitions of the homes they had occupied for 57 years. The Eswatini constitution requires evictions to be carried out with sufficient notice, and the payment of adequate compensation, in accordance with the law.

In July, the Eswatini Supreme Court ordered the forceful eviction within 21 days of another 150 long term residents of the Malterns farming settlement. The court did not address issues related to compensation, assistance during and after the eviction, or provision of alternative accommodation.

Rule of Law

King Mswati holds supreme executive power over the parliament and judiciary by virtue of a 1973 state of emergency decree. The country's courts have upheld the legality of the decree. This is contrary to the 2005 constitution, which in accordance with the 2007 African Charter on Democracy, Elections and Governance, provides for three separate organs of government—the executive, legislature, and judiciary. The prime minister theoretically holds executive authority, but in reality, King Mswati exercises supreme executive power and also controls the judiciary.

The 2005 constitution provides for equality before the law, but also elevates the king above the law. In 2018, in an apparent exercise of his absolute executive powers, the king renamed the country without parliamentary approval or the requisite constitutional change.

The Sedition and Subversive Activities Act, which restricts freedom of expression through criminalizing alleged seditious publications and the use of alleged seditious words, such as those which "may excite disaffection" against the king, remained in force in 2018. In February, then-Prime Minister Barnabas Dlamini said that a newspaper, *Swaziland Shopping*, was shut because it criticized the government. Its editor, Zweli Martin Dlamini fled the country in January after allegedly receiving death threats for implicating King Mswati in a corruption case.

Women's and Girls' Rights

The Eswatini government made some progress toward the promotion and protection of women's and girls' rights through amendments to the 1964 Marriage Act, and the passing of the Sexual Offences and Domestic Violence Act of 2018, which provides the framework to curb sexual and gender-based violence in the country. The amendments prohibit child marriages of persons under the age of 18.

Women are under-represented in leadership and decision-making positions in both public and private sectors. To fulfill the constitutional requirement for quotas for the representation of women and and marginalized groups in parliament, the government passed the Election of Women Act in 2018. Eswatini also committed to a number of regional and international instruments to promote gender equality, including the Convention for the Elimination of All Forms of Discrimination Against Women (CEDAW), which Eswatini ratified without reservation, and the Southern African Development Community (SADC) declaration on Gender and Development.

Article 20 of the Eswatini Constitution provides for equality before the law and non-discrimination, but does not prevent discrimination on the grounds of sex, language, sexual orientation, and gender identity. Eswatini's dual legal system, where both Roman Dutch common law and Eswatini customary law operate side by side, has resulted in conflicts leading to numerous violations of women's rights over the years.

Sexual Orientation and Gender Identity

A colonial-era law criminalizes "sodomy," with an unspecified sentence. Despite this law, lesbian, gay, bisexual, and transgender (LGBT) activists successfully held the first ever "Eswatini Pride" in June 2018, with hundreds marching in the streets of Mbabane in support of LGBT equality.

Key International Actors

Representatives of the Southern African Development Community (SADC) and the African Union (AU) observed Eswatini's national elections on September 21. After the elections, despite political parties being banned, SADC issued a statement saying it observed that the 2018 general elections were conducted successfully in a peaceful environment, in line with the constitution of the Kingdom of Eswatini, and the guiding legal framework.

The AU Observer Mission report on the Eswatini elections found that electoral process was conducted in a generally calm and peaceful environment, but raised concerns about the wage-related workers' strike that took place prior to election day and the resultant police intervention. The AU further noted that, although the 2005 constitution guarantees fundamental rights and freedoms, such as freedom of association, assembly, and expression, practical restrictions on civil and political rights remain. These relate to, among others, the formation and participation of political parties in the electoral process.

In his address to the United Nations General Assembly in New York on September 26, King Mswati noted the need to ensure that every citizen has access to basic goods, such as clean water, health, and free primary education. He listed the enactment of the sexual offences and domestic violence act, and the holding of "a very peaceful national election, which was free and fair," as some of the country's key successes.

HUMAN
RIGHTS
WATCH

"We are Like the Dead"
Torture and other Human Rights Abuses in Jail Ogaden,
Somali Regional State, Ethiopia

Ethiopia

After years of widespread protests against government policies, and brutal security force repression, the human rights landscape transformed in 2018 after Abiy Ahmed became prime minister in April. The government lifted the state of emergency in June and released thousands of political prisoners from detention, including journalists and key opposition leaders such as Eskinder Nega and Merera Gudina. The government lifted restrictions on access to the internet, admitted that security forces relied on torture, committed to legal reforms of repressive laws and introduced numerous other reforms, paving the way for improved respect for human rights.

In July, Ethiopia and Eritrea resolved a decades-long stalemate, signed a peace agreement and agreed to implement the 2002 international boundary commission decision. Relations between the countries had been violent or frozen since their troops clashed in the border town of Badme in 1998.

Parliament lifted the ban on three opposition groups, Ginbot 7, Oromo Liberation Front (OLF), and Ogaden National Liberation Front (ONLF) in June. The government had used the proscription as a pretext for brutal crackdowns on opposition members, activists, and journalists suspected of affiliation with the groups. Many members of these and other groups are now returning to Ethiopia from exile.

With the ruling Ethiopian People's Revolutionary Democratic Front (EPRDF) controlling 100 percent of the seats in parliament, the institutional and legal impediments for sustained political space remain a challenge. Accountability for years of abuses, including torture and extrajudicial killings, and opening the space for political parties and civil society remain significant challenges for the new administration. There are indications that the reform process may ultimately be hindered by a lack of independent institutions to carry forward changes.

In September, security forces shot and killed five people during demonstrations in the capital Addis Ababa. Protestors criticized the government for not protecting citizens from forced displacement and ethnically-based attacks, particularly allegations of rape and killings in Oromia earlier in the month. Ongoing ethnic violence and internal displacement continue to put lives at risk. More than 2 mil-

lion people are internally displaced due to intercommunal conflicts and violence, at times involving regional state and local security forces.

Freedom of Expression and Association

Ethiopia released journalists who had been wrongfully detained or convicted on
politically motivated charges, including prominent writers such as Eskinder Nega
and Woubshet Taye, after more than six years in jail. The federal Attorney General's Office dropped all pending charges against bloggers, journalists and diaspora-based media organizations, including the Zone 9 bloggers, Ethiopian
Satellite Television (ESAT), and Oromia Media Network (OMN), which had previously faced charges of violence inciting for criticizing the government.

OMN and ESAT television stations reopened in Addis Ababa in June, following
calls by Prime Minister Abiy for diaspora-based television stations to return. Additionally, the government lifted obstructions to access to more than 250 websites. The restriction on access to the internet and mobile applications
introduced during the 2015 protests was also lifted.

Many of Ethiopia's repressive laws used to silence dissent and restrict citizens'
meaningful engagement—including the Charities and Societies Proclamation,
the Media Law, and the Anti-Terrorism Proclamation—were being revised at time
of writing.

Impunity, Torture, and Arbitrary Detention

Government officials often dismissed allegations of torture, contrary to credible
evidence. But in a July speech to parliament, Abiy admitted that the government
used torture and other unlawful techniques on suspects, acknowledging that
such techniques amounted to terrorism by the state.

Earlier this year, Ethiopia closed Makaelawi detention center, known for torture
and mistreatment of political prisoners. After media reported significant complaints of abuse from prisoners in other federal detention centers, the federal Attorney General's Office dismissed administrators of five facilities in July but they
did not face criminal charges. Many detention centers run by regional administrations, some well-known for ill-treatment, rape, torture, and lack of access to
medical and legal aid, remain unaffected by the reform efforts.

In July, the federal attorney general told media that there would be investigations into torture and mistreatment in detention facilities. In November, a number of high-ranking security officials were arrested due to their alleged involvement in human rights abuses in detention, according to the attorney general. They had not yet been charged at time of writing.

The government did not take any steps to carry out investigations into the killings over 1,000 protesters by security forces during widespread protests in 2015 and 2016 in Oromia and other regions. Even though the legal and justice reform council under the Attorney General's Office announced that judicial independence is a key area of reform, Human Rights Watch is not aware of any concrete steps taken at either the federal or regional level. Courts continue to implement political decisions of the executive branch.

Abuses in Somali Region

In August, Mustapha Omer, an outspoken critic of Somali region's authoritarian leadership, was appointed regional president in place of Abdi Mohamoud Omar, known as Abdi Illey, who presided over a regime of abuses, especially since 2007, when armed conflict escalated between the insurgent Ogaden National Liberation Front (ONLF) and Ethiopia's Defense Force.

All sides committed war crimes between mid-2007 and early 2008, and the Ethiopian armed forces were responsible for crimes against humanity, including executions, torture, rape and forced displacement.

Ethiopian authorities created the Liyu ("special" in Amharic) police, which by 2008 had become a prominent counterinsurgency force reporting to Abdi Illey, regional security chief at the time, who went on to serve as the regional president for eight years. Liyu police continued to commit abuses in the region and, at times, killings in neighboring Oromia regional state.

Abdi Illey resigned and was arrested in August, two weeks after Liyu police and youth loyal to him attacked residents and burned property in the regional capital, Jijiga. He remains in government custody but has not been charged. Police head Abdirahman Abdillahi Burale (known as Abdirahman Labagole) resigned in August, but despite evidence of his involvement in committing human rights abuses, Abdirahman Labagole and other members of the Ethiopian army or Liyu police implicated in abuses against civilians have not faced any charges.

In Jail Ogden, a regional detention facility administered in part by Liyu police, prisoners were tortured, with no access to adequate medical care, family, lawyers, or even, at times, food. After the July publication of a Human Rights Watch report, many prisoners were released from Jail Ogaden. The prison was closed in August.

Internal Displacement

Ethiopia has over 2 million internally displaced people, including almost 1 million displaced in April and June due to inter-communal conflict between Guji and Gedio communities in Oromia and the Southern Nations, Nationalities and Peoples' Region (SNNPR). In early August, at least 145,000 more people were displaced in Somali and Oromia regional states due to renewed fighting. In September, ethnic violence displaced an estimated 15,000 people from the outskirts of Addis Ababa. Despite signs of possible clashes, the government failed to prevent attacks, resulting in further displacement. Except for humanitarian aid, Human Rights Watch is not aware of sustainable federal government efforts to address internal displacement and inter-ethnic violence.

Key International Actors

Ethiopia won international acclaim for its reform agenda this year and continues to enjoy strong support from foreign donors and most of its regional neighbors, due to its role as host of the African Union, its contributions to UN peacekeeping, regional counterterrorism efforts, and migration partnerships with Western countries.

Former UN High Commissioner for Human Rights Zeid Ra'ad Al Hussein visited Ethiopia in April, and conducted meetings with released political prisoners and government officials.He underlined the importance of making greater efforts to ensure the independence of the government-affiliated human rights commission.

In April, the US House of Representatives passed a resolution encouraging Ethiopia's government to increase respect for human rights, rule of law, and democracy. The US maintained its support for Ethiopia and announced that it supports the ongoing reform efforts.

Despite its role as a member of both the UN Security Council and, until the end of 2018, the UN Human Rights Council, Ethiopia maintains its history of non-co-operation with UN mechanisms. Other than the UN special rapporteur on Eritrea, no special rapporteur has been permitted to visit since 2006. The rapporteurs on torture, freedom of opinion and expression, and peaceful assembly, among others, all have outstanding requests to visit the country.

Ethiopia has been inconsistent on human rights-related issues on a number of country situations on the Security Council. It failed to support a long-awaited arms embargo on South Sudan in July. And while voting in favor of a chemical weapons probe in Syria, Ethiopia did not support a March Security Council briefing by the high commissioner for human rights on the situation in Syria.

"Sink or Swim"

Barriers for Children with Disabilities in the European School System

HUMAN
RIGHTS
WATCH

EUROPEAN
DISABILITY
FORUM

European Union

Despite falling numbers of migrants arriving at the borders of the European Union, populist leaders in EU states sought to use the issue of migration to stoke fear and increase their support at the polls. Their positions on migration frequently undermined the EU's moral standing and often had little to do with effective policy. However, EU institutions acted to address the Hungarian government's attacks on the country's democratic institutions and the Polish government's attacks on the rule of law.

Migration and Asylum

Despite arrivals of migrants and asylum seekers decreasing to pre-2015 levels, the often- opportunistic hardline approach of anti-immigrant European Union governments, including those of Italy, Hungary, and Austria, dominated the migration debate throughout the year.

With disagreements blocking agreements on reforms of EU asylum laws and fair distribution of responsibility for processing migrants and asylum seekers entering and already present in EU territory, the focus remained on keeping migrants and asylum seekers away from the EU, including through problematic proposals for offshore processing and migration cooperation with non-EU countries with fewer resources, uneven human rights records, and less capacity to process asylum claims.

By mid-November, 107,900 arrivals were registered by sea (the vast majority) and over land, compared to 172,300 in 2017. A combination of factors, including the EU's problematic migration cooperation with Libya and curbs on nongovernmental rescue efforts in the central Mediterranean, led to a marked decrease in arrivals to Italy, while crossings from Turkey to Greek islands and from Morocco to Spain increased.

The EU consolidated its partnership on migration control with Libya despite overwhelming evidence of brutality against migrants and asylum seekers there. Support to the Libyan Coast Guard, combined with the International Maritime Organization's recognition, in June, of a Libyan search-and-rescue zone, meant that increased numbers of people were intercepted at sea and subsequently detained in abusive conditions in Libya.

A United Nations High Commissioner for Refugees (UNHCR) program to evacuate vulnerable asylum seekers from Libya to Niger did not receive sufficient resettlement offers from EU countries. In September, UNHCR updated its non-return advisory for Libya, emphasizing that Libya is not a safe place to disembark rescued persons.

EU member states' efforts to obstruct rescue efforts by nongovernmental organizations (NGOs) and the increasing reliance on Libyan coast guard forces coincided with a skyrocketing death rate. By mid-November, the death toll had reached 2,043, a decrease compared to 2017. But the death rate per crossing increased from 1 in 42 in 2017 in the first eight months to 1 in 18 in the same period in 2018, according to UNHCR.

In early June, Italy began refusing or delaying disembarkation of rescued persons from NGO, commercial, and military ships. With Malta following suit, there were numerous incidents when hundreds of people had to remain aboard rescue ships until ad hoc disembarkation agreements could be reached. There were concerns that the actions could deter merchant vessels from carrying out rescues.

Instead of seeking a regional disembarkation agreement to ensure a fair and predictable system for sharing responsibility among EU countries, European leaders focused on creating so-called disembarkation platforms outside the EU where all rescued persons would be taken for processing of asylum claims. Egypt, Tunisia, and other North Africa states, and Albania were proposed as possible partners despite concerns about conditions, treatment, and meaningful access to asylum.

Proposed reforms to EU asylum laws, put forward in May 2016, remained largely blocked. Changes to the EU Dublin regulation needed to ensure a more equitable distribution of responsibility for asylum processing remained the most contested.

Belgium moved forward with plans to resume family immigration detention, completing the construction of new detention units for migrant families with children in mid-2018. It had abandoned immigration detention of children, whether unaccompanied or with families, in early 2016. EU countries do not systematically report data on immigration detention of children, the EU Agency for Fundamental Rights observed in a 2017 study. Elsewhere in the EU, 16 of the 28 member states held children in immigration detention in 2016, the last year for which complete data are available.

Discrimination and Intolerance

Populist extremist parties and ideas again exercised an outsize influence over European politics during the year. Parties aligned with radical right populism won re-election in Hungary, joined ruling coalitions in Italy and Austria, and gained ground in elections in Sweden and Slovenia, and in state elections in Germany. Poland's populist government remained in power, but lost momentum in local elections in 2018. Elements of the populists' anti-immigration, anti-refugee and anti-Muslim policy agenda continued to be embraced by some mainstream political parties in several EU countries, including in Germany.

Danish authorities introduced a series of measures during the year to enforce "Danish values," designating certain areas as "ghettos" based on a high proportion of residents with ethnic minority or immigrant backgrounds, and low social status. Children in those areas would be subject to mandatory daycare in the name of integration. In August, a ban on wearing face veils in public came into effect.

There were instances of racist intolerance or violent hate crimes in many EU states including Bulgaria, France, Germany, Greece, Hungary, Italy, Slovakia, Spain, and the United Kingdom. Anti-Semitism remained a concern in EU member states.

An April report by the EU Fundamental Rights Agency noted that Roma across the EU commonly faced harassment and experienced discrimination in accessing education, employment, and healthcare.

The European Commission launched a consultation to develop standards on disability inclusion in EU-funded humanitarian operations.

Discrimination on the grounds of gender and sex remained widespread. At time of writing, eight member states and the EU had yet to ratify the Istanbul Convention, a Council of Europe treaty on combatting and preventing violence against women. In July, Bulgaria's constitutional court found the treaty incompatible with its constitution.

In Ireland, a referendum in May overturned a near-total abortion ban; at time of writing, legislation legalizing access to abortion was pending before parliament. In Poland, a bill introduced in January to "stop abortion" was still pending at time of writing. The initiative aimed to restrict legal abortions carried out in situations of severe fetal anomaly, the grounds for over 95 percent of legal abortions performed in Poland.

In June, the EU Court of Justice ruled that the same-sex spouses of EU citizens are entitled to free movement to any member state in the EU, even if the member state's marriage laws (in this case Romania) did not authorize same-sex marriages.

Rule of Law

EU institutions stepped up their responses to conduct by EU governments that threatens the rule of law and other EU founding values. Poland and Hungary were subject to the political mechanism contained in article 7 of the EU treaty for posing such threats.

In December 2017, the European Commission activated article 7 over the rule of law crisis in Poland, following the adoption of 13 laws that undermined the country's entire judiciary. At time of writing, EU European affairs ministers had convened two hearings in June and September with the government of Poland to discuss the issues. In parallel, the commission pursued enforcement action against Poland over the Law on Ordinary Courts and the Law on the Supreme Court, referring the cases to the EU Court of Justice in December 2017 and September 2018. In October, the EU Court of Justice ordered Poland to suspend application of the Law on the Supreme Court that would remove sitting judges from their posts until a final decision on the case. At time of writing, the EU Court of Justice had yet to hear the merits of either case.

In July, the EU Court of Justice ruled that national courts can block otherwise automatic extradition requests made by Poland on a case by case basis if it is determined that the defendant would not receive fair trial guarantees.

In September, the European Parliament decided by a two-thirds majority to activate article 7 over the situation in Hungary. The parliament expressed concerns on a wide range of issues, including judicial independence, freedom of expression, freedom of association, academic freedom, and the rights of migrants and asylum seekers.

In December 2017, the European Commission referred Hungary's 2017 Higher Education Law and law on foreign-funded NGOs to the EU Court of Justice. In July 2018, the commission referred Hungary's 2017 asylum law to the court. It also began enforcement action over the anti-NGO law that Hungary adopted in May.

In November, the European Parliament adopted a resolution expressing concern over legislative reforms in Romania that undermine the independence of the judiciary and threaten the ability of NGOs to operate.

In May, the European Commission proposed that the next EU budget starting in 2021 should link distribution of EU funds to member states to their respect for rule of law.

The killing of three journalists in member states raised troubling questions about protection of media freedom in the EU. Maltese investigative journalist Daphne Caruana Galizia was killed in a car bomb in October 2017; Slovak investigative journalist Ján Kuciak was shot dead in February 2017; and Bulgarian TV journalist Viktoria Marinov was raped and killed in October 2018. All three were working on exposing corruption or fraud allegations. None of the cases had been resolved at time of writing.

Terrorism and Counterterrorism

In March, the European Commission announced a series of non-binding "operational measures" for states and internet companies to remove online content deemed terrorism-related or otherwise illegal, raising concerns about privacy and freedom of expression. In September, the commission published a draft regulation that, if passed, would turn these measures into law, including large fines for internet companies that failed promptly to remove content deemed illegal.

Two key judgments issued together in May by the European Court of Human Rights condemned Lithuania and Romania for their complicity in the CIA's torture and secret detention program in the 2000s. The court also determined that national investigations in both countries were ineffective, calling for a renewal of the investigations to identify and punish responsible officials.

In March, the European Court of Human Rights rejected a request by the Irish government to reconsider the landmark 1978 case *Ireland v UK* on prohibited interrogation techniques used by British security forces in Northern Ireland in the 1970s. Ireland had sought to reopen the case in light of evidence that the UK withheld information which could have altered the finding that the methods were ill-treatment rather than torture.

By September, at least 12 member states had reported transposing into domestic law the 2017 EU directive to combat terrorism. The directive contains provisions that undermine free expression and freedom of movement.

Croatia

According to the minister of interior, 3,200 migrants and asylum seekers crossed into Croatia between January and August, with 852 claiming asylum. Authorities granted 140 people asylum and 21 subsidiary protection during the same period.

In August, UNHCR reported allegations that since January around 2,500 asylum seekers and migrants had been pushed back by Croatian police to Bosnia and Herzegovina, hundreds of cases of denied access to asylum procedures, and over 700 allegations of police violence and theft. The same month, a group of members of the European Parliament from 11 EU states jointly requested the European Commission to urgently investigate the allegations, with the Council of Europe human rights commissioner echoing that call in October.

A decade after Croatia ratified the UN Convention on the Rights of Persons with Disabilities (CRPD), thousands of adults and children with disabilities remain trapped in segregated institutions. A draft law on foster care tabled by the government in May would prioritize placement of adults with disabilities in foster care, including without their consent, in contradiction to the CRPD. It remained pending at time of writing.

A government funded study published in July found that almost all Roma in the country live in poverty and less than a third finish primary school.

A campaign starting in May for a public referendum to reduce the number of seats for ethnic Serbs in the Croatian parliament and limit them from voting on the budget and government formation raised alarm among Serb community leaders and NGOs. Authorities were reviewing the proposal at time of writing.

Between January and September 2018, there were 14 war crimes cases before courts in Croatia. In the same period, courts convicted only four people for war-related crimes and the prosecution of other cases moved slowly.

France

In August, France adopted a flawed asylum and immigration law. The French Ombudsman, the Council of Europe Commissioner for Human Rights, the UN High Commissioner for Refugees and NGOs criticized the law for undermining access to asylum, including by weakening appeal rights and safeguards for those subject to accelerated asylum procedures. The law failed to ban detention of migrant children, despite six European Court of Human Rights rulings that such detention by France violated their rights.

In April and May, the French ombudsman warned of the dire living conditions of migrants and asylum seekers in the camp of La Villette, in Paris, and in Grande-Synthe in northern France, and called for the camps' dismantlement only if sustainable solutions respectful of fundamental rights are implemented. Authorities cleared the camps in late May and early September respectively. Living conditions for migrants and asylum seekers in the Calais area remain squalid and harassment of aid workers there by police continued.

Child protection authorities in Paris continued to use flawed age assessment procedures for unaccompanied migrant children, excluding many from care they need and are entitled to, leaving hundreds homeless.

In July, the Constitutional Council ruled that solidarity was among the highest values of the French republic and that assisting undocumented migrants should not therefore be criminalized "when these acts are carried out for humanitarian purposes." This ruling was enshrined in the August immigration and asylum law. NGOs remain concerned that judges could narrowly interpret the humanitarian exception in a way that permits prosecutions.

HUMAN
RIGHTS
WATCH

"Like a Lottery"
Arbitrary Treatment of Unaccompanied Migrant Children in Paris

Since late 2017, France's asylum office selected 458 refugees currently in camps in Niger and Chad for resettlement. France pledged to resettle 3,000 refugees from that region before October 2019.

In May, the NGO SOS Homophobie said it received 15 percent more reports of physical attacks on LBGT people for 2017 compared to 2016. In November, Prime Minister Edouard Philippe announced a 69 percent increase in antisemitic attacks in the first nine months of 2018 compared to 2017. The National Commission on Human Rights reported in March that violent anti-Muslim acts had increased in 2017 by 8 percent compared to 2016.

The welcome decision to include access to inclusive education in the national strategy for autism launched in April stood in contrast to a housing law adopted in October that would reduce the obligation to ensure that new housing is wheelchair accessible.

In August, France adopted a new sexual violence law aimed at tackling sexual harassment and sexual violence against children. The law makes street harassment an offense, raises the statute of limitation on sex crimes against children from 20 to 30 years, and gives judges the power to rule on a case by case basis that sex by an adult with a child under 15 is rape but falls short of criminalizing all such sex with a child under 15 as rape. In September, a man was convicted of sexual harassment for the first time under the new law and fined 300 euros (approximately $340).

France's Universal Periodic Review took place in January and the report was adopted in June. France accepted recommendations to stop ethnic profiling in identity checks but failed to take legislative steps to end such practices.

On a visit to France in May, the UN special rapporteur on human rights and counterterrorism expressed concerns about the 2017 counterterrorism law, which incorporates state of emergency powers into ordinary law and includes insufficient safeguards in the use of non-criminal measures against terrorism suspects.

Germany

Chancellor Angela Merkel announced in October she would not seek a fifth term after a poor showing in several state elections by her Christian Democratic Union party and its sister party, the Christian Social Union (CSU). Efforts by the CSU in the Bavarian elections to emulate the rhetoric and agenda of the anti-immigrant Alternative for Germany backfired as the CSU lost voters to AfD and the Greens, with the latter becoming that state's second largest party.

Arrivals of asylum-seekers and migrants fell for the third year in a row, and federal authorities made significant progress clearing a backlog of asylum claims during the year. By the end of July, 96,644 new asylum-seekers had been registered, decreasing by a sixth from the previous year.

Despite disagreements within the newly formed federal coalition government over Germany's approach to EU asylum and migration policy, Germany continued to play a leadership role in refugee resettlement. In April, the government announced that Germany would accept 4,600 resettled refugees in 2018 and 5,600 in 2019 as a contribution towards an EU program. In July, the government granted admission to up to 300 refugees evacuated to Niger from Libya.

NGOs criticized aspects of Germany's deportation system after reports of a series of cases in which asylum seekers were returned to their home countries while their cases were still pending, including a Tunisian deported despite a court order blocking the transfer on the grounds of risk of torture.

Although fewer than in previous years, attacks on refugees and asylum seekers remained a matter of concern. In the first half of 2018, police recorded 627 attacks on refugees and asylum seekers outside their home, and 77 attacks on refugee shelters.

Xenophobic demonstrations in the city of Chemnitz triggered by the killing of a German man, allegedly by two foreign nationals, in August and the exploitation of the killing by the far-right, saw violent scenes, including attacks on people perceived as "non-German."

In March, a Dresden judge found eight people from a far-right group guilty of terrorism offences and attempted murder for attacks in 2015 on refugee shelters and a local politician supporting newly arrived migrants. In July, a Munich judge found a man guilty of murder, terror offenses, and arson in a case relating to a series of murders carried out by a neo-Nazi group between 2000 and 2006. Four accomplices were found guilty of lesser charges.

The controversial Network Enforcement Act (NetzDG), came into effect on January 1. It compels social media companies to take down hate speech and other illegal content or face large fines. The act came under criticism after several high-profile social media users had their content or accounts blocked, either as a result of NetzDG or the companies' terms of use.

A group of foreign correspondents—with support from German journalists' unions and other press freedom groups—launched a challenge in January before the Federal Constitutional Court to the German domestic intelligence agency's power to surveil the communications of foreign nationals, arguing it infringes their right to free expression and privacy.

German judicial authorities continued their work investigating serious international crimes committed abroad, including in Syria.

Greece

Although Greece continued to host large number of asylum seekers, it failed to protect their rights. Overall numbers of arrivals increased compared to the same period in 2017. Deficiencies in the reception and asylum system escalated with severe overcrowding, unsanitary, unhygienic conditions, and lack of sufficient specialized care, including medical care, trauma counseling, and psychosocial support. Physical and gender-based violence were common in asylum camps, and NGOs reported deteriorating mental health conditions among asylum seekers. Most unaccompanied children continued to be placed in camps with adults, in so-called protective police custody or detention or risked homelessness, with authorities failing to resolve a shortage of juvenile shelters or foster care.

Greece's EU-backed policy of confining asylum seekers who arrived by sea to the Aegean islands trapped thousands in these conditions.

While the government transferred 18,000 asylum seekers from islands to mainland Greece following a concerted NGO campaign in November, it refused to implement a binding high court ruling to end the confinement policy for new arrivals, and instead adopted a new law in May to continue it. On Lesbos, a regional authority inspection in September concluded that the Moria camp, the largest of its kind, presented a danger to public health and the environment, and called on the government to address acute shortcomings or close the camp.

Some migrants and asylum seekers trying to cross the land border from Turkey into northeastern Evros region reported being summarily returned to Turkey dur-

ing the year, sometimes violently. Greece did not address reception needs of newly arriving asylum seekers in the region, despite an increase in arrivals starting in April. As a result, women and girls were housed with unrelated men in sites for reception or detention of asylum seekers and lacked access to essential services.

Less than 15 percent of asylum-seeking children had access to education on the islands, and only one in two on the mainland were enrolled in public schools.

Far-right groups continued to campaign against asylum seekers on the islands, and there were media reports of attacks across the country on persons perceived to be migrants or Muslims. Police statistics for hate crimes for 2017 released in March showed a marked increase compared to the previous year.

The Council of Europe's Committee for the Prevention of Torture visited Greece in April, and issued a preliminary report expressing concerns about inhuman and degrading treatment in psychiatric establishments and migrant detention centers.

Hungary

Hungary's ruling party Fidesz and its Prime Minister Viktor Orbán won a third consecutive term with a two-thirds majority in elections in April.

Ahead of the April elections, the government ran a smear campaign on TV, radio, and country-wide billboards targeting civil society organizations working on asylum and migration, and Hungarian-born philanthropist George Soros, a key funder.

During the election campaigning period, government officials, including Prime Minister Orbán, referred to civil society organizations, political opposition, and critical journalists as "agents of Soros."

In addition to the smear campaign, which continued after the elections in pro-government media, civil society organizations, particularly those working on asylum and migration, came under increasing government pressure in 2018.

In June, parliament approved government-proposed amendments to the constitution and other legislation, criminalizing services, advice, and support to migrants and asylum seekers, punishable by up to one-year imprisonment. The measures came into force in July. At time of writing, no prosecutions had taken place. The measures were adopted despite criticism from the Council of Europe commissioner for human rights in February, the UN Human Rights Committee in April, UNHCR in May, and the Council of Europe's constitutional advisory body in June.

EU institutions took various enforcement actions against Hungary during the year (see Rule of Law section).

In August, a special 25 percent tax on funding to organizations "supporting immigration" was introduced, exempting only political parties and international organizations with immunity.

No agreement was reached between Central European University and the Hungarian government to secure the university's operations in Hungary after the government introduced an abusive law in 2017 aimed at forcing the university out of the country.

A law on public assembly due to enter into force in October 2018 gives police more discretion to ban or disband demonstrations.

The country saw a significant decline in asylum applications in 2018 in large part because it became almost impossible for asylum seekers to enter the country to seek protection.

By August, authorities had limited daily entry of asylum seekers to 1-2 asylum seekers per day, leaving thousands stranded in poor conditions in Serbia. In early August, Hungarian authorities denied rejected asylum seekers in the transit zones food. Following an emergency intervention by the European Court of Human Rights, authorities resumed food distribution.

In July, a constitutional amendment entered into force further restricting access to asylum by explicitly banning the "settlement of foreign populations" in Hungary and refusing protection to any asylum seekers arriving in Hungary via any transit country that Hungarian authorities deem safe for asylum seekers. By August, a total of 3,119 people filed for asylum, and authorities granted international protection to a total of 320 people, of whom 54 received refugee status and 266 received subsidiary protection.

Roma continued to face discrimination in housing, education, and public health care.

The July constitutional amendment criminalized homelessness, ignoring criticism in June by the UN special rapporteur on the right to adequate housing that the plan was cruel and incompatible with human rights law. Homeless people were prosecuted after the law entered into force in October.

Italy

A coalition government between the anti-immigrant League and the populist Five Star Movement was inaugurated in June. In March, the UN high commissioner for human rights deplored the racism and xenophobia that characterized the election campaign.

By mid-November, only 22,435 migrants and asylum seekers had reached Italy by sea according to UNHCR, in large part because of measures to prevent arrivals already put in place by the outgoing government. In contrast, during the whole of 2017, 119,369 people arrived.

Almost immediately upon taking power, the new government intensified that approach and began blocking disembarkation of rescued persons in Italian ports. In November, a Sicilian prosecutor filed to close an investigation, launched in August, into Deputy Prime Minister and Interior Minister Matteo Salvini for unlawful detention and kidnapping, among other charges, for refusing to allow 177 asylum seekers from an Italian Coast Guard ship disembark, some for as long as 5 days.

In June, Italy began systematically handing over coordination of rescues in the Mediterranean to the Libyan Coast Guard, despite concerns over their capacity and the fate of individuals returned to Libya. In August, parliament approved the supply of 12 boats and training programs for Libyan crews.

In November, parliament approved a government decree limiting humanitarian visas and restricting access to specialized reception centers. One-quarter of asylum seekers in 2017 was granted permission to stay for humanitarian reasons, and up to 28 percent of decisions taken in January-February of 2018 granted humanitarian visas. In October, prosecutors charged the mayor of Riace, in southern Italy, with irregularities in what was widely held as a model integration project for asylum seekers and refugees.

Episodes of racist violence marked the year. In February, one month before the national elections, a former League candidate in local elections shot and wounded six immigrants in Macerata, central Italy. An anti-racism group recorded a sharp increase in attacks in the two months after the new government took power compared to the same period in 2017.

In July, authorities evicted several hundred Roma people from a settlement in Rome, despite an order from the European Court of Human Rights to delay the move. Minister Salvini called in June for a census of all Roma in Italy in order to deport those without Italian citizenship. There was no visible progress in a European Commission investigation, ongoing since 2012, into discrimination against Roma in access to housing and forced evictions.

In December 2017, the UN Committee against Torture urged Italy to ensure that the definition of the crime of torture in domestic law, introduced last year, conforms with international law.

Netherlands

The government moved to limit accommodation for newly arrived asylum seekers in the country, arguing that local authorities were increasingly meeting demand, and during the year closed multiple shelters, with the aim of reducing capacity from 31,000 to 27,000. The reduction in reception capacity for the second year in a row gave rise to concerns about the adequacy of provision for arriving asylum seekers.

In July, the government announced that it planned to improve procedures to assess asylum claims based on fear of persecution on grounds of lesbian, gay, bisexual, and transgender (LGBT) identity or religious conversion, by treating cases in a more individualized manner, following criticism by NGOs and parliamentarians.

Notwithstanding the results of a non-binding public referendum in March rejecting a sweeping new surveillance law passed the previous year by parliament, the law entered force in May. Domestic rights groups remained critical of the new bulk interception powers, the level of oversight of those powers to intercept bulk data, and controls over sharing material derived from the interception with other countries' intelligence agencies.

In June, the Minister of Justice and Security confirmed to parliament that the government continued to exercise powers to deprive terror suspects abroad of their Dutch citizenship, although he refused to confirm how many individuals had citizenship removed. The same month a Dutch court expressed concerns about whether the limited safeguards in the process are consistent with the EU Charter of Fundamental Rights,

A May ruling by Limburg district court found the Dutch law requiring people to identify as either male or female on official documents, including birth certificates, to be too restrictive and urged legislators to make statutory provision for a gender-neutral option.

Poland

The government's efforts to undermine the rule of law and human rights protections continued during the year.

Curbing judicial independence remained a focus, despite growing international criticism. In July, a law entered into effect which reduces the retirement age for Supreme Court judges, forcing 27 judges to retire—well over a third of all Supreme Court judges. The first president of the Supreme Court refused to step down and was, at time of writing, continuing her work. In August, the Supreme Court suspended the application of the law, requesting that the Court of Justice of the EU rule on whether it violates EU law, followed by similar requests in August and September in two cases by common courts. In October, the EU Court of Justice ordered Poland to suspend application of the Law on Supreme Court, following a request by the European Commission for interim measures.

The government's attack on the rule of law began to impact Poland's judicial cooperation with other EU states. In July, the EU Court of Justice ruled that Irish courts were entitled to refuse the extradition of a Polish national to Poland if they concluded there is a real risk of an unfair trial to that individual, citing the article 7 proceedings. In September, the European Network of Councils for the Judiciary suspended Poland over concerns about independence of its judicial appointments body.

In addition to the referrals to and rulings of the EU Court of Justice, other EU institutions took various actions against Poland during the year (see Rule of Law section).

In June, the government pushed through a law which makes it a crime to ascribe any responsibility or co-responsibility to Poland for Nazi-era atrocity crimes committed on Polish soil.

Following international condemnation, authorities removed the crime's three-year maximum sentence but maintained fines.

In mid-January, the Polish parliament enacted government legislation hampering the rights of environmental activists to protest at United Nations climate talks in December 2018 and allowing authorities to subject them to government surveillance.

NGOs working on issues related to asylum and migration, women's rights, or LGBT rights reported ongoing difficulties accessing previously available public funding and some were subject to smears in pro-government media.

Summary returns of asylum seekers to Belarus continued, the majority from the Russian republic of Chechnya and Central Asia. In May, the top administrative court found that border guards had failed to conduct a proper assessment of an asylum seeker's intent to seek asylum.

Spain

The Spanish Socialist Party assumed power in June after a no-confidence vote in parliament against the then-ruling Popular Party. The new government pledged to reform the controversial 2015 public security law and to adopt more humane immigration policies. At time of writing, no legal reforms had been tabled.

Over 49,300 people arrived by sea by mid-November. Almost 6,000 crossed land borders into the country's North African enclaves in Ceuta and Melilla from Morocco, many by scaling fences. Migrants faced substandard conditions in arrival facilities and obstacles to applying for asylum.

Summary returns from the enclaves continued, and the new government pursued an appeal initiated by the previous government against a European Court of Human Rights 2017 ruling that Spain violated the rights of two sub-Saharan

African migrants when border guards summarily returned them to Morocco from Melilla in 2013. The Council of Europe called on Spain in September to improve conditions and protection measures for migrants and asylum seekers, particularly unaccompanied children, in Ceuta and Melilla.

In January, a Ceuta judge closed the investigation into the February 2014 deaths of 15 migrants after Guardia Civil officers fired rubber bullets and tear gas into the water off the enclave's coast.

Protests erupted across Spain in April after a court acquitted five men of gang rape and convicted them on the lesser charge of sexual assault because the prosecution did not establish the use of violence or intimidation, prompting the government to examine possible changes to the criminal code. In July, a Supreme Court ruling enforced compliance with a 2014 decision by the UN committee on discrimination against women ordering the government to compensate a woman for gender-based discrimination.

At time of writing, no police officer had been convicted for excessive use of violence during the crack-down on the October 1, 2017, independence referendum in Catalunya. In March, 25 independence leaders were indicted on various charges ranging from rebellion to misuse of public funds.

In February, the Council of Europe's Commission against Racism and Intolerance called on Spain urgently to create an equality body to tackle racism, and recommended measures to integrate migrants and end school segregation for Roma children. Draft legislation to ensure the right to vote for persons with intellectual disabilities has remained under examination in the Spanish parliament since September 2017.

In February, the Supreme Court upheld a prison sentence for a rapper convicted of glorifying terrorism and slander against the Crown. The highest criminal court sentenced a different rapper in March to jail time on similar charges. In March, the Supreme Court overturned the 2017 conviction of a young woman for joking on Twitter about an assassination by the Basque separatist group ETA in 1973.

United Kingdom

The UK's planned exit from the EU (Brexit) in March 2019 continued to dominate public life and overshadow other pressing human rights concerns. The EU and

UK government reached provisional agreement in November on a treaty covering the transition period following the UK's departure from the EU in 2019. They also agreed a draft political declaration on future relations that included a commitment to human rights. But at time of writing it was not clear if the treaty would be approved by the UK parliament, leaving open the possibility the UK would leave in 2019 without an agreement, which would carry risks for human rights, including uncertainty regarding the future residence rights of EU citizens living in the UK and of UK citizens living in EU countries post-Brexit.

A June 2018 law to incorporate EU law into domestic law when the UK leaves the EU was criticized for omitting the EU Charter of Fundamental Rights, leaving it open to a future UK government to weaken employment and other rights protections derived from EU law.

There were significant developments regarding UK complicity in the CIA-led torture and secret detention. In May, the prime minister apologized unreservedly to a Libyan couple for the UK's role in their 2004 rendition to Libya. In June, a parliamentary committee published two reports containing its findings into allegations of UK complicity more widely. The committee found actions the UK took and tolerated between 2001 and 2010 to have been "inexcusable." There were fresh calls from NGOs and some politicians for a full judicial inquiry into the issue. At time of writing, no one in the UK had been charged with a crime in connection with the abuses.

The UK persisted in not imposing a maximum time limit for immigration detention, and continued to detain asylum-seeking and migrant children. Data published in November showed the government had relocated only 220 unaccompanied children from other EU countries out of a target 480. The UK had resettled only 417 refugee children under a 2016 pledge to accept 3,000 such children from conflict zones in the Middle East and Africa.

The UK Supreme Court ruled that Northern Ireland's strict abortion law violates the right to personal integrity protected by the European Convention on Human Rights, though the court dismissed the case in question on technical grounds. A private members bill introduced in the House of Commons in October called for decriminalization of abortion throughout England, Wales, and Northern Ireland.

The public inquiry into a 2017 fire that destroyed a London apartment block, killing 71 and leaving hundreds homeless, continued its work, amid concerns about whether victims can participate fully in the process. A criminal investigation into the fire was ongoing at time of writing.

A draft counterterrorism law approved by the parliament's lower house (the House of Commons) contained problematic measures that could harm people's human rights, including criminalizing the viewing of extremist material and proposing an offence of travel to a "designated area." The draft law remained pending before the unelected upper house (the House of Lords) at time of writing.

In September, the European Court of Human Rights ruled that the lack of safeguards in the now-lapsed surveillance powers under the Regulation of Investigatory Powers Act 2000 had violated the right to privacy, in a case brought by over a dozen NGOs, privacy organizations, and journalists. The court did not, however, find bulk interception necessarily unlawful. Privacy rights campaigners remained critical of the replacement powers.

The body established in 2017 to complete investigations into allegations of abuse by British forces in Iraq between 2003 and 2008, continued its work. At time of writing, no prosecutions had arisen from its work or that of its predecessor.

After a visit in November, the UN special rapporteur on extreme poverty concluded that changes to the welfare system and reductions in public services had entrenched negative outcomes for the rights of people living in poverty.

Foreign Policy

Despite shortcomings, the European Union remained a leading actor in promoting human rights globally.

In July, EU foreign ministers reaffirmed their continued strong support of the International Criminal Court (ICC) and a rules-based international order.

The EU and its member states remained strong supporters of international efforts to ensure accountability for atrocity crimes committed in Syria. Together they are the largest donors to the United Nations' International, Impartial and Independent Mechanism (IIIM), which has a mandate to collect and analyze information and evidence of international crimes committed in Syria to assist criminal proceedings before national or international courts.

The EU sought to mitigate the impact of decisions by the US to withdraw support for international agreements, human rights bodies and mechanisms: the EU's External Action Service (EEAS) fought to ensure the survival the Joint Comprehensive Plan of Action (JCPOA) with Iran, but the EU focused far less on the worrying human rights situation in the country and was unable to secure the release of jailed activists and journalists, including EU citizens. The EU and its member states significantly increased their financial contributions to the UN agency providing assistance to Palestinian refugees (UNRWA) following the Trump administration's decision to withdraw all US funding. The EU continued to press Israel to stop its illegal settlement policy.

The United States' decision to leave the UN Human Rights Council (UNHRC) pushed the EU to search for new allies at the UN's prime human rights body. In September, the EU stepped up its efforts to advance criminal justice for Myanmar armed forces' ruthless campaign of ethnic cleansing of more than 700,000 Rohingya Muslims and other serious violations of international humanitarian and human rights law elsewhere in the country.

Together with the Organisation for Islamic Cooperation (OIC), the EU pushed for a UNHRC resolution which established an accountability mechanism similar to the Syria IIIM. In June, the EU adopted targeted sanctions against seven individuals considered responsible for atrocities and serious human rights violations committed against the Rohingya population. In September, EU Trade Commissioner Cecilia Malmström warned Myanmar that the army and government's responsibility for serious human rights violations and continued impunity for human rights crimes could lead to the suspension of trade preferences conditioned on respect for human rights.

Similarly, and after repeated warnings, the EU initiated procedures to suspend trade preferences with Cambodia conditioned on respect for human rights, citing Cambodia's fraudulent elections and Prime Minister Hun Sen's and his government's failure to comply with international human rights norms.

The EU persistently called for the release of peaceful activists, lawyers, and dissenters detained in China and, together with Germany, played an important role in securing the freedom of Liu Xia, an artist and the widow of the late Nobel

Peace Prize laureate, Liu Xiaobo. Yet at a summit in June, the EU Council and Commission presidents failed to use the momentum generated by Liu Xia's release and relocation to Germany to publicly voice concerns over China's abysmal human rights record and press for further releases.

The EU took a firm stance against the continued crackdown on basic freedoms and dissent in Russia. The EU publicly pressed for the release of several human rights defenders and government critics and opponents detained for their peaceful activities. While the EU addressed rights violations in areas of Ukraine under the control of Russian backed rebels and in Russia-occupied Crimea, it has been more cautious when Ukraine's government curbed free speech in the rest of the country.

The EU and its member states largely failed to adequately respond to the brutal crackdown on dissent and the shrinking space for freedoms of expression, assembly, and association in the Arab states of the Gulf. For the most part, the EU failed to publicly press for the release of women rights activists, journalists, human rights defenders and government critics in the United Arab Emirates, Bahrain, Kuwait, and Saudi Arabia, including Sakharov Prize laureate, Raif Badawi. However, in response to the disappearance and killing of Saudi journalist, Jamal Khashoggi, in Saudi Arabia's Istanbul consulate, Germany placed 18 Saudi officials allegedly connected to the killing on an entry ban list to the Schengen Zone of 26 states, a unilateral move that subsequently was expressly supported by several other states.

The EU continued to largely mute its position on human rights violations in Turkey, Libya, Egypt, and Sudan because of its cooperation with those countries on preventing migration to Europe.

As a direct reaction to Venezuela's rigged May elections and continuing human rights violations, in June the EU added 11 individuals responsible for human rights violations and for undermining democracy and the rule of law in the country to its list of sanctions, bringing the total number of officials sanctioned by the EU to 18.

In October, the EU renewed its targeted sanctions against individuals responsible for serious human rights violations and acts to undermine democracy in Burundi.

Georgia

The October 2018 presidental election brought Georgia's past and current human rights problems to the forefront of political debates. Authorities took steps to establish a mechanism to investigate abuse by law enforcement, but did not give it full independence. Other areas of concern included unjustifiably harsh drug laws, occupational safety and labor rights, discrimination against lesbian, gay, bisexual, and transgender (LGBT) people, and threats to media pluralism.

Presidential Elections

The presidential elections, Georgia's last direct presidential vote, resulted in a runoff between the ruling party-backed candidate Salome Zurabishvili and the opposition candidate Grigol Vashadze. According to local and international observers "candidates were able to campaign freely and voters had a genuine choice," but there were instances of the ruling party's misuse of administrative resources. The second round was scheduled for late November.

Lack of Accountability for Police, Security Service Abuse

Impunity for abuse by law enforcement officials remained a persistent problem. Investigations, if launched, often led to charges that carry lesser, inappropriate sanctions and rarely resulted in convictions. Authorities routinely refused to grant victim status to those who alleged abuse, depriving them of the opportunity to review investigation files.

By September, the Ombudsman's Office received 149 complaints of ill-treatment by prison staff or police and petitioned the prosecutor's office to launch investigations in eight cases. None resulted in criminal prosecution.

In July, parliament adopted a law creating a State Inspector's Office, a separate body in charge of investigating abuses by law enforcement. The law grants the prosecutor a supervisory role over this body's investigations, including the right to give mandatory directives on any investigative procedure, or change investigative decisions, which compromises the body's independence.

In May, a court's partial acquittal of suspects in the stabbing to death of two 16-year-olds in a December 2017 brawl among 15 high school students prompted mass protests about law enforcement bias. The victims' families claimed that the Prosecutor's Office had deliberately concealed or manipulated evidence. The protests led to the chief prosecutor's resignation and the creation of an interim parliamentary commission. Opposition parliamentarians made up the majority of the commission.

In September, the commission concluded that a former employee of the Prosecutor's Office who is related to two of the brawl participants helped conceal some elements of the crime. In a dissenting opinion, the commission's ruling party members claimed that the investigation's flaws were due not to any individual, but rather to the "flawed system of investigation." Zaza Saralidze, father of one of the victims, criticized the ruling party's conclusion as an attempt to protect those who falsified the investigation. Public protests resumed. Authorities arrested Saralidze in October on charges of assaulting a police officer, after he struck an officer who tried to stop him from erecting a tent outside the parliament building. Released on bail, Saralidze could face up to seven years' imprisonment.

In December 2017, State Security Service (national intelligence agency) officers shot to death Temirlan Machalikashvili, 18, an alleged terror suspect, during an operation in Pankisi Gorge, which neighbors Russia's Chechnya. According to an official account, Machalikashvili tried to detonate a hand grenade during arrest, an allegation vehemently denied by his family, who claimed that he was sleeping when the officers entered his room and opened fire. Authorities eventually launched an investigation into Machalikashvili's killing, which was still pending at time of writing. Authorities refused to grant Machalikashvili's family victim status, limiting their access to the investigation files.

In May, three-day public protests took place over alleged heavy-handed police behavior during drug raids on two night clubs in the capital, Tbilisi. Two leading rights groups, the Georgian Young Lawyers' Association (GYLA) and the Human Rights Education and Monitoring Center (EMC), documented excessive use of police force against spontaneously gathered protesters outside the clubs immediately after the raids, and arbitrary detention of many.

In a commendable move, authorities created a human rights department under the Interior Ministry, overseeing investigations into domestic violence, hate crimes, and crimes committed by and against children.

Drug Policy

Although the overall numbers of drug-related prosecutions continued to decline, authorities continued to use harsh drug laws to prosecute people for mere consumption or possession of drugs for personal use. Drug-related felonies often result in long sentences, prohibitive fines, and deprivation of other rights, including the right to drive a vehicle or work in an array of professions. Police compelled thousands of people to take drug tests, in some cases by arbitrarily detaining them for up to 12 hours.

In response to a July Constitutional Court decision that struck down all remaining penalties for marijuana consumption, authorities proposed a bill that would legalize cannabis consumption at home, but impose penalties for public use. It also criminalized consuming marijuana in the presence of a child and while driving. Marijuana purchase or possession remained a crime.

Labor Rights

According to the Georgian Trade Union Confederation, 29 workers died and 24 were injured in work-related accidents through July. Eleven of them died in mining accidents. In March, parliament adopted a law on labor safety that applies to only high-risk areas of work. The law authorizes the labor inspectorate to inspect an employer without a court order following an accident, but limits its mandate to work safety issues, as opposed to other labor standards. All other inspections must be court-ordered.

Sexual Orientation and Gender Identity

According to the ombudsman, LGBT individuals often experience abuse, intolerance, and discrimination in every sphere of life. Homophobic statements by public officials feed widespread homophobia in society.

In June, Justice Minister Tea Tsulukiani tried to deflect generalized criticism of her tenure by invoking her conservative position on gender recognition, possibly to tap into public transphobia. A group of prominent nongovernmental groups (NGOs) had demanded Tsulukiani's resignation over her failure to implement key justice reforms, including in the judiciary. Tsulukiani responded by saying these groups held a grudge against her because she refused to register "a person with male organs as female" and vice-versa. Georgian law allows gender recognition for transgender people, however, transgender people are required to present proof of gender reassignment surgery.

Freedom of Media, Civil Society

In December 2017, parliament amended the broadcasting law, expanding the Public Broadcaster's powers to, among other things, allow it receive additional revenues from commercial advertising. Private television stations and NGOs criticized the move, citing concern that the publicly-funded television's entry to the already shrinking advertisement market, would threaten sustainability of smaller, regional broadcasters, and undermine media pluralism. The president vetoed the bill in January for those reasons, but the parliament overturned the veto.

The ownership dispute over Georgia's most-watched television broadcaster, Rustavi 2, remained pending before the European Court of Human Rights (ECtHR). A former owner alleged that he had been forced to sell the station below the market value and sought to restore his rights. Rustavi 2's current owners allege the lawsuit is government-orchestrated to take over the opposition-minded station. The dispute raised concerns over government interference with media.

In October, Iberia TV suspended broadcasting, alleging that the authorities were trying to shut down the critically-minded broadcaster by worsening the owner's financial problems. The owners alleged that the authorities proposed they forfeit the channel in exchange for resolving their tax debt. Authorities denied the allegations.

In October, several top officials made statements attacking NGOs, after 13 leading human rights groups published a joint statement criticizing high-level corruption. Georgia's public defender criticized the officials' statements.

International Actors

In its first implementation report on the European Union–Georgia Association Agreement, adopted in November, the European Parliament hailed the country's progress, but also called on authorities to address some outstanding concerns, such as labor standards, environmental protection, and discrimination against vulnerable groups and women.

In his July report, the United Nations (UN) independent expert on the enjoyment of all human rights by older persons noted, *inter alia*, the "frequent" nature of old age discrimination in the labor market, gender-based violence, lack of programs preventing violence against older persons, low pensions, and poverty. She called on authorities to devise a strategy addressing discrimination and ageism.

In October, following his country visit, the UN expert on the protection against violence and discrimination based on sexual orientation and gender identity, Victor Madrigal-Borloz, commended authorities' commitment to addressing violence against LGBT persons, but also urged authorities to address bullying, harassment, and public exclusion.

According to the US annual human trafficking report, released in June, although the government meets minimum standards for eliminating trafficking, the country remains a source, transit, and destination for trafficking for sex work and other forced labor.

The UN, EU, US, and Georgia's other bilateral and multilateral partners issued statements on the 10th anniversary of the Georgia-Russia war, some calling for an end to the occupation of Georgian territories.

The International Criminal Court continued its investigation into war crimes and crimes against humanity allegedly committed in the lead-up to, during, and after the August 2008 war between Russia and Georgia over South Ossetia.

Guatemala

Progress in prosecuting corruption and abuse made in recent years is at risk due to serious obstruction from the government. This progress was the result of the collaboration of the Attorney General's Office with the United Nations-backed International Commission against Impunity in Guatemala (CICIG), established in 2007 to investigate organized crime and reinforce local efforts to strengthen the rule of law. At time of writing, CICIG and the Attorney General's Office were prosecuting more than a dozen current and former Congress members, as well as former President Otto Pérez Molina and former Vice-President Roxana Baldetti, who were arrested on corruption charges in 2015.

In August, President Jimmy Morales announced that he would not renew CICIG's mandate when it expires in September 2019. In September, he prohibited CICIG Commissioner Velásquez from re-entering the country. At time of writing, the Constitutional Court had ordered that Velásquez should be allowed to return, but authorities indicated they would not comply with this order.

In August, the Guatemalan Congress approved in a preliminary vote a bill that contains provisions that would discriminate against lesbian, gay, bisexual, and transgender (LGBT) people and expand the criminalization of abortion. The bill remained pending in Congress at time of writing.

Public Security, Corruption, and Criminal Justice

Violence and extortion by powerful criminal organizations remain serious problems in Guatemala. Gang-related violence is an important factor prompting people, including unaccompanied children and young adults, to leave the country.

Guatemala suffers from high levels of impunity, partly because criminal proceedings against powerful actors often suffer unreasonably long delays due to excessive use of motions by criminal defendants. Those delays are compounded by courts often failing to respect legally mandated time frames and sometimes taking months to reschedule suspended hearings. Intimidation against judges and prosecutors and corruption within the justice system continue to be problems.

Despite these obstacles, investigations by CICIG and the Attorney General's Office have exposed more than 60 corruption schemes, implicating officials in all three branches of government, and prompting the resignation and arrest of the country's then-president and vice-president in 2015, for their alleged participation in a scheme to defraud the customs authority by collecting bribes instead of customs duties.

Prosecutors also pressed charges against scores of officials—including more than a dozen current and former members of Congress from six different political parties—for hiring people in Congress who never performed any work for the institution (or already received a salary from another employer) and pocketing the wages for those "phantom jobs."

In October 2018, former Vice-President Baldetti was sentenced to 15 years and six months in prison for her role in a scheme to defraud the state for US$18 million. At time of writing, other major corruption cases brought since 2015 were still in pretrial proceedings.

Accountability for Past Human Rights Violations

In May 2018, three former military officers were sentenced to 58 years each for the enforced disappearance of then 14-year old Marco Antonio Molina Theissen and the rape of his sister Emma in 1981. After Emma escaped from an army base where she was raped, officers went to her house and took away her younger brother in apparent retaliation. Among those convicted was Benedicto Lucas García, former top military officer and brother of former military dictator Romeo Lucas García. One officer was sentenced to 33 years for the rape.

The trial against former Guatemalan dictator Efraín Ríos Montt and a former soldier for their role in the 1982 Dos Erres massacre, in which Guatemalan army special forces killed around 200 civilians as part of their counterinsurgency policy during the armed conflict, had been scheduled for August 2018. It eventually started in October and was ongoing at time of writing. However, Ríos Montt died in April. In 2011 and 2012, five former members of the military were convicted for their roles in the massacre.

In May 2013, Ríos Montt was found guilty of genocide and crimes against humanity for the assassination of over 1,771 Mayan Ixil civilians in 105 massacres, when he was head of state in 1982 and 1983. He was sentenced to 80 years in prison, but 10 days later the Constitutional Court overturned the verdict on procedural grounds. The retrial began in March 2016 but was suspended two months later because of outstanding legal challenges. The trial restarted in October 2017 with just one session per week. Ríos Montt died before the trial concluded. In September 2018, the other defendant in the case, the former head of intelligence, was acquitted.

Violence Against Journalists

Journalists are targets of harassment and violence. In February 2018, the bodies of journalist Laurent Castillo and radio worker Luis de León were found bound with gunshot wounds to the head outside the town of Santo Domingo, in Guatemala's southwestern Suchitepéquez department. In June 2017, TV journalist Carlos Rodríguez survived a gunshot to the head. In June 2016, radio journalist Álvaro Aceituno was killed, and in March 2015, journalists Danilo López and Federico Salazar were assassinated. In January 2017, investigations by CICIG and the Attorney General's Office implicated Congressman Julio Juárez from government party FCN-Nación in the latter crime. At time of writing, the case was in pre-trial proceedings.

Women and Girls' Rights

In March 2017, 41 adolescent girls were killed in a fire in the Hogar Seguro government-run shelter. Fifty-six girls had been locked up for the night in a space that could safely hold only 11, without access to water or a restroom, following a protest against the poor living conditions and treatment received in the shelter—including reports of sexual violence stretching back years. After at least six hours in those conditions, one of the girls set a mattress on fire so guards would open the door—but they didn't. Three public officials were due to stand trial in February 2019 for involuntary manslaughter and breach of duty, among other charges. At time of writing, proceedings against nine others were ongoing.

Under current law, abortion is legal in Guatemala only when the life of a pregnant woman or girl is in danger. In August, Guatemalan Congress approved a preliminary version of the "Life and Family Protection" bill, which would expand the criminalization of abortion and could subject women who have miscarriages to prosecution. It would also raise the maximum sentence for abortion from 3 to 10 years and would make it a crime to engage in "the promotion of abortion," which could mean that the provision of sexual and reproductive information, counseling, or referrals might result in sentences of up to 10 years. The bill needs to pass another round of votes, as well as an approval per article, before the president can sign it into law.

Sexual Orientation and Gender Identity

The proposed "Life and Family Protection" bill that was approved in a preliminary version in August also contains provisions that discriminate against LGBT people. It prohibits same-sex marriage and defines marriage as a union between people who were a man and a woman "by birth," thus excluding many transgender people. The bill defines "sexual diversity" as "incompatible with the biological and genetic aspects of human beings."

The bill also establishes that "freedom of conscience and expression" protect people from being "obliged to accept non-heterosexual conduct or practices as normal." This provision could be interpreted to mean that people can be denied services on the basis of sexual orientation or gender identity, in violation of international human rights law.

Key International Actors

The UN-backed CICIG plays a key role in assisting Guatemala's justice system in prosecuting violent crime. CICIG works with the Attorney General's Office, the police, and other government agencies to investigate, prosecute, and dismantle criminal organizations operating in the country. It is empowered to participate in criminal proceedings as a complementary prosecutor, to provide technical assistance, and to promote legislative reforms.

In August 2018, CICIG and the attorney general presented a renewed request to strip President Jimmy Morales of his presidential immunity in order to investigate his role in illicit campaign financing. Two weeks later, Morales, flanked by military and police officers, announced that he would not renew CICIG's mandate when it expires in September 2019. The following week, he announced that he had prohibited CICIG Commissioner Iván Velásquez—who was on a work trip abroad—from re-entering the country.

Even though the Constitutional Court ordered that Velásquez be allowed to return, authorities refused, and in October 2018, the Foreign Ministry refused to receive the documents for the renewal of Velásquez's visa. At time of writing, proceedings against the president and migration authorities for allegedly disobeying the Constitutional Court's order were pending before the court. UN Secretary-General Antonio Guterres' spokesman has said that Velásquez would continue to oversee CICIG's work from outside Guatemala, adding that the move to block Velásquez from returning was inconsistent with the agreement to establish the commission.

The US Congress approved US$615 million in assistance for 2018 for the Plan of the Alliance for Prosperity in the Northern Triangle, a five-year initiative announced in 2014 that intends to reduce incentives to migrate from Guatemala, El Salvador, and Honduras by aiming to reduce violence, strengthen governance, and increase economic opportunity. Twenty-five percent of it is conditioned on the beneficiary countries taking steps to limit migration to the United States, and 50 percent on the US Department of State annually certifying progress by the beneficiary countries in strengthening institutions, fighting corruption and impunity, and protecting human rights.

In 2018, Guatemala received certification for continued full funding under the plan. The assistance for 2018 included $7 million for CICIG, but in May, a group of congressmen requested a hold on the disbursement of the outstanding $6 million following allegations of Russian influence with CICIG, even though the Department of State indicated that it had not found proof of those allegations. The hold was lifted in August.

Guinea

Guinea held long-delayed local elections in February 2018, but allegations of electoral fraud and ethnic and communal tensions led to deadly clashes between protesters and security forces. Popular frustration over economic inequality and the slow pace of economic development led to unrest, exemplified by often-violent protests against a fuel-price increase in July and long-running teachers' strikes. The government regularly banned demonstrations led by opposition and civil society groups, while security forces often resorted to excessive force and engaged in criminality and extortion in seeking to disperse often violent street protests. Violations of freedom of expression, including the arrest of and attacks against journalists, persisted.

The judiciary made some progress toward delivering justice for the 2009 stadium massacre, but largely failed to investigate and prosecute other state-sponsored violence. The government took steps to reduce lengthy pretrial detention by transferring all criminal cases to first instance courts but concerns over prison overcrowding and corruption continued to undermine the credibility and effectiveness of Guinea's justice system.

Guinea's mining sector—a key driver of economic growth—continued to grow rapidly, but the population saw few dividends and a lack of effective government oversight denied communities adequate protection from the negative social and environmental impacts of mining.

Security Force Abuses

Although the conduct of Guinea's security forces, which have a decades-long history of human rights abuses and criminality, has improved in recent years, in 2018 the police and gendarmerie were still implicated in excessive force, corruption, and criminality.

Consistent with a 2015 law on public order, civilian institutions largely dictated the timing and location of security force deployments in response to 2018's demonstrations, providing some civilian oversight of security forces' role in policing.

Nevertheless, the security forces on numerous occasions used excessive lethal force against protesters. At least 12 people were shot dead in Conakry in 2018 by

HUMAN
RIGHTS
WATCH

"What Do We Get Out of It?"
The Human Rights Impact of Bauxite Mining in Guinea

security forces during the often-violent protests that followed the disputed local elections and teachers' strikes. In several cases, deaths were a result of police or gendarmes firing deliberately at protesters, while others were killed by stray bullets, according to witness accounts. Two members of the security forces were killed by protesters. When patrolling opposition neighborhoods during the February and March protests, some police and gendarmes also vandalized homes and vehicles and stole money, mobile phones, and cash.

Then-minister for citizenship and national unity, Gassama Diaby, promised that the alleged killings by security forces in the aftermath of the 2018 local elections would be investigated. The Ministry of Justice said in July 2018 that investigations had been opened, but no member of the security forces had, at time of writing, been charged or even disciplined.

In June 2018, security forces reportedly opened fire on protesters in the northern mining town of Siguiri, injuring at least 10 and killing 2. In November 2017, border clashes over territory between artisanal gold miners from northeast Guinea and southwest Mali resulted in at least six deaths.

Guinean and international human rights groups reported credible allegations of torture to intimidate or to obtain confessions from detainees in police and gendarme custody in Conakry, including, in several cases, against minors.

Justice for the 2009 Stadium Massacre

There was meaningful progress in the investigation of the September 28, 2009 stadium massacre, in which security forces killed over 150 peaceful opposition supporters, and raped dozens of women. In December 2017, the panel of Guinean judges investigating the massacre concluded over seven years of investigations. At least 13 suspects are indicted, including Moussa Dadis Camara, the then leader of the military junta that ruled Guinea in September 2009, and two high-ranking officials currently serving in the security forces. The investigation ended before judges had located and exhumed mass graves believed to contain more than 100 victims. However, the trial had yet to start at time of writing.

In April 2018, the Ministry of Justice created a steering committee to prepare for the trial by securing funding and ensuring adequate security for witnesses and magistrates. The committee, which includes key figures in the national justice system, United Nations representatives, and international donors, at time of writing had only met three times over a seven-month period, but had identified a location and budget for the trial.

Accountability for Election-Related Crimes

Impunity largely continued for past human rights abuses committed by the security forces and government and opposition supporters.

A Conakry court in April 2018 began the trial of the former governor of Conakry, Sékou Resco Camara, and the former head of the army, Nouhou Thiam, for the 2010 torture of several detainees arrested for blocking a presidential motorcade. However, there has been little effort to investigate or prosecute other abuses dating back several years, including the dozens of people killed by security forces in street protests.

The trial of a police officer arrested in August 2016 for a shooting death during a protest began in December 2017, but the trial was quickly adjourned, and, for reasons unknown to Human Rights Watch, had yet to resume at time of writing. In the past year, there was little or no progress in prosecutions relating to the alleged killings of at least 10 people in the lead-up to the 2015 presidential poll, some 60 opposition supporters protesting the delay in holding parliamentary elections in 2013-2014, and more than 130 unarmed demonstrators in 2007.

In April, the Court of Justice for the Economic Community of West African States (ECOWAS Court) ruled against Guinea for the torture and death of Liberian refugee Jallah Morris while in custody of Guinean police in 2011, and for its failure to investigate and prosecute those responsible.

Judiciary and Detention Conditions

The judiciary continued to face various shortcomings, including lack of adequate court rooms and other physical infrastructure, as well as insufficient personnel to investigate and prosecute human rights violations and other crimes.

Guinean prisons and detention centers operate far below international standards, with severe overcrowding due to over-reliance on pretrial detention, weak case management, and the failure of the courts to sit regularly. Overcrowding and conditions in Guinea's largest detention facility in Conakry, built for 300 detainees, continued to worsen. The facility at time of writing accommodated around 1,650.

Freedom of Assembly

The government frequently prohibited opposition and popular protests, citing risks to public security. Security forces were regularly deployed to deter protesters from assembling and often dispersed demonstrators by tear gas and water cannons. Civil society leaders filed a lawsuit challenging the banning of protests, which they said violated the right to freedom of assembly.

Freedom of Expression

Threats to media freedoms, which have increased in the last several years, continued in 2018 with several journalists arrested and then released for coverage critical of the government, and several attacks against media institutions or journalists.

President Alpha Condé warned in November 2017 during a teachers' strike that any media outlets offering coverage to union leaders would be shut down. Two days later, a regional governor reportedly shut down a radio station for interviewing a union leader, and two journalists were reportedly briefly detained and interrogated by police. A RFI correspondent's accreditation was revoked by the press regulator on November 14 after he published an article describing allegations that soldiers were responsible for the November 7 killing of two protesters.

In January, 10 shots were fired outside the home of a journalist, who said he had received death threats for his work, including an article alleging security force involvement in the 2012 killing of the head of the treasury. In March, ruling party sympathizers in Conakry, angry at media coverage given to government critics, vandalized the offices of *Hadafo Media* (home of *Espace TV and radio*), throwing stones at the building and destroying cars. In June, an online journalist was arrested in Conakry on criminal defamation charges, detained for two weeks and released on conditional bail for publishing an article alleging that the Minister of Justice accepted bribes.

Extractive Industries

Guinea's natural resources, notably gold, bauxite, and diamonds, were a major driver of economic growth. China, an increasingly close economic and political partner, signed in September 2017 a US$20 billion infrastructure for bauxite deal with Condé's government. Inadequate supervision of mining's environmental and human rights impacts, however, including in the booming bauxite sector, resulted in thousands of farmers losing their land to mining, often for inadequate compensation. Mining roads have significantly damaged water sources, reducing access to water and creating health consequences for villagers.

Key International Actors

The European Union, France, and the United States remained major donors, including in the justice and security sector, and helped mediate between the government and opposition following the disputed February local elections.

The Office of the United Nations High Commissioner for Human Rights conducted training for the judiciary and security forces, but rarely publicly denounced human rights violations. UN Special Representative on Sexual Violence in Conflict Pramila Patten— whose office continued to support accountability for rapes and crimes committed during the 2009 stadium massacre—visited Guinea in March to encourage progress in the investigation. The International Criminal Court (ICC) also continued to play a significant positive role in promoting the September 28, 2009 investigation through its engagement with Guinean authorities.

Haiti

Political instability continued in 2018 to hinder the Haitian government's ability to meet the basic needs of its people, resolve long-standing human rights problems, or address humanitarian crises.

In July 2018, the government's announcement that it would eliminate subsidies, allowing fuel prices to increase by up to 50 percent, led to widespread protests and the worst civil unrest the country has seen in years.

Haitians remain susceptible to displacement by natural disasters, including tropical storms and hurricanes. In October, an earthquake left 17 people dead and over 350 injured. More than 140,000 households still need decent shelter, more than two years after Hurricane Matthew in which between 540 to 1,000 people died, according to different estimates.

As of May 2018, nearly 38,000 people, 70 percent of them women and children, lived in displacement camps formed after the 2010 earthquake. Authorities have not provided assistance to resettle them or return them to their places of origin. As of May, at least 17 of 26 remaining displacement camps lacked adequate sanitary facilities.

The country's most vulnerable communities continue to face environmental risks, such as widespread deforestation, pollution from industry, and limited access to safe water and sanitation. Low rainfall exacerbates food insecurity in the country.

Since its introduction by UN peacekeepers in 2010, cholera has infected more than 800,000 people and claimed nearly 10,000 lives. However, intensified control efforts—including an ambitious vaccination campaign—have resulted in a significant decline in cases, from more than 41,000 suspected cases and 440 deaths in 2016, to just over 3,000 suspected cases and 37 deaths from January through August 2018.

Criminal Justice System

Haiti's prison system remains severely overcrowded, with many inmates living in inhumane conditions. In 2016, the United Nations estimated that nearly all inmates in Haiti's national prison system have access to less than one square meter of space and most are confined for 23 hours a day. According to the former UN Independent Expert on Haiti, overcrowding is largely attributable to high numbers of arbitrary arrests and the country's large number of pretrial detainees. In July 2018, Haitian prisons housed nearly 12,000 detainees, 75 percent of whom were awaiting trial.

Illiteracy and Barriers to Education

Illiteracy is a major problem in Haiti. According to the UN Development Programme (UNDP), approximately one-half of all Haitians age 15 and older are illiterate. The quality of education is generally low, and 85 percent of schools are run by private entities that charge school fees that can be prohibitively expensive for low income families. At least 350,000 children and youth remain out of primary and secondary school throughout the country.

Accountability for Past Abuses

Accountability for past human rights abuses continues to be a challenge in Haiti. In August, a federal court in the United States ruled that a case alleging torture, murder, and arson—in the rural town of Les Irois in 2017 and 2018—could proceed against a former Haitian mayor now living in the US, Jean Morose Viliena. The lawsuit was filed on behalf of Haitian media activists and human rights defenders who survived a campaign of violence allegedly led by Viliena and his political supporters.

As of November 2018, a re-opened investigation into crimes committed by former President Jean-Claude Duvalier's collaborators remained pending. Duvalier died in 2014, six months after the Port-of-Prince Court of Appeal ruled that the statute of limitations could not be applied to crimes against humanity and ordered that investigations against him should continue for human rights crimes allegedly committed during his tenure as president from 1971-1986. Allegations of violations include arbitrary detentions, torture, disappearances, summary executions, and forced exile.

Women's and Girls' Rights

Gender-based violence is a widespread problem. Haiti does not have specific legislation against domestic violence, sexual harassment, or other forms of violence targeted at women and girls. Rape was only explicitly criminalized in 2005, by ministerial decree.

There has been little progress towards consideration of a criminal code reform submitted to parliament in April 2017 that would address some of these gaps in protection. The draft criminal code would also partially decriminalize abortion, which is currently prohibited in all circumstances, including in cases of sexual violence.

Sexual Orientation and Gender Identity

Lesbian, gay, bisexual, and transgender (LGBT) people continue to suffer high levels of discrimination.

In 2017, the Haitian Senate passed two anti-LGBT bills, which were under consideration by the Chamber of Deputies as of November 2018. One bill would regulate conditions for the issuance of the Certificat de Bonne Vie et Mœurs, a document that many employers and universities require. The bill lists homosexuality, alongside child pornography, incest, and commercial sexual exploitation of children, as a reason to deny a citizen a certificate.

The other bill calls for a ban on gay marriage, as well as any public support or advocacy for LGBT rights. Should the ban become law, "the parties, co-parties and accomplices" of a same-sex marriage could be punished by three years in prison and a fine of about US$8,000.

Children's Domestic Labor

Widespread use of child domestic workers—known as restavèks—continues. Restavèks, most of whom are girls, are sent from low-income households to live with wealthier families in the hope that they will be schooled and cared for in exchange for performing household chores. Though difficult to calculate, some estimates suggest that between 225,000 and 300,000 children work as restavèks.

These children often work for no pay, are denied education, and are physically or sexually abused.

Haiti's labor code does not set a minimum age for work in domestic services, though the minimum age for work in industrial, agricultural, and commercial enterprises is 15. In February 2016, the UN Committee on the Rights of the Child called on Haiti to criminalize the practice of placing children in domestic service.

Deportation and Statelessness for Dominicans of Haitian Descent

At least 250,000 Dominicans of Haitian descent and Haitian migrants working in the Dominican Republic re-entered Haiti between June 2015 and March 2018, after Dominican officials began deportations in accordance with a controversial 2015 Plan for the Regularization of Foreigners in the Dominican Republic. Many deportations did not meet international standards and many people have been swept up in arbitrary, summary deportations without any sort of hearing.

In addition to those deported, many people left the Dominican Republic under pressure or threat. Of more than 6,000 under investigation, the UN Refugee Agency (UNHCR) has verified legitimate Dominican nationality for more than 2,800 individuals now in Haiti.

During the first six months of 2018 alone, nearly 70,000 Haitians were returned to their country. After being renewed three times, the Plan for the Regularization of Foreigners ended in August 2018, leaving more than 200,000 Haitians who remain in the Dominican Republic without valid paperwork at continued risk of deportation.

Mining and Access to Information

In the past decade, foreign investors have pursued the development of Haiti's nascent mining sector. In July 2017, the Haitian government presented a draft mining law to parliament, prepared with assistance from the World Bank. According to the Center for Human Rights and Global Justice (CHRGJ), the draft law grants insufficient time for adequate environmental review, restricting the government's ability to thoroughly study the documentation and limiting opportunity for public participation or comment, and is silent on the rights of individuals displaced by mining activities. In addition, it contains provisions that could render all company documents confidential for 10 years, preventing affected communities from engaging in meaningful consultation about mining projects. As of November 2018, the draft law was awaiting consideration by parliament.

Key International Actors

At the end of the UN Stabilization Mission in Haiti's (MINUSTAH's) mandate in October 2017, the UN adopted a new, smaller peacekeeping mission, the UN Mission for Justice Support in Haiti (MINUJUSTH), intended to contribute to help promote rule of law, police development, and human rights. In April, the Security Council extended MINUJUSTH's mandate for one year. The council also affirmed its intention to consider the mission's drawdown and transition to a non-peacekeeping mission by October 2019.

In 2016, the secretary-general apologized for the UN's role in the cholera outbreak and announced a new approach to cholera in Haiti. This included intensifying efforts to treat and eliminate cholera and establishing a trust fund to raise $400 million to provide "material assistance" to those most affected by the epidemic. As of November 2018, only $17.7 million had been pledged to the effort.

The UN has concluded a pilot consultation in the area where cholera started, but has indicated that funds will be used for community projects, regardless of consultation outcomes. Victim advocates have criticized the UN for failing to put victims at the center of its response.

According to figures from the UN Office of Internal Oversight Services, at least 102 allegations of sexual abuse or exploitation were made against MINUSTAH personnel between 2007 and 2017. In December 2017, 10 Haitian mothers of 11 children fathered and abandoned by UN peacekeepers filed the first legal actions in Haiti for child support.

In June, Haiti announced that Oxfam Great Britain had lost its right to operate in the country, after a scandal involving sexual exploitation by staff engaged in relief activities following the 2010 earthquake.

In its April concluding observations on Haiti, the UN Committee on the Rights of Persons with Disabilities found that adults and children with disabilities face ill-treatment and chaining in institutions and that women with intellectual disabili-

263

ties may face contraceptive procedures without their consent. The committee also criticized the absence of legislation prohibiting discrimination based on disability; failure to promote independent living in the community; and laws that deny people with disabilities legal capacity.

In October, a federal judge issued a preliminary injunction temporarily blocking the decision by President Donald Trump's administration to terminate Temporary Protected Status (TPS) for Haitians effective July 2019, which would affect an estimated 60,000 Haitians who were permitted to stay in the US following the 2010 earthquake.

Honduras

Violent crime is rampant in Honduras. Despite a downward trend in recent years, the murder rate remains among the highest in the world. A crackdown on protests following the November 2017 national elections resulted in the death of at least 22 civilians and one police officer, and in more than 1,300 detentions. Journalists, environmental activists, and lesbian, gay, bisexual, and transgender (LGBT) individuals are vulnerable to violence. Efforts to reform the institutions responsible for providing public security have made little progress. Marred by corruption and abuse, the judiciary and police remain largely ineffective. Impunity for crime and human rights abuses is the norm.

The Mission to Support the Fight against Corruption and Impunity in Honduras (MACCIH), established in 2016 through an agreement between the government and the Organization of American States (OAS), advanced investigations in a small number of cases regarding corruption by senior officials.

Police Abuse and Corruption

In January 2018, President Juan Orlando Hernández announced that the Special Commission for Police Reform Restructuring would extend its mandate through January 2019. As of April 2018, more than 5,000 of the more than 10,000 police officers evaluated by the commission had been removed, and in June, the commission presented the Attorney General's Office with more than 1,300 case files of removed officers for further investigation into alleged criminal activities. However, the commission has been criticized for its opacity and came under fire in October 2018, when an officer whom the commission had promoted to deputy police commissioner, and who later became head of police, was arrested for illicit association and money laundering.

Eight former police officers faced prosecution or were convicted in the United States for involvement in organized crime.

Judicial Independence

Judges have faced interference from the executive branch and others, including private actors with connections in government. In June 2017, the former vice-president of the defunct Judiciary Council, Teodoro Bonilla, was found guilty of influence peddling.

In October 2018, the judiciary reinstated judges Tirza Flores Lanza and Guillermo López Lone. In 2015, the Inter-American Court on Human Rights determined that they had been fired arbitrarily after the 2009 coup in Honduras.

Crackdown on Protests

Following reports from both international observers and national actors of irregularities in the November 2017 national elections, protests erupted and authorities decreed a state of emergency, which the Office of the UN High Commissioner on Human Rights (OHCHR) and the Inter-American Commission on Human Rights (IACHR) criticized for its lack of compliance with international human rights standards.

According to the UN High Commissioner's Office, at least 22 civilians were killed during the protests, of whom at least 16 were shot by security forces. A police officer was also killed after being hit by a Molotov cocktail filled with shrapnel. More than 1,300 people were detained, many of them in military detention centers. The UN High Commissioner's Office documented "credible and consistent testimonies" that detainees had been subject to ill-treatment and said that security forces had indiscriminately opened fire on protesters on several occasions.

Freedom of Expression, Association, and Assembly

Journalists are targets of threats and violence. During the protests following Honduras' elections, discussed above, the OHCHR documented physical attacks on at least six journalists, threats against journalists who were covering the protests, and the interruption of broadcasts critical of the government.

According to a 2016 report from the human rights ombudsman, CONADEH, 25 journalists were murdered between 2014 and 2016. Ninety-one percent of killings of journalists since 2001 remain unpunished.

In April 2018, Congress approved a preliminary version of a cybersecurity bill that would severely harm free speech by compelling companies providing internet services to censor content. At time of writing, the bill, which was criticized by the OAS' special rapporteur for freedom of expression, faced another round of discussion and voting before it could become law.

In February 2017, Congress approved a new penal code making it a criminal of-fense—punishable by four to eight years in prison—for individuals or media out-lets to engage in the "apology, glorification, [or] justification" of terrorism. The new code also contained a vague and broad definition of terrorism that could conceivably be used to bar peaceful protests and group meetings as terrorism. Following criticism from the OHCHR in Honduras and the IACHR, Congress re-pealed the provision on "apology, glorification, [or] justification" of terrorism in June 2018. But the broad definition of terrorism remained in force.

Attacks on Lawyers, Human Rights Defenders, and Environmental Activists

Lawyers, human rights defenders, and environmental activists suffer threats, at-tacks, and killings. In 2016, CONADEH registered 16 violent attacks against lawyers, including 13 killings. The IACHR described Honduras in August 2016 as one of the "most hostile and dangerous countries for human rights defenders" in the Americas.

At time of writing, nine men had been charged with the murder in March 2016 of environmental and indigenous rights activist Berta Cáceres, including an army major and the president, as well as the former environment manager of Desar-rollo Energético S.A. (DESA), the company behind the Agua Zarca dam project that Cáceres was campaigning against at the time of her assassination. When the trial against eight of the suspects started in September 2018, the Cáceres family lawyers filed legal appeals questioning the proceedings and seeking a new panel of judges. In October, the existing panel started the trial while the ap-peals remained pending.

Local activists criticized the Mechanism for the Protection of Journalists, Human Rights Defenders and Operators of Justice, created in 2015, for lacking uniform criteria in awarding protection measures. Activists also claimed the measures are not always effective.

Sexual Orientation and Gender Identity

Violence based on gender identity or sexual orientation is a major problem in Honduras. Several UN agencies working in Honduras have noted that violence against LGBT individuals forces them into "internal displacement" or to flee the country in search of international protection.

In August 2018, Honduran Congress approved several articles of a preliminary version of a new adoption law that would prohibit same-sex couples from adopting children. Final approval of the law remained pending at time of writing.

Women's Sexual and Reproductive Rights

Under the criminal code, abortion is illegal without any exceptions in Honduras, and women and girls who terminate pregnancies can face prison sentences of up to six years. Emergency contraception is also prohibited. In May 2017, Congress voted against modifying the existing criminal code to allow abortion in cases of rape, grave risks to the life and health of the woman, or fetal complications incompatible with life outside the womb. The law that remains in force also sanctions abortion providers and those who assist with procedures.

Children's Rights

In July 2017, the Honduran Congress unanimously passed a bill making all child marriage illegal. The new bill replaces legislation that previously allowed for girls to marry at 16 with permission from family. According to UNICEF, a third of Honduran girls marry before 18.

In May 2017, President Hernández created a commission to revise the criminal code to allow children as young 12 to be prosecuted as adults, rather than through the existing juvenile justice system, in violation of international standards. However, at time of writing no proposal had been put forward.

Prison Conditions

Inhumane conditions, including overcrowding, inadequate nutrition, and poor sanitation, are endemic in Honduran prisons. Designed to hold up to 10,600 inmates, the country's penal institutions held almost 20,500 in August 2018, according to news reports.

Key International Actors

The Mission to Support the Fight against Corruption and Impunity in Honduras (MACCIH), has been active in the country since April 2016. It has assisted in the creation of an anti-corruption jurisdiction in the country and in the approval of the Law on Clean Politics, which aims to prevent organized crime from contributing to political campaigns and hold parties and candidates accountable for financing their campaigns illegally. It also contributed to several anti-corruption investigations, together with the Attorney General's Office.

Amongst these is a case regarding fraud in the country's social security office (IHSS) for which, at time of writing, 14 people had been convicted—including the institute's former director and three former deputy ministers. Five members of Congress of three different opposition parties were being investigated for the alleged embezzlement of HNL 8,3 million (US$ 345,000), as was a former first lady, for the alleged embezzlement of HLN 16 million (US$ 680,000).

However, in January 2018, a month after MACCIH and UFECIC indicted the members of Congress, the legislature passed legal reforms that established that the country's court of auditors was the only entity allowed to audit public funds, effectively halting the investigation. In May 2018, the Constitutional Court ruled that although MACCIH was constitutional, elements of the anti-corruption prosecutorial unit (UFECIC) might not be, potentially undermining its work.

In February 2018, MACCIH head Juan Jiménez stepped down, citing a lack of support from the OAS secretary general. After the appointment of his replacement was held up for several months by the Honduran government, Luiz Antonio Guimarães Marrey started his work in June 2018.

In May 2018, the Committee on Enforced Disappearances recommended Honduras bring its legislation regarding disappearances in line with international law and improve search efforts, including for those who disappeared in the 1980s and 1990s.

For fiscal year 2018, US Congress allotted $67.85 million in bilateral aid to Honduras.

India

In 2018, the government led by the Bharatiya Janata Party (BJP) harassed and at times prosecuted activists, lawyers, human rights defenders, and journalists for criticizing authorities. Draconian sedition and counterterrorism laws were used to chill free expression. Foreign funding regulations were used to target non-governmental organizations (NGOs) critical of government actions or policies.

The government failed to prevent or credibly investigate growing mob attacks on religious minorities, marginalized communities, and critics of the government—often carried out by groups claiming to support the government. At the same time, some senior BJP leaders publicly supported perpetrators of such crimes, made inflammatory speeches against minority communities, and promoted Hindu supremacy and ultra-nationalism, which encouraged further violence.

Lack of accountability for past abuses committed by security forces persisted even as there were new allegations of torture and extrajudicial killings, including in the states of Uttar Pradesh, Tamil Nadu, and Haryana.

The Supreme Court decriminalized homosexual sexual relations, striking down a colonial-era law, paving the way for full constitutional protections for lesbian, gay, bisexual, and transgender (LGBT) people.

Impunity for Security Forces

There were repeated allegations of violations by government forces in Jammu and Kashmir during security operations. In 2018, there was increased violence involving militants that many attributed to political failures to ensure accountability for abuses. Militants killed at least 32 policemen in 2018. In August, in retaliation for the arrest of their relatives, militants in South Kashmir kidnapped 11 relatives of several policemen. The militants released all relatives of police personnel after authorities released the family members of the militants. In November, militant group Hizbul Mujahideen killed a 17-year-old boy in Kashmir on suspicion that he was a police informer, and released the video of the killing as a warning to others. Militants killed several other people in 2018 on suspicions of being police informers. In June, unidentified gunmen killed prominent journalist Shujaat Bukhari, editor of the *Rising Kashmir*, outside the newspaper's office in Srinagar.

The Office of the United Nations High Commissioner for Human Rights released its first-ever report on the human rights situation in Kashmir in June. The report focused on abuses since July 2016, when violent protests erupted in response to the killing of a militant leader by soldiers. The government dismissed the report, calling it "fallacious, tendentious and motivated."

The report described impunity for human rights violations and lack of access to justice, and noted that the Armed Forces (Jammu and Kashmir) Special Powers Act (AFSPA) and the Jammu and Kashmir Public Safety Act (PSA) impede accountability for human rights violations.

The AFSPA, which is also in force in several states in India's northeast, provides soldiers effective immunity from prosecution for serious human rights abuses. The government has failed to review or repeal the law despite repeated recommendations from several government-appointed commissions, UN bodies and experts, and national and international rights groups.

In March, in a welcome step, the government removed AFSPA from the northeastern state of Meghalaya and from 8 out of 16 police stations in Arunachal Pradesh.

In May, police shot at demonstrators protesting a copper plant in Tamil Nadu state, killing 13 people and injuring 100. Police said they were compelled to respond with live ammunition after demonstrators stoned the police, attacked a government building, and set vehicles on fire. A fact-finding report by activists and civil society groups said police failed to follow standard operating procedures for crowd control.

After the BJP formed the government in Uttar Pradesh state, 63 people died in alleged extrajudicial killings by state police between March 2017 and August 2018. The National Human Rights Commission and the Supreme Court sought responses from the state government. The killings in Uttar Pradesh highlighted the lack of accountability for police abuses and the need for police reforms.

Dalits, Tribal Groups, and Religious Minorities

Mob violence by extremist Hindu groups affiliated with the ruling BJP against minority communities, especially Muslims, continued throughout the year amid rumors that they traded or killed cows for beef. As of November, there had been 18 such attacks, and eight people killed during the year.

In July, the government in Assam published a draft of the National Register of Citizens, aimed at identifying Indian citizens and legitimate residents following repeated protests and violence over irregular migration from Bangladesh. The potential exclusion of over four million people, many of them Muslims, from the register raised concerns over arbitrary detention and possible statelessness.

Dalits, formerly "untouchables," continued to be discriminated against in education and in jobs. There was increased violence against Dalits, in part as a reaction to their more organized and vocal demands for social progress and to narrow historical caste differences.

In November, farmers protested against debt and lack of state support for rural communities, and called for establishing rights of women farmers and protecting the land rights of Dalits and tribal communities against forcible acquisition.

In April, nine people were killed in clashes with police after Dalit groups protested across several north Indian states against a Supreme Court ruling to amend the Scheduled Castes and the Scheduled Tribes (Prevention of Atrocities) Act. In response to a complaint of alleged misuse of the law, the court had ordered that a senior police official should conduct a preliminary inquiry before a case is registered under the law. Following the widespread protests, the parliament passed amendments to the law in August, overturning the Supreme Court order.

In July, police in Ahmedabad city raided an area, home to 20,000 members of the vulnerable and marginalized Chhara tribe, a denotified tribe. According to residents, police allegedly brutally beat up scores of people, damaged property, and filed false cases against many of them.

A January report by a government-appointed committee on denotified tribes— tribes that were labeled as criminal during British colonial rule, a notification repealed after independence—said they were the most marginalized communities, subject to "social stigma, atrocity and exclusion."

Tribal communities remained vulnerable to displacement because of mining, dams, and other large infrastructure projects.

In September, the Supreme Court upheld the constitutionality of the biometric identification project, Aadhaar, saying the government could make it a requirement for accessing government benefits and filing income tax, but restricted it for other purposes. Rights groups raised concerns that Aadhaar registration requirements had prevented poor and marginalized people from getting essential services that are constitutionally guaranteed, including food and health care.

Freedom of Expression

Authorities continued to use laws on sedition, defamation, and counterterrorism to crack down on dissent.

In April, police in Tamil Nadu state arrested a folk singer for singing a song at a protest meeting that criticized Prime Minister Narendra Modi. In August, state authorities detained an activist for sedition, allegedly for describing police abuses against protesters opposing a copper factory at the UN Human Rights Council. When a magistrate refused to place him in police custody, police arrested him in an older case and added sedition to the charges against him. Police have also added charges under the Unlawful Activities Prevention Act (UAPA), the key counterterrorism law.

In September, Tamil Nadu state authorities arrested a woman for calling the BJP government "fascist" on board a flight in the presence of the state's BJP president.

In June, police arrested eight people in Bihar state, including five under the age of 18, for sedition, for playing and dancing to an "anti-India" song.

Journalists faced increasing pressure to self-censor due to threat of legal action, smear campaigns and threats on social media, and even threats of physical attacks. In August, the government withdrew its controversial proposal to monitor social media and online communications and collect data on individuals after the Supreme Court said it would turn India into a "surveillance state."

State governments resorted to blanket internet shutdowns either to prevent violence and social unrest or to respond to an ongoing law and order problem. By

November, they had imposed 121 internet shutdowns, 52 of them in Jammu and Kashmir and 30 in Rajasthan.

Civil Society and Freedom of Association

Authorities increasingly used the Unlawful Activities Prevention Act to target civil rights activists and human rights defenders. Police in Maharashtra state arrested and detained 10 civil rights activists, lawyers, and writers, accusing them of being members of a banned Maoist organization and responsible for funding and instigating caste-based violence that took place on January 1, 2018. At time of writing, eight of them were in jail, and one was under house arrest. A fact-finding committee, headed by Pune city's deputy mayor, found that the January 1 violence was premeditated by Hindu extremist groups, but police were targeting the activists because of pressure from the government to protect the perpetrators.

In Manipur state, police threatened and harassed activists, lawyers, and families pursuing justice for alleged unlawful killings by government security forces.

The Indian government also continued to use the Foreign Contribution Regulation Act (FCRA) to restrict foreign funding for NGOs critical of government policies or protesting the government's large development projects. Cases filed by NGOs challenging government decisions to suspend or cancel their FCRA were pending in court.

Women's Rights

Numerous cases of rape across the country once again exposed the failures of the criminal justice system. Nearly six years after the government amended laws and put in place new guidelines and policies aimed at justice for survivors of rape and sexual violence, girls and women continue to face barriers to reporting such crimes. Victim-blaming is rampant, and lack of witness and victim protection laws make girls and women from marginalized communities even more vulnerable to harassment and threats.

Starting in September, numerous women in India's media and entertainment industries shared their accounts on social media of workplace sexual harassment and assault, as part of the #MeToo movement. These public accounts, naming the accused, highlighted the failures of due process, lack of mental health services and support for survivors, and the urgent need to fully implement the Sexual Harassment of Women at Workplace Act of 2013, which prescribes a system for investigating and redressing complaints in the workplace.

In September, the government launched a national registry of sexual offenders, which would store the name, address, photo, fingerprints, and personal details of all arrested, charged, and convicted of sexual offenses. The database, available only to law enforcement agencies, raised concerns regarding data breaches and violations of privacy protections, including for individuals never convicted of a sexual offense.

In September, the Supreme Court lifted the ban on entry of women of menstruating age—between 10 and 50—to a temple in southern India, on grounds of nondiscrimination, equality, and women's right to practice religion. This prompted protests from devotees, including women, who tried to stop girls and young women from entering the temple. The same month, the top court struck down an archaic law that criminalized adultery.

Children's Rights

In April, the government passed an ordinance introducing capital punishment for those convicted of raping a girl under 12 years of age. The new ordinance also increased minimum punishment for rape of girls and women.

The ordinance was a response to the widespread criticism and protests after two prominent cases. In one, some leaders and supporters of the ruling BJP defended alleged Hindu perpetrators of the abduction, ill-treatment, rape, and murder of an 8-year-old Muslim child in Jammu and Kashmir state. The second was in Uttar Pradesh state, where authorities not only failed to arrest a BJP legislator accused of raping a 17-year-old girl, but also allegedly beat her father to death in police custody.

The ordinance was widely criticized by rights groups. However, in August, with parliament's approval, the ordinance became law.

Child labor, child trafficking, and poor access to education for children from socially and economically marginalized communities remained serious concerns throughout India.

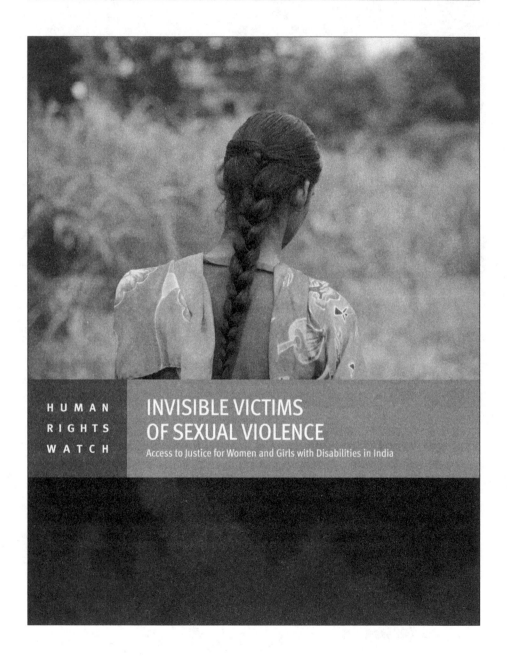

HUMAN
RIGHTS
WATCH

INVISIBLE VICTIMS
OF SEXUAL VIOLENCE
Access to Justice for Women and Girls with Disabilities in India

Sexual Orientation and Gender Identity

In September, India's Supreme Court struck down section 377 of India's penal code, decriminalizing consensual adult same-sex relations. The ruling followed decades of struggle by activists, lawyers, and members of LGBT communities. The court's decision also has significance internationally, as the Indian law served as a template for similar laws throughout much of the former British empire.

In August, the union cabinet approved revisions to the Transgender Persons (Protection of Rights) Bill, introduced in parliament in August 2016. Rights groups and a parliamentary committee criticized the draft law for contradicting several provisions laid down in a 2016 Supreme Court ruling, including transgender people's right to self-identify. The revised bill incorporates many of the committee's recommendations, but falls short of ensuring that transgender people receive needed education and employment benefits.

Disability Rights

Women and girls with disabilities continue to be at a heightened risk of abuse. Even though the laws on sexual violence include several provisions to safeguard the rights of women and girls with disabilities and facilitate their participation in investigative and judicial processes, girls and women with disabilities face serious barriers in the justice system.

Foreign Policy

The Indian government spoke out against Maldives President Abdulla Yameen's crackdown on opposition leaders and declaration of a state of emergency, despite concerns that criticism of the Maldives' leader would push the country further toward China. This led to tense relations between the two countries. India aimed to repair ties with the Maldives after Yameen was defeated in elections held in September 2018.

In June, India joined 119 other countries in voting in favor of a United Nations General Assembly resolution that deplored Israel's "excessive, disproportionate and indiscriminate" use of force against Palestinian civilians in Gaza after the United States vetoed a similar resolution at the UN Security Council.

In May, Foreign Minister Sushma Swaraj visited Myanmar and said India would help to ensure a "safe, speedy and sustainable" return of hundreds of thousands of Rohingya Muslim refugees who had fled to Bangladesh during a campaign of ethnic cleansing by security forces in late 2017. Swaraj reaffirmed India's commitment to socioeconomic development projects in Myanmar's Rakhine State, but did not call on the Myanmar government to check abuses by its security forces or amend its discriminatory citizenship law that effectively keeps the Rohingya stateless. In October, the Indian government deported seven Rohingya to Myanmar, where they are at grave risk of abuse, prompting condemnation from rights groups at home and abroad.

A public call on rights protections did not feature during bilateral engagement with other neighbors including Bangladesh, Nepal, Sri Lanka, and Afghanistan. Relations with Pakistan were marked by angry allegations and counter-allegations of sponsoring violent groups.

Key International Actors

In September, US Secretary of State Mike Pompeo and Secretary of Defense James Mattis visited India to hold talks with their counterparts to strengthen trade, economic, and defense cooperation between the two countries, but there was no public discussion of the human rights situation in either country.

Throughout the year, the UN special procedures issued several statements raising concerns over a slew of issues in India including sexual violence, discrimination against religious minorities, targeting of activists, and lack of accountability for security forces.

The UN special rapporteur on racism called the decision to deport seven Rohingya back to Myanmar a "flagrant denial of their right to protection."

Indonesia

Indonesian President Joko "Jokowi" Widodo's administration took small steps in 2018 to protect the rights of some of Indonesia's most vulnerable people. In April, Jokowi announced that he would ban child marriage, but failed to provide a timetable for abolition. In August, the government moved eight Moluccan political prisoners more than 2,000 kilometers from a remote high-security prison in Nusa Kambangan to a prison much closer to their families.

Although Jokowi issued a plea for religious tolerance in his annual State of the Nation address on August 16, his administration has failed to translate his rhetorical support for human rights into meaningful policies during his first term in office. Religious and gender minorities continue to face harassment. Authorities continue to arrest, prosecute, and imprison people under the blasphemy law. Indonesian security forces continue to pay little price for committing abuses, including past unlawful killings of Papuans, and authorities continue to place far-reaching restrictions on foreign journalists seeking to report from Papua and West Papua provinces. There is little sign that Jokowi is willing to extend the necessary political capital to make human rights a meaningful component of his campaign for re-election in 2019.

The surge in police killings of alleged criminal suspects in the run-up to the Asian Games in Jakarta in July followed public expressions of support by senior officials for Philippines-style "drug war" methods and explicit police authorization for use of deadly force against criminal suspects who resist arrest. The Jokowi administration also publicly backpedaled from a commitment to provide accountability for the mass killings of 1965-66. Following a 2016 deluge of government-driven anti-lesbian, gay, bisexual, and transgender (LGBT) rhetoric, authorities in 2018 continued to target private gatherings and LGBT individuals—a serious threat to privacy and public health initiatives in the country.

Freedom of Religion

In 2018, Indonesian courts sentenced six individuals to prison terms of one to five years for violations of the country's dangerously ambiguous blasphemy law. They included an ethnic Chinese Buddhist in Tanjung Balai in North Sumatra who received an 18-month prison sentence in August for complaining about noise levels at a local mosque. The previous month, the Supreme Court dismissed a legal challenge to the blasphemy law filed by the Ahmadiyah religious minority.

In March, a Christian association in Jayapura, the capital of Papua province, issued a stark 14-day ultimatum to municipal authorities: dismantle the minaret of the city's Al-Aqsa mosque by the end of February or the group would "take their own action." The group did not take any action, however, when the 14-day period passed.

On March 26, Indonesia's Supreme Court rejected former Jakarta Governor Basuki Purnama's appeal of his 2017 blasphemy conviction for which he is serving a two-year prison sentence.

On May 19, militant Islamists attacked and damaged eight Ahmadiyah houses on Lombok Island, forcing 24 people from seven families to seek refuge at the East Lombok police precinct.

Freedom of Expression and Association

Journalist Muhammad Yusuf died on June 10 in police custody in Kotabaru, South Kalimantan, while being detained for criminal defamation. Yusuf's family members alleged that his death was the result of intentional police neglect to provide him medical attention for "breathing difficulties."

In September 2018, the Bireuen Regency government banned unmarried couples from sitting at the same table in restaurants. That prohibition was in a Sharia (Islamic law) regency circular that also forbids such businesses from serving female customers after 9 p.m. or hiring LGBT people as servers.

Women's and Girls' Rights

Indonesia's National Police and Armed Forces continued to inflict abusive, unscientific, and discriminatory "virginity testing" on female applicants despite mounting public pressure to abolish the practice.

In April, Jokowi announced that he was preparing a presidential decree that would ban child marriage. Indonesia's 1974 Marriage Law allows girls to marry at 16 and men to marry at 19 with parental permission. Around 14 percent of girls in

Indonesia are married before age 18, and 1 percent marry before age 15. No timetable was mentioned for abolition.

In July, Indonesia's official Commission on Violence against Women sought assistance from the Presidential Executive Office in combating discrimination against women. The commission has been advocating for the revocation of discriminatory Sharia-based regional ordinances proliferating nationwide.

Papua and West Papua

A measles outbreak in Asmat regency killed an estimated 100 Papuan children in January 2018, underscoring the Indonesian government's neglect of indigenous Papuans' basic health care.

In March, the mysterious death in police custody of Rico Ayomi, a 17-year-old student, for alleged "alcohol poisoning" underscored the lack of accountability for deaths of Papuans by police. Security forces have been responsible for an estimated 95 deaths in 69 incidents from 2010-2018 in which 39 were related to peaceful political activities such as demonstrations or raising the Papuan independence flag. No security force personnel have been convicted in civilian courts for those deaths, with only a handful of cases leading to disciplinary measures or military trials.

Two foreign journalists were harassed in Papua in 2018 for alleged "illegal reporting." They include BBC correspondent Rebecca Henschke, arrested in February, and Polish freelancer Jakub Fabian Skrzypski, arrested in August. Henschke, who had a legitimate travel document, was questioned for a total of 17 hours before being freed. Five Papuan men, including a graduate student, were arrested separately in the Skrzypski case (Skrzypski did not have a travel permit for Papua).

In June, then-UN High Commissioner for Human Rights Zeid Ra'ad Al Hussein said he was "concerned that despite positive engagement by the authorities in many respects, the Government's invitation to my Office to visit Papua—which was made during my visit in February—has still not been honored."

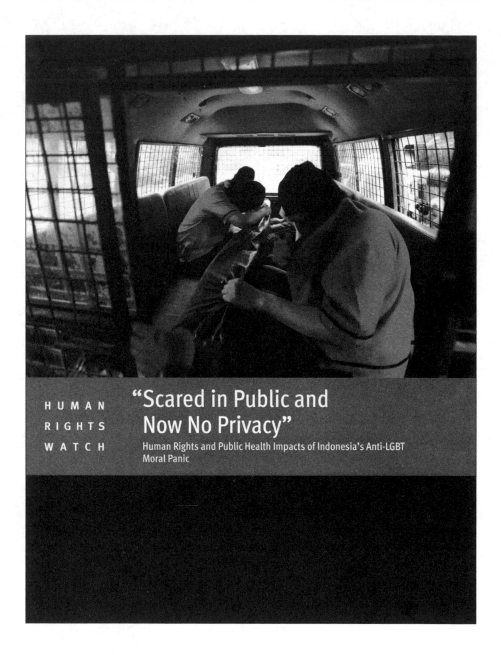

HUMAN
RIGHTS
WATCH

"Scared in Public and
Now No Privacy"
Human Rights and Public Health Impacts of Indonesia's Anti-LGBT
Moral Panic

Sexual Orientation and Gender Identity

Indonesian authorities continued to fail to uphold basic rights of LGBT people, fueling a spike in the country's HIV epidemic. Police arbitrary and unlawful raids on private LGBT gatherings, assisted by militant Islamists, has effectively de-railed public health outreach efforts to vulnerable populations. HIV rates among men who have sex with men (MSM) have consequently increased five-fold since 2007 from 5 to 25 percent.

In January 2018, police and Sharia police in North Aceh detained 12 transgender women and forced them to disrobe. National Police Chief Tito Karnavian ordered an investigation into the raids.

A criminal code bill, designed to replace the 1918 Dutch-colonial era criminal code, underwent several rounds of debate and revision in parliament. Some law-makers pushed to include criminal sanctions for adult consensual same-sex con-duct—a law Indonesia has never previously had—justifying it on the grounds that such provisions "protect" LGBT people from vigilante violence. The govern-ment representative on the drafting committee said he opposed criminalizing same-sex conduct, but at time of writing the process had stalled and language referring to undefined "deviant sex" remained in the draft.

Terrorism and Counterterrorism

On May 13-14, three Indonesian families intentionally used their own children, who were between the ages of 9 and 18, to detonate explosives or to accompany their parents carrying out suicide attacks against three churches in Surabaya. The bombings killed at least 12 people, plus 13 attackers, and wounded at least 50 others. The families were linked to the Jamaah Ansharut Daulah, an affiliate of the Islamic State, which claimed responsibility for the bombings.

On May 25, parliament amended the 2003 counterterrorism law, which relies on an overbroad definition of terrorism, extends capital punishment crimes, and ex-tends pre-charge detention periods to 21 days. The law also grants potentially disproportionate surveillance powers. It extends military deployment in coun-terterrorism operations, a move that carries potential risks, in part because mili-tary personnel typically do not receive law enforcement training. The Indonesian

HUMAN
RIGHTS
WATCH

INDONESIA: SHACKLING REDUCED, BUT PERSISTS

Oversight Crucial to End Abuse of People with Disabilities

military justice system has an egregious track record investigating and prosecuting human rights violations by military personnel.

Children's Rights

Children in Indonesia continue to work in hazardous conditions on tobacco farms, where they are exposed to nicotine, toxic pesticides, and other dangers. Though the government bans hazardous work for children under 18, authorities have not changed Indonesian labor law or regulations to explicitly prohibit children from handling tobacco.

Disability Rights

The government has taken promising steps to end shackling, reducing the number of people with psychosocial disabilities who are shackled or locked up in confined spaces from nearly 18,800, the last reported figure, to 12,800 in July 2018, according to government data.

The Ministry of Health rolled out a community outreach program to collect data, raise awareness, and provide services on 12 issues, including mental health. As of November 2018, the program had reached 21.5 million households but the data collected indicates that only 17 percent of people with psychosocial disabilities surveyed had received access to mental health services. Despite the progress, people with psychosocial disabilities continue to be detained in institutions where they face abuse, including physical and sexual violence, involuntary treatment, restraints, and forced seclusion.

Extrajudicial Killings

In February, the Indonesian government awarded Philippine National Police Director-General Ronald dela Rosa its highest honor. Rosa has been implicated in possible crimes against humanity for inciting and instigating killings linked to the Philippine government's "war on drugs" that killed more than 12,000 people since June 2016.

Jakarta police data indicate that police killed 11 suspects and wounded 41 others from July 3 to July 12 for "resisting arrest" during an anti-crime campaign linked to the city's preparations to host the 2018 Asian Games in August. The surge in killings followed public expressions of support by senior officials for abusive "drug war" methods promoted by Philippine President Rodrigo Duterte and explicit police authorization for use of deadly force against criminal suspects who resist arrest.

In August, Indonesia's national police chief, Gen. Tito Karnavian, announced that police would reopen their investigation into the murder in 2004 of human rights defender Munir Thalib. Investigations and prosecutions in the case to date have failed to uncover the full circumstances of Munir's killing or target the most senior officials believed responsible.

Environmental Rights

In January, a court in eastern Java sentenced Heri Budiawan, a leader of the grassroots environmental group Banyuwangi People's Forum, to 10 months' imprisonment for violating Indonesia's draconian anti-communism laws. Prosecutors alleged that Budiawan and his supporters displayed banners bearing the hammer and sickle symbol during an April 4, 2017 protest against pollution by a local gold mine.

In February, with World Bank support, Jokowi launched the One Map program to register all land in Indonesia, including disputed areas, by 2025. In September, he announced a moratorium on oil palm plantations, instructing his ministries to stop issuing new plantation permits on state forests till 2021. Many indigenous and peasant rights groups argued that moratoriums and land certification alone are not sufficient to resolve land disputes. In 2017, the Agrarian Reform Consortium documented 659 land-related conflicts over a total area of 520,490 hectares, affecting more than 650,000 households. Land clearing for plantations has resulted in loss of forest cover and forest fires that both cause air pollution and aggravate climate change.

Key International Actors

In January, Indonesia's Defense Minister Ryamizard Ryacudu and US Defense Secretary James Mattis discussed the possible resumption of US assistance to Indonesia's Kopassus special forces. Assistance to the unit had been halted in large part because of the US "Leahy Law," which bars US assistance and training to foreign military units known to have committed gross human rights abuses unless the government has taken steps to address the abuses and hold those responsible to account.

UN Special Rapporteur on the Right to Food Hilal Elver visited Indonesia in April 2018, reporting that "over 80 million" Indonesians remain vulnerable to food insecurity in certain areas.

On April 28, Jokowi met Myanmar President Win Myint and asked him to implement the recommendations of a commission led by the late United Nations Secretary-General Kofi Annan to resolve the humanitarian crisis in Myanmar's Rakhine State.

On February 7, UN High Commissioner for Human Rights Zeid met President Jokowi, urging his government to scrap proposed clauses in the draft Criminal Code that discriminate against LGBT people. Zeid also discussed the plight of Rohingya refugees in Bangladesh.

On May 31, Zulfiqar Ali, a Pakistani citizen, died of cancer in a Jakarta prison, spending his final days on death row despite promises by leaders of both Pakistan and Indonesia to return him to his family in Lahore.

In September, the Indonesian government pledged it would "not interfere" in the Chinese government's arbitrary detention of more than 1 million Uighur Muslims in "re-education" camps in China's Xinjiang region. The government expressed hope that China would "uphold the rule of law and human rights" despite mounting evidence of egregious ongoing abuses in Xinjiang.

Iran

Iranians participated in numerous protests across the country amid deteriorating economic conditions, perceptions of systematic government corruption, and popular frustration over lack of political and social freedoms. Security forces and the judiciary have responded to these protests with arbitrary mass arrests and serious due process violations. While at least 30 people, including security forces, have been killed during the protests, officials have not conducted credible investigations into protesters' deaths, or into security agencies' use of excessive force to repress protests. Authorities have also tightened their grip on peaceful activism, detaining lawyers and human rights defenders who face charges that could lead to long jail terms.

Rights to Peaceful Assembly and Free Expression

Since protests first occurred in December 2017, authorities have systematically violated the right of citizens to peaceful assembly, arbitrarily arresting thousands of protesters. According to Alireza Rahimi, a parliamentarian, authorities arrested 4,900 people, including 150 university students, during the December and January protests. According to Iranian media, at least 21 people were killed during the December and January protests, including law enforcement agents.

On February 19 and 20, several media reported that clashes between security forces and protesters from the Dervish community, a Muslim minority group, had left several dozen Dervishes severely injured and four law enforcement agents dead, including three who were struck by a bus. On March 4, authorities informed the family of Mohammad Raji, one of those arrested, that he had died in custody. Authorities have refused to provide any explanation for Raji's death and have threatened reprisals against his family if they speak publicly about it.

On March 18, after a rapid trial that concluded only a few weeks after his arrest and allegations of police torture, a court sentenced Mohammad Sallas, a Dervish member who was arrested during the clashes, to death for allegedly driving the bus that ran over and killed three officers. Authorities executed Sallas on June 18. Since May 2018, revolutionary courts have sentenced at least 208 members of the Dervish religious minority to prison terms and other punishments in trials that violate their basic rights.

On July 31, a new wave of anti-government protests began in the city of Esfahan and quickly spread to other cities, including Karaj in Alborz province, and Tehran, the capital. Since August 3, authorities have detained more than 50 men and women they arrested during the protests and held them in Fashafuyeh and Qarchack prisons in Tehran.

On April 30, 2018, the prosecutor of the second branch of Tehran's Culture and Media Court ordered all internet service providers to block access to the popular messaging application of Telegram, which has more than 40 million Iranians users. Authorities had temporarily blocked Telegram during the January protests. Facebook and Twitter remain blocked, along with hundreds of other websites.

Death Penalty

According to rights groups, Iran executed at least 225 as of November 9, compared to 507 in 2017.

The decrease in number is largely due to an amendment to Iran's drug law that went into force in November 2017. Since November 2017, the judiciary has halted most executions of individuals convicted of drug offenses in order to review their cases in accordance with an amendment to Iran's drug law that raised the bar for imposing mandatory death sentences. On January 15, Hassan Norouzi, the parliamentary judicial spokesperson, told domestic media that authorities are reviewing some 15,000 cases as part of this process. However, rights organizations have since documented four executions related to drug offenses and armed robbery.

The judiciary also executed at least five individuals who were sentenced to death for crimes they allegedly committed as children. Under Iran's current penal code, which went into force in 2013, judges can use their discretion not to sentence individuals who committed the alleged crime as children to death. However, several individuals who were retried under the new code for crimes they allegedly committed as children have been sentenced to death again.

On September 8, authorities executed Zanyar and Loghman Moradi, and Ramin Hossein Panahi, three Kurdish men convicted in unfair trials of participating in armed struggle against the government. Their executions took place despite serious allegations of torture and due process violations and on the same day that

Iranian forces carried out an attack on the headquarters of the Kurdistan Democratic Party-Iran and the Democratic Party of Iranian Kurdistan, two opposition groups in the town of Koya, in northern Iraq.

Iranian law considers acts such as "insulting the prophet," "apostasy," same-sex relations, adultery, and certain non-violent drug-related offenses as crimes punishable by death. The law also prescribes the inhumane punishment of flogging for more than 100 offenses, including drinking alcoholic beverages and extramarital sex, which are prohibited in Iran.

Human Rights Defenders and Political Prisoners

While scores of human rights defenders and political activists remain behind bars for their peaceful activism, Iran's Ministry of Intelligence and Islamic Revolutionary Guard Corps (IRGC) Intelligence Organization increased their targeting of human rights defenders and activists.

Since January 24, the Revolutionary Guards' Intelligence Organization has detained Taher Ghadirian, Niloufar Bayani, Amirhossein Khaleghi, Houman Jokar, Sam Rajabi, Sepideh Kashani, Morad Tahbaz, and Abdolreza Kouhpayeh, eight environmental activists accused of using environmental projects as a cover to collect classified strategic information, without providing any evidence of wrongdoing.

On February 10, the family of Kavous Seyed Emami, a well-known Iranian-Canadian environmentalist and professor also arrested, reported that he had died in detention in unknown circumstances. Authorities claimed Seyed Emami committed suicide, but they have not conducted an impartial investigation into his death. They have also placed a travel ban on Seyed Emami's wife, Maryam Mombeini.

Since 2014, the IRGC Intelligence Organization has arrested at least 14 dual and foreign nationals who authorities allegedly perceived to have links with western academic, economic, and cultural institutions. They remain behind bars on vague charges such as "cooperating with a hostile state," deprived of due process, and routinely subjected to pro-government media smear campaigns.

Since June, Ministry of Intelligence authorities intensified their crackdown against human rights defenders. Those arrested include prominent human rights lawyer Nasrin Sotoudeh and her husband Reza Khandan, as well as Farhard Meysami, another human rights defender, for their peaceful activism in opposing compulsory hijab laws. The Ministry of Intelligence also arrested four other human rights lawyers, Qasem Sholehsadi, Arash Keykhosravi, Farokh Forouzan, and Payam Derafshan. On September 6, authorities released Derafshan and Forouzan on bail.

In the first days of September, authorities also arrested Hoda Amid and Najmeh Vahedi, two women's rights defenders who teach workshops for women on realizing equal rights in marriage, at their homes in Tehran.

Due Process Rights and Treatment of Prisoners

Iranian courts, and particularly the revolutionary courts, regularly fell short of providing fair trials and used confessions likely obtained under torture as evidence in court. Authorities routinely restrict detainees' access to legal counsel, particularly during the investigation period. In June, the judiciary reportedly restricted the right of legal representation for defendants facing national security crimes' charges to a judiciary-approved list of just 20 lawyers who can represent them during the investigation phase in Tehran. The list includes no women or human rights lawyers.

Several individuals charged with national security crimes suffered from a lack of adequate access to medical care in detention. On August 31, the family of Arash Sadeghi, a 30-year-old human rights defender, reported that he had been diagnosed with a rare kind of cancer and is in urgent need of specialized care. Authorities reportedly allowed Sadeghi to undergo surgery at a hospital on September 13, but returned him to prison against his doctor's medical advice.

Revolutionary courts handed down long prison sentences to at least 17 student activists arrested during the December and January protests.

Women's Rights

Iranian women face discrimination in personal status matters related to marriage, divorce, inheritance, and child custody. Iranian women cannot pass on their nationality to their foreign-born spouses or their children like men. A married woman may not obtain a passport or travel outside the country without the

"I Am Equally Human"
Discrimination and Lack of Accessibility for People with Disabilities in Iran

HUMAN
RIGHTS
WATCH

Center for
HUMAN
RIGHTS
in Iran

written permission of her husband. Under the civil code, a husband is accorded the right to choose the place of living and can prevent his wife from having certain occupations if he deems them against "family values."

In December 2017 and January 2018, several women took their headscarves off while standing on electric utility boxes across the country to protest Iran's compulsory hijab law. Court have sentenced several of these women to imprisonment ranging from a few months to 20 years (18 years of which is suspended). Authorities have filed a complaint against Nasrin Sotoudeh for her work in defending Shaparak Shajarizadeh, a woman arrested for protesting these discriminatory laws.

In June, authorities opened Azadi stadium's doors to women and men to watch a live screening of the last two games of Iran's national football team at the 2018 World Cup. Despite authorities' promise to allow women to watch the games however, women are still banned from attending several men's sports tournaments, such as Iran's football league matches.

Iranian law vaguely defines what constitutes acts against morality, and authorities have long censored art, music, and other forms of cultural expression, as well as prosecuted hundreds of people for such acts. These laws often disproportionally target women and sexual minorities. On July 9, Iranian state television broadcasted several women's apologies briefly detained in May for posting videos of themselves dancing on their popular Instagram accounts.

Treatment of Religious Minorities

Iranian law denies freedom of religion to Baha'is and discriminates against them. At least 79 Baha'is were held in Iran's prisons as of November 2018. Iranian authorities also systematically refuse to allow Baha'is to register at public universities because of their faith.

The government also discriminates against other religious minorities, including Sunni Muslims, and restricts cultural and political activities among the country's Azeri, Kurdish, Arab, and Baluch ethnic minorities.

According to Article 18, an Iranian NGO, as of September 30, Iran has sentenced 37 Christians who converted from Muslim backgrounds to imprisonment for "missionary work."

On July 21, after a long legal and legislative battle between Iran's Guardian Council and the parliament, Sepanta Niknam, a Zoroastrian member of the Yazd City Council whose membership had been suspended because of his religion, was reinstated as a councilor.

Disability Rights

In 2018, Human Rights Watch and the Center for Human Rights in Iran documented how people with disabilities face stigma, discrimination, and lack of accessibility when accessing social services, healthcare, and public transportation. People with disabilities may receive medical treatment, including electroshock therapy, without their informed consent. In March, parliament passed a disability law that increases disability pensions and insurance coverage of disability-related healthcare services but does not explicitly prohibit discrimination against persons with disabilities. Under election law, people who are blind or deaf may not run for parliament.

Key International Actors

Iran continues to provide the Syrian government with military assistance and plays an influential role alongside Russia and Turkey in the Syria negotiations currently taking place in Astana, Kazakhstan.

On May 8, President Donald Trump announced the US withdrawal from the nuclear agreement signed in 2015 between Iran and the five permanent members of the United Nations Security Council, plus Germany and the European Union. The US has re-imposed several sanctions that had been lifted as a result of the agreement. President Trump sharply criticized Iran and the nuclear deal during a UN Security Council summit meeting on nonproliferation in September, although other council members defended the deal, including France, Britain, Russia, China, and the Netherlands.

On October 3, the International Court of Justice ordered a provisional measure in a complaint made by Iran that the United States must remove any obstacles arising from its economic sanctions to "the free exportation to the territory of the Islamic Republic of Iran of medicines and medical devices; foodstuffs and agricultural commodities; and spare parts, equipment and associated services necessary for the safety of civil aviation." After the ruling, the US announced that it would withdraw from the 1955 Treaty of Amity, Economic Relations, and Consular Rights, which Iran used to file the complaint.

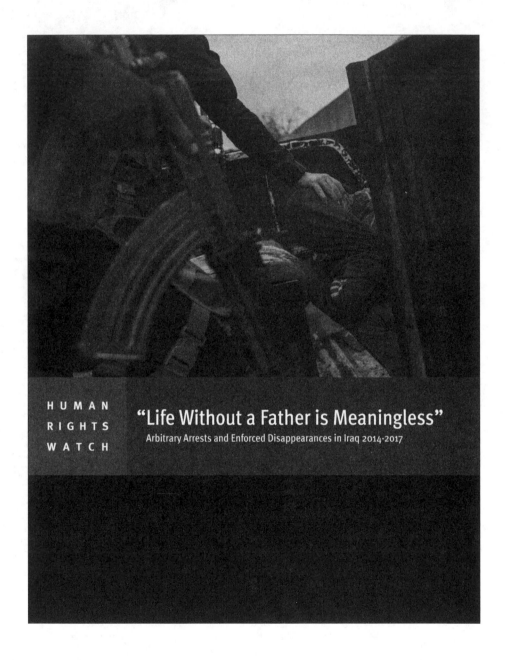

HUMAN
RIGHTS
WATCH

"Life Without a Father is Meaningless"
Arbitrary Arrests and Enforced Disappearances in Iraq 2014-2017

Iraq

While many of the active battlefronts between Iraqi forces and the Islamic State (ISIS) had quieted by 2018, military operations continued against sleeper cells and rural ISIS holdouts. ISIS continued to capture and extrajudicially kill civilians and Iraqi armed forces throughout the year. Under the guise of fighting terror, Iraqi forces arbitrarily detained, ill-treated and tortured, and disappeared mostly Sunni men from areas where ISIS was active and failed to respect their due process and fair trial rights. The years of fighting across the country left at least 1.8 million Iraqis still displaced in 2018. Iraqi authorities imposed security measures against individuals and families perceived as having relatives who supported ISIS in the past in what amounted to collective punishment.

Other human rights violations persisted, including violations of freedom of assembly and expression, women's rights, and the continued use of the death penalty.

May parliamentary elections led to Adil Abd Al-Mahdi taking up the post of prime minister from Haidar al-Abadi in October and forming a new government.

Justice for ISIS Abuses

In 2018, ISIS fighters captured and extrajudicially killed civilians, often targeting community leaders and Iraqi armed forces. They carried out dozens of explosive attacks on civilian-populated areas. Under international law some of the brutal crimes perpetrated by ISIS since 2014 amounted to war crimes and may amount to crimes against humanity or genocide. In 2018, Iraq failed to pass legislation to make war crimes and crimes against humanity specific offenses under Iraqi law.

Iraqi judges instead prosecuted ISIS suspects with the single charge of ISIS affiliation, under Iraqi counterterrorism legislation. The trials were generally rushed, based on a defendant's confession, and did not involve victim participation. Authorities did little to protect, gather, and use in criminal prosecutions evidence found at mass gravesites left by ISIS.

The Iraqi government and Kurdistan Regional Government (KRG) conducted thousands of trials of ISIS suspects without a strategy to prioritize the worst abuses under Iraqi and international law.

Based on a United Nations Security Council resolution adopted in September 2017, a UN investigative team was created to document serious crimes committed by ISIS in Iraq. By the end of 2018, the team had yet to properly launch investigations in Iraq.

Iraq passed Law No. 20, Compensating the Victims of Military Operations, Military Mistakes and Terrorist Actions in 2009, creating governmental commissions to compensate Iraqis affected by terrorism, military operations, and military errors. Compensation commissions in areas that fell under ISIS control in 2014 have received thousands of compensation requests but have yet to pay out any claims from 2014 onwards.

Arbitrary Detention, Due Process, and Fair Trial Violations

Iraqi forces arbitrarily detained some ISIS suspects, predominately Sunni men, many of them for months. According to witnesses and family members, security forces regularly detained suspects without any court order, arrest warrant, or other document justifying arrest and often did not provide a reason for the arrest.

During March protests launched by civil servants in the Kurdistan Region of Iraq for unpaid wages, KRG security forces also arbitrarily detained dozens of protesters and journalists.

Authorities systematically violated the due process rights of ISIS suspects and other detainees, such as guarantees in Iraqi law for detainees to see a judge within 24 hours, to have access to a lawyer throughout interrogations, and to have families notified of their detention and to able to communicate with them.

Judges also ignored claims made by foreign women charged with ISIS affiliation for having entered Iraq and lived in ISIS-controlled areas that their husbands brought them against their will. Children above the ages of nine were also prosecuted for illegal entry into the country despite statements in court that their parents brought them to Iraq without their consent.

Despite requests, the government of Iraq failed to release information on which security and military structures have a legal mandate to detain and in which facilities.

Torture and Other Forms of Ill-Treatment

Detainees in Nineveh gave graphic accounts of torture during interrogations in Mosul's prisons under the control of the Ministry of Interior, in some cases leading to the deaths of detainees. These allegations are consistent with reports of widespread use of torture by Iraqi forces as a method to extract confessions instead of carrying out robust criminal investigations. Authorities detained ISIS suspects in overcrowded, and in some cases inhumane, conditions.

Despite commitments by the prime minister in September 2017 to investigate allegations of torture and extrajudicial killings, authorities seemingly took no steps to investigate these abuses.

In 16 terrorism trials Human Rights Watch monitored in 2018, defendants alleged torture, including to extract confessions, but most judges did not take any action to investigate the allegations, and in only one instance was an officer investigated and sanctioned.

Enforced Disappearances

The International Center for Missing Persons, which has been working in partnership with the Iraqi government to help recover and identify the missing, estimates that the number of missing people in Iraq could range from 250,000 to 1 million people. Since 2014,

Iraqi military and security forces have forcibly disappeared predominately Sunni Arab males in the context of counterterrorism operations, as well as in other cases. A range of military and security actors are responsible for the enforced disappearances, many of which took place at checkpoints or the homes of suspects. Despite requests from the families of the disappeared for information, Iraqi authorities have given none. Authorities did not respond to queries from Human Rights Watch as to which channels were available to families searching for loved ones. An initiative in 2015 and in 2017 to pass a new law that prohibits enforced disappearances as a distinct crime has been stalled in parliament.

Collective Punishment of Families of Suspected ISIS-Affiliates

Iraqi families with perceived ISIS affiliation, usually because of their family name, tribal affiliation, or area of origin, were denied security clearances required to obtain identity cards and all other civil documentation. This impacted their freedom of movement, right to education, right to work, and right to apply for welfare benefits and obtain birth and death certificates needed to inherit property or remarry.

Denial of security clearances also blocked families with perceived ISIS affiliation from being able to make claims to the governmental commission to compensate Iraqis affected by terrorism, military operations, and military errors; to bring court cases; or to challenge the seizure of property by Iraqi security forces or other local families. In Nineveh, families with perceived ISIS affiliation also said they were sometimes denied access to humanitarian assistance, usually by community leaders.

Lawyers providing legal services to ISIS suspects and, their families, or those perceived to be, reported that security forces threatened, and in some instances, detained, them for providing these services.

Despite joint government and humanitarian efforts to facilitate the return of displaced persons to areas once held by ISIS, local decrees and other preventative measures prevented families with perceived ISIS affiliation from returning home to some areas, including in Anbar, Diyala, Nineveh, and Salah al-Din. In some instances, these families were forced from their homes into camps by Iraqi armed forces or were forced into secondary displacement.

Freedom of Assembly and Expression

KRG security forces arbitrarily detained dozens of protesters and journalists at March protests by civil servants demanding unpaid wages. Some protesters alleged security forces also beat them.

Protests that began in central and southern Iraq in July demanding improved access to water, jobs, and electrical power turned violent in some areas, particularly in Basra, with Ministry of Interior forces injuring dozens of protesters, and killing a few through their excessive use of force when trying to disperse crowds and detain protesters. The protests in Basra continued through September, with violence increasing on both sides leading to protesters burning down buildings and leaving at least 15 dead.

Women's Rights, Sexual Orientation, Morality Laws

Human Rights Watch and other organizations documented a system of organized rape, sexual slavery, and forced marriage by ISIS forces of Yezidi women and girls. However, no ISIS member has been prosecuted or convicted for those specific crimes.

Women have few legal protections to shield them from domestic violence. Iraq's criminal code includes provisions criminalizing physical assault but lacks any explicit mention of domestic violence. While sexual assault is criminalized, article 398 provides that such charges be dropped if the assailant marries the victim. While no recent national studies on domestic violence have been carried out, women's rights organizations reported a high rate of domestic violence.

Iraq's criminal code does not prohibit same-sex sexual relations, although article 394 makes it illegal to engage in extra-marital sex. Paragraph 401 of the penal code holds that any person who commits an "immodest act" in public can be put in prison for up to six months, a vague provision that could be used to target sexual and gender minorities, although such cases have not been documented.

Death Penalty

Iraq has long had one of the highest rates of executions in the world, ranked in the top four alongside China, Iran, and Saudi Arabia. Iraqi law permits the death penalty against adults for a range of crimes. Iraqi authorities handed down hundreds of death sentences to those convicted under counterterrorism legislation and carried out executions without publicizing any official numbers or sharing this information with international actors. After an ISIS attack in June, the prime minister called for the "immediate" execution of all convicted "terrorists" on death row, after which authorities publicly announced the execution of 12 men.

In the Kurdistan Region of Iraq, the KRG implemented a de facto moratorium on the death penalty in 2008, banning it "except in very few cases which were considered essential," according to a KRG spokesperson. The Iraqi criminal code prohibits the use of the death penalty against children.

Foreign Military Operations

While the United States-led Global Coalition against ISIS continued its military operations in Iraq, Turkey increased its operations in northern Iraq against the armed Kurdistan Workers' Party (PKK). The PKK, an outlawed armed group active in Turkey, has long maintained a presence in northern Iraq near the Turkish, Iranian, and Syrian borders.

Turkish forces have conducted operations against the PKK in Iraq at various times for over two decades. Starting in March, Turkish forces extended their presence into northern Iraq by at least 30 kilometers, establishing multiple outposts, including in rural areas of Dohuk and Erbil governorates. In March and June, two Turkish military operations in the area killed five non-combatants in attacks where there were no apparent military objectives.

In September, Iranian forces reportedly carried out an attack on the headquarters of the Kurdistan Democratic Party of Iran and the Democratic Party of Iranian Kurdistan, two opposition groups in the northern town of Koya, in northern Iraq, killing at least 13 individuals and wounding another 39.

Key International Actors

The US-led Global Coalition against ISIS, including Australia, Belgium, Canada, Denmark, France, the Netherlands, and the United Kingdom, as well as Iranian and Turkish forces, have supported Iraqi and Kurdish troops in the war against ISIS since 2014. This support includes billions of dollars spent training, equipping, and supporting a range of Iraqi military and security forces. The countries were generally vague as to what they published publicly on the scale, nature, and parameters of their assistance in 2018, as well as the exact recipients.

In 2018, Iraq also purchased weapons worth millions of dollars through foreign military sales from US-coalition members as well as Iran and Russia reportedly.

In February, North Atlantic Treaty Organisation (NATO) defense ministers agreed to a bigger "train-and-advise" mission in Iraq. The US-led coalition has also committed to staying in Iraq indefinitely, and continued to carry out military operations against ISIS targets in Iraq.

In light of the rampant impunity of Iraqi security forces, Human Rights Watch called on foreign governments to end military assistance to units involved in laws of war violations and explain publicly any suspension of military assistance, including the grounds for doing so.

In January, European Union foreign ministers adopted a new EU strategy on Iraq that seeks to address Iraq's humanitarian, stabilization, reform, and reconciliation needs. In July, the European Parliament gave its consent to the EU-Iraq Partnership and Cooperation Agreement.

In July 2018, US Secretary of State Mike Pompeo held his first ever ministerial, which focused on religious liberties. Senior US government officials highlighted the plight of Christians, Yezidis, and other religious minorities in Iraq and pledged $17 million for landmine clearance in the Nineveh plains.

Israel and Palestine

The Israeli government continued to enforce severe and discriminatory restrictions on Palestinians' human rights; restrict the movement of people and goods into and out of the Gaza Strip; and facilitate the unlawful transfer of Israeli citizens to settlements in the occupied West Bank.

Israeli forces stationed on the Israeli side of the fences separating Gaza and Israel responded to demonstrations for Palestinian rights on the Gaza side with excessive lethal force. Between March 30 and November 19, security forces killed 189 Palestinian demonstrators, including 31 children and 3 medical workers, and wounded more than 5,800 with live fire. Demonstrators threw rocks and "Molotov cocktails," used slingshots to hurl projectiles, and launched kites bearing incendiary materials, which caused significant property damage to nearby Israeli communities, and, in at least one instance, fired towards soldiers. Officers repeatedly fired on protesters who posed no imminent threat to life, pursuant to expansive open-fire orders from senior officials that contravene international human rights law standards. In May, the United Nations Human Rights Council set-up a commission of inquiry to investigate the events in Gaza, with a view to identifying those responsible, including in the chain of command, and ensuring accountability.

The Israeli army also launched intermittent air and artillery strikes in the Gaza Strip, killing 37 Palestinians between March 30 and November 19, including at least five civilians. Palestinian armed groups fired 1138 rockets and mortars indiscriminately toward Israel from Gaza as of November 13, according to the Meir Amit Intelligence and Terrorism Information Center, a major increase over previous years, killing one person and injuring at least 40, including civilians.

Attempts to reconcile did not end the rivalry between Palestinian groups Fatah and Hamas. Both the Fatah-dominated Palestinian Authority (PA) in the West Bank and Hamas in Gaza arrested opposition supporters and other critics, and mistreated and tortured some in their custody. The Independent Commission for Human Rights in Palestine (ICHR), a statutory commission charged with monitoring human rights compliance by the Palestinian authorities, received 180 complaints of arbitrary arrest, 173 complaints of torture and ill-treatment, and 209 complaints of administrative detention pursuant to orders from a regional governor by PA security forces as of October 31. In the same period, the body recorded

81 complaints of arbitrary arrest and 146 complaints of torture and ill-treatment against Hamas security forces.

Israel continued to maintain its more than decade-long effective closure of Gaza, exacerbated by Egyptian restrictions on its own border with Gaza, limiting access to water and electricity (households in Gaza received power between four and five hours a day on average during most of the year). Israel also restricted access to medical care and educational and economic opportunities. In July, in response to the launching of incendiary kites from Gaza, Israeli authorities banned the shipment of most goods out of Gaza, limited entry to "humanitarian" items and temporarily reduced the fishing zone off the Gaza coast from six to three nautical miles, measures that amount to collective punishment. Gaza's unemployment rate stood at 55 percent during the third-quarter of 2018, according to the Palestinian Central Bureau of Statistics, and 80 percent of Gaza's nearly 2 million people depend on humanitarian aid.

Israeli authorities continued to expand settlements in the occupied West Bank and to discriminate systematically against Palestinians and in favor of settlers, in providing services, allowing freedom of movement, and issuing building permits, among other actions. During 2017 and the first eight months of 2018, Israeli authorities approved plans for 10,536 housing units in West Bank settlements, excluding East Jerusalem, and issued tenders for 5,676, as compared to approving plans for 4,611 units and issuing tenders for 592 units in all of 2015 and 2016, according to the Israeli group Peace Now.

Meanwhile, Israeli authorities destroyed 390 Palestinian homes and other property, forcibly displacing 407 people as of November 19, the majority for lacking construction permits that Israel makes nearly impossible for Palestinians to obtain in East Jerusalem or in the 60 percent of the West Bank under its exclusive control (Area C).

Gaza Strip

Closure

Israel's near-total closure of the Gaza Strip continued to severely harm the civilian population.

The Israeli army limits travel out of Gaza to what it calls "exceptional humanitarian cases," meaning mostly medical patients, their companions, and prominent businesspersons with permits. In the first eight months of 2018, the army approved only 60 percent of permit applications from Palestinians seeking medical treatment outside Gaza. In August, the Israeli Supreme Court found unlawful Israel's practice of denying exit permits to "first-degree relatives of Hamas members."

During the first 10 months of 2018, an average of about 274 Palestinians exited the Erez crossing each day, compared to the daily average of more than 24,000 in September 2000, according to the Israeli rights group Gisha. Outgoing goods in the same period, mostly destined for the West Bank and Israel, averaged 201 truckloads per month, less than 20 percent of the average 1,064 truckloads per month prior to the June 2007 tightening of the closure.

The limited supply of electricity in Gaza compromised the water supply, sewage treatment, and hospital operations. Shortages of fuel, needed to operate generators during power outages, stemming from various factors including disputes over payment for the power between the PA and Hamas and exacerbated by Israel blocking entry of fuel in July, led to the partial closure of several hospitals. As of October 31, 44 percent of "essential" medicines were completely depleted, according to Gaza's Central Drug Store.

Israeli restrictions on the delivery of construction materials to Gaza and a lack of funding have impeded reconstruction of homes severely damaged or destroyed during Israel's 2014 military operation in Gaza. About 17,700 Palestinians who lost their homes remain displaced. The Israeli government said that to prevent construction materials from being diverted by Hamas for military purposes, it would allow in only limited quantities under the supervision of international organizations.

Egypt also restricts the movement of people and goods at its border with Gaza at Rafah. Between January and April, an average of about 2,500 persons monthly crossed through Rafah in both directions, according to the United Nations Office for the Coordination of Humanitarian Affairs (OCHA). Egyptian authorities opened Rafah on a more regular basis beginning in May, with an average of 11,746 crossing monthly in both directions between May and October, but still a fraction of the average of 40,000 per month in the first half of 2013.

Israeli Actions in Gaza

As of November 19, lethal force by Israeli forces resulted in the killing of 252 and injuring of 25,522 Palestinians in Gaza, OCHA reported. Many of the injuries were life-changing, including hundreds of cases of severe soft tissue damage, some necessitating amputation of limbs. Most of the killings took place in the context of protests, where Israeli forces, following orders from senior officials, used live ammunition against people who approached or attempted to cross or damage fences between Gaza and Israel. Israeli officials rejected the international human rights law standard in policing situations that prohibits the intentional use of lethal force except as a last resort to prevent an imminent threat to life. They argued that live ammunition was necessary to stop breaches of the fences, which they claimed was a Hamas strategy to enable militants to kill or capture Israelis, without sufficiently addressing why lesser measures would not have worked.

Hamas and Palestinian Armed Groups' Actions in Gaza

Attacks by Palestinian armed groups in Gaza, mainly indiscriminate rocket attacks, led to the injuries of more than 40 Israelis as of November 19. Hamas authorities continue to disclose no information about two Israeli civilians with psychosocial disabilities, Avera Mangistu and Hisham al-Sayed, whom they have apparently held for several years, in violation of international law.

In addition to regular arbitrary arrests of dissidents and torture of those in its custody, Hamas authorities have carried out 25 executions since they took control in Gaza in June 2007, though none in 2018, following trials that lacked appropriate due process protections. Courts in Gaza have sentenced 125 people to death in this period, according to the Palestinian Center for Human Rights.

Laws in Gaza punish "unnatural intercourse" of a sexual nature, understood to include same-sex relationships, with up to 10 years in prison.

West Bank

Israeli Actions in the West Bank

In the West Bank, including East Jerusalem, Israeli security forces fatally shot 27 Palestinians and wounded at least 5,444, including those suspected of attacking

HUMAN
RIGHTS
WATCH

BANKROLLING ABUSE
Israeli Banks in West Bank Settlements

Israelis, but also passersby and demonstrators, as of November 19. In many cases, video footage and witness accounts strongly suggest that Israeli forces used excessive force. As of November 19, attacks by settlers injured 61 Palestinians and damaged property in 147 incidents, according to OCHA. Palestinians killed 10 Israelis, including six civilians, and wounded at least 58 in the same period in the West Bank in acts that Hamas sometimes praised; in one killing, its military wing claimed responsibility.

In April, an Israeli court sentenced to nine months in prison an Israeli border policeman caught on camera in 2014 shooting 17-year-old Palestinian Nadim Nuwarah from about 60 meters away when he appeared to pose no imminent threat to them. The conviction marked a rare exception to the pattern by which security forces and settlers who attack Palestinians and destroy or damage their homes and other property do not face prosecution.

Settlements, Discriminatory Policies, Home Demolitions

Israel continued to provide security, administrative services, housing, education, and medical care for more than 628,000 settlers residing in unlawful settlements in the West Bank, including East Jerusalem. International humanitarian law bars an occupying power's transfer of its civilians to occupied territory. Palestinians in much of the West Bank have access to water, electricity, and other state services that are either more limited or costlier than the same services that the state makes available to Jewish settlers there.

The difficulty in obtaining Israeli-issued building permits has driven Palestinians to construct housing and business structures that are at constant risk of demolition or confiscation by Israel on the grounds of being unauthorized. The UN considers 46 Palestinian communities at "high risk of forcible transfer," including Khan al-Ahmar, a village of 180 residents east of Jerusalem with a school serving 160 children from the community and five surrounding villages, whose demolition Israel's High Court authorized in May. International law prohibits an occupying power from destroying property unless "absolutely necessary" for "military operations."

Israeli authorities have also demolished the homes of families in retaliation for attacks on Israelis allegedly carried out by a family member, a violation of the international humanitarian law prohibition on collective punishment.

Freedom of Movement

Israel maintained onerous restrictions on the movement of Palestinians in the West Bank. OCHA documented 705 permanent obstacles such as checkpoints across the West Bank in July. Israeli-imposed restrictions designed to keep Palestinians far from settlements forced them to take time-consuming detours and restricted their access to their own agricultural land.

Israel's separation barrier, which Israel said it built for security reasons but 85 percent of which falls within the West Bank rather than along the Green Line separating Israeli from Palestinian territory, cuts off Palestinians from their agricultural lands and isolates 11,000 Palestinians on the western side of the barrier who are not allowed to travel to Israel and must cross the barrier to access their own property and other services.

Arbitrary Detention and Detention of Children

As of October 31, according to Prison Services figures, Israeli authorities held 5,426 detainees for "security" offenses, including 3,224 convicted prisoners, 1,465 pretrial detainees, and 481 in administrative detention based on secret evidence without charge or trial. Almost all are Palestinian. Apart from those detained in East Jerusalem, most of the Palestinians detained in the West Bank, including those held for nonviolent expression, were tried in military courts. Those courts have a near-100 percent conviction rate. Israel incarcerates many West Bank and Gaza Palestinian detainees and prisoners inside Israel, violating international humanitarian law requiring that they not be transferred outside the occupied territory and complicating family visits.

As of October 31, Israel was detaining 220 Palestinian children, many suspected of criminal offenses under military law, usually stone-throwing. Israel denied Palestinian children arrested and detained in the West Bank legal protections granted to Israeli children, including settlers, such as protections against nighttime arrests and interrogations without a guardian present. Israeli forces frequently used unnecessary force against children during arrest and physically abused them in custody. In July, Israel released 17-year-old activist Ahed Tamimi after she served an eight-month sentence for slapping a soldier.

Palestinian Authority's Actions in the West Bank

PA security services arrested dozens of journalists, activists and opposition members, tortured detainees, and dispersed nonviolent protests. On June 13, they violently broke up a protest in Ramallah against its policy towards Gaza, arresting dozens of demonstrators, beating some of them in custody before releasing them.

In April, the PA amended a cybercrime law passed the previous year following complaints by civil society groups. The amended law continues to grant the government vast authority to monitor and restrict online activity. The PA also blocked more than two dozen websites affiliated with Hamas and rival Fatah factions.

In March, the PA repealed legal provisions that stopped prosecutions of alleged rapists, or allowed convicted rapists to escape punishment, if they married their victims. The PA also prohibited reducing sentences for serious crimes against women including murder done in the name of "honor." However, discrimination against women in personal status laws and gaps in accountability for domestic violence persisted.

Israel

In July, the Knesset passed the Nation State Law, a law with constitutional status that articulates for Jews alone the right of self-determination, makes it a national priority to build homes for Jews but not others, and revokes the status of Arabic as an official language of Israel. Israeli authorities continued to narrow the space for criticism of its policies toward Palestinians, denying entry into Israel of foreign nationals critical of Israeli policies. In May, Israel announced it was revoking the work visa of a Human Rights Watch official based in Jerusalem, claiming that he supported boycotts of Israel. Human Rights Watch, which takes no position on boycotts of Israel but urges businesses to end their involvement in West Bank settlements, challenged the revocation in a court case that as of early December was still pending. In May, Israeli police beat Jafer Farah, head of Mossawa, an advocacy group for Palestinians, while in custody after participating in a protest, breaking his leg.

Israel demolished homes of Palestinian Bedouin citizens who live in "unrecognized" villages in the Negev claiming that their homes were built illegally, even though most of those villages existed before the state of Israel was established or were created in the 1950s on land that Israel moved them onto.

The Israeli government continued the policy described by the interior minister at the time of making "miserable" the lives of the roughly 40,000 Eritrean and Sudanese asylum seekers present in the country who refused to depart. The government did so through restrictions on movement, work permits, and access to health care. After the UN High Commissioner for Refugees condemned Israel's failure to properly process asylum claims, Israeli authorities in January said they would indefinitely detain thousands of Eritrean and Sudanese men if they refused to leave for Rwanda and Uganda. In March, the High Court confirmed that such a policy would be illegal as neither Rwanda nor Uganda had agreed to receive deportees. In response, Israel released all those detainees whom they were holding on the basis that they had refused deportation.

Key International Actors

In May, the US moved its embassy from Tel Aviv to Jerusalem, which it declared the capital of Israel, triggering Palestinian protests. The US slashed funding to the PA, though it allocated US$60 million in nonlethal assistance to PA security forces, and $3.1 billion in military aid to Israel for the 2018 fiscal year. In August, the US cut all funding to the United Nations Relief and Works Agency (UNRWA)—previously up to $350 million per year—which provides critical services, including education and health care, to children in the West Bank and Gaza.

The European Union called on Israeli authorities not to demolish Khan al-Ahmar and to use restraint in the Gaza protests.

The prosecutor for the International Criminal Court Office is conducting a preliminary examination into the situation in Palestine to determine whether the criteria have been met to merit pursuing a formal investigation. In May, Palestinian authorities formally referred the situation in Palestine to the court's prosecutor.

The global tourism company Airbnb announced it would stop listing properties in Israeli settlements in the occupied West Bank, as part of a new policy to bar listings that contribute to "existing human suffering."

The Office of UN High Commissioner for Human Rights continued its work to establish a database of businesses that have enabled or profited from settlements, which its due to publish before the March 2019 UN Human Rights Council session.

Japan

Japan is a liberal democracy with the world's third largest economy, an established rule of law, and a vibrant civil society. In September, the ruling Liberal Democratic Party again chose Shinzo Abe as its leader, putting him on track to be Japan's longest-serving prime minister.

Japan remains one of only three of the Organisation for Economic Co-operation and Development's 36 member countries that retains the death penalty. It has no law against racial, ethnic, or religious discrimination, or discrimination based on sexual orientation or gender identity, and accepts an extremely small number of refugees each year. Japan also has no national human rights institutions.

Death Penalty

In July, Japan executed by hanging 13 members of Aum Shinrikyo, the group behind the sarin chemical attack in the Tokyo subway in 1995 that killed 13 people and injured thousands. Among those executed was the group's leader, Shoko Asahara. Anti-death penalty advocates have long raised concerns about death row inmates having inadequate access to legal counsel and being notified of their execution only on the day it takes place.

Disability Rights

Persons forcibly sterilized under the Eugenic Protection Act between 1948 and 1996 sued the government for compensation. Under the law, approximately 84,000 persons, mostly with genetic disorders (including at least around 16,500 persons forced to have sterilization surgery), were victimized. In May, a bipartisan committee was established to create a law that is expected to address both compensation and apologies to the victims.

In August, a scandal erupted in major government agencies, including the National Tax Agency and the ministries of justice, foreign affairs, and transport, when officials admitted they had inflated the number of disabled employees they had hired by around 3,700 in an attempt to meet the quota set by the Act on Employment Protection of Persons with Disablities. Prime Minister Abe apologized for the scandal during a parliamentary session in early November.

Women's Rights

In May, Japan passed the first national law that encourages political parties to field an equal number of male and female political candidates during elections.

In August, one of Japan's most prestigious medical universities admitted it had altered female applicants' entrance exam scores to suppress the number of qualifying women. The university had received billions of yen in government subsidies while the school was discriminating against women, a blow to Prime Minister Abe's plans to make Japan a country "where women can shine." In response, the Education Ministry investigated 81 universities, and found other potential cases of discrimination. There is only one comprehensive law in Japan prohibiting sexual discrimination and it applies only to employment.

Over 95 percent of incidents of sexual violence in Japan are not reported to police, according to government figures, partly because discussing rape is perceived to be "embarrassing" in Japan and many victims feel reporting it would not make a difference. In 2017, parliament passed reforms to Japan's rape law, but it still falls far short of international standards. Rather than focusing on consent, the law requires "violence or intimidation" as a basis for prosecution, except when guardians abuse children in their care.

Sexual Orientation and Gender Identity

The Tokyo Municipal Government (TMG) in October passed a LGBT non-discrimination law, which requires the TMG and encourages private organizations such as companies, schools, and private groups to act to address discrimination based on sexual orientation and gender identity.

In doing so, it became the first prefectural level non-discrimination law regarding sexual orientation and gender identity. No such law exists at the national level.

Japan continues to enforce an outdated and discriminatory legal gender recognition law. Transgender people who want to change their legal gender in the family register and on official documents must submit themselves to psychiatric evaluations and diagnosis of "Gender Identity Disorder," as well as surgeries that sterilize them.

Foreign Laborers

Prime Minister Abe is expanding Japan's "Foreign Technical Intern Training Program" to recruit more foreign workers—many from Southeast Asia—amid a chronic labor shortage. The program has drawn criticism for human rights violations, including payment of sub-minimum wages, illegal overtime, forced return of whistleblowers to their home countries, and dangerous or unhygienic working conditions.

"Paradise on Earth" Campaign

Five victims of the "Paradise on Earth" campaign, which recruited Koreans in Japan to North Korea on false premises that North Korea was a "Paradise on Earth" and "anything needed for life including housing, food, clothes are fully guaranteed," sued the North Korean government in a Japanese court in August 2018, part of a larger effort to get the Japanese government to press North Korea harder to let all "Paradise on Earth" victims and relatives leave the country. While approximately 93,000 ethnic Koreans (Zainichi) and Japanese migrated from Japan to North Korea under the program's auspices between 1959 and 1984, authorities never allowed them to return.

Children's Rights

In July, the government notified all relevant local governments to implement the "family-based care" principle of the 2016 Child Welfare Act, which guarantees a family setting, such as adoption and foster care, for children unable to live with their birth parents. Placement in child welfare institutions is limited to cases in which family-based care is "not appropriate," and even in such cases institutions should provide "the best possible family-like settings." The government aims to place more than 75 percent of pre-school children needing alternative care into foster care within the next seven years.

Public scrutiny of the child welfare system intensified after reports that a five-year-old girl was abused and killed by her parents in March. In response, the government revealed emergency measures, including increasing the number of child welfare officers by approximately 2,000 before 2022.

Refugees

Japan's asylum and refugee determination system remains strongly oriented against granting refugee status. In the first half of 2018, the Justice Ministry received 5,586 applications for refugee status largely by people from Asia. The ministry only granted refugee recognition to 22 people, while another 21 asylum seekers were classified as needing humanitarian assistance, allowing them to remain in Japan.

Tokyo 2020 Olympic and Paralympic Games

In June, the Tokyo 2020 Organizing Committee declared its commitment to the United Nations Guiding Principles on Business and Human Rights (UNGPs), becoming the first Olympic host to do so. Under the UNGPs, the organizing committee will need to investigate, know and prevent human rights risks, provide remedy, and be transparent about the entire process.

Foreign Policy

Japan states that it pursues "diplomacy based on the fundamental values of freedom, democracy, basic human rights, and the rule of law." However, some important diplomatic actions were inconsistent with this commitment.

In June, Japan welcomed Myanmar's creation of an "independent commission of inquiry" into abuses by Rohingya militants and Myanmar security forces in late 2017. Establishment of the commission, which includes Japanese former diplomat Kenzo Oshima, was widely seen as an attempt by Myanmar to sideline the UN fact-finding mission examination of the same events and deflect attention from the need for a genuinely independent international investigation mechanism.

Unlike other leading democracies, Japan continued its election assistance to Cambodia, despite the Cambodian government's dissolution of the main opposition party ahead of the July 29 general election, and a severe crackdown on civil society, opposition politicians, and independent media. Japan provided Cambodia ¥800 million (around US$7 million), including funds for Cambodia's biased National Election Committee.

Days before the vote, under increased international pressure not to legitimize a sham election, Tokyo announced it would not deploy an official election observer mission. Unlike several other governments, Japan did not criticize the vote, which left all parliament seats with the ruling party, effectively creating a one-party state.

Jordan

In late May 2018, Jordan's national trade syndicates called a general strike to protest a new income tax law and other austerity policies proposed by the government of then-Prime Minister Hani al-Mulki. The strike developed into largely peaceful mass street protests across the country, leading to the resignation of al-Mulki on June 4 and the appointment of Omar al-Razzaz as the new prime minister.

Jordan continued to violate human rights, including restrictions on free expression, free assembly, and women's rights. Bassel Tarawneh, Jordan's governmental human rights coordinator, facilitated government interaction with local and international nongovernmental organizations (NGOs) and held open consultation sessions on human rights issues.

Freedom of Expression

Jordanian law criminalizes speech deemed critical of the king, foreign countries, government officials and institutions, and Islam, as well as speech considered to defame others.

On January 17, authorities detained Omar al-Mahrama and Shadi al-Zinati, editor and editor-in-chief respectively of the Jfranews website, over an article the website published which accused the minister of finance of tax evasion. The editors were released on bail on January 18.

In 2018, Jordan's cabinet sent for parliamentary approval controversial amendments to the country's 2015 Electronic Crimes Law that criminalize hate speech, defining it vaguely as "any word or action that incites discord or religious, sectarian, ethnic, or regional strife or discrimination between individuals or groups." The amendments could stifle free expression online by branding controversial views as "hate speech." They require parliamentary approval and the king's endorsement to become law.

Freedom of Association and Assembly

In 2018, Jordan's public prosecutor pursued charges against Nidal Mansour, director of the Center for Defending Freedom of Journalists (CDFJ), a regional media freedom organization, over the organization's receipt of foreign funding and financial irregularities. In June, a lower court convicted Mansour and sentenced him to one year in prison and a fine of 200 Jordanian Dinars (US$282), but in November an appeals court threw out the lower court ruling and cleared Mansour and CDFJ of any wrongdoing. The group works on behalf of journalists detained across the region and hosts annual workshops and events on media freedom.

Since the amended Public Gatherings Law took effect in March 2011, Jordanians no longer require government permission to hold public meetings or demonstrations. However, organizations and venues continued to seek permission from Jordan's Interior Ministry to host public meetings and events. In some cases, the ministry cancelled public events without explanation.

Refugees and Migrants

Between 2011 and 2018, over 670,000 persons from Syria had sought refuge in Jordan, according to the United Nations High Commissioner for Refugees (UNHCR). Over 85 percent of Syrians lived outside refugee camps. In 2018, Jordan did not permit Syrians to enter the country to seek asylum but made an exception for over 400 Syrian White Helmet rescue workers and their dependents to enter Jordan in July to await resettlement in a third country.

On March 4, 2018, Jordanian authorities began to regularize the status of many Syrian refugees who had been living in towns and cities without permits, offering thousands of vulnerable refugees protection from arrest for being outside refugee camps illegally and increasing their access to jobs, aid, and education. On January 24, however, the government revoked the eligibility for subsidized health care for Syrians living outside refugee camps.

Jordanian officials stated that the country did not receive enough international financial assistance in 2018 to cope with the effects of the refugee crisis on its public infrastructure, especially in the areas of public education and health. The UNHCR Jordan office, which coordinates the refugee response, said that by November it had raised only 36 percent of its US$1 billion budget goal for 2018. As of September, UNICEF announced that because of an $8.6 million shortfall in its requested budget for 2018, it had to cut back a program that subsidized school-related costs to only 10,000 Syrian refugee children out of about 55,000 in need.

HUMAN
RIGHTS
WATCH

"I Just Want Him to Live
Like Other Jordanians"
Treatment of Non-Citizen Children of Jordanian Mothers

In 2018, authorities continued the implementation of the Jordan Compact, which aims to improve the livelihoods of Syrian refugees by granting new legal work opportunities and improving the education sector. By 2018, labor authorities had issued or renewed at least 160,000 work permits for Syrians. Most professions, however, remained closed to non-Jordanians, and many Syrians continued to work infornal sector without labor protections.

In January, Jordanian authorities allowed one delivery of humanitarian aid by crane to the tens of thousands of Syrians at Rukban, an unorganized camp along Jordan's border with Syria. According to UN satellite analysis, the number of shelters at Rukban increased by 12 percent between January and July. The Syrians there face limited access to food, water, and medical assistance. Authorities had previously announced in October that they would no longer allow aid to reach the camps from Jordan and did not allow further deliveries after January.

Women's and Girls' Rights

Jordan's personal status code remains discriminatory, despite a 2010 amendment that included widening women's access to divorce and child custody. Marriages between Muslim women and non-Muslim men, for instance, are not recognized.

Article 9 of Jordan's nationality law does not allow Jordanian women married to non-Jordanian spouses to pass on their nationality to their spouse and children. In 2014, Jordanian authorities issued a cabinet decision purporting to ease restrictions on non-citizen children of Jordanian women's access to key economic and social rights, but the easing of restrictions has fallen short of expectations. In September, authorities announced that they would waive the five-year residency requirement for mothers of non-citizen children to benefit from the 2014 cabinet decision, and that the special ID card for non-citizen children of Jordanian women would be considered a valid ID card.

Article 98 of Jordan's penal code, amended in 2017, states that perpetrators of crimes "against women" cannot receive mitigated sentences. The provision leaves a loophole, however, under article 340 of the same law, which allows for mitigated sentences for those who murder their spouses discovered committing adultery.

In July, authorities opened a new shelter for women at risk of "honor"-related violence from family members. The Minister of Social Development announced that 29 women held in "protective custody" in Amman's Juwieda Prison would be "gradually" moved into the new shelter.

Criminal Justice System and Police Accountability

By September, authorities had not carried out any executions in 2018, but Jordan's National Center for Human Rights (NCHR) reported that there were 128 people on death row by the end of 2017.

Authorities detained five policemen from the Criminal Investigations Directorate (CID) after a Jordanian man died in custody on June 8. According to the medical report he had "bruising injuries on different areas of his body, especially in the area of his testicles." On June 13, Jordan's Public Security Directorate (PSD) denied reports that a man died in Birayn prison as a result of beating, stating that his death was from natural causes.

The "torture" trial of five policemen in the Police Court relating to the September 2015 death in detention of 49-year-old Omar al-Nasr remained ongoing as of November 2018.

In January, the NCHR reported that it had carried out the first-ever unannounced visit to the General Intelligence Directorate (GID)'s detention center in Amman to monitor conditions for detainees, but the NCHR did not disclose the results of its visit.

Local governors continued to use provisions of the Crime Prevention Law of 1954 to place individuals in administrative detention for up to one year, in circumvention of the Criminal Procedure Law. The NCHR reported that 34,952 persons were administratively detained in 2017, some for longer than one year, marking an increase of over 4,000 from the number of administrative detainees in 2016.

Key International Actors

On February 14, 2018, the United States and Jordan signed a new Memorandum of Understanding on US foreign assistance to Jordan. The agreement commits the US to provide $1.275 billion in aid each year over a five year period for a total of $6.375 billion. The US did not publicly criticize human rights violations in Jordan in 2018, except in annual reports.

Officials feared that the US administration's cuts in $300 million in aid to UNRWA, the UN agency that provides education and healthcare to Palestinian refugees, could leave thousands of children out of school in Jordan's 10 Palestinian refugee camps.

Jordan's King Abdullah II rejected an alleged US-sponsored proposal to join the Palestinian West Bank to Jordan as a "confederation" as part of a peace plan, calling the proposal a "red line."

In 2018, Jordan appealed a December 2017 decision by International Criminal Court judges that it had failed to uphold its obligations as a member of the court by not arresting Sudanese President Omar al-Bashir when he visited Jordan in March 2017 for the Arab League summit.

Jordan is a member of the Saudi-led coalition fighting the Houthis in Yemen. Human Rights Watch has documented 87 apparently unlawful coalition attacks in Yemen, some of which may be war crimes, which have killed nearly 1,000 civilians. Jordan did not respond to Human Rights Watch inquiries regarding what role, if any, it has played in unlawful attacks in Yemen and if it was undertaking investigations into the role its own forces played in any of these attacks.

Kazakhstan

There was no meaningful improvement to Kazakhstan's poor human rights record in 2018. Authorities did not allow peaceful protests that criticized government policies. Trade unions remained restricted from freely determining their structures. Despite government promises to amend the 2014 Trade Union Law, it remained unchanged. Some activists were released from prison, but politically motivated prosecutions continued. Rights activist Maks Bokaev remained incarcerated. A court banned an opposition movement as "extremist" and authorities targeted its supporters. Impunity for torture and ill-treatment in detention persisted. Free speech was suppressed, and independent journalists harassed or prosecuted for their work.

Civil Society

Maks Bokaev, who was imprisoned for peacefully protesting proposed land code amendments in May 2016, continued to serve a wrongful five-year sentence. In September, authorities transferred Bokaev to a prison in Aktobe, 1,000 kilometers closer to his home. In April, authorities released on parole Talgat Ayan, an activist jailed with Bokaev in 2016.

In June, Vadim Kuramshin, an activist imprisoned for extortion, became eligible for parole after a court shortened his 12-year sentence by three years. On August 17, he was released.

Authorities continued to misuse the vague and overbroad criminal charge of "inciting discord" against outspoken critics. According to the Prosecutor General's Office, 57 people were charged with "inciting discord" in the first half of 2018. In March, authorities charged the Shymkent-based activist, Ardak Ashim, with "inciting discord" for her critical social media posts, and put her into court-sanctioned psychiatric detention. In May, a court ruled to excuse her from criminal liability and freed her. In April, police closed the criminal case against atheist writer Aleksandr Kharlamov, pending since 2013 on bogus charges of "inciting religious discord." Kharlamov sued authorities for abuse during his forced detention in a psychiatric facility. On July 10, a court granted him compensation worth approximately US$2,700.

In July, authorities in Pavlodar opened a criminal investigation on charges of "disseminatining false information" against the human rights activist Elena Semenova, and placed her under house arrest. Semenova had earlier in July spoken to European Parliament members in Strasbourg about prison conditions. At time of writing, the investigation is ongoing. On October 8, authorities prevented Semenova from traveling to Strasbourg for a meeting with European officials. On October 9, assailants attacked her house with Molotov cockails.

In September, a court ruled to transfer Natalya Ulasik, a government critic whom a court had found to be mentally incompetent in October 2016, from forced psychiatric detention to "general regime" conditions, allowing her weekend home visitations.

In July, authorities charged Baurzhan Azanov, a lawyer, with "disseminating false information" after Azanov took up a high-profile case of a sexual assault on a seven-year-old child. Kazakhstan's Ombudsman's Office issued a statement expressing concern about the "legitimacy of initiating a criminal case against a lawyer in the exercise of his professional rights and obligations." The case was dropped in October, on grounds that no crime had been committed.

Freedom of Media

Independent and opposition journalists continued to face harassment, arbitrary detention, and spurious criminal prosecutions. Authorities blocked websites, including social media. Between January and July, AdilSoz, a local media watchdog, recorded 18 detentions, arrests, convictions, or limits on freedoms of journalists. In March, a court denied parole to Aset Mataev, an imprisoned journalist, despite his eligibility after serving one-third of his six-year prison sentence. In April, problematic media and information law amendments entered into force.

In March, the Almaty City Prosecutor's Office opened a criminal investigation on "disseminating false information," into Forbes Kazakhstan and Ratel.kz, an analytical news portal, and interrogated journalists. In March, an Almaty court preliminarily approved blocking Ratel.kz and its affiliated websites. At time of writing, both cases were ongoing.

Arrest and Harassment of Opposition Members

In March, a court banned the unregistered opposition movement Democratic Choice of Kazakhstan (DVK), finding the group's activities "extremist." Authorities increased harassment of perceived or actual DVK supporters. Between March and November, authorities prosecuted at least 12 individuals for allegedly supporting or financing the DVK. Murat Tungishbaev, an activist wrongfully extradited from Kyrgyzstan in August, was charged in April with financing DVK. The investigation is ongoing. Tungishbaev is in pre-trial detention in Almaty. In August, Tungishbaev's wife expressed concern that authorities were not providing Tungishbaev adequate medical treatment for his eye, which was operated on before his arrest.

Torture

Despite government claims to have zero-tolerance for torture, impunity for torture, and ill-treatment of prisoners and suspects remained the norm. Seven years after violent clashes brought an end to an extended oil sector labor strike in Zhanaozen, Kazakh authorities have failed to credibly investigate the torture allegations made by those subsequently detained and prosecuted.

In early 2018, Iskander Yerimbetov, the businessmen tied to Mukhtar Ablyazov, an exiled former banker and government critic, credibly alleged ill-treatment and torture in detention. After public outcry, including petitions by human rights groups to Kazakhstan's prosecutor general, authorities opened a preliminary investigation. In May, the Almaty Prosecutor's Office claimed they found no evidence of a crime and closed the case. In October, Yerimbetov was sentenced to seven years' imprisonment on charges of large-scale fraud.

Freedom of Assembly

Authorities routinely deny permits for peaceful protests against government policies. Police break up even single-person unauthorized protests, and arbitrarily detain organizers and participants. On May 10, police detained dozens of people in cities across the country peacefully protesting against torture and politically motivated imprisonment. In June, a court in Taldikorgan sentenced a man to three days' arrest for his unsanctioned protest against police abuse.

Freedom of Religion

In September, parliament adopted government-proposed amendments to the religion law, which would increase restrictions and sanctions on religious teaching, proselytizing, and publications. At time of writing, the amendments were pending final adoption in parliament. Rights and religious groups expressed concern about the amendments.

In the first half of 2018, authorities brought 79 administrative cases against individuals or religious communities, leading to fines or short-term bans on worship, in violation of their right to freedom of religion or belief, according to the religious freedom watchdog Forum 18. Three other individuals were criminally convicted on charges of "organizing activities of a banned religious organization" and received three-year prison sentences.

Teimur Akhmedov, the Jehovah's Witness imprisoned in May 2017, was released in April after a presidential pardon.

Labor Rights

Authorities took no meaningful steps to restore freedom of association rights for independent trades unions in 2018. The Confederation of Independent Trade Unions of Kazakhstan (KNPRK) remained closed. In May, Nurbek Kushakbaev and Amin Eleusinov, trade union activists imprisoned in 2017 on politically motivated charges, were released on parole, but remained banned from trade union activities. Larisa Kharkova, the former KNPRK president, similarly remained banned from leading trade unions.The Ministry of Justice three times refused to register the Congress of Independent Trade Unions of Kazakhstan (formerly KNPRK). In September, authorities in Shymkent opened a criminal investigation on charges of embezzlement against trade union leader Erlan Baltabay. The investigation was ongoing at time of writing.

Kazakhstan's labor rights record came under increased scrutiny in 2018. In May, a high-level tri-partite International Labour Organization (ILO) mission visited Kazakhstan. Also in May, the International Trade Union Confederation filed a complaint before the ILO. In June, the United States Trade Representative (USTR) considered a complaint against Kazakhstan filed by the American Federation of Labor and Congress of Industrial Organizations, which claimed that Kazakhstan was violating international labor rights standards, and urged the USTR to suspend trade benefits. The outcome of each complaint was pending at time of writing.

Sexual Orientation and Gender Identity

In March, Feminita, an Almaty-based lesbian, gay, bisexual, and transgender (LGBT) group, issued a report that documented abuses against LGBT women in Kazakhstan, including insults, humiliation, harassment, illegal dismissals, and forced resignations. In August, Zhanar Sekerbaeva, a Feminita co-chair, was charged with petty hooliganism after participating in a photoshoot aimed at destigmatizing menstruation, and fined.

Children with Disabilities

Despite commitments to expand inclusive education, whereby children with and without disabilities study together, progress is slow. Many children with disabilities remain segregated in special schools, or isolated at home with little or no quality education. Children with disabilities in mainstream schools typically study in separate classrooms and may face stigma and discrimination.

Asylum Seekers and Refugees

In July, a court convicted an ethnic Kazakh Chinese citizen, Sayragul Sauytbai, a primary school teacher who spoke publicly about China's abusive "political re-education" camps in Xinjiang, of illegal border crossing, but did not deport her to China. Sauytbai had fled China in early 2018. In October, Kazakhstan denied her asylum.

Key International Actors

In January, President Nursultan Nazarbaev met US President Donald Trump in Washington. Public readouts of the meeting indicate there was no discussion of human rights by either president. In its 2017 annual human rights report, published in April, the US identified arbitrary arrest and detention, and restrictive trade union registration requirements among Kazakhstan's notable human rights problems.

330

In December 2017, the European Parliament ratified the EU-Kazakhstan Enhanced Partnership and Cooperation Agreement, signed in December 2015, and called on Kazakhstan to end harassment of journalists, activists, trade union leaders, and human rights defenders, release those unfairly jailed, and revise its Trade Union Law and Labour Code.

The Extractive Industries Transparency Initiative, a coalition of governments, companies, and nongovernmental groups, granted Kazakhstan "meaningful progress" status in February, missing the opportunity to push for improvements in the restrictive space for civil society.

Kenya

Lack of accountability for serious human rights violations, perpetrated largely by security forces, remains a major concern in 2018. The 2017 presidential election period saw abusive police operations in opposition strongholds, with police beating and shooting to death at least 100 opposition protesters and by-standers. Many women and girls were raped and sexually harassed by police during these operations.

A March 2018 peace deal between President Uhuru Kenyatta and main opposition leader, Raila Odinga, eased political tensions, but at time of writing, authorities had not taken any significant steps to ensure accountablity for police brutality.

Kenyatta on numerous occasions publicly promised to respect freedom of expression and media. However, the working environment for journalists and activists remains hostile. In 2017 and early 2018, police threatened journalists and bloggers, arrested and detained journalists, and shut down at least three television stations.

Abuses by Security Forces

Human Rights Watch research found that police and pro-government militia were responsible for the deaths of more than 100 opposition supporters in Nairobi and western Kenya during elections protests. Although these killings and other abuses have been well documented by human rights groups, Kenyan authorities have rarely investigated them.

In November 2017, the Independent Policing Oversight Authority (IPOA), a civilian police oversight institution, said it had investigated at least two cases relating to the 2017 elections, but could not identify the killers due to lack of evidence. IPOA recommended a public inquest for the killing of six-month-old Samantha Pendo in Kisumu, and compensations for the families of baby Pendo and nine-year-old Stephanie Moraa, who witnesses said was shot by police as she stood on the balcony of her home in Nairobi.

In July, the director of public prosecutions charged an administration police officer with the killing of a Meru University student, Evans Njoroge, following investigations by IPOA. The officer was awaiting trial at time of writing. Evans was shot on March 10, 2018, at close range at the back of his head during protests by Meru university students in eastern Kenya over poor management of the institution. Such investigations were few and far between, as authorities have overwhelmingly failed to investigate and prosecute cases of widespread police killings across the country.

In early 2018, investigations by Kenyan human rights organizations, found that Kenya Forest service officers used excessive force against members of the Sengwer, an indigenous community in the Rift Valley region. Authorities forcefully evicted them from Embobut forest in late 2017 in an effort to preserve the Mau water catchment area.

Freedom of Expression and Media

Despite public promises by President Kenyatta to safeguard press freedom, police and senior state officials attacked and threatened journalists writing on "sensitive issues" such as elections, corruption and security.

Around the 2017 elections, police and other government officials threatened and intimidated journalists and bloggers. In early 2018, the Communications Authority of Kenya switched off at least three television stations – KTN, NTV, Citizen and Inooro – for defying government order against covering Odinga's mock swearing in ceremony on January 30.

On January 6, David Mugonyi, the spokesperson of Deputy President William Ruto, threatened to have a *Daily Nation* journalist, Justus Wanga, sacked for a story that exposed a rift between Kenyatta and Ruto over cabinet appointments.

On March 26, Kenyan media reported that anti-riot police physically attacked journalists, including Citizen TV's Stephen Letoo and NTV cameraman, Robert Gichira, as they reported on the airport scuffle that ensued during deportation of opposition lawyer, Miguna Miguna. One of the police officers slapped,Sophia Wanuna of KTN News. Kenyatta's director of digital communications, Dennis Itumbi, later that day tweeted to commend the police officers for "acting firm" at the airport.

On May 16, Kenyatta signed a new law on cybercrime that criminalized "false or fictitious" news and imposed hefty fines. Although the High court later struck down that provision as unconstitutional, other provisions introduce new offences and harsh penalties, thus stifling freedom of expression and media.

Threats to Activists and Political Opposition

Human rights organizations and activists critical of the government, especially those working on accountability, security forces abuses, and elections, continue to face threats and restrictions, including on freedom to assemble. Human Rights Watch found that between August 2017 and March 2018, police and other officials targeted at least 15 activists and victims of police brutality in Nairobi and the western county of Kisumu. They faced threats of arrest, warnings not to post information on the internet about police brutality during the elections period, home and office raids, and confiscation of laptops and other equipment.

In September, an activist who documented police brutality in Nyalenda, Kisumu said that police warned him by phone not to share photos and video clips of the violence and accused him of tarnishing their image. Police raided his office in October and ordered him to hand over photos and videos of police abuses during the election period.

On January 30, authorities designated the National Resistance Movement (NRM), an activist wing of Odinga's NASA coalition, a criminal group. This step set the stage for a crackdown on politicians and lawyers who took part in Odinga's oath ceremony, with arbitrary arrests and detentions and, in at least one case, deportation.

In February, 2018, the authorities stripped opposition lawyer, Miguna Miguna, of Kenyan citizenship and forcefully deported him to Canada despite numerous court orders to restore Miguna's citizenship, and rescind the decision to deport him. The authorities arrested and charged other opposition politicians Tom Kajwang, Babu Owino and George Aladwa with participating in an illegal assembly and further revoked passports for over 100 opposition legislators.

Following Supreme Court nullification of August presidential election, senior government officials, including Kenyatta threatened and intimidated judges.

The government continues to ignore civil society appeals to implement the Public Benefits Organizations (PBO) Act, 2013, signed into law by then-President Mwai Kibaki in February 2013 to streamline the regulation of the NGO sector and enhance accountability. Instead, the Kenyatta administration twice attempted to introduce amendments to the law restricting the work of NGOs that receive more than 15 percent of their funding from foreign sources. The first amendments were rejected by parliament in December 2014 and the second were shelved in the lead up to the 2017 elections, but there remains the possibility of the authorities reintroducing the amendments.

Lack of Accountability for Rape and Sexual Violence

Human Rights Watch documented rape and sexual harassment during police operations in western Kenya and Nairobi during the elections period.

Most women said they were raped by policemen or men in uniform, many of whom carried guns, batons, teargas carnisters, whips and wore anti riot gear. In at least one case, a girl died after being raped. A 27 year old woman, interviewed, who had given birth on August 27 was raped four days later. Many women and girls said they suffered incapacitating physical injury or experienced other health consequences.

Although both Kenya Police Service and IPOA, had promised to investigate these cases, there has been little progress in holding the perpetrators to account. Many survivors did not receive post-rape medical care or counselling support.

Threats to Livelihoods and Lake Turkana

Dropping water levels in Kenya's Lake Turkana following the development of dams and plantations in Ethiopia's lower Omo Valley continues to threaten the livelihoods of half-a-million indigenous people in Ethiopia and Kenya. In June, United Nations Educational, Scientific and Cultural Organization (UNESCO) placed Lake Turkana's National Parks on the list of endangered World Heritage Sites. The UNESCO's World Heritage Committee expressed concern about the "disruptive effect of Ethiopia's Gibe III dam on the flow and ecosystem of Lake Turkana".

Sexual Orientation and Gender Identity

Kenya punishes consensual same-sex relations with up to 14 years in prison. A constitutional challenge to the ban remains pending before the High Court. In

"They Just Want to Silence Us"
Abuses Against Environmental Activists at Kenya's Coast Region

HUMAN
RIGHTS
WATCH

National
Coalition
of Human Rights Defenders - Kenya

October, a court ordered the seven-day suspension of a ban that the Kenya Film Classification Board had slapped on "Rafiki," a love story about two young women whose fathers are political opponents.

Key International Actors

Kenya continues to play a major role in east Africa and has maintained close political and economic ties with the United States, China and European nations.

While there are no pending International Criminal Court (ICC) cases concerning alleged crimes against humanity committed during the 2007-2008 post-election violence in Kenya, the government has yet to surrender three persons wanted by the ICC on allegations of witness tampering.

As in 2007, the contested presidential elections in August 2017 attracted global concern. In January 2018, the UN secretary general Antonio Guterres dispatched former Nigeria president, Olusegun Obasanjo, to meet Kenyatta and Odinga, in a bid to de-escalate the political tension. On March 9, Kenyatta and Odinga agreed to work together to ease the tension.

Between October and March 2018, US Ambassador to Kenya Robert Godec, and other heads of missions in Kenya, publicly urged both the ruling Jubilee party and Odinga's NASA alliance to take measures to end the violence and political tension following the disputed presidential election.

Civil society groups criticized diplomats for siding with the ruling party by urging the opposition to concede defeat and end protests, and for failing to condemn what they described as the manipulation of the electoral process in favour of Kenyatta.

Kuwait

Kuwaiti authorities continue to use provisions in the constitution, the national security law, and other legislation to restrict free speech, prosecute dissidents, and stifle political dissent.

In July, Kuwait's Court of Cassation convicted 16 people and sentenced them to between two to three-and-a-half years in prison with labor for storming parliament during a 2011 protest.

Despite recent reforms, migrant workers do not have adequate legal protections, and remain vulnerable to abuse, forced labor, and deportation for minor infractions.

Kuwait continues to exclude thousands of stateless people, known as Bidun, from full citizenship despite their longstanding roots in Kuwaiti territory.

Unlike many of its Gulf neighbors, Kuwait continues to allow Human Rights Watch access to the country and engages in constructive dialogue with the organization on a range of human rights issues.

Migrant Workers

Two-thirds of Kuwait's population is comprised of migrant workers, who remain vulnerable to abuse despite recent reforms. In January, the Philippines temporarily banned Filipinos from migrating to Kuwait for work, pending an investigation into the deaths of seven domestic workers. In May, the two countries agreed on additional legal protection for Filipino workers in Kuwait.

In 2015, Kuwait issued a new standard contract for migrant workers, and a 2016 administrative decision allowed some migrant workers to transfer their sponsorship to a new employer after three years of work, without their employer's consent. However, these reforms do not include migrant domestic workers.

In 2015, the National Assembly passed a law granting domestic workers the right to a weekly day off, 30 days of annual paid leave, a 12-hour working day with rest, and an end-of-service benefit of one month salary for each year of work at the end of the contract, among other rights. In 2016 and 2017, the Interior Ministry passed implementing regulations for the law, and mandated that employers must pay overtime compensation. The ministry also issued a decree establishing a minimum wage of KD60 (US$200) for domestic workers.

Protections for domestic workers are still weaker than those in Kuwait's labor law. The domestic worker law also falls short by failing to set out enforcement mechanisms, such as inspections of working conditions in households. The law also does not set out sanctions against employers who confiscate passports or fail to provide adequate housing, food, and medical expenses, work breaks, or weekly rest days.

Migrant domestic workers remain vulnerable to abuse and exploitation and can be arrested for "absconding" from an employer largely because of the kafala system, which ties their visas to their employers.

Freedom of Expression

Kuwaiti authorities have invoked several provisions in the constitution, penal code, Printing and Publication Law, Misuse of Telephone Communications and Bugging Devices Law, Public Gatherings Law, and National Unity Law to prosecute journalists, politicians and activists for criticizing the emir, the government, religion, and rulers of neighboring countries in blogs or on Twitter, Facebook, or other social media.

In July, Kuwait's Court of Cassation convicted 16 people and sentenced them to from two to three-and-a-half years in prison with labor for storming parliament during a 2011 protest.

Prosecutions for protected speech are ongoing in Kuwaiti courts. Kuwaiti officials and activists reported that many, if not most, initial complaints in these cases are filed by individuals, underscoring the need to further amend broadly written or overly vague Kuwaiti laws to ensure adequate protections for speech and expression.

In 2016, Kuwait amended the election law to bar all those convicted for "insulting" God, the prophets, or the emir from running for office or voting in elections. The law is likely to bar some opposition members of parliament from contesting or voting in future elections.

The Cybercrime Law, which went into effect in 2016, includes far-reaching restrictions on internet-based speech, such as prison sentences, and fines for insulting religion, religious figures and the emir.

Treatment of Minorities

Kuwait has a population of about 100,000 stateless persons, known as Bidun, whose predicament dates back to the foundation of the Kuwaiti state.

After an initial registration period for citizenship ended in 1960, authorities shifted Bidun citizenship claims to administrative committees that for decades have avoided resolving the claims. Authorities claim that many Bidun are "illegal residents" who deliberately destroyed evidence of another nationality in order to receive benefits.

Members of the Bidun community have taken to the streets to protest the government's failure to address their citizenship claims, despite government warnings that Bidun should not gather in public. Article 12 of the 1979 Public Gatherings Law bars non-Kuwaitis from participating in public gatherings.

Terrorism and Security

In 2017, Kuwait's Constitutional Court found that an overbroad 2015 law that had required all Kuwaiti citizens and residents to provide DNA samples to authorities violated the right to privacy. The law was introduced after the June 2015 suicide bombing of the Imam Sadiq Mosque. Authorities reported to local media at the time that anyone failing to comply with the law would be subject to sanctions, including cancelling their passports and a possible travel ban. In 2016, the United Nations Human Rights Committee found the law imposed "unnecessary and disproportionate restrictions on the right to privacy."

In May, Kuwaiti authorities arrested and extrajudicially deported dual Qatari-Saudi national Nawaf al-Rasheed, a poet and university student who lives in Qatar, to Saudi Arabia on unclear grounds, ostensibly "under bilateral mutual security arrangements."

Women's Rights, Sexual Orientation, and Gender Identity

Kuwaiti personal status law, which applies to Sunni Muslims who make up the majority of Kuwaitis, discriminates against women. For example, some women require a male guardian to conclude their marriage contracts; women must apply to the courts for a divorce on limited grounds, unlike men who can unilaterally divorce their wives; and women can lose custody of their children if they remarry someone outside the former husband's family. Men can marry up to four wives, without the permission or knowledge of the other wife or wives. A man can prohibit his wife from working if it is deemed to negatively affect the family interests. The rules that apply to Shia Muslims also discriminate against women.

Kuwait has no laws prohibiting domestic violence or marital rape. A 2015 law establishing family courts set up a center to deal with domestic violence cases, but requires the center to prioritize reconciliation over protection for domestic violence survivors. Article 153 of the Kuwaiti penal code stipulates that a man who finds his mother, wife, sister or daughter in the act of adultery and kills them is punished by either a small fine or no more than three years in prison. Article 182 also allows an abductor who uses force, threat or deception with the intention to kill, harm, rape, prostitute, or extort a victim to avoid punishment if he marries the victim with her guardian's permission. Kuwaiti women married to non-Kuwaitis, unlike Kuwaiti men, cannot pass citizenship to their children or spouses.

Adultery and extramarital intercourse are criminalized, and same-sex relations between men are punishable by up to seven years in prison. Transgender people can be arrested under a 2007 penal code provision that prohibits "imitating the opposite sex in any way."

Death Penalty

Kuwait maintains the death penalty for non-violent offenses, including drug-related charges. In 2017, it carried out seven executions by hanging, the first executions since 2013. Human Rights Watch has documented due process violations in Kuwait's criminal justice system that have made it difficult for defendants to get a fair trial, including in capital cases.

Key International Actors

Kuwait joined the Saudi-led coalition that began attacking Houthi forces in Yemen on March 26, 2015, with media reporting that Kuwait had deployed 15 aircraft. Human Rights Watch has documented about 90 apparently unlawful coalition attacks in Yemen, some of which may amount to war crimes, that repeatedly hit markets, schools, and hospitals. The coalition's investigative mechanism has failed to meet international standards regarding transparency, impartiality, and independence. Kuwait has not responded to Human Rights Watch inquiries regarding what role, if any, it has played in unlawful attacks in Yemen and if it was undertaking investigations into the role its own forces played in any of these attacks.

Kyrgyzstan

Long-term human rights concerns persisted in the first year of Soronbai Jeen-bekov's presidency, even as blatant attacks on media freedoms became less fre-quent, and the president appeared to seek more constructive engagement with civil society. Violence against women, including bride-kidnapping, and impunity for torture persisted. Kyrgyzstan has not released the wrongfully imprisoned human rights defender Azimjon Askarov. As authorities have stepped up counter-extremism measures, criminalizing possession of extremist materials, the overbroad definition of extremism, and breaches of due-process have led to human rights violations. In September, Kyrgyzstan's prime minister signed a de-cree initiating ratification of the United Nations Convention on the Rights of Per-sons with Disabilities (CRPD), which Kyrgyzstan signed in 2011.

Access to Justice

Eight years after the June 2010 interethnic violence, victims continued to wait for justice. Ethnic Uzbeks were disproportionately affected by the violence, which left more than 400 dead and destroyed thousands of homes, and was followed by numerous cases of arbitrary detention, ill-treatment, and torture. Authorities did not review torture-tainted convictions delivered in the aftermath of the June 2010 events.

In its May 2018 concluding observations, the UN Committee on the Elimination of all forms of Discrimination (CERD) noted with concern "the persistence of … tensions, notably between the Kyrgyz majority and the Uzbek minority" in Kyr-gyzstan, and cautioned that the government's official inter-ethnic relations pol-icy "focused on creating a national identity that is not explicitly inclusive of all ethnicities and may tend to reignite past conflicts."

Civil Society

Kyrgyzstan continued to ignore its obligation to fulfill a 2016 UN Human Rights Committee (HRC) decision to release the imprisoned human rights defender, Az-imjon Askarov. In May, the CERD "expressed concern about the State party's con-tinuing failure to restore the rights of Azimjan Askarov."

In early 2018, five human rights organizations discovered that two of their reports, a 2015 report on labor migrants submitted to the UN Committee on the Rights of Migrant Workers and "A Chronical of Violence," detailing the June 2010 violence, published in 2012, had been included on a government list of banned "extremist" material following a January 2017 court ruling. The court also banned ADC Memorial, a Brussels-based rights organization and co-author of one of the reports, from conducting activities in Kyrgyzstan. In October, Kyrgyzstan's Surpreme court overturned the ruling and returned the case for consideration to a lower court.

A July meeting with Kyrgyzstan's president gave rights defenders the opportunity to directly present key rights concerns. Activists spoke about domestic violence, limits on freedom of expression, the entry bans on Chris Rickleton, an Agence-France Presse journalist, and Mihra Rittmann, Human Rights Watch Central Asia senior researcher, among many issues. Defenders present said that President Jeenbekov promised to follow up on several of these issues.

Freedom of Media

In February and May, Kyrgyzstan's current and former presidents withdrew their respective claims to significant damages that courts had awarded in unfounded defamation lawsuits against journalists in 2017, somewhat lessening the impact of the 2017 media crackdown. President Jeenbekov withdrew his claim to compensation only after Kabay Karabekov, the journalist he sued, issued a formal apology. In June, travel bans imposed in 2017 on journalists Narynbek Idinov and Dina Maslova, and rights defender Cholpon Djakupova, were lifted.

Prosecutors in April dropped charges of "illegal receipt of commercial secrets" and "disclosing secret commercial information" in the criminal case against freelance journalist Elnura Alkanova. Charges were brought against Alkanov in 2017 after the Moscow-based Ferghana News, an independent news website, published her investigative reports on alleged corruption in the sale of government-owned prime real estate.

In February, prosecutors brought charges of "disseminating false information" against satirist poet Temirlan Ormukov, whose writings were critical of the former president. The case was ongoing at time of writing.

Terrorism and Counterterrorism

The government continued counterterrorism crackdowns following deadly attacks abroad that investigators link to armed extremists of Central Asian origin. At least 358 people have been convicted in Kyrgyzstan since 2010 for possessing videos, literature, and other material alleged to fall under a broad and vague definition of extremism, many in cases where prosecutors presented no evidence that suspects intended to incite violence or distribute the material. One hundred of those convictions were handed down during the first eight months of 2018. Prosecutors opened 174 additional criminal cases involving possession of extremist material during that period. Suspects in extremism-related investigations have alleged abuses such as planting of evidence, beatings to extract confessions, or payoffs.

Violence Against Women

Impunity for widespread domestic violence persists, despite a 2017 domestic violence law that mandates police and judicial response to domestic violence and guarantees greater legal protections for victims. In July, the Prosecutor General's Office commented in the media that "in the last two years" it had registered more than 9,000 cases of violence against women and children and had opened 5,456 administrative cases and 784 criminal cases.

In May, 18-year-old Burulai Turdaaly Kyzy was stabbed to death in a police station by a man who had kidnapped her for marriage. In response, UN agencies in Kyrgyzstan called on authorities "to take all appropriate measures to stop [bride kidnapping, forced marriage, and child religious marriages] and fulfil its domestic legislation and international treaties." Twenty-three law enforcement officers were sanctioned in the case, including five who were fired. Prosecutors charged the perpetrator and an accomplice with "forcing a woman to marry," and brought an additional murder charge against the perpetrator. Their trial was ongoing at time of writing.

The UN Committee on the Elimination of Discrimination against Women found after an inquiry published in September into "bride kidnapping" that a "culture of abduction, rape and forced marriage violates women's rights in Kyrgyzstan," and called on Kyrgyzstan "to strengthen its legislation and law enforcement, in

HUMAN
RIGHTS
WATCH

"We Live in Constant Fear"
Possession of Extremist Material in Kyrgyzstan

particular by preventing, investigating, punishing and providing reparation for all crimes of abduction and related sexual violence."

Torture

Impunity for ill-treatment and torture remains the norm, with criminal cases into allegations of ill-treatment or torture rare, and investigations and trials delayed or ineffective. On June 25, the International Day to Support Victims of Torture, at national anti-torture consultations hosted by the National Center for the Prevention of Torture, the prosecutor general's office reported that it had registered 418 cases of torture in 2017, and brought charges of "torture" against 15 law enforcement officers.

After a visit to Kyrgyzstan in September, the UN Subcommittee on Prevention of Torture found that most of its recommendations from 2012 had yet to be implemented and that safeguards against torture "are not protecting [apprehended people] appropriately."

Asylum Seekers and Refugees

In May, Kyrgyzstan flouted the principle of nonrefoulement in extraditing to Kazakhstan Murat Tungishbaev, an activist, despite the serious risk of ill-treatment and torture and politically motivated prosecution he faced there. Tungishbaev fled Kazakhstan in 2012, after Kazakh security services summoned him for reporting on an oil workers' strike and violent clashes in Zhanaozen town in 2011. His asylum claim was pending at the time of his extradition.

Sexual Orientation and Gender Identity

Lesbian, gay, bisexual, and transgender (LGBT) rights groups reported that LGBT people continue to face ill-treatment, extortion, and discrimination by state and non-state actors. In August, following a local newspaper's publication of a photograph of four Kyrgyz LGBT activists participating in a pride parade in Europe, the activists received anonymous death threats and were subject to online hate speech. The activists reported the threats to the State National Security Committee; an investigation is underway. There is widespread impunity for such abuses. Consideration of an anti-LGBT bill, which would ban "propaganda of nontraditional sexual relations," remained stalled in parliament.

A January 2018 European Union-commissioned "Gender Study for Kyrgyzstan" found that "adequate measures to protect the fundamental rights of LGBT people as guaranteed by the Constitution and the International Covenant on Civil and Political Rights (ICCPR) do not exist."

Key International Actors

In December 2017, the EU and Kyrgyzstan launched negotiations for an enhanced partnership and cooperation agreement. In April, High Representative/Vice-President Federica Mogherini met President Jeenbekov to discuss negotiations and cooperation. In a draft recommendation on the negotiation, the European Parliament called for Azimjon Askarov's release, and respect for human rights in the context of countering terrorism.

At the annual EU-Kyrgyzstan human rights dialogue in June, the two sides discussed freedom of expression, judicial reforms, torture prevention, and women's rights.

The EU in January issued its two-year interim report on Kyrgyzstan's compliance with GSP+ requirements, noting with respect to human rights standards that "successful implementation [of the legal framework] is often hindered by inactivity or non-compliance with the law by local investigators, law enforcement bodies and courts."

In its 2017 annual human rights report, published in April, the US identified use of torture and arbitrary arrest by law enforcement officials, increasing pressure on independent media, and politically motivated prosecutions as being among Kyrgyzstan's "most significant human rights issues."

In April, the Organization for Security and Co-operation in Europe (OSCE) Parliamentary Assembly president, George Tsereteli, expressed concern about media freedoms and freedom of expression in Kyrgyzstan.

Following his May visit, UN Special Rapporteur on the Right to Health Dainius Pūras acknowledged Kyrgyzstan's political will to invest in primary healthcare and good efforts towards improving maternal health, but criticized discrimination in the healthcare system, informal payments for services, and cited the need for improved mental healthcare services.

Lebanon

Lebanon held parliamentary elections in May 2018, the first such elections since 2009. Most political parties failed to make public commitments to strengthen human rights protections. Longstanding human rights violations persisted throughout the year.

Lebanese authorities continue to prosecute individuals for peaceful speech, police and soldiers have beaten protesters, and detainees continue to report torture by security forces.

Women still face discrimination under 15 separate religion-based personal status laws, and both child marriage and marital rape remain legal in Lebanon. Unlike men, women cannot pass their citizenship to their children and foreign spouses.

Lebanon's waste management crisis has led to widespread open burning of waste, risking a range of health effects among local residents.

There are approximately 1.5 million Syrian refugees in Lebanon; however, 74 percent lack legal status. Authorities heightened calls for the return of refugees in 2018 and municipalities have forcibly evicted thousands of refugees.

Children with disabilities are often denied admission to schools. In 2018, 300,000 refugee children were out of school.

Security forces shut down Beirut Pride events and disrupted a gender and sexuality conference, but in a positive development, for the first time a district court of appeal found that consensual sex between people of the same sex is not unlawful.

Ill-Treatment and Torture

Human Rights Watch continued to document reports of torture by Lebanese security forces, including Internal Security Forces, State Security, and the Lebanese Armed Forces. A prominent actor who was falsely accused of spying for Israel said in March that State Security held him for six days in 2017 at what appeared to be an unofficial detention site, where men tortured him. A military judge closed the case against him in May, but did not investigate his allegations of torture.

In 2017, parliament passed a new anti-torture law that, while a positive step, falls short of Lebanon's obligations under international law. In 2016, parliament passed legislation creating a national preventative mechanism to monitor and investigate the use of torture. However, Lebanon has still not established the mechanism or allocated funding.

Freedom of Assembly and Freedom of Expression

A pattern of prosecutions for criticizing officials is threatening freedom of speech and opinion in Lebanon. In 2018, authorities continued to detain and charge individuals for speech critical of government officials. The Internal Security Forces' cybercrimes bureau has summoned activists for interrogations for social media posts criticizing officials and compelled them to sign commitments to cease their criticisms.

Defaming or criticizing the Lebanese president or army is a criminal offense carrying penalties of up to three years in prison. The Lebanese penal code also criminalizes libel and defamation, authorizing imprisonment of up to three months, and up to one year in the case of public officials.

In recent years, Lebanon's army and police have used force to disperse demonstrations, and videos show security forces beating people.

Military Courts

Lebanon continues to try civilians, including children, in military courts, in violation of their due process rights and international law. Military trials take place behind closed doors, and military judges are not required to have law degrees. Those who have stood trial in the military courts describe incommunicado detention, the use of confessions extracted under torture, decisions issued without an explanation, seemingly arbitrary sentences, and a limited ability to appeal.

In 2018, the United States handed over eight Lebanese Islamic State suspects from northern Syria to Lebanese Military Intelligence to be prosecuted before military courts. According to local media, Military Intelligence held them for over a month without any communication with their families or judicial authorities.

Women's Rights

Women continue to face discrimination under the 15 distinct religion-based personal status laws. Discrimination includes inequality in access to divorce, child custody, and property rights. Unlike men, Lebanese women also cannot pass on their nationality to foreign husbands and children, and are subject to discriminatory inheritance laws.

In 2017, Lebanon's parliament repealed article 522, which had allowed rapists to escape prosecution by marrying the victim, but left a loophole with regard to offences relating to sex with children aged 15-17 and sex with virgin girls with promises of marriage.

A lack of coordination in the government's response to sex trafficking continues to put women and girls at risk.

Lebanon has no minimum age for marriage for all its citizens. Instead, religious courts set the age based on the religion-based personal status laws, some of which allow girls younger than 15 to marry. Parliament has failed to take up draft bills that would set the age of marriage at 18.

A 2014 Law on the Protection of Women and Family from Domestic Violence established important protection measures and introduced policing and court reforms. But it failed to criminalize all forms of domestic violence, including marital rape. Some women continued to face obstacles in pursuing criminal complaints of domestic violence.

Sexual Orientation and Gender Identity

Adultery is criminalized under Lebanon's penal code. Furthermore, article 534 of the penal code punishes "any sexual intercourse contrary to the order of nature" with up to one year in prison.

In July, a district court of appeal issued a groundbreaking ruling that consensual sex between people of the same sex is not unlawful. This follows four similar judgments from lower courts declining to convict gay and transgender people under article 534 since 2007.

In May, the Lebanese Internal Security Forces arrested a prominent LGBT rights activist and pressured him to cancel Beirut Pride events. On September 29, Gen-

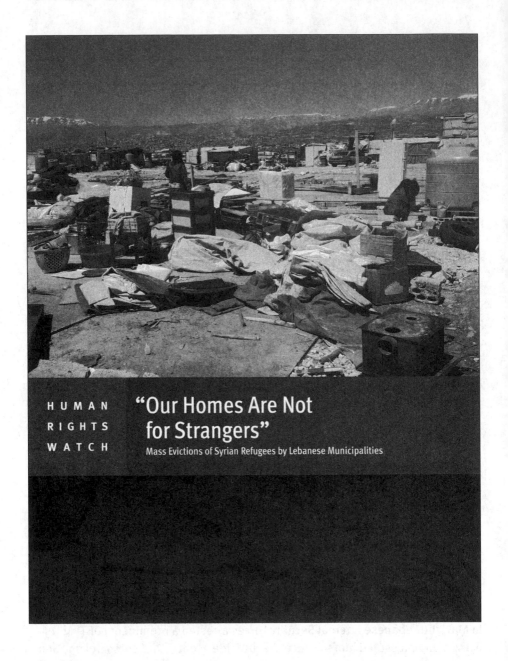

HUMAN
RIGHTS
WATCH

"Our Homes Are Not
for Strangers"
Mass Evictions of Syrian Refugees by Lebanese Municipalities

eral Security forces disrupted an LGBT conference, directing organizers to cease any conference activities.

Migrant Workers

An estimated 250,000 migrant domestic workers, primarily from Sri Lanka, Ethiopia, the Philippines, Nepal, and Bangladesh, are excluded from labor law protections.

The kafala (sponsorship) system subjects them to restrictive immigration rules under which they cannot leave or change employers without permission of their employer, placing them at risk of exploitation and abuse.

Civil society organizations frequently document complaints of non-payment or delayed payment of wages, forced confinement, refusal to provide time off, and verbal and physical abuse. Migrant domestic workers seeking accountability for abuse face legal obstacles and inadequate investigations, risking imprisonment and deportation due to the restrictive visa system. Migrant domestic workers in Lebanon have committed suicide, attempted to commit suicide, or have attempted dangerous escapes in 2018.

Refugees

More than 1 million Syrian refugees are registered with the United Nations High Commissioner for Refugees (UNHCR) in Lebanon. The government estimates the true number of Syrians in the country to be 1.5 million.

Lebanon's residency policy makes it difficult for Syrians to maintain legal status, heightening risks of exploitation and abuse and restricting refugees' access to work, education, and healthcare. Seventy-four percent of Syrians in Lebanon now lack legal residency and risk detention for unlawful presence in the country. In March, Lebanon lifted some restrictions to residency for Syrian refugee children age 15-18.

In 2017, Lebanese authorities stepped up calls for refugees to return to Syria and put pressure on UNHCR to organize returns despite the ongoing conflict in Syria and well-founded fears of persecution held by many refugees.

HUMAN
RIGHTS
WATCH

"I Would Like to Go to School"
Barriers to Education for Children with Disabilities in Lebanon

Lebanese authorities estimated that from July to November, between 55,000 and 90,000 refugees returned to Syria under localized agreements not overseen by UNHCR. Refugees have said they are returning because of harsh policies and deteriorating conditions in Lebanon, not because they think Syria is safe. On November 3, the Minister for Refugee Affairs said that about 20 refugees, including at least 2 children, have been killed by Syrian regime forces since their return.

Municipalities in Lebanon have forcibly evicted thousands of refugees in mass expulsions without a legal basis or due process. Tens of thousands remain at risk of eviction.

In 2018, Lebanon continued to impose entry regulations on Syrians that effectively barred many asylum seekers from entering Lebanon.

There are also approximately 174,000 Palestinian longstanding refugees living in Lebanon, where they continue to face restrictions, including on their right to work and own property. In addition, approximately 45,000 Palestinians from Syria have sought refuge in Lebanon.

Education

More than 300,000 school-age Syrian children were out of school during the 2017-2018 school year, largely due to parents' inability to pay for transport, child labor, school directors imposing arbitrary enrollment requirements, and lack of language support. Secondary-school age children and children with disabilities faced particular barriers.

Children with disabilities are often denied admission to schools and for those who manage to enroll, most schools do not take reasonable steps to provide them with a quality education. On May 22, the Ministry of Education and Higher Education launched an inclusive education pilot program targeting 30 public schools, the terms of the program however only included children with certain types of disabilities.

Open Burning of Waste

Lebanon continues to face a waste management crisis but, in a positive development, parliament passed a national solid waste management law in September. There are hundreds of open dumps across the country, many of which are being burned, posing a range of health risks to residents, especially children and older persons. Open burning disproportionately affects poorer areas of the country.

In January, Cabinet passed a summary waste management plan and, in February, it allocated US$20 million to begin closing or rehabilitating some open dumps.

Legacy of Past Conflicts and Wars

An estimated 17,000 Lebanese were kidnapped or "disappeared" during the 1975-1990 civil war. On November 12, parliament passed a landmark law creating an independent national commission to investigate the fate of the disappeared. Article 27 of the law states that those found responsible for the disappearances will be held accountable.

Key International Actors

Syria, Iran, and Saudi Arabia maintain a strong influence on Lebanese politics through local allies and proxies.

The international community has given Lebanon extensive, albeit insufficient, support to help it cope with the Syrian refugee crisis and to bolster security amid spillover violence.

Lebanese armed forces and police also receive assistance from a range of international donors, including the United States, European Union, United Kingdom, France, and Saudi Arabia.

Libya

Unaccountable militias—some linked to the interior and defense ministries of the United Nations-backed Government of National Accord (GNA), and others linked to the Libyan National Army (LNA) affiliated with the rival Interim Government—continued to clash with each other in various parts of the country, as efforts to reconcile main parties in the east and west failed. In Libya's south, Tebu, Tuareg, and Arab armed groups continued to clash for control of territory and resources.

Despite the UN's support for holding elections in 2018, prospects for a nationwide vote remained dim due to the political impasse.

The violence, including frequent attacks on oil installations, disrupted the economy and public services. Around 200,000 people remained internally displaced, as of October.

Armed groups, some of them affiliated with the GNA or the Interim Government, carried out extrajudicial executions, attacked civilians and civilian properties, and abducted, tortured, and disappeared people.

The extremist armed group Islamic State (also known as ISIS) carried out several attacks that killed both civilians and members of the security forces.

Although the number of migrants and asylum seekers who transited Libya en route to Europe dropped dramatically compared to 2017, the number of those who died trying to reach Europe via the so-called Central Mediterranean Route soared. Those who ended up in detention in Libya faced ill-treatment and inhumane conditions at the hands of guards in official detention centers run by one of the competing governments, and in unofficial places of detention controlled by militias or traffickers and smugglers.

Political Transition and Constitution

The GNA struggled to gain control over territory and institutions in western Libya. The LNA, under the command of General Khalifa Hiftar and allied with the Interim Government, expanded control over territory in the east and south.

Libya's legislative body, the House of Representatives (HOR), allied with the LNA and Interim Government, approved on September 25 amendments to the 2011 Constitutional Declaration, paving the way for a referendum on the draft constitution, and gave the High National Elections Commission (HNEC) 90 days to organize the referendum.

Armed Conflict and War Crimes

On January 23, unidentified armed groups detonated two car bombs in front of Baya'at al-Radwan mosque in Benghazi, killing at least 34 people and wounding over 90. Video recordings appeared to show LNA commander Mahmoud al-Werfalli, wanted for war crimes by the International Criminal Court (ICC) since August 2017, allegedly executing 10 individuals on January 24 in front of the same mosque.

Between February and June, clashes in the southern town of Sebha between armed groups loyal to the Awlad Suleiman and Tebu groups killed at least 16 civilians.

On May 2, ISIS claimed responsibility for an armed attack on the HNEC in Tripoli that, according to news reports, resulted in the killing of 14, most of them staff members, and the wounding of least 19 others.

In May, after a nearly 20-month-long siege of Derna, the LNA started a land and air operation to wrest control of the eastern city from the Derna Mujahedeen Shura Council (DMSC), an armed group that includes Islamists that opposes the LNA. As of September, resistance was reduced to one neighborhood, where some families remained trapped by the fighting. According to GNA-linked local council officials and members of the Derna Committee for Displaced, at least 1,000 families had been displaced by the fighting to other towns. Local officials also alleged cases of extrajudicial executions, appropriation of private property, looting, and arbitrary detention by the LNA as it overran the city.

Clashes erupted on August 26 in the capital, Tripoli, between armed groups vying for control of state institutions and lasted one month. While the southern parts of the city bore the brunt, indiscriminate shelling in neighborhoods elsewhere also killed civilians and destroyed infrastructure. At least 120 people were killed and 400 wounded over the course of the month-long fighting, according to the UN Support Mission in Libya (UNSMIL). The fighting involved destruction of civilian property, looting, abductions, and the displacement of thousands.

ISIS claimed responsibly for an attack on October 29, on al-Foqha, a town in central Libya, that resulted in the killing of four civilians—including two who were executed in public—in addition to at least nine who were abducted, according to UNSMIL.

Judicial System and Detainees

Civilian and military courts operated at reduced capacity and were closed down entirely in some parts of the country

Prison authorities, often only nominally under the authority of one or another of the two rival governments, continued to hold thousands of detainees in long-term arbitrary detention without charges.

Pursuant to a ceasefire agreement between warring factions, the Special Deterrence Force (SDF), which is linked with the GNA Interior Ministry, released in September from Mitiga Prison, one of its prisons in Tripoli, 120 prisoners who had been held beyond the expiration of their sentences. In October, the SDF transferred 120 prisoners accused or sentenced for minor infractions, from Mitiga to Jdeida Prison, which is controlled by the GNA Justice Ministry. According to UN-SMIL, authorities released 255 detainees in the aftermath of the crisis as of November 8.

Over 100 mostly non-Libyan women and children remain held without charge in two prisons in Tripoli and Misrata, and 24 orphaned children were at time of writing being held separately in a facility run by the Libyan Red Crescent in Misrata, all of them because of their suspected familial relationship to alleged ISIS fighters. There are few prospects for their release, either because it is not clear where they are from or because their governments will not accept their repatriation. Prisons in Libya are marked by overcrowding, bad living conditions, widespread ill-treatment and the lack of specialized services for women and children, such as educational and leisure activities and medical care.

International Criminal Court

On July 4, a second arrest warrant was issued at the International Criminal Court (ICC) against LNA Commander al-Werfalli. Al-Werfalli's whereabouts were unknown at time of writing.

The ICC unsealed in April 2017 an arrest warrant that it had issued in 2013 for Mohamed Khaled al-Tuhamy, who, under ousted Libyan leader Muammar Gaddafi, headed the Internal Security Agency, for serious crimes committed during the 2011 uprising. His whereabouts were unknown at time of writing.

Saif al-Islam Gaddafi, a son of former Libyan leader Muammar Gaddafi, who was sentenced to death in absentia by a Libyan court in 2015, continued to be subject to an ICC arrest warrant to face charges of crimes against humanity. Gaddafi's current whereabouts cannot be confirmed; independent international observers have not seen or heard from him since 2014.

In her November update to the Security Council, ICC Prosecutor Fatou Bensouda responded to a challenge brought by Saif al-Islam Gaddafi disputing the admissibility of his case in front of the ICC and affirmed that he should be arrested and surrendered to the court.

Death Penalty

The death penalty is stipulated in over 30 articles in Libya's penal code, including for acts of speech and association. An unknown number of people were sentenced to death by Libyan civil and military courts since 2011, often after trials marred by due process violations. No death sentences have been carried out since 2010.

On August 15, and despite allegations of serious due process violations, a Tripoli court convicted 99 suspected Gaddafi supporters in a mass trial, sentencing 45 to death and 54 to five years in prison, in relation to the alleged killing of 146 people during the 2011 uprising.

Internally Displaced Persons

The International Organization for Migration (IOM) estimated that around 200,000 people were internally displaced in Libya as of October.

A few hundred of the 40,000 residents of Tawergha whom armed groups and authorities based in Misrata forcibly displaced in 2011, began to return to their hometown after authorities representing Misrata and Tawergha signed a reconciliation memorandum in June. Authorities in the city of Misrata accused Tawerghans of having committed serious crimes as alleged Gaddafi supporters during the 2011 uprising that ousted him. Misrata-linked armed groups ransacked, looted, burned, and destroyed the town after the departure of the population in 2011.

Fighting in eastern Libya since May 2014 has displaced thousands of civilians from Benghazi and Ajdabiya. They have sought shelter in the west of the country after militias affiliated with the LNA accused them of being terrorists and detained them, and attacked, burned or appropriated their homes. Since 2014, authorities in Misrata and Tripoli have detained tens of people displaced from Benghazi, often on dubious terrorism allegations. Since the fighting started in May in Derna, at least 1,000 families fled the fighting, according to Derna officials.

Freedom of Speech and Expression

Armed groups intimidated, threatened, and physically attacked activists, journalists, bloggers, and media professionals.

On April 29, the SDF arrested Suleiman Qashout and Ahmed Yaacoubi, organizers of an annual media award in Libya. They were both released in July, after being held without charge. Relatives and colleagues speculated that the SDF might have targeted the men because it disapproved of revealing clothing and the mixing of men and women at the award ceremony.

Musa Abdul Kareem, a journalist with the newspaper *Fasanea,* which is based in the south of Libya, was found dead on July 31 in Sebha, after unidentified individuals abducted him. According to news reports, Kareem had written reports critical of militias in Sebha.

On August 1, an armed group linked with the GNA Interior Ministry detained at the Tripoli Naval Base four Libyan journalists and photographers from Reuters and Agence France-Presse who were covering migration-related issues and held them for 10 hours without explanation.

Freedom of Religion

Since 2011, militias and forces affiliated with several interim authorities, as well as ISIS fighters, have attacked religious minorities, including Sufis, Ibadis, and Christians, and destroyed religious sites in Libya with impunity.

On November 28, 2017, unidentified assailants set fire to Zawiyat Sheikha Radiya, a historic Sufi mosque in Tripoli, heavily damaging it. This attack follows the destruction by unidentified assailants in October 2017 of Sidi Abu Gharara, another historic Sufi mosque in Tripoli.

In July, unidentified armed groups attacked and damaged at least four Sufi sites in Al-Majouri and Al-Kish neighborhoods of Benghazi.

Women's Rights, Sexual Orientation, and Gender Identity

Libyan law does not criminalize domestic violence. Personal status laws discriminate against women, particularly with respect to marriage, divorce, and inheritance. The penal code allows for a reduced sentence for a man who kills or injures his wife or another female relative because he suspects her of extramarital sexual relations. It also allows rapists to escape prosecution if they marry their victim.

The penal code prohibits all sexual acts outside marriage, including consensual same-sex relations, and punishes them with flogging and up to five years in prison.

According to human rights activists, armed groups have continued to detain people because of their sexual orientation.

Migrants, Refugees, and Asylum Seekers

Libya remained a major hub for refugees, asylum seekers, and migrants on their way to Europe. Human Rights Watch interviewed migrants and asylum seekers who reported a litany of abuses at the hands of smugglers, and members of militias and gangs including rapes, beatings, and killings, with no intervention or protection provided by Libya's weak law enforcement agencies.

As of August, the International Organization for Migration (IOM) recorded around 20,000 arrivals to Italy and Malta by sea since January, most of whom departed

AUDACITY IN ADVERSITY
LGBT Activism in the Middle East and North Africa

HUMAN
RIGHTS
WATCH

from Libya. According to the UN High Commissioner for Refugees (UNHCR), at least 1,111 died or went missing while crossing the central Mediterranean route to Europe. As of August, the IOM reported that there were 669,176 migrants in Libya, including more than 60,000 children.

Libya is not a party to the 1951 Refugee Convention and does not have a refugee law or procedure. UNHCR registers some asylum seekers but they—and those unable to register—are not effectively protected and assisted in Libya.

To discourage and prevent arrivals in Europe from Libya, the European Union has provided training, equipment, and funds to Libyan coast guard forces to intercept boats both in Libyan coastal waters and international waters, and to return migrants and asylum seekers to Libyan territory.

Migrants and asylum seekers who are captured at sea and returned to Libyan territory, are placed in detention, where many suffer inhumane conditions, including beatings, sexual violence, extortion, forced labor, inadequate medical treatment, and insufficient food and water.

The Department for Combating Illegal Migration (DCIM), under the GNA Interior Ministry, manages the formal migrant detention centers, while smugglers and traffickers run informal ones. As of July, DCIM estimated that official detention centers were holding 9,000 migrants and asylum seekers in Libya.

Key International Actors

The United States continued to conduct what it calls "precision airstrikes" against purported ISIS and Al-Qaeda targets in the south and west of the country. The United States did not report any civilian casualties

In a report issued on May 10, Cecilia Jimenez-Damary, the special rapporteur on the human rights of internally displaced persons (IDPs) and the first expert under the UN Special Procedures mechanisms to visit Libya after 2011, criticized in a report issued May 10 the lack of a legal framework for addressing the rights and needs of IDPs, and the absence of a comprehensive policy in line with international standards.

In June, the UN Security Council renewed the arms embargo on Libya, effective since 2011, for another 12 months, and added measures to inspect vessels suspected of violating the embargo. On June 7, the Libya Sanctions Committee responsible for overseeing sanctions imposed by the Security Council, approved the addition of six individuals—including two Eritrean and six Libyan nationals—to the Libya Sanctions List subjecting them to asset freezes and travel bans in relation to alleged serious human rights abuses of migrants and participation in illicit human trafficking and smuggling.

On September 5, the UN Panel of Experts, established pursuant to UN Security Council resolution 1973 (2011), issued its final 2018 report on threats and attacks on Libyan state institutions, human rights abuses, violations of the arms embargo, illicit exports of petroleum and implementation of asset freezes and travel bans. The report found that most armed groups involved in human rights violations were affiliated with the GNA or LNA.

According to the panel, weapons transfers to eastern Libyan such as armored vehicles, rifles, mortar, and rocket launchers have increased most notably in eastern Libya, which indicated that member states were not sufficiently enforcing the arms embargo.

In September, the UN Sanctions Committee imposed an asset freeze and travel ban on Ibrahim Jadhran, a Libyan militia commander, for his repeated attacks against the oil crescent region in Libya that resulted in civilian casualties and for his attempts to export oil illegally.

The mandate of the European Union's anti-smuggling naval operation in the central Mediterranean, Operation Sophia, runs until December 2018. It aims to disrupt migrant smugglers and human traffickers; it also has provided training to Libyan Coastguard and Navy forces and contributed to the enforcement of the UN arms embargo in international waters off Libya's coast.

Malaysia

In May 2018, Malaysians voted out the ruling coalition led by the United Malays National Organization (UMNO) that had governed Malaysia since independence in 1957, and elected the Pakatan Harapan alliance led by former Prime Minister Mahathir Mohamad. Anwar Ibrahim, a leader of one party in the alliance who was imprisoned on politically motivated charges by the prior administration, was pardoned and released in May.

Pakatan Harapan ran on an election manifesto promising to abolish oppressive laws, ensure accountability for police abuses, improve the situation for refugees, ratify international human rights treaties, and make Malaysia's human rights record "respected by the world." By the end of the year, the new government had begun to take steps to fulfil some of those promises. However, progress on legal reform has been slow and the negative rhetoric directed toward the country's lesbian, gay, bisexual, and transgender (LGBT) population raises questions about whether the new government will ensure equal rights for all.

Freedom of Expression

Prior to the election, the government of Prime Minister Najib Razak intensified suppression of freedom of speech. In February, graphic artist Fahmi Reza was sentenced to one month in jail and a fine for posting a caricature of the prime minister as a clown, and opposition member of parliament Rafizi Ramli was sentenced to 30 months in prison for leaking bank details as part of an effort to expose corruption, highlighting weaknesses in Malaysia's protection of whistle-blowers.

In March, the government passed the Anti-Fake News law, broad legislation imposing up to seven years in prison for anyone who maliciously spreads "fake news," deliberately defined vaguely to allow maximum discretion for the government to target critics of UMNO and the government. In April, a Danish citizen was sentenced to one week in prison and a RM10,000 (US$2,384) fine for posting a video criticizing the police's response to a targeted killing in Kuala Lumpur.

Since the Pakatan Harapan government took office, the situation for freedom of speech has improved dramatically. The Attorney General's Office has dropped politically motivated sedition charges against a number of activists and politicians and ended government appeals of adverse rulings in a number of other expression-related cases. In August, the government introduced and passed legislation to repeal the Anti-Fake News Law. However, the Malaysian Senate, which is controlled by allies of the previous government, blocked repeal of the law in September.

Use of the sedition act continues, with at least three new sedition investigations opened in July and August against individuals accused of insulting Malaysia's royalty. Despite its election manifesto promising to repeal the Sedition Act, the government had not yet moved to do so at time of writing. The government also backed away from an election commitment to repeal the Official Secrets Act, saying it would instead be amended.

Criminal Justice System

In October, the government announced its intention to abolish the death penalty and placed a moratorium on executions pending that action. Malaysia currently permits the death penalty for various crimes, and makes the sentence mandatory for 11 offenses. In December 2017, parliament passed an amendment to the Dangerous Drugs Act that allows the court the discretion to impose life imprisonment instead of death for drug trafficking offenses in a limited set of circumstances.

Malaysia continues to detain individuals without trial under restrictive laws. Both the 1959 Prevention of Crime Act and the 2015 Prevention of Terrorism Act give government-appointed boards the authority to impose detention without trial for up to two years, renewable indefinitely, to order electronic monitoring, and to impose other significant restrictions on freedom of movement and association. No judicial review is permitted for these measures. The similarly restrictive Security Offences (Special Measures) Act allows for preventive detention of up to 28 days with no judicial review for a broadly defined range of "security offenses." The new government has committed to "abolish draconian provisions" in these laws, but had yet to do so at time of writing.

Police Abuse and Impunity

Police torture of suspects in custody, in some cases resulting in death, continues to be a serious problem, as does a lack of accountability for such offenses. The standard of care for those in detention is also problematic, with suspects and prisoners dying from treatable illnesses.

However, in September, the prime minister announced that the Enforcement Agencies Integrity Commission (EAIC) would be strengthened and transformed into the long-sought Independent Police Complaints and Misconduct Commission (IPCMC), which will have authority to investigate and punish abusive police officers.

Refugees, Asylum Seekers, and Trafficking Victims

Malaysia is not a party to the 1951 Refugee Convention, although the new government has committed to ratify that convention. Over 150,000 refugees and asylum seekers, most of whom come from Myanmar, are registered with the United Nations refugee agency, UNHCR, in Malaysia but have no legal status and are currently unable to work, travel, or enroll in government schools.

Asylum seekers arrested by authorities are treated as "illegal migrants" and locked up in overcrowded and unhealthy immigration detention centers. The new government has committed to improve the situation for refugees and asylum seekers, but had not yet taken concrete steps to do so at time of writing.

Malaysia denied requests from China for the return of 11 Uyghurs who were detained in March after fleeing immigration detention in Thailand. They were released from custody after Malaysia dropped immigration charges against them and ultimately made their way to Turkey.

No Malaysians have been held responsible for their role in the deaths of over 100 ethnic Rohingya trafficking victims whose bodies were found in 2015 in remote jungle detention camps on the Thai-Malaysian border. The 12 policemen initially charged in the case were all exonerated and released in March 2017.

The Malaysian government has failed to take necessary administrative steps to provide assistance and work authorization to all trafficking victims who desire it, as mandated by amendments passed in 2014 to Malaysia's 2007 anti-trafficking law.

Freedom of Assembly and Association

Prior to the May election, Malaysian authorities regularly prosecuted individuals who held peaceful assemblies without giving notice or participated in street protests. Under the new government, police have continued to open new investigations for violation of the Peaceful Assembly Act, despite a manifesto promise to "abolish draconian provisions" of that law. For example, on June 11, the police lodged reports against S. Arutchelvan of Parti Sosialis Malaysia and 50 others for gathering outside the prime minister's office to submit a direct appeal to him. On July 12, lawyer Fadiah Nadwa Fikri was called in for questioning about a solidarity rally that took place outside the police station when she was being questioned for sedition. On September 16, eight student activists were arrested during a Malaysia Day protest in Sabah.

The Societies Act restricts freedom of association by requiring that organizations with seven or more members register with the registrar of societies. The law gives the minister of home affairs "absolute discretion" to declare an organization illegal and grants the Registrar of Societies authority over political parties.

In the run-up to the election, the Registrar of Societies threatened to dissolve the political party founded by Mahathir Mohamed, and seriously delayed efforts by Pakatan Harapan to register as a coalition.

Freedom of Religion

Malaysia restricts the rights of followers of any branches of Islam other than Sunni, with those following Shia or other branches subject to arrest for deviancy. In September, 50 Shia, including children, were arrested in Kelantan for practicing their religion. In April, a high court ruled that members of the Ahmadiyya community, which has been declared "deviant" in Malaysia, cannot be charged with offenses under the Shariah laws governing Muslims in the country.

Sexual Orientation and Gender Identity

Discrimination against LGBT people remains pervasive in Malaysia. Federal law punishes "carnal knowledge against the order of nature" with up to 20 years in prison, while numerous state Sharia laws prohibit both same-sex relations and non-normative gender expression, resulting in frequent arrests of transgender people. While the new minister for religious affairs called for an end to workplace discrimination against LGBT people, he also made clear any visible expression of an alternative sexuality or gender identity will be prosecuted under existing laws, and that he supports programs, broadly discredited, designed to change personal sexual orientation.

In August, the religious affairs minister ordered the removal of portraits of transgender activist Nisha Ayub and LGBT activist Pang Khee Teik from an exhibit in Penang celebrating influential Malaysians, claiming the government's policy is to not promote LGBT activities. The controversy unleashed a wave of verbal abuse against transgender people. On August 18, eight men brutally beat a transgender woman in Negeri Sembilan, causing internal injuries, broken ribs, and injuries to her head and back.

In September, a Sharia court in Terengganu state ordered two women be given six strokes of the cane for alleged same-sex conduct. The sentence was carried out in a courtroom in front of 100 witnesses, prompting global criticism.

On September 21, Prime Minister Mahathir stated that Malaysia "cannot accept LGBT culture," raising concern about the government's commitment to protect the rights of LGBT people.

Women's and Children's Rights

Malaysia permits child marriage under both civil and Islamic law, but there is movement to restrict the practice. Girls age 16 and older can marry with permission of their state's chief minister. For Muslims, most state Islamic laws set a minimum age of 16 for girls and 18 for boys, but permit marriages below those ages, with no apparent minimum, with the permission of a Sharia court.

In July, a 41-year-old man was reported to have married an 11-year-old Thai Muslim girl whose parents were working in Malaysia. He was fined RM1800 (US$429) for failing to get approval for the marriage and the girl was ultimately sent back to Thailand. In September, a 44-year-old man was permitted to marry a 15-year-old girl in Kelantan.

In August, the state of Selangor announced that it was raising the minimum age of marriage for Muslim girls from 16 to 18 and setting tighter rules for marriage of those under 18 but would not ban such marriages. In October, media reported that Prime Minister Mahathir had directed state governments to raise the minimum age of marriage to 18 for both Muslims and non-Muslims, and some states have moved to do so while retaining exceptions to the minimum age. In October, the government announced that it does not intend to criminalize marital rape due to the difficulty of proving such cases in court.

Key International Actors

US Secretary of State Mike Pompeo, who visited Kuala Lumpur in August, said he looked forward to deepening the partnership between the two countries on a range of issues, including trade and countering Islamic extremism, but said nothing publicly about human rights reform.

Prime Minister Mahathir visited China, the country's largest trading partner, in August, where he received a warm public welcome despite having suspended major Chinese-backed infrastructure projects endorsed by his predecessor.

Anwar Ibrahim, a leader of the Pakatan Harapan alliance and likely contender for prime minister, criticized China's treatment of its Muslim Uyghur population.

The new government has indicated it wishes to play a more active role in the Association of Southeast Asian Nations (ASEAN), the Organisation of Islamic Cooperation (OIC), and the United Nations. Malaysia was the only one of ASEAN's 10 country members that has spoken out strongly against Myanmar's mistreatment of Rohingya Muslims.

Maldives

There was hope for improvement in the human rights situation in the Maldives after joint opposition candidate Ibrahim Mohamed Solih defeated then-President Abdulla Yameen Abdul Gayoom by a wide margin in September 2018. Solih took office on November 17 and vowed to implement judicial reform, restore fundamental rights, and investigate the murder of a political activist and the forced disappearance of a prominent journalist.

Solih's election followed a sharp deterioration in rights protections in the first half of 2018 after the Yameen government imposed a state of emergency for six weeks, arrested two Supreme Court justices, and detained scores of opposition activists under counterterrorism laws. The Yameen government had also expanded its use of an overly broad anti-defamation law, as well as laws aimed at curbing peaceful protests to arrest and intimidate media and government critics. Religious extremists and thugs, some linked to prominent politicians, targeted dissenters and those perceived as deviating from Islamic teachings.

Ahead of presidential elections on September 23, the government blocked opposition candidates from running and severely limited the ability of opposition parties to hold rallies. Although Yameen conceded shortly after his loss, he later challenged the results. In a unanimous ruling on October 21, the Maldives Supreme Court denied his petition to annul the election.

State of Emergency

On February 1, 2018, the Supreme Court overturned the convictions of nine members of the opposition, including former President Mohamed Nasheed, who had been sentenced to 13 years in prison on terrorism charges in a 2015 trial widely condemned as unfair. Then-President Yameen denounced the ruling as "illegal," and on February 5 declared a 15-day state of emergency that was later extended until March 22. The decree suspended constitutional protections, banned public assemblies, and granted security forces sweeping powers to arrest and detain.

Supreme Court Justices Abdulla Saeed and Ali Hameed were arrested, along with former President Maumoon Abdul Gayoom, Yameen's half-brother; all were convicted of "terrorism" and obstructing justice. The remaining three Supreme Court justices reinstated the convictions of the opposition leaders. Scores of opposition figures and activists were detained during the state of emergency, mostly for alleged "acts of terrorism" despite the fact that protests were overwhelmingly peaceful.

Following the September elections, authorities began releasing jailed opposition figures. On October 18, the High Court overturned former President Gayoom's conviction on obstruction of justice charges. On November 18, Justices Saeed and Hameed were released on house arrest pending a review of the charges.

Targeting Political Opposition

In May, the Election Commission nullified the candidacy of all nominees convicted of a criminal offense within the past three years. Since all senior opposition party leaders were facing spurious terrorism charges at the time, the ruling left only the incumbent president, Yameen, eligible to run. In June, an opposition party alliance agreed to support one candidate who was not facing charges, Ibrahim Mohamed Solih, in his challenge to Yameen.

Before the election, the Election Commission made multiple changes regulating voter registration, including limiting the number of ballot boxes for local workers at tourism resorts, the biggest source of employment in the Maldives, and requiring that civil servants re-register at their workplace. Civil society groups reported that ruling party officials submitted re-registration forms only from their supporters. Police also repeatedly closed opposition party offices, detained their supporters, and seized opposition flags and banners. Human rights groups documented efforts by ruling party officials to manipulate voter registration lists in their favor.

Freedom of Expression

Using the 2016 Anti-Defamation and Freedom of Expression Act, the government in 2018 imposed heavy fines on media that published content critical of the president. After the government declared a state of emergency in February, the regulatory Maldives Broadcasting Commission warned media stations that they could face closure if they were deemed "a threat to national security, incited un-

HUMAN
RIGHTS
WATCH

"An All-Out Assault on Democracy"
Crushing Dissent in the Maldives

rest with false information or endangered the public interest." After the September elections, parliament repealed the anti-defamation law.

In February 2018, Raajje TV, a popular opposition network, said that it was suspending its regular broadcast "amid continued harassment, threats and intimidations." Journalists were arrested after anti-government protests in March, and some reported threats by criminal gangs apparently hired by ruling party politicians. Three Raajje TV journalists were arrested after an anti-government protest on March 16.

Extremists that endorse an Islamist ideology, including some gangs linked to prominent politicians, harassed and attacked media and civil society groups. The targets included individuals who criticized the government on social media, published material deemed offensive to Islam, or promoted the rights of lesbian, gay, bisexual, and transgender (LGBT) people.

The Yameen government had made no progress in investigating the abduction of journalist Ahmed Rilwan, who was last seen in August 2014, or the murder of Yameen Rasheed, a blogger and activist who was stabbed to death in April 2017. At a campaign rally on August 7, 2018, Yameen declared that Rilwan was dead—a claim he later retracted. On November 18, President Solih established a commission to investigate both cases, chaired by a former attorney general, Husnu Al Suood.

Women's Rights

Gender-based violence is endemic in the Maldives. In January 2018, a women's rights organization, Uthema, criticized the government for failing to carry out adequate investigations into hundreds of cases of sexual assault. In some cases, the alleged perpetrators included ruling party officials. Maldivian law bans sexual harassment in the workplace, but the law is seldom enforced. In late 2017, civil society groups launched an online social media campaign, #nufoshey (Don't Harass), to raise awareness about sexual harassment.

Trafficking of Women and Children

The Maldives is both a destination and a source country for women and children subjected to forced labor and sex trafficking. Some women are forced into prostitution after being recruited for domestic labor or the tourism industry. Children are trafficked from outlying islands to the capital, Malé, some of whom are reportedly subjected to sexual abuse and forced labor.

In 2018, the US State Department downgraded the Maldives on its watchlist for human trafficking, citing its failure to take steps to effectively investigate and combat trafficking.

Sexual Orientation and Gender Identity

The Maldivian penal code criminalizes adult, consensual same-sex sexual conduct; the punishment can include imprisonment of up to eight years and 100 lashes. Extremist groups in the Maldives have used social media to harass and threaten those who promote the rights of LGBT people.

Human Rights Defenders

Social media trolls and thugs, some with links to the ruling party, have threatened human rights defenders because of their work. In January 2018, Shahindha Ismail, the executive director of the Maldivian Democracy Network, received threats on social media after an online news site branded her an apostate for a statement promoting religious freedom.

Key International Actors

The February 2018 declaration of a state of emergency was widely condemned internationally. The United Nations high commissioner for human rights, among the first to speak out, described the crackdown as "an all-out assault on democracy." Following warnings and a strong European Parliament resolution, European Union member states adopted a legal framework for EU sanctions, including travel bans and asset freezes, against individuals and entities responsible for undermining the rule of law, committing human rights violations, or obstructing an inclusive political solution. After the elections, the EU congratulated the Maldives and said the results reflected the commitment of the Maldivian people to democracy.

Ties with India deteriorated after New Delhi criticized the government crackdown on the opposition and the declaration of a state of emergency. After the election, President-elect Solih vowed to restore good relations with India.

In December 2017, China and the Maldives government signed agreements to promote Beijing's "One Belt, One Road" initiative. Following the election, China called for "continuity and stability" in its relations with the Maldives. During the campaign, Solih had vowed to review all Chinese projects in the Maldives.

HUMAN
RIGHTS
WATCH

"We Used to Be Brothers"
Self-Defense Group Abuses in Central Mali

Mali

Mali's human rights situation seriously deteriorated in 2018 as attacks by armed Islamist groups against civilians spiked, the army committed atrocities during counterterrorism operations, and intercommunal violence killed hundreds and precipitated a humanitarian crisis.

The peace process envisioned to end the 2012-2013 political-military crisis in the north made scant progress, including on disarmament and the restoration of state authority. Rampant banditry continued amid a deepening security vacuum.

In central Mali, Islamist group attacks, including with explosive devices on road-ways, increased from 2017, killing many villagers. State counterterrorism operations resulted in dozens of summary executions and ill-treatment.

During 2018, at least 300 civilians were killed in over 100 incidents of communal violence in central and northern Mali. The violence pitted ethnically aligned self-defense groups against communities accused of supporting Islamist armed groups, resulting in the pillage and destruction of dozens of villages and displacement of tens of thousands.

In September, President Ibrahim Boubacar Keita was sworn in for a second term after winning elections marred by insecurity, allegations of irregularities, and some rights violations, including banned demonstrations and the closure of a local radio station.

Little effort was made toward providing justice for victims of abuses, and rule of law institutions remained weak. However, the military opened investigations into allegations of extrajudicial killings by their forces. Humanitarian agencies suffered scores of attacks, mostly by bandits, which undermined their ability to deliver aid.

During 2018, Mali's international partners focused on containing the regional spread of Islamist group attacks and ensuring legitimate presidential elections. These actors demonstrated increased willingness to denounce abuses by Malian security forces.

Abuses by Armed Groups in North and Central Mali

Islamist armed groups allied to Al-Qaeda, and to a lesser extent the Islamic State, dramatically increased their attacks on Malian security services, peacekeepers, and international forces in northern and central Mali throughout 2018.

Scores of civilians were killed in these attacks, primarily by the indiscriminate use of improvised explosive devices planted on major roads, including an attack in Mopti Region that killed 26. At time of writing, 11 United Nations peacekeepers with the Multidimensional Integrated Stabilization Mission in Mali (MINUSMA) were killed during 2018, bringing the total to 103 killed since MINUSMA's creation in 2013.

Islamist armed groups continued to threaten, and sometimes kill, villagers deemed to have collaborated with authorities and beat those engaged in cultural practices they had forbidden. They also imposed their version of Sharia (Islamic law) via courts that did not adhere to fair trial standards.

During the elections, they burned polling stations and election materials, killed at least three election workers, and threatened voters, forcing the closure of hundreds of polling stations in north and central Mali.

Abuses by State Security Forces

The number of serious violations of international human rights and humanitarian law by state security forces in the context of counterterrorism operations increased significantly in 2018, notably in the first half of the year.

During 2018, Malian soldiers allegedly killed and buried in common graves over 60 men suspected of supporting armed Islamists, while numerous others were subjected to enforced disappearance or torture during interrogations. Numerous men accused of terrorism-related offenses were detained by the national intelligence agency without respect for due process.

The military opened up investigations into at least three incidents, including the extrajudicial killing of 12 suspects near Diourra in April; 12 men in Boulikessi in May; and 25 suspects near Nantaka in June.

Progress in the professionalization of the security forces was also evident in the increased presence of military police responsible for ensuring discipline during military operations, patrols to protect civilians, and operationalization of the Military Justice Directorate in Bamako.

Children's Rights

Over 25 children in central and northern Mali were killed and others injured by explosive devices, in crossfire and during intercommunal clashes. Numerous children who fled their villages during attacks by ethnic militias, including Boumbo and Gueourou, remain missing. Thousands of children suffered from malnutrition as a result of conflict and intercommunal violence.

In February, Mali adopted the Safe Schools Declaration, a political commitment to reduce attacks on education. However, over 735 schools remained closed and 225,000 children were denied the right to education because of insecurity and displacement. Numerous teachers were threatened, and schools vandalized, destroyed, or occupied by armed groups.

Accountability for Abuses

Judicial authorities made scant progress in investigating over 100 complaints filed by victims of alleged abuses during the 2012-2013 armed conflict, and few investigations into more recent communal violence and security force abuse were opened.

In June, the government passed a "national consensus" law extending amnesty to members of armed groups involved in the 2012-2013 hostilities who had not been accused of violent crimes. Human rights groups called for the postponement of the law's passage pending impartial investigations into abuses committed since 2012.

The trial of former coup leader Gen. Amadou Haya Sanogo and 17 other members of the Malian security services for the 2012 killing of 21 elite "Red Beret" soldiers was suspended in December 2016.

Judiciary and Human Rights Legal Framework

The Malian judiciary was plagued by neglect and mismanagement, and insecurity led many judicial personnel to abandon their posts in northern and central

Mali. Hundreds of detainees were held in extended pretrial detention due to the courts' inability to adequately process cases.

However, the judiciary made efforts to improve its case management system, increased hearings in conflict-prone areas, and improved prison conditions. The Specialized Judicial Unit against Terrorism and Transnational Organized Crime, created by law in 2013, saw its first case brought to trial; at time of writing, the unit had tried at least six cases.

In October, the cabinet extended for one year the state of emergency, first declared in 2015.

Independent Human Rights Commission and Truth and Reconciliation Mechanism

The National Commission for Human Rights (CNDH) made significant progress in fulfilling its mandate. With improved funding and personnel, the CNDH investigated abuses, issued numerous communiques and visited detention centers to advocate on victims' behalf.

The Truth, Justice and Reconciliation Commission, established in 2014 with a mandate to investigate crimes and root causes of violence dating back to 1960, made meaningful progress. The 25-member commission has taken over 9,300 victim and witness statements, but its credibility has been weakened by the inclusion of nine armed group members and the exclusion of victims' representatives.

Key International Actors

The United Nations, France, European Union, and United States put respect for human rights in Mali more squarely on the agenda in 2018 through numerous public statements denouncing abuse by state forces and non-state armed groups and calls for accountability.

France, together with the US, led on military matters, the EU on training and security sector reform, and the UN on rule of law and political stability.

The operationalization of the 2017 G5 Sahel multinational counterterrorism military force, comprised of forces from Mali, Mauritania, Burkina Faso, Niger, and

Chad, suffered delays and its headquarters was destroyed by armed Islamist groups in June. In 2017 and 2018, international donors pledged over US$500 million for the force, including €116 million (approximately $132 million) from the EU.

Operation Barkhane, the 4,000-member French regional counterterrorism force, conducted numerous operations in Mali. In May, the EU Training Mission in Mali (EUTM) and the EU Capacity Building Mission (EUCAP)'s mandate was expanded to include training for the G5 Sahel force.

MINUSMA meaningfully supported the organization of presidential elections, training government forces and judicial officers, and community reconciliation efforts. While the forces increased patrols, MINUSMA struggled to implement its more robust 2016 civilian protection mandate, largely due to persistent attacks against peacekeepers and lack of equipment.

In January, the UN secretary-general established the International Commission of Inquiry envisioned by the 2015 peace accord to investigate serious violations of international human rights and humanitarian law between 2012 and January 2018.

In December 2017, the UN Security Council approved a resolution enabling MINUSMA to provide some operation and logistical support to the G5 Force, and implementation of the UN's Human Rights Due Diligence Policy, with support from the OHCHR, is progressing in this context. Such support could effectively make MINUSMA a party to the conflict in Mali and lose peacekeepers' protection as non-combatants.

In January, Mali underwent its third review under the UN's Universal Periodic Review mechanism. In March, the UN Human Rights Council decided to continue the mandate of the UN independent expert on Mali for another year. The independent expert visited the country before and after the presidential elections, in June and October.

In August, the UN Security Council renewed for one year the 2017 asset freeze and travel ban against those who obstruct the 2015 peace accord and commit human rights abuses. The August report of the panel of experts strongly condemned rights violations by both state and non-state actors, but the Security

Council has failed to sanction anyone for alleged human rights violations and abuses by state and non-state actors.

The International Criminal Court Prosecutor's Office continued its Mali investigation and in March, issued an arrest warrant for former Ansar Dine leader, Al Hassan Ag Abdoul Aziz Ag Mohamed Ag Mahmoud, for crimes against humanity and war crimes in Timbuktu in 2012 and 2013. However, it had not yet sought arrest warrants for any state actors at time of writing.

Mauritania

Mauritanian authorities restricted freedom of expression and assembly, especially when independent activists protested racism and ethnic discrimination, the persistence of slavery, and other sensitive issues. They imprisoned activists on dubious charges and refused to free blogger Mohamed Cheikh Ould Mkhaitir after he had completed his term for blasphemy. Opposition Senator Mohamed Ould Ghadda spent most of 2018 in pretrial detention on vague corruption charges.

Slavery has declined but has not been eliminated entirely.

In addition to social pressures, a variety of state policies and laws that criminalize adultery and morality offenses render women vulnerable to gender-based violence, making it difficult and risky for them to report sexual assault to the police.

Mauritania's laws impose the death penalty for a range of offenses, including, under certain conditions, blasphemy, adultery, and homosexuality. A de facto moratorium remains in effect on capital punishment and on corporal punishments that are inspired by Islamic Sharia law and found in the penal code.

Freedom of Expression

Local online news media provide a range of views and reportage, some of it virulently critical of President Mohamed Ould Abdel Aziz, who completes his second term in 2019 amid speculation that he may seek a constitutional amendment or other arrangement that will enable him to retain power. However, prosecutors use repressive legislation that includes criminal defamation and broad definitions of terrorism and "inciting racial hatred" to censor and prosecute critics for nonviolent speech. A new anti-discrimination law adopted in 2017 added to the arsenal; article 10 states, "Whoever encourages an incendiary discourse against the official rite of the Islamic Republic of Mauritania shall be punished by one to five years in prison."

In November 2017, an appeals court reduced the blasphemy sentence of blogger Mohamed Cheikh Ould Mkhaitir from death to two years in prison, deeming that he had "repented" sufficiently to qualify for the lighter sentence. Mkhaitir's of-

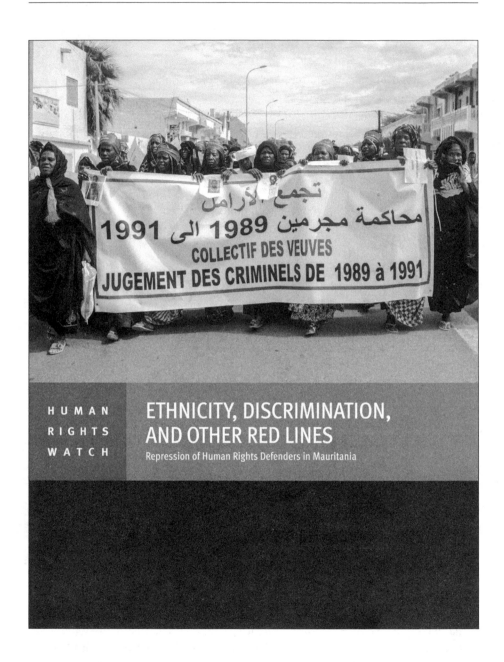

HUMAN
RIGHTS
WATCH

ETHNICITY, DISCRIMINATION,
AND OTHER RED LINES
Repression of Human Rights Defenders in Mauritania

fense was an article in which he argued that his countrymen should not use the discrimination that the Prophet Muhammad was said to have practiced in his day to justify their own discrimination against vulnerable groups, including the M'alimin caste to which Mkhaitir belongs. Imprisoned since his arrest in January 2014, the appeals court should have released Mkhaitir upon reducing his sentence.

However, authorities have since detained him in an undisclosed location, despite his declining health and offers reportedly made by other countries to grant him political asylum. Mkhaitir was in "administrative detention for his own safety," authorities told a United Nations committee on May 2, an apparent reference to street protests in which some Mauritanians have demanded his execution.

The National Assembly on April 27 voted to make the death penalty mandatory for anyone convicted of "blasphemous speech." This toughened punishment seemed to be a response to the reduction of Mkhaitir's sentence.

On August 7, authorities arrested Biram Dah Abeid, president of the Initiative for the Resurgence of the Abolitionist Movement (IRA), an anti-slavery association. The activist, who while jailed won a seat in the 2018 National Assembly elections, remained in pre-trial detention as of this writing, under investigation for reportedly insulting and threatening a journalist.

Activist Abdallahi Yali has been in jail since January 2017, facing a trial that opened October 29, 2018, on charges of incitement to violence and racial hatred under the penal code, counterterrorism law, and cybercrime law. The basis for the charges are WhatsApp messages in which Yali called on his fellow Haratines to resist discrimination and demand their rights. The Haratines, who are Arabic-speaking, dark-skinned descendants of slaves, are one of Mauritania's largest ethnic groups.

Freedom of Association

The 1964 Law of Associations requires associations to obtain permission to operate legally and allows the Ministry of Interior to refuse such permission on vague grounds such as "anti-national propaganda" or exercising "an unwelcome influence on the minds of the people." The ministry has withheld recognition from several associations that campaign on controversial issues, such as IRA and "Hands Off My Nationality," which accuses the government of discriminating against blacks in the national civil registration process.

In July, IRA activists Abdallahi Saleck and Moussa Bilal Biram completed two-year prison terms. They were the last of 13 IRA members freed after conviction in an unfair trial for their purported role in violence that erupted when police tried to dismantle an informal settlement in Nouakchott in 2016. The appeals court had convicted Saleck and Biram of incitement to an unlawful gathering and administering an unrecognized association.

On July 22, Mauritanian authorities blocked the departure for Geneva of five activists who lead organizations of widows and orphans that demand accountability for the state-sponsored repression that targeted Afro-Mauritanians between 1989 and 1991 and oppose the amnesty that the government decreed for those events in 1993. Maimouna Alpha Sy, Aïssata Mamadou Anne, Aïssata Alassane, Diallo Yaya Sy, and Baba Traoré were to participate in the UN Committee Against Torture's periodic review of Mauritania.

Human Rights Watch representatives entered and conducted research in Mauritania several times in 2018 without obstacles, but were unable to get government permission to hold a press conference in a Nouakchott hotel in February, holding it instead in the office of a local organization.

Political Opposition

Early in 2017, Senator Mohamed Ould Ghadda helped to defeat a motion before the Senate supported by President Abdel Aziz to dissolve that body, which is the upper chamber of parliament. In response, the president called a referendum to abolish the chamber, which Ghadda also opposed. In August 2017, five days after voters approved the measure, authorities arrested Ghadda and charged him with taking bribes from Mohamed Bouamatou, an exiled financier and critic of the president. (A foundation created by Bouamatou, the Fondation pour l'Egalité des chances en Afrique, supports the work of Human Rights Watch.) In August 2018, authorities released Ghadda after he had spent one year in pretrial detention. Four months earlier, on April 25, the UN Working Group on Arbitrary Detention determined Ghadda's detention to be arbitrary. The charges against him are pending.

Authorities have refused legal recognition to a political party, the Forces of Progress for Change, that is outspoken on racial discrimination. The party appealed the refusal to the Supreme Court in 2015 but has not received a decision since.

Slavery

Mauritania abolished slavery in 1981 and criminalized it in 2007. The government claims that there is no longer any slavery, only its legacy, in the form of extreme poverty and exclusion, which it is addressing. The Global Slavery Index estimates that there are 90,000 slaves in Mauritania, or 2 percent of the population, including those who endure "modern" forms of the practice, such as forced or bonded labor.

Three special courts that prosecute slavery-related crimes have tried a handful of cases since their creation under a 2015 law. In March 2018, the special court in Nouadhibou reportedly sentenced a father and son to 20 years in prison and, in a separate case, a woman to 10 years in prison for enslaving others.

Women's Rights

In 2017, parliament adopted a law on reproductive health that recognized it to be a universal right but that maintained the ban on abortion. It also adopted a general code on children's protection, which criminalizes female genital mutilation.

In addition to societal pressure to keep silent, women who endure sexual violence confront institutional barriers that include police and judicial investigative procedures that are not gender-responsive. Mauritanian law does not adequately define the crime of rape and other forms of sexual assault, although a draft law on gender-based violence with more specific definitions was pending before parliament. The criminalization of consensual adult sexual relations outside marriage likely deters girls and women from reporting assaults, because they can find themselves charged if the judiciary views the sexual act in question as consensual. During 2018, there were women in prison for adultery who said they had in fact been raped.

Mauritania's laws on divorce, child custody, and inheritance discriminate against women.

HUMAN
RIGHTS
WATCH

"They Told Me to Keep Quiet"
Obstacles to Justice and Remedy for Sexual Assault Survivors
in Mauritania

Sexual Orientation

Article 308 prohibits homosexual conduct between Muslim adults and punishes it with death for males. There were no known cases of persons imprisoned or sentenced to death in 2018 for homosexual conduct.

Civil Registration

Mauritania continued to implement a biometric national civil registration process for all citizens and others present in the country. Many citizens, particularly the poor or poorly educated, struggled to fulfill the arduous documentation requirements. Some had reportedly given up trying. Schools sometimes prevented unregistered children from enrolling, even though school is compulsory from ages 6 to 14. Even when education authorities allowed unregistered pupils to enroll, they prevented them from taking the national exams they must pass to continue their education, causing many to drop out of school.

Key International Actors

Mauritania is a member of the G5 Sahel, an alliance of five countries that cooperate on security, including counterterrorism. The G5 is headquartered in Nouakchott. In his most significant official meeting during 2018 with a Western head of state, President Abdel Aziz received French President Emmanuel Macron on July 2 and 3 during a G5 summit. There was no public indication that the two had discussed human rights issues.

On November 3, the US notified Mauritania that as of January 2019, it would lose bilateral trade preference benefits under the African Growth and Opportunity Act (AGOA). The White House justified the decision stating, "Mauritania has made insufficient progress toward combating forced labor, in particular the scourge of hereditary slavery…. [and] continues to restrict the ability of civil society to work freely to address anti-slavery issues." In 2017, the US exported to Mauritania goods valued at US$128 million and imported $62 million worth of goods.

Mexico

President Andrés Manuel López Obrador, who took office in December 2018, inherited a human rights catastrophe rooted in extreme violence by organized crime and widespread abuse by the military, police, and prosecutors. The administration of his predecessor, former President Enrique Peña Nieto (2012-2018), made little progress in improving human rights practices. Security forces continued to commit extrajudicial killings, enforced disappearances, and torture. Impunity for these crimes remained the norm. Laws enacted in 2017 could help address the problems of torture and disappearances, but implementation has lagged.

Criminal Justice System

The criminal justice system routinely fails to provide justice to victims of violent crimes and human rights violations. Causes of failure include corruption, inadequate training and resources, and complicity of prosecutors and public defenders with criminals and abusive officials.

In 2013, Mexico enacted a federal victims law intended to ensure justice, protection, and reparations for crime victims. Reforms aimed at reducing bureaucracy and improving access to reparations were approved in January 2017. However, victims report that bureaucratic delays continue to hinder access.

Military Abuses and Impunity

Mexico has relied heavily on the military to fight drug-related violence and organized crime, leading to widespread human rights violations by military personnel. Between December 2012 and January 2018, the National Human Rights Commission (CNDH) received more than 4,600 complaints regarding alleged abuses by the military.

In 2014, Congress reformed the Code of Military Justice to require that abuses committed by members of the military against civilians be handled by the civilian criminal justice system rather than the military system, which had a history of failing to hold members of the military accountable for abuses. However, the pursuit of justice for these violations remains elusive. An investigation by the

Washington Office on Latin America (WOLA) found that civilian prosecutors had opened 505 investigations between 2012 and 2016 into crimes and human rights violations committed by soldiers but only obtained 16 convictions.

In November 2018, the Supreme Court struck down the Interior Security Law, which had entered into force in December 2017, because it "[normalized] the use of the armed forces in public security issues," which the court ruled unconstitutional and in violation of Mexico's international obligations. The law would have granted the armed forces broad authority to engage in public security operations, including the ability to operate without effective civilian control, and would have deemed information generated by these "internal security" activities to be matters of "national security," thereby limiting public access. However, the same week of that ruling, López Obrador announced that his government would seek to change the constitution to create a military-controlled National Guard to preserve public security.

Torture

Torture is widely practiced in Mexico to obtain confessions and extract information. It is most frequently applied in the period between when victims are detained, often arbitrarily, and when they are handed over to civilian prosecutors—a period in which they are often held incommunicado at military bases or illegal detention sites.

According to a survey of more than 64,000 people incarcerated in 338 Mexican prisons located throughout the country in 2016, performed by Mexico's national statistics office (INEGI), 64 percent of the prison population reported having suffered some type of physical violence at the time of their arrest: 19 percent reported receiving electrical shocks; 36 percent being choked, held underwater, or smothered; and 59 percent being hit or kicked. In addition, 28 percent reported that they were threatened that their family would be harmed.

Between December 2012 and January 2018, the Attorney General's Office opened more than 9,000 investigations into torture. However, torturers are rarely brought to justice.

Investigations suffer from serious shortcomings. In March, the Mexican Office of the UN High Commissioner for Human Rights published an investigation that stated it had found "solid grounds to conclude" that at least 34 detainees had been tortured during the investigation of the 2014 disappearance of 43 students from Ayotzinapa. In May, a federal judge established that prosecutors had not adequately investigated evidence of torture of detainees in the Ayotzinapa case. At least 10 government agencies filed appeals against the ruling, which, at time of writing, remained pending.

In April 2017, the Mexican legislature approved the Law to Investigate, Prevent, and Sanction Torture, aimed at curbing torture and excluding testimony obtained through torture from judicial proceedings. At time of writing, implementation of the law remained pending. Although the law required the Attorney General's Office to have the infrastructure for a national torture registry in place by December 2017, it had not done so as of August 2018.

Enforced Disappearances

Since 2006, enforced disappearances by security forces has been a widespread problem. Criminal organizations have also been responsible for many disappearances.

In October 2018, the interior minister stated that the whereabouts of more than 37,400 people who had gone missing since 2006 remain unknown. According to the CNDH, more than 3,900 bodies have been found in over 1,300 clandestine graves since 2007.

Prosecutors and police routinely neglect to take basic investigative steps to identify those responsible for enforced disappearances, often telling the missing people's families to investigate on their own. Since 2013, the Attorney General's Office has had a specialized office to investigate and prosecute disappearances. As of August 2018, it had opened 1,255 investigations but only pressed charges in 11 cases. It did not report any convictions.

In November 2017, Congress passed a law on disappearances that established a single nationwide definition for the crime and mandated the creation of entities to facilitate the investigation and prosecution of disappearances. These include the National Search Commission (CNB) that was created in March 2018 to coordinate search efforts in the field, and the National Search System (SNB), established in October 2018 to coordinate state institutions involved in the search for the disappeared.

However, at time of writing these entities were not yet fully operational. In July 2018, the Citizen Council of the National Search System, an advisory body created by the disappearances law, reported that the CNB was not receiving the resources it needs to fulfill its mandate. The council also criticized the lack of coordination between institutions, and expressed its concern that most states lag behind in implementing the law. Only 13 out of 32 states had created a specialized prosecutor's office and only nine out of 32 states had local search commissions or offices, even though the law mandated the creation of those entities by February and April 2018, respectively.

Victims' families have repeatedly denounced serious shortcomings regarding the identification and storage of bodies. In September, media reported that in Jalisco state, neighbors complained about smells of decaying bodies and leaks of blood after the state prosecutor's office parked a refrigeration trailer packed with unidentified bodies in their neighborhood because the morgue was full. The former director of forensic services stated that authorities had used refrigeration trailers for at least two years to store more than 250 bodies. The human rights prosecutor asserted that authorities had taken proper information and samples to enable identification of only 60 bodies.

In May 2018, the UN High Commissioner for Human Rights denounced a "wave of enforced disappearances" of at least 23 people in Nuevo Laredo, Tamaulipas state, between February and May. The Executive Commission for Assistance to Victims (CEAV) indicated that Navy personnel were likely involved in the disappearances. However, prosecutors conducted limited search efforts, and only after a federal judge—acting on an appeal from victims' families—ordered them to do so. At time of writing, the judge had imposed 10 fines on the Navy and five on the Attorney General's Office because they failed to respond to her inquiries.

Extrajudicial Killings

Unlawful killings of civilians by Mexican security forces "take place at an alarmingly high rate" amid an atmosphere of "systematic and endemic impunity," according to the United Nations special rapporteur on extrajudicial, summary, or arbitrary executions in 2014.

However, there is no reliable information about the number of extrajudicial executions. The vast majority of homicides are never prosecuted. Government authorities only register the number of homicides and not the circumstances in which these took place. The Defense Department stopped registering the numbers of civilians it killed as of 2014.

Attacks on Journalists

Journalists, particularly those who report on crime or criticize officials, often face harassment and attack by both government authorities and criminal groups. Many journalists are driven to self-censorship as a result. A 2017 study by researchers from the University of Miami and the Iberoamerican University in Mexico City showed that almost 70 percent of journalists said they had engaged in self-censorship out of fear for their personal safety.

Between January 2000 and August 2018, 110 journalists were killed and 25 disappeared, according to the Attorney General's Office. The CNDH put that number even higher: it reported 148 journalists killed since 2000 and 21 disappeared since 2005. Media reports indicated that eight journalists were killed between January and September 2018.

In 2012, the federal government established the National Protection Mechanism to issue and coordinate the implementation of protective measures for journalists and human rights defenders under threat. Between October 2012 and July 2018, 418 journalists requested and 357 were authorized to receive protection measures. However, protection has been slow to arrive and, in some cases, has been insufficient. In August 2018, the CNDH and the Mexican Office of the UN High Commissioner for Human Rights expressed their concern about the lack of resources for the mechanism.

Authorities routinely fail to investigate crimes against journalists adequately, often preemptively ruling out their profession as a motive. The CNDH reported in 2016 that 90 percent of crimes against journalists in Mexico since 2000 have gone unpunished, including 82 percent of killings and 100 percent of disappearances. Since its creation in July 2010, the federal Special Prosecutor's Office opened more than 1,000 investigations into crimes against journalists. As of August 2018, it brought charges in 152 cases and obtained only seven convictions, of which just one was for homicide.

Women's and Girls' Rights

Mexican laws do not adequately protect women and girls against domestic and sexual violence. Some provisions, including those that make the severity of punishments for some sexual offenses contingent upon the "chastity" of the victim, contradict international standards.

Eighteen of Mexico's 32 states establish in their constitutions that there is a right to life from the moment of conception. Although the Supreme Court ruled in 2010 that all states must provide emergency contraception and access to abortion for rape victims, many women and girls face serious barriers accessing abortions after sexual violence, including official intimidation. According to a study by the Group for Information about Elective Reproduction (GIRE), between 2007 and 2016, Mexico convicted 98 women for abortions.

In July, the UN Committee on the Elimination of Discrimination against Women urged the state to take measures to combat the discrimination of women—including in the workplace—and to prevent gender-based violence and the trafficking of women and girls.

Migrants and Asylum Seekers

Migrants traveling through Mexico are frequently subject to abuses and human rights violations. In some of these cases there are allegations that government authorities are involved. Between December 2012 and January 2018, the CNDH received more than 3,000 complaints of abuses against migrants. And a 2017 WOLA report, citing official numbers, indicated that there had been 5,294 reports of crimes against migrants between 2014 and 2016 in five states alone.

It is very likely that such crimes are severely underreported due to fear of authorities, of reprisals, and for practical reasons: the prosecutor's offices where reports can be made tend to be far from the places where crimes are committed.

According to government statistics, apprehensions of unaccompanied children from the Northern Triangle countries of El Salvador, Guatemala, and Honduras were significantly lower in 2017 and 2018 compared to 2016, and asylum recognition rates for unaccompanied children from these countries have risen in recent years. Even so, less than 1 percent of those apprehended each year received international protection, far short of the likely need: the UN High Commissioner for Refugees (UNHCR) has estimated that as many as half of the unaccompanied children who arrive in Mexico from the Northern Triangle have plausible asylum claims that should be seriously considered.

Sexual Orientation and Gender Identity

Mexico City and 11 additional states have legalized same-sex marriage. In other states, same-sex couples must file a constitutional challenge (*amparo*) to be allowed to marry; a 2015 Supreme Court decision holding that the definition of marriage as being only between a man and a woman violates the constitution, means that rulings in such cases should be in their favor. In September 2018, a same-sex couple in Michoacán was able to obtain a birth certificate for their child on which the two mothers were listed as the parents.

In 2016, President Peña Nieto instructed the Secretariat of Education to include the topic of sexual diversity in its new educational materials, with which it complied in 2018.

In October 2018, the Supreme Court ruled in favor of a transgender applicant who sought to change their gender marker through administrative means at the Civil Registry in Veracruz. The ruling, which cited an Inter-American Court on Human Rights advisory opinion on the right to legal gender recognition, suggested the court might uphold transgender rights in an upcoming case that may create binding jurisprudence.

Disability Rights

In its 2014 concluding observations on Mexico, the UN Committee on the Rights of Persons with Disabilities found that, despite new laws and programs protecting the rights of people with disabilities, serious gaps remained, including in access to justice, legal standing, and the right to vote; access to buildings, transportation, and public spaces; violence against women; and education.

Mexico made no progress in implementing the right to legal capacity for persons with disabilities.

In October 2018, the second chamber of Mexico's Supreme Court ruled that failing to admit a group of children with disabilities to community schools and placing them in separate special schools violated Mexico's Constitution.

Key International Actors

In September 2017, the UN Committee on Migrant Workers expressed its concern about the "grave irregularities" in the identification of the victims and those responsible for the mass murders of migrants committed between 2010 and 2012 in the states of Nuevo León and Tamaulipas. It also urged the state to guarantee the rights of migrants in transit and called on Mexican authorities to "only use the detention of migrants as a measure of last resort," to improve conditions of detention, and to "immediately put an end to" the detention of migrant children.

In April 2018, the UN Committee on Economic, Social, and Cultural Rights urged Mexico to improve its protection of human rights defenders, as well as to implement measures to address poverty, inequality, and discrimination, and in July 2018, the UN Committee on the Elimination of Discrimination against Women expressed concern about reports of forced sterilization of women with disabilities in Mexico.

Since 2007, the United States has allocated nearly US$2.9 billion in aid through the Mérida Initiative to help Mexico combat organized crime. In 2015, the US secretary of state withheld $5 million in security aid, saying the State Department could not confirm that Mexico had met the agreement's human rights criteria, but Mexico has received its full Mérida aid the following years. In 2018, Congress appropriated $145 million for Mérida aid.

Morocco/Western Sahara

Demonstrating increasing intolerance of public dissent, Moroccan authorities in March responded to protests in the mining town of Jerada with weeks of repression, using excessive force against protesters and arresting protest leaders, who were later sentenced to months in prison. In June, a Casablanca court sentenced leaders of the "Hirak," a protest movement that demonstrated regularly in the Rif region for months, to sentences of up to 20 years in prison after unfair trials. A court sentenced a prominent journalist and government critic to three years in prison on a dubious security charge, while he was already serving a sentence for inciting unauthorized demonstrations.

Though Human Rights Watch staff were able to operate in Morocco and Western Sahara in a relatively free manner, authorities continued throughout 2018 to restrict the activities of other NGOs, including Morocco's biggest independent human rights organization.

Laws on violence against women and on domestic work took effect in the fall, offering modest new protections to victims of violence and labor abuse.

Freedom of Assembly, Police Violence, and the Criminal Justice System

Morocco's Ministry of Human Rights stated that security services broke up only three percent of the 17,511 demonstrations that protesters organized in Morocco in 2017. The dispersals, the ministry said, were conducted in a manner consistent with the "respect of basic freedoms and the rule of law." However, in both 2017 and 2018, Human Rights Watch documented several instances of excessive use of force in breaking up protests, as well as arrests of peaceful protesters on grounds such as demonstrating without a permit and assaulting police.

The Code of Penal Procedure gives a defendant the right to contact a lawyer after 24 hours in police custody, extendable to 36 hours. But detainees do not have the right to a have a lawyer present when police interrogate or present them with their statements for signature.

Starting on March 14, authorities met socioeconomic protests in the impoverished northeastern mining town of Jerada with a crackdown that went well beyond an effort to bring allegedly violent protesters to justice. In one incident captured on video, a police vehicle on March 14 sped into a protest, hitting 16-year-old Abdelmoula Zaiqer and severely injuring him. Police agents broke into houses without showing warrants, beat several men upon arrest, and broke doors and windows, local activists and a lawyer said. Between March 14 and May 31, authorities arrested and prosecuted at least 69 protesters in Jerada; four protest leaders received between three and nine months in prison.

The "Hirak," a socioeconomic protest movement in the Rif region that started in 2016, staged several largely peaceful mass protests until a police crackdown in May 2017 led to the arrest of more than 450 activists. Fifty-three of them, including the movement's main leaders, were transferred to a prison in Casablanca, where they faced a year-long mass trial. The court of first instance rejected defendants' claims that their confessions were obtained through torture and coercion, despite medical reports that gave some support to their claims. On June 26, the court convicted all of the defendants. The charges included rebellion, violence against police forces, staging unauthorized protests, and receiving foreign funding. The court sentenced them to prison terms from one to 20 years.

In August 2018, King Mohamed VI pardoned 188 sentenced Hirak activists, including 11 of the Casablanca group, but none of the leaders. The appeals trial of the Casablanca group opened November 14.

On September 25, the coastguard fired on a boat in the Mediterranean, killing student Hayat Belkacem, 20, and wounding three other passengers, who were apparently trying to migrate to Europe. Morocco's state news agency said that the coastguard opened fire after the boat acted "suspiciously" in Moroccan waters and the pilot disobeyed orders. Authorities pledged to investigate the killing but had not disclosed their findings at time of writing.

On October 17, a Tetouan court of first instance sentenced Soufian al-Nguad, 28, to two years in prison for incitement to insurrection, spreading hate, and insulting Morocco's flag and symbols, after he criticized the killing of Belkacem on Facebook and encouraged people to march in protest at the incident.

Freedom of Association

Authorities frequently impeded events organized by local chapters of the Moroccan Association for Human Rights (AMDH) by denying access to planned venues. In a typical instance, on March 12, security forces in the city of Beni Mellal blocked the entrance of a community center where the local branch had planned a conference. Authorities provided no written justification for the interdiction. Between January 2017 and July 2018, 16 events organized by AMDH were cancelled throughout Morocco, after authorities either directly denied access to participants or pressured the venue's operator to cancel the events, according to the AMDH.

The government has continued to impose a de facto ban on research missions by Amnesty International since 2015, despite relatively unimpeded access of the organization for nearly 25 years before then. Human Rights Watch researchers were able to conduct research missions in 2018 to Jerada and El-Ayoun in Western Sahara, but were frequently followed by cars containing men in civilian clothes.

Freedom of Expression

The Press and Publications Code, adopted by parliament in July 2016, eliminates prison sentences for speech-related offenses. Meanwhile, the penal code maintains prison as a punishment for a variety of nonviolent speech offenses, including for "causing harm" to Islam, the monarchy, and "inciting against" Morocco's "territorial integrity," a reference to its claim to Western Sahara.

Authorities prosecuted journalists and social media activists for criminal offenses that, while not ostensibly journalism-related, were pursued apparently in reprisal for their speech activities.

On November 14, an appeals court in Sale, near Rabat, confirmed the five-year prison term for Elmortada Iamrachen, 32, one of the main spokespeople for the Rif's "Hirak" protest movement. A court convicted Iamrachen in November 2017 of inciting and praising terrorism in Facebook posts, based on a confession to police that he had sought, via these posts, to incite readers to engage in terrorism. Iamrachen repudiated the confession shortly after he signed it, and told the court it was coerced.

On June 28, a Casablanca court of first instance sentenced journalist Hamid El Mahdaoui to three years in prison for failing to report a security threat. The conviction was based on a phone call he received from a man who said he intended to create armed strife in Morocco. The court did not accept El Mahdaoui's main line of defense—that he had concluded the caller's declarations to be idle chatter. A noted critic of the government, El Mahdaoui was already serving a one-year sentence for "inciting people to participate in an unauthorized protest."

Western Sahara

The United Nations-sponsored process of negotiations between Morocco and the Polisario Front for self-determination of Western Sahara, most of which is under de facto Moroccan control, remained stalled despite visits to the region of Horst Kohler, envoy of the UN secretary-general. Morocco proposes a measure of autonomy under its rule but rejects a referendum on independence.

For several weeks in March and April, and again between September and November, three prisoners sentenced to life and one sentenced to 30 years, all part of the "Gdeim Izik" group, conducted a hunger strike in Kenitra prison, to demand that they be moved to prisons nearer to their families in Western Sahara, about 1,200 kilometers south. The demand was not met at the time of writing. Along with some 20 co-defendants, the three were convicted in unfair trials in 2013 and 2017 of responsibility in the deaths of 11 security force members during clashes that erupted after authorities forcibly dismantled a large protest encampment in Gdeim Izik, Western Sahara, in 2010. Both courts relied almost entirely on their confessions to police to convict them, even though the defendants repudiated those confessions and said they signed under torture without being permitted to read them.

Moroccan authorities systematically prevent gatherings in Western Sahara supporting Sahrawi self-determination, obstruct the work of some local human rights NGOs, including by blocking their legal registration, and on occasion beat activists and journalists in their custody and on the streets.

On June 28, pro-independence activists organized a protest in El-Ayoun coinciding with the visit of UN envoy Kohler. Police beat at least seven activists, including members of the Sahrawi Association of Victims of Grave Human Rights Violations Committed by the Moroccan State (*ASVDH*) , according to the ASVDH,

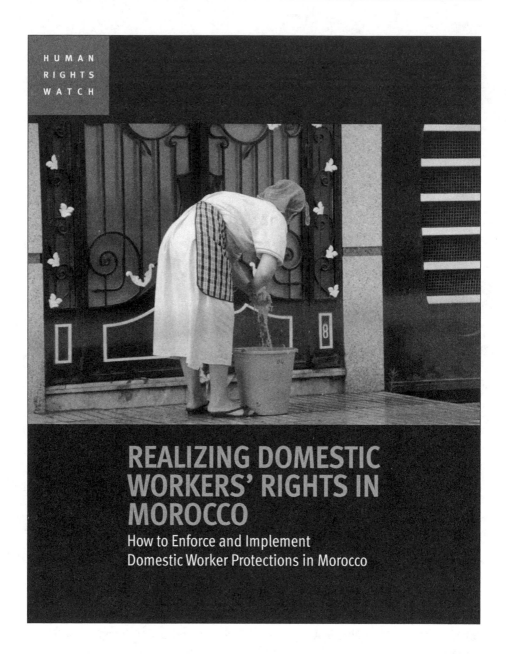

HUMAN
RIGHTS
WATCH

REALIZING DOMESTIC WORKERS' RIGHTS IN MOROCCO

How to Enforce and Implement
Domestic Worker Protections in Morocco

which sent complaints to El-Ayoun's prosecutor. No investigation was opened, to Human Right Watch's knowledge.

On June 25, Mohamed Salem Mayara and Mohamed El Joumayi, two journalists for the website Smara News and correspondents of the pro-Polisario RASD TV, were accused of throwing stones and blocking a street. The charges came months after they published pictures of a policeman with his gun drawn in the city of Smara in Western Sahara. Police arrested Mayara and El Joumayi on March 27 in Smara, then the same policeman beat them in a van on their way to El-Ayoun, their lawyer, Mohamed Aboukhaled, told Human Rights Watch. At time of writing, they remained in detention while their trial continued.

Migrants and Refugees

The government has yet to approve a draft of Morocco's first law on the right to asylum. Between 2013 and 2017, a Moroccan ad hoc inter-ministerial commission granted refugee cards and one-year renewable residency permits to 745 persons, most of them sub-Saharan Africans, whom the UN High Commissioner for Refugees (UNHCR) recognized as refugees. Since then, Morocco allowed another 1,106 UNHCR-recognized refugees access to essential public services, such as education and health, but not the right to work.

In September, Amnesty International reported on a "large-scale crackdown on thousands of sub-Saharan migrants, asylum seekers, and refugees without due process." The group said that security forces have carried out raids in several cities in the northern provinces of Tangiers, Nador, and Tetuan, rounding up sub-Saharans and bussing them to cities in the interior and releasing them there.

Women's and Girls' Rights

The 2004 Family Code discriminates against women with regard to inheritance and procedures to obtain divorce. The code sets 18 as a minimum age of marriage but allows judges to marry children below this age in certain circumstances. They routinely do so.

Criminalization of adultery and sex outside marriage has a discriminatory gender impact, in that rape victims risk prosecution if they file charges that are not later sustained. Women and girls also face prosecution if they are found to be pregnant or bear children outside marriage.

A new law on violence against women, adopted on February 14, took effect six months later. It criminalizes some forms of domestic violence, establishes prevention measures, and provides new protections for survivors. But it does not set out duties of police, prosecutors, and investigative judges in domestic violence cases, or fund women's shelters.

Domestic Workers

A 2016 law on domestic worker rights took effect on October 2. The law provides domestic workers with minimal labor protections from which they have long been excluded. It requires written labor contracts for domestic workers, sets 18 as the minimum age for such employment, after a five-year interim period during which 16 and 17-year-olds are allowed to work, limits weekly working hours, guarantees a weekly day off and paid vacation, and sets a minimum wage. It imposes fines on employers who violate the law, and prison sentences for some repeat offenders. While the law came into force, authorities have yet to ensure adequate implementing mechanisms to ensure that domestic workers can realize their rights.

Sexual Orientation and Gender Identity

Morocco's penal code still discriminates against LGBT persons. Article 489 of the penal code stipulates prison terms of six months to three years for "lewd or unnatural acts with an individual of the same sex."

Key International Actors

In a challenge to Morocco's efforts to win international recognition of its unilateral annexation of the Western Sahara, the European Court of Justice on February 27 ruled that a fishing agreement between Morocco and the European Union did not apply to the waters off the coast of Western Sahara, due to the separate and distinct status that the UN assigned to that territory.

Two new EU-Morocco agreements, crafted in response to the decision and alluding to "benefits to the population of Western Sahara and the consultation of this population," are pending votes by the parliaments of the European Union and Morocco.

Mozambique

The government of Mozambique under President Filipe Nyusi struggled to protect people's rights in 2018. State security forces were implicated in serious human rights violations in their response to attacks by suspected Islamist armed groups in the northern province of Cabo Delgado. Thousands were displaced as armed men attacked villages, burned houses and killed people.

Mozambican law enforcement failed to hold anyone to account for serious abuses documented by Human Rights Watch and other organizations, including threats and intimidation against activists and human rights defenders. The work of the press, especially private media and correspondents, was under threat after the government issued a decree that imposed high fees on media organizations seeking to operate in the country.

Violations and Attacks in the North

Attacks by a suspected armed Islamist group in the northern province of Cabo Delgado killed at least 39 people and left more than 1,000 displaced between May and July 2018. The wave of attacks on civilians began in October 2017, when suspected armed Islamists attacked a police station in the Mocimboa da Praia district, causing two days of lockdown in the area and a military response that led to the evacuation of villages. Despite the police presence in the region and the establishment of a special military operation to fight the armed groups, attacks on villages continued sporadically in 2018.

Human Rights Watch documented killings, arson, destruction of property, and other abuses committed by the group locally known as both Al-Sunna wa Jama'a and Al-Shabab. In one village of Macomia district, the group burned 164 houses and five cars, and killed scores of cattle during a night attack on June 5. Residents said the attackers beheaded a local Islamic leader inside a mosque before burning down the mosque, which housed copies of the Quran and prayer mats. In June, Human Rights Watch witnessed dozens of families carrying their belongings and fleeing their villages. On June 6, the group raided the village of Namaluco, in Quissanga district, killing six people and burning more than 100 houses. On June 12, the group attacked the village of Nathuko, in the Macomia district, where they beheaded an elderly man and burned down at least 100 homes. Between May and July, the group attacked at least three districts of Cabo

HUMAN
RIGHTS
WATCH

THE NEXT ONE TO DIE
State Security Force and Renamo Abuses in Mozambique

Delgado province and burned down more than 400 homes, leaving thousands homeless. In August, the United Nations World Food Programme (WFP) began distributing food aid to 10,000 people who fled the attacks and sought refuge in makeshift camps set up by local authorities.

Security forces were also implicated in serious human rights abuses during their response to the violence in Cabo Delgado province. Following the first attack in October 2017, authorities closed down seven mosques and detained more than 300 people without charge, including religious leaders and foreigners suspected of having links to the armed attacks in Palma and Mocimboa da Praia districts. Security forces also prevented suspected members of the armed group from receiving medical treatment.

In August, a South African businessman, Andre Hanekon, was kidnapped by security forces and was later found injured in a local hospital in Pemba, Cabo Delgado. On September 11, he was detained, accused of involvement in attacks by armed groups in the region, but no formal charges have been brought against him.

Accountability for Past Crimes

Mozambican law enforcement failed to hold anyone to account for serious abuses documented by Human Rights Watch and other organizations. The case of journalist and lawyer Ericino De Salema, who was kidnapped and beaten in Maputo in March, remains unresolved, as well as the cases of 10 high-profile figures, including senior opposition members, state prosecutors, and prominent academics, who were either killed or injured in politically motivated attacks in 2016.

Authorities failed to investigate human rights abuses committed by government security forces during military clashes with armed men from the opposition Renamo. Human Rights Watch documented cases of enforced disappearances, arbitrary detention, and the destruction of private property by government forces, as well as political killings, attacks on public transport, and looting of health clinics by the Renamo political party's armed group, between November 2015 and December 2016. Since the ceasefire was declared in December 2016, fighting and related human rights abuses have ceased. But authorities have not held anyone accountable.

Freedom of Expression

Activists and human rights defenders continued to live in fear in the face of threats and intimidation from unknown individuals. On March 27, Salema was abducted by two unidentified gunmen outside the headquarters of the National Union of Journalists in the capital, Maputo. They beat him with AK-47 assault rifles, leaving him unconscious just outside the city. Salema was a resident political commentator on one of Mozambique's leading television shows. Two other former commentators from the same show said they decided to cut ties with the program after receiving frequent threats from unidentified people who claimed to work for the state security and intelligence services.

Following the incident, six activists said they received threatening messages for criticizing the government. Two said they had been forced to move, use different cars, and change their routines after noticing vehicles without license plates following them in the city or parked outside their homes for hours.

Freedom of Media

Press freedom, especially for private media and correspondents, was threatened by the Mozambican government's issuance on July 23 of Decree 40/2018, which required foreign journalists to pay US$2,500 per trip to Mozambique for media accreditation. Freelancers and foreign correspondents based in the country would be charged $500 and $8,300 per year, respectively.

The new regulations also established new fees for the establishment of Mozambican media organizations, imposing a $3,300 fee for new publications and an $800 fee for new community radio stations. Local journalists' groups and other nongovernmental organizations criticized the government for approving the controversial decree without consultations. In August, the director of the Mozambican Information Office, Emilia Moiane, said the decision to increase the fees had been put on hold pending further consultations.

Disability Rights

There is little data available on the exact number of persons with albinism in Mozambique, but civil society organizations estimate there are from 20,000 to 30,000 people with albinism across the country. Kidnappings and physical attacks against people with albinism continued. In Mozambique and some neighboring countries, people with albinism are hunted for their body parts, which are used for witchcraft.

In January 2018, police stopped an attempt to kidnap an 11-year-old boy in the central province of Zambezia. The boy had been attacked by five people, who cut off his ears and shaved his head before the police arrived. In July 2018, a 10-year-old boy was abducted from his home in Niassa province in northern Mozambique. In early September, two children with albinism, ages 4 and 11, were reportedly abducted in separate incidents in Niassa province.

Key International Actors

The Mozambique group of 14 donor countries, including the United Kingdom and European Union, and multilateral institutions, including the International Monetary Fund and World Bank, continued the freeze on direct support to the state budget because of corruption concerns. Some international partners continued to support crucial sectors. The United States, for example, maintained its support for malaria and HIV programs, while the European Union is supporting the strengthening of civil society groups and protection of human rights defenders.

In March, the US criticized the kidnapping of Salema and defended the importance of a free and independent media as a pillar of Mozambican democracy. In April, the UN special rapporteur on freedom of opinion and expression and the UN special rapporteur on human rights defenders sent a communication to Mozambique echoing the US's concerns. They also expressed their concern at the absence of thorough investigations and accountability for any alleged perpetrators of attacks against activists, and stated that the ensuing impunity contributes to the recurrence of these crimes.

On June 25, President Nyusi announced that Russia and the US had offered to help fight terrorist attacks in northern province of Cabo Delgado, but did not provide further details.

HUMAN
RIGHTS
WATCH

"Nothing for Our Land"
Impact of Land Confiscation on Farmers in Myanmar

Myanmar

Myanmar security forces continued to commit grave abuses against Rohingya Muslims throughout 2018, deepening the humanitarian and human rights catastrophe in Rakhine State. More than 730,000 Rohingya have fled to neighboring Bangladesh since the military campaign of ethnic cleansing began in August 2017. The government denied extensive evidence of atrocities, refused to allow independent investigators access to Rakhine State, and punished local journalists for reporting on military abuses.

In August, a United Nations-mandated fact-finding mission found that the military abuses committed in Kachin, Rakhine, and Shan States since 2011 "undoubtedly amount to the gravest crimes under international law," and called for senior military officials, including Commander-in-Chief Sr. Gen. Min Aung Hlaing, to face investigation and prosecution for genocide, crimes against humanity, and war crimes.

The ruling National League for Democracy (NLD) under de facto leader Aung San Suu Kyi increasingly stifled dissent using a slew of repressive laws. Democratic space diminished, with the NLD doing little to address the country's weak rule of law, corrupt judiciary, or impunity for security force abuses. The 2008 constitution places the Ministries of Defense, Home Affairs, and Border Affairs under the control of the military.

Over 30,000 civilians were newly displaced by fighting in Kachin and Shan States in 2018, and left increasingly vulnerable by government restrictions on humanitarian access.

Grave Crimes Against Rohingya

More than 14,500 Rohingya fled to Bangladesh between January and November 2018 to escape ongoing persecution and violence in Myanmar, joining almost 1 million others from 2017 and previous years in precarious, overcrowded camps. Conditions remain dire for the estimated 500,000-600,000 Rohingya still in Rakhine State. Refugees who arrived in Bangladesh in 2018 reported continuing abuses by Myanmar security forces, including killings, arson, enforced disappearances, extortion, severe restrictions on movement, and lack of food and health care. They also reported sexual violence and abductions of women and girls in villages and at checkpoints along the route to Bangladesh. Returnees to Myanmar faced arrest and torture by authorities. Over 4,500 Rohingya remained stuck in the Bangladesh-Myanmar border "no-man's land," subject to harassment by Myanmar officials and regular threats via loudspeaker to induce them to cross into Bangladesh.

Rohingya refugees who fled in 2018 reported that Myanmar authorities had ordered them to accept the National Verification Card (NVC)—which does not provide citizenship—or leave Myanmar. Successive governments have for decades deprived Rohingya of nationality through systematic and institutionalized marginalization, rendering them stateless.

From January to March 2018, at least 34 villages in Myanmar were completely or partially destroyed, bringing the total number of predominantly Rohingya villages destroyed between August 2017 and March 2018 to 392, most by fire. The government also seized and bulldozed dozens of Rohingya villages, destroying evidence of crimes. Authorities began construction over the demolished villages, including new security force bases.

More than 128,000 Muslims—about 125,000 Rohingya and 3,000 Kaman—remain in detention camps in central Rakhine State, where they have been confined since 2012, arbitrarily deprived of their liberty. The government announced several camp "closures" in 2018, but its plans entail constructing permanent structures in the current camp locations, further entrenching segregation and denying Rohingya the right to return to their original areas of residence or move elsewhere.

The government barred the UN fact-finding mission and special rapporteur on Myanmar from the country. Authorities have repeatedly denied that significant security force abuses took place, setting up successive investigations that lacked independence or credibility. A commission of inquiry with international members was established in July, which the fact-finding mission determined "will not and cannot provide a real avenue for accountability."

Myanmar claimed throughout 2018 that it was ready to accept repatriated refugees, yet showed no willingness to create conditions for safe and dignified returns or address the root causes of the crisis. The government built two "reception centers" and a "transit camp," surrounded by perimeter fences, to process and house returnees, based on a November 2017 agreement with Bangladesh.

In June 2018, UNHCR, the UN Development Programme, and the Myanmar government signed a memorandum of understanding on returns which lacked guarantees of citizenship. The UN agencies began limited assessments in Rakhine State in September.

Bangladesh and Myanmar announced in October that the first round of repatriation of 2,260 Rohingya refugees would begin in mid-November, a proposal opposed by the UN refugee agency (UNHCR) and Rohingya refugee community, neither of which had been consulted. Returns were suspended following widespread opposition; no official repatriations had taken place at time of writing.

Ethnic Conflicts and Forced Displacement

Armed conflicts between the Myanmar military and ethnic armed groups intensified over the course of 2018 in Kachin, Shan, and Karen States, stoked by large-scale development projects and disputes over natural resources. Civilians were endangered by the military's indiscriminate attacks, forced displacement, and aid blockages. Reports emerged of the military using civilians as human shields. The UN fact-finding mission determined that the military's actions in Shan and Kachin States since 2011 amounted to war crimes and crimes against humanity.

In January 2018, clashes broke out between the military and the Kachin Independence Army (KIA) in several townships in Kachin State, with the military employing aerial bombing and heavy artillery shelling. More than 3,500 civilians attempting to flee the fighting were trapped, some for over two weeks, without access to adequate food or basic supplies. Hostilities in Kachin State resumed in April. Government shelling and airstrikes killed at least 10 civilians and forced approximately 2,000 to flee into the jungle, where they were stranded for nearly a month without access to aid, in dire conditions.

An estimated 106,000 civilians remain in long-term displacement camps in Kachin and northern Shan States, many near areas of active conflict, while more than 30,000 were temporarily displaced in 2018. Thousands were also displaced by fighting in Karen State in March, and in Chin State in May.

Authorities continued throughout 2018 to bar the UN and international organizations from delivering aid in areas controlled by ethnic armed groups. Access was also restricted in government-controlled areas and for local organizations. The resulting shortages of food, medicine, and shelter have had a ruinous effect on displaced populations, contributing to a rise in exploitative practices including portering and trafficking. Aid workers who traveled to a non-government-controlled area in 2018 to provide humanitarian support were threatened with arrest under the Unlawful Associations Act.

In July, following clashes in northern Shan State, the military allegedly detained six female medics from the Ta'ang National Liberation Army (TNLA), who were found dead from gunshot and stab wounds shortly thereafter.

Ongoing fighting has fostered conflict-related sexual violence, with internally displaced women and girls especially vulnerable to sexual exploitation and abuse.

Trafficking of women and girls remains a serious problem in Kachin and northern Shan States, where conflict and economic desperation has made them vulnerable to being lured to China under false promises and sold as "brides." The Myanmar government has failed to take sufficient steps to prevent trafficking, recover victims, bring perpetrators to justice, or assist survivors.

In February, authorities in Muse township, Shan State, issued an announcement that wounded ethnic armed group soldiers found by the army should be brought immediately to the nearest military base and not be provided medical treatment, a practice that amounts to torture.

In July, Aung San Suu Kyi presided over the third session of the 21st Century Panglong Conference, the government's peace process forum, which has largely stagnated, failing to gain trust or traction among ethnic armed groups.

Freedom of Speech

The government in 2018 increased its use of overly broad and vaguely worded laws to arrest and imprison individuals for peaceful expression deemed critical of the government or military. Journalists' ability to cover conflict areas steadily declined, while the rise in prosecutions had a chilling effect on the country's media. A September UN report on legal and judicial harassment of reporters in

Myanmar concluded that it had become "impossible for journalists to do their job without fear or favour."

In September, a Yangon court sentenced Reuters journalists Wa Lone and Kyaw Soe Oo to seven years in prison under the colonial-era Official Secrets Act for their reporting on a military massacre of Rohingya in Rakhine State's Inn Din village. They were arrested in December 2017, in what witness accounts revealed to be a police setup, held incommunicado for two weeks, and subjected to mistreatment during interrogation. The prosecution's case was marked by evidence of police misconduct and conflicting official accounts.

Prosecutions for criminal defamation increased in 2018, particularly under section 66(d) of the 2013 Telecommunications Act, with most complainants state, military, or political party officials; over 60 percent of defendants were journalists, activists, or others addressing matters of public interest. Acquittals were rare. In May, a human rights defender from the Ayeyarwady Region was sentenced to three months in prison under 66(d) for broadcasting a video of a satirical play about armed conflict on Facebook.

In March, authorities sentenced Aung Ko Htwe, a former child soldier, to two years in prison with hard labor for an interview he gave to journalists detailing his forced recruitment into the army at age 14. Two supporters who protested his case were sentenced to one year in prison in September.

Authorities began using section 8(f) of the Privacy Law, enacted in March 2017, to prosecute critics for criminal defamation. In January, a Mon State official sued a man in Thaton under the new law for social media posts deemed critical of the Mon State chief minister; he was sentenced to one year in prison in September.

More than 45 activists were charged in April and May for peaceful protests held throughout the country calling for the protection of civilians displaced by military offensives in Kachin State. Authorities in Yangon attempted to ban a May 12 anti-war protest, citing a November 2017 order prohibiting protests in 11 Yangon townships, even though organizers had notified authorities in advance. Police in riot gear violently dispersed the protest and arrested 17 demonstrators. In Kachin State, a lieutenant colonel filed criminal defamation complaints against three Kachin human rights defenders who had helped organize protests in Myitkyina. The three activists were officially charged in September and sentenced to six months in prison in December.

In July, police violently quelled a demonstration in Karenni State, tasing and baton-charging protesters who were marching against plans to erect a statue of Myanmar's independence leader, General Aung San. Ten Karenni youth activists were arrested and charged with alarming the public and incitement.

In January, police shot and killed seven ethnic Rakhine protesters in Mrauk U, Rakhine State, among a crowd that had converged at a local government building after authorities shut down an annual event.

An estimated 27 political prisoners were serving prison sentences and 262 facing trial in Myanmar as of November 2018.

Land Rights

While the NLD government has made efforts to address the military's legacy of land grabbing, thousands of land claims remain unresolved. Farmers continue to face threats and arrests for protesting unresolved confiscation claims and for farming the land they claim. In May 2018, 33 farmers were found guilty of criminal trespass for farming land near a special economic zone that had been seized in 1996. In September, parliament passed amendments to the Vacant, Fallow and Virgin Lands Management Law requiring anyone occupying land classified as "vacant, fallow, or virgin" to apply for permits or face up to two years in prison. The government issued a March 2019 deadline for permit applications.

Key International Actors

Myanmar faced international condemnation in 2018 for military atrocities against the Rohingya. In June, the European Union and Canada sanctioned seven military officials for their involvement in the Rakhine State operations. In August, the United States imposed financial and travel sanctions against four security force commanders and two military units.

The UN Human Rights Council adopted a resolution in September, presented jointly by the EU and Organisation of Islamic Cooperation (OIC), establishing a mechanism to collect, preserve, and analyze evidence of grave crimes committed in Myanmar, and prepare case files for prosecution. The UN General Assembly passed a resolution on Myanmar in November affirming the establishment of the mechanism and calling for its prompt initiation.

In September, the International Criminal Court (ICC) prosecutor launched a full preliminary examination into Myanmar's deportation of the Rohingya, following a panel ruling affirming the court's jurisdiction over the crime on the grounds that it was completed in Bangladesh, an ICC member state. Several countries voiced support for a UN Security Council referral to the ICC, including council members Sweden and the Netherlands, to address the full range of alleged international crimes in Kachin, Rakhine, and Shan States.

Myanmar and Bangladesh continued repatriation discussions in 2018 following their November 2017 agreement. Tensions between the countries grew, with repatriation delays and mounting challenges in Bangladesh from the mass influx of refugees. Bangladesh Prime Minister Sheikh Hasina urged international actors, including the Security Council and Islamic Development Bank, to exert pressure on Myanmar.

Facebook was criticized by the UN fact-finding mission and other investigations for its failure to prevent the spread of anti-Muslim hate speech and incitement to violence. In response, the company announced new measures to review Myanmar language content and identify abusive posts. Facebook banned 20 individuals and organizations in August, including Sr. Gen. Min Aung Hlaing, and removed a further 10 accounts in October. The company commissioned an assessment of its human rights impact in Myanmar, which found that it had failed to prevent use of the platform to "foment division and incite offline violence."

China continued to shield Myanmar from accountability and scrutiny, obstructing international action and weakening UN measures. While many foreign governments cut funding to Myanmar in 2017 and 2018, China expanded its investment in the country. In September, the two countries signed an agreement on the China-Myanmar Economic Corridor, a development project under China's "One Belt, One Road" initiative linking Yunnan Province to the Indian Ocean. Attempting to compete with China for influence, Japan broke with other democracies and called for the international community to avoid criticizing the Myanmar government.

The UN Committee on the Elimination of Discrimination against Women requested in November 2017 that the Myanmar government submit a report on violence against Rohingya women and girls by May 2018—only the fourth time the committee had made an "exceptional report" request—to which the government did not respond. The UN secretary-general included the Myanmar military for the first time in his annual list of parties that have committed sexual violence in armed conflict. Myanmar also remains on the UN's list of parties that use and recruit child soldiers.

In September, the US State Department quietly released the findings from its $1.4 million investigation into the crackdown on the Rohingya, which detailed the military's atrocities but did not reach legal conclusions about the abuses committed. Members of Congress followed up with a call for a legal determination to be made. The State Department downgraded Myanmar in its 2018 Trafficking in Persons report to Tier 3, the lowest tier. It also restored Myanmar to its annual list of governments using child soldiers, following its removal in 2017.

Nepal

Following local, provincial, and national elections through late 2017, Khadga Prasad Oli of the Unified Marxist-Leninist party was sworn in as Nepal's new prime minister in February 2018. Oli swiftly combined forces with the Communist Party of Nepal–Maoist to form a majority in parliament. There were ongoing discussions about the devolution of power, including on law enforcement and justice, after a new federal structure was adopted under the 2015 constitution.

The attorney general, appointed by the new prime minister, promised to amend flawed legislation on transitional justice mechanisms to bring them in line with Supreme Court directives and international law.

Transitional Justice and Accountability

The Truth and Reconciliation Commission (TRC) and the Commission of Investigation on Enforced Disappeared Persons (CIEDP) held extensive hearings throughout Nepal during 2018, meeting victims of the country's decade-long conflict between government and Communist Party of Nepal–Maoist (CPN-M) forces. Although the terms of the two commissions were extended in 2018, concerns lingered over their independence and impartiality, particularly with the CPN-M, a vested party in the conflict, joining the ruling party in the new government in early 2018.

Due to flaws in the legislation setting up the transitional justice mechanisms, the international community had withdrawn support for the commissions, beginning in 2014. In June 2018, the attorney general pledged to amend the laws to bring them into compliance with international laws, and in particular to withdraw clauses allowing amnesties for perpetrators credibly accused of war crime violations.

However, the proposed amendments did not properly address concerns around entrenched impunity. Perpetrators who face credible allegations against them continue to remain in positions of power. Over several years, including as recently as 2018, the government held consultations with various groups, including international agencies. However, there had been no progress made at time of writing.

Cases filed before the courts remained stalled as the police and relevant authorities refused to conduct investigations that would enable indictments and prosecutions to proceed. The main political parties continued to insist that these are political cases and should not be handled by regular courts.

Earthquake Reconstruction

Nepal's two earthquakes in 2015 led to an estimated 9,000 deaths, and the destruction of nearly a million homes across the affected areas. According to a report by the United Nations, most victims have had to rely on money-lenders to rebuild their homes, although the government remains in charge of the over US$4 billion of aid that poured in for victims of earthquake relief. Most victims survived through several monsoons and winters without any proper shelter.

New Criminal Code

The government replaced the outdated national legal code, known as the Muluki Ain, with a new criminal code that came into effect in August, although implementation laws still must be passed to bring it fully into effect.

Activists and journalists were concerned that certain regressive provisions in the new law criminalize normal news-gathering activities, such as reporting on public figures, including through satire. Even important media houses came under scrutiny and threat. *Himal Southasian*, a monthly magazine, was forced to relocate its headquarters from Nepal to Sri Lanka in 2018 following threats from the government to shut it down.

Although the constitution recognizes sexual orientation and gender identity as protected through fundamental rights, the criminal code failed to repeat the protection clause, which contradicts the constitution. Additionally, although Nepal has in many ways been at the forefront of protecting the rights of sexual minorities—including by legally recognizing a third gender category based solely on self-identification—the new law only recognizes marriage rights as being between a man and woman.

Migrant Workers

Nepal continued to send migrant workers to several different destinations. Most Nepali migrant workers are in India, where Nepali citizens can freely travel and work. However, they often remain under the radar due to unofficial migration, which can mean they have little access to legal aid or help from Nepali authorities.

The government continued to report on a steady number of deaths of migrant workers in the Middle East and Southeast Asia, many of whom labor under harsh conditions and without access to proper health care. An August report by the Ministry of Labour, Employment and Social Security stated that, on average, two migrant workers have died every day during the last seven years, primarily, but not exclusively, in the Gulf states.

Although the government has provided some restitution to families of migrant workers who died or suffered severe injury, it has failed to implement its stated policy of providing legal aid to workers accused of crime in host countries.

Failure to properly combat the exorbitant fees charged by migration agencies means that many Nepalis remain in debt.

Disability Rights

Many children with mental and physical disabilities study in separate schools or classrooms and do not receive quality inclusive education because schools lack physical accessibility, teachers trained in inclusive education, accessible educational materials, and other supports. In 2017, Nepal adopted the Disability Rights Act and an Inclusive Education Policy, which calls for children with disabilities to study without discrimination in their communities.

Women's and Girls' Rights

Nepal has the third highest rate of child marriage in Asia—37 percent of girls marry before 18, and 10 percent by 15. In 2016, the government launched a national strategy to end child marriage by 2030, but action on operationalizing and implementing the plan has since stalled. A new law in 2017 criminalized *chaupadi*, a practice that forces menstruating women and girls from their homes into sheds or isolated dark rooms, although it continues in remote areas due to lack of enforcement.

Key International Actors

The Nepal government continued talks with India to renegotiate trade and border treaties to prevent blockade on essential goods. In April, China offered infrastructure and development assistance under its One Belt, One Road initiative, including a railway link from Lhasa in Tibet all the way through Nepal to the border with India. While the railway could offer significant opportunities, many in civil society voiced concerns over the impact on communities that would be displaced as a result, and its lack of key human rights safeguards.

Restrictions on free assembly and expression rights for the Tibetan community continued under sustained political pressure from China.

In 2017, Nepal was elected to the UN Human Rights Council for a three-year term, pledging to "contribute to the work of the Human Rights Council for the promotion and protection of human rights and fundamental freedoms in a fair and equitable manner, without distinction of any kind." However, its voting record since shows that it is squarely voting with its regional block and failing to take a strong stance on important human rights initiatives at the council.

The Office of the UN High Commissioner for Human Rights and the international community were largely silent on the transitional justice process, with several states arguing that they could not be involved until Nepal's laws on transitional justice were brought into line with international norms and practices.

Nicaragua

An enormous concentration of power by the executive has allowed President Daniel Ortega's government to commit egregious abuses against critics and opponents with complete impunity. A crackdown by national police and armed pro-government groups in 2018 left 300 dead, over 2,000 injured, and hundreds arbitrarily arrested and prosecuted.

Since taking office in 2007, Ortega's government has aggressively dismantled all institutional checks on presidential power. Stacked with his supporters, the Electoral Council barred political parties and removed opposition lawmakers. The Supreme Court of Justice has upheld Electoral Council decisions undermining political rights and allowed Ortega to circumvent a constitutional prohibition on re-election and run for a second term. His party secured a 79 percent majority in Congress in 2016, enabling it to fast-track institutional reforms that gave the president direct personal control over the police and army, allowed him to legislate by decree, and run for indefinite re-election.

Crackdown on Dissent

In April, massive anti-government protests broke out countrywide. Police, in coordination with armed pro-government groups, brutally repressed them, killing hundreds, and injuring several thousand. Government forces were responsible for most of the 324 people killed as of September, a figure that included 23 children, and for most of the over 2,000 injured. Some killings constituted extrajudicial executions. Public hospitals under the purview of the Ministry of Health denied or obstructed medical care for wounded protesters.

Police arbitrarily arrested, and pro-government groups kidnapped, hundreds of people as part of "a policy" to "eradicate the structural conditions that support opposition voices and critics," according to the United Nations Office of the High Commissioner for Human Rights (OHCHR). In some cases, the whereabouts of detainees were not confirmed for up to two weeks, constituting enforced disappearances during the time they were missing.

National Police subjected protesters to abuses that at times amounted to torture, including beatings, waterboarding, electric shocks, and rape. Many told the press and Human Rights Watch that they were forced to record self-incriminating videos.

As the crackdown intensified, some individuals responded violently and 22 police officers died between April and September, according to official statistics. The OHCHR found that demonstrators did not make a coordinated effort to use violence.

High level officials repeatedly accused protesters of being "terrorists" or "attempting to overthrow the government."

Though some detainees have been released, Nicaraguan nongovernmental organizations providing legal counsel to detainees reported that 320 people were being prosecuted in connection with the protests. Among these were 136 people accused of terrorism-related offenses, some under the new counterterrorism law that the legislature enacted in July.

In September, the attorney general accused Félix Maradiaga, a chief opposition figure and director of a research center, of "financing terrorism" under the new law. According to press reports, the indictment states that Maradiaga trained people to participate in "destabilizing" activities by creating a Civil Society Leaders Institute; the institute's stated mission is to impart values of democracy and human rights to youth.

According to the OHCHR, defendants are subject to due process rights violations that include being denied access to legal representation of their choice, being unable to meet privately with their lawyers while in detention, and having closed trial hearings.

Abuses that authorities perpetrated remain unpunished. The Attorney General's Office and the Supreme Court obstructed international human rights bodies' efforts to document and investigate these cases.

Human Rights Defenders

Human rights defenders and other critics of the government's human rights record have increasingly become the targets of death threats, intimidation, online defamation campaigns, harassment, surveillance, assault, and judicial persecution.

Public officials repeatedly made stigmatizing statements to undermine the credibility of defenders. In July, during a public address, Ortega referred to prominent Catholic bishops who have denounced government abuses as "assassins" and "coup-plotters."

Freedom of Expression

Authorities and armed pro-government groups harassed, threatened, intimidated, attacked, robbed, and confiscated equipment from journalists and bloggers who reported on the protests. In October, police briefly arbitrarily detained journalists from *La Prensa* newspaper and reporters from TV channel 100% Noticias while they covered a peaceful protest; authorities also searched their vehicles, according to media accounts. Reporters who are critical of the government often face online smear campaigns.

Foreign correspondents have at times been detained and deported. In August, for example, police detained Emilia Mello, a Brazilian-American documentary filmmaker in Carazo, confiscated her equipment, interrogated her for several hours, and deported her the next day.

Political Discrimination

During the crackdown, the Nicaraguan Health Ministry authorities fired at least 135 doctors, nurses, and other health workers from several public hospitals in apparent retaliation for participating in protests or otherwise expressing disagreement with government policy. At least 40 professors from the National University of Nicaragua (UNAN), a public institution, were fired since the start of the protests for supporting or taking part in anti-government demonstrations, according to media. The Inter American Commission on Human Rights (IACHR) also found public officials were threatened with dismissal if they did not participate in pro-government demonstrations.

Nicaraguan Asylum Seekers

Between April and October 19, the number of Nicaraguans applying for asylum in neighboring Costa Rica increased to 15,584 from only 22 in the previous three months before the crackdown began, according to the UN High Commissioner for

Refugees (UNHCR). As of November, another 11,383 people had been given an appointment to seek asylum.

Thousands more fled to Mexico, Panama, and the United States.

Women and Girls' Sexual and Reproductive Rights

Nicaragua prohibits abortion in all circumstances, even if a pregnancy is life-threatening or resulted from rape or incest. The 2006 total abortion ban penalizes women and girls who have abortions with prison terms of up to two years. The penalties for medical professionals range from one to six years in prison for providing abortions. A 2008 legal challenge submitted to the Supreme Court argued that the ban was unconstitutional. The court never ruled on this case, nor on a similar one regarding the 2014 constitution. The abortion ban remains in place and forces women and girls facing unwanted pregnancies to have clandestine abortions, at great risk to their health and lives.

Key International Actors

After an in-country visit in May, the IACHR released a report concluding that Nicaraguan authorities had perpetrated widespread abuses in responding to anti-government protests that were not isolated actions by rogue agents. The IACHR then created a Special Monitoring Mechanism for Nicaragua (MESENI) to remain in country. The government has refused to cooperate with MESENI and has restricted its operations, including by barring its staff from inspecting detention sites.

Shortly after, the Organization of American States (OAS), the IACHR, and the Nicaraguan government agreed to create an Interdisciplinary Group of Independent Experts (GIEI) that would support the Attorney General Office's investigations into human rights abuses. The GIEI's mandate expired in November; in its final press conference it announced judicial authorities had not cooperated in any way foreseen in the agreement. The GIEI also stated it received no information on any investigation or sentence against police officers or members of armed pro-government groups implicated in abuses. Lastly, the GIEI called for a special prosecutorial unit to be created in the Attorney General's Office to investigate gross rights violations in the context of protests.

In August, the Supreme Court of Justice ordered MESENI and GIEI to seek authorization from the Foreign Affairs Ministry to enter trial hearings that the law requires to be public. Neither MESENI nor GIEI have been allowed in courthouses; they have repeatedly submitted the requests to the ministry, but these have gone unanswered.

The OAS Permanent Council held several meetings to address the crisis. In August, it created a Working Group on Nicaragua made up of 12 OAS member countries to search "for peaceful and sustainable solutions." In September, at the behest of the Working Group, the council adopted a resolution calling on its members and permanent observers to take all "appropriate diplomatic measures to support the reinstatement of the rule of law and human rights in Nicaragua." Only four countries—Venezuela, Bolivia, Saint Vincent, and Nicaragua—voted against it.

The government allowed the OHCHR into the country in June, after months of refusing its requests for an invitation. Authorities consistently obstructed its work, and in August, two days after the OHCHR released a scathing report, the Nicaraguan government expelled its representatives.

In September, the UN Security Council held a public meeting on Nicaragua. Two-thirds of its members underscored their concern for ongoing human rights violations, the refugees they have generated, and the expulsion of the OHCHR team. Days later, UN High Commissioner for Human Rights Michelle Bachelet called on the UN Human Rights Council (HRC) to "strengthen its oversight" on Nicaragua and to "take all available measures to address the serious human rights violations which have been documented in recent reports."

During the September HRC sessions, Argentina, on behalf of a group of 47 countries, delivered a joint statement demanding an immediate halt to extrajudicial executions, forced disappearances, judicial harassment of activists, and arbitrary arrests. Numerous other states, including Australia, Costa Rica and Iceland, raised similar concerns during their statements in their individual capacity.

Between June and July, the US State Department revoked visas for some Nicaraguan officials allegedly responsible for abuses and "undermining democracy." The Treasury sanctioned Francisco Díaz, then deputy chief of police and an official from the mayor's office in Managua under the 2012 Magnitsky Act, "for being responsible for, or the leaders of, entities involved in serious human rights abuse." Previously, in December 2017, the US had also sanctioned Roberto Rivas, president of the Electoral Council, for his alleged involvement in electoral fraud and embezzling public funds.

At time of writing, the US Senate was considering a bill that would impose additional sanctions on Nicaraguan officials and restrict the country's access to international credit.

In July, the Netherlands suspended an €18.4 million project (US$21,200) in the health sector due to "grave human right violations committed by government officials and parapolice groups." Shortly after, Luxembourg froze aid disbursements, underlining its "deep concern for the deterioration of the situation" and calling for accountability.

Nigeria

Heightened political tensions ahead of the 2019 elections in which President Muhammadu Buhari is seeking re-election defined Nigeria's rights landscape in 2018. Despite notable military advances, and apparently premature proclamations of Boko Haram's defeat by government forces, the group remained a threat to security in the northeast region.

Abductions, suicide bombings, and attacks on civilian targets by Boko Haram persisted. At least 1,200 people died and nearly 200,000 were displaced in the northeast in 2018. In June, at least 84 people were killed in double suicide bomb attacks attributed to Boko Haram at a mosque in Mubi, Adamawa State.

Decades old communal conflict between nomadic herdsmen and farmers in the Middle Belt intensified in 2018 and further exacerbated the security situation in the country. At least 1,600 people were killed and another 300,000 displaced as a result of the violence.

Civil society led campaigns against arbitrary arrests, detention, and torture exposed human rights abuses by security agencies, including by the Department of State Security Services (DSS) and the Police Special Anti-Robbery Squad (SARS).

Abuses by Boko Haram

Although Boko Haram's territorial control shrank to small pockets of villages around Lake Chad as a result of sustained government military action, factions of the insurgency group continued to carry out attacks against civilians in the region.

In February, insurgents abducted 110 schoolgirls from Dapchi, Yobe State, in a style reminiscent of the 2014 abduction of 276 Chibok school girls. One hundred and four of the Dapchi girls were released two weeks later after negotiations with the government. Five of the remaining girls reportedly died in captivity and one girl, Leah Sharibu, continues to be held hostage allegedly for refusing to deny her Christian faith. About 100 of the Chibok schoolgirls remain unaccounted for.

In September and October, Boko Haram insurgents executed Saifura Ahmed and Hauwa Liman, both aid workers with the International Committee of the Red Cross (ICRC). The group kidnapped them in March.

In June, twin suicide bomb attacks and grenade explosions by suspected Boko Haram fighters killed 31 people and injured 48 others during Muslim religious celebrations in Damboa, Borno State. The attack occurred in the wake of Chief of Army Staff Tukur Buratai's speech encouraging displaced people to return to their communities.

Over 35,000 internally displaced people returned to northeast communities despite security concerns and lack of basic necessities, including food and shelter. Within two months of the return of 25,000 people to Gudumbali Borno State in July, suspected members of Boko Haram's Islamic State's West Africa franchise killed eight people and temporarily took control of the town.

Between October 2017 and July 2018, authorities conducted three rounds of trials of over 1,500 Boko Haram suspects in a military base in Kainji Niger State. Some defendants had been in detention since 2009 and the majority faced charges of material and non-violent support to Boko Haram. The trials were fraught with irregularities, including lack of interpreters, inadequate legal defense, lack of prosecutable evidence or witnesses and non-participation of victims.

Conduct of Security Forces

In August, Vice President Yemi Osinbajo dismissed DSS Director General Lawal Daura for the unauthorized sealing of the National Assembly. The National Human Rights Commission reported that under Daura's three-year leadership, the agency repeatedly violated rights, including carrying out unlawful arrests, prolonged detention without trial, and torture of detainees. Osinbajo took the action while he was acting president.

Despite court orders, the DSS refused to release a former national security adviser, Sambo Dasuki, as well as the Shia Islamic Movement of Nigeria (IMN) leader, Sheik Ibrahim El Zakzaky and his wife, Ibraheemat, all of whom have been in detention pending trial since 2015.

Police continued their crackdown on protests by members of the Shia IMN and the Indigenous People of Biafra (IPOB) separatist group with arrests and detention. In April, 115 Shia IMN members were arrested in Abuja during a protest for the release of their leader Sheik Zazaky and his wife. Soldiers killed at least 42 more in Abuja during similar protests in October.

On August 17, 112 women were arrested and prosecuted in Owerri, Imo State, for protesting the disappearance of IPOB leader, Nnamdi Kanu. They were discharged and released by a court six days later.

A December 2017 social media campaign against human rights abuses by SARS, including extortion, illegal arrests, torture, and extra-judicial killing continued in 2018.

Inter-Communal Violence

Recurring violence between herdsmen and farmers, as well as related cattle theft and banditry in many northern states, including Zamafara and Kaduna, posed serious threats to peace and security. Although the violence is increasingly described in religious terms, competing claims to land and other resources are at its core.

In June, a typical reprisal attack began after farmers allegedly killed five herdsmen for allegedly trespassing on farms in Plateau state. In apparent retaliation, herdsmen attacked villages in the area, killing 86 and injuring hundreds, including women and children. In September, suspected herdsmen killed 51 people and abducted about 24 others in Numan, Adamawa State.

Uncoordinated and inadequate responses by state and federal authorities deepened mistrust and perception of authorities' bias and complicity in the violence.

In May, at least 45 people were killed in an attack by bandits in Gwaska village, Kaduna State. Zamfara state was perhaps the worst affected by frequent bandit attacks, who killed at least 400 people and displaced over 38,000 in 2018. In July, the government deployed 1,000 military troops to the state to tackle insecurity.

Public Sector Corruption

The Economic and Financial Crimes Commission (EFCC) recorded notable strides in its fight against corruption. In June, serving senator and former governor of Plateau State, Joshua Dariye, was found guilty and sentenced to 14 years' imprisonment for fraud and misappropriation of the state's US$3 million ecological fund. The EFCC in May secured the conviction and 14 years' imprisonment of Jolly

Nyame, a former governor of Taraba State, for fraud and misappropriation of over US$4million in state funds.

Sexual Orientation and Gender Identity

In May, the Benue State House of Assembly passed the Same Sex Marriage Prohibition (SSMP) Law. Like the federal law adopted in 2014, the law criminalizes public show of same sex amorous relationships, same sex marriages, and the registration of gay clubs, societies, and organizations.

Elsewhere in the country, scores were arrested, detained, and prosecuted based on their real or perceived sexual orientation and gender identity. In June, more than 100 people partying at a hotel in Asaba, Delta State, were arrested on allegations of being gay. In August, 57 people were arrested at a Lagos hotel based on information provided by a vigilance group that the victims had gathered to perform gay initiation rites.

In November, an Abuja Federal High Court dismissed the Lesbian Equality and Empowerment Initiative's lawsuit challenging its non-registration. The court held that the Corporate Affairs and Allied Matters Act and the Same Sex Marriage Prohibition Act prohibited the registration of groups considered "undesirable, offensive and contrary to public policy."

Freedom of Expression, Media, and Association

Although the Nigerian press remains largely free, several arrests and detention of journalists and activists in 2018 suggest a disturbing trend toward repression of freedom of expression and media.

In August, a social media campaign for the release of Jones Abiri, a journalist and publisher of *Weekly Source* newspaper forced the DSS to bring him before an Abuja Magistrate court, more than two years after his detention in 2016. The court discharged him of the charges because the prosecution failed to substantiate them. Another court awarded him $270, 000 in damages for breach of his human rights.

Similarly, an Abuja court conditionally released *Premium Times* journalist, Samuel Ogundipe, amid protests and campaigns for his freedom. He was arrested and prosecuted by SARS for allegedly refusing to disclose the source for a story about a police inspector general, Ibrahim Idris.

Key International Actors

International actors, notably the United States and the United Kingdom, continued to support the Nigerian government's effort to tackle security challenges and provide humanitarian aid to vulnerable communities.

In August, Nigerian Air Force urged the US to expedite delivery of 12 A-29 Super Tucano light attack aircraft worth $496 million. The Trump administration approved the sale in 2017, lifting the freeze imposed by the Obama administration over human rights concerns. The US also provides training to the Nigerian military, and in June, announced $102 million in humanitarian assistance for people affected by the northeast conflict.

During a visit to Abuja in August, United Kingdom Prime Minister Theresa May signed the first ever security and defense pact between both countries. Under the agreement, the UK will expand provision of protective equipment and training to Nigerian soldiers and deliver a £13 million ($14.7 million) program to educate 100,000 children living in conflict zones. She also unveiled a series of measures to tackle illegal migration and human trafficking in Nigeria, including a new UK and France-led project to strengthen border security and cooperation.

In July, French President Emmanuel Macron pledged to increase cooperation between Nigeria and France to tackle security challenges posed by activities of Boko Haram and ISIS in Nigeria and the Sahel.

During a joint visit to Nigeria in July, the United Nations Office on Counter Terrorism and the Counter Terrorism Executive Directorate pledged continued technical assistance, including support for criminal justice processes that comply with human rights and rule of law, to help Nigeria to counterterrorism.

In September, Germany, Nigeria, Norway and the United Nations co-hosted a high-level conference on the Lake Chad Region in Berlin that raised over $2 billion in support, and $467 million in concessional loans for humanitarian, peace-building, and development activities in Cameroon, Chad, Niger, and Nigeria. The European Union also announced the release of €138 million ($157 million) to assist vulnerable communities in the region affected by prolonged violence, insecurity, and environmental degradation.

Foreign Policy

Nigeria, which currently sits on the UN Human Rights Council, in July abstained from voting on a resolution on the human rights situation in Syria, Venezuela, Yemen, and Burundi; and another resolution urging states to respect and protect basic human rights and civil society space.

In November, under the HRC's Universal Periodic Review mechanism, states made 290 recommendations to Nigeria, including to combat all forms of discrimination, especially against women and lesbian, gay, bisexual, transgender, and intersex persons; combat impunity; and abolish the death penalty.

The Office of the Prosecutor of the International Criminal Court (ICC) continued its preliminary examination into the situation in Nigeria, with a focus on alleged international crimes committed in the Niger Delta, the Middle-Belt states and in the Boko Haram conflict. The preliminary examination also focuses on the status of national proceedings regarding these crimes.

In August, President Buhari delivered the keynote address at the 20th Anniversary of the ICC's Rome Statute event at The Hague and used the opportunity to mark Nigeria's strong support for the ICC's mandate.

Nigeria, a member of the African Union Peace and Security Council (PSC), in April led the PSC on a South Sudan field mission aimed at fostering peace talks in the nation, which entered its fifth year of armed conflict.

In a letter to President Buhari in March, the African Commission on Human and Peoples' Rights (ACHPR) declared the government's proscription of IPOB as a terrorist group and attacks against its members as prima facie violation of the African Charter on Human and People's Rights. In April, Nigeria's sixth periodic report on the implementation of the charter was considered at the ACHPR's 62nd Ordinary Session in Mauritania.

In July, President Buhari was elected chairperson of the Authority of Heads of State and Government of the Economic Community of West African States.

North Korea

North Korea remains one of the world's most repressive states. In his seventh year in power, Kim Jong-un—who serves as chairman of the States Affairs Commission and head of the ruling Workers' Party of Korea—continues to exercise almost total political control. The government restricts all civil and political liberties, including freedom of expression, assembly, association, and religion. It also prohibits all organized political opposition, independent media, civil society, and trade unions.

The government routinely uses arbitrary arrest and punishment of crimes, torture in custody, and executions to maintain fear and control over the population. The government and security agencies systematically extract forced, unpaid labor from its citizens— including women, children, detainees, and prisoners—to build infrastructure, implement projects, and carry out activities and events extolling the ruling Kim family and the Workers' Party of Korea (WPK).

The government continued its tight restrictions on unauthorized cross-border travel to China, collaborated with Chinese authorities to capture and return North Korean refugees, and punished North Koreans making contact with the outside world. The government fails to protect or promote the rights of numerous at-risk groups, including women, children, and people with disabilities.

In 2017, the Democratic People's Republic of Korea (DPRK) fired 23 missiles during 16 tests and conducted a sixth nuclear test, raising tensions on the Korean peninsula to their highest level in decades. But starting February 2018 at the Pyeongchang Winter Olympics, North Korea engaged in new diplomatic efforts with South Korea, the United States, China, Russia, and others. Kim Jong-un had previously not met with any major world leaders, but between March and September, he met once with US President Donald Trump, three times each with South Korean President Moon Jae-in and Chinese President Xi Jinping, and once with Russian Foreign Minister Sergei Lavrov.

International Human Rights Mechanisms

North Korea has ratified five human rights treaties: the Convention on the Rights of the Child (CRC), the Convention on the Elimination of All Forms of Discrimina-

"You Cry at Night but Don't Know Why"
Sexual Violence against Women in North Korea

tion against Women (CEDAW), the Convention of the Rights of Persons with Disabilities (CRPD), the International Covenant on Civil and Political Rights (ICCPR), and the International Covenant on Economic, Social and Cultural Rights (ICESCR), though in some cases (such as the ICCPR and ICESCR) North Korea's state report is more than a decade overdue.

The international community has continued to press the North Korean government to engage with UN human rights mechanisms and to accept and act on the findings of the 2014 United Nations Commission of Inquiry (COI) report on human rights in the Democratic People's Republic of Korea (DPRK, North Korea), which found the government committed crimes against humanity, including extermination, murder, enslavement, torture, imprisonment, rape and other forms of sexual violence, and forced abortion.

On December 11, 2017, for the fourth consecutive year, the UN Security Council put North Korea's egregious human rights violations on its formal agenda as a threat to international peace and security. On December 19, 2017, the UN General Assembly adopted a resolution without a vote condemning human rights abuses in North Korea. On March 23, the Human Rights Council adopted without a vote a resolution emphasizing the need for advancing mechanisms to ensure that North Korean officials responsible for crimes against humanity are held to account. On November 15, the UN General Assembly's Third Committee adopted a human rights resolution on North Korea, setting the stage for the full UN General Assembly to adopt the resolution in December, marking the 14th year in a row the UN has called on North Korea to significantly improve its rights record.

North Korea refuses to cooperate with the Office of the High Commissioner for Human Rights in Seoul or with Tomas Ojea Quintana, the UN special rapporteur on the situation of human rights in North Korea.

Rights of Women, Other At-Risk Groups

Women in North Korea suffer a range of sexual and gender-based abuses, in addition to facing violations of their rights common to the rest of the population. These include rape and other sexual violence and torture in detention facilities, sexual exploitation, or forced marriage of North Korean women in China, and sexual and gender-based violence and discrimination.

Gender-based discrimination begins at childhood, where schools favor boys and men in leadership roles, and girls are socialized to uphold stereotyped, subservient gender roles. Women face greater difficulty than men in being admitted to university and in joining the military and the ruling WPK, which serves as the gateway to any position of power. State authorities perpetrate abuses against women, and systematically fail to offer any protection or justice to women and girls facing sexual abuse.

North Korea also discriminates against individuals and their families on political grounds in key areas such as employment, residence, and schooling by applying *songbun*, a socio-political classification system that, from its creation, grouped people into "loyal," "wavering," or "hostile" classes. However, pervasive corruption among officials enables some room to maneuver around the strictures of the songbun system, with government officials accepting bribes to grant permissions, permit market activities, and allow travel domestically or abroad.

Forced Labor

The government uses forced labor from ordinary citizens, including children, to control its people and sustain its economy. A significant majority of North Koreans must perform unpaid labor at some point in their lives.

Ordinary North Korean workers are not free to choose their own job. The government assigns jobs to both men and unmarried women from cities and rural areas. In many cases, these enterprises do not compensate them, forcing them to find other jobs to survive and pay bribes to be absent at their assigned workplace. Failing to show up for work without permission is a crime punishable by three to six months in forced labor training camps (*rodong dallyeondae*).

Former North Korean students told Human Rights Watch their schools forced them to work for free on farms twice a year, for one month at a time. Some sources reported that their schools forced students aged between 10 and 16 to work every day to generate funds to pay teachers and school administrators, maintain school facilities, and carry out government campaigns.

The government also compels many North Koreans to join paramilitary forced labor brigades. These brigades (*dolgyeokdae*) are controlled and operated by the ruling party and work primarily on buildings and infrastructure projects. Prisoners in political prisons (*kwanliso*), ordinary prison camps (*kyohwaso*), and short-term detention facilities also face back-breaking forced labor in dangerous conditions, sometimes in winter weather, without proper clothing.

Border-Tightening

Kim Jong-un's government bolstered efforts to prevent people from leaving North Korea without permission by increasing the number of border guards, CCTV cameras, and barbed wire fences on its border with China. Other tactics included jamming Chinese mobile phone services at the border and targeting for arrest those communicating with people outside the country.

Guiding networks that help North Koreans to escape to a safe third country said they continued to face limited capacity to help those fleeing, following an apparent intensified crackdown in the summer of 2017, by the Chinese government and North Korea. In 2011, before the rise of Kim Jong-un, 2,706 North Koreans arrived in South Korea, compared to 1,127 in 2017, and only 808 between January and September 2018.

The Ministry of People's Security considers defection to be a crime of "treachery against the nation." Harsh punishments apply to North Koreans forcibly returned by China. The severity of punishment depends on authorities' assessments of what returnees did while in China. North Koreans caught working or living in China are sent to long term ordinary prisons (*kyohwaso*) or short-term detention facilities (*rodong danryeonda*). Those discovered trying to reach South Korea are treated more harshly and may be sent to North Korea's horrific political prison camp system (*kwanliso*), where prisoners face torture, sexual violence, forced labor, and other inhuman treatment.

North Koreans fleeing into China should be protected as *refugees sur place* because of the certainty of punishment on return. China fails to meet its obligation to protect refugees as a state party to the 1951 Refugee Convention and its 1967 protocol. Beijing denies permission to the staff of the UN Refugee Agency to travel to border areas where North Koreans are present.

Key International Actors

South Korea's Moon administration has not made its policy clear on North Korean human rights issues. The North Korean Human Rights Act, which came into effect in September 2016, requires Seoul to implement the recommendations of the COI report, assist North Koreans who escaped their country and South Korean nationals detained in North Korea, and research and publish status reports on human rights conditions in North Korea. To date, South Korea has still not implemented provisions of that law mandating the creation of a North Korea Human Rights Foundation to fund further investigations and action on rights abuses. Moon met with Kim in April, May, and September, but did not address the human rights situation in North Korea.

Japan continues to demand the return of 12 Japanese citizens whom North Korea abducted in the 1970s and 1980s. Some Japanese civil society groups insist the number of abductees is much higher. On August 19, five victims of the "Paradise on Earth" campaign, which used false promises to recruit approximately 93,000 ethnic Koreans (Zainichi) and Japanese nationals in Japan to go to North Korea between 1959 and 1984, sued the North Korean government for damages.

The United States government is still the only government in the world that imposes human rights-related sanctions, including on government entities, on Kim Jong-un, and on several other top officials. US President Donald Trump, despite inviting a defector to his 2018 State of the Union and raising North Korea's human rights abuses in both that speech and a November speech in Seoul, did not raise human rights issues publicly when he met with Kim Jong-un at their summit in Singapore in June, and there is little indication that US negotiators raised human rights issues in subsequent counterproliferation negotiations with North Korea.

China is the most influential international actor in North Korea. Most of North Korea's energy supplies come from China and it is the country's largest trading partner. China has the ability to pressure North Korea on human rights, but has declined to do so, including during President Xi Jinping's three meetings with Kim in 2018—in March, May, and June.

Oman

Sultan Qaboos bin Said al Said, 78, has ruled Oman since 1970. He holds an array of senior government positions, including prime minister, supreme commander of the Armed Forces, minister of defense, minister of finance, and minister of foreign affairs. Omani authorities continued in 2018 to block local independent newspapers and magazines critical of the government, confiscate books, and harass activists.

Freedom of Expression

Security agencies, particularly the Internal Security Service (ISS), continued to target pro-reform activists, often for views they expressed on social media platforms like Facebook and Twitter. Courts sentenced activists to prison terms using vaguely defined laws that limit free speech, including crimes such as "insulting the Sultan" and "undermining the prestige of the state."

Issued on January 14, 2018, Oman's revised penal code increases the punishment for committing slander against the sultan and his authority from between six months and three years in prison to between three and seven years in prison under article 97. Article 269 has also increased the penalty for committing blasphemy or insulting Islam from between 10 days and 3 years to between 3 to 10 years in prison.

According to the Omani Center for Human Rights (OCHR), the Court of First Instance in Muscat sentenced former media presenter Khaled al-Rashdi on January 2, 2018, to one year in prison under article 19 of the Cyber Crimes Law and a $2,600 fine for tweeting about "official institutions."

On April 18, the ISS summoned internet activist Yousif Sultan al-Arimi and later detained him at the Special Division of the Omani Police General Command in Muscat. Al-Arimi did not have access to a lawyer or his family, according to reports received by the Gulf Center for Human Rights (GCHR), and authorities arrested him based on views expressed on his Twitter account. Authorities released al-Arimi on April 22.

On June 13, writer and online activist Abdullah Habib was released from Samail Central Prison while serving a six-month prison sentence on charges under article 19 of the Information Technology Crimes Act for "using the internet in what would prejudice the state public order" in addition to "contempt of religions." Habib was due for release in October 2018, however was pardoned under Sultan Qaboos' amnesty on the occasion of the Muslim holiday of Eid al-Fitr.

On October 5, 2017, Oman's Supreme Court issued its final ruling on *Azamn* newspaper to permanently close. Editor-in-chief Turki bin Ali al-Balushi of *Al-Balad* decided to close down this online newspaper following *Azamn's* consistent harassment by ISS, according to reports received by GCHR.

The main domain of the online magazine, Mowaten, remains blocked throughout Oman, though it can be accessed through alternative domains.

During the 23rd Muscat International Book Fair held between February 21, 2018, and March 3, 2018, authorities confiscated more than 20 books. Saeed al-Hashimi, Suleiman al-Maamari, Nabhan al-Hanashi, Hamoud Saud, Mohammed al-Fazari, Zaher al-Mahrouqi, and Abdulaziz Baraka, a writer from Sudan, are all authors whose books were banned.

Freedom of Assembly and Association

According to article 121 of the 2018 Omani penal code, participants in a public gathering of 10 individuals or more can be deemed liable to cause a breach of security or public order and can be imprisoned for up to one year and fined up to OR500 (US$1,300). However, if the gathering turns violent, those participating are subject to imprisonment of up to three years and a fine of up to OR1,000 ($2,600). One can risk imprisonment of between three to 10 years for establishing an association, according to article 116, and one to three years if one joins an association that seeks to "to contest the political ... principles of the State." If an established religious association is deemed to "contest or harm" Islam, according to article 270, punishment includes three to seven years in prison.

Protesters gathered in mid-January 2018 in Muscat urging the government to address the country's high unemployment, and on January 29 protesters gathered in front of the Ministry of Manpower and its directorates in Muscat, Salalah, and Sur. Security forces arrested a number of those protesting; there were reports they were released.

Women's Rights, Sexual Orientation, and Gender Identity

Article 17 of the Basic Law states that all citizens are equal and bans gender-based discrimination. In practice, however, women continue to face discrimination. The Personal Status Law discriminates against women on matters such as divorce, inheritance, child custody, and legal guardianship. For instance, women can lose child custody if they re-marry, and men continue to hold guardianship of the child, regardless of whether they have custody.

Oman promulgated a new penal code in January 2018, which for the first time criminalizes non-normative gender expression. Article 266 provides for a prison sentence of one month to one year, a fine of 100 to 300 riyals (US$260-780), or both, for any man who "appears dressed in women's clothing."

While the previous penal code punished same-sex relations only if they led to a "public scandal," article 261 of the new penal code punishes any consensual sexual intercourse between men with six months to three years in prison.

The 2018 penal code has no provisions prohibiting domestic violence, instead explicitly allowing parents to chastise underage children. It also does not explicitly criminalize marital rape although the language that previously excluded marital rape from the offence of rape has been removed. Cases can only be brought under general provisions that criminalize assault.

Under article 259 of the 2018 penal code, consensual intercourse outside marriage is punishable with between six months to three years' imprisonment, and at least two years if either person is married. Criminalization of such offenses apply disproportionately to women whose pregnancy can serve as evidence of the offense.

The United Nations Committee on the Elimination of Discrimination Against Women in its 2017 review of Oman concluded that Oman has made "very little progress in removing discrimination from marriage and family related law and practice, while numerous forms of discrimination remained in the Personal Status Law."

Migrant Workers

Oman has yet to make any significant reform to its *kafala* (visa sponsorship) system which ties migrant workers visas to their employers and prohibits them from leaving or changing jobs without their employer's agreement, but officials in a response to Human Rights Watch in November 2017, said that they are studying alternatives to the system. Oman is also now the last Gulf Cooperation Council state to not provide labor law protections to domestic workers. Its labor law excludes domestic workers, and its 2004 regulations on domestic workers provide guidance on the employment relationship but fail to provide any sanctions against employers or agents for breaches.

Oman's more than 154,000 female migrant domestic workers, according to official statistics from November 2017, are left exposed to abuse and exploitation by employers, whose consent they need to change jobs. Workers have few avenues for redress and risk imprisonment and deportation for "absconding," even when fleeing exploitation or abuse. Frequent abuses include employers confiscating workers' passports despite a legal prohibition; not paying workers their salaries, in full or at all; forcing them to work excessively long hours without breaks or days off; denying them adequate food and living conditions; beatings, sexual abuse, unpaid wages, and excessive working hours.

Workers reported that police at times returned them to their employers despite complaints of abuse, and Ministry of Manpower officials sided with employers during dispute-resolution processes despite workers' complaints of severe abuse.

Key International Actors

Both the US and UK provide significant economic and military aid to Oman. Oman's Western allies offered muted, if any criticism, of its human rights abuses in 2018, except in annual reports. In 2018, the United States Trafficking in Persons Report maintained Oman's Tier 2 Watch List category, recommending that Omani government continues "to increase efforts to investigate, prosecute, and convict traffickers, especially for forced labor offenses; expand labor law protections to, and enforce legal protections for, domestic workers; [and] amend the sponsorship-based employment scheme that renders expatriate workers vulnerable to exploitative labor."

Pakistan

Imran Khan's Pakistan Tehreek-e-Insaf party won the highest number of seats in parliamentary elections in July, and Khan took office as prime minister in August. It was the second consecutive constitutional transfer of power from one civilian government to another in Pakistan. In the campaign, Khan pledged to make economic development and social justice a priority.

Attacks by Islamist militants resulted in fewer deaths in Pakistan in 2018 than in recent years. However, strikes primarily targeting law enforcement officials and religious minorities killed hundreds of people. The Taliban and other armed militants killed and injured hundreds of people in a failed effort to disrupt the elections.

The government continues to muzzle dissenting voices in nongovernmental organizations (NGOs) and media on the pretext of national security. Militants and interest groups also threaten freedom of expression through threats and violence.

Women, religious minorities, and transgender people face violent attacks, discrimination, and government persecution, with authorities failing to provide adequate protection or hold perpetrators accountable.

Freedom of Expression and Attacks on Civil Society

A climate of fear continues to impede media coverage of abuses both by government security forces and militant groups. Journalists increasingly practiced self-censorship in 2018, after threats and attacks from militant groups. Media outlets came under pressure from authorities to avoid reporting on several issues, including criticism of government institutions and the judiciary. In several cases, government regulatory agencies blocked cable operators from broadcasting networks that had aired critical programs.

Gul Bukhari, a journalist in Lahore, was abducted in June by unknown assailants and released after a few hours. On the same night, Asad Kharal, a broadcast journalist, was assaulted and injured in Lahore.

Kadafi Zaman, a Norwegian journalist, was arrested by police in July while covering a political rally and was beaten up. Zaman was released after three days.

Human Rights Watch received several credible reports of intimidation, harassment, and surveillance of various NGOs by government authorities in 2018. The government used its "Regulation of INGOs in Pakistan" policy to impede the registration and functioning of international humanitarian and human rights groups.

Freedom of Religion and Belief

At least 17 people remain on death row in Pakistan after being convicted under the draconian blasphemy law, and hundreds await trial. Most of those facing blasphemy allegations are members of religious minorities.

In October, Pakistan's Supreme Court quashed the conviction and ordered the release of 47-year-old Aasia Bibi, a Christian woman from a village in Punjab province who had been on death row for eight years. Groups supporting the blasphemy law took to the streets to protest the decision of Aasia's release, damaged public and private property, and threatened judges of the Supreme Court, government officials, and military leadership with violent reprisals.

Blasphemy allegations and related rhetoric from both private actors and officials increased in 2018. However, the government did not amend the law and instead encouraged discriminatory prosecutions and other abuses against vulnerable groups.

In February, Patras Masih, 18, and Sajid Masih, 24, were charged with blasphemy in Lahore. Sajid Masih alleged that the police torture he endured while being held led him to attempt suicide, by jumping out of the interrogation room window. He was badly injured but survived.

In May, then-Interior Minister Ahsan Iqbal was shot in an assassination attempt by an individual affiliated with an anti-blasphemy group at an election rally in Narowal district, Punjab.

In May, a mob led by anti-blasphemy clerics attacked and destroyed two historic Ahmadiyya religious buildings.

Members of the Ahmadiyya religious community continue to be a major target for prosecutions under blasphemy laws, as well as specific anti-Ahmadi laws across Pakistan. They face increasing social discrimination as militant groups and the Islamist political party Tehreek-e-Labbaik (TLP) accuse them of "posing as Mus-

lims." The Pakistan penal code continues to treat "posing as Muslims" by Ahamdis as a criminal offense. They were effectively excluded from participating in the 2018 parliamentary elections: to vote, Ahmadis are required to declare they are not Muslims, which many see as a renunciation of their faith.

In September, the new Imran Khan government appointed Atif Mian, a prominent academic belonging to the Ahmadiyya community, to join the government as economic adviser and then, almost immediately after, asked him to step down after the TLP and other Islamist groups objected to his appointment because of his religion. Atif Mian said he stepped down because of "adverse pressure regarding my appointment from the mullahs and their supporters."

Women's and Children's Rights

Violence against women and girls—including rape, so-called honor killings, acid attacks, domestic violence, and forced marriage—remains a serious problem. Pakistani activists estimate that there are about 1,000 "honor" killings every year.

In June, the murder of 19-year-old Mahwish Arshad in Faisalabad district, Punjab, for refusing a marriage proposal gained national attention. According to media reports, at least 66 women were murdered in Faisalabad district in the first six months of 2018, the majority in the name of "honor."

Justice Tahira Safdar was appointed as the chief justice of Balochistan High Court, becoming the first woman ever appointed chief justice of a high court in Pakistan.

Women from religious minority communities remain particularly vulnerable to abuse. A report by the Movement for Solidarity and Peace in Pakistan found that at least 1,000 girls belonging to Christian and Hindu communities are forced to marry Muslim men every year. The government has done little to stop such forced marriages.

Early marriage remains a serious problem, with 21 percent of girls in Pakistan marrying before the age of 18, and 3 percent marrying before age 15.

The Taliban and affiliated armed groups continued to attack schools and use children in suicide bombings in 2018. In August, militants attacked and burned down at least 12 schools in Diamer district of Pakistan's Gilgit-Baltistan region.

At least half were girls' schools. Pakistan has not banned the use of schools for military purposes, or endorsed the Safe Schools Declaration as recommended by the United Nations Committee on Economic, Social and Cultural Rights in 2017.

Over 5 million primary school-age children in Pakistan are out of school, most of them girls. Human Rights Watch research found girls miss school for reasons including, lack of schools, costs associated with studying, child marriage, harmful child labor, and gender discrimination.

Child sexual abuse remains disturbingly common in Pakistan with 141 cases reported in just Lahore, Punjab, in the first six months of 2018. At least 77 girls and 79 boys were raped or sexually assaulted in the first half of 2018, according to police reports, but none of the suspects had been convicted at time of writing and all had been released on bail.

In January, the rape and murder of 7-year-old Zainab Ansari in Kasur, Punjab, led to nationwide outrage and prompted the government to promise action. On June 12, the Supreme Court upheld the convictions of Imran Ali for the rape and murder of Zainab Ansari and at least eight other girls. Imran Ali was executed on October 17. On August 8, the body of a 5-year-old girl who was raped and murdered was found in Mardan district, Khyber-Pakhtunkhwa. The rape of a 6-year-old girl in Sukkur district, Sindh, was confirmed by a medical report on August 10.

According to the organization Sahil, an average of 11 cases of child sexual abuse are reported daily across Pakistan. Zainab Ansari was among the dozen children to be murdered in Kasur district, Punjab in 2018. In 2015, police identified a gang of child sex abusers in the same district.

Terrorism, Counterterrorism, and Law Enforcement Abuses

Suicide bombings, armed attacks, and killings by the Taliban, Al-Qaeda, and their affiliates targeted religious minorities, security personnel, and politicians, resulting in hundreds of deaths.

Taliban and other militant groups targeted candidates and their supporters in the lead-up to the July election. On July 13, in one of the most deadly suicide bombings in Pakistan's history, at least 128 people were killed during an election rally held by the Balochistan Awami Party (BAP) in Mastung district, Balochistan. BAP politician Nawabzada Siraj Raisani was killed in the attack. A faction of the Taliban claimed responsibility, media reported. The same day, four people were killed and at least 32 injured, when the convoy of Akram Khan Durrani, a senior political leader of Muttahida Majlis-e-Amal (MMA), was targeted in a remote-controlled blast in Bannu district, Khyber-Pakhtunkhwa. Durrani survived.

On July 10, Haroon Bilour, a senior leader of the Awami National Party (ANP), was killed along with at least 20 others in a suicide bombing targeting his election meeting in Peshawar, Khyber-Pakhtunkhwa. The militant group Tehrik-e-Taliban Pakistan (TTP) claimed responsibility for the attack.

On election day on July 25, 31 people were killed in a suicide attack targeting a polling station in Quetta. The militant group Islamic State (ISIS) claimed responsibility for the attack.

On November 23, gunmen attacked the Chinese consulate in Karachi, killing four people, including two police officers. The militant group Baloch Liberation Army claimed responsibility for the attack. On the same day, a suicide attack claimed by ISIS in Orakzai tribal district killed at least 33 people.

During counterterrorism operations, Pakistani security forces often are responsible for serious human rights violations including torture, enforced disappearances, detention without charge, and extrajudicial killings, according to Pakistan human rights defenders and defense lawyers. Counterterrorism laws also continue to be misused as an instrument of political coercion. Authorities do not allow independent monitoring of trials in military courts and many defendants are denied the right to a fair trial.

Sexual Orientation and Gender Identity

Violence against transgender and intersex women in Pakistan continues.

According to the local group Trans Action, 479 attacks against transgender women were reported in Khyber-Pakhunkhwa province in 2018. At least four transgender women were killed there in 2018, and at least 57 have been killed there since 2015. On May 4, the fatal shooting of Muni, a transgender woman in Mansehra district, Khyber-Pakhtunkhwa province, attracted national attention.

In a major development, Pakistan's parliament in May, passed a law guaranteeing basic rights for transgender citizens and outlawing discrimination by employers. The law grants individuals the right to self-identify as male, female, or a blend of genders, and to have that identity registered on all official documents, including National Identification Cards, passports, driver's licenses, and education certificates.

Pakistan's penal code criminalizes same-sex sexual conduct, placing men who have sex with men and transgender women at risk of police abuse, and other violence and discrimination.

Death Penalty

Pakistan has more than 8,000 prisoners on death row, one of the world's largest populations facing execution. Pakistani law mandates capital punishment for 28 offenses, including murder, rape, treason, certain acts of terrorism, and blasphemy. Those on death row are often from the most marginalized sections of society.

In April, the Pakistan Supreme Court suspended the execution of Imdad Ali and Kaniz Fatima, prisoners with psychosocial disabilities and ordered a bench of the Supreme Court to examine the issue. The court said that a person with psychosocial disabilities cannot be executed. Imdad Ali and Kaniz Fatima, however, remained on death row at time of writing.

Key International Actors

In March, the UN Human Rights Council (HRC) adopted the outcome of Pakistan's third Universal Periodic Review (UPR), which was conducted in November 2017. The Pakistani government rejected a large number of key recommendations that states made to it during the UPR.

Since Pakistan was elected to the Human Rights Council in 2017, it has generally failed to take a strong stance on serious human rights situations. However, in September 2017, it led Organisation for Islamic Cooperation member states at the council in expressing concerns about the ethnic cleansing campaign against the Rohingya by the Myanmar military.

Pakistan's volatile relationship with United States, the country's largest development and military donor, deteriorated in 2018, amid signs of mistrust. In August, the US stopped payment of US$300 million in military reimbursements to Pakistan for not taking adequate action against the Haqqani network, a Taliban-affiliated group that is accused of planning and carrying out attacks on civilians, government officials, and NATO forces in Afghanistan.

In June, the Office of the United Nations High Commissioner for Human Rights (OHCHR) released the first-ever report by the United Nations on human rights in Kashmir. The report noted that human rights abuses in Pakistani Kashmir were of a "different caliber or magnitude" to those in Indian Kashmir and included misuse of anti-terrorism laws to target dissent, and restrictions on the rights to freedom of expression and opinion, peaceful assembly, and association.

In July, the EU deployed an election observation mission to Pakistan that later issued a report highlighting significant curtailment of freedom of expression, allegations of interference in the electoral process by the military-led establishment, and politicization of the judiciary.

Pakistan and China deepened extensive economic and political ties in 2018, and work continued on the China-Pakistan Economic Corridor, a project consisting of construction of roads, railways, and energy pipelines.

Historically tense relations between Pakistan and India have shown no signs of improvement, with both countries accusing each other of facilitating unrest and militancy.

Papua New Guinea

Papua New Guinea (PNG) is a resource-rich country, yet almost 40 percent of the population lives in poverty. Former United Nations High Commissioner for Human Rights Zeid Ra'ad Al Hussein visited PNG in February 2018 and called on the government to tackle a long list of abuses, including corruption, land rights abuses, gender-based violence, and attacks on activists and journalists.

In June, authorities confirmed that the country was facing its first polio outbreak in 18 years, prompting an emergency vaccination campaign.

Chronic problems continued to plague the criminal justice system in PNG, including abuses by police. Overcrowding and dire prison conditions led to prison breakouts.

PNG continues to see high levels of violence and political unrest since the 2017 election, which was marred by widespread electoral irregularities and violence. In June, in the Southern Highlands, a mob set alight a passenger plane in an election-related protest.

Women's and Girls' Rights

Sorcery-related violence continued unabated, with women and girls the primary targets. In May, in the Southern Highlands, one woman was killed and another two seriously injured after a mob attacked the women following accusations they had used sorcery to kill a man. The government's 2013 Sorcery National Action Plan is inadequately funded and has yet to be implemented.

In December 2017, the PNG government announced A$4 million (US$2.9 million) of funding for sorcery awareness and education programs. In July, the National Court sentenced eight men to death for their involvement in a sorcery-related killing of seven people. PNG continued to impose the death penalty, although authorities have not carried out any executions since 1954.

In 2013, the Family Protection Act was passed, which criminalizes domestic violence and allows victims to obtain protection orders. In 2017, the government passed regulations to implement the law, but enforcement remains weak and inconsistent.

Police and prosecutors rarely pursued investigations or criminal charges against people who commit family violence—even in cases of attempted murder, serious injury, or repeated rape—and instead prefer to resolve such cases through mediation and/or payment of compensation.

There is also a severe lack of services for people requiring assistance after having suffered family violence, such as safe houses, qualified counselors, case management, financial support, or legal aid.

PNG continues to have one of the highest rates of maternal death in the Asia-Pacific, and the number of women and girls who give birth in a health facility or with the help of a skilled birth attendant has reduced in the last five years. Although the PNG government supports universal access to contraception, two out of three women and girls still are unable to access and use it due to geographic, cultural, and economic barriers. Abortion remains illegal in PNG, except in cases where the mother's life is at risk.

Police Abuse

The PNG government failed to address abuses by security forces. Few police are ever held to account for beating or torturing criminal suspects, a common occurrence. In September, the government indicated it would introduce new measures to give immunity to police and defense force soldiers on special operations supposedly to "curb lawlessness."

Despite the ombudsman and police announcing investigations into the 2016 police shooting of eight student protesters in Port Moresby, at time of writing no police had been charged or disciplined and neither body had issued a report.

In July, prison officers shot and killed four men who escaped from Buimo prison in Lae. This followed a similar escape in 2017, in which 17 prisoners were killed. Corrective Services ordered an inquiry in 2017, but at time of writing no investigation had begun, allegedly due to lack of funding.

Children's Rights

Police often beat children in lock-ups and house them with adults, despite a child justice law that states children should be kept separate from adults during all stages of the criminal justice process.

In August, a video showing two PNG police officers brutally assaulting a teenage boy in West New Britain was widely circulated on social media. Minister for Police Jelta Wong ordered an immediate investigation and promised to hold those responsible to account. The two officers have reportedly been suspended and charged under the Criminal Code Act, but neither had been prosecuted at time of writing.

Children's access to education improved from 2012 to 2016 following the introduction of the Tuition Fee Free Policy in 2012 but was still low, with only 76 percent of children enrolled in primary school and 33 percent in secondary.

Land Rights

More than 5 million hectares of land has been awarded to PNG-based subsidiaries of foreign companies on Special Agricultural Business Leases, resulting in loss of ancestral land and forest for rural Papua New Guineans. The leases represent over 10 percent of the country's total landmass and potentially impact more than 700,000 people.

Government Corruption

Corruption in PNG is widespread. In December 2017, the Supreme Court quashed a long-standing arrest warrant for corruption against Prime Minister Peter O'Neill, finding that the warrant failed to meet a number of requirements and was issued without jurisdiction.

That same month, anti-corruption police arrested and charged the country's deputy chief electoral commissioner with corruption for allegedly manipulating votes, for perjury and making a false declaration.

In April, media reported that anti-corruption police are investigating the Governor of Port Moresby Powes Parkop, after a former official revealed the city council was paying A$1.2 million (approximately US$870,000) a year to a yoga and health company run by his alleged partner.

Asylum Seekers and Refugees

About 570 male asylum seekers and refugees live in PNG, most on Manus Island. Nearly all were forcibly transferred to PNG by Australia in 2013. Following a 2016 PNG Supreme Court decision that detaining asylum seekers is unconstitutional, in November 2017, the Australian and PNG government closed the main center on Manus and relocated refugees and asylum seekers to other accommodation facilities on the island.

Many asylum seekers and refugees suffer complex health problems including mental health conditions that have been exacerbated by long periods in detention and uncertainty about their futures. In May, a Rohingya refugee died by apparent suicide having jumped from a moving bus, the seventh asylum seeker or refugee to die on Manus Island since 2013. The Australian Department of Home Affairs has acknowledged that medical services have been reduced since the men were forcibly removed from the main center in 2017. There have been urgent calls, including by Australian doctors, to improve healthcare standards on Manus Island.

Australia pays for refugees' living expenses but refuses to resettle them in Australia, insisting they must settle in PNG or third countries, such as the United States. US resettlement from Manus remains slow, with 163 resettled as of October.

Refugees and asylum seekers do not feel safe on Manus due to a spate of violent attacks by locals in the town of Lorengau and ongoing disputes with the local community. In January, neighboring residents blocked access to living compounds in a protest about leaking sewage. In May, a fire in Hillside Haus forced the relocation of 120 residents. Since June, a 12-hour curfew has been imposed on the refugees and asylum seekers in violation of their freedom of movement, following a car accident in which a woman died; an allegedly drunk refugee was driving the car. In October, a local man violently assaulted an Iranian refugee who was hospitalized with serious injuries to his head and eyes.

In June, following a class action settlement, the Australian government paid A$70 million (approximately US$51million) in compensation to asylum seekers and refugees for their illegal detention on Manus Island.

In July, the Queensland Coroner ruled that the death of Manus detainee and Iranian asylum seeker Hamid Khazaei in September 2014 was preventable and the result of "compounding errors" in health care provided under Australia's offshore immigration detention system.

Disability Rights

Despite the existence of a national disability policy, people with disabilities are often unable to participate in community life, go to school, or work because of lack of accessibility, stigma, and other barriers. Access to mental health care is limited, and many people with psychosocial disabilities and their families often consider traditional healers to be the only option.

Sexual Orientation and Gender Identity

The PNG criminal code outlaws sex "against the order of nature," which has been interpreted to apply to consensual same-sex acts, and is punishable by up to 14 years' imprisonment.

Key International Actors

In March, then-Australian Foreign Minister Julie Bishop visited Port Moresby and met with PNG Foreign Minister Rimbink Pato to discuss health and immigration. In November, Australian Prime Minister Scott Morrison and PNG Prime Minister Peter O'Neill signed a joint defense agreement to deepen relations and security cooperation, partly to curb China's growing influence in the Pacific.

China is set to overtake Australia as the largest donor to PNG, though most assistance is in the form of infrastructure loans rather than aid. China is committing approximately US$4 billion to developing a national road network. Australian government aid to PNG for the year 2018-19 is A$572 million (approximately US$411.3 million).

In November, PNG hosted the annual Asia-Pacific Economic Cooperation (APEC) forum which was overshadowed by growing tensions between China and Australia for regional dominance in the Pacific. China provided significant infrastructure support—including the A$35million (approximately US$25.4 million) convention center—and President Xi Jinping invited Pacific Island leaders to a special summit ahead of APEC.

Australia spent A$130 million (approximately US$94.2 million) on security costs for APEC, and provided 1,500 Australian Defence Force personnel.

The PNG government drew criticism for its purchase of 40 new Maserati cars for visiting APEC dignitaries, when the impoverished country struggles to pay teachers and faces a health crisis. The summit ended in disarray when Chinese officials physically forced their way into the office of the PNG foreign minister and refused to sign the final joint statement.

Peru

In March, President Pedro Pablo Kuczynski offered his resignation ahead of a congressional impeachment vote linked to allegations of corruption and a vote-buying scandal. Congress accepted his resignation, and Vice President Martin Vizcarra was sworn in as president.

In December 2017, then-President Kucynski granted former President Alberto Fujimori an "humanitarian pardon" based on claims of illness. Fujimori had been sentenced in a landmark trial in 2009 to 25 years in prison for killings, enforced disappearances, and kidnappings committed in 1991 and 1992. There are strong reasons to believe that his release was due to a negotiation in response to growing pressure from Fujimori supporters in Congress, including a December attempt to impeach Kuczynski. In October 2018, a Supreme Court judge overturned the pardon and ordered the imprisonment of Fujimori. An appeal remained pending at time of writing, and Fujimori had not been sent back to prison.

In July, President Vizcarra announced a referendum to reform the political and justice system after Peruvian media released audio recordings presumably implicating members of the National Magistrate Council—the body charged with appointing and removing judges and prosecutors—in corruption. The referendum, set for December 9, proposed a single-term limit for congressmen, establishing a bicameral legislature, reforms of financing rules for political parties, and changes to the composition of the National Magistrate Council.

Confronting Past Abuses

Efforts to prosecute grave human rights abuses committed during the 20-year armed conflict that ended in 2000 have had mixed results.

Peru's Truth and Reconciliation Commission estimated that almost 70,000 people died or were subject to enforced disappearance during the country's armed conflict between 1980 and 2000. Many were victims of atrocities by the Shining Path and other insurgent groups; others were victims of human rights violations by state agents.

Authorities have made limited progress in prosecuting wartime abuses by government forces, in part due to lack of collaboration from the Defense Ministry.

According to Peruvian human rights groups, prosecutors had only achieved rulings in 78 cases related to abuses committed during the armed conflict, as of May 2017, and only 17 convictions.

Although then-President Kucynski granted former President Fujimori an "humanitarian pardon" in December 2017 based on claims of illness, on October 3, 2018, a Supreme Court judge overturned the pardon and ordered Fujimori's imprisonment. An appeal remained pending at time of writing, and Fujimori had not been sent back to prison.

On October 12, 2018, Fujimori supporters in Congress passed a bill that would have granted prisoners who are over a certain age and have served a third of their sentences the right to serve the remainder under "electronic surveillance." Proponents of the bill said it was intended to ease prison conditions for elderly prisoners, but the timing and language in the bill showed its objective was to ensure Fujimori's freedom. On October 22, President Vizcarra vetoed the bill.

In April 2018, a senior prosecutor ordered that Fujimori and three of his health ministers be indicted in connection with forced sterilizations of mostly poor and indigenous women. At time of writing, Fujimori and his ministers had not been charged.

In September, the National Penal Chamber of Peru sentenced leaders of Shining Path, including its founder Abimael Guzmán, to life in prison for terrorist acts. Guzman was already serving life in prison for the 1983 killing of 69 peasants in the town of Santiago de Lucanamarca.

In 2017, new evidence surfaced corroborating longstanding allegations that former President Humala ordered egregious human rights violations, including torture, enforced disappearances, and killings, committed by security forces in the early 1990s at the Madre Mía military base in the Alto Huallaga region. In September, a commission of lawmakers charged with investigating allegations of extrajudicial killings at the Madre Mía base in 1992 concluded there was sufficient evidence against Humala to warrant reopening criminal investigations.

In 2015, the government created a national registry of victims of forced sterilizations committed between 1995 and 2001. More than 5,000 victims had been registered at time of writing.

Courts have made much less progress in addressing violations, including extra-judicial killings, disappearances, and torture, committed during the earlier administrations of Fernando Belaúnde (1980-1985) and Alan García (1985-1990).

In August, the National Criminal Chamber sentenced two retired military agents to up to 30 years in prison for their role in the forced disappearances and extrajudicial killings of 53 people at the Cabitos military base, in Ayacucho, in 1983. In August, the remains of several victims were exhumed from a nearby clandestine cemetery and given to their relatives.

Peruvian authorities estimate that some 20,000 people disappeared during the country's armed conflict. In September, President Vizcarra ordered the establishment of a genetic profile bank that will help in the search for those disappeared.

Police Abuse

Security forces sometimes use excessive force when responding to occasional violent protests over mining and other large-scale development projects. In January 2018, Irineo Curiñaupa Campos and Celestino Flores Ventura died from gun shots fired by Peruvian national police while they were protesting during the national agricultural strike. Since 2002, security forces have reportedly killed 155 people during protests throughout Peru, according to human rights groups. These killings have significantly declined since 2016.

In August 2015, then-President Humala issued Decree 1186 that limited the use of force by police. Under the decree, police are permitted to employ lethal force only when it is "strictly necessary" in the face of a "serious and imminent risk" of grave harm. However, Law 30151, passed in January 2014, grants legal immunity to "armed forces and police personnel who in fulfillment of their duty and using their weapons or other means of defense, cause injury or death." The law may make it impossible to hold accountable police officers who use lethal force unlawfully. According to local human rights groups, no member of the armed forces or police has been convicted for excessive use of force by armed forces and police personnel during protests since 2002.

In 2016, the Interior Ministry announced an investigation into a group of 28 policemen, including a general, who had allegedly committed at least 20 extrajudicial killings between 2009 and 2015, and falsely reported the victims as criminals killed in combat, in order to receive promotions and awards. A trial on these crimes against 11 policemen, including 8 who are fugitive from justice, remained pending at time of writing.

Freedom of Expression

Threats to freedom of expression continued to be a concern in Peru.

In June, Congress passed a law forbidding the government from purchasing media advertisement in private outlets. In October, the country's Constitutional Tribunal ruled that the law was unconstitutional because it undermines Peruvians' right to access information of public interest.

In July, the media outlets IDL-Reporteros and Panomara released audio recordings purportedly showing that judges, prosecutors, and members of the National Magistrates Council negotiated judicial decisions and judicial appointments.

On July 10, a prosecutor visited the offices of IDL-Reporteros and requested the reporters' work materials and documents. The prosecutors left, without the documents and materials, after the director of IDL-Reporteros requested to see their warrant. On July 12, lawmakers summoned the journalists and required them to inform them how they obtained the audios and provide the original audios and documents.

Women's and Girls' Rights

Gender-based violence is a significant problem in Peru. In 2017, 368 women were victims of "femicides" (the killing of a woman in certain contexts, including domestic violence and gender-based discrimination). Courts in Peru convicted 54 people on "femicide" charges between January 2015 and March 2016.

In August, Congress amended the definition of the crime of rape in the criminal code, making "lack of consent" the defining element of the crime, irrespective of whether there was violence.

Women and girls in Peru have the right to access abortions only in cases of risk to their health or lives. A bill introduced in October 2016 to decriminalize abortion in cases of rape or if the fetus suffers severe conditions not compatible with life outside the womb remained pending in Congress at time of writing. But also pending in Congress since 2016 is a bill that would recognize the "right" of a fetus conceived as a result of rape to receive "protection from the state" until it is "adopted."

Sexual Orientation and Gender Identity

Same-sex couples in Peru are not allowed to marry or engage in civil unions. In February 2017, a group of lawmakers introduced a bill to legalize same-sex marriage. It remained pending in Congress at time of writing.

People in Peru are required to appear before a judge in order to revise the gender marker on their identification documents. A bill introduced in 2017 allowing people to revise the gender noted on their identification documents without prior judicial approval remained pending in Congress at time of writing.

In March 2018, Peru's National Institute of Statistics published the results of a survey showing that over 60 percent of LGBT people surveyed had suffered some type of discrimination or violence.

Disability Rights

September changes to the civil code eliminated guardianship for persons with disabilities. Under the new rules, people with mental and physical disabilities have the same legal capacity as any other Peruvian, including the power to decide whether to undergo medical treatment, get married, or have children. The reform allows people with disabilities the option of appointing a supporter to assist them in decision-making.

Refugees, Asylum Seekers, and Migrants

More than 126,000 Venezuelans are seeking asylum in Peru, the largest number of registered Venezuelan asylum seekers in any country.

More than 430,000 Venezuelans live in Peru. In 2017, President Kuczynski decreed a special permission process for Venezuelans to stay in the country. Under the decree, Venezuelans who arrived in the country before February 2, 2017—the date it entered into force—whose legal permission to stay in the country has expired, and who do not have a criminal record, may request a year-long temporary residency permit. In August, the government extended the permit, allowing people who arrived in the country before October 31, 2018, to apply for it. Those who obtain the permit are allowed to work, enroll their children in school, and access health care.

At time of writing, more than 93,000 Venezuelans had benefited from the permit. In October, President Vizcarra said that his government would carry out an "assessment" after October 31 into whether the country had the means to grant more special permits to Venezuelans.

In August, authorities announced that they would require Venezuelans entering the country to present a passport, a move that would have effectively closed the door to many Venezuelan migrants, as the process for obtaining a passport in Venezuela is extremely difficult. But on August 25, Peru's foreign minister announced that Venezuelans could enter with an expired passport, that children and older people could enter without passports, and that people without a passport could still seek asylum.

Foreign Policy

Peru has played a leading role in regional efforts to help address the human rights crisis in Venezuela. In August 2017, then-President Kuczynski convened a meeting at which foreign affairs ministers of 12 nations signed the Lima Declaration—a comprehensive statement that condemns the rupture of democratic order and the systematic violation of human rights in Venezuela.

In June 2018, Peru delivered a statement on behalf of a cross-regional group of 53 countries, expressing concern about the human rights and humanitarian crisis in Venezuela, and calling for continued reporting by the UN High Commissioner for Human Rights.

On September 26, the governments of Peru, Argentina, Canada, Chile, Colombia, and Paraguay referred the situation in Venezuela to ICC Prosecutor Fatou Bensouda for investigation.

As a member of the Human Rights Council, Peru has supported resolutions to spotlight human rights abuses, including in Myanmar, Iran, and Venezuela.

Key International Actors

In June, the Inter-American Court of Human Rights (IACtHR) requested that Peruvian courts review the December 2017 "humanitarian pardon" of former President Fujimori by October 29, to determine whether Peru has complied with its duty to investigate, prosecute, and sanction the grave human rights violations.

In July, in response to the requests made to the journalists of IDL-Reporteros and Panorama by a prosecutor and lawmakers, the Organization of American States special rapporteur on freedom of expression expressed concern, noting that any measure to seize journalistic material that may reveal sources or cite journalists as witnesses has a restrictive effect on freedom of expression.

In September, the IACtHR condemned Peru for the enforced disappearance of five people committed between 1984 and 1992.

Philippines

The human rights crisis in the Philippines unleashed since President Rodrigo Duterte took office in June 2016 deepened in 2018 as Duterte continued his murderous "war on drugs" in the face of mounting international criticism.

In March, Duterte announced that the Philippines would withdraw from the International Criminal Court (ICC) "effective immediately" in response to the ICC's move in February to launch a preliminary examination of "drug war" killings to determine whether to open a full-blown investigation.

Duterte sought to silence his critics via various means. His most prominent critic, Senator Leila de Lima, remained in detention on politically motivated drug charges. In May, the Philippine Supreme Court took unprecedented action to remove Chief Justice Maria Lourdes Sereno, apparent reprisal for her criticism of Duterte's "drug war" and other abusive policies. In September, Duterte revoked the amnesty given to Senator Antonio Trillanes IV, another Duterte critic, by the previous administration for leading mutinies in 2003 and 2007 when he was a naval officer; in October, a Manila court denied a Department of Justice petition to issue a warrant for his arrest.

In November, in a rare triumph of accountability in the Philippines, a Manila court found three police officers guilty for the murder of 17-year-old Kian delos Santos in August 2017. The killing, which was caught on surveillance camera, sparked outrage against the "drug war." In September, a court in Bulacan province convicted ex-army Maj. Gen. Jovito Palparan and two other military men for the kidnapping and illegal detention of Karen Empeño and Sherlyn Cadapan, two student activists who were allegedly abducted, raped, and tortured by military agents in 2006. The two women remain missing.

Extrajudicial Killings

The Duterte administration's "war on drugs" continued in 2018 and expanded into areas outside the capital, Metro Manila, including to the provinces of Bulacan, Laguna, Cavite, and the cities of Cebu and General Santos.

According to the Philippine Drug Enforcement Agency (PDEA), 4,948 suspected drug users and dealers died during police operations from July 1, 2016 to September 30, 2018. But this does not include the thousands of others killed by unidentified gunmen. According to the Philippine National Police (PNP), 22,983 such deaths since the "war on drugs" began are classified as "homicides under investigation."

The exact number of fatalities is difficult to ascertain because the government has failed to disclose official documents about the "drug war." It has issued contradictory statistics and, in the case of these "homicides under investigation," stopped releasing the figures altogether.

Masked gunmen taking part in killings appeared to be working closely with police, casting doubt on government claims that most killings have been committed by vigilantes or rival drug gangs.

Duterte has vowed to continue his anti-drug campaign until his term ends in 2022. In July 2018, he again pledged to continue the "war on drugs," saying "it will be as relentless and chilling as on the day it began."

Duterte has also vowed to protect police officers and agents carrying out the "drug war" from prosecution. Except for a few high-profile cases, the killings have not been investigated.

Human Rights Defenders

Since February 2017, Senator Leila de Lima has been jailed on politically motivated drug charges filed against her in apparent retaliation for leading a Senate inquiry into the "drug war" killings. Her plight has prompted international expressions of support.

In September, Duterte ordered the arrest of a colleague of de Lima's, Senator Antonio Trillanes IV, by revoking his amnesty, forcing him to remain at the Senate premises for weeks. In October, a Manila court dismissed the government's petition to issue the arrest warrant against Trillanes. Trillanes has been Duterte's most vocal critic since de Lima, accusing the president and his family of corruption.

In February, the Department of Justice issued a petition that labeled more than 600 people—among them Victoria Tauli-Corpuz, the United Nations special rapporteur on the rights of indigenous peoples, and dozens of leftist activists—as members of the Communist Party of the Philippines (CPP) and its armed wing, the New People's Army (NPA). That action put those individuals at risk of extrajudicial execution. Tauli-Corpuz called the allegation "baseless, malicious and irresponsible." In August, a Manila court removed her name from the petition.

Philippine presidential spokesman Harry Roque alleged in March that "some human rights groups have become unwitting tools of drug lords to hinder the strides made by the administration." That echoed comments made days prior by Foreign Affairs Secretary Alan Peter Cayetano equating efforts of some unnamed human rights organizations to stop Duterte's murderous "war on drugs" with "being used by drug lords."

Children's Rights

The Philippine Drug Enforcement Agency (PDEA) announced in June that it was seeking to impose annual unannounced drug screening tests on teachers and schoolchildren starting in the fourth grade. PDEA sought to justify the move as an attempt to identify 10-year-old potential drug users so they "can get intervention while they are still young."

Imposing drug testing on schoolchildren when Philippine police are summarily killing alleged drug users endangers children should they fail such a drug test. Mandatory testing may also violate children's right to bodily integrity, constitute arbitrary interference with their privacy and dignity, and may deter children from attending school for reasons unrelated to any potential drug use.

Police have killed dozens of children since the start of the "war on drugs" in June 2016, deaths which Duterte has dismissed as "collateral damage." In February, police arrested three police officers implicated in the execution-style summary killing of 17-year-old Kian Lloyd delos Santos in August 2017.

Attacks on Journalists

The Duterte administration ratcheted up its attack on media freedom in January 2018 by threatening the closure of Rappler.com, an online news outlet critical of the "war on drugs." In November, the Department of Justice indicted Rappler and its editor and founder, Maria Ressa, for tax evasion. This followed months of attacks and harassment of Rappler by the Duterte government and its supporters.

New draft regulations by the Philippine House of Representatives in May would allow Congress to ban reporters who "besmirch" the reputation of lawmakers from covering the national legislature. Journalists and some members of Congress have denounced the proposed rule as dangerously ambiguous and stifling.

The killings of journalists continued in 2018, with six murdered by unidentified gunmen in different parts of the country.

HIV Epidemic

The Philippines faces the fastest-growing epidemic of HIV in Asia. According to the Joint United Nations Programme on HIV/AIDS (UNAIDS), the number of new HIV cases jumped from 4,400 in 2010 to 12,000 in 2017, the last year for which data were available. Most new infections—up to 83 percent—are among men and transgender women who have sex with men. There are now an estimated 68,000 Filipinos living with HIV.

This increase has been attributed to government policy failures to respond to the epidemic. Human Rights Watch research shows that many sexually active young Filipinos have little or no knowledge about the role of condoms in preventing sexually transmitted diseases because the government fails to promote condoms vigorously, among other factors.

Human Rights Watch documented that workers and employees in the Philippines living with HIV may suffer workplace discrimination including refusal to hire, unlawful firing, and forced resignation of people with HIV. Some employers may also disregard or actively facilitate workplace harassment of employees who are HIV positive. In February, Duterte suggested to a group of returning overseas migrant workers that they avoid using condoms because they "aren't pleasurable."

In October, the Senate and House of Representatives approved a bill that would amend the country's 20-year-old AIDS law. The new law outlines a rights-based response to the epidemic and prohibits discrimination against people with HIV in the workplace and other settings. It also makes it unlawful to disclose the HIV status of an individual without their consent. However, the law does not include specific provisions directing the government to promote condom use.

Sexual Orientation and Gender Identity

The Philippine Supreme Court heard a long-awaited argument in June that could open the door to same-sex marriage in the overwhelmingly Catholic country. In May, the city of Mandaluyong approved an ordinance to protect the rights of lesbian, gay, bisexual, and transgender (LGBT) people—the latest in a slew of similar local laws passed across the country.

The House of Representatives unanimously passed a federal nondiscrimination bill protecting LGBT people in September 2017, but opponents have stalled a companion bill in the Senate. Representatives also introduced a bill that would create civil partnerships and give same-sex couples rights in adoption, insurance, inheritance, property, and medical decision-making.

Key International Actors

In January 2018, the European Commission expressed strong concerns about the Philippines' compliance with the human rights obligations related to the trade preferences scheme from which it benefits.

In February, the prosecutor of the International Criminal Court (ICC) announced that she would open a preliminary examination into the "drug war" killings in the Philippines. The Duterte administration responded by withdrawing from the Rome Statute, which takes effect in one year. In April, the European Parliament adopted a resolution calling on the Philippines to put an end to the drug war and ensure accountability, and on the EU to use all available mean—including suspending trade benefits if necessary—to persuade the Philippines to reverse its abusive trend.

Asian governments have expressed implicit or explicit support for the anti-drug campaign. The Indonesian government in February awarded then-Philippine National Police Director-General Ronald dela Rosa its highest honor, the Medal of Honor, for his "rock star-like inspiration to the Indonesian national police and the Indonesian people on how to fight the war on drugs."

In May, the South Korean Embassy in Manila and the Korean Police National Agency donated more than 130 vehicles to the Philippines National Police despite its role in the "drug war" killings.

The US Congress regularly appropriates assistance to the Philippine government, including substantial financing for arms sales as well as funds for law enforcement and military training. Law enforcement funding is restricted to drug user treatment projects and marine and international interdiction programs. The US military also routinely provides the Philippines military with second-hand military vehicles, ships, and non-lethal equipment.

Iceland led a joint statement on behalf of 32 states at the June session of the United Nations Human Rights Council (HRC), building on two previous joint statements, condemning the extrajudicial killings and calling for "a more formal Council initiative" if needed to hold the Philippines to its obligations as a member of the Council. It also called for the Philippines to "cooperate with the international community" to ensure investigations into these deaths. On October 12, the Philippines was elected to serve a second three-year term on the UN HRC, starting January 2019.

Qatar

Qatar passed a number of important human rights reforms in 2018 but failed to deliver on several other promised reforms. While Qatar acceded to two core human rights treaties, it made reservations, depriving migrants and women of some of their protections. Qatar passed the Gulf region's first refugee asylum law, but it fell short of the country's international obligations. Qatari laws continue to discriminate against migrants, women, and lesbian, gay, bisexual, and transgender (LGBT) individuals. Throughout 2018, the diplomatic crisis persisted between Qatar on one side and Saudi Arabia, Bahrain, Egypt, and the United Arab Emirates (UAE) on the other, over Qatar's alleged support of terrorism and ties with Iran, impacting the rights of Qataris.

Women's Rights

Qatar does not allow dual nationality and discriminates against women by not allowing them to pass nationality to their children on the same basis as men. Qatar allows men to pass citizenship to their spouses and children, whereas children of Qatari women and non-citizen men can only apply for citizenship under narrow conditions.

In September, Qatar passed a law on permanent residency that would be available for the first time to children of Qatari women married to non-Qatari men. The permanent residency allows qualified children to receive government health and educational services, to invest in the economy, and own real estate. However, the law falls short of granting women equal rights to men in conferring nationality to their children and spouses.

Qatar's personal status law also discriminates against women in marriage, divorce, child custody, and inheritance. The law provides that women can only marry if a male guardian approves of the marriage; men have a unilateral right to divorce while requiring women to apply to the courts for divorce on limited grounds; and a wife is responsible for looking after the household and obeying her husband. Under inheritance provisions, female siblings receive half the amount their brothers get.

The penal code does not criminalize domestic violence or marital rape, other than one article of the family law forbidding husbands from hurting their wives physically or morally, and general provisions on assault.

Migrant Workers

Qatar has a migrant labor force of over 2 million people, who comprise approximately 95 percent of its total labor force. Approximately 800,000 workers are employed in construction while another 100,000 are domestic workers. Qatar's *kafala* (sponsorship) system governing the employment of migrant workers gives employers excessive control over them, including the power to deny them the right to leave the country or change jobs.

In October 2017, the International Trade Union Confederation announced Qatar's agreement with the International Labour Organization (ILO) to extensive reforms of the current *kafala* (sponsorship) system, institute a nondiscriminatory minimum wage, improve payment of wages, end document confiscation or the need for an exit permit for workers wanting to leave the country, enhance labor inspections and occupational safety and health systems—including by developing a heat mitigation strategy—refine the contractual system to improve labor recruitment procedures, and step up efforts to prevent forced labor.

In November 2017, Qatar implemented a temporary minimum wage of QR750 (US$206) per month for migrant workers. Also in 2017, the emir ratified Law No.15, granting labor protections to domestic workers for the first time. The new law guarantees domestic workers a maximum 10-hour workday, a weekly rest day, three weeks of annual leave, an end-of-service payment of at least three weeks per year, and healthcare benefits. However, the new law is still weaker than the Labor Law and lacks provisions for enforcement.

In September, Qatar passed a law allowing most migrant workers to leave the country without an exit permit, but excluding workers not covered by the Labor Law including those in the military, public sector, and domestic work, and allowing employers to apply to exclude some other workers.

Qatar has failed to implement other promised reforms. On April 30, 2018 the ILO inaugurated its first project office in Qatar for a three-year cooperation program to help Qatar achieve its commitments on migrant rights.

Human Rights Treaties

In May 2018, Qatar joined the International Covenant on Civil and Political Rights and the International Covenant on Economic, Social and Cultural Rights with a range of formal reservations depriving women and migrant workers of some of the treaties' protections.

It rejected gender equality provisions in marriage, divorce, and child custody on grounds that they contravene Islamic law. It also declared it would interpret several provisions in line with Islamic law, including on defining cruel, inhuman, or degrading punishment— avoiding bans on capital and corporal punishment— minimum marriage ages, and freedom of religion.

In its reservations, Qatar also said it would interpret the term "trade unions" in accordance with its national law. Article 116 of Qatar's Labor Law allows only Qatari nationals the right to form workers' associations or trade unions, depriving migrant workers of their rights to freedom of association and to form trade unions.

Refugee Rights

In September, Qatar's emir signed into law the Gulf region's first refugee asylum law. The law demonstrates Qatar's commitment to refugee rights but falls short of its international obligations, particularly with regard to its restrictions on freedom of movement and expression. Qatar is not a signatory to the 1951 Refugee Convention and its 1967 Protocol.

Sexual Orientation and Morality Laws

Qatar's penal code criminalizes "sodomy," punishing same-sex relations with imprisonment between one to three years. Muslims convicted of *zina* (sex outside of marriage) can also be sentenced to flogging (if unmarried) or the death penalty (if married). Non-Muslims can be sentenced to imprisonment.

Qatar, in addition to banning sex outside marriage for Muslims, provides penalties for any male, Muslim or not, who "instigates" or "entices" another male to commit an act of sodomy or immorality. The law does not provide for a penalty for the person who is "instigated" or "enticed." Under article 296 of the penal

476

code, "[l]eading, instigating or seducing a male anyhow for sodomy or dissipation" and "[i]nducing or seducing a male or a female anyhow to commit illegal or immoral actions" is punishable by up to three years. It is unclear whether this law is intended to prohibit all same-sex acts between men, and whether only one partner is considered legally liable.

Journalists and printers operate under section 47 of the 1979 Press and Publications Law, which bans publication of "any printed matter that is deemed contrary to the ethics, violates the morals or harms the dignity of the people or their personal freedoms." Throughout 2018, private publishing partners in Qatar, including the partner of the *New York Times*, censored numerous articles that touched on LGBT topics, in line with the country's anti-LGBT laws.

Key International Actors

In response to the Gulf crisis in 2017, in order to prevent food shortages, Qatar cultivated new supply chains through Oman and received assistance from Turkey and Iran, among other countries.

Many Emirati, Egyptian, Bahraini, and Saudi nationals affected by the diplomatic crisis chose to remain in Qatar for family or work reasons or because they fear persecution in their home countries.

In June 2018, Qatar filed a case at the International Court of Justice (ICJ) arguing that UAE-imposed measures violated the International Convention on the Elimination of All Forms of Racial Discrimination. On July 23, 2018, in a provisional ruling, the ICJ said that the UAE must allow Qatari families separated by its measures to reunite, allow Qatari students to complete their education in the UAE or obtain their educational records, and allow affected Qataris access to the UAE's courts. After the ruling, the UAE's foreign affairs minister tweeted that the UAE has already implemented the required measures.

Russia

The government increased its crackdown on political opposition and other critics before and after presidential elections that Vladimir Putin won, and that lacked real competition. Authorities continued to stifle critical voices, particularly online, through criminal prosecutions on extremism charges. In November, the European Court of Human Rights (ECtHR), amongst other violations, found that the repeated arrests of opposition figure Alexei Navalny were unlawful and for the purpose of suppressing political pluralism. The Kremlin did not stop authorities in Chechnya from threatening and imprisoning human rights defenders.

The 2017 decriminalization of first battery offenses within the family weakened protections for survivors of domestic violence.

A shocking video of the torture of a prisoner forced the government to acknowledge the use of torture in Russian prisons.

Torture and Cruel and Degrading Treatment

In July, *Novaya Gazeta* published a leaked video of penitentiary staff in Yaroslavl viciously beating a prisoner. Responding to public indignation, Russia's criminal investigation agency arrested 15 suspects by November. One suspect testified that staff recorded the video to demonstrate that they had carried out an order by senior officials to punish the prisoner.

The swift, effective investigation was unprecedented in Russia, where authorities typically dismiss prisoners' complaints of ill-treatment.

In August, Meduza, an independent online media outlet, published data on more than 50 other publicly reported torture cases in 2018. The alleged perpetrators included police, investigators, security agents, and penitentiary officials. Authorities opened only a few criminal investigations into the allegations, and only one case advanced to trial.

Freedom of Assembly

Police arbitrarily detained thousands of protesters in several nationwide peaceful demonstrations. Courts routinely sentenced protesters to fines and short-term arrests for violating restrictive regulations on demonstrations. Authorities pressured universities, schools, and parents to discourage students from participating in protests.

In January, in response to authorities barring Alexei Navalny, a leading opposition politician, from running for president, his supporters organized nationwide rallies at which police detained over 370 people. Police also raided Navalny's campaign offices, and in some cities made home visits to warn people who had indicated on social media that they would attend rallies.

In May, police detained at least 1,600 people, including 158 children, in 27 cities during peaceful protests against Putin's inauguration. In some cases, police officers used excessive force.

In September, police detained at least 1,195 people, including at least 60 children, in 39 cities at peaceful protests against plans to raise the pension age. Police also detained at least 14 journalists covering the protests and beat three of them. Numerous peaceful protesters sustained injuries, including bruising and fractures from police beatings.

In October, authorities did not disperse a two-week mass protest in Ingushetia, over the demarcation of the republic's administrative border with Chechnya. Unidentified security officials kidnapped and beat an Amnesty International researcher who was observing the protests, and subjected him to mock executions. At time of writing, authorities were carrying out an inquiry into his complaint.

Freedom of Association

Authorities continued their large-scale smear campaign against independent nongovernmental organizations (NGOs). The prosecutor general banned four more foreign organizations from Russia as "undesirable."

In July, the Andrei Rylkov Foundation, a Russian group dedicated to responsible drug policy, filed a complaint with the ECtHR arguing that the law on "undesirable organizations" interferes with freedoms of expression and association. In 2017, a court fined the group 50,000 rubles (at the time, approximately US$862) over an article on its website that contained a hyperlink to the website of a banned US organization. It was one of at least 11 Russian groups sanctioned over "undesirable" hyperlinks.

In August, the Justice Ministry proposed legislation further restricting foreign funding for Russian NGOs, introducing a procedure for the swift extrajudicial suspension of Russian NGOs on very broad grounds, and further broadening the grounds on which the government may ban foreign organizations as "undesirable."

Freedom of Expression Online

Authorities continued to use vague anti-extremism legislation to criminally prosecute independent voices for social media posts and reposts. Russia's ombudsperson and Communications Ministry supported draft legislation, introduced in June, to eliminate criminal liability for reposts.

A November 2017 law empowered the prosecutor's office to extrajudicially block content shared by foreign "undesirable" organizations and websites disseminating materials from these organizations.

In December 2017, the Justice Ministry designated Voice of America and eight Radio Free Europe outlets as "foreign media foreign agent" under a law adopted in November 2017.

In April, a court in Moscow ruled to block Telegram, a popular messaging service with almost 10 million users in Russia, for refusing to give encryption keys to security services. In restricting access to Telegram, authorities also temporarily blocked millions of unrelated IP addresses.

In October, a court in Moscow fined The New Times, an independent online magazine, the unprecedented sum of 22.25 million rubles (US$337,000) for supposed failure to report foreign funding, putting it at risk of closure.

In October, President Putin proposed a draft law decriminalizing a first offense of inciting hatred against ethnic, religious, or social groups. At time of writing, the draft law was pending parliamentary review.

Chechnya

In Chechnya, authorities arbitrarily detained, tortured, and disappeared suspected jihadists and local dissenters, and imposed collective punishment against their families.

In January, Chechen police arrested Oyub Titiev, the Grozny director of Memorial, on bogus marijuana possession charges. Memorial was the only human rights organization left which maintained a presence in Chechnya. Soon after, two separate arson attacks targeted Memorial's property in neighboring regions. Memorial's staff and Titiev's lawyers received anonymous threats and experienced surveillance by Chechen security officials, and the head of Chechnya, Ramzan Kadyrov, publicly threatened human rights defenders, promising to "break the backs of our enemies." In the ensuing months, he repeatedly called Titiev a "drug addict" and a traitor. Titiev's trial was ongoing at time of writing.

In August, several Chechen youths attacked local police, allegedly killing one and wounding three. Following the attacks, police carried out abusive raids, involving arbitrary detentions and ill-treatment of dozens of young men, some of whom were under 18. Kadyrov stated he would inflict collective punishment on relatives of alleged insurgents and threatened human rights defenders who "have the audacity to ask why we resort to collective responsibility." He equated human rights defenders with terrorists and said they would be banned from Chechnya after Titiev's trial.

Sexual Orientation and Gender Identity

Federal authorities failed to carry out an effective investigation into the 2017 anti-gay purge in Chechnya, during which local police tortured dozens of men presumed to be gay. Authorities did not launch a criminal investigation into a complaint filed in autumn 2017 by an ethnic Russian victimized in the purge and did not grant his request for state protection.In May, during its universal periodic review before the United Nations Human Rights Council (UNHRC), the Justice Minister said, "[we] failed to confirm not only the existence of facts of violations of these rights, we were unable to even find members of the LGBT (lesbian, gay, bisexual and transgender) community in Chechnya."

Rights activists documented new attacks on LGBT people by relatives and officials in Chechnya. Chechen singer Zelim Bakaev, whom security officials abducted in Grozny in August 2017, remained disappeared. In January, Kadyrov hinted that Bakaev died in an "honor killing."

481

HUMAN
RIGHTS
WATCH

NO SUPPORT
Russia's "Gay Propaganda" Law Imperils LGBT Youth

In July, a group of individuals in St. Petersburg, of Chechen origin, including at least one security official, attempted to kidnap Zelimkhan Akhmadov, who had fled Chechnya in 2017 because of threats over his presumed sexual orientation. An investigation was ongoing at time of writing.

In spring, police kept in incommunicado detention for over two months and ill-treated a young woman because of her presumed sexual orientation, and eventually released her to her family. Several women fled Chechnya under threat of honor killings over their presumed sexual orientation.

Authorities continued to enforce the discriminatory "gay propaganda" law. In May, authorities ordered the blocking of ParniPlus, a website that raises awareness about the HIV epidemic among gay men. In August, a governmental commission on minors' affairs in Biisk found a 16-year-old boy in violation of the law because he had posted four images exhibiting males hugging and modeling underwear. The commission fined him and his family 50,000 rubles (US$745). In October, Biisk City Court overturned the commission's decision.

In February, a court in Yekaterinburg ruled a 40-year-old woman unfit to foster two children with disabilities, claiming that because she allegedly projected a "style of male behavior," she violated Russian family legislation, as well as Russian society's "traditions and mentality." The boys had been living with the woman and her husband for several years.

World Cup 2018

In 2018, Russia hosted the Fédération Internationale de Football Association (FIFA) World Cup, which put several human rights issues in an international spotlight.

In February, workers in Nizhny Novgorod working on World Cup-related metro construction held strikes to protest wage and contract abuses. Workers on World Cup construction sites in other cities had reported similar abuses in previous years.

The same month, FIFA confirmed Chechnya's capital, Grozny, as the Team Base Camp for Egypt's national team. Kadyrov exploited Grozny's selection to boost his prestige.

HUMAN
RIGHTS
WATCH

HUMAN RIGHTS GUIDE
FOR REPORTERS
2018 FIFA World Cup in Russia

Authorities used a presidential decree on security around the World Cup to put additional restrictions on demonstrations from May 25 to July 25. Officials used the decree to deny protest permits and detain protesters, including those carrying out single-person pickets, which under regular circumstances do not require authorization.

Attacks on Human Rights Defenders

In December 2017, three assailants in Krasnodar assaulted Andrei Rudomakha, the head of the leading environmentalist group in southern Russia, and three of his colleagues. Rudomakha spent several weeks in a hospital with traumatic brain injury and multiple facial fractures. Authorities failed to carry out an effective investigation.

In March, in Makhachkala, an unidentified assailant attacked the director of Memorial's Dagestan office, Sirazhutdin Datsiev, hitting him on the back of the head with a heavy object. Datsiev was hospitalized with a head injury. The investigation into his attack yielded no tangible results.

In June, a court acquitted Yuri Dmitriev, head of the Karelia branch of Memorial, of bogus child pornography charges regarding his adopted daughter. However, police re-arrested him in June on criminal charges of sexual abuse of a child. Memorial asserted that Dmitriev's prosecution is politically motivated as part of the broader smear campaign against the organization.

Disability Rights

In its March review of Russia, the United Nations Committee on the Rights of Persons with Disabilities welcomed the legislative prohibition of discrimination based on disability and inclusion of more children with disabilities in mainstream education, but expressed concerns about the institutionalization of people with disabilities; violence, restraints, and sedation in institutions; segregated education; and the failure to guarantee full legal capacity, or the right to make decisions, to all people with disabilities.

HUMAN
RIGHTS
WATCH

"I Could Kill You and
No One Would Stop Me"
Weak State Response to Domestic Violence in Russia

Freedom of Religion

In 2018, police launched a sweeping campaign against Jehovah's Witnesses. It included dozens of home searches, raids, and interrogations stemming from a 2017 Supreme Court ruling that banned as extremist all Jehovah's Witnesses organizations in Russia.

By November, authorities were investigating 85 Jehovah Witnesses worshippers on criminal extremism charges, 26 of whom were in pretrial detention.

Domestic Violence

Domestic violence remained widely under-reported, and services for survivors inadequate. Survivors reported police failure to register or respond to domestic violence reports, and significant barriers to accessing the few available shelters.

The implementation of the 2017 amendments which decriminalized first offenses of battery among family made it harder for women to seek criminal prosecution if they are subject to domestic violence. Russian law does not provide for protection orders, which could help keep women safe. A comprehensive domestic violence draft law has been stalled in parliament since 2014.

Russia and Syria (see also Syria chapter)

Russia continued to play a key military role alongside the Syrian government in offensives on anti-government-held areas, indiscriminately attacking schools, hospitals, and civilian infrastructure. The Syrian-Russian military campaign to retake Eastern Ghouta in February involved the use of internationally banned cluster munitions as well as incendiary weapons, whose use in populated areas is restricted by international law.

In June, the Syrian-Russian offensive to regain control of Daraa province displaced more than 320,000 people. Russia remains the biggest weapons supplier to the Syrian government.

Russia continued to use its veto power at the UN Security Council to block accountability for Syrian crimes. After a chemical weapons attack on Douma killed dozens in April, Russia vetoed a UN resolution to create a new inquiry on chemical weapons use in Syria. In February, Russia blocked a UN resolution to establish a ceasefire and allow humanitarian deliveries in Eastern Ghouta. At time of writing, Russia had used its veto 12 times to protect Syria from condemnation and international pressure, six of those on chemical weapons. States parties to the Chemical Weapons Convention in June voted to establish an attribution mechanism at the Organisation for the Prohibition for Chemical Weapons (OPCW) in The Hague, thereby bypassing the deadlocked Security Council.

Russia hosted the Syrian People's Congress in Sochi, aiming for agreement on a new constitution, and created a working group in Astana on detentions and disappearances alongside Turkey and Iran. Both initiatives failed to make concrete progress. Russian officials urged Western countries to launch reconstruction efforts in order to facilitate the return of refugees, but failed to address key obstacles to return.

Russia and Ukraine (see also Ukraine chapter)

The government continued to provide political and material support to armed groups in eastern Ukraine, but took no measures to rein in their abuses, including arbitrary detention and ill-treatment of detainees. Russian authorities also continued to repress critics, primarily Crimean Tatars, in occupied Crimea.

In June, a court in Moscow sentenced Roman Sushchenko, a Ukrainian journalist, to 12 years in prison on highly dubious espionage charges.

Oleg Sentsov, a filmmaker from Crimea and an opponent of Russia's occupation of it, continued to serve a 20-year sentence on bogus terrorism charges. From May through October, he held a 145-day hunger strike demanding the release of dozens of Ukrainian nationals jailed in Russia and Crimea. In October, the European Parliament awarded Sentsov its annual Sakharov Prize for Freedom of Thought.

Key International Actors

Many of Russia's international partners urged the government to free Titiev, Sentsov, and others. The European Union repeatedly called for the release of Oleg Sentsov and other jailed Crimea activists and pressed Russia to drop the cases against Titiev and Dmitriev and release them. A European Parliament resolution demanded the release of Oleg Sentsov and more than 70 "Ukrainian political prisoners in Russia" and Crimea. Also in June, at a meeting with President Putin in St. Petersburg, French President Emmanuel Macron advocated for the release of Sentsov and Titiev. FIFA informed human rights groups that the organization's leadership was "personally invested in engagements" on Titiev's case.

Following a debate among EU foreign ministers on the block's relations with Russia, the EU's foreign policy chief noted the shrinking space for independent voices and "waning" respect for human rights and the rule of law.

In April, Secretary General of the Council of Europe (CoE) Thorbjørn Jagland, said that Russia's threats to pull out of the CoE would be a "disaster." Russia has not resumed funding contributions to the CoE, which it suspended in 2017.

During Russia's Universal Periodic Review at the UNHRC in May, Russia faced criticism for failure to end harassment, physical violence and killing of lawyers, journalists, human rights defenders and opposition politicians, attacks on and discrimination of LGBT people, torture, and ill-treatment of suspects and prisoners, and other serious abuses.

In June, the CoE Parliamentary Assembly unanimously adopted a resolution calling on Russia to allow an international investigation into the anti-gay purge and ongoing persecution of LGBT people in Chechnya.

In July, the UN Committee against Torture (CAT) reviewed Russia's sixth periodic report under the Convention Against Torture. While acknowledging the progress Russia made in "amending legislation on the penitentiary system and criminal justice," it emphasized that there was "reliable information that torture was practiced widely" and credible torture allegations "rarely resulted in criminal prosecutions." The committee stressed the need for accountability and underscored that the definition of torture in Russian law still was not in compliance with the convention. In September, Russia's ombudsperson spoke in support of amending the definition and increasing criminal sanctions against perpetrators.

In August, 15 participating states of the European and North American Organization for Security and Co-operation in Europe (OSCE) invoked the organization's Vienna Mechanism to raise concerns about abuses in Chechnya. Russia had 10 days to outline its actions to stop the abuses, but its written response did not satisfy the other governments. In November, they followed up by invoking the Moscow Mechanism to start an inquiry on Chechnya.

Russia's relations with the US and EU hit a new low in March, after the attempted killing of former Russian security official Sergei Skripal and his daughter in the UK, allegedly orchestrated by Russia with the use of a chemical nerve agent. The US introduced new sanctions in response to the Skripal incident.

The International Criminal Court (ICC) continued its investigation into war crimes and crimes against humanity allegedly committed in the lead-up to, during, and after the August 2008 war between Russia and Georgia over South Ossetia. The ICC prosecutor also continued a preliminary examination as to whether it should open an investigation into abuses committed during the armed conflicts in eastern Ukraine and Crimea. Although Ukraine is not an ICC member country, it has accepted the court's jurisdiction over alleged crimes committed on its territory since November 2013.

Rwanda

The ruling Rwandan Patriotic Front (RPF) and President Paul Kagame continued to exert control over the political landscape in Rwanda, as political opposition leaders have been intimidated and silenced, arrested, or forced into exile. The RPF won an overwhelming victory in legislative elections in September, following Kagame's re-election with a reported 98.8 percent of the vote in the 2017 presidential elections. A 2015 referendum changed the constitution and allowed Kagame to run for additional terms.

In July, the United Nations Subcommittee on Prevention of Torture (SPT) cancelled its visit to Rwanda, due to a lack of cooperation from Rwandan authorities, making it the first time in 11 years the SPT would cancel a visit. The National Commission for Human Rights is yet to publish a report on the killing of Congolese refugees by police in the Western Province.

Civil society groups, local and international media, international human rights organizations, and political opponents cannot operate independently or criticize government policy. A Human Rights Watch researcher was denied access to the country in January 2018. That same month, a Rwandan consultant working with Human Rights Watch was detained and arbitrarily held for six days, the first twelve hours of which were incommunicado.

Freedom of Expression

While some private radio stations occasionally broadcast programs on "sensitive" issues, most print and broadcast media continued to be heavily dominated by pro-government views. Most journalists were unable or unwilling to engage in investigative reporting on politically sensitive issues and rarely criticized government policies, because of intimidation, threats, and prosecutions in previous years.

The BBC Kinyarwanda service remained suspended, as it has been since 2014.

After many years of state intimidation and interference, independent civil society organizations are very weak and few document and expose human rights abuses by state agents.

Political Pluralism

The RPF won parliamentary elections in September, with 40 of the 53 elected seats. The Democratic Green Party of Rwanda won at least 5 percent of the vote, granting the party two parliamentary seats. This will be the first independent voice in Rwandan parliament in several years.

The trial of former would-be 2017 presidential candidate Diane Rwigara and her mother, Adeline Rwigara, opened in May 2018. The women, along with four others tried in absentia, were charged with "inciting insurrection or trouble among the population." Diane Rwigara was also charged with "forging or alteration of documents" and "use of counterfeited documents," and Adeline Rwigara with "discrimination and sectarian practices." On October 5, the High Court ordered their release on bail. The women were acquitted of all charges on December 6.

Diane Rwigara, her sister Anne, and their mother were arrested in September 2017, after Diane Rwigara had been barred from filing her candidacy for the August presidential elections. In the days leading up to her arrest, she spoke with international media outlets and criticized police actions and accusations against her. Hours before her arrest, Rwigara told one outlet that her family was being "persecuted for criticizing the government." Anne Rwigara was later released, and the charges against her dropped.

The charges of inciting insurrection were related to comments Diane Rwigara made at a press conference in July 2017 in which she was critical of the government. The charges related to forged documents and their use stemmed from allegations from the National Electoral Commission that many of the signatures supporting her candidacy were invalid. The incitement and discrimination charges against Adeline Rwigara appeared to be based on private WhatsApp messages. Some of these messages that leaked to pro-government Rwandan press were critical of the government.

Disproportionate Use of Force at Kiziba Refugee Camp

In February 2018, Rwandan police used excessive force and fired live ammunition to suppress a demonstration of several thousand Congolese refugees protesting camp conditions and a cut in food rations in Karongi district, Western Province. Some of the refugees, who were unarmed, threw stones at the police.

While the police stated that five refugees were killed, the United Nations refugee agency (UNHCR) publicly stated that at least 11 refugees were shot dead and called for an independent investigation. Human Rights Watch received testimony from survivors indicating that at least 15 refugees were killed, with several others still missing and feared dead.

Police arrested 15 refugees during the incident, and others were arrested in the days and weeks after the protest. Tensions boiled again at the Kiziba refugee camp in May, leaving one refugee dead and leading to the arrest of at least 42 others. At time of writing, many of those refugees remain in detention, accused of organizing protests or throwing stones at police officers, among other charges.

In March, the National Commission for Human Rights issued a statement deploring the injuries and deaths that resulted from the protests and stating that a public detailed report would follow an investigation. At time of writing, the commission has not published the report.

In April, the Ministry of Disaster Management and Refugee Affairs, the government agency that manages Kiziba, dissolved the refugees' executive committee in Kiziba, blaming the committee for the "unrest." This move, coupled with the arrests, prompted many members of the executive committee to flee the country.

Most of the refugees, ethnic Banyamulenge from neighboring Democratic Republic of Congo, have been in Rwanda since 1996.

Arbitrary Detention, Ill-Treatment, and Torture

Without access to the country, allegations of continued cases of unlawful detention in 2018 were difficult for Human Rights Watch to confirm. Ugandan media reported on the high-profile cases of Dennis Karera, a businessman and brother of the current justice minister, and Karenzi Karake, a former intelligence chief, who were allegedly victims of enforced disappearances following arrest by state security agents on July 25. Karera was released on August 6. Karake remains missing. When asked by Ugandan media, state authorities have denied holding Karake.

People previously arrested and accused of crimes against state security remained in unlawful detention centers. In July, the trial started in Nyanza, Southern Province, for a group of 25 people accused of state security crimes. They had been arrested in 2017 and held in a police station in Gikondo, a residential suburb of Kigali, commonly called "Kwa Gacinya." Some of the accused shared information with Human Rights Watch about beatings and torture in Kwa Gacinya.

The detention of street vendors, sex workers, street children, and other poor people in so-called transit centers continued across the country. Detention at these centers is arbitrary and conditions are harsh and inhumane.

In April, Rwandan lawyer Donat Mutonzi was found dead in police custody in suspicious circumstances, 10 days after he was arrested.

Justice for the Genocide

In June 2017, the UN International Residual Mechanism for Criminal Tribunals (IRMCT) in Arusha granted Augustin Ngirabatware's request for a review of his appeals judgment. His request was based on the grounds of "new information of an evidentiary nature" of relevance to the case. The International Criminal Tribunal for Rwanda (ICTR) sentenced Ngirabatware, a former planning minister in the government of former Rwandan President Juvénal Habyarimana, to 35 years' imprisonment in 2012 for genocide, incitement to commit genocide, and rape as a crime against humanity.

In 2014, the ICTR's appeals chamber reduced his sentence to 30 years' imprisonment. Ngirabatware was arrested in 2007 in Germany and transferred to the ICTR in 2009. The review of the appeals judgment, previously slated to begin on September 24, 2018, was adjourned until further notice.

Linked to Ngirabatware's case, five Rwandans were arrested and transferred to Arusha, Tanzania, in September in relation to an indictment issued by the chief prosecutor of the IRMCT. The court said in a statement that the five had "offered bribes and exerted pressure to influence the evidence of protected witnesses" in the case. The five are accused of contempt of court, incitement to commit contempt, and interfering with the administration of justice.

In June, an appeals court in Brussels, Belgium, ruled that the Belgian state was not responsible for the massacre of some two thousand ethnic Tutsis at Kigali's Ecole Technique Officielle (Official Technical School, ETO) during the 1994 genocide. The court said that the UN was responsible, given that the Belgian soldiers who evacuated the site and failed to protect the Rwandan civilians were serving as part of a UN force. The Rwandan National Commission for the Fight against Genocide (Commission nationale de lutte contre le génocide, CNLG) denounced this ruling as politically motivated.

Key International Actors

In July, the SPT, which oversees enforcement of the Optional Protocol to the Convention against Torture (OPCAT), ratified by Rwanda in 2015, terminated its visit to Rwanda. The visit had been suspended in October 2017 due to obstruction by the Rwandan government. In its decision to terminate the visit, the SPT cited a lack of cooperation from the government and concluded "there was no realistic prospect of the visit being successfully resumed and concluded within a reasonable timeframe." This is the first time the SPT has taken such action in its 11 years of existence.

The government rejected the allegations of lack of cooperation and declared they were made in bad faith.

An annual report by the UN secretary-general released in September identified Rwanda as one of 38 countries where human rights defenders face reprisals for cooperating with the UN on human rights.

"Caught in a Web"
Treatment of Pakistanis in the Saudi Criminal Justice System

HUMAN
RIGHTS
WATCH

JUSTICE
PROJECT
PAKISTAN

Saudi Arabia

Saudi Arabia came under intense criticism in 2018 following the October 2 murder of prominent Saudi journalist Jamal Khashoggi inside the Saudi consulate in Istanbul by Saudi agents. After weeks of denials and obfuscations, Saudi Arabia admitted to Khashoggi's murder and announced the arrest of 18 individuals and firing of senior officials, but the statements appeared to be designed to insulate Crown Prince Mohammad bin Salman from further scrutiny over the murder.

Saudi authorities stepped up their arbitrary arrests, trials, and convictions of peaceful dissidents and activists in 2018, including a large-scale coordinated crackdown against the women's rights movement beginning in May. In June, Saudi Arabia ended the long-standing ban on women driving, but authorities continued to discriminate against women and religious minorities.

Through 2018, the Saudi-led coalition continued a military campaign against the Houthi rebel group in Yemen that has included scores of unlawful airstrikes that have killed and wounded thousands of civilians.

Yemen Airstrikes and Blockade

As the leader of the coalition that began military operations against Houthi forces in Yemen on March 26, 2015, Saudi Arabia has committed numerous violations of international humanitarian law. As of August, at least 6,592 civilians had been killed and 10,471 wounded, according to the Office of the United Nations High Commissioner for Human Rights (OHCHR), although the actual civilian casualty count is likely much higher. The majority of these casualties were a result of coalition airstrikes.

Since March 2015, Human Rights Watch has documented about 90 apparently unlawful attacks by the coalition that have hit homes, markets, hospitals, schools, and mosques. Some of these attacks may amount to war crimes. An April coalition attack on a wedding killed 22 people and wounded more than 50. An August attack on a bus killed and wounded dozens of children. Saudi commanders face possible criminal liability for war crimes as a matter of command responsibility.

The conflict exacerbated an existing humanitarian crisis. The Saudi-led coalition has imposed an aerial and naval blockade since March 2015 and restricted the flow of life-saving goods and the ability for Yemenis to travel into and out of the country to varying degrees throughout the war.

The Joint Incidents Assessment Team (JIAT), which the coalition established in 2016 after evidence mounted of coalition violations of the laws of war, has so far failed even in its limited mandate to assess "claims and accidents" during coalition military operations. Its work has fallen far short of international standards regarding transparency, impartiality, and independence. As of September 2018, JIAT cleared the coalition of wrongdoing in most of the strikes investigated. There is no evidence JIAT investigated alleged abuses by coalition forces beyond unlawful airstrikes, such as mistreatment of detainees. Despite the coalition's promises, there is no clear way for civilian victims or relatives to obtain redress from coalition forces. The coalition's continuing unlawful airstrikes and failure to adequately investigate alleged violations puts weapons' suppliers to the coalition at risk of complicity in future unlawful attacks.

Freedoms of Expression, Association, and Belief

Saudi authorities in 2018 intensified a coordinated crackdown on dissidents, human rights activists, and independent clerics.

On May 15, 2018, just weeks before the Saudi authorities lifted the ban on women driving on June 24, authorities launched arrests of prominent women's rights activists and accused several of them of grave crimes like treason that appear to be directly related to their activism. By November at least nine women remain detained without charge, though some anticipated charges could carry prison terms of up to 20 years. The nine included Loujain al-Hathloul, Aziza al-Yousef, Eman al-Nafjan, Nouf Abdelaziz, Mayaa al-Zahrani, Hatoon al-Fassi, Samar Badawi, Nassema al-Sadah, and Amal al-Harbi. Human rights organizations reported in November that Saudi interrogators tortured at least four of the women, including by administering electric shocks, whipping the women on their thighs, and forcible hugging and kissing.

Saudi prosecutors escalated their longstanding campaign against dissidents in 2018 by seeking the death penalty against detainees on charges that related to nothing more than peaceful activism and dissent. By November those on trial facing the death penalty included prominent cleric Salman al-Awda, whose charges were connected to his alleged ties with the Muslim Brotherhood and public support for imprisoned dissidents, as well as Israa al-Ghomgham, a Shia activist from Saudi Arabia's Eastern Province whose charges related to her support for and participation in protests.

Saudi Arabia continued to use counterterrorism regulations to suppress political expression and dissent. In 2017, Saudi Arabia passed a new counterterrorism law that included definitions of specific acts of terrorism and their corresponding sentencing guidelines. It included criminal penalties of 5 to 10 years in prison for portraying the king or crown prince, directly or indirectly, "in a manner that brings religion or justice into disrepute," and criminalized a wide range of peaceful acts that bear no relation to terrorism.

Over a dozen prominent activists convicted on charges arising from their peaceful activities were serving long prison sentences. Prominent activist Waleed Abu al-Khair continued to serve a 15-year sentence that the Specialized Criminal Court imposed on him after convicting al-Khair in 2014 on charges stemming solely from his peaceful criticism in media interviews and on social media of human rights abuses.

By 2018 Saudi Arabia had jailed nearly all the founders of the banned Saudi Civil and Political Rights Association (ACPRA). Members of the group imprisoned in 2018 included Mohammad al-Bajadi and Abdulaziz al-Shubaily. In June, the authorities arrested Amal al-Harbi, the wife of imprisoned ACPRA activist Fowzan al-Harbi.

With few exceptions Saudi Arabia does not tolerate public worship by adherents of religions other than Islam and systematically discriminates against Muslim -religious minorities, notably Twelver Shia and Ismailis, including in public education, the justice system, religious freedom, and employment. Government-affiliated religious authorities continued to disparage Shia and Sufi interpretations, versions, and understandings of Islam in public statements and documents.

Saudi Arabia has no written laws concerning sexual orientation or gender identity, but judges use principles of uncodified Islamic law to sanction people suspected of committing sexual relations outside marriage, including adultery, extramarital, and homosexual sex.

Criminal Justice

Saudi Arabia applies Sharia (Islamic law) as its national law. There is no formal penal code, but the government has passed some laws and regulations that subject certain broadly-defined offenses to criminal penalties. In the absence of a written penal code or narrowly-worded regulations, however, judges and prosecutors can convict people on a wide range of offenses under broad, catch-all charges such as "breaking allegiance with the ruler" or "trying to distort the reputation of the kingdom." Detainees, including children, commonly face systematic violations of due process and fair trial rights, including arbitrary arrest.

Judges routinely sentence defendants to floggings of hundreds of lashes. Children can be tried for capital crimes and sentenced as adults if they show physical signs of puberty.

During 2018, authorities continued to detain arrested suspects for months, even years, without judicial review or prosecution. Saudi Arabia's online prisoner database revealed in May that authorities were holding 2,305 individuals who are under investigation for more than six months without referring them to a judge, including 251 for over three years.

As of November, Ali al-Nimr, Dawoud al-Marhoun, Abdullah al-Zaher, Abdulkareem al-Hawaj, and others remained on death row for allegedly committing protest-related crimes while they were children. Saudi judges based the capital convictions primarily on confessions that the defendants retracted in court and said had been coerced, and the courts did not investigate the allegations that the confessions were obtained by torture.

According to Interior Ministry statements, Saudi Arabia executed 139 persons between January and December, mostly for murder and drug crimes. Fifty-four of those executed were convicted for non-violent drug crimes. Most executions are carried out by beheading, sometimes in public.

Women's and Girls' Rights

Women in Saudi Arabia face formal and informal barriers when attempting to make decisions or take action without the presence or consent of a male relative.

In 2018, Saudi Arabia's discriminatory male guardianship system remained intact despite government pledges to abolish it. Under this system, adult women must obtain permission from a male guardian—usually a husband, father, brother, or son—to travel abroad, obtain a passport, marry, or be discharged from prison. They may be required to provide guardian consent to work or access healthcare.

Saudi authorities opened to women some sectors of work that were previously closed such as air traffic control, passport control, and as investigators in the public prosecution. In June, Saudi Arabia passed a law on sexual harassment with a sentence for offenders of up to two years imprisonment or a fine of up to 100,000 Saudi riyals (US$26,666), which can be increased in certain circumstances. However, the law also provides that anyone who falsely reported a crime of harassment or falsely claimed to have been a victim shall be sentenced to the same punishment that they alleged took place. This article as such could be used to punish victims where the authorities do not believe the crime took place and could deter victims from coming forward if they fear that authorities will not believe them.

On February 26, Saudi authorities came before the UN Committee on Discrimination against Women to defend their record on women's rights. The committee called on Saudi Arabia to accelerate efforts to abolish the male guardianship system, adopt an anti-discrimination law, and adopt a written unified family code based on the principles of equality and non-discrimination.

During the first months of 2018 Saudi Arabia allowed women to obtain driver's licenses and on June 24 lifted the longstanding ban on women driving. In the weeks leading up to the lifting of the ban, however, Saudi authorities carried out a wave of arrests of prominent women's rights advocates. Authorities accused several of those detained of serious crimes, including "suspicious contact with foreign parties" under dubious legal pretenses. Government-aligned media outlets then carried out an alarming campaign against them, publishing their photos branded with the word "traitor."

Migrant Workers

Over 12 million migrant workers fill manual, clerical, and service jobs in Saudi Arabia, constituting more than eighty percent of the private sector workforce, though government efforts to nationalize the workforce in addition to the imposition of a monthly tax on foreign workers' dependents in mid-2017 led to an exodus of at least 667,000 migrant workers between January 2017 and July 2018.

Some migrant workers suffer abuses and exploitation, sometimes amounting to conditions of forced labor. The *kafala* (visa sponsorship) system ties migrant workers' residency permits to "sponsoring" employers, whose written consent is required for workers to change employers or leave the country under normal circumstances. Some employers confiscate passports, withhold wages, and force migrants to work against their will. Saudi Arabia also imposes an exit visa requirement, forcing migrant workers to obtain permission from their employer to leave the country. Workers who leave their employer without their consent can be charged with "absconding" and face imprisonment and deportation.

In November 2017, Saudi Arabia launched a campaign to detain foreigners found in violation of existing labor, residency, or border security laws, including those without valid residency or work permits, or those found working for an employer other than their legal sponsor. On November 23, 2018, authorities announced that the campaign had netted over 2.1 million arrests, including for over 1.6 million residency law violations and over 328,000 labor law violations.

The campaign had referred over 553,000 individuals for deportation. Of the estimated 12 million migrant workers in Saudi Arabia, up to 500,000 are Ethiopian, a significant number of whom arrived after fleeing serious Ethiopian government abuses. International agencies reported that between November 2017 and June 2018 Saudi Arabia had deported at least 160,000 Ethiopians, around 10,000 individuals per week.

Saudi Arabia is not party to the 1951 Refugee Convention and does not have an asylum system under which people fearing persecution in their home country can seek protection, leading to a real risk of deporting them to harm.

Domestic workers, predominantly women, faced a range of abuses including overwork, forced confinement, non-payment of wages, food deprivation, and psychological, physical, and sexual abuse without the authorities holding their employers to account.

Key International Actors

As a party to the armed conflict in Yemen, the US provided logistical and intelligence support to Saudi-led coalition forces, including refueling coalition planes on missions in Yemen. In March, the US State Department approved a $1 billion new arms sale to Saudi Arabia, which included $670 million for anti-missile tanks, $106 million for helicopter maintenance, and $300 million for spare parts for military vehicles.

The UK government continued to back the Saudi-led coalition in 2018 and has allowed the sale of £4.6 billion ($5.9 billion) of military equipment to Saudi Arabia since the beginning of the armed conflict.

In June, the UN secretary-general released his annual "list of shame" for violations against children in armed conflict. This list included many of Yemen's warring parties—the Houthis, Al-Qaeda in the Arabian Peninsula, pro-government militias, and Security Belt forces, but the Saudi-led coalition was treated differently. Instead, the secretary-general placed the coalition on a special list for countries that put in place "measures to improve child protection."

Saudi Arabia faced intense scrutiny by countries across the globe for its role in the murder of prominent journalist Jamal Khashoggi, but only a handful of countries, including Germany and Switzerland, announced they would halt further arms sales. Prominent US and European officials called for an independent investigation into Khashoggi's murder.

Serbia

There was little improvement in human rights protection in Serbia in 2018. War crimes prosecutions in domestic courts progressed slowly and lacked necessary political support. The asylum system remained flawed and conditions for asylum seekers failed to improve. The situation for journalists remained precarious, including attacks, threats, and lawsuits for reporting on sensitive issues.

Migrants, Asylum Seekers, and Long-Term Displaced Persons

Between January and end of July, Serbia registered 4,715 asylum seekers, compared to 3,538 during the same period in 2017. Pakistanis comprised the largest national group in 2018, followed by Afghans and Iranians. By end of July, UNHCR estimated that there were approximately 6,098 asylum seekers and other migrants present in Serbia, compared to 4,700 in August 2017. Asylum seekers and some other migrants are accommodated in 18 government-run facilities across Serbia, including reception centers, asylum centers and transit centers, with a total capacity of 5,880.

In late March, Serbia adopted a new law on asylum and temporary protection. The law aims to align Serbian legislation to international and EU standards and includes victims of gender, gender identity and gender-based violence in the refugee definition and improved provisions for unaccompanied and separated asylum-seeking children. However, it also provides for detention of asylum seekers, restriction of free movement and accelerated asylum procedures.

The process for asylum determination remained inadequate with low recognition rates and long delays before decisions are made. Between January and August, only 151 asylum seekers lodged applications in Serbia, and authorities granted refugee status to only nine and subsidiary protection to 14. Over the past decade, Serbia has only granted refugee status to a total of 53 people and subsidiary protection to 74.

By end of July, 257 unaccompanied children were registered with Serbian authorities, most from Afghanistan, compared to 101 during the same period in 2017. Serbia lacks formal age assessment procedures for unaccompanied children, putting older children at risk of being treated as adults instead of receiving special protection. Only three institutions exist for unaccompanied children, with a total of 43 places. Other unaccompanied children stay in open asylum centers, such as reception and transit centers, often with unrelated adults, making them vulnerable to abuse and exploitation.

There was little progress towards durable solutions for refugees and internally displaced persons from the Balkan wars living in Serbia. According to the Serbian Commissioner for Refugees and Migration, as of July, there were 26,702 such refugees in Serbia, compared to 27,802 during the same period in 2017, most from Croatia, and 199,584 internally displaced people, majority from Kosovo, as of July, compared to 201,047 the previous year.

Freedom of Media

Journalists continued to experience attacks and threats and an inadequate response from Serbian authorities. Pro-government media outlets continued to smear independent outlets and journalists.

Between January and mid-August, the Independent Journalists' Association of Serbia (NUNS) registered 50 incidents of violence, threats or intimidation against journalists, including four physical attacks and 18 cases of intimidation of journalists by state officials.

In June, blogger and independent journalist Stefan Cvetkovic was reported missing following his reporting on the killing of Kosovo Serb politician Oliver Ivanovic in January. Two days after he went missing, Cvetkovic reappeared and told authorities he had been kidnapped by three unknown men for reasons he did not know. The public prosecutor launched criminal charges against Cvetkovic for falsely reporting a kidnapping. The criminal investigation into his case was ongoing at time of writing. Cvetkovic had reported several threats in previous years linked to his journalism.

In August, the independent online daily Juzne Vesti reported that tax authorities launched a procedure to force the website to pay 8,500 euro in damages. Juzne Vesti had been subject to several tax inspections in the past without any indication of wrongdoing.

A commission established to investigate the murders of three prominent journalists, Dada Vujasinovic in 1994, Slavko Curuvija in 1999, and Milan Pantic in 2001, made no progress. In June, the Higher Court in Belgrade dismissed evidence allegedly placing former Serbian state security officers at the scene of the murder of Curuvija. In July, however, the same court decided to allow the previously rejected evidence. The Vujasinovic and Pantic killings remained unsolved.

In August, the commission's mandate expanded to include murders of journalists in Kosovo between 1998-2001, and Bosnia-Herzegovina and Croatia between 1991-1995.

Accountability for War Crimes

War crimes prosecutions remained hampered due to a lack of political will, adequate resources, and weak witness support mechanisms.

Few high-ranking officials implicated in serious wartime abuses have been held to account in Serbian courts. By August 2018, 11 war crimes cases were still at investigation stage and 19 were pending before Serbian courts. The Office of Serbia's War Crimes Prosecutor issued two new indictments during the same period. In the first eight months of 2018, first instance courts delivered no judgments in war crimes cases. The appeals court acquitted six persons and returned one case to the first instance court for retrial.

Since the establishment of the War Crimes Prosecutor in 2003, 44 final judgments have been issued, 74 people convicted, and 50 acquitted.

The first trials in Serbia for war crimes in Srebrenica restarted in November 2017 after being plagued by delays. Eight Bosnian Serb former police officers resident in Serbia were charged with the killing in a warehouse of more than 1,300 Bosniak civilians from Srebrenica in July 1995. In June, a witness quit the trial, stating he received threats despite having a protected identity.

In June, the Appeals Court in Belgrade acquitted six former members of a paramilitary group, referred to as the Sima's Chetniks Unit, of killing 27 Roma in the village of Skocic, Bosnia and Herzegovina, in 1992. The court however found three of the six defendants guilty of inhuman treatment, violations of physical integrity, sexual humiliation and rape and sentenced them to between 6-10 years imprisonment.

In January, the Appeals Court in Belgrade confirmed jail sentences of eight former Vukovar Territorial Defence fighters for the massacre of approximately 200 people at Ovcara following the fall of Vukovar, Croatia, in 1991. The court sentenced the accused to between 5 and 20 years' imprisonment.

Chief Prosecutor Serge Brammertz at the Mechanism for International Criminal Tribunals (MICT) urged Serbia in June to officially acknowledge the crimes committed in Srebrenica in 1995 as genocide.

The MICT in The Hague in April sentenced Vojislav Sejelj to 10 years' imprison-ment for inciting crimes through nationalist speeches in the Vojvodina, Serbia during the 1992 war. The Tribunal cleared Seselj of war crimes in Bosnia and Herzegovina and Croatia. Seselj has already served his time, having been in cus-tody in The Hague since 2003.

After their 2013 acquittal was overturned, the retrial of former Serbian state se-curity officials Jovica Stanisic and Franko Simatovic at the MICT started in June. Stanisic and Simatovic are charged with crimes against humanity and genocide committed by Serbian forces in Bosnia and Herzegovina and Croatia during the Balkan wars.

Human Rights Defenders

Human rights defenders continued to operate in a hostile environment. Online threats against human rights activists occurred regularly and investigations were slow.

In August, a misdemeanor court in Ruma fined eight activists from the Youth Ini-tiative for Human Rights €420 ($US 476) each for interrupting a speech by con-victed war criminal Veselin Sljivancanin in January 2017. The activists were attacked and ejected during the event.

Sexual Orientation and Gender Identity

Attacks and threats of lesbian, gay, bisexual, and transgender (LGBT) people and activists continued. Between January and mid-August, the Serbian LGBT rights organization DA SE ZNA! recorded nine incidents against LGBT people, including four physical attacks, and five cases of threats and intimidation. Investigations are often slow and prosecutions rare. The Pride parade in September took place without major incidents.

Disability Rights

In 2018, the Serbian government continued to promote access to education for all children with disabilities. Children and adults with disabilities continued to be placed in institutions. The government has yet to adopt a time-bound plan to move people with disabilities out of institutions and to support them to live in the community.

Key International Actors

During an April visit to Belgrade, European Union High Representative for Foreign Affairs and Security Policy Federica Mogherini focused on Serbia's EU accession and the Belgrade-Pristina process but did not publicly address the need to improve human rights.

In its April 2018 report in the context of the Serbia's accession negotiations, the European Commission stressed that the lack of progress on freedom of expression is "a matter of increasing concern" and the council of the EU pressed Serbia in June to step up efforts to investigate cases of attacks against journalists.

In January, the UN Human Rights Council reviewed Serbia through its Universal Periodic Review mechanism. Serbia accepted 175 out of 190 recommendations made to it by states, but rejected important recommendations to refrain from prosecuting journalists, human rights defenders and other civil society members as a means of deterring them from freely expressing their opinions, and to ratify the International Convention on the Protection of the Rights of All Migrant Workers and Members of Their Families.

In January, the UN Committee on the Elimination of All Forms of Racial Discrimination, after having reviewed Serbia, expressed concerns about the low percentage of Roma children attending all levels of education, as well as segregation of Roma children in schools, and forced evictions of Roma without due process and alternative accommodation provided.

The Council of Europe Committee for the Prevention of Torture and Inhuman and Degrading Treatment or Punishment (CPT) in May published a report raising concerns of ill-treatment of persons in police custody and called on authorities to combat police ill-treatment.

In February, then-Council of Europe Human Rights Commissioner Nils Muižnieks called on Serbia not to glorify war criminals and expressed concerns regarding the state of media freedom and the hostile environment in which journalists work.

Kosovo

Progress on improving human rights protection was slow during the year. Serb and Kosovo leaders in August announced a controversial plan to redraw the borders between Serbia and Kosovo as part of a peaceful settlement between the countries. The plan sparked concerns about human rights consequences of population transfers that would be required under the plan. In March, the Kosovo parliament ratified a border demarcation agreement with Montenegro, an EU requirement for visa liberalization for Kosovo. The operation of the special court to try serious war crimes committed during the 1998-1999 Kosovo war was delayed due to a change in the special prosecutor. Journalists faced threats and intimidation, and prosecutions of crimes against journalists were slow. Tensions between Serbs and Kosovo Albanians continued, particularly in the north. Roma, Ashkali, and Balkan Egyptian communities continue to face discrimination.

Accountability for War Crimes

In March, special prosecutor David Schwendiman at the Hague-based Specialist Chambers and Prosecutor's Office trying serious war crimes committed during the 1998-1999 conflict resigned his post. In May, Jack Smith, was appointed as the new special prosecutor. At time of writing, no indictments had been issued.

The court is set to adjudicate cases investigated by the Special Investigative Task Force, prompted by a 2011 Council of Europe report accusing some Kosovo Liberation Army (KLA) members of abductions, beatings, summary executions, and the forced removal of human organs in Kosovo and Albania during and after the Kosovo war. Senior KLA fighters are expected to be indicted and stand trial. The court will operate under Kosovo laws, with 19 international judges.

In August, the special prosecution office in Kosovo charged a former Serb police officer with war crimes for his alleged participation in the killing of two Albanian civilians in 1998.

In July, the Kosovo Appeal's court upheld the indictment against Darko Tusic, an ex-reservist in the Yugoslav army, for war crimes committed in the village of Mala Krusa in 1999.

By mid-June, the European Rule of Law Mission (EULEX) ceased its executive functions in the Kosovo judiciary. By that time, mixed panels of EULEX and local judges had handed down four decisions related to war crimes. Formal investigations were underway in 33 cases and 374 cases were pending at a preliminary investigation stage. EULEX was involved in a total of 46 verdicts since its establishment in 2008. At time of writing, EULEX was set to hand over 900 unresolved cases to the local Special Prosecutor's Office, working with only two prosecutors on war crimes.

The Human Rights Review Panel, an independent body set up in 2009 to review allegations of human rights violations by EULEX staff, ruled in six cases between January and September and found all inadmissible. Twenty-five cases were pending before the panel at time of writing.

Accountability of International Institutions

No progress was made by the United Nations to follow recommendations made in 2016 by the Human Rights Advisory Panel (HRAP), an independent body set up in 2006 to examine complaints of abuses by the UN Interim Administration Mission in Kosovo (UNMIK), that the UN apologize and pay individual compensation to lead poison victims forced to live in UNMIK-run camps in northern Kosovo after the 1998-1999 war. Victims of the poisoning are displaced members of the Roma, Ashkali, and Balkan Egyptian communities. The special rapporteur on the implications for human rights of the environmentally sound management and disposal of hazardous substances and wastes sent a letter to UN Secretary General Gueterres in July 2018, emphasizing that the "need to provide the victims, who continue to face economic and social hardship in addition to grave health concerns, with individual compensation remains as critical as ever."

Treatment of Minorities

Roma, Ashkali, and Balkan Egyptians continue to face problems acquiring personal documents, affecting their ability to access health care, social assistance, and education. There was no visible or reported progress towards integration of these minority communities.

Inter-ethnic tensions continued during 2018 particularly in Kosovo's divided north. In January, unknown assailants shot dead Kosovo-Serb politician Oliver Ivanovic outside his office in Mitrovica, northern Kosovo. Kosovo police were investigating at time of writing. In October, unknown assailants threw stones at two buses carrying pilgrims from Serbia to an Orthodox-Christian monastery in the north west of Kosovo. No one was injured and Kosovo police were investigating at time of writing. Kosovo police registered six cases of inter-ethnic violence between January and July 2018, that included incidences categorized as ethnic defamatory graffiti, incitement of religious, ethnic and racial hatred, and damaging of a commemorative plaque.

Women's Rights

Domestic violence remained widespread in Kosovo with weak police response, few prosecutions, and judges seemingly reluctant to issue restraining orders against abusive spouses. In January, eight of nine shelters for victims of domestic violence were forced to shut down temporarily due to budgetary delays but reopened later that month when authorities provided emergency funding. In May, rules stating that organizations receiving government support were required to receive 50 percent of funds from elsewhere, put domestic violence shelters under renewed financial pressure. In November, one of the nine shelters, located in Gjilan, reported that the new rules had created budget instability and were limiting the capacity of shelters to provide needed services to victims of domestic violence. In February, authorities officially launched the application process for wartime survivors of sexual violence to be granted legal status as war victims and to seek financial compensation.

Asylum Seekers and Displaced Persons

During the first 10 months of the year, the United Nations High Commissioner for Refugees registered 232 voluntary returns of members of ethnic minorities to Kosovo down from 343 during that period in 2017.

The Kosovo Ministry of Internal Affairs registered 628 forced returns to Kosovo between January and September. The Ministry of Internal Affairs reported that it does not have ethnic data for the returnees. Among those deported to Kosovo were 39 children. Most of these forced returns were from Germany. The state provides returnees with limited assistance upon return.

Sexual Orientation and Gender Identity

Hate speech online against lesbian, gay, bisexual, and transgender (LGBT) rights activists continued, particularly around the Kosovo Pride in October. In May, authorities rejected a transgender man's request to change his first name and legal gender. The legal gender recognition request was the first case of its kind in Kosovo. At time of writing, an appeal of the decision was being prepared. Kosovo Pride in October took place without significant incidents.

Freedom of Media

Threats and attacks against journalists continued in 2018, while investigations and prosecutions were slow. Between January and September, the Association of Journalists of Kosovo registered 13 cases of threats and violence against journalists, including one physical attack, one case of property damage, one death threat, and 10 other threats. Police were investigating at time of writing.

In June, Valon Rashiti, a reporter at TV-station *T7*, was physically attacked by the family member of a person he was interviewing for a news story in Pristina. He suffered light injuries. Police were investigating at time of writing.

Unknown assailants twice damaged the car of Radio Kosova news editor, Serbeze Haxhiaj, in March, after Balkan Investigative Reporting Network published her story on political assassinations after the war. Haxhiaj reported the damage to her car to police who were investigating at time of writing.

In July, *Gazeta Metro* journalist Shkumbin Kajtazi received a threat over the phone from Mitrovica Mayor Agim Bahtiri. Bahtiri allegedly told Kajtazi that "I will f**k your relatives. You stepped on my morals." The threat came following Kajtazi's publication of a story about an alleged improper appointment of the mayor's new cabinet chief. Police were investigating the attack at time of writing.

Key International Actors

During the year, European Union High Representative for Foreign Affairs and Security Policy Federica Mogherini met with Kosovo President Hashim Thaci and Serbian President Aleksandar Vucic on several occasions, often focusing on the normalization of Kosovo's relations with Serbia but did not raise human rights concerns adequately.

In February, the European Commission adopted a new strategy for EU engagement with the Western Balkans, which stated that without effective normalization of relations between Belgrade and Pristina, there could not be lasting stability in the region.

In April, the European Commission confirmed that Kosovo had met two outstanding criteria to qualify for visa liberalization; the ratification of the demarcation agreement with Montenegro and the strengthened fight against crime and corruption. In September, the European Parliament voted in favour of visa liberalization for Kosovo.

The Organization for Security and Cooperation in Europe (OSCE) Representative on Freedom of the Media Harlem Desir in March expressed concerns about the safety of journalists reporting on a police intervention in Mitrovica in northern Kosovo and stressed the need for journalists to be able to operate safely without fear.

In March, six Turkish citizens with legal residency in Kosovo were summarily deported to Turkey without due process, and in violation of safeguards against refoulement. Kosovo Prime Minister Ramush Haradinaj denied knowledge of the deportation and stated that it had been undertaken by Kosovo Intelligence Agency and police. In April, Turkish media reported that the six Turkish citizens had been imprisoned upon arrival in Turkey pending trial.

In his May report on the situation in Kosovo, UN Secretary-General Antonio Guterres expressed concerns about the slow progress of the investigation into the murder of Kosovo-Serb politician Oliver Ivanovic and called on authorities to intensify their investigation efforts.

Singapore

Prime Minister Lee Hsien Loong stated in a June 2018 interview that Singapore-ans were free to say or publish whatever they wanted, "subject to the laws of sedition, libel and contempt." In reality, those laws, along with a range of regulatory measures, impose severe restrictions on the right to freedom of speech inn Singapore. Critics of the courts are targeted for "scandalizing the judiciary" and in April, those critical of a government proposal to pass a law criminalizing "fake news" were subjected to harassment at parliamentary hearings on the subject.

Freedoms of Peaceful Assembly and Expression

The government maintains strict restrictions on the right to peaceful assembly through the Public Order Act, requiring a police permit for any "cause-related" assembly if it is held in a public place, or in a private venue if members of the general public are invited.

The definition of what is treated as an assembly is extremely broad and those who fail to obtain the required permits face criminal charges. Activist Jolovan Wham was prosecuted in 2018 for three counts of violating the Public Order Act for organizing two peaceful protests and a candlelight vigil. On October 3, 2018, performance artist Seelan Palay was convicted of violating the Public Order Act by walking from Hong Lim Park to parliament carrying a piece of art to commemorate the 32 years, since 1989, that Chia Thye Poh was detained under the Internal Security Act. Seelan was sentenced to two weeks in prison after refusing to pay a fine of S$2,500 (US$1,800).

Applications for permits for cause-related assemblies are regularly denied. For example, in April Terry Xu's application to hold a one-man silent protest against a law recently passed by parliament was denied. The refusal came even though he proposed to hold it late at night on a weekend in the Central Business District. The denial cited the "risk of causing public disorder, as well as damage to property."

In March 2018, the government passed the Public Order and Safety (Special Powers) Act, which provides Singapore's home affairs minister with sweeping powers if a "serious incident" has been, is being, or is likely to be committed.

While the law purports to be aimed at "serious violence and large-scale public disorder," illustrations in the law of what may be considered a "serious incident" make clear it can be used against peaceful protesters.

In April 2018, a parliamentary committee held hearings on dealing with "deliberate online falsehoods" and invited several activists and critics of the government to testify. Those who agreed to appear were harangued and asked questions unrelated to the issue of "fake news." A number of the witnesses who testified subsequently filed complaints stating that the official record of the hearing seriously misrepresented their testimony.

In the same month, the Accounting and Corporate Regulatory Authority (ARCA) refused to permit PJ Thum and Kirsten Han to register a private company to organize discussions and provide editorial services to the website New Naratif, saying that to do so would be "contrary to national interests." ARCA justified the decision as necessary to prevent foreigners from interfering in Singaporean affairs because the company received funding from the US-based Open Society Foundations.

In May 2018, the government charged activist Jolovan Wham with "scandalizing the judiciary" for posting on Facebook that "Malaysia's judges are more independent than Singapore's for cases with political implications." Authorities also charged John Tan, the vice-chairman of the opposition Singapore Democratic Party, with contempt for commenting on his Facebook page that Wham's prosecution "only confirms that what [Wham] said is true." On October 9, both were found guilty of contempt of court. They were awaiting sentencing at time of writing.

The Board of Film Censors must pre-approve all films and videos shown in Singapore, and exhibiting unapproved films is a criminal offense. The newly enacted Films (Amendment) Act broadened the law to include films received on a computer monitor or mobile phone and gives sweeping enforcement powers, including the power to conduct warrantless searches, to various individuals tasked with enforcing the law.

Criminal Justice System

In February 2018, Singapore's parliament once again extended the Criminal Law (Temporary Provisions) Act, which allows detention without trial for up to 12 months if the home affairs minister is satisfied that the person "has been associated with activities of a criminal nature," and "that it is necessary that the person be detained in the interests of public safety, peace and good order." There appears to be no limit to the number of times detention can be extended. Singapore also continues to detain individuals without trial under the Internal Security Act. There is little publicly available information about the number of people detained, their identities, or the basis for their detention.

Singapore retains the death penalty, which is mandated for many drug offenses and certain other crimes. However, under provisions introduced in 2012, judges have some discretion to bypass the mandatory penalty and sentence low-level offenders to life in prison and caning. There is little transparency on the timing of executions, which often take place with short notice. Singapore executed seven people in October. At least two other individuals were executed for drug offenses earlier in the year.

Use of corporal punishment is common in Singapore. For medically fit males ages 16 to 50, caning is mandatory as an additional punishment for a range of crimes, including drug trafficking, violent crimes (such as armed robbery), and even some immigration offenses.

Sexual Orientation and Gender Identity

The rights of lesbian, gay, bisexual, and transgender (LGBT) people in Singapore are severely restricted. Sexual relations between two male persons remains a criminal offense under criminal code section 377A, and there are no legal protections against discrimination on the basis of sexual orientation or gender identity.

The Media Development Authority effectively prohibits all positive depictions of LGBT lives on television or radio. In April, the movie Love Simon, which is about a teenager coming to terms with his sexuality, was given a rating that precludes viewing by anyone under the age of 21, even though it contains no sexual scenes or violence and is rated PG-13 or PG in most other countries.

In July 2018, the research and advocacy director of the Inter-University LGBT Network, who had been invited to speak about her experience as a young person concerned about LGBT issues at a TEDxYouth event at St. Joseph's Institute, was informed by event organizers that she would not be permitted to speak due to unspecified Ministry of Education regulations.

In the wake of India's Supreme Court repealing Section 377 in September, a British colonial-era law that imposed criminal penalties for same-sex relations, a Singaporean disc jockey filed a constitutional challenge to the similarly worded Section 377A, and tens of thousands of people submitted a parallel petition to the government urging its repeal.

Migrant Workers and Labor Exploitation

Foreign migrant workers are subject to labor rights abuses and exploitation through debts owed to recruitment agents, non-payment of wages, restrictions on movement, confiscation of passports, and sometimes physical and sexual abuse. Foreign women employed as domestic workers are particularly vulnerable to abuse.

Work permits of migrant workers in Singapore are tied to a particular employer, leaving them extremely vulnerable to exploitation. Foreign domestic workers are still excluded from the Employment Act and from many key labor protections, such as limits on daily work hours and mandatory days off. Labor laws also discriminate against foreign workers by barring them from organizing and registering a union or serving as union leaders without explicit government permission.

Key International Actors

Singapore is a regional hub for international business and maintains good political and economic relations with both the United States, which considers it a key security ally, and China. Singapore hosted the summit between US President Donald Trump and North Korean leader Kim Jong-Un in June 2018, before which Prime Minister Lee met with President Trump. Singapore was also the chair of the Association of Southeast Asian Nations (ASEAN) in 2018, hosting the 32nd ASEAN summit in April. Singapore's allies focused their priorities on trade and business, and did not publicly criticize Singapore's poor human rights record.

HUMAN
RIGHTS
WATCH

"It's Like We're Always
in a Prison"
Abuses Against Boys Accused of National Security Offenses in Somalia

Somalia

Fighting, insecurity and lack of state protection, and recurring humanitarian crises had a devastating impact on Somali civilians in 2018. The number of internally displaced people, many living unassisted and at risk of serious abuse, reached an estimated 2.7 milllion.

The Islamist armed group Al-Shabab subjected people living under its control to harsh treatment, forced recruitment, and carried out deadly attacks targeting civilians.

The United Nations Assistance Mission in Somalia (UNSOM) reported 982 civilian casualties by October, over half from Al-Shabab attacks. Inter-clan and intra-security force violence, along with sporadic military operations against Al-Shabab by Somali government forces, African Union Mission in Somalia (AMISOM) troops, and other foreign forces, resulted in deaths, injuries, and displacement of civilians.

While federal and regional authorities made some progress in clarifying roles and responsibilities in the security and justice sectors, political infighting diverted from greatly needed reforms. Tensions between the former speaker of parliament, Mohamed Osman Jawari, and the executive brought parliament to a standstill for a month, resulting in the speaker's eventual resignation.

The government has yet to endorse the list of nominees for the country's first independent Human Rights Commission and has made no tangible progress reining in abusive security forces, notably the intelligence agency, or ending repeated forced evictions of the country's displaced people.

Abuses by Government and Allied Forces

Security forces unlawfully killed and wounded civilians during infighting over land, control of roadblocks, and disarmament operations, particularly in Mogadishu and Lower Shabelle. Dozens of government and security officals and former electoral delegates were assassinated; Al-Shabab claimed responsibility for some of the killings.

Intelligence agencies at the federal level, in Puntland and Jubaland, arbitrarily arrested and detained many individuals for prolonged periods without charge or access to legal counsel or family members. Somali authorities and Somalia's international partners committed to building an accountable national security sector, but the federal government failed to pass legislation clarifying the mandate of the intelligence agency.

While military prosecutors handed over some files implicating security force members to civilian judges, military courts continue to try a broad range of cases and defendants, including for terrorism-related offenses, in proceedings falling far short of international fair trial standards. According to media reports and the United Nations, the government in 2018 carried out at least four executions of security force personnel mainly convicted of murder of other members of the security forces.

Tensions between Somaliland and Puntland in the contested Sool border region led to armed clashes, including in January when Somaliland took over the strategic town of Tukaraq. The UN said the fighting resulted in the displacement of 12,500 civilians.

Civilians were targeted or faced indiscriminate attacks during clan violence, notably in Ceel Afweeyn in Sanaag region, Galgaduud, and Hiraan.

In July, media reported that Kenyan forces deployed outside of AMISOM forces had raped three women and two girls in Belet-Hawo town along the Kenyan border.

In a December 2017 report, the UN highlighted the lack of transparency around AMISOM investigations and prosecutions, and raised concerns about the lack of formal efforts to protect victims and witnesses from reprisals.

Abuses by Al-Shabab

Al-Shabab committed serious abuses, including forcibly recruiting children and adults; arbitrary executions, notably of those it accused of spying for the government and foreign forces; and extorting "taxes" through threats. Al-Shabab attacks against civilians and civilian infrastructure using improvised explosive devices (IEDs), suicide bombings, and shellings in Mogadishu resulted in hundreds of civilian deaths and injuries.

Al-Shabab continues to prohibit most nongovernmental organizations and all UN agencies from working in areas under its control. The group continued to block-

ade government-controlled towns and attacked civilians who broke the block-
ades, destroying goods and vehicles.

Abuses Against Children

All Somali parties to the conflict continued to commit serious abuses against
children, including killings, maiming, recruitment and use in military operations.

Al-Shabab pursued an aggressive child recruitment campaign with retaliation
against communities refusing to hand over children, particularly in Galmudug
and South West State. As a result, hundreds of children, many unaccompanied,
fled their homes to escape. According to the UN, in July residents of Xaradheere,
a locality that has repeatedly come under pressure to provide children to Al-
Shabab, fought back, resulting in deaths and significant civilian displacement.

On January 18, Somali and US military forces rescued 36 children from an Al-
Shabab-run camp in Middle Shabelle. They were handed over to the UN for rehabilitation one week later.

Somali authorities, particularly the National Intelligence and Security Agency
(NISA), unlawfully detained, and at times prosecuted in military courts, children
with alleged ties to Al-Shabab. On appeal, Puntland judges reduced, but did not
overturn, prison sentences determined by its military court in 2016 to 40 children who fought for Al-Shabab.

Displacement and Access to Humanitarian Assistance

About 2.6 million Somalis live in protracted internal displacement according to
the UN, facing serious abuses, including indiscriminate killings, forced evictions, sexual violence, and limited access to basic services.

According to humanitarian actors, over 204,000 people had been forcibly
evicted in the first eight months of 2018, including by government forces, primarily in Mogadishu and Bay region.

In December 2017, security forces demolished dozens of informal settlements,
including humanitarian infrastructure, without sufficient warning or providing
residents with alternative settlements, leaving around 30,000 people homeless.

The Benadir regional administration investigated the evictions, and in April suggested how to tackle forced evictions but did not press for accountability.

Humanitarian agencies faced serious challenges in accessing vulnerable populations due to insecurity, restrictions imposed by parties to the conflict, illegal checkpoints, and extortion. Targetted attacks on aid workers persist. On May 2, a staff member of the International Committee of the Red Cross (ICRC) was kidnapped from an ICRC residence in Mogadishu; she had not been released at time of writing.

Sexual Violence

Internally displaced women and girls remain at particular risk of sexual and gender-based violence by armed men, including government soldiers and militia members, and civilians.

Positively, federal and some regional authorities have adopted measures and legislation to improve their capacity to prosecute sexual violence. In May 2018, the federal cabinet endorsed a progressive Sexual Offences Bill; at time of writing, the bill is before parliament. Impact and implementation, including of the 2016 Puntland sexual offenses law, have been limited.

The Somali penal code, currently being revised, classifies sexual violence as an "offence against modesty and sexual honor" rather than as a violation of bodily integrity, punishes same-sex intercourse, and imposes criminal penalties for speech considered insulting to authorities.

Freedom of Expression

Targeted attacks on media, including harassment and arbitrary detentions, continued. The Somali authorities seldom investigate cases of killings or attacks on journalists.

On July 26, a police officer shot dead Abdirizak Kasim Iman, a cameraperson for a privately owned television station, at a checkpoint in Mogadishu. According to the UN, the Somali Police launched an investigation, but at time of writing no arrest has been made.

Somaliland

In December 2017, Muse Bihi Abdi was sworn in as president of Somaliland. The Somaliland government arbitrarily arrested numerous journalists and critics—targeting people who spoke out on "controversial issues," notably the ongoing border tensions with Puntland and unity with Somalia.

In April, Naima Ahmed Ibrahim, a popular poet; Mohamed Kayse Mohamud, a blogger; and Boqor Osman Aw-Mohamud, an outspoken traditional elder, were convicted under vague and overly broad criminal provisions for public criticism of government policies and public officials. Police officials and judges violated due process rights during their detention and trials. All three subsequently received a presidential pardon. According to the independent nongovernmental organization, Human Rights Center, since the inauguration of Somaliland's new president, 18 journalists have been arrested and five convicted under similar provisions. In four cases, prison terms were later converted into fines.

Positively, in July the Somaliland House of Representatives rejected problematic amendments made by the Upper House (Guurti) to the Rape and Sexual Offences Bill that defined an adult as 15 years of age and above, and removed criminal responsibility of close male relatives for forced marriage. In August, the president signed the bill into law.

Key International Actors

International support focused on building Somalia's security sector, including the integration of regional forces, including through implementation of the government's transition plan; attention to ensuring accountability for abuses remained limited.

AMISOM troop-contributing countries expressed concern over the capacity of Somali government forces to assume key security responsibilities. In July the UN Secuity Council heeded African Union calls to delay the withdrawal of 1,000 AMISOM troops by several months.

The United States Defense Department continued to conduct airstrikes and joint operations with an increase in strikes in the Jubaland region. The department concluded without substantiation that there were no civilian casualties in its operations in 2018. However, in May, media and the UN reported five civilians casualities during a joint US-Somali raid in Afgooye district; the Pentagon announced in June that it found the allegations "not credible." After media reported the alleged killings of 10 civilians in Barire, the US Naval Criminal Investigative Service committed to a second investigation into the August 2017 incident, but results have not been made public at time of writing.

The diplomatic crisis between Qatar and other Gulf countries continued to exacerbate tensions in Somalia, between Mogadishu and federal states, with Somaliland, as well as among Mogadishu's political elite, over a United Arab Emirate company's development of key ports.

South Africa

In 2018, South Africa's record on respect for human rights and the rule of law remained poor under new president, Matamela Cyril Ramaphosa, who took office in February following Jacob Zuma's resignation. Corruption, poverty, high unemployment, and violent crime significantly restricted South Africans' enjoyment of their rights. Cuts to health and education services also compromised quality and access to these rights.

Former President Zuma appeared in court three times on charges that include fraud, corruption, and racketeering. On November 16, ahead of the beginning of his criminal trial on corruption charges, Zuma applied to the KwaZulu-Natal High Court seeking a permanent stay in the court case citing bias of the prosecution. At time of writing, the court had not ruled on the matter.

The government did not fulfil the right to education for many of South Africa's children and young adults with disabilities. Under-reporting of rape, challenges in the criminal justice system, and the absence of a comprehensive national strategy remained challenges to combatting high rates of violence against women throughout the year. In 2018, the government continued to send mixed signals about its position on the International Criminal Court (ICC) and international justice following a domestic court's rejection of the government's withdrawal notice to the ICC as unconstitutional and invalid. In September, the international relations minister indicated the government would review its previous decision to withdraw from the ICC.

In August, South Africa ended its one-year term as chairperson of the Southern African Development Community (SADC), during which it did not use the role to promote or support human rights improvements in the region.

Disability Rights

In 2018, almost 600,000 children with disabilities remained out of school. Most children with disabilities attend specialized schools or classes. Children with psychosocial disabilities are frequently placed in poorly regulated special service centers, based on long-term institutionalization, often located far from their families and communities, and lack properly trained staff. No legislation exists to give full effect to the right to inclusive education for all children with disabilities.

Across South Africa, a high number of cases continued to be reported of corporal punishment, violence, abuse, neglect, and inequality involving children with disabilities, especially children with autism spectrum disorder and children with psychosocial and/or intellectual disabilities, by teachers and peers in schools and school hostels.

As in previous years, the government still did not implement key aspects of the 2001 national policy to provide inclusive education for all children with disabilities, nor adopt legislation to guarantee the right to inclusive education. However, the government continued to implement the Screening, Identification, Assessment, and Support (SIAS) policy designed to ensure that children with disabilities are provided full support when accessing education. The majority of the government's limited budget for learners with disabilities continued to be allocated to special schools rather than to inclusive education.

In February, retired Judge Dikgang Moseneke concluded an arbitration hearing over the 2016 mass transfers of mentally ill patients that resulted in the death of at least 144 after their forced removals from Life Esidimeni facilities. Moseneke highlighted poor accountability on the part of state authorities as mental health care patients were transferred to 27 centers operating without valid licenses by nongovernmental organizations. Judge Moseneke ordered that the government to compensation of various sums to families of the Life Esidimeni tragedy, and to provide counselling and support services.

Accountability for Xenophobic Attacks on Foreign Nationals

African foreign nationals in South Africa, including refugees and asylum-seekers, continued to face xenophobic violence and threats of violence in 2018. In May, the KwaZulu-Natal Premier Willies Mchunu met with foreign shop owners after the Northern Region Business Association ordered them to close their businesses or face attacks. The provincial government leadership promised to increase police protection to prevent another wave of xenophobic violence.

In August, at least four people died when xenophobic violence erupted in Soweto, south of Johannesburg. Mobs of protesting locals beat foreign nationals, mostly Somalis, and looted their shops. The protesters accused foreign nationals of selling fake and expired food products. A few days after the Soweto violence, a new anti-foreigner political group marched in Johannesburg, demanding the deportation of all undocumented foreigners in South Africa by the end of the year.

Virtually no one has been convicted over past outbreaks of xenophobic violence, including for the Durban violence of April 2015 that displaced thousands of foreign nationals, or the 2008 attacks, which resulted in the deaths of more than 60 people across the country. The government has yet to finalize the draft national action plan to combat racism, racial discrimination, xenophobia and related intolerance, or provide a mechanism for justice and accountability for xenophobic crimes.

Women's Rights

Widespread and mostly underreported gender based violence, including rape and domestic violence, continued across the country in 2018.

South Africa's law criminalizes the sale and purchase of sex, as well as related activities, such as keeping a brothel or living on the earnings of sex work. However, in part because criminalization may be interpreted as being at odds with South Africa's constitution, decriminalization has been under active discussion for nearly a decade.

The Choice on Termination of Pregnancy Act, a progressive abortion law, has not translated into unhindered access for women seeking to terminate pregnancies. Barriers included health workers' refusal to provide abortions mostly on the grounds of religious or moral beliefs, including the unregulated practice of conscientious objection.

Land Reform

The government continued to debate land reform. In July, the ruling African National Congress indicated its intent to seek an amendment of the constitution to clarify constitutional provisions that grant the government powers to expropriate without compensation. The proposed legislation would set out conditions under which land expropriation without compensation could occur.

In September, President Ramaphosa created a 10-member advisory panel that would support an Inter-Ministerial Committee on Land Reform to lead public consultations on the proposed amendments. The committee had not made any proposals at time of writing.

Environmental Activists' Rights

During 2018, community environmental rights activists were harassed for demanding their rights to health and a healthy environment. South Africa is one of the world's biggest coal producers, and a leading producer of a wide range of metals. The serious environmental, health, and social impacts of mining, coupled with a lack of transparency, accountability, and consultation, have increased public opposition to mining projects.

No one has been identified or arrested for the murder of Sikhosiphi Rhadebe, a Xolobeni community activist who was killed in 2016. His family said the investigation into his murder has stalled. Community activism against harmful impact of mining, like Rhadebe's, has often been met with harassment, intimidation, and violence. On July 11, for example, unidentified gunmen shot and killed Panza and Shange, two activists who opposed relocation of the community in KwaDube in KwaZulu Natal (KZN).

Sexual Orientation and Gender Identity

In an October speech in Cape Town, President Ramaphosa strongly supported the rights of the LGBTI community, stating that "the violation of the rights and equal worth of lesbian, gay, bisexual, transgender or intersex people demeans our common humanity as South Africans. Not only does it expose individuals to pain, suffering and even violence, but it often limits access to social services and economic opportunities for LGBTI people in our country."

South Africa has a progressive constitution that prohibits discrimination on the basis of sexual orientation and protects the human rights of LGBTI people. The Department of Justice and Constitutional Development has taken significant steps to improve coordination between government and civil society in combatting violence (including rape and murder) against lesbians and transgender men.

For instance, in March 2011, the Minister of Justice and Constitutional Development mandated the establishment of a National Task Team (NTT) to develop a National Intervention Strategy that will address "corrective rape." The department initiated engagements with other key government departments and institutions to develop the National Task Team. The department established a Rapid Response Team on pending cases relating to gender and sexual orientation-based crimes in the criminal justice system.

Foreign Policy

August marked the end of South Africa's one-year leadership of the Southern African Development Community (SADC), but it missed key opportunities to press Eswatini (formerly Swaziland) and Zimbabwe to improve their poor human rights records.

In June, the United Nations General Assembly, for the third time, elected South Africa to serve as a non-permanent member of the UN Security Council for 2019-2020. The seat is a chance for President Ramaphosa to restore South Africa's human rights-based foreign policy and take a leadership role in resolving conflicts throughout Africa.

During its summit in January, the African Union (AU) endorsed the candidature of South Africa for the UNSC, the only country to receive the backing of the regional body. In announcing its bid for the non-permanent seat, the South African government declared its intention to promote an African Agenda of peace and security in the region, and to end armed conflict by 2020.

In November, International Relations Minister Lindiwe Sisulu said she intends to review South Africa's guidelines on how the country casts its vote in international fora and ensure they are underpinned by South Africa's values and constitutional principles. She also expressed deep concern about the deteriorating human rights situation in Myanmar. Her spokesperson said South Africa will vote in December in the UN General Assembly for a resolution strongly condemning human rights abuses—including alleged genocide—by the Myanmar military against the Muslim minority Rohingya people—a reversal of its position.

In September, the government indicated it was reviewing its withdrawal from the ICC. Minister Sisulu told media that South Africa may have taken the decision to withdraw from the ICC in a pique of anger, but now felt that, "we are actually better off in the ICC to transform it from inside rather than standing outside and hurling a whole lot of expletives from outside." The ICC debacle had severely dented South Africa's international image as a champion of human rights and international justice.

Also in September, the UN Committee on the Rights of Persons with Disabilities, the body of independent experts that monitors implementation of the Convention on the Rights of Persons with Disabilities, noted with concern the high number of children with disabilities who remain out of school and the continuing growth of special schools. It called on South Africa to develop a "comprehensive plan to extend it throughout its territory, where children can stay in their local school, not be removed from their families and live in hostels." It also called on the government to prepare a time-bound plan of action to address the high levels of physical, sexual, verbal, and emotional abuse, including bullying, in special schools.

In October, the government said it would declare special schools for children with disabilities as no-fee schools during its first review by the UN Committee on Economic, Social and Cultural Rights, the body that monitors the implementation of the International Covenant on Economic, Social and Cultural rights. In October, the committee called on South Africa to "immediately roll out the no-fee schools programme to state-run schools for children with disabilities who cannot be accommodated in mainstream schools," and to "ensure that inclusive education is a guiding principle in all education plans and programmes, including by the provision of reasonable accommodation for children with disabilities."

South Korea

The Republic of Korea (South Korea) is a democracy that generally respects civil and political liberties. However, it maintains unreasonable restrictions on freedom of expression, association, and assembly. Discrimination against lesbian, gay, bisexual, and transgender (LGBT) persons, women, racial and ethnic minorities, and foreigners—especially refugees and migrants—continued to be a major problem in 2018.

Freedom of Expression

South Korea has a free press and a lively civil society. However, successive South Korean governments and large corporations (chaebol) have limited critical scrutiny of themselves through a variety of laws.

Criminal defamation actions can result in up to seven years' imprisonment and a fine. The law focuses solely on whether what was said or written was in the public interest and does not allow for truth as a complete defense.

The National Security Law criminalizes any dissemination of anything that the government classifies as North Korean "propaganda." The law imposes severe criminal penalties on anyone who joins, praises, or induces others to join an "anti-government organization," a term not clearly defined in law.

Worker's Rights

The government has not ratified the International Labour Organization's fundamental conventions on freedom of association (C.87), and on the right to organize and collectively bargain (C.98). Government officials are legally prohibited from exercising their right to form a union. The South Korean government refuses to legally recognize the Korean Teachers and Education Workers' Union (KTU). Migrant workers from many countries in Asia flock to South Korea, but continue to face discrimination, harassment, and labor rights abuses.

In May, the government released former Korean Confederation of Trade Unions (KCTU) President Han San-gyun from prison on parole. In June, former KCTU Secretary-General Lee Young-joo was also released with a suspended sentence. Both had been jailed for organizing worker protests in 2015.

Women's Rights

The #MeToo movement against sexual harassment and abuse in South Korea caused an outpouring of complaints and resignations, along with one acquittal, although it is too soon to say whether the protests will change a widespread culture of impunity for sexual assault and harassment in the country.

In January 2018, public prosecutor Seo Ji-hyeon accused a former senior Justice Ministry official of sexual harassment, and a steady stream of women followed her example the following month. A number of prominent men, including a theater director, a film director, a politician, a professor, and a Catholic priest, were accused. Some apologized for sexual misconduct and resigned from their positions.

In March, Kim Ji-eun, former secretary to Ahn Hee-jung, governor of South Chungcheong province, accused him of repeatedly raping her. He stepped down as governor and was indicted by prosecutors for abusing his supervisory power to force her into an unwanted sexual relationship. However, the court acquitted Ahn in August, after questioning the credibility of Kim's statements and determining Ahn did not abuse his power.

Between June and August 2018, tens of thousands of women demonstrated to demand the government take action against spycams in women's public toilets and other violations of women's privacy involving cameras.

At time of writing, the Constitutional Court was reviewing South Korea's laws on abortion. Abortion is considered to be a crime punishably by up to one year in prison or fines up to 2 million won (US$1,794). Healthcare workers who provide abortions can face up to two years in prison. Some exceptions are provided on grounds of rape or incest, the pregnant woman's health, or presence of hereditary disorders or communicable diseases. Married women must have their spouse's permission to get an abortion. All abortions are prohibited after 24 weeks of pregnancy.

In February , the UN Committee on the Elimination of Discrimination Against Women reviewed South Korea, and raised concerns regarding the absence of the comprehensive anti-discrimination laws and the low levels of reporting of domestic violence.

Sexual Orientation and Gender Identity

The growing lesbian, gay, bisexual, and transgender (LGBT) movement triggered increased resistance by conservative groups. In July, more than 210,000 people signed a petition on the South Korean president's website demanding that the Seoul Pride Parade be cancelled. The event took place as planned. In September, anti-LGBT protesters blocked the first-ever Queer Culture Festival in Incheon and attacked festival participants, leading to eight arrests.

Government education guidelines on sexual education discriminate against LGBT youth, by omitting any mention of sexual minorities in the suggested curriculum.

The Constitutional Court is also currently reviewing the 1962 Military Criminal Act (Article 92-6), which punishes sexual acts between soldiers with up to two years in prison under a "disgraceful conduct" clause.

Refugees and Asylum Seekers

South Korea is a party to the 1951 UN Refugee Convention and its 1967 protocol but continues to reject the vast majority of non-North Korean asylum seekers.

In 2017, the Ministry of Justice reviewed 6,015 asylum seekers' claims and only accepted 91 as refugees. In some cases, the government issued humanitarian visas to allow continued stay in the country, but in most instances, applicants were rejected outright. Asylum seekers complained about widespread discrimination and lack of basic social assistance.

Between January and May, more than 500 Yemeni asylum seekers arrived on Jeju island, gaining entry through a visa free policy designed to promote tourism. Their presence sparked an intense debate and rise of an anti-refugee movement, with Islamophobic overtones on the island and elsewhere in the country. On June 1, the Moon government excluded Yemen from the visa-free policy.

Between June and July, more than 700,000 people signed a petition calling on the government to revoke the Yemenis' refugee applications and expel them. Justice Minister Park Sang-ki reaffirmed South Korea's international obligations toward refugees, but added there would be efforts to root out "fake refugees," and announced additional penalties for "refugee brokers who promote illegalities." On October 17, 2018, the government announced a decision denying the refugee claims of 373 Yemeni asylum seekers. Thirty-four were ordered to be deported and plan to appeal, while another 339 received humanitarian visas to remain in the country for a year because their "right to life and personal liberty" could be at risk if they were returned to Yemen.

Policy on North Korean Human Rights

In February 2018, North Korea jointly participated with South Korea at the Pyeongchang Winter Olympics. President Moon subsequently met with North Korea's leader Kim Jong-un three times between May and September.

President Moon's administration has still not clearly enunciated its policy on North Korean human rights issues in the context of its new diplomatic opening with Pyongyang. South Korea has yet to fully implement the North Korean Human Rights Law that came into effect in September 2016, and failed to establish the North Korea Human Rights Foundation, designed to support research on North Korea's rights situation and fund groups working on these rights issues. The foundation is also supposed to help the government develop a strategy to promote rights in the North. A Center for North Korean Human Rights Records was created under the Ministry of Unification (MOU) to act as an archive of North Korean human rights violations for possible use in future prosecutions.

Key International Actors

South Korea has a mutual defense treaty and close bilateral relations with the United States, yet the country's continued economic growth is highly dependent on maintaining close trading relationships with countries around the world, including Japan and China—which accounts for approximately one-quarter of South Korea's exports.

Despite both being democracies and allies of the US, tensions born of historical differences make the Japan-South Korea relationship fraught with tension and divisions. The Singapore summit meeting between US President Donald Trump and North Korean leader Kim Jong-un in June, reached an agreement to start a process of de-nuclearization, but failed to include any human rights issues.

Following the Singapore summit, rapprochement between South Korea and North Korea picked up speed with a focus on de-escalating military tensions and making plans for closer economic cooperation in the event that international sanctions are lifted. For the first time since 2015, reunions of Korean families separated during the Korean War took place in August. However, at the end of the year, tensions grew between Washington—unhappy about progress on denuclearization—and Seoul over the rapidly growing North-South ties.

South Sudan

A "revitalized" peace agreement signed by government and opposition leaders in September did not end the fighting between government forces and various rebel forces. The agreement envisions a transitional government led by President Salva Kiir, with Riek Machar as first vice president and four additional vice presidents. It provides for an eight-month pre-transitional period, followed by a 36-month transitional period.

All parties to the conflict committed serious abuses, including indiscriminate attacks against civilians including aid workers, unlawful killings, beatings, arbitrary detentions, torture, sexual violence, recruitment and use of child soldiers, looting and destruction of civilian property. Some of the abuses constitute war crimes or crimes against humanity. All parties to the conflict restricted access for the United Nations mission, those providing humanitarian assistance, and ceasefire monitors.

Since the conflict started in December 2013, more than 4 million people have fled their homes, with 2.47 million taking refuge in neighboring countries. Close to 200,000 people are living in six UN "protection of civilians" sites across the country. Seven million people need humanitarian assistance, most of whom faced acute food shortages.

Lack of accountability continued to fuel the violence, while progress on establishing the hybrid court envisioned in the 2015 peace agreement remains stalled. The government continued to restrict media and civil society and arbitrarily detain perceived critics and opponents.

Attacks Against Civilians and Civilian Property

All parties attacked civilians and civilian properties, but government forces were responsible for most documented abuses. People with disabilities and older people continued to be particularly vulnerable during attacks due to difficulties fleeing.

In Northern Jonglei, clashes between government and rebel forces in Yuai, Pieri, Motot, and Waat displaced thousands of civilians to Akobo, Lankien, the UN site in Bor and Ethiopia. In June, four civilians were killed and another five injured, in a government attack in Kuernyuong in former Jonglei State.

The UN mission in South Sudan (UNMISS) documented how, in April and May, government and aligned fighters attacked 40 villages in opposition-controlled parts of southern Unity, killing at least 232 civilians and injuring many more, looted and burned homes, and used rape "as a weapon of war," against at least 120 women and girls, and ordered civilians to leave their villages. Thousands fled their homes or hiding places.

Forces also vandalized, destroyed, and looted schools and health facilities. In Western Bahr El Ghazal region, witnesses from the greater Bagari area outside Wau told Human Rights Watch that government forces, between June and August, attacked civilians, looted and burned property, and occupied schools, health centers, and churches. Thousands fled into the bush and to Wau.

In the Greater Equatoria region, clashes between government and rebel forces and criminality along the main roads continued throughout the year, killing civilians and forcing people to flee to refugee settlements in Uganda or the bush. An October UN report documented the abduction of 900 civilians and other abuses by rebel and government forces in Western Equatoria between April and August.

Members of all parties committed acts of sexual violence against women and girls during armed attacks on their homes, while they were fleeing attacks or when they went to buy or search for basic necessities such as food and firewood around UN sites. Perpetrators of sexual violence crimes were rarely held accountable.

All sides recruited and used children despite repeated promises to stop. In January, the Ceasefire and Transitional Security Arrangements Monitoring Mechanism (CTSAMM) released a report indicating that "the recruitment and employment of child soldiers goes on throughout the country." The UN reported that 6,500 children were recruited and used as fighters by armed groups between October 2014 and June 2018, and were victims of other abuses such as abductions, killing, maiming and sexual abuse.

Attacks on and Restrictions of Humanitarian Aid

South Sudan remains one of the most dangerous places to be an aid worker. All parties have attacked aid workers, and restricted access to populations in need. At least 12 aid workers were killed in 2018, bringing the toll to over 100 since December 2013. In February, rebel forces detained 29 aid workers in greater Baggari area and released them after one day. In April, 10 aid workers were abducted for five days In Yei, in the former Central Equatoria state.

In July, armed youth in Maban county, in Upper Nile, looted and burned UN and humanitarian facilities to protest lack of job opportunities, forcing aid groups to suspend operations.

UNMISS peacekeepers were attacked by armed actors on several occasions; a Bangladeshi soldier was killed in June and a Nepalese soldier was injured in September. Armed groups and government soldiers continued to attack UNMISS compounds, including in Juba Bor, Bentiu, Malakal, Wau, Akobo, and Melut.

Arbitrary Detentions and Enforced Disappearances

Government security forces, especially the National Security Service (NSS), detained perceived government opponents and critics, including human rights activists and academics. In July, NSS officials detained activist Peter Biar Ajak, who at time of writing was being held without charge at the NSS Juba headquarters, reportedly in solitary confinement. Kerbino Wol, a businessman, remained in detention without charge since April.

National security and military officials have subjected civilian detainees to harsh conditions including beatings, electric shocks and other ill-treatment. Since the start of the conflict, countless people have disappeared or died in custody.

In January 2017, lawyer Dong Samuel and opposition member Aggrey Idri were abducted in Nairobi, Kenya and resurfaced in national security headquarters in Juba later that month. The government has not acknowledged their detention or investigated their enforced disappearance. Similarly, the fate of two UN staff, Anthony Nyero and James Lual, who were held in the NSS Riverside detention facility in Juba in December 2016, remained unknown.

The government announced the release of 21 detainees in August and another five in October. None of the former detainees who spoke to Human Rights Watch had been charged with crimes despite being detained for months. The government also released William Endley and James Gatdet Dak, the spokesperson of Riek Machar, both of whom had been sentenced to death in February on trumped up charges.

Freedom of Expression and Association

National security officials summoned, questioned, and harassed journalists and editors and censored newspaper articles. In February, the UN published a report identifying 60 incidents including killings, arbitrary arrests and detentions of journalists and editors, closure, suspension, or censorship of newspapers and blocking of websites from July 2016-Dec 2017.

In February and May, the NSS summoned the editor-in-chief of *Juba Monitor* and repeatedly warned her against publishing articles deemed critical of the government. In March, the Media Regulatory Authority suspended UN Radio Miraya from operating, but the station defied the authority and continued to broadcast.

Authorities, particularly the NSS, continued to harass and intimidate members of civil society. Government measures including a requirement to obtain prior NSS authorization for the conduct of public meetings, bureaucratic registration processes and surveillance, have eroded the exercise of freedoms of speech and association.

In February, Jonglei authorities issued a ministerial order dissolving all youth associations in the state for allegedly engaging in activities disrupting public order.

Civil society activists participating in the peace process faced intimidation and threats. In June, one female activist was threatened by a government representative in Addis and another surveilled. Similarly, four activists in exile in neighboring countries reported facing intimidation, threats and surveillance by authorities.

In August, a civil society activist was arrested and detained in Yambio and transferred to NSS headquarters in Juba. He was released without charge in late October.

In an annual report released in September, the United Nations secretary-general put South Sudan on a blacklist of 38 states where individuals faced intimidation or reprisals for cooperating with the UN on human rights.

Justice and Accountability

In September, a South Sudanese military tribunal found nine soldiers guilty of crimes committed during a July 2016 attack on a compound housing international aid workers. Dozens of soldiers attacked the compound, killed a journalist, raped, gang-raped, and assaulted aid workers, and looted and destroyed property. The court acquitted one of ten soldiers prosecuted, sentenced nine others to imprisonment, and awarded financial compensation to rape and gunshot victims and 51 cows to the family of deceased journalist, John Gatluak. However, the government did not address impunity for widespread conflict related sexual and gender-based violence against South Sudanese.

South Sudan did not make progress on establishing the hybrid court envisioned in the 2015 peace agreement, included in the revitalized agreement. It has yet to sign the memorandum of understanding with the African Union or promulgate legislation to establish the court.

In May, Kiir appointed Gen. Gabriel Jok Riak as chief of defense forces of the SPLA. Riak is subject to targeted sanctions by the UN, European Union, and United States.

In August, Kiir announced an amnesty for Machar and other rebel commanders, a move Human Rights Watch criticized as contravening international law prohibitions on amnesties for war crimes.

Key International Actors

International and regional actors condemned ongoing violations of ceasefires and threatened punitive action. The US imposed a unilateral arms embargo on South Sudan in February and sanctioned 15 South Sudanese oil-related entities.

In July, by a vote of nine in favor and six abstentions, the UN Security Council imposed a globally enforceable arms embargo and targeted sanctions—travel bans and asset freezes—on two of three individuals already subject to EU unilateral sanctions in February, bringing the total number of South Sudanese individuals under UN sanctions to eight.

In March, the UN Human Rights Council renewed the mandate of the Commission on Human Rights in South Sudan for another year. The commission submitted names of individuals and groups who bear responsibility for abuses to the High Commissioner for Human Rights.

Under the auspices of the regional trade bloc, Intergovernmental Authority on Development (IGAD), Sudan, Ethiopia and Kenya played key roles in mediation of the revitalized peace agreement. In September, IGAD requested that the UN Security Council include troops from Sudan, Uganda, Djibouti, and Somalia in the "Regional Protection Force" that it mandated in the summer of 2016, and which has only partially deployed.

In September, South Sudan acceded to the Optional Protocol to the Convention on the Rights of the Child on the involvement of children in armed conflict.

The AU Commission has the authority to establish the hybrid court without the engagement of the South Sudanese government under the terms of the 2015 peace agreement, and the revitalized agreement, but has yet to move ahead in the face of lack of progress by South Sudanese authorities.

HUMAN
RIGHTS
WATCH

LOCKED UP WITHOUT EVIDENCE
Abuses under Sri Lanka's Prevention of Terrorism Act

Sri Lanka

Sri Lanka plunged into a constitutional crisis after President Maithripala Sirisena abruptly dismissed the prime minister on October 26, 2018, and replaced him with Mahinda Rajapaksa—the former president linked to widespread abuses whom Sirisena defeated in the January 2015 presidential elections. Sirisena then dissolved parliament and called for new elections. There were protests and lawsuits to challenge his decision. The crisis ended after the Supreme Court, on December 13, ruled that Sirisena's actions were unconstitutional. Rajapaksa stepped down as prime minister.

The political crisis further slowed progress on ensuring truth and justice for grave rights violations during the 27-year-long civil war between the separatist Liberation Tigers of Tamil Eelam (LTTE) and government forces.

In September, the newly formed Office of Missing Persons (OMP) recommended interim relief for victims and witnesses. However, recent political changes renders their viability uncertain.

Promise of security sector reform remained elusive. The government forwarded several drafts of new counterterrorism legislation, which local groups and the international community criticized for being overbroad, despite some genuine reforms.

Violence against minority communities, particularly against Muslims, led to at least two deaths.

Sri Lanka acceded to the 2008 Convention on Cluster Munitions on March 1, 2018, becoming the first South Asian country to ban these indiscriminate weapons. This followed its accession to the 1997 Mine Ban Treaty on December 13, 2017.

Transitional Justice

President Sirisena's sudden decision to appoint Mahinda Rajapaksa as prime minister raised fears about a return to past abusive practices in the country and a further delay in transitional justice. Rajapaksa stepped down only after the Supreme Court ruled that the president's actions were illegal.

HUMAN
RIGHTS
WATCH

"Why Can't We Go Home?"
Military Occupation of Land in Sri Lanka

After the defeat of the LTTE in 2009, instead of addressing allegations of serious violations by both sides, the Rajapaksa government suppressed media, targeted rights activists, and continued to arbitrarily detain and torture perceived opponents. The new government that took office after Rajapaksa's electoral defeat in 2015, pledged at the United Nations Human Rights Council to ensure accountability for conflict-related abuses.

By 2018, however, while Sri Lanka had acted on some of the human rights-related undertakings, it failed to make much progress on transitional justice. Of the four mechanisms adopted at the Human Rights Council—an office on missing persons; a truth and reconciliation commission; reparations and non-recurrence; and a special court to ensure accountability through prosecutions—only the first had been established, three years later.

The OMP published its interim report in September, urging the government to provide interim relief to families of the missing while they wait for the investigations to be completed. The interim report importantly acknowledged that families of the disappeared were having difficulty trusting the OMP, given the government's long history of failed commissions, and called on the government to strengthen the OMP's authority and independence to work free from government interference. Importantly, the OMP pledged to set up 12 regional offices throughout the country, and emphasized the need for redress, through a proposed Office for Reparations, to families of the disappeared.

The government stated it had drafted a bill on reparations for victims, under the terms of the Human Rights Council resolution. However, given the ongoing political uncertainty, it is unclear what future any of the transitional justice mechanisms will have.

While the government made progress in returning land occupied by security forces or other state agencies, usually after protests by communities, vast areas remain under government control. Some of the land was seized during the conflict, while some new land was occupied after the conflict ended. Although the government claims it needs to hold onto areas occupied by the military for national security reasons, activists say in some places the land is being instead used for commercial gain through farms, businesses, and tourism.

Sri Lanka has not endorsed the international Safe Schools Declaration, which encourages armed forces to refrain from using schools for military purposes, as occurred during the conflict.

Security Sector Reform

Despite pledges, the government failed to repeal and replace the Prevention of Terrorism Act (PTA), a draconian law widely condemned for including an overly broad definition of terrorism and lengthy administrative detention provisions that have facilitated due process violations, including the use of torture, to obtain confessions.

Sri Lanka's Human Rights Commission had unfettered access to places of detention, which has helped lower the levels of abuse against those in custody.

In July, Ben Emmerson, former UN special rapporteur on the promotion and protection of human rights and fundamental freedoms while countering terrorism, released a report on Sri Lanka that concludes progress on overhauling the PTA has "ground to a virtual halt."

Violence Against Minorities

In March, local altercations burst into anti-Muslim riots, leading to the death of at least two people. Following the incidents, the government announced a 10-day nationwide state of emergency.

In recent years, Sri Lanka has witnessed a spate of anti-Muslim violence linked to ultra-nationalist Sinhalese Buddhist groups. The current wave began in late February in the eastern district of Ampara, followed by clashes in Kandy. Observers reported that two mosques and dozens of homes, small businesses, and vehicles were destroyed. Authorities arrested several suspects in the attacks, but concerns remained about police inaction during the violence.

Women's and Girls' Rights

The government failed to respond to the many recommendations made during the 2017 hearings before the UN Committee on the Elimination of Discrimination against Women (CEDAW). These included concerns about protection issues for victims and witnesses who might appear before the transitional justice mechanisms or the courts, and the lack of women appearing before various consultations on the constitution and the transitional justice mechanisms.

As also raised by CEDAW, the government has yet to take steps to address institutional barriers and law enforcement prejudice to help ensure that women and girls are able to access justice, including in cases of sexual or domestic violence.

No discernable progress was made on reforming laws affecting Muslim women on issues concerning inequalities around marriage and divorce.

Sexual Orientation and Gender Identity

Sri Lanka has not revoked sections 365 and 365A of the penal code, which criminalize consensual same-sex conduct. Some lesbian, gay, bisexual, and transgender (LGBT) people—particularly those who are visibly gender non-conforming—face arbitrary arrest, police mistreatment, and discrimination in accessing health care, employment, and housing. The Health Ministry established a Gender Recognition Certificate in 2016, that allows people to change their legal gender, but requires psychiatric evaluation first. The government accepted recommendations to protect LGBT people from discrimination in the report of its Universal Periodic Review, adopted in March, but did not accept recommendations to decriminalize same-sex conduct.

Key International Actors

Following the political upheavals in November, many governments called on the Sri Lankan government to abide by its constitution.

In her first update to the Human Rights Council in September 2018, the UN High Commissioner for Human Rights called on Sri Lanka for speedier and more meaningful implementation of its traditional justice commitments, and underlined the importance of "more progress in advancing accountability and truth-seeking".

The mandate of the Human Rights Council resolution on Sri Lanka will expire in March 2019, when a further resolution will be needed to ensure the HRC holds Sri Lanka to its commitments on accountability issues.

The United States claims it will continue to engage on concerns around human rights accountability despite pulling out of the Human Rights Council. The US conducted joint exercises and training with Sri Lankan military as part of an effort to send members of the forces to UN peacekeeping operations.

China remained engaged with Sri Lanka through the "One Belt, One Road" initiative, which will draw significant infrastructural development through the country, although concerns remained about political compromises that the Sri Lankan government may make to enable this, including control of a Chinese-built port.

Sudan

Sudan's rights record showed little change in 2018. Conflicts in Darfur, Southern Kordofan, and Blue Nile continued. The National Intelligence and Security Service (NISS) used excessive force to break up protests and arbitrarily detained dozens of activists and opposition party members. Authorities censored media, confiscated newspapers, detained outspoken critics, and barred key opposition figures from traveling outside the country.

Amid Sudan's ongoing economic crisis, President Omar al-Bashir reshuffled the government twice and the ruling National Congress Party endorsed him to run for another term in 2020. Sudan has made no meaningful attempt to provide accountability for past or current abuses in conflict zones or other serious human rights violations. It has not cooperated with the International Criminal Court (ICC) cases on charges against the president and four other men, of genocide, crimes against humanity and war crimes committed in Darfur.

Conflict and Abuses in Darfur, Southern Kordofan, and Blue Nile

Although in July Sudan extended its unilateral ceasefire in conflict zones until the end of the year, its forces, including the paramilitary Rapid Support Forces, attacked over a dozen villages in the Jebel Mara region of Darfur between March and May. Attackers killed at least 23 civilians, destroyed and looted civilian property, and caused thousands to flee their homes.

Sudanese forces blocked United Nations-African Union Hybrid Operation in Darfur, UNAMID, peacekeepers and aid groups' access to displaced people and conflict-affected areas on several occasions. More than 2 million people remain displaced due to the conflict between armed opposition and government forces that started in 2003.

Seven years into the armed conflict in Southern Kordofan and Blue Nile, the government and armed opposition have failed to agree on modalities for supplying life-saving aid to civilians in need. Sudanese human rights monitors reported government-aligned militia attacks on civilians in Blue Nile in April.

Crackdown on Protesters

In January and February, security forces violently broke up anti-austerity protests in Khartoum, Omdurman, and other towns, arresting hundreds, beating protesters with sticks and hoses, and using tear gas, according to rights monitors.

Security officials dispersed several university student protests across the country, detaining and injuring many throughout the year. In January, security forces shot at student protesters in El Geneina, West Darfur, killing one, and at displaced persons at a camp in Zalingei, in Central Darfur, killing five.

Arbitrary Detentions, Torture

During the wave of protests in January and February, security agents detained hundreds of rights activists, protesters and opposition party members and held dozens for weeks without charge.

Rudwan Daoud, a Sudanese-American activist, was detained for six weeks without charge after security agents arrested him during a protest against government land expropriations.

Activist and vocal critic Husham Ali has been detained without charge by security officials following his deportation in May from Saudi Arabia, where he had been detained since November 2017.

In July, security agents arrested social media activist and sports commentator, Ahmed al-Dai Bushara, at his home in Omdurman and held him incommunicado, without charge, for over two months, releasing him in mid-September.

Detainees were subjected to torture and ill-treatment. A Darfuri student leader, released in late January after five months of solitary confinement, was repeatedly beaten, subjected to electric shocks, threatened with death and rape, and held in harsh conditions. In October, student activist Asim Omer Hassan, who faces charges of killing a policeman during protests in May 2016, was hospitalized after being beaten in Kober prison.

Sudan has failed to investigate allegations of torture by national security officials and has yet to ratify the Convention Against Torture, which it signed in 1986. It retains the death penalty and corporal punishment for numerous crimes.

Malicious Prosecutions, Harassment

In February, a group of nine police in plainclothes raided an apartment where activist Wini Omer—a vocal critic of the public order regime—was meeting three friends, arrested the group, detained them for five days, and accused them of prostitution. On July 24, a prosecutor brought eight additional charges against Omer, including crimes against the state, punishable by death.

A religious teacher in Central Darfur, Matar Younis, arrested in April for criticizing human rights violations by government forces in Darfur, was accused of crimes against the state and espionage. In July, authorities dropped charges and released him.

In November, security officials charged activist Mohamed Boshi with espionage and crimes against the state after he was forcibly disappeared and then extrajudicially returned from Egypt to Sudan in October.

Authorities also barred opposition politicians and activists from traveling out of Sudan and confiscated passports, including of a Darfur Bar Association lawyer returning from an award ceremony in the United States in August.

Freedom of Media

In the first week of January alone, security officials seized print runs of eight newspapers because they had covered the anti-austerity protests. Throughout the year they suspended, delayed, or confiscated editions of newspapers for running pieces critical of the president or ruling party, its economic policies, corruption, or other sensitive topics.

During January protests, at least 18 journalists, including correspondents of Reuters and AFP, were arrested. Most were released the same day but four were held for several weeks without charge; journalist Amal Habani was severely beaten during interrogation. Security officials arrested a group of journalists for protesting a ban on coverage of Omdurman's parliament in October.

Security officials summoned and interrogated editors and journalists, confiscated laptops, and warned them not to cross "red lines." At least one columnist was banned from writing for *al-Saiha* newspaper. Authorities prosecuted an al-Jareeda editor and journalist for criminal defamation because they had written about corruption in March. Officials sentenced the former editor-in-chief of al-Mustagila newspaper to prison for "false news" for articles published in 2015.

Sexual Violence and Discrimination

Government forces used sexual violence against women and girls with impunity, particularly in Darfur where they have been implicated in widespread sexual violence in the past. In February, the United Nations expert on sexual violence in conflict noted following her visit to Sudan that there is a deep-seated culture of denial around rape.

Sudan's morality and public order laws, which make dress code violations and other personal choice crimes punishable by humiliation and flogging, discriminate against women and girls. In 2016, Human Rights Watch documented how these laws, in combination with security officials' abuses, can be used to silence those who challenge authority.

Sudan's laws allow marriage of girls as young as 10 and despite 2015 amendments to the criminal code that clarified the definition of rape, judicial authorities do not recognize marital rape as a crime. In May, Noura Hussein, a 19-year-old woman forced into marriage at 16, was sentenced to death for killing her husband when he tried to rape her. In June, a court commuted the sentence to five years in prison with a heavy fine.

Freedom of Religion

Authorities imposed Sharia law on non-Muslims and brought apostasy charges against those who converted to Christianity and minority, or non-Sunni, Muslims. In October, security officials in South Darfur detained a group of Christians for several days and forced them to renounce their faith. They charged a priest with apostasy. On February 11, authorities demolished an evangelical church building in Khartoum without notice, after previously threatening to demolish 25 churches.

Refugees and Migrants

Sudan hosts refugees and migrants from the region and received nearly 200,000 more refugees from South Sudan, bringing the total over 770,000. The notoriously abusive Rapid Support Forces lead its response to migration. Authorities have deported Eritreans, often without giving them an opportunity to apply for asylum. Hundreds of thousands of Sudanese refugees from Darfur, Southern Kordofan, and Blue Nile live in camps in Chad, South Sudan, and Ethiopia. Sudanese living in Cairo, including refugees, were subjected to harassment, interrogations, and warned of deportation by Egyptian and Sudanese officials.

Key International Actors

Sudan hosted peace talks on conflicts in the Central Africa Republic and South Sudan, and continued participation in the Arab coalition fighting in Yemen. The US, which lifted economic sanctions in 2017, continued counterterrorism cooperation and granted visas to the current and former heads of Sudan's draconian national security agency, responsible for torture and other abuses.

The European Union continued to support controversial migration programs, widely criticized for encouraging abuses by security forces.

In July, the UN security council adopted plans to dramatically downsize UNAMID and limit the area of operations to Jebel Mara region. The downsizing limits the mission's operational area but does not extinguish its responsibility for human rights monitoring and protection of civilians in the whole of Darfur. The mission is expected to draw down its presence and has yet to test the Sudanese government's willingness to allow it to return to its former areas of operation to try to fulfill these duties.

In September, the UN Human Rights Council adopted a resolution to continue the work of the independent expert on human rights in Sudan for another year, or until a country office of the Office of the High Commissioner for Human Rights is operational.

The UN Security Council failed to press Sudan to cooperate with the ICC in the surrender of the five fugitives sought on alleged Darfur crimes, despite having referred the situation to the court in 2005. The ICC first announced charges in 2007.

Syria

In 2018, the Syrian government, supported by Russia and Iran, recaptured areas in Eastern Ghouta in Damascus countryside and Daraa governorate. Government forces used a combination of unlawful tactics, including prohibited weapons, indiscriminate strikes, and restrictions on humanitarian aid, to force anti-government groups to surrender in these areas, resulting in mass displacement. Anti-government armed groups indiscriminately attacked neighboring government-held areas and restricted civilians' ability to flee hostilities.

At the time of writing, a tenuous ceasefire was holding in Idlib between the Syrian-Russian military alliance and anti-government armed groups. Anti-government groups in Idlib detained individuals attempting reconciliation with the government, media activists, and restricted humanitarian aid. After several reported chemical attacks during the first half of the year, in an unprecedented step, the Organisation for the Prohibition of Chemical Weapons (OPCW) was authorized to attribute responsibility for attacks in Syria.

In areas re-taken from the Islamic State (also known as ISIS), the high toll of the war in civilian casualties and damaged infrastructure became clearer. Landmines planted by ISIS before fleeing continued to kill and maim civilians. Little progress has been made in providing the necessary resources for recovery, and/or compensation for civilian victims of attacks. ISIS and Al-Qaeda affiliates in Syria continued to perpetrate abuses, ranging from summary executions and kidnappings to interference in aid delivery.

The Syrian Observatory for Human Rights (SOHR), a monitoring group based in the UK, estimated the death toll since the start of the war to be as high as 511,000 as of March 2018. Years of relentless fighting left 6.6 million displaced internally and 5.6 million around the world, according to the United Nations High Commissioner for Refugees (UNHCR).

At the end of the year, the Geneva-led political process remained at a standstill, and a new UN special envoy was appointed.

As active conflict partially decreases, Russia and Syria called for refugees to return and Syria passed laws to facilitate reconstruction. Despite this, government forces continued to violate human rights and international humanitarian law, arbitrarily detaining and mistreating people, and imposing onerous restrictions on freedom of movement.

Syrian-Russian Indiscriminate Attacks

Indiscriminate attacks on civilians and civilian objects by the Syrian-Russian military alliance persisted in 2018. In February, government forces launched a military campaign to retake Eastern Ghouta, an urban suburb of Damascus. Over 1,600 civilians were reportedly killed between February 18 until March 21. The Syrian-Russian military alliance struck at least 25 medical facilities, 11 schools, and countless civilian residences.

Similarly, on June 16, the alliance led an offensive in Daraa and Quneitra governorates, southwest of Syria, triggering massive displacement towards Jordan and the Israeli-occupied Golan Heights.

Use of Unlawful Weapons, including Chemical Weapons

Parties to the conflict continued to use unlawful weapons. The Syrian-Russian military alliance used internationally banned cluster munitions and chemical weapons in re-taking areas. Human Rights Watch investigated 36 cluster munition attacks between July 2017 and June 2018 and another two-dozen more possible cluster munition attacks. Evidence suggests the alliance used incendiary weapons in Ghouta and Daraa.

Between 2013 and 2018, Human Rights Watch and seven other independent, international organizations investigated and confirmed at least 85 chemical weapons attacks – the majority perpetrated by Syrian government forces. The actual number of chemical attacks is likely higher.

After a chemical attack on Douma in Eastern Ghouta, there were renewed international efforts to deter use of chemical weapons. Russia used its veto in the Security Council in February and April, preventing the creation of a UN-led investigatory mechanism. However, in June, states parties to the Chemical Weapons Conventions granted the OPCW permanent authorization to investigate and assign responsibility for chemical weapons attacks.

Abuses by Non-State Armed Groups

Between February and April, anti-government groups based in Ghouta – including Jaysh al-Islam, Ahrar al-Sham, and Faylaq al-Rahmane – killed and maimed hundreds of civilians in indiscriminate attacks on Damascus. According to the UN Commission of Inquiry, the armed groups regularly arbitrarily arrested and tortured civilians in Douma, including members of religious minority groups.

Hay'at Tahrir al-Sham (HTS), an Al-Qaeda affiliate present in Idlib, carried out arbitrary arrests and kidnappings that targeted local political opponents and journalists. Infighting left civilians dead, as did recurring assassinations and car bombings. The group continued to interfere with humanitarian access and aid distribution in areas under its control.

On July 25, ISIS led simultaneous incursions in al-Suweida governorate, killing at least 200 individuals and kidnapping 27 people. ISIS unlawfully executed one of the hostages in August. In November, all the remaining hostages were freed according to the state news agency. In the meantime, the fate of thousands of those kidnapped by ISIS in the east of Syria before they lost the territory remains unknown, with little effort by the Syrian Democratic Forces and US-led coalition to uncover their whereabouts.

Though the Syrian Democratic Forces (SDF) and the US-led coalition pushed ISIS out of Raqqa in October 2017, homemade landmines and explosive devices planted by ISIS before fleeing continued to kill and maim civilians. Between October 2017 and April 2018, more than 1,000 people have been injured or killed by mines, according to local medical workers.

Turkish Offensive on Afrin

On January 20, Turkey launched a military offensive in Afrin district in northwest Syria, previously under the control of the Kurdish-majority Autonomous Administration. As of March, the Turkish offensive reportedly resulted in the deaths of dozens of civilians, and displaced tens of thousands according to the United Nations. Turkish media reported the YPG launched indiscriminate attacks on Turkish border towns and killed at least seven civilians.

Turkish-supported non-state armed groups affiliated with the Free Syrian Army also seized, destroyed, and looted properties of Kurdish civilians in Afrin, while

556

local activists reported at least 86 incidents of abuse that appeared to amount to unlawful arrests, torture, and disappearances by those groups.

Violations by US-Backed Forces and the US-Led Coalition

While the United States-led coalition re-opened investigations into civilian casualties from its strikes and admitted to inadvertently killing civilians, it did not provide transparency around these investigations nor compensation for victims. Although exhumation of mass grave sites began in Raqqa city, little support has been provided to develop clear protocols to preserve or forensically identify the dead.

The US assisted the SDF in northern Syria to detain hundreds of foreign ISIS suspects, and has begun returning suspected fighters to their countries, without transparency, raising human rights concerns.

The Syrian Democratic Council, a civilian authority operating in areas retaken from ISIS, and the Kurdish-majority Autonomous Administration overseeing displacement camps in the northeast, confiscated identification documents of displaced persons and arbitrarily prevented them from leaving the camps and moving freely. In a positive step, in September, the Syrian Democratic Forces pledged to stop recruiting children.

Since January, the Autonomous Administration and the Asayish, the local police, detained at least 20 members of the Kurdish National Council, a coalition of opposition Kurdish parties, and in some cases appear to have forcibly disappeared them.

Arbitrary Detention and Enforced Disappearances

As of August 30, more than 90,000 individuals were forcibly disappeared in Syria, most at the hands of the Syrian government, according to the Syrian Network for Human Rights (SNHR), a local monitoring organization. The Violations Documentation Center (VDC), a local monitoring group, has compiled 60,000 names of those detained by the government since 2011 whose fate remains unknown.

In July, the Syrian government updated civil registries to include death certificates for hundreds of individuals previously detained or disappeared by the government. The updates provided no specific details other than date and, occasionally, cause of death, and the government failed to provide the remains to the families. Meanwhile, the Syrian government continues to detain and mistreat individuals in areas under its control.

Russia, Iran, and Turkey have repeatedly made commitments to resolve arbitrary detention and enforced disappearances as guarantors of the Astana talks. In December 2017, the guarantors established a working group on detentions and abductions in the Syrian conflict. Yet, little progress has been made.

In March, the UN Commission of Inquiry on Syria issued a report on sexual and gender-based violence from March 2011 to December 2017 finding that the rape and sexual violence committed by government forces and associated militias amounted to war crimes and crimes against humanity.

Displacement Crisis

From January to April 2018 more than 920,000 individuals had been newly displaced inside of Syria, according to the UN. Neighboring countries – including Turkey, Jordan, and Lebanon – continued to prevent Syrians from seeking asylum at their borders, despite serious risks of violence. By September 2018, 5.6 million Syrians have taken refuge outside the country, the majority in neighboring countries.

More than a million Syrian refugees are registered with UNHCR in Lebanon. Lebanon's residency policy makes it difficult for Syrians to maintain legal status. Seventy-four percent of Syrians in Lebanon lack legal residency and risk detention for being in the country unlawfully. In 2017, Lebanese authorities stepped up calls for refugees to return, despite the ongoing conflict and well-founded fears of persecution. A small number of refugees have returned to Syria under localized agreements, however these are not overseen by UNHCR. Some refugees have said they are returning because of harsh policies and deteriorating conditions in Lebanon, not because they think Syria is safe. Municipalities in Lebanon forcibly evicted thousands of refugees in mass expulsions without a legal basis or due process. Tens of thousands remain at risk of eviction.

As of May, Turkey had registered almost 3.6 million Syrian refugees in the country. Since January, however, ten provinces – including Istanbul and Hatay – suspended Syrian asylum seeker registration. Turkish security forces intercepted and deported thousands of newly arrived Syrian asylum seekers at the Turkey-Syrian border during the year, and summarily deported them to the war-ravaged Syrian governorate of Idlib. Turkey has stated that it will not open its border to asylum seekers fleeing hostilities in Idlib. Instead, Turkish authorities have opened several displacement camps in areas under their control in Syria.

As of June 2018, Jordan has registered around 666,294 Syrian refugees. Jordan categorically refused to open the border – closed since June 2016 – to incoming asylum seekers fleeing hostilities in the southwest. However, Jordan helped evacuate members of the Syrian Civil Defense, a humanitarian emergency re-sponse team affiliated with the opposition, whom Germany, the United Kingdom and Canada, among others, agreed to resettle. In 2018, Jordan began regulariz-ing the stay of refugees without residency permits.

Russia refused to grant asylum to a Syrian national, claiming that his case was baseless given "the ongoing events on [Syria's] territory have specific character-istics of a counterterrorist operation, not a classical military confrontation."

The US renewed its grant of Temporary Protected Status (TPS) to almost 7,000 Syrians living in the United States, but did not extend the status to any new Syrians. It also maintained a ban on Syrian citizens entering the United States. The European Union's response to the Syrian refugee crisis continued to fall short, with its emphasis on preventing arrivals from Turkey and confining those who do in overcrowded, unsanitary camps on Greek islands.

Reconstruction and Property Rights

The Syrian government passed Law 10 of 2018, empowering it to establish rede-velopment zones for rehabilitation and reconstruction projects. The law empow-ers the government to confiscate residents' property without due process or adequate compensation. In November, in response to international pressure, the Syrian parliament amended the law. However, there are still significant con-cerns in the law that remain unaddressed. In Qaboun and Darayya the govern-ment has restricted access for civilian residents seeking to return to their homes, and has unlawfully demolished residents' private homes, without providing no-tice, alternative housing, or compensation.

Russia has called on the European Union and Western states to support reconstruction in Syria, currently predicted to cost at least US$250 billion. The European Union and the United States have maintained that they will not fund reconstruction in government-held Syria in the absence of a political transition along the lines of the UN Security Council resolution 2254. However, several European states, including France and Switzerland have opened humanitarian offices in Damascus and are seeking to support rehabilitation and stabilization efforts in areas re-taken by the government.

In areas controlled by anti-government groups and the Syrian Democratic Forces, most Western donors continue to provide humanitarian aid. However, the United Kingdom and Netherlands have withdrawn their support for stabilization and resilience in northwest Syria. The United States also froze its funding for recovery and stabilization in areas captured from ISIS, asking the UAE and Saudi Arabia to step in to support local authorities, which they did.

Key International Actors

The UN-led political negotiations remained at a standstill, while Russia continued its attempts to politically legitimize the government's military gains. In January, Russia hosted a Syrian People's Congress in Sochi to agree on a new constitution. Though it failed to achieve its stated objective, the congress mandated the UN Special Envoy with the creation of a constitutional committee. The committee has not been created yet.

Russia, Turkey, and Iran continued their tripartite meetings on Syria, holding three summit-level meetings in 2018 and three rounds of talks in the Astana process, negotiations on de-escalation held regularly in Astana, Kazakhstan since 2017. Russia remains the primary arms supplier to the Syrian government.

The United States' policies on Syria oscillated. In August, the US announced it would pull back hundreds of millions of dollars in funding allocated to rebuild parts of Syria previously held by ISIS. In September, the US announced that it intended to maintain a military presence in Syria, despite having announced a pullback earlier in the year.

The United States, United Kingdom, and France conducted airstrikes on April 14 in response to the reported chemical weapons attack on Douma. Israel also reportedly conducted several strikes on government-held areas.

In April, EU foreign ministers reiterated their joint commitment to "relentlessly" pursue the release of civilians detained and disappeared, and alongside the UN, co-chaired the Brussels II conference on Syria. It will host a third in March 2019.

In June, Germany's chief federal prosecutor reportedly issued an arrest warrant for a senior Syrian military official on charges of war crimes. France issued its own arrest warrants in November.

UN Security Council and General Assembly

In late 2017, the UN Security Council renewed the mandate for cross-border aid delivery. The humanitarian aspect of the Syrian conflict is one of few where the council maintains consensus. On accountability, the council remains deadlocked due to Russia's use of the veto.

Meanwhile, the International, Impartial and Independent Mechanism (IIIM), a quasi-special prosecutor's office established by the UN General Assembly in December 2016, continued to gather and preserve evidence for future criminal prosecutions. The body is reportedly opening two cases in 2018.

Tajikistan

Tajikistan's abysmal human rights record deteriorated further in 2018. Tajik authorities jailed government critics, including opposition activists, journalists, and relatives of peaceful dissidents abroad, for lengthy prison terms on politically motivated grounds. The crackdown on freedoms of expression, association, and religion extended to virtually any manifestation of dissent, even social media users who expressed mild criticism of government policy. Extremely worrying was the emergence of a government registry of persons identified as belonging to the lesbian, gay, bisexual, and transgender (LGBT) community, exposing hundreds of individuals to the risk of detention and extortion by police.

Authorities intensified their campaign to forcibly return political opponents from abroad, relying on politically motivated extradition requests made via INTERPOL, the international police organization, as well as on alliances with police and security services in Turkey and Russia. The most frequent targets of the reportedly hundreds of INTERPOL "red notices" and other extradition requests lodged by the Tajik government are members of the Islamic Renaissance Party of Tajikistan (IRPT) and opposition movement Group 24, both banned and labeled "extremist" in Tajikistan.

However, 2018 also witnessed a few positive steps by the government in individual cases of abuse following social media campaigns by Tajik and international civil society activists.

Harassment of Dissidents Abroad

Pursuant to a Tajik red notice, Greek migration officials detained IRPT activist Mirzorakhim Kuzov on October 9, 2017, while he was in transit at Athens International Airport after attending a human rights conference in Poland. Kuzov was detained until November 30 when a Greek court rejected Tajikistan's extradition request with Greek and international human rights groups having intervened.

On February 16, police in Istanbul detained Namunjon Sharipov, a businessman and IRPT member who fled Tajikistan in 2015. For several days prior to his detention, Tajik officials in Istanbul visited the teahouse Sharipov owned, pressuring him to return to Tajikistan. Following an 11-day detention, Tajik officials forced him to board a plane to Dushanbe. On February 20, Sharipov resurfaced on Tajik public television, stating that his return to the country had been "voluntary." Relatives and Sharipov himself later told Human Rights Watch he had been detained by Tajik security services. Following a public outcry, Tajik officials allowed Sharipov to return to Turkey in June.

In April, Turkish police also detained Group 24 chairman Suhrob Zafar and member Nasimjon Sharipov (unrelated to Namunjon Sharipov) pursuant to an extradition request by Tajik authorities. Their lawyers filed a stay of extradition with Turkey's Constitutional Court, citing the high risk of torture both could face if returned to the country. The court granted the stay and later released Sharipov in July. Zafar remains in detention.

Tajikistan also detained or forcibly returned to the country other opposition activists in various countries, including Naimjon Sameev, the former IRPT head in the Sughd region in northern Tajikistan, who was detained in Russia on November 30 and immediately forced his return to Tajikistan, where relative reported he had been detained by Tajik security services and faces a high risk of torture.

Dushanbe's pressure on the IRPT reached a zenith after a July 30 attack that killed four cyclists, two American, one French, and one Dutch, in southern Tajikistan. The Islamic State, also known as ISIS, claimed responsibility for the attack and disseminated a video that depicted the attackers pledging allegiance to the group. Despite ISIS's claim of responsibility and absent any credible evidence, the Tajik government accused the IRPT, now based in Europe, of organizing the attack. The IRPT denied responsibility. The IRPT said the allegations were "baseless and irrational" and called for a thorough investigation.

Dissidents' Families

Authorities also harassed the relatives of peaceful dissidents abroad. Activists based in France, Germany, and Poland told Human Rights Watch that their relatives in Tajikistan are regularly visited by security services, who pressure them to denounce their relatives and provide information on their whereabouts or activities and threaten them with imprisonment if their relatives continue their peaceful opposition work.

563

The government also imposed travel bans on the immediate relatives, including children and grandchildren, of opposition activists. For several years, authorities refused to allow Ibrohim Hamza Tillozoda, the four-year old grandson of exiled IRPT leader Muhiddin Kabiri, to leave the country to receive potentially life-saving medical treatment for testicular cancer. Authorities relented, however, on July 29, following international pressure.

A similar development happened with Fatima Davlyatova, the 10-year-old daughter of activist Shabnam Khudoydodova, whom border guards removed from a flight on August 4 when she and her relatives attempted to leave the country to reunite with her mother in Europe. Following a social media campaign, authorities allowed her and her relatives to leave Tajikistan on August 11.

In September, a Dushanbe court sentenced Rajabali Komilov, the brother of Germany-based IRPT member Janatullo Komilov brother, to 10 years in prison for alleged party membership and unspecified crimes committed during Tajikistan's 1992-1997 civil war. Komilov told Human Rights Watch that the case against his brother was brought to coerce his return to the country.

Freedom of Expression

Authorities persistently block access to popular social media and news sites, including Facebook, YouTube, and Radio Free Europe/Radio Liberty (RFE/RL), and periodically cut access to mobile and messaging services when critical statements about the president, his family, or the government appear online.

On August 22, a Tajik appellate court overturned the 12-year prison sentence of independent journalist Khayrullo Mirsaidov, arrested in December 2017 after he wrote a public letter to President Emomali Rahmon that revealed corruption by local officials. Mirsaidov's sentence was replaced on appeal with a fine of 80,000 somoni (approximately US$8,500) and one year of community service. An international campaign, #FreeKhayrullo, had earlier highlighted his case.

In August, a court sentenced Umar Murodov to five-and-a-half years' imprisonment for "insulting" President Rahmon on the social media site Odnoklassniki. A fall 2017 law amendment provided for criminal liability for "public insult or slander against [the President], the Founder of Peace and National Unity, the Leader of the Nation."

Also in August, a court sentenced Bezhan Ibragimov, a National Guard soldier, to seven years' imprisonment for "extremism" after he had allegedly posted a photograph of the flag of an Islamic group Ansarullah and had allegedly chatted online with a former classmate living in Syria or Iraq.

In September, human rights lawyer Shuhrat Kudratov and government critic Abubakr Azizkhojaev, whose imprisonment in 2014 and 2015 human rights groups had labelled as politically motivated, were released from prison having completed their prison terms.

Freedom of Religion or Belief

The Tajik government severely curtails freedom of religion or belief, proscribing certain forms of dress, including the hijab for women and long beards for men. Salafism, a fundamentalist strand of Islam, has been officially banned in Tajikistan since 2011 and authorities regularly arrest individuals for alleged membership in Salafi groups.

In August, authorities charged opposition blogger Junaydullo Khudoyorov over his alleged ties to Salafi armed extremists. He was sentenced to five years in prison. Following his sentencing, Khudoyorov told journalists in the courtroom that his case was politically motivated retaliation for articles he had written accusing local officials of involvement in corruption and that "these publications have nothing to do with Salafiya [Salafism]." In August, Tajikistan amnestied seven Salafis, previously extradited from Russia, after they announced their withdrawal from the movement.

In 2018, the Ministry of Culture published a "Book of Recommendations," outlining in detail "approved" dressing styles for women aged 7 to 70. Authorities banned Barbie dolls in hijabs, promoting "national dress" instead. Devout Muslim men had to shave their beards to have their documents returned from confiscation.

Domestic Violence

By late 2018, authorities had taken several steps to combat domestic violence against women and children, operating more than 15 police stations staffed by female police inspectors who underwent training in gender-sensitive, community policing. The Ministry of Internal Affairs also developed further guidelines on the implementation of Tajikistan's 2013 law on the prevention of violence in the family. However, survivors of domestic violence, lawyers, and service providers reported that the law remains largely unimplemented and that victims of domestic violence continue to suffer inadequate protection, including a critical lack of access to domestic violence shelters.

Sexual Orientation and Gender Identity

LGBT people face discrimination in Tajikistan, although same-sex conduct is not criminalized. In October 2017, authorities announced the creation of a special registry including 367 "proven" LGBT persons, after conducting law enforcement operations called "Morality" and "Purge," purportedly to protect sexual minorities and halt the spread of sexually transmitted diseases. The creation of the registry exposed hundreds of individuals to the risk of detention and extortion by police and severe social stigma.

Key International Actors

The US, European Union, and other international actors largely resisted imposing any serious policy consequences for Tajikistan's abysmal rights record, reluctant to alienate Dushanbe given its geostrategic position along the border with Afghanistan.

Following the sentencing of Khayrullo Mirsaidov to 12 years' imprisonment, the US, UK, Germany, France, and the EU delegation in Tajikistan issued a joint statement condemning his sentence, calling it "extremely harsh." They said that "[t]his sentencing will have a negative impact on the freedom of media and expression in Tajikistan." The sentence was overturned on appeal following an international campaign in support of the journalist.

Harlem Desir, the Organization for Security and Co-operation in Europe's (OSCE) Representative for Freedom of the Media, stated that he was "alarmed by the stringent and disproportionate sentence handed down to the journalist."

On March 9, the EU and Tajikistan held their sixth Cooperation Committee meeting in Brussels. Highlighting worsening conditions for civil society in Tajikistan, the EU noted that its strategy would promote "reforms and respect for human rights."

In its 2018 annual report, the US Commission on International Religious Freedom recommended the State Department re-designate Tajikistan a "country of particular concern" for its severe violations of religious freedom.

In May, the UN Working Group on Arbitrary Detention released an opinion finding IRPT deputy chairman Mahmadali Hayit's detention and imprisonment since September 2016 a violation of Tajikistan's international human rights obligations and called for his immediate release. In a similar ruling in July, the UN Human Rights Committee declared unlawful the continued imprisonment of another opposition figure, Zayd Saidov, urging his immediate release.

In its third periodic report on Tajikistan in June 2018, the UN Committee on Torture expressed concern with reports of torture in prisons and pretrial detention, including deaths in custody. It further pointed to serious problems of domestic violence and persecution of LGBT persons. The committee urged Tajikistan to investigate allegations that imprisoned IRPT figures Mahmadali Hayit, Rahmatullo Rajab, and Saidumar Husaynov were tortured.

Tanzania

Since the election of President John Magufuli in December 2015, Tanzania has witnessed a marked decline in respect for free expression, association, and assembly. Rhetorical Attacks on rights by authorities are increasingly accompanied by implementation of repressive laws and the harassment and arrest of journalists, opposition members and critics. Self-censorship and fear of reprisals have stifled criticism. Women and girls, particularly young mothers seeking to study, continue to face discriminatory policies.

Freedom of Expression

In March, Tanzania adopted regulations for online content as part of the 2010 Electronic and Postal Communications Act, giving the Tanzania Communications Regulatory Authority (TCRA) wide discretionary powers to license internet-based content, including blogs, which are now subject to fees of up to US$900, curtailing access for many. Non-compliance is a criminal offence.

The 2015 Cybercrimes Act continues to impede free expression and privacy rights. In March, student activist Abdul Nondo was charged with publishing false information after sending a WhatsApp message alerting friends and family that he had been abducted. Nondo said he was accused by his abductors of being used by opposition parliamentarians and activists to organize student protests. He was released on bail, and at time of writing, his trial was ongoing. Nondo had previously been critical of police conduct during a rally in February in which a student was killed. Police dispute that he was abducted. On November 5, Nondo was acquitted.

At the end of the year, Bob Chacha Wangwe was appealing his 2017 conviction for publication of false information under the Cybercrimes Act for critiquing the conduct of elections in Zanzibar in 2015 on a Facebook page. A Dar es Salaam court sentenced him to 1.5 years' imprisonment, or a fine of 5 million Tanzania shillings (US$2,185).

In June, a court acquitted Maxence Melo and Micke William, founders of popular whistleblowing site Jamii Forums, on charges of failure to comply with a police order to disclose the identity of platform users under the Cybercrimes Act. Two remaining charges, of management of a domain not registered in Tanzania under the Online Content regulations and of obstructing investigation under the Cyber-crimes Act, remained pending at time of writing.

In January, the TCRA fined five television stations 60 million Tanzania shillings ($27,000) for broadcasting a press conference by the Legal and Human Rights Centre, in which the organization alleged abuses by government security forces during the November 2017 by-elections. The regulator argued the content was "seditious" and contrary to the Broadcasting Act.

On August 8, police arrested Sitta Tumma, a journalist with Tanzania Daima newspaper, as he reported on police dispersing an opposition rally in Tarime. He was detained overnight but not charged. At a separate event on the same day in Dar es Salaam, anti-riot police beat Silas Mbise, a radio sports reporter, caught on video, as he lay on the ground with his hands in the air.

In September, parliament adopted an amendment to the 2015 Statistics Act making it a crime to publish statistics without the approval of the National Bureau of Statistics (NBS) and prohibiting dissemination of statistics that are meant to "invalidate, distort or discredit" NBS' statistics. The implementation of this law could curtail legitimate independent research across a broad range of sectors.

Opposition party members have faced multiple arrests and criminal charges for criticizing the government. Joseph Mbilinyi, a parliamentarian in Mbeya, and Emmanuel Masonga, a party official, were sentenced to five months' imprisonment in February for "insulting" Magufuli during a political rally.

On June 21, the East African Court of Justice held that Tanzania must annul the ban on a weekly newspaper, Mseto, in 2016 by then-Minister of Information, Youth, Culture and Sports Nape Nnauye, for reporting corruption allegations in Magufuli's presidential campaign.

Freedom of Assembly

On March 9, Magufuli promised a crackdown on demonstrations the government deems illegal. Prior to nationwide anti-government protests called for April 26 by United States-based Tanzanian activist Mange Kimambi, Dodoma Regional Police Commander Gilles Muroto told journalists that protesters would "seriously suffer" and would be "beaten like stray dogs." The demonstrations did not occur.

Political rallies resulted in the arrest of many opposition members. In March, police arrested and charged CHADEMA parliamentarians Freeman Mbowe, Vincent Mashinji, John Mnyika, Peter Msigwa, Esther Matiko, Salum Mwalimu, and later Halima Mdee, with participating in an illegal demonstration in Dar es Salaam. CHADEMA chairperson, Mbowe, was accused of "inciting hatred and rebellion" reportedly for saying during a public speech that Magufuli would not last long as president.

Disappearances and Politically Motivated Attacks

Within a fortnight, unknown assailants brutally killed two CHADEMA officials, in attacks that appeared to be politically motivated. On February 13, the body of Daniel John, an official for Hananasif ward Kinondoni in Dar es Salaam, was discovered along the coast with machete wounds to the head. On February 23, Godfrey Luena, a councilor for Nemawala ward in Morogoro, was found dead outside his home. Luena also worked as a human rights monitor, documenting illegal land appropriation. While police have said that investigations into the deaths are ongoing, there have been no arrests.

In June, police said that there would be no further investigations into the killing of 21-year-old Akwilina Awkilini, who was shot on a bus in February as police attempted to disperse a CHADEMA demonstration.

Police have made no arrests in two 2017 killings that drew significant outcry. In September 2017, unknown assailants shot opposition parliamentarian Tundu Lissu, a prominent critic of Magufuli's government, outside his home in the capital Dodoma. Mwananchi journalist Azory Gwanda has been missing, and presumed dead, since November 2017. Gwanda is reported to have been working on a story about a spate of killings in Kibiti, south of Dar es Salaam.

Refugees

On January 23, the government announced its withdrawal from the Comprehensive Refugee Response Framework (CRRF) for reasons of "security and lack of funds," ending an ongoing exercise to integrate refugees into host communities.

The government also stated that it would discourage new asylum applications. Between September 2017 and end July 2018, authorities and the United Nations High Commissioner for Refugees (UNHCR) facilitated the return of just over 40,000 Burundian refugees to their country, setting a returns target in March of 2,000 a week. However, since late 2017, UNHCR has expressed concern about numerous factors making refugees' lives difficult and in August pressed the Tanzanian authorities to ensure that refugees were not pressured to return home.

Children's Rights

Girls in Tanzania continue to face discrimination in education following Magufuli's 2017 ban on pregnant girls and young mothers in schools. Many secondary school officials routinely subject girls to forced pregnancy testing as a disciplinary measure to expel pregnant students from schools.

Corporal punishment remains a serious problem in Tanzanian schools. In August, a 13-year-old schoolboy died after being beaten severely by his teacher.

Women's Rights

In September, the government announced that it was suspending United States Agency for International Development-supported birth control-related messaging. Magufuli has argued women should give up contraception, that family planning information is unnecessary and that people should work harder to provide for their families.

Thousands of Tanzanian women working as domestic workers in the Middle East face pervasive labor rights violations and other abuses. Tanzania has no legal framework to protect migrant workers from being recruited into abusive employment situations overseas, facilitating the abuse of workers.

Sexual Orientation and Gender Identity

Tanzanian law makes consensual adult same-sex conduct punishable by up to life in prison. The crackdown on lesbian, gay, bisexual, and transgender (LGBT) people initiated by Magufuli's government in July 2016 continues unabated. On October 31, Dar es Salaam Regional Commissioner Paul Makonda announced plans to round-up suspected gays and subject them to forced anal examinations and conversion therapy. Four days later, the Ministry of Foreign Affairs said in a statement that the campaign by Makonda represented "his opinion and not the position of the government" and pledged to "continue to respect and protect" internationally recognized human rights.

Key International Actors

Tanzania continues to play a critical role in the United Nations peacekeeping mission in the Democratic Republic of Congo and hosts the East African Court of Justice and the African Court of Human and Peoples' Rights in Arusha.

The European Union, Germany, the United Kingdom, and the Netherlands, Tanzania's international partners, remain muted in their criticism of the ongoing threats to free expression and assembly and the implementation of increasingly repressive laws.

The US Embassy in Dar es Salaam raised concerns about politically related violence, irregularities in the conduct of by-elections, and the "deterioration of civil liberties and human rights," following the arrests and harassment of lesbian, gay, and transgender people.

In October, the World Bank criticized amendments to the 2015 Statistics Act, for being out of line with international standards.

In November, Denmark announced that it was withholding $US10 million of funding to Tanzania because of "unacceptable homophobic comments" by a government official, believed to be Makonda.

Thailand

The National Council for Peace and Order (NCPO) military junta delayed lifting severe restrictions on free expression, association, and assembly, despite announcing a national election in February 2019. There are serious concerns that political parties, media, and voters will not be given the opportunity to participate in a genuinely democratic process. Prime Minister Gen. Prayuth Chan-ocha still wields power unhindered by administrative, legislative, or judicial oversight or accountability, including for serious human rights violations.

Freedom of Expression

Acting on the junta's orders, authorities have routinely enforced censorship, and threatened media outlets with punishment and closure if they publicize information critical of military rule and the monarchy or raised issues considered to be sensitive to national security. Peace TV was temporarily shut down in February and May 2018 for failing to comply with such regulations. Voice TV's outspoken news talk programs "Tonight Thailand" and "Wake Up News" were forced off the air for 15 days in March and for 30 days in September.

Thai authorities often disrupted academic seminars and public discussions about the state of human rights and democracy in Thailand. In August, prominent academic Chayan Vaddhanaphuti and four other participants from the International Conference on Thai Studies, held on July 2017 in Chiang Mai province, were brought to court and charged with violating the NCPO's ban on public assembly by more than five persons and for displaying symbolic opposition to the NCPO by making *The Hunger Games* three-finger salute and holding banners criticizing the military's heavy-handed surveillance of the conference.

In December 2018, Thai authorities blocked access to the Human Rights Watch Thailand web page, saying that the contents were inappropriate and constituted a threat to public order and national security.

Authorities in Pathum Thani province forced the cancellation of a seminar organized by the Rohingya Peace Network of Thailand to mark the one-year anniversary of violence in Myanmar's Rakhine State on August 25, claiming the event would undermine relations between Thailand and Myanmar. On September 10,

HUMAN
RIGHTS
WATCH
|

HIDDEN CHAINS
Rights Abuses and Forced Labor in Thailand's Fishing Industry

the NCPO forced the closure of a panel event, "Will Myanmar's Generals Ever Face Justice for International Crimes?" at the Foreign Correspondents' Club of Thailand (FCCT) on the same grounds.

In 2018, at least 130 pro-democracy activists in Bangkok and other provinces faced illegal assembly charges—and in some cases, sedition—for peacefully demanding the junta's promised election to be held without further delay and that all restrictions on fundamental freedoms be immediately lifted.

In October, army chief, Gen. Apirat Kongsompong, announced that a coup remained an option for the military to quell political upheavals.

The junta continued to prosecute its critics under the sedition law and the Computer-Related Crime Act (CCA). Since the 2014 coup, at least 92 people have been charged with sedition. In February, authorities charged an outspoken politician, Watana Muangsook, with sedition and for violating the CCA for his Facebook posts in support of pro-democracy activists' demands for a free and fair election.

The CCA provides overly broad grounds for authorities to prosecute anyone for their internet postings critical of government agencies and officials. In June, authorities issued an arrest warrant against London-based Watana Ebbage for posting information on her Facebook page—KonthaiUK—alleging corruption in military procurement programs. At least 29 people in Thailand were arrested for sharing Watana's posts. In September, authorities arrested 12 Facebook users for sharing information about an alleged rape of a British tourist on Koh Tao island. Arrest warrants were also issued against Suzanne Emery, the British publisher of the online newspaper *Samui Times*, and Pramuk Anantasin, the Thai-American administrator of the CSI LA Facebook page, for reporting the story and criticizing the quality of police work in this case.

In 2018, the NCPO continued to summon members of the opposition Pheu Thai Party and the United Front for Democracy against Dictatorship (UDD, also known as the "Red Shirts"), as well as anyone accused of opposing military rule, for "attitude adjustment" sessions to compel them to stop expressing political opinions against the junta. Failure to report when summoned is a criminal offense.

Authorities have arrested more than 100 people on *lese majeste* (insulting the monarchy) charges since the 2014 coup, mostly for posting or sharing critical commentary online. Some have been convicted and sentenced to decades of imprisonment.

Military Detention and Military Courts

Under NCPO Orders 3/2015 and 13/2016, military authorities can secretly detain people for a wide range of offenses and hold them for up to seven days without charge, access to lawyers, or any safeguards against mistreatment. The government also regularly uses military detention under the 1914 Martial Law Act and the 2005 Emergency Decree on Public Administration in State of Emergency—in which abuses during interrogation occur with impunity—during operations against suspected separatist insurgents in the southern border provinces of Pattani, Yala, and Naradhiwat.

The NCPO rejected calls to disclose information about persons held in military detention and summarily dismissed all allegations that soldiers tortured or otherwise mistreated detainees.

The junta has failed to transfer 369 criminal cases, involving more than 1,800 civilians, from military courts to civilian courts as international law requires.

Enforced Disappearances and Torture

Thailand signed the International Convention for the Protection of All Persons from Enforced Disappearance in January 2012 but has yet to ratify the treaty. The penal code does not recognize enforced disappearance as a criminal offense. After the junta-appointed National Legislative Assembly suddenly suspended its consideration of the Prevention and Suppression of Torture and Enforced Disappearance Bill in February 2017, the government has not provided a clear timeframe when the bill will be reintroduced.

The Department of Special Investigations has made little progress in investigating enforced disappearance cases, including the two high-profile cases of Muslim lawyer Somchai Neelapaijit and ethnic Karen activist Porlajee "Billy" Rakchongcharoen. Meanwhile, the government-appointed Committee to Receive Complaints and Investigate Allegations of Torture and Enforced Disappearance has little authority or political will to take serious action.

Thailand does not have a law that criminalizes torture as required by the UN Convention against Torture, which it ratified in 2007. In 2018, authorities regularly failed to conduct serious and credible inquiries into torture allegations. When accused of using torture, government agencies often retaliated against accusers with libel and computer crime lawsuits for allegedly damaging their reputation and making false statements. In February 2018, the Internal Security Operations Command (ISOC) filed criminal and civil defamation complaints against Ismae Teh for making allegations on Thai PBS TV that he was tortured in military custody in Pattani province in 2008. The military also filed a criminal defamation complaint and sought 10 million Thai baht (US$286,000) in damages from MGR Online news for its reports about torture allegations related to Ismae and other ethnic Malay Muslims in Thailand's southern border provinces.

Lack of Accountability for Politically Motivated Violence

Despite evidence showing that soldiers were responsible for most casualties during the 2010 political confrontations with the UDD, or "Red Shirts," that left at least 90 dead and more than 2,000 injured, no military personnel or officials from the government of former Prime Minister Abhisit Vejjajiva have been charged for killing and wounding civilians at the time. At the same time, numerous UDD leaders and supporters have been prosecuted on criminal charges related to the "Red Shirt" street protests in 2010.

Human Rights Defenders

Government pledges to develop measures to protect human rights defenders remained unfulfilled in 2018. The killings of more than 30 human rights defenders and civil society activists since 2001 remained unresolved. Military cover-up and shoddy police work hampered the efforts to prosecute soldiers who shot dead teenage ethnic Lahu activist Chaiyaphum Pasae in March 2017 in Chiang Mai province.

Authorities and private companies used civil and criminal defamation lawsuits to retaliate against individuals reporting human rights abuses. In March 2018, Bangkok's Prakanong Court ordered labor rights activist Andy Hall to pay 10 million Thai baht (US$313,000) in damages, plus legal and court fees to Natural Fruit Co., Ltd. regarding an interview he gave to Al Jazeera English in April 2013 alleging abuses of Burmese workers in the company's pineapple processing factory. The company continued to press for imprisonment of Hall for criminal defamation and computer crimes related to FinnWatch's 2013 "Cheap Has a High Price" report.

Authorities are continuing the criminal cases against Sirikan Charoensiri of the Thai Lawyers for Human Rights, who was accused of sedition and other serious offenses for her professional activities representing 14 student activists arrested in June 2015 after staging peaceful protests in Bangkok.

In May, six United Nations human rights experts called on Thailand—where defamation laws have frequently been used to retaliate against whistle blowers who report labor abuses—to revise its laws and prosecution processes to prevent the "misuse of defamation legislation by companies."

In an annual report released in September, the UN secretary-general named Thailand on a list of 38 states where individuals faced intimidation or reprisals for cooperating with the UN on human rights.

After the revised law on the National Human Rights Commission of Thailand was enacted in August 2017, the agency has been seriously weakened. The government has required that the commission issue rebuttals to reports by international human rights groups and foreign governments about Thailand's human rights problems.

Violence and Abuses in Southern Border Provinces

Since January 2004, Barisan Revolusi Nasional (BRN) insurgents have committed numerous laws-of-war violations. More than 90 percent of the 6,800 people killed in the ongoing armed conflict in Thailand's southern border provinces have been civilians, including children, from both ethnic Malay Muslim and ethnic Thai Buddhist communities.

In June and July, at least five ethnic Thai Buddhists were seriously wounded from landmines that BRN insurgents laid in rubber plantations in Yala province.

The government has failed to prosecute members of its security forces responsible for torture and unlawful killings of ethnic Malay Muslims. In many cases, authorities provided financial compensation to the victims or their families in exchange for their agreement not to speak out or file criminal cases against officials.

Refugees, Asylum Seekers, and Migrant Workers

Thailand is not a party to the 1951 Refugee Convention and its 1967 protocol. Thai authorities continued to treat asylum seekers, including those recognized by the UN as refugees, as illegal migrants subject to arrest and deportation. The January 2017 cabinet resolution to set up a national screening mechanism for asylum seekers still has not been implemented.

Starting in August, the government has launched a nationwide crackdown on illegal migrants and arrested more than 200 refugees and asylum seekers from Vietnam, Cambodia, and Pakistan. They have since been detained in squalid immigration lockups. More than 50 children have been separated from their parents.

The government refused to let the UN refugee agency conduct refugee status determinations for Rohingya asylum seekers and holds at least 105 in indefinite immigration detention. Over 60 ethnic Uighurs reportedly from China remained in indefinite immigration detention at time of writing after they were arrested in March 2014.

Migrant workers from Myanmar, Cambodia, Laos, and Vietnam are vulnerable to physical abuses, indefinite detention, and extortion by Thai authorities; severe labor rights abuses and exploitation by employers; and violence and human trafficking by criminals who sometimes collaborate with corrupt officials. The situation worsened as many missed the registration deadline under the Decree Concerning the Management of Foreign Workers' Employment in June. Migrant workers remained fearful of reporting abuses to authorities due to fears of retaliation. Under the Labor Relations Act, migrant workers are legally barred from organizing or leading trade unions.

In July, a magistrates court in Bangkok acquitted 14 Burmese migrant workers of criminal defamation charges for filing a complaint against their employer—Thammakaset Company Limited, a chicken farm in Lopburi province—with the National Human Rights Commission of Thailand, ruling that the workers took action in good faith in order to protect their rights as guaranteed by the Thai constitution and international conventions. However, the company still pursues retaliatory prosecution of the workers and human rights activists involved in this case with defamation charges.

Government reforms in the fishing industry fell fall far short of resolving serious labor rights abuses. Many migrant workers still face forced labor in the fishing industry, in conditions of debt bondage to recruiters, unable to change employers, not paid on time, and paid well below the minimum wage.

The influential National Fisheries Association of Thailand (NFAT) campaigned against ratification and implementation of the International Labour Organization (ILO) Work in Fishing Convention (No. 188), which would ensure vulnerable fishing workers are sufficiently protected. The NFAT's opposition to a standalone law to criminalize forced labor also stalled Thailand's progress to meet its commitments after ratifying in June the Protocol of 2014 to the Forced Labor Convention.

The United States State Department ranked Thailand in Tier 2 (of three tiers) in its annual Trafficking in Persons Report. The European Commission raised concerns about human trafficking and forced labor on Thai fishing boats and put Thailand on formal notice for possible trade sanctions connected to illegal, unreported, and unregulated fishing.

Gender Equality

While Thailand enacted the Gender Equality Act in 2015, implementation remains problematic. For example, the government's pledges to the UN Committee on the Elimination of Discrimination against Women (CEDAW) about its commitment to improve gender equality were undermined by the decision in September to end the enrollment of women in the Police Cadet Academy.

Anti-Narcotics Policy

The government failed to pursue criminal investigations of extrajudicial killings related to anti-drug operations, especially the more than 2,800 killings that accompanied then-Prime Minister Thaksin Shinawatra's "war on drugs" in 2003.

The Interior Ministry and military continued to operate boot camp-style forced rehabilitation of drug users.

Key International Actors

The UN and Thailand's major allies continued to express concerns regarding violations of fundamental rights and freedoms since the 2014 coup. The United States, European Union, and other countries maintained that relations will only be fully restored after the junta returns the country to democratic civilian rule through free and fair elections.

In December 2017, all 28 EU foreign ministers decided to resume political contacts at all levels with Thailand and expressed its readiness to strengthen relations and cooperation once a democratically elected civilian government is in place.

The EU decried Thailand carrying out its first execution in nearly 10 years, in June, and urged the Thai government to refrain from any future executions and to work towards a moratorium and the eventual abolition of the death penalty.

Tunisia

Tunisia stalled during 2018 on reforming repressive laws and establishing key institutions to protect human rights. Although freedom of expression was generally respected, with a variety of independent media able to operate freely, Tunisian authorities continued to prosecute speech considered offensive to "public morals" or "public decency." The state of emergency, which was declared in November 2015 following a deadly attack on the presidential guard, was last extended in October 2018 for a period of one month. Authorities used the state of emergency to impose house arrest on hundreds of people accused of threatening state security.

On May 6, Tunisia held its first municipal elections since a popular uprising ousted authoritarian president Zine el-Abidine Ben Ali in 2011. Independent lists came first nationwide, followed by lists from Ennahdha, the main Islamist party.

On June 12, a commission on Individual Freedoms and Equality, appointed by President Beji Caid Essebsi, delivered its report recommending decriminalizing sodomy, ensuring equality between men and women in inheritance, eliminating "morality" laws, and abolishing the death penalty. The president publicly endorsed the recommendation for legal equality in inheritance but has so far remained silent on the other recommendations.

Implementation of the Constitution

Because parliament had failed to elect its allotted quota of Constitutional Court members, the body could not begin to perform its function, affirmed in the constitution, of scrutinizing and invalidating existing laws that do not conform with human rights standards. Several other constitutional authorities, such as the Human Rights Commission and Commission on Corruption and Good Governance, have yet to be established.

Authorities made progress in harmonizing legislation with the constitution. In 2016, parliament revised the Code of Criminal Procedure to grant suspects the right to a lawyer from the onset of detention, and shortened the maximum duration of pre-charge detention to 48 hours, renewable once, for all crimes except for terrorism cases, where pre-charge detention can last up to 15 days. Defense lawyers welcomed the new law for making it easier for them to visit their detained clients and monitor their treatment. Nevertheless, spotty implementation meant that lawyers did not always get prompt access, and detainees still suffered from violations of their due-process rights while in pre-charge custody.

Freedom of Expression, Association, and Assembly

Tunisian authorities continued to prosecute civilians in military courts based on articles in the code of military justice prohibiting the defamation of the army. A military court sentenced parliamentary deputy, Yassine Ayari, to three months in prison on June 26, 2018, for a Facebook post criticizing the army. He was also sentenced on March 27 to 16 days in prison for another blog post. On November 1, the military appeals court increased his sentence in this last case to three months in prison. The decision was not enforced and Ayari had not been imprisoned at time of writing.

Tunisian authorities continued to use articles in the penal code and other laws that criminalize freedom of speech, despite adopting, in November 2011, Decree Law 115 on freedom of the press that liberalizes the legal framework applicable to written media. On September 13, 2018, a first instance court in Ben Arous gave Amina Mansour, a blogger, a suspended two-month prison sentence for a Facebook post in which she declared the head of government's "war on corruption" to be "fake." She was sentenced on the basis of article 86 of the Telecommunications Code, which criminalizes the offense of "harming others or disturbing their well-being through the internet," and article 128 of the penal code, which penalizes defaming public servants.

In trying to quell the social protests that gripped much of Tunisia during January 2018, police beat those arrested and denied their right to a lawyer under Tunisian law. They also arrested and held for up to two days some people for blogposts or for distributing leaflets that peacefully criticized government policy and called for social justice. The United Nations special rapporteur on the rights to peaceful assembly and association expressed concern about reports of arbitrary arrests and disproportionate use of force during the protests.

Parliament adopted, on July 27, a new law creating a National Registry of Organizations that encroaches on Decree Law 88, adopted in 2011, which liberalized the legal framework governing associations. Under the new law, an association

الشرطة
POLICE

HUMAN
RIGHTS
WATCH

"YOU SAY YOU WANT A LAWYER?"
Tunisia's New Law on Detention, on Paper and in Practice

is required to file a "registration receipt," a document the government is required to deliver to the association once it submits its bylaws and constitutive documents.

Unlike Decree law 88, which provides that the registration receipt is presumed received if the government does not respond within 30 days, the new law does not provide for automatic registration when authorities withhold it, thus making legal recognition dependent on the administration's good will. In a December 2017 report, the International Financial Action Task Force (FATF) listed Tunisia as among the countries deficient in combating money laundering and terrorism financing. It recommended enhancing transparency of the non-profit sector. The law creating a national registry is seen in part as addressing the FATF's recommendations.

Transitional Justice

Tunisia adopted legislation in 2013 to deal with the crimes of the past, which included the creation of a Truth and Dignity Commission. The commission was mandated to investigate all serious human rights violations from 1955 to 2013 and is designed to provide accountability for torture, forced disappearances, and other abuses of the past. It has received more than 62,000 complaints and held confidential hearings for more than 50,000 of these.

Parliament undermined the process of transitional justice by voting not to allow the Truth and Dignity Commission to exercise its prerogative to extend its mandate by one year.

The Transitional Justice Law mandates the commission to transfer serious crimes to specialized chambers to be established within the country's court system that "will have jurisdiction over widespread or systematic human rights violations, including deliberate killing, rape and sexual violence, torture, enforced disappearance, and execution without fair trial guarantees."

On May 29, the first trial of past violations in a specialized chamber opened in the city of Gabes. The trial related to the forced disappearance of Kamel Matmati, an Islamist activist whom the police arrested in 1991.

The commission transferred to the specialized courts 16 other cases of human rights violations, including cases of torture, enforced disappearances, and arbitrary detentions. As of November, no verdicts had been reached.

Security and State of Emergency

The state of emergency President Essebsi declared after a 2015 suicide attack on a bus that killed 12 presidential guards remained in effect at time of writing. It is based on a 1978 decree that empowers authorities to ban strikes or demonstrations deemed to threaten public order, and to prohibit gatherings "likely to provoke or sustain disorder." Under the decree, authorities have placed hundreds of Tunisians under house arrest. Conditions of the house arrests were eased in 2018, but many who remained under house arrest were also placed under a travel ban procedure called "S17," which applied to anyone the state suspects of intending to join a fighting group abroad. The procedure allows restrictions on movement both abroad and inside Tunisia. A person placed under the S17 procedure risks lengthy questioning whenever they are stopped at a routine police check. The procedure is based on vague language in the law regulating the work of the Ministry of Interior.

Women's Rights

A Commission on Individual Freedoms and Equality, appointed by President Essebsi in 2017, issued its final report on June 12, 2018. The commission recommended, among other things, equality between men and women in inheritance.

On August 13, the president endorsed this recommendation, pledging to introduce a bill to amend the personal status code that would eliminate discrimination against women on inheritance except when a person opts out of the equality rule by formally expressing such a wish in his will. On November 28, a draft law on equality in inheritance was submitted to parliament.

Gender Identity and Sexual Orientation

Despite accepting a recommendation during its Universal Periodic Review at the UN Human Rights Council in May 2017 to end the discredited police practice of administering anal testing to "prove" homosexuality, the government has not yet taken any steps to carry out this pledge. Authorities have continued to prosecute and imprison presumed gay men under article 230 of the penal code, which provides up to three years in prison for "sodomy."

Key International Actors

In February, the European Parliament failed to override the classification of Tunisia as a high-risk country for money-laundering and terror funding by the European Commission. The actions of the European Union bodies followed the critical reports on Tunisia by the Financial Action Task Force (FATF).

The UN special rapporteur on freedom of religion or belief conducted a visit to Tunisia in April 2018. He noted that there are few explicit restrictions on freedom of religion or belief, but that some groups—such as Tunisia's small Bahai community—face indirect restrictions, especially through failure to obtain registration as associations that would grant them the legal status they need to carry out several institutional functions or display their faith publicly.

Turkey

Parliamentary and presidential elections in Turkey in June 2018 saw President Recep Tayyip Erdoğan re-elected president and the ruling Justice and Development Party (AKP) retain control of parliament through a coalition.

The June 2018 election campaign took place under a state of emergency imposed after the July 2016 attempted military coup and in a climate of media censorship and repression of perceived government enemies and critics that persisted throughout the year, with many journalists as well as parliamentarians and the presidential candidate from the pro-Kurdish opposition in jail.

The election brought into force the presidential system of governance agreed in a 2017 referendum. The system lacks sufficient checks and balances against abuse of executive power, greatly diminishes the powers of parliament and consolidates presidential control over most judicial appointments.

In January 2018, Turkey launched a military offensive on the northwest Syrian Kurdish-populated district of Afrin and at time of writing continued to control the territory (see Syria chapter for further information).

State of Emergency and After

The two-year state of emergency formally lapsed in July but was replaced with new counterterrorism legislation, approved by parliament in August. The legislation contains many measures similar to the extraordinary powers the authorities enjoyed under emergency rule. They include widening already broad powers of appointed provincial governors to restrict assemblies and movement; executive authority for three years to dismiss public officials, including judges, by administrative decision; and increased police powers including custody periods extendable for up to 12 days.

The commission reviewing the dismissal of more than 130,000 public officials over alleged association with terrorist groups continued its work. Most are alleged to be associated with the Fethullah Gülen religious movement that the government and courts accuse of masterminding the coup attempt and deem a terrorist organization (FETÖ).

At time of writing, the commission, established in 2017 following Council of Europe advice, had issued decisions in 36,000 cases, with 2,300 reinstated in their jobs or similar measures of redress, and at least another 88,660 appeals to review.

Terrorism charges continued to be widely used. As of June, almost one-fifth (48,924) of the total prison population (246,426) had been charged with or convicted of terrorism offences, according to the Ministry of Justice. Those prosecuted and convicted included journalists, civil servants, teachers, and politicians, as well as police officers and military personnel.

Of the 48,924, 34,241 were held for alleged Gulenist (FETÖ) links, and 10,286 for alleged links to the outlawed Kurdistan Workers' Party (PKK), and 1,270 for alleged links to the extremist Islamic State (ISIS) group.

Many terrorism trials in Turkey lack compelling evidence of criminal activity or acts that would reasonably be deemed terrorism, and the practice of holding individuals charged with terrorism offenses in prolonged pretrial detention raised concerns its use has become a form of summary punishment.

Trials continued of military personnel and others for involvement in the July 2016 attempted coup in which 250 people died. As of June, 2,177 defendants were convicted and 1,552 acquitted at first instance, according to the Ministry of Justice. There were no finalized verdicts at time of writing.

Freedom of Expression, Association, and Assembly

Turkey remained the world leader in jailing journalists. An estimated 175 journalists and media workers are in pretrial detention or serving sentences for terrorism offenses at time of writing. Hundreds more are on trial but at liberty.

Most media lack independence and promote the government's political line.

During the year courts issued verdicts in several major politically motivated trials of journalists, based on evidence consisting of writing and reporting which does not advocate violence alongside unsupported allegations of connections with terrorist organizations or the coup attempt. Most cases are now at appeal.

In February, writers and commentators Ahmet Altan, Mehmet Altan, and Nazlı Ilıcak were sentenced to life imprisonment without parole on trumped up coup charges. A court bailed Mehmet Altan in June, after a January Constitutional Court ruling and a March European Court of Human Rights ruling ordering his release. Ahmet Altan and Nazli Ilicak remain jailed. After the regional appeal court upheld the convictions on October 2, all defendants appealed to the Court of Cassation.

The trial of staff from *Cumhuriyet* newspaper, including journalists, executives, and the editor, ended in April. Fourteen were convicted on trumped up terrorism charges, and given sentences ranging from two to eight years, and three acquitted.

In a separate case, the Court of Cassation in September upheld a prison sentence against serving Republican People's Party (CHP) parliamentarian Enis Berberoğlu for providing video footage that *Cumhuriyet* published showing weapons Turkey allegedly supplied to Syrian opposition groups, but also ordered his release after 16 months in pretrial detention.

Verdicts in trials on terrorism charges of 31 journalists and media workers from the shuttered *Zaman* newspaper concluded in July with writers Ahmet Turan Alkan, Şahin Alpay, and Ali Bulaç who spent up to two years in pretrial detention but were at liberty at time of writing, receiving eight-year-nine-month sentences and Mustafa Ünal and Mümtazer Türköne, who remain jailed, receiving 10-year-6-month sentences.

Journalists working for Kurdish media in Turkey continued to be arrested and jailed repeatedly, obstructing critical reporting from the southeast of the country.

After a police raid in March on the pro-Kurdish newspaper *Free Democracy* (*Özgürlükçü Demokrasi*), its journalists and other workers were detained and its printing works and assets turned over to the state. The newspaper was closed by decree in July, and 21 printworkers and 14 journalists are being prosecuted in separate trials. A total of 13 printworkers and journalists were being held in pretrial detention at time of writing.

The blocking of websites and removal of online content continued, and thousands of people in Turkey faced criminal investigations and prosecutions for their social media posts. Wikipedia remained blocked in Turkey.

In 2018 there was an increase in arbitrary bans on public assemblies, particularly evident after the end of emergency rule when governors assumed greater powers to restrict assemblies.

Police detained students from leading universities for peaceful protests on campus against Turkey's offensive on Afrin and for holding up banners critical of the president. At least 18 students were held in pretrial detention for such protests and many more prosecuted for crimes such as "spreading terrorist propaganda" and "insulting the president."

In August, the Interior Minister banned the long-running peaceful weekly vigil at a central location in Istanbul by the Saturday Mothers, relatives of victims of enforced disappearances seeking accountability. Police violently dispersed and briefly detained 27 of the organizers. The ban on holding the vigil at the traditional location remained in effect at this writing. A Saturday Mothers' vigil in Diyarbakir was also banned, as were all public assemblies organized by the Diyarbakir branch of the Human Rights Association from September onwards.

On September 15, police detained hundreds of construction workers who protested poor work and living conditions on the building site of the third airport in Istanbul. Courts ordered 37, including trade union officials, into pretrial detention, with six later released. Many more are under criminal investigation accused of offenses such as staging an unauthorized protest and resisting dispersal.

Human Rights Defenders

After more than 13 months behind bars, in August an Izmir court released Amnesty International Turkey's honorary chair Taner Kılıç from prison. He remains on trial on bogus terrorism membership charges, together with eight other prominent defenders from Turkey and two foreign nationals working on human rights arrested in July 2017 and later bailed.

Osman Kavala, a businessman and well-known figure in civil society in Turkey, has been held in pretrial detention since November 2017. At time of writing Kavala had not been indicted for any crime but the prosecutor's investigation widened in November 2018 with the detention of 13 individuals, including some connected with the nongovernmental organization Kavala runs, and a focus on their activities after the 2013 Gezi Park mass protests in Istanbul. Twelve were promptly released but at time of writing human rights defender Yiğit Aksakaloğlu was jailed pending trial.

A related media smear campaign, and public comments by Turkey's president, also targeted US-based philanthropist George Soros. Soros's Open Society Foundation announced in November that it would dissolve its Turkish foundation and cease operations in the country.

Human rights lawyers are among over 1,500 lawyers on trial on terrorism charges at time of writing. Their cases underscore the dramatic erosion of defendants' rights and due process in Turkey. In September, an Istanbul court released on bail 17 lawyers who had spent up to a year in pretrial detention for membership of an armed leftist group, but reversed its own decision a day later, ordering the rearrest of 12 of them. At time of writing their case was ongoing.

A November 2017 ban on public events by lesbian, gay, bisexual, and transgender (LGBT) rights groups by the Ankara governor was enforced throughout 2018, and inspired bans of assemblies and events in other cities and revealed Turkey's increasingly repressive approach to LGBT groups. In July, the Istanbul governor banned the city's annual Pride march for a fourth year, citing security and public order concerns.

Torture and Ill-Treatment in Custody, Abductions

Continued allegations of torture, ill-treatment, and cruel and inhuman or degrading treatment in police custody and prison and the lack of any meaningful investigation into them remained a deep concern. These issues were raised by the UN special rapporteur on torture in a February statement.

There have been no effective investigations into the 2017 abductions allegedly by state agents of at least six men who were held in undisclosed places of detention before their release months later in circumstances that amount to possible enforced disappearance.

The Turkish authorities continued to seek the extradition of alleged Gülen supporters, many of them teachers, from countries around the world. Without adhering to legal due process, security services in countries including Kosovo and Moldova cooperated with Turkish agents during the year to apprehend and transfer Turkish citizens to Turkey where they were detained and prosecuted.

Kurdish Conflict and Crackdown on Opposition

Armed clashes between the military and the armed Kurdistan Workers' Party (PKK) in the southeast continued through 2018, mainly in rural areas. The government continued its repressive measures against elected parliamentarians, mayors and municipalities from pro-Kurdish parties, although the Peoples' Democratic Party (HDP) secured 67 parliamentary seats (11.9 percent of the vote) in the June election.

Serving HDP deputy Leyla Güven and nine former HDP parliamentarians remained in prolonged pretrial detention on politically motivated terrorism charges, including former party co-leader and presidential candidate Selahattin Demirtaş. Eleven deputies were stripped of their parliamentary seats in the period before the June election and were barred from standing again as candidates.

In the southeast, the suspension of local democracy continued as the government maintained control of 94 municipalities won in the 2014 local elections by the HDP's sister party, the Democratic Regions Party (DBP). At time of writing, 50 co-mayors remained jailed on politically motivated terrorism charges after their removal from elected office and the assignment of government appointees to their positions.

Refugees and Migrants

Turkey continued to host the world's largest number of refugees, around 3.5 million from Syria. Turkey also hosts asylum seekers from Afghanistan, Iraq, and other countries. A migration deal with the EU that offers aid in exchange for preventing onward migration to the EU continued. The border with Syria is effectively closed to new asylum seekers. Border guards intercepted and deported thousands of newly arrived Syrians during the year and sometimes shot at those trying to cross. Since November 2017, 10 provinces have suspended registration of Syrians who manage to get passed the border guards and reach Turkey's cities. There remained high rates of child labor and large numbers of child refugees and asylum seekers not attending school. In September, Turkey assumed full responsibility for deciding refugee claims. But authorities do not grant refugee status and third-country resettlement is available only to a fraction of those determined to be refugees.

Following extensive international coverage of gross human rights violations of Uyghurs and other Turkic Muslims in China, in October Turkey admitted 11 Uyghurs who had fled repression after Malaysia declined to return them to China and released them from custody.

Key International Actors

EU-Turkey relations remained poor and accession negotiations stalled. The EU External Action Service spoke out on some rights issues, including detention of human rights defenders, journalists, parliamentarians and academics, but continuing the migration deal remained the EU's paramount objective.

The United States government in October secured the release of US pastor Andrew Brunson detained for over two years on terrorism charges but did not speak out forcefully about the wider misuse of terrorism laws against Ankara's perceived enemies and critics. Relations were also marked by tensions over the US conviction of a Turkish banker for US sanctions violations, the application between August and November of sanctions against Turkey's interior and justice ministers over the detention of Brunson, the presence on US soil of Turkish cleric Fethullah Gülen, and US support for PKK- associated Kurdish forces in northern Syria.

President Erdoğan's September state visit to Germany was intended to re-establish links between the countries after deep tensions over the arbitrary detention in 2017 of German nationals, including journalist Deniz Yücel who was released in February. Germany's chancellor and president both made clear reference to the arbitrary detention of Turkey's own citizens as well as German nationals.

During Erdoğan's January visit to Paris, France's President Emmanuel Macron spoke out on human rights in Turkey and asserted that there was no prospect of Turkey joining the EU at present.

In March, the Office of the UN High Commissioner for Human Rights published a report on violations under the state of emergency, describing the detention of an estimated 600 women and their babies or young children in connection with their husbands' alleged association with terrorist organizations as an "alarming pattern."

In November, the European Court of Human Rights ruled that Turkey's repeated prolonging of the pre-trial detention of opposition politician Selahattin Demirtaş violated his rights and had the "ulterior purpose of stifling pluralism and limiting freedom of political debate, which is at the very core of the concept of a democratic society." The court ordered his release.

Turkmenistan

Turkmenistan is one of the world's most isolated and oppressively governed countries. All aspects of public life are controlled by President Gurbanguly Berdymukhamedov and his associates.

In 2018, Turkmenistan faced a severe economic crisis that experts believe was caused in part by state mismanagement of hydrocarbon revenues. Yet authorities blocked people from regions most affected by the crisis from traveling so they could seek work elsewhere.

All forms of religious and political expression not approved by the government are brutally punished. Access to information is strictly controlled, and no independent monitoring groups are allowed. Dozens of victims of enforced disappearance allegedly are in Turkmen prisons.

Parliamentary Elections

The Organization for Security and Co-operation in Europe (OSCE) concluded that the March 2018 parliamentary elections "lacked important prerequisites of a genuinely democratic election process." The election campaign was barely visible. All candidates aligned themselves with Berdymykhamedov's policies.

Freedom of Media and Information

Turkmenistan continued to exercise tight control over all print and electronic media. Foreign media outlets have almost no access to the country, and the government often retaliates against people who provide them information.

Internet access is very limited and controlled by the state. In February, Berdymukhamedov met a vice president of a German technology firm, from which Turkmenistan had been allegedly seeking technology that could enable the government to monitor and block mobile and satellite communications and internet access.

In May, Saparmamed Nepeskuliev, a freelance contributor to an exile-run news website, Alternative News of Turkmenistan (ANT), and Radio Free Europe/Radio Liberty (RFE/RL), was released after serving a three-year prison term on fabricated narcotics charges.

RFE/RL reporter, Soltan Achilova, who has been assaulted numerous times in previous years, was attacked on multiple occasions. In May, plainclothed security agents threatened her and blocked her access to a public memorial event, which she had sought to photograph. In June, two men punched Achilova when she was visiting relatives in Yoloten, knocking her over and injuring her. On the same day, the police seized her relatives' car, saying that they would not return it until Achilova left for Ashgabat. The car was returned two days after Achilova left.

Civil Society

Independent groups can carry out human rights work openly only in exile. It is illegal for unregistered nongovernmental organizations (NGOs) to operate, and strict regulations create severe challenges for groups to register. The government constantly threatens civil society activists with reprisal.

ATN activist Gaspar Matalaev continued to serve a three-year prison sentence on false fraud charges in retaliation for monitoring state-sponsored forced labor in the cotton harvest. In May, the United Nations (UN) Working Group on Arbitrary Detention found that the government's detention of Gaspar Matalaev was "an attempt to censor" his human rights activities and recommended his immediate release.

In June, an activist for Baloch minority rights, Mansur Mingelov, sentenced in 2012 to 22 years in prison on bogus narcotics and other charges, was denied adequate medical help when he experienced chest pain and high blood pressure. Mingelov was taken to a prison medical unit, but according to Amnesty International he was provided with treatment only in July, after his family brought medications and insisted that doctors administer them.

Authorities kept Turkmen students abroad under heavy surveillance. In February, they lured Omruzak Omarkulyev, who created an informal Turkmen students club at a university in Turkey, into returning to Turkmenistan. In March, Omarkulyev went missing after migration authorities banned him from returning to Turkey for his studies. RFE/RL and the Turkmen Initiative for Human Rights (TIHR), an exile group, reported that Omarkulyev was sentenced to 20 years in prison on unknown charges, and was being held at the maximum security prison in Ovadandepe.

In June, Turkmenistan's ombudsperson published a report on the first year of the institution's work, stating that she had resolved 25 of the 254 complaints filed. Among them was the case of a woman whom authorities had banned from leaving Turkmenistan. After the ombudsperson's intervention, she was allowed to travel to Russia so her child, who has multiple disabilities, could receive medical treatment.

Police harassed Batyr Batyrov, a history teacher who had filed official complaints about corruption in education. In August, TIHR reported that police issued death threats to Batyrov and his family if he did not stop writing complaints.

Freedom of Movement

According to TIHR, in August, the number of people whom the Turkmen authorities banned from leaving the country for foreign travel reached at least 30,874.

The government arbitrarily bans from foreign travel families of dissidents and prisoners whom it considers disloyal. For example, the Ruzimatov family, relatives of a government official in exile, remained banned from traveling abroad.

Authorities also arbitrarily barred citizens from the most economically distressed regions from leaving the country. Security officials reportedly summoned people who faced repeated denials to remind them that they may not travel abroad. According to the exile group Rights and Freedoms of Turkmen Citizens, local authorities in some regions place families of people living abroad on a special register.

Turkmen authorities also pressured people to persuade their relatives living abroad to return. In April, RFE/RL reported that authorities threatened a woman that they would press criminal charges against her brother if he did not return.

Housing and Property Rights

The government continued to expropriate and demolish homes in Ashgabat and its suburbs without providing adequate compensation, and in some cases harassing and intimidating residents. Homeowners were offered poor-quality compensation housing. Some had very little time to move out because of late demolition notification, and were offered compensation apartments in buildings still under construction, forcing them to rent interim apartments without compensation. Others received no explanation as to why their property was expropriated and what compensation they would receive.

Freedom of Religion

Unregistered religious groups and congregations are banned in Turkmenistan. Authorities censor religious literature and severely punish unauthorized religious activity.

Conscientious objection to military service is not allowed. At least 10 objectors were jailed, all of them Jehovah's Witnesses.

In July, the Supreme Court upheld the 12-year prison terms of five men sentenced in 2017 for studying the works of the late Turkish Muslim theologian Said Nursi. The men were charged with incitement, financing criminal activity, and related offenses.

Political Prisoners, Enforced Disappearances, and Torture

Turkmenistan's prison system remains rife with human rights abuses. The number of political prisoners is impossible to determine because the government does not provide numbers and does not allow independent human rights work. The justice system lacks transparency, and in sensitive cases trials are closed.

Authorities continued to hold dozens of prisoners in full isolation from family, lawyers, and the outside world, some for as long as 16 years, and denied their families information about their whereabouts and fate, including whether they are dead or alive. These amount to enforced disappearances. According to Prove They Are Alive, an international campaign dedicated to ending enforced disappearances in Turkmenistan, 121 people remained forcibly disappeared. Many are believed to be held in Ovadandepe prison, notorious for conditions that amount to torture. In February, Begmurad Otuzov, a former Turkmen security official imprisoned in 2002, died. His family had had no news of him for 15 years when they received his corpse, weighing about 45 kilograms (roughly 99 pounds).

Starting at the end of 2017, authorities for the first time allowed some family visits to Ovadandepe. In June, more than 30 relatives of prisoners held there, convicted on religious charges in or after 2016, were allowed to visit.

Sexual Orientation and Gender Identity

Homosexual conduct is a criminal offense under Turkmen law, punishable by a maximum two-year prison sentence. The Turkmen government rejected recommendations, made during Turkmenistan's Universal Periodic Review at the United Nations Human Rights Council (UNHRC) in May, to decriminalize homosexual conduct.

Key International Actors

In an opinion issued in April, the UN Human Rights Committee (HRC) found Turkmenistan responsible for the 2006 torture and death of human rights activist Ogulsapar Muradova. She died in Ovadandepe, shortly after her arrest and trial on politically motivated charges.

In its periodic review of Turkmenistan, the UN Committee on the Elimination of Discrimination against Women noted the adoption of various laws to ensure gender equality, but found these laws inadequate to protect women from discrimination. The committee also noted the "prevalence of child/forced marriage," dress, and travel restrictions for women, and numerous, profound gaps in protections for women from gender-based violence.

During Turkmenistan's Universal Periodic Review at the UNHRC in May, more than a dozen delegations urged Turkmenistan to address allegations of enforced disappearances, but the government representative refused to acknowledge the problem.

In May, the US banned the import of Turkmen cotton and products produced with it. The ban came two years after ATN and the International Labor Rights Forum petitioned US Customs and Border Protection to do so, due to forced labor in Turkmenistan's cotton sector.

During its annual human rights dialogue with Turkmenistan, the European Union urged the Turkmen government to recognize the problem of enforced disappearances and to take effective measures to solve this issue. The EU also recommended that Turkmenistan issue invitations to UN monitors.

Uganda

Uganda's Constitutional Court upheld parliament's 2017 constitutional amendment to remove age limits for presidential candidates, paving the way for President Yoweri Museveni, in power since 1986, to run in all future elections. Allegations of widespread repression and intimidation of parliamentarians during debates marred the amendment process.

Violations of rights to freedoms of association, expression, and assembly persisted, as security forces beat and, at times, tortured and arbitrarily detained protesters, journalists, and opposition members. Thirty-three people, including six parliamentarians, arrested during by-election campaigns in Arua, northwest Uganda, faced treason charges and alleged torture by security forces. Police and soldiers beat and detained journalists reporting in Arua and at ensuing protests.

Despite various government commitments to hold security forces accountable for their conduct, many investigations into military and police abuses of civilians failed to progress, including into the November 2016 killing of more than 100 civilians in Kasese, western Uganda, and the killings of protesters in September 2009 and April 2011.

Freedom of Expression and Assembly

In July, the government implemented a social media tax requiring users of WhatsApp, Twitter, and Facebook, among other sites, to pay a daily fee of 200 Ugandan Shillings (US$0.05). At a protest march against the tax in Kampala on July 11, police fired live bullets and tear gas to disperse the demonstration, which police deemed "illegal." Protesters argued the tax violated Ugandans' rights to free expression and information.

In June, security officials in Kitgum, northern Ugandan, banned a song by musician Bosmic Otim that was critical of government officials for being "misleading" and "inciting violence." The song criticized four parliamentarians for allegedly being sycophants of the government and for being unresponsive to citizens' problems in northern Uganda.

On June 5, police arrested six people as they attempted to petition police leadership at Naguru Police Headquarters in Kampala as part of a protest over numerous kidnappings and unresolved murders of women and children. Anti-terrorism and anti-riot police were deployed to block the activists from accessing the premises.

Freedom of Media and Attacks on Journalists

On February 14, five unidentified men wearing military uniforms seized Charles Etukuri, an investigative journalist for *New Vision*, outside the newspaper's Kampala offices days after he published an article linking Internal Security Organisation agents to the death of a Finnish businessman. Etukuri said his abductors demanded he reveal his sources. He was released after six days following a court ruling.

On August 13, security personnel arrested journalists Herbert Zziwa and Ronald Muwanga as they covered the Arua by-election and the military's fatal shooting of Yasin Kawuma, parliamentarian Robert Kyagulanyi's (aka Bobi Wine) driver. Security forces tied and beat Zziwa and Muwanga before holding them overnight in Gulu, charging them with malicious damage to property and incitement of violence. They were later released on bond.

On August 20, soldiers beat and detained journalists covering protests, including photojournalist James Akena, confiscating and damaging his equipment. In September, police detained at least eight journalists and confiscated their equipment as they sought to report on Kyagulanyi's return from the United States for medical treatment following his alleged torture by soldiers. Despite the military's stated commitment to investigate soldiers for beating journalists, no one had been held accountable at time of writing.

On April 29, the Uganda Communications Commission ordered internet service providers to shut down all unauthorized news sites following a directive requiring online data communication service providers, including publishers, news platforms, radio and television operators to obtain authorization.

Lack of Accountability for Torture, Extrajudicial Killings

In March, John Martin Okoth Ochola was appointed inspector general of police. His predecessor, Kale Kayihura, was arrested three months later, brought before a military court and charged with failing to protect war materials, failing to supervise police officers, and abetting the kidnap and forced repatriation of Rwandan refugees. He has been released on bail but charges remain pending. No charges have been brought against him for commanding units involved in torture or extrajudicial killings, despite credible allegations of such crimes during his leadership.

In April, Okoth Ochola ordered that the Nalufenya detention facility in Jinja, Eastern Uganda, be redesignated from a special force operation base to a standard police station. This was significant because Nalufenya had been notorious as a place of torture and long-term detention without trial. In May, Okoth Ochola disbanded the police Flying Squad Unit, established in 2013 to counter armed robberies, but which has been implicated in multiple serious allegations of extortion and torture.

On August 13, Ugandan police and military arrested and beat six opposition members of parliament, including Francis Zaake and Kyagulanyi, and 28 other people in advance of the August 15 by-elections in Arua. Prosecutors charged all 34 with treason for allegedly throwing stones at a presidential convoy on August 13. Media reported that men in military uniform took Zaake, who was unconscious, to a hospital in Kampala and abandoned him. Kyagulanyi alleged Special Forces Command soldiers tortured him while was detained for 10 days by the military. He was also charged before a military court for illegal possession of firearms and ammunition, but the charges were later dropped. Authorities promised to investigate Kyagulanyi's allegations of torture.

Police and military shot and killed at least six people in Kampala, Mityana, Katwe, and Gomba, during protests related to security forces' abusive conduct at the time of the Arua by-election.

Freedom of Association

In recent years, offices of over two dozen nongovernmental organizations (NGOs) have been robbed, and some of their security guards killed, but police failed to credibly investigate the attacks. The targeted groups worked on "sensitive issues" including human rights, land, and resource governance and corruption.

On February 8, unknown assailants broke into the offices of Human Rights Awareness and Promotion Forum, which provides legal services to marginalized groups such as LGBTI people, and disabled its security system. Two guards were severely injured. On August 6, unidentified people broke into Isis-WICCE, a women's rights organization, and stole computer processors, hard drives, and cash. In September, Twerwaneho Listeners Club, a human rights organization in Fort Portal, western Uganda, reported three forced entries into its offices in a single month.

Prosecutions for Serious Crimes

In April, International Criminal Court (ICC) prosecutors in The Hague, completed their case against alleged former Lord's Resistance Army (LRA) commander Dominic Ongwen, charged with 70 counts of war crimes and crimes against humanity. Ongwen's defense began its case in September. Two ICC warrants remain outstanding for the arrest of Joseph Kony, long-time LRA leader and Vincent Otti, who is presumed dead. The LRA remains active in central Africa, but there have been fewer media reports of killings and abductions.

On August 30, the International Crimes Division (ICD) of Uganda's High Court confirmed charges against alleged former LRA commander Thomas Kwoyelo, in custody since his capture in the Democratic Republic of Congo (DRC) in 2009.The trial began in September but was quickly adjourned until November, when Kwoyelo pled not guilty to all 93 counts against him.

Pre-trial sessions in the case against Jamil Mukulu, alleged leader of the rebel Allied Democratic Forces (ADF), captured in Tanzania in April 2015, started at the ICD. Mukulu and 34 others are charged with terrorism, multiple murders, aggravated robbery and crimes against humanity over several years.

Sexual Orientation and Gender Identity

Uganda's colonial-era law continues to prohibit "carnal knowledge" among people of the same sex and crackdowns on lesbian, gay, bisexual, transgender, and intersex activists continued. On May 17, police and Minister of Ethics and Integrity Simon Lokodo shut down a celebration of the International Day Against Homophobia, Biphobia, and Transphobia organized by the NGO Sexual Minorities Uganda. In May, Lokodo vowed to block the Health Ministry's first annual conference on Key and Priority Populations, arguing it would promote "homosexuality and other dirty things." The conference did not take place.

Forced Evictions

Years of security forces' forced evictions in Apaa, Northern Uganda gained attention in June when 200 residents traveled 100 kilometers to seek refuge at the UN Office of the High Commissioner for Human Rights (OHCHR) in Gulu after soldiers allegedly torched homes, beating and killing a resident. Following a month of negotiations between OHCHR, the community and government, residents elected to return home, but reported that forced evictions have continued.

Key International Actors

The United States, United Kingdom, and the European Union continue to provide funding for logistics and training to the African Union Mission in Somalia, where Uganda contributes troops. The United States has been a significant donor to Uganda's military, providing training to thousands of soldiers, through the *Africa Contingency Operations Training and Assistance* (ACOTA) program, among other funding streams.

International donors echoed domestic criticism of security forces' conduct during and after the Arua by-election. The US State Department said it was "gravely concerned" by reports of torture, and that "such human rights abuses are unacceptable." In September, the European Parliament in a 14-point resolution called for the investigation and prosecution of security officers for torture and extrajudicial killings. However, neither the US nor EU announced specific changes regarding support for Uganda's security forces.

Uganda hosts over 1 million refugees, primarily from South Sudan and the Democratic Republic of Congo. In June, the United Nations, and Uganda sought at least $2 billion to support refugee assistance but raised significantly less.

Ukraine

The armed conflict in eastern Ukraine between the Ukrainian government and Russia-backed armed groups entered its fifth year. Total impunity for conflict-related abuses persisted in 2018. The government took further steps to restrict freedom of expression and association. Violence by radical groups promoting hatred put ethnic minorities, lesbian, gay, bisexual, and transgender (LGBT) people, activists, and journalists at risk. In Crimea, Russian authorities continued targeting pro-Ukraine activists and Crimean Tatars for their vocal opposition to Russia's abuses and occupation of the peninsula.

Hostilities in Eastern Ukraine

According to the Organization for Security and Co-operation in Europe (OSCE) Special Monitoring Mission, as of October, at least 212 civilians were injured or killed in 2018, mostly from shelling and light weapons fire.

Shelling across or near the contact line separating the two sides continued to damage civilian homes and infrastructure and to threaten civilian lives. Since 2014, 740 education facilities were damaged during the conflict, 16 from January to October 2018. Both sides carried out indiscriminate or deliberate attacks on schools and used them for military purposes.

Authorities continued to enforce discriminatory policies requiring pensioners from armed group-controlled parts of eastern Ukraine to register as internally displaced persons (IDPs) and maintain residency in government-controlled areas to access their pensions. Rules prohibit them from spending more than 60 consecutive days in armed group-controlled regions, or risk suspension of their pensions.

In two separate cases, Ukrainian courts found several provisions of decrees regulating pension payments to be discriminatory and ordered authorities to cease restricting access to pensions. However, authorities did not observe these rulings.

Older people and people with disabilities eligible for priority crossing and assistance at the contact line faced difficulty accessing these services. Authorities on duty at the contact line often did not identify those eligible nor ensure they were provided with assistance.

Basic facilities and sanitary infrastructure at crossing points along the line of contact remained inadequate, particularly on the side controlled by Russia-backed armed groups in Donetsk and Luhansk regions. Long waits at all crossing points in extreme temperatures continued to cause civilians undue hardship.

Cruel and Degrading Treatment and Arbitrary Detention

Ukraine's Security Service (SBU) continued to deny the secret and prolonged detention of 18 civilians in its Kharkiv secret detention facility from 2014 to 2016. All 18 were unofficially freed by the end of 2016 and their detention was never acknowledged.

In February, one of the former detainees, Konstantyn Beskorovaynyi, was reinstated as a plaintiff in a case he filed with the prosecutor's office in July 2016. In March, a court ruled to reopen the criminal investigation. Investigations are stalled in the cases of four others who filed complaints.

Pro-Ukraine blogger and Radio Free Europe/Radio Liberty (RFE/RL) contributor Stanyslav Aseev, who was forcibly disappeared in Donetsk in June 2017, remained held by Russia-backed armed groups on dubious espionage charges.

Rule of Law, Accountability for Past Abuses

Justice for conflict-related abuses and crimes committed during the 2014 Maidan protests and mass disturbances in Odesa remained unaddressed several years later, despite numerous pledges from Ukrainian authorities to ensure justice. Law enforcement failed to preserve evidence after the events and to prevent suspects from fleeing the country.

In April, appeals hearings began against the acquittal of 19 anti-Maidan activists who were on trial for offenses related to the May 2, 2014 Odessa mass disturbances, which pitted pro-Maidan and anti-Maidan groups against each other, and in which 48 people died and more than 200 were injured. At time of writing, no progress was made in the appeal proceedings.

Criminal proceedings continued against former members of the Berkut riot police battalion, charged with killing and injuring protesters in the February 2014 Maidan protests. In April, charges against a pro-Maidan protester, Ivan Bubenchik, for killing two police officers in February 2014 were dropped after the prosecutor general cited a 2014 law exempting protesters from prosecution for certain crimes committed during the Maidan protests. Bubinchik remains under investigation for illegal use of weapons and endangering law enforcement.

Freedom of Expression and Media

The Ukrainian government continued restrictions on freedom of expression, freedom of information, and media freedom, seeking to justify them by citing the need to counter Russia's military aggression in eastern Ukraine and anti-Ukraine propaganda. According to the Institute for Mass Information, a media freedom watchdog, as of October, 201 press freedom violations took place in 23 regions. These ranged from threats and intimidation to restricting journalists' access to information.

In May, an appellate court upheld a regional court's decision to suspend the re-trial of Ruslan Kotsaba, a journalist who had been prosecuted on treason charges for calling for boycotting conscription. The court concluded that the prosecution failed to properly formulate the indictment.

In May, the SBU deported two journalists from the main Russian-state television channel, Channel 1, alleging that they had planned to spread disinformation about Ukraine. Also in May, the Ukraine editor of the Russian state wire service, RIA Novosti, in Ukraine, Kirill Vyshinsky, was arrested on treason charges for his alleged participation in "propaganda campaigns" to legitimize Russia's actions in Crimea. Security services raided the outlet's office in Kyiv.

In October, the European Court of Human Rights (ECtHR) extended indefinitely its September 18 ruling requesting that Ukrainian authorities refrain from reviewing 17 months' worth of cellphone data of RFE/RL reporter Natalia Sedletska. Authorities requested the data as evidence in a criminal investigation against National Anti-Corruption Bureau Director Artem Sytnyk, who is accused of disclosing state secrets to journalists.

A March 2017 law requiring activists and journalists investigating corruption to publicly declare their personal assets remained in effect. Although many refused to comply, at time of writing none were prosecuted.

Authorities did not conduct effective investigations into numerous assaults against anti-corruption and other community activists. In November 2018, Kateryna Handzyuk, an anti-corruption activist, died from burn wounds inflicted in a July acid attack.

Palliative Care

Patients with advanced cancer and other life-limiting illnesses continued to face barriers to effective pain relief. The regulatory reforms adopted in recent years to make opioid pain medications more accessible to those who need it have yet to be fully implemented. Healthcare workers lack proper education and training in pain treatment, or simply refuse to change their practices. HIV/AIDS and tuberculosis patients faced obstacles to accessing pain relief due in part to stereotypes surrounding drug addiction.

Hate Crimes

Members of groups advocating hate and discrimination carried out at least two dozen violent attacks, threats, or instances of intimidation against Roma people, LGBT people, and rights activists in several Ukrainian cities. In most cases, police failed to respond or effectively investigate.

In March, hate groups attacked events to promote women's rights in Kyiv, Lviv, and Uzhgorod. In Kyiv, they physically assaulted participants while police looked on.

In June, members of a far-right group attacked a Roma settlement in Lviv, killing a man and seriously injuring several others. In October, court hearings began for four of the nine suspects in the case, eight of whom are minors.

In April, members of a radical group in Kyiv, authorized by the local municipality to carry out patrolling, attacked a Roma settlement. They torched tents and chased women and children with rocks and pepper spray. Two criminal investigations were launched, but at time of writing, those investigations had not led to any prosecutions.

In May, hate groups disrupted an equality festival in Chernivtsi while local police failed to effectively protect participants. Also in May, hate groups in Kyiv disrupted an Amnesty International LGBT rights event in Kyiv. Police present took no action and made homophobic comments.

However, in June, police briefly detained dozens of radicals who sought to interfere with the Kyiv Pride March, and a robust police presence at the march ensured marchers' safety. LGBT equality marches in Krivyi Rih and Odessa also took place without major violence.

In March, a petition to stop "propaganda" of homosexuality was removed from the president's website.

Crimea

Russia has occupied Crimea since 2014 and continues to perpetrate grave human rights violations against people there for expressing pro-Ukrainian views.

On October 6, imprisoned Ukrainian filmmaker Oleg Sentsov ended his 145-day hunger strike to avoid force-feeding. Senstov was arrested in 2014 in Crimea on bogus terrorism charges and is serving a 20-year prison sentence (See Russia chapter). On May 14, he went on a hunger strike to demand the release of 64 Ukrainians held in Russia and Crimea on politically motivated charges.

Russian authorities targeted Crimean Tatars who criticized the occupation with false terrorism and criminal incitement charges. They harassed Crimean Tatars, searching their homes, sometimes detaining residents for questioning.

In January, authorities arrested Ismail Ramazanov, a Crimean Tatar, on incitement charges for comments he made online. In court the next day, he stated that security officers beat him. Authorities refused to investigate his allegations of torture. In July, he was released from custody pending trial.

In May, Russian authorities in Crimea arrested Server Mustafayev and Edem Smailov for their alleged involvement with the Islamist movement Hizb ut-Tahrir, banned as a terrorist organization in Russia but not in Ukraine. Twenty-one men arrested in 2016 and 2017 on terrorism-related charges, based on allegations of involvement with Hizb-ut-Tahrir, remained in pretrial custody.

Also in May, a court upheld a suspended two-year sentence for Suleyman Kady-rov, a Crimean Tatar activist, on separatism charges for a comment posted to Facebook.

In June, Elina Mamedova was charged with incitement to hatred for sharing content in 2014 and 2015 from a pro-Ukraine social media page. In October, Crimea's Supreme Court upheld a lower court's decision to dismiss a complaint filed by Mamedova's lawyer against investigative authorities for refusing to provide information on the qualifications of an expert it summoned to examine the materials of the case. Mamedova is at liberty as the investigation continues.

In March, a court dismissed a lawsuit against police for failing to investigate the disappearance of Ervin Ibragimov, a Crimean Tatar activist who went missing in May 2016.

The number of students in Crimea in classes with Ukrainian as the language of instruction plummeted from 12,694 in 2014 to 318 in 2018, according to the United Nations.

Key International Actors

In January, the Parliamentary Assembly of the Council of Europe (PACE) issued a resolution calling on Ukraine to facilitate the "delivery of humanitarian assistance to the war-affected territories." It also called on the Russian occupying authorities to respect human rights in Crimea.

Following a May visit to conflict areas in eastern Ukraine, US Special Representative for Ukraine Negotiations Kurt Volker expressed concern for the conflict's impact on public health, infrastructure, and the safety of civilians living close to the contact line.

In June, the Council of Europe's (CoE) commissioner for human rights urged Ukrainian authorities to step up efforts to prevent attacks against Roma and human rights defenders and prosecute those responsible for any attacks. In July, a group of UN experts called on the government to protect Roma from attacks and ensure adequate compensation for victims.

The UN working group on enforced disappearances and the UN special rapporteur on torture paid separate working visits to Ukraine in June, and both raised concerns about impunity for continuing cases of enforced disappearances and torture.

During the July European Union-Ukraine summit, European Council President Donald Tusk commended Ukraine's efforts to establish a High Anti-Corruption Court and encouraged the country to adopt legislation to ensure the court's effectiveness. Tusk also called for the release of "all those illegally detained in Crimea and in Russia." But EU officials rarely publicly engage the government of Ukraine on non-conflict related concerns like media freedom and civil society issues.

Although Ukraine is not a member of the International Criminal Court (ICC), it has accepted the court's jurisdiction over alleged crimes committed on its territory since November 2013. The ICC prosecutor's preliminary examination as to whether it should open an investigation into abuses committed during the armed conflict remained ongoing; it also reviewed additional information it received related to the Maidan protests. It had previously determined that crimes allegedly committed in connection with events in Maidan would not fall within the ICC's mandate.

United Arab Emirates

The United Arab Emirates' intolerance of criticism continued in 2018 as authorities in May sentenced Ahmed Mansoor, an Emirati award-winning human rights activist, to a 10-year prison sentence for exercising his right to free expression. The government continues to arbitrarily detain and forcibly disappear individuals who criticize authorities.

The UAE maintains their leading role in the Saudi-led military coalition, which has conducted scores of unlawful attacks in Yemen. The UAE was implicated in detainee abuse at home and abroad.

Labor abuses persist. Migrant construction workers face serious exploitation. The UAE introduced a domestic workers law providing them labor rights for the first time in September 2017, but some provisions are weaker than those provided to other workers under the labor law.

The UAE continued to block representatives of international human rights organizations from visiting.

Freedom of Expression

UAE authorities have launched a sustained assault on freedom of expression and association since 2011. The UAE arbitrarily detains and forcibly disappears individuals who criticize the authorities within the UAE's borders. UAE residents who have spoken about human rights issues are at serious risk of arbitrary detention, imprisonment, and torture. Many are serving long prison terms or have left the country under pressure.

In March 2017, the UAE detained Ahmed Mansoor, an award-winning human rights defender, on speech-related charges that included using social media websites to "publish false information that harms national unity." Before his arrest, Mansoor had called for the release of Osama al-Najjar, who remains in prison despite having completed a three-year prison sentence on charges related to his peaceful activities on Twitter. Authorities held Mansoor in an unknown location for more than a year with no access to a lawyer and only very limited family visits before being sentenced to 10 years in prison for crimes that appear to violate his right to free expression on May 29, 2018.

In March 2017, the UAE imposed a 10-year prison sentence on prominent academic Nasser bin-Ghaith, whom authorities forcibly disappeared in August 2015, for charges that included peaceful criticism of the UAE and Egyptian authorities. The Gulf Centre for Human Rights reported that bin-Ghaith initiated a hunger strike in February to protest poor conditions in Al-Razeen prison and he ended it in April after Emirati authorities threatened to restrict visits.

On May 5, 2018, security forces arrested British citizen Matthew Hedges at Dubai International Airport as he was preparing to leave the country following a two-week trip to the UAE. Authorities held Hedges, a PhD candidate at Durham University, in incommunicado detention for the first two weeks and did not allow him access to legal counsel until October 10, at his second court hearing, more than five months after his arrest. According to a relative, authorities held him in solitary confinement in an undisclosed location in Abu Dhabi for the majority of his time in pretrial detention. On October 16, UAE's public prosecutor referred Hedges to the Abu Dhabi Federal Court of Appeal on state security charges of "spying for a foreign state" based partly on his confession. On November 21, the Abu Dhabi Federal Court of Appeal sentenced Hedges to life in prison. Five days later, following growing diplomatic pressure and international outrage, the UAE pardoned him.

Unlawful Yemen Attacks and Detainee Abuse

The UAE is a leading member of the Saudi-led coalition operating in Yemen. Human Rights Watch has documented about 90 apparently unlawful coalition attacks, some likely war crimes, since March 2015.

Coalition members have provided insufficient information about the role their forces are playing in the campaign to determine which are responsible for unlawful attacks. In March 2015, the Emirati State news agency reported that the UAE had deployed 30 aircraft to take part in coalition operations. In March 2017, after a helicopter attacked a boat carrying Somali migrants and refugees off Yemen's coast, killing and wounding dozens, a member of the UAE armed forces said UAE forces were operating in the area but denied carrying out the attack.

The UAE leads coalition efforts in southern Yemen, including by supporting Yemeni forces carrying out security campaigns. Human Rights Watch has documented abuses by UAE proxy forces, including use of excessive force during arrests, detaining family members of wanted suspects to pressure them to "voluntarily" turn themselves in, arbitrarily detaining men and boys, detaining children with adults, and forcibly disappearing dozens. Former detainees and family members reported abuse or torture inside facilities run by the UAE and UAE-backed forces. Yemeni activists who have criticized these abuses have been threatened, harassed, detained, and disappeared.

Emirati commanders face possible criminal liability as a matter of command responsibility. The United Nations Security Council should consider imposing targeted sanctions on senior coalition commanders who share the greatest responsibility for serious repeated violations.

Migrant Workers

Foreign nationals account for more than 88.5 percent of the UAE's population, according to 2011 government statistics. Many low-paid migrant workers remain acutely vulnerable to forced labor, despite some reforms.

The kafala (visa-sponsorship) system continues to tie migrant workers to their employers. Those who leave their employers can face punishment for "absconding," including fines, prison, and deportation.

The UAE's labor law excludes domestic workers, who face a range of abuses, from unpaid wages, confinement to the house, workdays up to 21 hours with no breaks, to physical or sexual assault by employers, from its protections. Domestic workers face legal and practical obstacles to redress.

The UAE has made some reforms to increase domestic worker protection. In September 2017, the president signed a bill on domestic workers that guarantees domestic workers labor rights for the first time including a weekly rest day, 30 days of paid annual leave, sick leave, and 12 hours of rest a day. In some cases, the law allows for inspections of recruitment agency offices, workplaces, and residences, and sets out penalties for violations.

But the 2017 law does not prohibit employers from charging reimbursement for recruitment expenses and requires that workers who terminate employment without a breach of contract compensate their employers with one month's salary and pay for their own tickets home. In June, while authorities set out new

615

fixed recruitment fees that included some packages of fixed salaries for domestic workers, these salaries discriminate by nationality.

Women's Rights

Discrimination on the basis of sex and gender is not included in the definition of discrimination in the UAE's 2015 anti-discrimination law.

Federal Law No. 28 of 2005 regulates personal status matters. Some of its provisions discriminate against women. For a woman to marry, her male guardian must conclude her marriage contract; men have the right to unilaterally divorce their wives, whereas a woman must apply for a court order to obtain a divorce; a woman can lose her right to maintenance if, for example, she refuses to have sexual relations with her husband without a lawful excuse; and women are required to "obey" their husbands. A woman may be considered disobedient, with few exceptions, if she decides to work without her husband's consent.

UAE law permits domestic violence. Article 53 of the penal code allows the imposition of "chastisement by a husband to his wife and the chastisement of minor children" so long as the assault does not exceed the limits of Islamic law. Marital rape is not a crime. In 2010, the Federal Supreme Court issued a ruling, citing the penal code, that sanctions husbands' beating and infliction of other forms of punishment or coercion on their wives, provided they do not leave physical marks.

Sexual Orientation and Gender Identity

Article 356 of the penal code criminalizes (but does not define) "indecency" and provides for a minimum sentence of one year in prison. UAE courts use this article to convict and sentence people for *zina* offenses, which include consensual heterosexual relations outside marriage.

Different emirates within the UAE's federal system have laws that criminalize same-sex sexual relations, including Abu Dhabi, where "unnatural sex with another person" can be punished with up to 14 years in prison.

Similarly, article 177 of the penal code of the Emirate of Dubai punishes consensual sodomy by imprisonment of up to 10 years.

Additionally, the UAE's federal penal code punishes "any male disguised in a female apparel and enters in this disguise a place reserved for women or where entry is forbidden, at that time, for other than women" with one year's imprisonment, a fine of up to 10,000 dirhams (US$2,723), or both. In practice, transgender women have been arrested under this law even in mixed-gender spaces.

Key International Actors

In October, the European Parliament adopted a resolution condemning the UAE's harassment of human rights defenders, calling for the release of Ahmed Mansoor, and calling for an EU-wide ban on the export to the UAE of security equipment which can be used for internal repression. It remains the only EU body to have openly called for Mansoor's release.

HUMAN
RIGHTS
WATCH

ACLU

"YOU MISS SO MUCH
WHEN YOU'RE GONE"
The Lasting Harm of Jailing Mothers
Before Trial in Oklahoma

United States

The United States continued to move backward on human rights at home and abroad in the second year of President Donald Trump's administration. With Trump's Republican party controlling the legislative branch in 2018, his administration and Congress were able to pass laws, implement regulations, and carry out policies that violate or undermine human rights.

Despite Trump signaling support for minimal reforms, his administration rolled back initiatives meant to reduce over-incarceration in the US, implemented an array of anti-immigration policies, and worked to undermine a national insurance program that helps Americans obtain affordable health care, including important reproductive care for women.

The Trump administration also continued to support abusive governments abroad militarily, financially, and diplomatically. Though it has expressed support for some international initiatives aimed at sanctioning individuals and governments committing human rights abuses, overall administration policy undermined multilateral institutions and international judicial bodies seeking to hold people accountable for egregious human rights violations.

Harsh Criminal Sentencing

State and federal jails and prisons continue to hold over 2 million people, with another 4.5 million on probation or parole. Women are the fastest growing correctional population nationwide, increasing by more than 700 percent between 1980 and 2016. Oklahoma incarcerates more women per capita than any other US state. In September, Human Rights Watch documented the lasting harm of jailing mothers pretrial, many of whom simply cannot afford bail in that state.

Former US Attorney General Jeff Sessions rescinded policies instructing prosecutors to avoid charging crimes that would trigger long mandatory minimum sentences and were aimed at curtailing racial disparities in the federal system. Sessions also rescinded a Justice Department directive giving federal prosecutors discretion to not prosecute marijuana offenses in the 10 states where marijuana has been legalized for adult consumption.

Millions of people still cannot vote due to a patchwork of felony disenfranchisement laws across the country. However, in November, Florida voters approved a ballot initiative during the mid-term elections that restored the right to vote for 1.4 million residents with felony convictions. The initiative was one of several that states passed that advanced criminal justice reform, including an initiative in Colorado that removed language in the state constitution that permitted convicted criminals to be forced to work in prison without pay or restitution; an initiative in Florida, allowing sentencing reforms to be retroactive; one in Michigan that legalized marijuana for recreational use; and another in Washington state that strengthened police accountability.

The death penalty is still permissible in 30 states. According to the Death Penalty Information Center, 21 people in eight states had been executed by the end of November, all in the south and midwest of the country. There were 11 executions in Texas. All but one of these executions were committed by lethal injection, the other by electric chair. Trump and administration officials have called for the death penalty for drug sellers.

Racial Disparities, Drug Policy, and Policing

Racial disparities permeate every part of the US criminal justice system. Black people are 13 percent of the population but close to 40 percent of those in prisons. They are incarcerated at more than five times the rate of white people. Black people use illegal drugs at similar rates to white people, but suffer drug arrests at significantly higher rates.

According to the *Washington Post,* police reportedly shot and killed 876 people in the US as of the beginning of October. Of those killed, whose race is known, 22 percent were black. Of the unarmed people killed by police, 39 percent were black. The Justice Department rolled back efforts to investigate local police departments following credible reports of systemic constitutional violations. Some state governments have taken on this oversight role. Racial disparities in police use of force, arrests, citations, and traffic stops continue to exist.

LIVING AT RISK

Transgender Women, HIV, and Human Rights in South Florida

Children in the Criminal and Juvenile Justice Systems

According to the Justice Department, the juvenile arrest rate has been declining but dramatic racial disparities persist: children of color are disproportionately represented at every stage, and in 37 states rates of incarceration were higher for black children than for white, according to the Sentencing Project.

According to the Citizens Committee for Children, roughly 32,000 children under 18 are admitted annually to adult jails. All 50 states continue to prosecute some children in adult criminal courts. Approximately 1,300 people have life without parole sentences for crimes committed under 18, according to the Campaign for the Fair Sentencing of Youth.

In October, the Washington State Supreme Court ruled that life sentences without parole for crimes committed below age 18 violated the state constitution. In all, 21 states and the District of Columbia now prohibit juvenile life without parole. California passed a law in October that ends the sentencing of 14 and 15-year-olds in adult court. And in April, New York ended the automatic trial of 16 and 17-year-olds in adult court, although children of these—or younger—ages, who are accused of violent crimes, will still begin their cases in adult court with the possibility of transfer to the juvenile system.

Poverty and Criminal Justice

Poor people accused of crimes are often jailed because judges require money bail as a condition of release, forcing people not convicted of any crime to stay behind bars for long periods of time awaiting trial, and resulting in coerced guilty pleas. A movement to reduce the use of money bail is growing but many states, including California—which passed a bill eliminating money bail in August—are replacing money bail with risk assessment tools that could entrench discrimination while failing to lower rates of pretrial incarceration.

Many local jurisdictions impose excessive fees and fines for even minor violations of law. If unpaid, these debts can result in arrests that feed a cycle of incarceration and increased poverty. Similarly, some states privatize misdemeanor probation services, which penalizes poor people who commit minor violations and leads to abuses.

HUMAN
RIGHTS
WATCH

IN THE FREEZER
Abusive Conditions for Women and Children
in US Immigration Holding Cells

HUMAN
RIGHTS
WATCH

IMMIGRANT CRIME FIGHTERS
How the U Visa Program Makes US Communities Safer

In June 2018, the United Nations (UN) special rapporteur on extreme poverty and human rights issued a report sharply *criticizing the US for its policies towards the poor.*

Incidents of Hate Crimes

During one week in October, men espousing far right and white supremacist views allegedly committed three separate violent acts: one carried out a mass shooting at a synagogue in Pittsburgh, killing 11 worshipers and injuring more; another mailed deadly pipe bombs to leading Democratic figures; and another shot two African-Americans in a Louisville grocery store, killing both. Multiple organizations and the government, which use different methodologies to collect different types of information about hate crimes, reported an increase in the number of hate-motivated incidents from prior years.

Rights of Non-Citizens

More than 2,500 families were forcibly separated at the US border as the Trump administration targeted parents traveling with children for criminal prosecution. As part of this policy, children with disabilities were separated from their families, including in one case, a 10-year-old girl with Down Syndrome from her mother.

Though a federal court and tremendous public outcry put a stop to mass separations in late June, reunifications of hundreds of families lagged for months. According to media reports, families continued to be separated on a smaller scale after Trump issued an executive order supposedly ending the practice. Reportedly, many of these continued separations were based on vague or unsubstantiated allegations of wrongdoing or minor violations against the parents. Ramped-up criminal prosecutions for illegal entry continued. Mental health professionals warned that separation was very likely to cause trauma, both immediate and long-lasting.

Hundreds of parents were deported separately from their children, including many whose asylum claims were improperly dismissed by US border agents. A June administrative ruling by former Attorney General Jeff Sessions sought to restrict access to asylum for people claiming persecution by non-state actors, in-

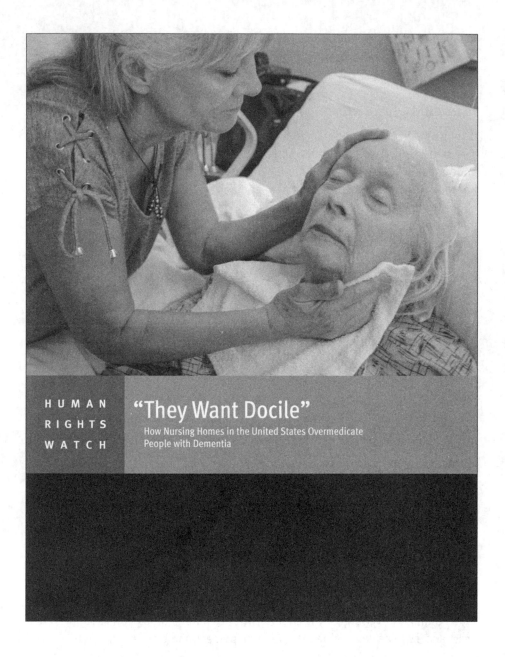

HUMAN
RIGHTS
WATCH

"They Want Docile"
How Nursing Homes in the United States Overmedicate
People with Dementia

cluding victims of domestic and gang violence. In November, the administration issued an interim final rule barring migrants who enter between ports of entry from asylum, in violation of US and international law; it was temporarily enjoined by a federal judge. A peaceful march by migrants on November 26 seeking asylum at the US-Mexico border ended with US border agents lobbing teargas projectiles at migrants, including young children.

The US Supreme Court upheld an executive order issued by Trump banning travel to the US from several predominantly Muslim countries, which Human Rights Watch and those challenging the ban said was discriminatory. The administration also announced Temporary Protected Status would expire for almost 400,000 deeply-rooted immigrants from Sudan, Haiti, El Salvador, Nicaragua, Honduras, and Nepal from late 2018 to early 2020, placing them at risk of deportation and separation from home and family. Arrests and deportations of undocumented people arrested in the interior of the United States mainly through minimal contact with the criminal justice system or in large-scale workplace raids continued to mount, without regard to their rights to home and family.

Immigration authorities sought to detain more people—including vulnerable populations like children and pregnant women—in the already-sprawling immigration detention system. Immigration authorities sought to remove legal limits to detaining children in families indefinitely. Of 15 recent deaths in immigration detention, Human Rights Watch found that eight were linked to poor medical care.

The fate of almost 800,000 young immigrants who hold work permits and protection from deportation under Deferred Action for Childhood Arrivals (DACA) remained uncertain as court challenges continued around the administration's 2017 decision to end the program. Proposed regulatory changes to the definition of "public charge" under US immigration law threatened to disrupt essential public health and benefit programs supporting citizen children of non-citizens.

Right to Health

To date, attempts in Congress to repeal the Affordable Care Act (ACA)—legislation that has greatly expanded access to health care for millions of Americans—have failed. However, a tax reform eliminated the individual mandate penalties for not participating in the program required in the law. The Congressional Budget Office estimated this could leave 13 million people without insurance coverage. In addition, the Medicaid program, private insurance subsidies, non-discrimination protections for lesbian, gay, bisexual, and transgender (LGBT) people, and other key elements of the ACA were targets of federal and state action that threaten to restrict access to health care. Many states with federal support have imposed work requirements, drug testing, and other barriers to Medicaid eligibility for low income individuals.

In 2017, a record 72,000 Americans died of drug overdose. The Trump administration's response to the continuing crisis was increasingly punitive, as criminal penalties were enhanced for fentanyl sale and distribution. In many states, criminal laws block expansion of proven public health interventions, such as syringe exchange programs and supervised consumption sites, which reduce transmission of infectious disease and prevent overdose. Reduced access to Medicaid threatens to put drug treatment out of reach for millions of Americans.

Older People's Rights

Human Rights Watch reported in February 2018 that nursing homes across the US routinely give antipsychotic drugs to residents with dementia to control their behavior, often without individuals' consent. This abusive practice remains widespread and can amount to cruel, inhumane or degrading treatment.

Women's and Girls' Rights

Revelations related to sexual harassment and misconduct by high-profile men continued to be made as the #MeToo movement expanded virally, highlighting abuses suffered by women at work and in public places. The Senate confirmed Brett Kavanaugh for a seat on the US Supreme Court, a lifetime appointment, without thoroughly investigating credible allegations of sexual assault or other aspects of his record, about which Human Rights Watch expressed serious concern.

Congress passed legislation in 2017 making it easier for states to restrict Title X grants by creating eligibility requirements that could exclude certain family planning providers, like Planned Parenthood. Title X is a national family planning program that funds services to more than 4 million Americans. The Department of Health and Human Services (HHS) proposed a "gag" rule in May to stop doctors receiving Title X funding from giving women the full range of pregnancy options and to eliminate a requirement that doctors give neutral and factual information to pregnant women. HHS received more than half-a-million comments in response to the notice of rule-making. At time of writing, a final rule had not been issued.

In 2017, HHS issued a rule exempting nearly any employer claiming religious or moral objections to birth control from the ACA's requirement that they provide contraceptive coverage as part of their employee health insurance plans. In March 2018, it proposed another rule that would dramatically expand healthcare providers' ability to turn away patients based on religious or moral objections, including women seeking reproductive health services and lesbian, gay, bisexual, and transgender people. At time of writing, the rule had not been finalized.

A few states took steps to proactively protect or expand protections for women's health. However, several states adopted highly restrictive laws on abortion and reproductive health. Two states—Delaware and New Jersey—in 2018 banned all marriage before age 18, but child marriage remains legal in the remaining 48 states.

Sexual Orientation and Gender Identity

The Department of Health and Human Services announced plans to roll back a federal rule clarifying that the Affordable Care Act's prohibition on sex discrimination includes discrimination based on gender identity.

In 2018, Oklahoma, Kansas, and South Carolina enacted laws permitting adoption and foster care providers asserting a religious objection to refuse to place children with LGBT people. A similar provision was added to an appropriations bill in the US House of Representatives but did not become law.

At time of writing, 19 states have laws expressly banning discrimination based on both sexual orientation and gender identity in employment, housing, and

HUMAN
RIGHTS
WATCH

"All We Want is Equality"

Religious Exemptions and Discrimination against LGBT People
in the United States

public accommodations. Wisconsin and New York prohibit discrimination based on sexual orientation but not gender identity, and Utah only prohibits discrimination in employment and housing. Michigan, New York, and Pennsylvania interpret their statutory prohibition on sex discrimination to include discrimination based on sexual orientation and/or gender identity.

National Security

In March, the US Senate confirmed Gina Haspel as director of the Central Intelligence Agency (CIA). In 2002, Haspel ran a CIA detention center in Thailand where she oversaw torture, and in 2005 advocated for, and helped to destroy, videotaped evidence of CIA torture.

The US is assisting Syrian Democratic Forces (SDF) run and secure detention facilities in northern Syria where the SDF were holding nearly 600 men from 47 countries accused of being Islamic State (ISIS) fighters or members. At time of writing, the US had also transferred at least eight detainees from SDF custody to Lebanon, seven to Macedonia, and other foreign nationals to Iraq. One dual US-Saudi citizen was held in US custody for over a year until October, when the US was finally pressured through litigation to release him. The US was also reportedly considering transferring hundreds more from SDF custody to Iraq, Tunisia, and other countries for detention. It was not clear what kind of process to safeguard against abuse the US was providing detainees transferred, but the transfers raised concerns that detainees may face torture or unfair trial, and not have an opportunity to challenge their transfers before they occur.

The US was also reportedly considering transferring two detainees whom the SDF was holding in northern Syria to the Guantanamo Bay detention facility. The men, both British-accused ISIS members who have had their British citizenship withdrawn, were accused of killing US citizens among others in territory once held by ISIS in Syria.

The US continues to hold 31 men indefinitely without charge at Guantanamo, all of whom have been there for 12 years or more. It also continued to prosecute 7 men for terrorist offenses, including the September 11, 2001 attacks on the US, in Guantanamo's military commissions system— which does not meet international fair trial standards and has been plagued by procedural problems and years of delay—and held two men who have already been convicted by the commissions.

Following reports that US forces interrogated detainees in secret prisons run by foreign forces in Yemen who had tortured detainees, which built on similar reports from 2017, the US enacted a law requiring the US Defense Secretary to determine whether US forces or their coalition partners in Yemen violated the laws of war or US laws barring the provision of US assistance to foreign forces that commit gross human rights violations.

Surveillance and Data Protection

In January, Congress re-authorized Section 702 of the Foreign Intelligence Surveillance Act, a law permitting the warrantless surveillance of foreign people and entities overseas, as well as the capture and search of Americans' communications in the process.

In January, Human Rights Watch reported that US authorities may be failing to notify other defendants about the way intelligence or other information used in their criminal cases was obtained, instead deliberately concealing its origins by finding alternative ways to obtain the same information, a practice known as "parallel construction."

The director of National Intelligence reported in May that the number of telephone call records that intelligence authorities collect under the USA Patriot Act more than tripled in 2017, to more than 534 million. The next month, the National Security Agency revealed that it was deleting years' worth of these records after receiving data it "was not authorized to receive."

Congress adopted the Clarifying Lawful Overseas Use of Data ("CLOUD") Act, which allows authorized foreign governments to demand data from US companies under weak and incomplete rights standards. At time of writing, the US was negotiating an agreement with the United Kingdom under the law, which would empower the UK to demand data under standards lower than those required by the US Constitution. The UK would then be able to pass this data back to the US, enabling US authorities to evade domestic privacy laws.

In a positive development, the Supreme Court decided in *Carpenter v. United States* that police need a warrant for access to extensive historic mobile phone

location data, which reveals a person's past movements and may be highly sensitive. However, evolving technology created new rights risks, as illustrated by revelations about Amazon's marketing of facial recognition technology to police departments. In the US, legal protections for personal data held by companies remained insufficient, as demonstrated by data analysis firm Cambridge Analytica's massive access to Facebook users' data.

Freedom of Expression and Assembly

President Trump continued to launch public attacks on news media throughout 2018, including by characterizing "a large percentage of the media" as "the enemy of the people." His remarks prompted hundreds of media outlets to publish coordinated defenses of press freedom in August. Journalists also experienced deadly violence and threats, including the shooting of five staff of an Annapolis, Maryland, newspaper in June.

Several police efforts to monitor protesters, including people of color, were reported or litigated during the year. US technology companies faced increased pressure from lawmakers to restrict speech on their platforms. In April, a new law aimed at curbing online sex trafficking made websites liable for what users say and do on their platforms. It also threatened to silence speech about consent-based sex work and other sexual activity.

Foreign Policy

The United States continued to withhold or reprogram humanitarian aid and funding to international bodies, eliminating all contributions to the United Nations Relief and Works Agency that aids Palestinian refugees, and significantly cutting US financial contributions to the UN Population Fund.

On February 7, the State Department released a six-month review of the Trump administration's Mexico City Policy, which blocks federal funding for non-governmental organizations that provide abortion counseling or referrals or advocate to decriminalize abortion or expand services, was silent on how it impacted women and girls.

In March, the State Department approved a weapons sale of nearly $1 billion to Saudi Arabia, which was ultimately cleared by Congress. Also that month, the Senate narrowly failed to pass a measure to end US military support to Saudi that would have restricted US participation in the Yemen conflict on grounds that it was unlawful.

The US continued to sell weapons to the coalition as well as provide targeting information and, in September, certified to Congress that the Saudi-led coalition had taken steps to reduce the risk to civilians. In November, the US announced it would stop refueling Saudi aircraft fighting in Yemen. The US response to the murder of Washington Post columnist and Virginia resident Jamal Khashoggi by Saudi state agents was inconsistent, with President Trump initially issuing a harsh rebuke but then questioning the reported CIA findings that the crown prince ordered Khashoggi's murder. The administration sanctioned 17 Saudis who were allegedly involved in Khashoggi's murder, but Secretary of State Mike Pompeo asserted that the US-Saudi partnership remained vital.

President Trump fired Secretary of State Rex Tillerson in March and nominated then-CIA Director Pompeo to be his successor. In April, the Senate confirmed Pompeo.

In March, the State Department's annual human rights country reports were released with reduced references to reproductive rights and violence against women. In May, Trump announced the US would withdraw from the Iran nuclear deal, despite the UN's confirmation that Iran continues to uphold its end of the agreement.

During weeks of protests at the Gaza border with Israel, the United States celebrated its embassy relocation to West Jerusalem on May 14, 2018. The move coincided with one of the deadliest days of the protests, with more than 60 Palestinian demonstrators killed. The US did not publicly condemn Israel's excessive use of force.

In June, Trump met with North Korean leader Kim Jong-un in Singapore. The following month, he met with Russian President Vladimir Putin. In August, he met with Kenyan President Uhuru Kenyatta, only his second meeting with an African leader. He publicly said nothing about the three governments' poor human rights records.

The United States officially withdrew from the UN Human Rights Council in June 2018 citing bias against Israel and the body's failure to reform, making it the first country ever to withdraw from the body. Shortly after, US Ambassador to the UN Nikki Haley wrote to Human Rights Watch and 16 other groups blaming them for the US' decision to withdraw, citing attempts to undermine efforts to improve the council.

Overall, Haley's record on human rights at the UN was mixed. She defended Israeli abuses but pushed the Security Council to approve an arms embargo for South Sudan and kept pressure on the Democratic Republic of Congo. Haley announced she would resign at the end of 2018.

The United States continued to impose visa restrictions and asset freezes on perpetrators of grave human rights violations and corruption. At time of writing, according to the Treasury Department, the United States had sanctioned 101 people under Executive Order 13818 "Blocking the Property of Persons Involved in Serious Human Rights Abuse or Corruption," which expands upon the Global Magnitsky Human Rights Accountability Act, in addition to the numerous other designations under different sanctions programs. Using this authority, as well as others, the United States has expanded human rights sanctions against the Iranian government, Venezuelan officials, and a number of Myanmar military officials and entities.

The State Department hosted its inaugural "Ministerial to Advance Religious Freedom" in Washington in July 2018—an event attend by foreign governments, civil society, and religious leaders, aimed at advancing religious liberties around the world. Iraq, Myanmar, and China, among other countries, were discussed. The US rhetorically condemned and pursued sanctions in response to China's abuses, but those efforts were undercut by President Trump's strong rhetorical support of President Xi Jinping.

In August, the State Department released a long-awaited report on the abuses committed by Myanmar's military against the Rohingya population since August 2017, but included no legal determinations or policy recommendations.

Also in September, National Security Advisor John Bolton announced that the Trump administration would not cooperate with the International Criminal Court (ICC) and threatened a number of retaliatory measures should ICC investigations reach US, Israeli, or other allied country citizens. He made clear that one of the reasons for this position was a pending ICC prosecutor request to open an investigation in Afghanistan that could include crimes of torture allegedly committed by US military and CIA personnel. President Trump reiterated this position in a speech to the UN General Assembly.

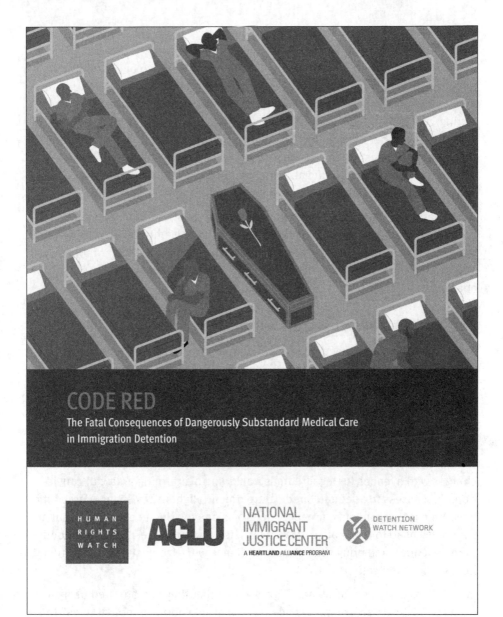

CODE RED

The Fatal Consequences of Dangerously Substandard Medical Care in Immigration Detention

HUMAN RIGHTS WATCH

ACLU

NATIONAL IMMIGRANT JUSTICE CENTER
A HEARTLAND ALLIANCE PROGRAM

DETENTION WATCH NETWORK

Uzbekistan

Two years after assuming the presidency following the death of Uzbekistan's long-serving leader Islam Karimov, President Shavkat Mirziyoyev continued to take some promising steps to reform the country's awful human rights record. During 2018, a detained journalist and other long-serving political prisoners were released, there was an increasingly vibrant media environment, evidence the government was working to combat forced labor in the cotton sector, and several cases where local officials were held accountable for abusive or corrupt actions following vigorous online debate.

At the same time, the Uzbek government remained authoritarian and many promising reforms have yet to be implemented. The security services' powers remain deep and vast, free elections and political pluralism are distant dreams, and there are still thousands of people in prison on politically motivated charges.

Politically Motivated Imprisonment and Criminal Justice

Authorities have released more than 30 people imprisoned on politically motivated charges since September 2016, including human rights activists Akzam Turgunov, Mehrinisso and Zulhumor Hamdamova, Isroiljon Kholdorov, Gaybullo Jalilov, Chuyan Mamatkulov, Fahriddin Tillaev and journalists Gayrat Mikhliboev, Yusuf Ruzimuradov, and Dilmurod Saidov.

While the releases raised hopes that the Uzbek government was making efforts to reform, authorities did not provide people released on politically motivated charges with avenues for legal redress, including overturning unlawful convictions, nor access to adequate medical treatment. Rights activists also urged the government to amend its criminal code provisions relating to extremism that are commonly used to criminalize dissent (articles 159, 216, 244-1, and 244-2 of the Criminal Code), and bring them into compliance with Uzbekistan's international human rights obligations.

In March, authorities told Human Rights Watch that they had stopped using article 221 of Uzbekistan's criminal code regarding "violations of prison rules" to arbitrarily extend the sentences of political prisoners. They have also reportedly released from prison hundreds of "independent" Muslims, individuals who practice Islam outside of strict state controls, but did not provide access to a list of all persons serving sentences on charges of extremism to verify who had been released or not.

Also in March, President Mirziyoev issued a decree transferring responsibility for a range of issues from the repressive National Security Service (SNB) to the Interior Ministry (MVD) and the Ministry of Defense. This decree came after the January dismissal of SNB Chairman Rustam Inoyatov, one of the most powerful officials in Uzbekistan, and head of the SNB since 1995. The SNB was renamed the State Security Service (SGB).

In May, following a trial observed by journalists and human rights monitors, a court conditionally released but still fined independent journalist Bobomurod Abdullaev, who had been detained in September 2017 and then allegedly tortured in pre-trial detention on charges of attempting to overthrow the government. While the trial set a precedent for its degree of openness and transparency, authorities have not investigated Abdullaev's credible allegations of severe torture. He has also reported being subjected to surveillance by security services on several occasions since the trial.

Thousands of individuals imprisoned on politically motivated charges remained behind bars. Among them are scholars Andrei Kubatin, Akrom Malikov, Rustam Abdumannapov, Jamoliddin Abdurakhmanov; Mirsobir Hamidkariev, a film producer; Aramais Avakyan, a fisherman; Ruhiddin Fahriddinov (Fahrutdinov), an independent cleric; Jahongir Kulidzhanov, a religious believer; Ravshan Kosimov, Viktor Shin, and Alisher Achildiev, soldiers; Nodirbek Yusupov, a deportee from the US; and Aziz Yusupov, the brother of a Radio Free Europe/Radio Liberty (RFE/RL) journalist. Some of them, including Kubatin, Fahriddinov, and Abdulhamid have been subjected to torture.

In June, several security agency officers were sentenced for their role in the torture and death in custody of Ilhom Ibodov, a Bukhara entrepreneur, in 2015.

Civil Society and Freedom of Expression

Freedom of speech and of the press have improved under Mirziyoyev but remain restricted. With 56 percent of the population under 30 years old and increasing

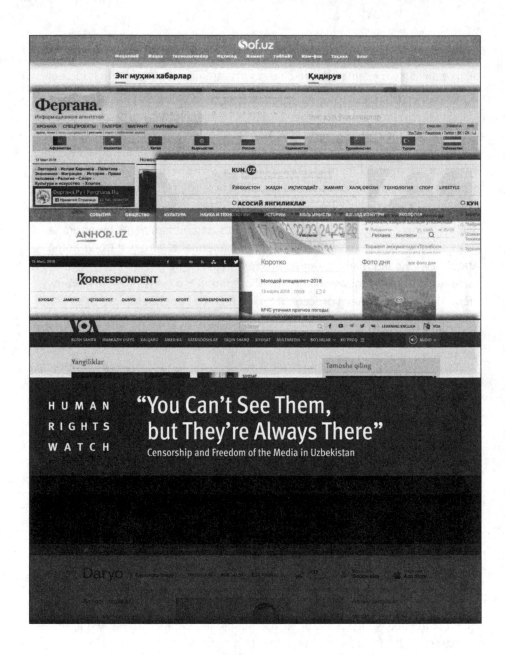

numbers of mobile internet users, both Uzbek and Russian-language online media are experiencing a period of growth and change. The president has urged the media not to hold back in addressing urgent social issues. Some journalists are now covering sensitive issues, such as forced labor and corruption, which were previously taboo, helping bring to the fore cases of injustice or wrongdoing by officials.

Yet much of the media remained under state control, and censorship is the norm. Journalists self-censor, unclear where the "red lines" are. Much of the internet remains blocked, and several pioneering online outlets such as kun.uz, xabar.uz, and qalampir.uz, were unavailable for a period in June and July. Facebook and YouTube were blocked for periods in August through November.

Voice of America's correspondent received accreditation in June. But at time of writing the government had still not granted accreditation for the BBC's local correspondent, despite promising to extend it to him since June 2017. RFE/RL remained unable to operate in Uzbekistan. In September, authorities detained at least eight conservative bloggers, allegedly for their views advocating a greater role for Islam in Uzbek society. Authorities denied several of them access to lawyers and sentenced some up to 15 days of administrative detention.

Authorities have slightly relaxed restrictions on the holding of modest peaceful demonstrations. But several participants in small-scale demonstrations held near the president's residence or the prosecutor-general's office were detained. In July, a group of 30 women were detained outside the president's residence during a peaceful protest. Six of the 30 were charged with "hooliganism" and held for 10 days.

In June, the Justice Ministry announced a new law on nongovernmental organizations (NGOs) that would relax procedures for registration, including by eliminating the requirement NGOs receive and hold funds in only two state-approved banks. The NGO law also purported to overturn the June 2015 law that severely restricted NGO activities by requiring organizations to receive advanced permission from authorities when holding virtually any activity or meeting. However, even under the amendments registered NGOs are still required to provide advanced notice before holding events or meetings, and civil society activists reported that during the year the law was not effectively implemented. They reported that local Justice Ministry officials have discouraged the registration of new organizations that focus on politically-sensitive issues.

In August, the Justice Ministry registered the American educational exchanges NGO ACCELS, the first American NGO to receive registration in 15 years. While able to freely visit the country and conduct research, Human Rights Watch remained unable to register due to a 2011 Supreme Court decision which remained in effect. Rights activists have urged the Uzbek government to overturn the decision.

In September, authorities fined rights activist Agzam Turgunov and refused him an exit visa, allegedly for filming police action during a peaceful protest.

Forced Labor

Forced labor in Uzbekistan's cotton sector in 2018 remained widespread. The government took measures to enforce a public decree prohibiting the forced mobilization of public sector workers, including teachers and medical personnel.

In October, the president dismissed the deputy prime minister Zoyir Mirzayev after an image appeared on social media of local officials and farmers apparently being forced to stand knee-deep in the cold water of an irrigation ditch. Mirzayev was present when an official punished the men for poor harvest results, prompting online anger at their humiliation. An eyewitness told RFE/RL's Uzbek service that Mirzayev had "berated the men, saying 'If you can't water the wheat, then I'll water you!' then forced them into the ditch, where they remained for half-an-hour for failing to water the wheat fields on time." At the same time, a social media campaign began where Facebook users posted photographs of themselves standing in irrigation ditches in order to raise awareness of the abuse. Mirzayev was reappointed to a lesser position of the head of a district in the Jizzak region several weeks later.

Various authorities continued to mobilize some public sector workers, students, and employees of private businesses to pick cotton on threat of punishment or loss of employment. In various regions such as Khorezm, public sector workers were forced to sign forms that they would pick a minimum amount of cotton.

The International Labour Organization (ILO), which found that over 300,000 people had picked cotton involuntarily during the 2017 harvest, continued to conduct monitoring in the country's cotton fields. It excluded from its monitoring teams officials from Uzbekistan's state-aligned Federation of Trade Unions, whose participation in previous monitoring led to concerns that the monitoring may have not been genuinely independent.

Key International Actors

In February, following an earlier mission to Uzbekistan, Ahmed Shaheed, the United Nations special rapporteur on freedom of religion or belief, issued a report that expressed concerns over limits on religious freedom and "extreme surveillance" of all religious practices that lead to bogus charges of terrorism. He urged authorities to substantially revise the 1998 religion law, make registration of religious organizations optional, "respect the liberty of parents to provide a religious education to their children," and review the arbitrary jail sentences of alleged "religious extremists." Following the issuance of the report, the Uzbek government adopted a roadmap to implement his recommendations.

In May, Uzbekistan underwent the third cycle of the Universal Periodic Review at the UN Human Rights Council (UNHRC). Several delegations called on Uzbekistan to release wrongfully imprisoned persons, to address torture and ill-treatment in detention and to revise the criminal code to bring it in line with international standards, including by repealing the provision that criminalizes consensual sexual relations between men.

In July, the US State Department's trafficking-in-persons report elevated Uzbekistan from a "Tier III" to "Tier II watch list" country, citing the government's efforts to combat forced and child labor in the country's cotton sector. The US State Department also designated Uzbekistan, for the 12th year in a row, a "country of particular concern," due to its serial violations of religious freedom.

The EU stated in its annual report on human rights and democracy that Uzbekistan's human rights record has been following a "positive trajectory." The EU welcomed Uzbek authorities' increased efforts to fight corruption, strengthen transparency, cease malpractices in prisons and detention centers, grant citizenship to stateless persons, and called for improvements in certain areas including the "arbitrary extension of prison sentences," "restrictions in the areas of freedom of expression, information, religion, assembly and association," excessive regulation of NGO activities, and the prevalence of forced labor.

In July, the EU decided to negotiate an Enhanced Partnership and Cooperation Agreement with Uzbekistan that would upgrade political and economic relations with the EU. The future agreement would also cover issues like rule of law, justice, and human rights.

Uzbek officials indicated a willingness to issue an invitation to the UN special rapporteur on the independence of lawyers and the judiciary in 2018 or early 2019, but at time of writing the visit had not been scheduled. Twelve other requests by UN special rapporteurs for access to visit Uzbekistan, such as the UN special rapporteur on torture, also remained outstanding.

Venezuela

In May, President Nicolás Maduro won presidential elections against an opposition badly weakened by years of government repression, and amid widespread allegations that the polls had not met international standards of freedom and fairness.

No independent government institutions remain today in Venezuela to act as a check on executive power. A series of measures by the Maduro and Chávez governments stacked the courts with judges who make no pretense of independence. The government has been repressing dissent through often-violent crackdowns on street protests, jailing opponents, and prosecuting civilians in military courts. It has also stripped power from the opposition-led legislature.

Severe shortages of medicines, medical supplies, and food leave many Venezuelans unable to feed their families adequately or access essential healthcare. The massive exodus of Venezuelans fleeing repression and shortages represents the largest migration crisis of its kind in recent Latin American history.

Other persistent concerns include poor prison conditions, impunity for human rights violations, and harassment by government officials of human rights defenders and independent media outlets.

Refugee Crisis

The United Nations High Commissioner for Refugees reported that, as of November, more than 3 million of an estimated 32 million Venezuelans had fled their country since 2014. Many more not registered by authorities have also left.

The political, economic, human rights, and humanitarian crises in Venezuela combine to compel Venezuelans to leave and make them unable or unwilling to return. Some qualify for refugee status. Others do not, but would face severe hardship if returned to Venezuela and are in urgent need of humanitarian assistance in the countries to which they have migrated.

Many Venezuelans in other countries remain in an irregular situation, which severely undermines their ability to obtain work permits, send their children to school, and access health care. This makes them vulnerable to exploitation and abuse.

Persecution of Political Opponents

The Venezuelan government has jailed political opponents and disqualified them from running for office. At time of writing, Venezuelan prisons and intelligence services offices held more than 230 political prisoners, according to the Penal Forum, a Venezuelan network of pro-bono criminal defense lawyers.

At time of writing, opposition leader Leopoldo López was serving a 13-year sentence under house arrest on charges of inciting violence during a demonstration in Caracas in February 2014, despite a lack of credible evidence against him. Several others arrested in connection with the 2014 protests or subsequent political activism remain under house arrest or in detention, awaiting trial. Others have been forced into exile.

Crackdown on Protest Activity

In two crackdowns in 2014 and 2017, Venezuelan security forces and armed pro-government groups called *"colectivos"* attacked demonstrations—some attended by tens of thousands of protesters. Security force personnel shot demonstrators at point-blank range with riot-control munitions, brutally beat people who offered no resistance, and staged violent raids on apartment buildings.

More than 12,500 people have been arrested since 2014 in connection with protests, according to the Penal Forum. These include not only demonstrators but bystanders, and people taken from their homes without warrants. Around 7,300 had been conditionally released at time of writing, but they remained subject to criminal prosecution. In 2017, military courts prosecuted more than 750 civilians, in violation of international human rights law. The practice continued with less frequency in 2018.

Security forces have committed serious abuses against detainees that in some cases amount to torture—including severe beatings, electric shocks, asphyxiation, and sexual abuse.

While no massive demonstrations have taken place since August 2017, security forces continue repressing spontaneous protests and carrying out targeted, arbitrary arrests of opponents or perceived opponents throughout the country.

Alleged Extrajudicial Killings

In January, security forces and members of a *colectivo* surrounded a house in the town of El Junquito, near Caracas, where Oscar Pérez—a rogue police officer who threw a grenade from a helicopter to the Supreme Court building after calling on the Venezuelan people to rebel against the government—and six others were hiding. Government authorities said the seven men died in a confrontation, and that they were "terrorists." Two security agents and a *colectivo* member also died.

Evidence suggests, however, that Pérez may have been extrajudicially executed. Prior to his death, he posted several videos on social media saying they were under attack and he was negotiating with authorities to surrender. A copy of his death certificate shows the cause of death as a single shot to the head.

In 2015, the government launched "Operation Peoples' Liberation" (OLP), supposedly to address rising security concerns. Police and members of the Bolivarian National Guard carried out raids that led to widespread allegations of such abuses as extrajudicial killings, mass arbitrary detentions, maltreatment of detainees, forced evictions, destruction of homes, and arbitrary deportations.

In November 2017, the attorney general said more than 500 people had been killed during OLP raids. Government officials typically said they died during "confrontations" with armed criminals, claims challenged in many cases by witnesses or families of victims. In several cases, victims were last seen alive in police custody.

Impunity for Abuses

Since former Attorney General Luisa Ortega Díaz was fired in August 2017, no official information has been available about prosecutions of officials implicated in human rights violations. The United Nations Office of the High Commissioner for Human Rights (OHCHR) reported in June 2018 that impunity for human rights abuses in Venezuela was "pervasive."

In July 2017, Ortega Díaz's office was investigating nearly 2,000 cases of people injured during the 2017 crackdown. In more than half of the cases, prosecutors had evidence suggesting fundamental rights violations, according to official sources. The OHCHR reported that 357 security officers were under investigation for alleged extrajudicial killings during OLPs. The OHCHR said that security forces suspected of extrajudicially killing protesters had in some cases been released, despite judicial detention orders, and that the prosecutors had issued at least 54 arrest warrants for security agents implicated in the killing of 46 people during protests. A trial, though, had started in only one case.

Humanitarian Crisis

Venezuelans are facing severe shortages of medicine, medical supplies, and food, seriously undermining their rights to health and food. In 2017, the Venezuelan health minister released official data for 2016, indicating that, during that year, maternal mortality had increased 65 percent, infant mortality 30 percent, and cases of malaria 76 percent. Days later, the health minister was fired. The government has not since published epidemiological bulletins.

The Pan American Health Organization has reported increasing numbers of patients with such diseases as malaria, tuberculosis, measles, and diphtheria. Until 2016, measles and diphtheria, which are preventable through vaccination, had been eliminated in Venezuela.

The estimated percentage of children under five suffering moderate or severe malnutrition increased from 10 in February 2017 to 17 in March 2018, according to Cáritas Venezuela, in Caracas and several states. Cáritas reported the average dipped to 13.5 in July, but figures were significantly higher in Caracas (16.7) and Vargas state (19.7). A 2018 nationwide study by three prestigious Venezuelan universities found that 80 percent of Venezuelan households were food insecure, and interviewees each had lost an average of 11 kilograms in 2017.

Judicial Independence

Since former President Hugo Chávez and his supporters in the National Assembly conducted a political takeover of the Supreme Court in 2004, the judiciary has ceased to function as an independent branch of government. Members of the Supreme Court have openly rejected the principle of separation of powers and publicly pledged their commitment to advancing the government's political agenda. The court has consistently upheld abusive policies and practices.

Constituent Assembly

In 2017, President Maduro convened a "Constituent Assembly" by presidential decree, despite a constitutional requirement that a public referendum be held before any effort to rewrite the Constitution. The assembly is made up exclusively of government supporters chosen through an election that Smartmatic, a British company hired by the government to verify the results, called fraudulent. The Constituent Assembly has, in practice, replaced the opposition-led National Assembly as the country's legislative branch.

Freedom of Expression

For more than a decade, the government has expanded and abused its power to regulate media and has worked aggressively to reduce the number of dissenting media outlets. The government can suspend or revoke concessions to private media if "convenient for the interests of the nation," arbitrarily suspend websites for the vaguely defined offense of "incitement," and criminalize expression of "disrespect" for high government officials. While a few newspapers, websites, and radio stations criticize the government, fear of reprisals has made self-censorship a serious problem.

In May, members of the Bolivarian Service of National Intelligence (SEBIN) detained Pedro Jaimes Criollo for mentioning the presidential plane's route, which was public information, on Twitter. Criollo has been charged with crimes including espionage and revealing political secrets. Neither his family nor lawyers from the Venezuelan group Espacio Público who are working on the case were allowed to see or talk to him for more than a month. He has told his family that security agents have brutally beaten him. At time of writing, he remained in an overcrowded cell, without access to medical treatment.

In November 2017, the Constituent Assembly adopted a Law Against Hatred that includes vague language undermining free speech. It forbids political parties that "promote fascism, hatred, and intolerance," and imposes prison sentences of up to 20 years on those who publish "messages of intolerance and hatred" in media or social media. In 2018, prosecutors charged several people with these crimes, including three children detained after voicing opposition to the government on social media.

Human Rights Defenders

Government measures to restrict international funding of nongovernmental organizations—combined with unsubstantiated accusations by government officials and supporters that human rights defenders are seeking to undermine Venezuelan democracy—create a hostile environment that limits the ability of civil society groups to promote human rights.

In 2010, the Supreme Court ruled that individuals or organizations receiving foreign funding can be prosecuted for treason. That year, the National Assembly enacted legislation blocking organizations that "defend political rights" or "monitor the performance of public bodies" from receiving international assistance.

Political Discrimination

People who supported referendums on Chávez's and Maduro's presidencies have been fired from government jobs. A government program that distributes food and basic goods at government-capped prices has been credibly accused of discriminating against government critics.

In April, President Maduro said he would "give a prize" to Venezuelans who voted in the May elections and presented their "carnet of the Fatherland," a government-issued ID required for accessing housing, pensions, certain medical procedures, and boxes of food subject to government-set prices. During the presidential campaign, participants who attended government rallies got bags of food.

Prison Conditions

Corruption, weak security, deteriorating infrastructure, overcrowding, insufficient staffing, and poorly trained guards allow armed gangs to exercise effective control over inmate populations. Excessive use of pretrial detention contributes to overcrowding. In March, at least 66 detainees and two visitors died during a fire following a riot in a police station used as a jail in Carabobo state.

Key International Actors

In February, International Criminal Court (ICC) Prosecutor Fatou Bensouda announced a preliminary examination to analyze whether since at least 2017 crimes occurring within the court's jurisdiction have taken place, including allegations of use of excessive force against demonstrators and detention of thousands of actual or perceived opponents, some of whom claim to have suffered serious abuse in detention. In September, six countries—all ICC member countries—requested an ICC investigation. Two other countries supported the states' referral since then.

In May, an expert panel appointed by OAS Secretary General Luis Almagro compiled a damning assessment of Venezuela's human rights record, concluding that crimes against humanity may have been committed. In September, after 14 neighboring governments agreed to coordinate responses to the Venezuelan exodus, Almagro created a working group to evaluate emigration and adopt recommendations to address it.

Many South American governments have made considerable efforts to welcome Venezuelans. In 2018, however, some adopted restrictive measures such as requiring passports, which are nearly impossible to get in Venezuela, making it harder for Venezuelans to apply for legal status.

In the Caribbean, no country has created a special permit for Venezuelans to stay legally, and most lack laws to regulate the asylum-seeking process. Some Venezuelans with asylum-seeker documents in Trinidad and Tobago and Curaçao have reportedly been detained or deported to Venezuela, a violation of international law. Venezuelans seeking refuge in places including Caribbean countries and northern Brazil have also faced xenophobic harassment.

In June, the OHCHR released a follow-up report concluding that Venezuelan authorities had failed to hold accountable perpetrators of such serious abuses as killings, excessive use of force, arbitrary arrests, and torture. The report highlights the health and nutrition crises, not only systemic shortages of foods and medicine, but such complicating factors as doctors leaving the country and government threats against, and detention of, healthcare workers and critics. The report concludes crimes against humanity may have been committed in

Venezuela, and calls on members of the Human Rights Council to create a commission of inquiry into violations committed in the country.

The Lima Group—consisting of 13 Latin American governments and Canada—has monitored the situation in Venezuela closely, criticizing abuses by Venezuelan authorities and offering humanitarian aid. During the June Human Rights Council session in Geneva, the Lima Group's joint statement on Venezuela's crisis attracted support from 53 states cross-regionally. In September, the group, with the exception of Brazil, presented the council's first ever resolution on Venezuela, condemning the human rights and humanitarian crisis and calling for continued reporting on the situation by the High Commissioner throughout 2019. The resolution was adopted by a vote of 23 in favor, 7 against, and 17 abstentions. It received support from delegations from every continent.

The United States, Canada, the European Union, Switzerland, and Panama have imposed targeted sanctions on more than 50 Venezuelan officials implicated in human rights abuses and corruption. The sanctions include asset freezes and the cancelling of visas. In 2017, the United States imposed financial sanctions, including a ban on dealings in new stocks and bonds issued by the Venezuelan government and its state oil company.

In January, the EU put seven individuals holding official positions under restrictive measures for their involvement in the non-respect of democratic principles or the rule of law as well as in the violation of human rights. The European Parliament condemned the negative developments in the country in resolutions adopted in February, May, and July, calling for the holding of credible, free and fair elections and for an effective response to the humanitarian and human rights crisis in the country. In May, the EU highlighted serious shortcomings in the Venezuelan electoral process, stressing that its results lack any credibility. In June, the EU added 11 individuals to its list of sanctions, bringing the total number to 18.

The Venezuelan government withdrew from the American Convention on Human Rights in 2013, leaving citizens and residents unable to request intervention by the Inter-American Court of Human Rights when local remedies for abuses are ineffective or unavailable. The Inter-American Commission on Human Rights continues to monitor Venezuela, however, applying the American Declaration of Rights and Duties of Man, which is not subject to states' ratification.

In September 2018, the UN Security Council held an informal "Arria Formula" meeting on corruption in Venezuela and world leaders led by Costa Rica convened a special "high-level" meeting on Venezuela during the annual UN General Assembly.

As a member of the UN Human Rights Council, Venezuela has regularly voted to prevent scrutiny of human rights violations in other countries, opposing resolutions spotlighting abuses in countries including Syria, Belarus, Burundi, and Iran. They also refuse to cooperate with council mechanisms, including rejecting visit requests by most special procedure mandate holders.

Vietnam

Vietnam's appalling human rights record worsened in 2018 as the government imprisoned dissidents for longer prison terms, sanctioned thugs to attack rights defenders, and passed draconian laws that further threaten freedom of expression.

The Communist Party of Vietnam monopolizes power through the government, controls all major political and social organizations, and punishes people who dare to criticize or challenge its rule.

Basic civil and political rights including freedom of expression, association, and peaceful public assembly are severely restricted. Independent media is not allowed as the government controls TV, radio, newspapers, and other publications. Vietnam prohibits the formation of independent labor unions, political associations, and human rights organizations. Police frequently use excessive force to disperse peaceful public protests that criticize the government.

Activists questioning government policies or projects, or seeking to defend local resources or land, face daily harassment, intrusive surveillance, house arrest, travel bans, arbitrary detention, and interrogation. Thugs, apparently collaborating with police, have increasingly launched physical attacks against activists with impunity.

Police subject dissidents to lengthy and bullying interrogations, and detain them incommunicado for months without access to family members or legal counsel. Communist Party-controlled courts receive instructions on how to rule in criminal cases, and have issued increasingly harsh prison sentences for activists convicted on bogus national security charges.

In September 2018, Vietnam's President Tran Dai Quang, former minister of the notorious Ministry of Public Security, died. In October, the National Assembly voted to elect Communist Party Secretary Nguyen Phu Trong to be the new president, merging two top positions into one.

Freedom of Expression, Opinion, and Speech

Vietnamese rights bloggers face regular harassment and intimidation. Officials often arrest political critics for their posts on the internet. In 2018, Vietnam put on trial at least 12 people for "conducting propaganda against the state." Sentences ranged from 4 to 12 years in prison, including for blogger Ho Van Hai (also known as Dr. Ho Hai), and activists Nguyen Dinh Thanh, Bui Hieu Vo, Tran Hoang Phuc, Vu Quang Thuan, Nguyen Van Dien, Nguyen Viet Dung, and Vuong Van Tha.

Activists and bloggers face frequent physical assaults by officials or government connected thugs, who are not punished for these attacks. In June and July 2018 in Lam Dong province, unidentified men threw rocks and a handmade incendiary device into the house of a labor activist and former political prisoner, Do Thi Minh Hanh. In August, security agents brutally beat rights activists Pham Doan Trang, Nguyen Tin, and Nguyen Dang Cao Dai after a raid on a concert in Ho Chi Minh City. Also in August, police in Khanh Hoa province detained activist Ngo Thanh Tu and beat him repeatedly. In September, men in civilian clothes assaulted activist Huynh Cong Thuan in Ho Chi Minh City as he was driving home from work on a motorbike. Also in September, unknown thugs attacked and broke the arm of former political prisoner Truong Van Kim in Lam Dong.

Police place activists under house arrest or briefly detain them to prevent them from participating in meetings and protests or attending the trials of fellow activists. The government prohibited many dissidents and human rights defenders from traveling abroad. In March, police barred dissident poet Bui Minh Quoc from leaving Vietnam for the United States. In May, police barred human rights activist Father Dinh Huu Thoai from leaving Vietnam for a personal trip to the US, and labor activist Do Thi Minh Hanh from leaving for Germany. In June, police prohibited Father Nguyen Duy Tan from leaving for Malaysia. In August, the police denied the issuance of a passport to former political prisoner Le Cong Dinh without explanation. In September, police detained Dr. Nguyen Quang A for hours to prevent him from leaving for Australia. According to him, this was his 18th detention by police since March 2016.

Repression of Freedom of Press and Access to Information

The Vietnamese government continues to prohibit independent or privately owned media outlets from operating. It exerts strict control over radio and TV stations and printed publications. Criminal penalties apply to those who disseminate materials deemed to oppose the government, threaten national security, or promote "reactionary" ideas. Authorities block access to politically sensitive websites, frequently shut down blogs, and require internet service providers to remove content or social media accounts deemed politically unacceptable.

In June 2018, Vietnam's National Assembly passed a highly problematic law on cybersecurity that was widely criticized in Vietnam and internationally. Under the new law, which will go into effect in January 2019, service providers must take down offending content within 24 hours of receiving a request from the Ministry of Public Security or the Ministry of Information and Communications. Internet companies are also required to store data locally, verify user information, and disclose user data to authorities on demand without a court order, all of which threaten the right to privacy and could facilitate further suppression of online dissent or activism.

In August, police arrested Nguyen Ngoc Anh in Ben Tre province for allegedly using Facebook to urge people to protest. In September, various courts in Can Tho province convicted Bui Manh Dong, Doan Khanh Vinh Quang, Nguyen Hong Nguyen, and Truong Dinh Khang for their posts and shares on Facebook for "abusing freedom and democracy to infringe upon the interests of the state" under article 331 of the penal code. The four were given sentences ranging from one year to two-and-a-half years in prison.

Freedom of Association and Assembly

Vietnam continues to prohibit the establishment and operation of independent labor unions, human rights organizations, and political parties. Organizers trying to establish independent unions or workers' groups face harassment, intimidation, and retaliation. Authorities convicted and sentenced labor activist Truong Minh Duc to 12 years in prison in April 2018 and activist Hoang Duc Binh to 14 years in February.

Communist Party-controlled courts severely punished people who were accused of being affiliated with political groups or parties that the Communist Party of Vietnam views as threatening its monopoly on power. In April, five members of a group that called itself the Brotherhood for Democracy—Nguyen Van Tuc, Nguyen Trung Ton, Nguyen Bac Truyen, Tran Thi Xuan, and Pham Van Troi—were sentenced to between 7 and 13 years in prison. In August, activist Le Dinh Luong received a 20-year prison sentence for his alleged involvement with Viet Tan, a banned overseas political party. In September, the People's Court of Quang Binh sentenced Nguyen Trung Truc to 12 years in prison for participating in various human rights activities and being a member of the Brotherhood for Democracy. In October, Luu Van Vinh, Nguyen Quoc Hoan, Nguyen Van Duc Do, Tu Cong Nghia, and Phan Trung were convicted under article 79 of the penal code for their alleged affiliation with the Vietnam National Self-Determination Coalition, an independent political group, and sentenced to between 8 and 15 years in prison.

Authorities require approval for public gatherings and systematically refuse permission for meetings, marches, or public gatherings they deem to be politically unacceptable. In June 2018, authorities harassed, detained, and assaulted dozens of people who participated in demonstrations throughout Vietnam to protest against a draft law on special economic zones and the draconian law on cybersecurity. As of October, the government convicted at least 118 protesters for disrupting public order. Many were sentenced to prison, some serving as long as four-and-a-half years.

Freedom of Religion

The government restricts religious practice through legislation, registration requirements, and surveillance. Religious groups are required to get approval from, and register with, the government, and operate under government-controlled management boards. While authorities allow many government-affiliated churches and pagodas to hold worship services, they ban religious activities that they arbitrarily deem to be contrary to the "national interest," "public order," or "national unity," including many ordinary types of religious functions.

Police monitor, harass, and sometimes violently crack down on religious groups operating outside government-controlled institutions. Unrecognized branches of the Cao Dai Church, Hoa Hao Buddhist Church, independent Protestant and Catholic house churches, Khmer Krom Buddhist temples, and the Unified Buddhist Church of Vietnam face constant surveillance, harassment, and intimidation.

Followers of independent religious group are subject to public criticism, forced renunciation of faith, detention, interrogation, torture, and imprisonment. In February 2018, authorities tried and convicted five independent Hoa Hao Buddhist practitioners including Bui Van Trung and his son Bui Van Tham, and sentenced them to between three and six years in prison for criticizing the government and staging a public protest against religious repression.

In June, men in civilian clothes broke into the house of Cao Dai religious activist Hua Phi in Lam Dong province, where they beat him and cut off his beard. In September, under police pressure, 91-year-old prominent religious leader Venerable Thich Quang Do was forced to leave Thanh Minh Zen Monastery in Ho Chi Minh City to return to his hometown in Thai Binh province.

Montagnards in the Central Highlands face constant surveillance and other forms of intimidation, arbitrary arrest, and mistreatment in custody. In detention, authorities question them about their religious and political activities, accuse them of allegiance to exile organizations, and discourage any efforts to flee Vietnam.

Key International Actors

China remains the most important international actor influencing Vietnam. Maritime disputes continue to complicate the bilateral relationship of these Communist Party governments with similar repressive approaches to human rights.

The United States continues to expand ties with Vietnam. In March, USS Carl Vinson arrived in Da Nang, the first US aircraft carrier to visit Vietnam since 1975. In July, US Secretary of State Mike Pompeo visited Vietnam and urged North Korea to follow Vietnam's steps to achieve economic growth, while ignoring Vietnam's systemic rights abuses. In January and October, US Defense Secretary James Mattis visited Vietnam to push for bilateral military ties between the two countries.

As the third largest trade partner with Vietnam, the European Union has growing leverage over the country. Negotiations for a free trade agreement reached their final stage. Over the year, the EU raised concerns over convictions of some rights activists. In September, 32 members of the European Parliament called on Vietnam to improve its rights record.

Australia and Vietnam upgraded ties under a new strategic partnership in March 2018. Australia's concerns about Hanoi's human rights violations are relegated to an annual bilateral human rights dialogue, without any promising signs from Hanoi.

As the most important bilateral donor to Vietnam, Japan continues to remain silent on Vietnam's long history of rights repression. In May, Prime Minister Shinzo Abe welcomed the now-late President Tran Dai Quang in Tokyo. In September, Japanese Foreign Minister Taro Kono visited Vietnam. In both cases, human rights were not mentioned in any meeting.

Yemen

The armed conflict in Yemen has killed and injured thousands of Yemeni civilians since it began. As of November 2018, 6,872 civilians had been killed and 10,768 wounded, the majority by Saudi Arabia-led coalition airstrikes, according to the Office of the United Nations High Commissioner for Human Rights (OHCHR). The actual civilian casualties are likely much higher. Thousands more have been displaced by the fighting and millions suffer from shortages of food and medical care.

In September 2014, Houthi forces and forces loyal to former president Ali Abdullah Saleh took control of Yemen's capital, Sanaa, and much of the country. On March 26, 2015, the Saudi-led coalition attacked Houthi-Saleh forces in support of Yemeni President Abdu Rabbu Mansour Hadi. The US supported coalition attacks with targeting intelligence and air refueling. As the war has continued, alliances have fractured. Houthi forces killed Saleh in December 2017 after clashes broke out in Sanaa. In January 2018, fighting broke out between Yemeni government forces and United Arab Emirates (UAE)-backed Yemeni forces in Aden. Across the country, civilians suffer from a lack of basic services, a spiraling economic crisis, and broken governance, health, education, and judicial systems.

Parties to the conflict have exacerbated what the UN has called the world's largest humanitarian catastrophe, including by unlawfully impeding delivery of desperately needed humanitarian aid.

The armed conflict has taken a terrible toll on the civilian population. The coalition has conducted scores of indiscriminate and disproportionate airstrikes killing thousands of civilians and hitting civilian objects in violation of the laws of war, using munitions sold by the United States, United Kingdom, and others, including widely banned cluster munitions. Houthi forces have used banned antipersonnel landmines, recruited children, and fired artillery indiscriminately into cities such as Taizz and Aden, killing and wounding civilians, and launched indiscriminate rockets into Saudi Arabia.

Both sides have harassed, threatened, and attacked Yemeni activists and journalists. Houthi forces, government-affiliated forces, and the UAE and UAE-backed Yemeni forces have arbitrarily detained or forcibly disappeared scores.

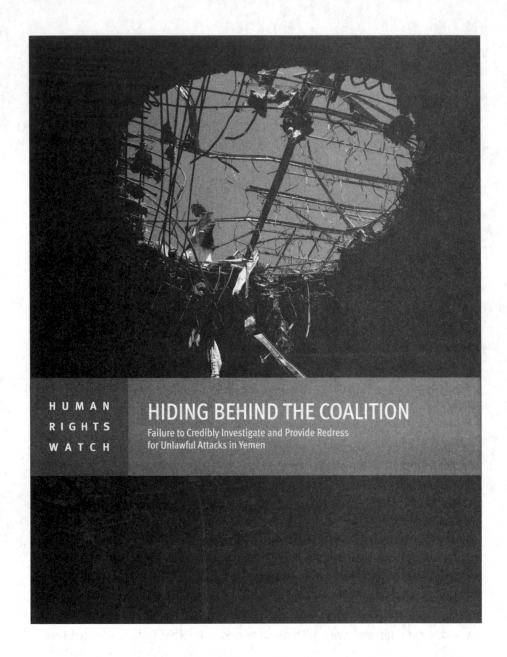

HUMAN
RIGHTS
WATCH

HIDING BEHIND THE COALITION

Failure to Credibly Investigate and Provide Redress
for Unlawful Attacks in Yemen

Houthi forces have taken hostages. Forces in Aden beat, raped, and tortured detained migrants.

Despite mounting evidence of violations of international law by the parties to the conflict, efforts toward accountability have been woefully inadequate.

Unlawful Airstrikes

Since 2015, Human Rights Watch has documented about 90 apparently unlawful coalition airstrikes, which have hit homes, markets, hospitals, schools, and mosques. Some of these attacks may amount to war crimes. In 2018, the coalition bombed a wedding, killing 22 people, including 8 children, and in another strike bombed a bus filled with children, killing at least 26 children. Human Rights Watch has identified remnants of US-origin munitions at the site of more than two dozen attacks, including the 2018 attacks on the wedding and the bus.

Indiscriminate Artillery Attacks

Houthi forces have repeatedly fired artillery indiscriminately into Yemeni cities and launched indiscriminate ballistic missiles into Saudi Arabia. Some of these attacks may amount to war crimes. Houthi attacks have struck populated neighborhoods in Yemen, having a particularly devastating impact on Taizz, Yemen's third largest city.

Banned Weapons

Landmines have killed and maimed civilians, disrupted civilian life in affected areas, and will pose a threat to civilians long after the conflict ends. Houthi forces have used landmines in governorates across Yemen, killing and wounding civilians and preventing their return home. Yemen is a party to the 1997 Mine Ban Treaty. The Saudi-led coalition has used at least six types of widely banned cluster munitions produced in Brazil, the US, and the UK. Yemen, Saudi Arabia, and other coalition states are not party to the 2008 Convention on Cluster Munitions.

Arbitrary Detentions, Torture, and Enforced Disappearances

Houthi forces, the Yemeni government, and the UAE and UAE-backed Yemeni forces have arbitrarily detained people, including children, abused detainees and held them in poor conditions, and forcibly disappeared people perceived to be political opponents or security threats. Yemeni human rights groups and lawyers have documented hundreds of cases of arbitrary detention and enforced disappearance.

Since late 2014, Human Rights Watch has documented dozens of cases of the Houthis and forces loyal to the late president Saleh carrying out arbitrary and abusive detention, as well as forced disappearances and torture. Houthi officials have used torture and other ill-treatment. Former detainees described Houthi officers beating them with iron rods and rifles, and being hung from walls with their arms shackled behind them.

The Houthis have also taken hostages, which is a war crime. Human Rights Watch documented 16 cases in which Houthi authorities held people unlawfully primarily to extort money from relatives or to exchange for people held by opposing forces. The Houthis have released only some of those held.

Human Rights Watch has also documented the UAE, UAE proxies, and Yemeni government forces arbitrarily detaining, torturing, and forcibly disappearing scores of people in areas of southern Yemen, which is nominally under government control.

In Aden, guards tortured, raped, and executed migrants and asylum seekers, including children, from the Horn of Africa in a detention center. The authorities denied asylum seekers an opportunity to seek refugee protection and deported migrants en masse to dangerous conditions at sea. The government shut down the facility where Human Rights Watch documented abuse, but Human Rights Watch continued to receive information of migrants and asylum seekers being arbitrarily and abusively detained in both the north and south of the country.

In 2018, the UN Group of Eminent Experts on Yemen concluded that the Houthi, Yemeni, Saudi, and UAE forces were credibly implicated in detainee-related abuse that might amount to war crimes. The UAE has run informal detention facilities in Yemen, but has not acknowledged any role in detainee abuse nor conducted any apparent investigations. Senior officials implicated in abuse remain in positions of authority across the country.

Attacks on Civil Society

One cost of Yemen's war has been the closing of space for civil society. Yemeni activists, journalists, lawyers, and rights defenders worry about arrest, harassment, targeted violence, and joining the list of Yemen's "disappeared." The risk is greatest when the target of criticism is a party to the conflict, who often retaliate.

The Houthis have detained students, human rights defenders, journalists, perceived political opponents, and members of the Baha'i religious community. A group of local journalists have been detained in Sanaa for more than three years. In January, a Sanaa court sentenced a Baha'i man to death on charges related to his religious beliefs. After Houthis killed former president Saleh, Houthi authorities cracked down further on dissent in areas under their control.

The Saudi-led coalition and Yemeni government forces have also harassed, intimidated, and arrested activists and journalists. Since May 2017, the coalition has restricted travel routes for journalists and international human rights organizations, including Human Rights Watch, to areas of Yemen under Houthi control, including via UN flights. The coalition has kept Sanaa International Airport closed since August 2016.

Blocking and Impeding Humanitarian Access

The UN considers Yemen to be the world's largest humanitarian crisis, with 14 million people at risk of starvation and repeated outbreaks of deadly diseases like cholera. This crisis is linked to the armed conflict.

The Saudi-led coalition's restrictions on imports have worsened the dire humanitarian situation. The coalition has delayed and diverted fuel tankers, closed critical ports, and stopped goods from entering Houthi-controlled seaports. Fuel needed to power generators to hospitals and pump water to homes has also been blocked.

Houthi forces have blocked and confiscated food and medical supplies and denied access to populations in need. They have imposed onerous restrictions on aid workers and interfered with aid delivery.

As thousands of civilians were displaced as fighting moved up Yemen's western coast in 2017 and 2018, Houthis and UAE-backed fighters restricted the flight of some families seeking to flee frontline areas.

Aid workers have been kidnapped, arbitrarily detained, and killed while conducting humanitarian operations in Yemen.

Children and Armed Conflict

Houthi forces, government and pro-government forces, and other armed groups have used child soldiers. In 2017, the UN verified 842 cases of recruitment and use of boys as young as 11, nearly two-thirds of which were attributable to Houthi forces. Under Yemeni and international law, 18 is the minimum age for military service.

In June, the UN secretary-general released his annual "list of shame" for violations against children in armed conflict. This list included many of Yemen's warring parties—the Houthis, Al-Qaeda in the Arabian Peninsula, pro-government militias, and UAE-backed Yemeni forces, but the Saudi-led coalition was treated differently.

The secretary-general placed the coalition on a special list for countries that put in place "measures to improve child protection," despite noting that the coalition continued to kill and maim children and attack schools and hospitals. In October, the UN Committee on the Rights of the Child found that children "are being killed, maimed, orphaned, and traumatized" by the coalition's military operations, "aggravated by an aerial and naval blockade" that had made many children food insecure.

In October, Yemen endorsed the Safe Schools Declaration, thereby committing to do more to protect students, teachers, and schools during conflict, including by implementing the Guidelines for Protecting Schools and Universities from Military Use During Armed Conflict.

Terrorism and Counterterrorism

Both Al-Qaeda in the Arabian Peninsula (AQAP) and the Islamic State in Yemen have claimed responsibility for suicide and other bombings. Until 2016, AQAP controlled major swathes of territory and, at times, governed cities.

The US continued to carry out drone attacks in Yemen against both groups. The US has also worked closely with the UAE, which leads coalition efforts in southern Yemen, including by supporting Yemeni forces carrying out security campaigns. Human Rights Watch has documented abuses by the UAE and UAE proxy forces, including arbitrary detentions, forced disappearances and torture.

Women's and Girls' Rights

Women activists have played a prominent role during the conflict advocating for better rights protection and protesting mistreatment. Some have been threatened, subjected to smear campaigns, beaten and detained in retaliation.

Women in Yemen face severe discrimination in law and practice. Violence against women in Yemen has increased—an estimated 3 million women and girls were at risk of violence by 2018, according to the UN. Forced marriage rates, including child marriage, have increased. Yemen has no minimum age of marriage. They cannot marry without the permission of their male guardian and do not have equal rights to divorce, inheritance, or child custody. Lack of legal protection leaves them exposed to domestic and sexual violence.

Accountability

None of the warring parties carried out credible investigations into their forces' alleged laws-of-war violations.

The coalition's Joint Incidents Assessment Team (JIAT) did not conduct credible investigations. JIAT failed to release full investigation reports or detailed information on their methodology, including how they determine which strikes to investigate, which state's forces participated in attacks they investigated, or what steps, if any, coalition states have taken to prosecute individuals responsible for war crimes. While JIAT has recommended the coalition pay civilian victims some form of assistance in more than a dozen attacks, the coalition does not appear to have made any concrete progress toward creating a fair, effective redress or condolence payment system.

The US is not known to have conducted investigations into any alleged unlawful attacks in which its forces have taken part.

In September, despite attempts by the Saudi-led coalition to terminate the mandate, the UN Human Rights Council voted by a substantial margin to renew the mandate of the Group of Eminent Experts to conduct international investigations into violations and abuses in Yemen.

Yemen has not joined the International Criminal Court.

Key International Actors

Coalition member countries have sought to avoid international legal liability by refusing to provide information on their forces' role in unlawful attacks. By early 2018, meetings of the coalition included representatives from Saudi Arabia, the UAE, Jordan, Bahrain, Sudan, Egypt, Kuwait, and Morocco, as well as Pakistan, Djibouti, Senegal, Malaysia, and Yemen, according to the Saudi state news agency.

The United States has been a party to the conflict and may be complicit in unlawful coalition attacks in which it took part. The US has provided in-air refueling and other tactical support to coalition forces, but has not provided detailed information on the extent and scope of its engagement. In November, the US said it was ending in-air refueling to the coalition.

The UK has provided training and weaponry to members of the coalition.

The US, UK, France, and others have continued to sell munitions and other arms to Saudi Arabia and other coalition states, despite the coalition's frequent unlawful attacks. A number of US and UK lawmakers have challenged their governments' continuation of these sales. UK arms sales to Saudi Arabia face ongoing litigation.

In October, the European Parliament called on EU member states to suspend weapons sales to Saudi Arabia due to its conduct in Yemen, decried coalition war crimes, and called for sanctions against those responsible for obstructing humanitarian assistance.

The Netherlands, Canada, Belgium, Ireland, and Luxembourg jointly presented the resolution at the UN Human Rights Council to continue the mandate of an independent international investigation.

The UN Security Council, in Resolutions 2140 (2014) and 2216 (2015), established a sanctions regime in Yemen whereby individuals that have violated international human rights law or international humanitarian law, or obstructed the delivery of humanitarian assistance, are potentially subject to travel bans and asset freezes.

Zimbabwe

Relatively peaceful national elections marred by disputed results and post-election violence signified that little had changed in Zimbabwe in 2018. The declaration of Emmerson Mnangagwa as winner of the July 30 presidential race, which for the first time in 30 years did not have former President Robert Mugabe on the ballot, was followed by a military crackdown on political opponents. Mugabe's ouster by the military in November 2017 paved the way for his erstwhile deputy, Mnangagwa, to take over the reins of power as interim president, and then as ruling ZANU-PF flagbearer in the national elections.

On August 1, soldiers shot and killed at least six people during opposition protests in the capital, Harare. Mnangagwa later established a commission of inquiry into the post-election violence, chaired by former South African President Kgalema Motlanthe. At time of writing, the commission had not published its findings.

Throughout the year, Mnangagwa and other high-level government officials made numerous promises to deliver governance reforms to mark the post-Mugabe era, but took few steps to demonstrate commitment to accountability, justice for human rights abuses, and respect for the rule of law. Mnangagwa, who has his own long record of human rights abuses, called on Zimbabweans in December 2017 "to let bygones be bygones," paving the way for continued widespread impunity for abuses by the military and state security agents.

The administration has also struggled to revive the economy, and to effectively respond to the outbreak of cholera in August, which killed at least 50 people and infected thousands in Harare.

Freedom of Expression and Media

On October 29, state security agents briefly detained and harassed journalist Violet Gonda at State House where she was officially accreditated to report on President Mnangagwa's meeting with business leaders. On September 21, police briefly detained Pauline Chateuka, a Community Radio Harare journalist, for filming police officers as they arrested street vendors in Harare. On September 19, police also briefly detained Gilbert Nyambavhu, editor of the online publication, New Zimbabwe, and his colleague Idah Mhetu.

On September 24, a group of publishers, editors, and journalists met with senior officials of the ruling ZANU-PF party in the Midlands city of Kwekwe to register complaints over cases of intimidation and threats issued against local journalists by some party members. ZANU-PF officials urged journalists to report any cases of intimidation involving party supporters to them.

The Mnangagwa administration failed to amend or repeal repressive laws such as the Access to Information and Protection of Privacy Act (AIPPA), the Public Order and Security Act (POSA), and the Criminal Law (Codification and Reform) Act. These laws were used under Mugabe to severely curtail basic rights through vague defamation clauses and draconian penalties. Partisan policing and prosecution worsened the impact of the repressive provisions in the AIPPA and POSA laws.

Women's and Girls' Rights, Sexual Orientation, and Gender Identity

Three years after Zimbabwe's Constitutional Court declared child marriage unconstitutional and set 18 as the minimum marriage age, the government has not put structures in place to implement the court decision and ensure that girls under 18 are not forced into marriage. Although Zimbabwe's 2013 constitution stipulates that "no person may be compelled to enter marriage against their will" and required authorities to ensure that children are not pledged into marriage, the government has yet to amend or repeal all other existing marriage laws that still allow child marriage.

During his State of the Nation address on September 18, Mnangangwa said that the current parliament is expected to consider the Child Justice Bill and the Marriages Bill, which seek to provide a child justice system and outlaw child marriages. The parliament has yet to consider these bills at time of writing.

Critical steps have not been taken to address the routine eviction of widows from their marital homes and confiscation of their property by in-laws with little recourse to the formal justice system, which Human Rights Watch documented in 2017. Many of the victims continue to struggle to claim rights for reasons unique to their status as widows. Few women formally own the property held during their marriage. As a result, they were unable to keep jointly held property upon the death of their husband.

Section 73 of the Criminal Law (Codification and Reform) Act, 2004 punishes consensual same-sex conduct between men with up to one year in prison or a fine or both. This restrictive legislation contributes to stigma and discrimination against lesbian, gay, bisexual, and transgender (LGBT) people. In September, a teacher at a Harare school who came out as gay resigned after he received death threats from members of the public over his sexual orientation.

Ahead of the July 2018 national elections, representatives of the LGBT community in Zimbabwe met with top ruling ZANU-PF party officials. The Gays and Lesbians of Zimbabwe (GALZ) advocacy group thanked Mnangagwa for this unprecedented meeting and for "understanding" them better than his predecessor Mugabe and the opposition parties.

Right to Health

The Ministry of Health on September 6 declared a cholera outbreak in Harare after confirmation of 11 cases. The government subsequently declared a national emergency after scores had died and thousands became infected. Between August 2008 and July 2009 Zimbabwe experienced Africa's worst cholera epidemic in 15 years when more than 4,000 people died and over 100,000 were infected. The conditions that allowed the devastating epidemic to flourish in 2008 persisted in 2018: little access to potable water, inadequate sanitation services, and limited information on water quality.

Rule of Law

Authorities continued to ignore human rights provisions in the country's 2013 constitution. The government did not enact new laws or amend existing legislation to bring them in line with the constitution and Zimbabwe's international and regional human rights obligations.

The Zimbabwe Human Rights Commission on August 7 strongly condemned the use of live ammunition and excessive force against unarmed protesters in Harare in August when the military fatally shot at least six people. Security forces have intensified a crackdown on supporters of the opposition Movement for Democratic Change Alliance (MDCA) in the aftermath of post-election protests in Harare. They also beat up and harassed scores of people in Harare as they searched for opposition party officials.

The whereabouts of pro-democracy activist and human rights defender Itai Dzamara remains unknown. He was abducted on March 9, 2015.

In October, prominent activist and director of Zimbabwe Peace Project, Jestina Mukoko, a victim of enforced disappearance and torture for three weeks by state agents in December 2008, finally received compensation after a Zimbabwe High Court ordered the state to pay her US$150,000.

Key International Actors

Following the November 2017 military coup, the leadership of the Southern African Development Community (SADC) called on Zimbabweans to peacefully resolve the nation's political challenges. SADC leaders welcomed Mugabe's decision to resign under military pressure, pledging to support future national elections. The African Union initially condemned the military takeover, but later welcomed Mugabe's resignation.

The AU and SADC adjudged the July 2018 elections as peaceful and in accordance with the SADC Principles and Guidelines Governing Democratic Elections, which were established to promote regular free and fair, transparent, credible and peaceful democratic elections in the region.

International observer missions, including those of the European Union, the AU, SADC and the Commonwealth, issued a joint statement on August 2 appreciating the generally peaceful and orderly pre-electoral and voting day environment, but expressing grave concern about the post-election violence. They condemned vandalism and destruction of property and called on political party supporters to abide by the law. They also denounced the excessive use of force to quell protests and urged the police and army to exercise restraint.

On August 8, United States President Donald Trump signed into law the amended Zimbabwe Democracy and Economic Recovery Act, which renewed sanctions against the Mnangagwa administration.